Minkove

The Fate of Others

1 October 2013

To Judy –

With great appreciation for your interest and kind words –

Nan Lefenfeld

The Fate of Others:

Rescuing Jewish Children on the French-Swiss Border

Nancy Lefenfeld

TIMBREL PRESS
Clarksville, Maryland

Published in the United States of America by
TIMBREL PRESS
5800 Clipper Lane, Number 304, Clarksville, MD 21029

ISBN (paperback): 978-0-9890319-0-5

for Bob

Abbreviations

AC	Amitié chrétienne
AFSC	American Friends Service Committee
ADHS	Archives départementales de la Haute-Savoie
AEG	Archives d'État de Genève
AIU	Alliance israélite universelle
ARJF	Anciens de la Résistance juive en France
Arr. ter. GE	Arrondissement territorial de Genève
CC	Consistoire central
CDJC	Mémorial de la Shoah, Musée/Centre de documentation juive contemporaine
CGQJ	Commissariat général aux questions juives
CIMADE	Comité d'intermouvements auprès des évacués
EIF	Éclaireurs israélites de France
FSJF	Fédération des sociétés juives de France
JDC	American Jewish Joint Distribution Committee
MAU	Mauthausen Memorial
MJS	Mouvement de jeunesse sioniste
ORT	Obschestvo Remeslenovo i zemledelcheskovo Trouda
OSE	Oeuvre de secours aux enfants
SIG	Schweizerischer Israelitischer Gemeindebund
UGIF	Union générale des Israélites de France
USHMM	United States Holocaust Memorial Museum
YIVO	YIVO Institute for Jewish Research
YV	Yad Vashem
VSJF	Verband Schweizerischer Jüdischer Fürsorgen

"A Klee painting named 'Angelus Novus' shows an angel looking as though he is about to move away from something he is fixedly contemplating. His eyes are staring, his mouth is open, his wings are spread. This is how one pictures the angel of history. His face is turned toward the past. Where we perceive a chain of events, he sees one single catastrophe which keeps piling wreckage and hurls it in front of his feet. The angel would like to stay, awaken the dead, and make whole what has been smashed. But a storm is blowing in from Paradise; it has got caught in his wings with such a violence that the angel can no longer close them. The storm irresistibly propels him into the future to which his back is turned, while the pile of debris before him grows skyward. This storm is what we call progress."

Walter Benjamin, "Theses on the Philosophy of History IX," 1940.

Contents

FRANCE, June 1940—November 1942

BELGIUM
LUX
GERMANY
SWITZERLAND
ITALY
SPAIN
Turin
Pas-de-Calais
Nord
Seine-Inférieure
Somme
Aisne
Ardennes
Meuse
Moselle
Manche
Calvados
Eure
Paris
Seine-et-Oise
Seine-et-Marne
Marne
Meurthe-et-Moselle
Bas-Rhin
Finistère
Côtes-du-Nord
Orne
Aube
Vosges
Mayenne
Eure-et-Loir
Haute-Marne
Haut-Rhin
Morbihan
Ille-et-Vilaine
Sarthe
Loiret
Yonne
Haute-Saône
Belfort
Côte d'Or
Loir-et-Cher
Loire-Atlantique
Maine-et-Loire
Indre-et-Loire
Nièvre
Doubs
Cher
Saône-et-Loire
Jura
Vendée
Deux-Sèvres
Indre
Vienne
Allier
Haute-Savoie
Vichy
Ain
Rhône
Lyon
Creuse
Charente-Maritime
Haute-Vienne
Loire
Isère
Savoie
Puy-de-Dôme
Charente
Corrèze
Cantal
Haute-Loire
Dordogne
Haute-Alpes
Drôme
Ardeche
Gironde
Lot
Lot-et-Garonne
Lozère
Basses-Alpes
Alpes-Maritimes
Aveyron
Gard
Vaucluse
Landes
Tarn-et-Garonne
Nice
Bouches-du-Rhône
Gers
Toulouse
Tarn
Var
Haute-Garonne
Hérault
Marseille
Basses-Pyrénées
Hautes-Pyrénées
Ariege
Aude
Pyrenees-Orientales
Demarcation line
German-Occupied Zone
Zone annexed to Germany
Departmental boundary
International border
0
150 Miles
0
200km

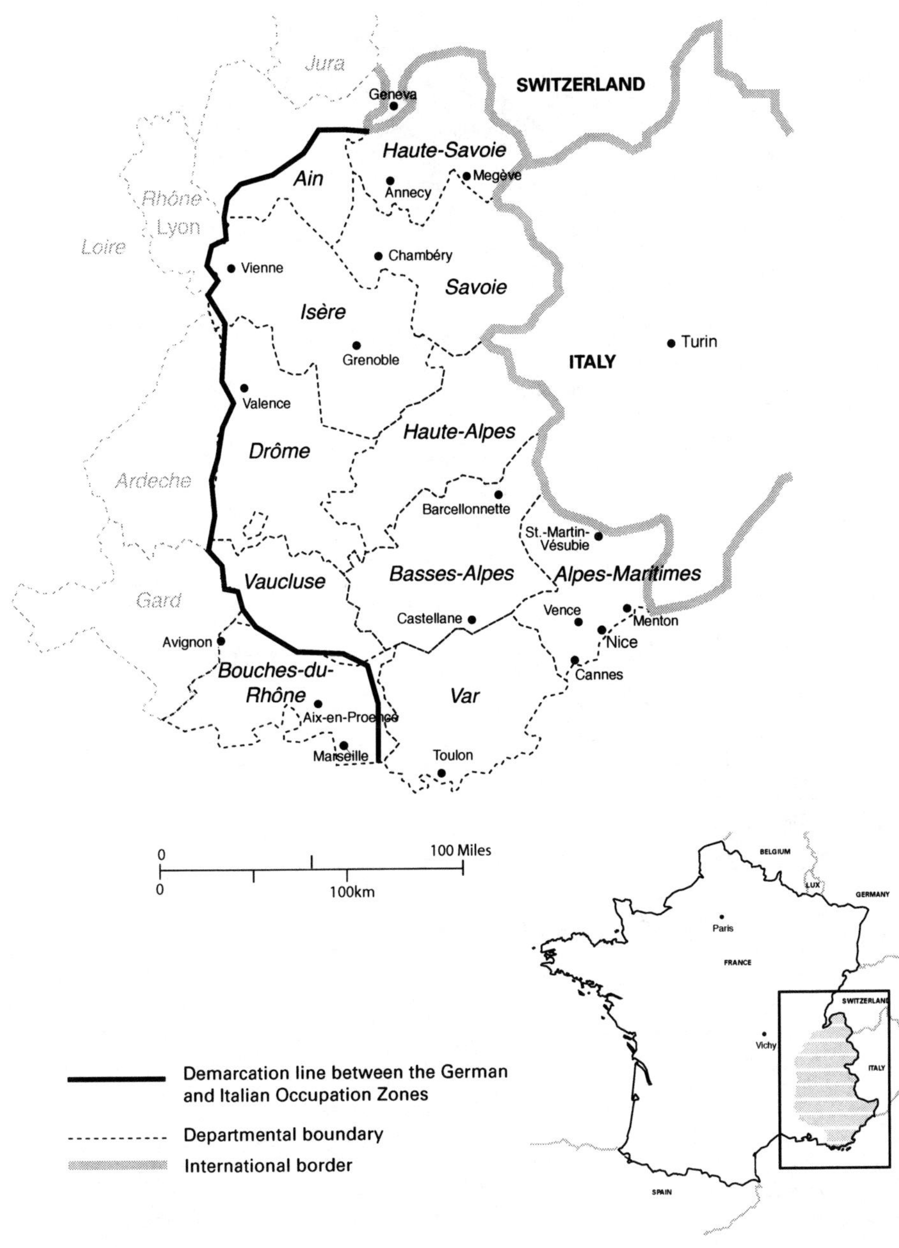
THE ITALIAN OCCUPATION ZONE
December 1942—September 1943
Jura
Geneva
SWITZERLAND
Haute-Savoie
Ain
Megève
Annecy
Rhône
Lyon
Loire
Chambéry
Vienne
Savoie
Isère
Turin
Grenoble
ITALY
Valence
Haute-Alpes
Drôme
Ardeche
Barcellonnette
St.-Martin-
Vésubie
Basses-Alpes
Alpes-Maritimes
Vaucluse
Gard
Vence
Castellane
Menton
Avignon
Nice
Cannes
Bouches-du-
Rhône
Var
Aix-en-Proence
Toulon
Marseille
0
100 Miles
0
100km
BELGIUM
LUX
GERMANY
Paris
FRANCE
SWITZERLAND
Vichy
ITALY
SPAIN
Demarcation line between the German and Italian Occupation Zones
Departmental boundary
International border

DEPARTMENT OF THE HAUTE-SAVOIE, FRANCE

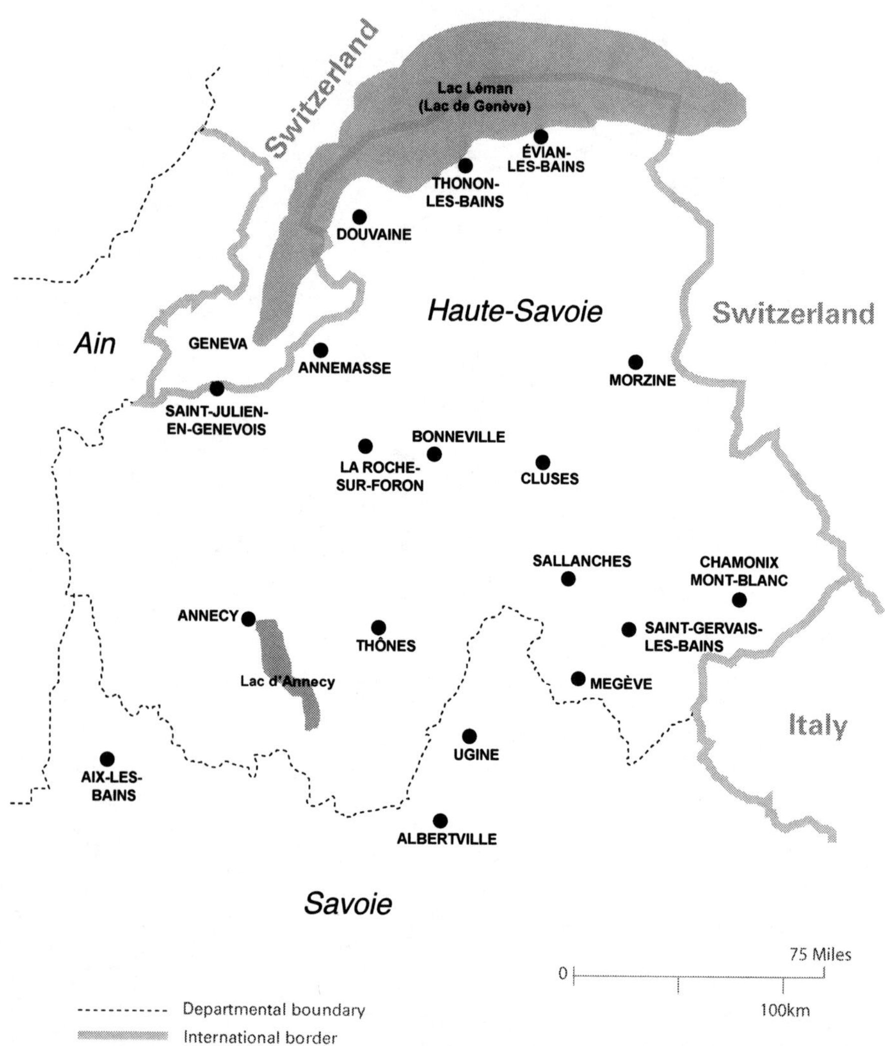

BORDER AREA BETWEEN THE CANTON OF GENEVA, SWITZERLAND, AND THE DEPARTMENT OF THE HAUTE-SAVOIE, FRANCE

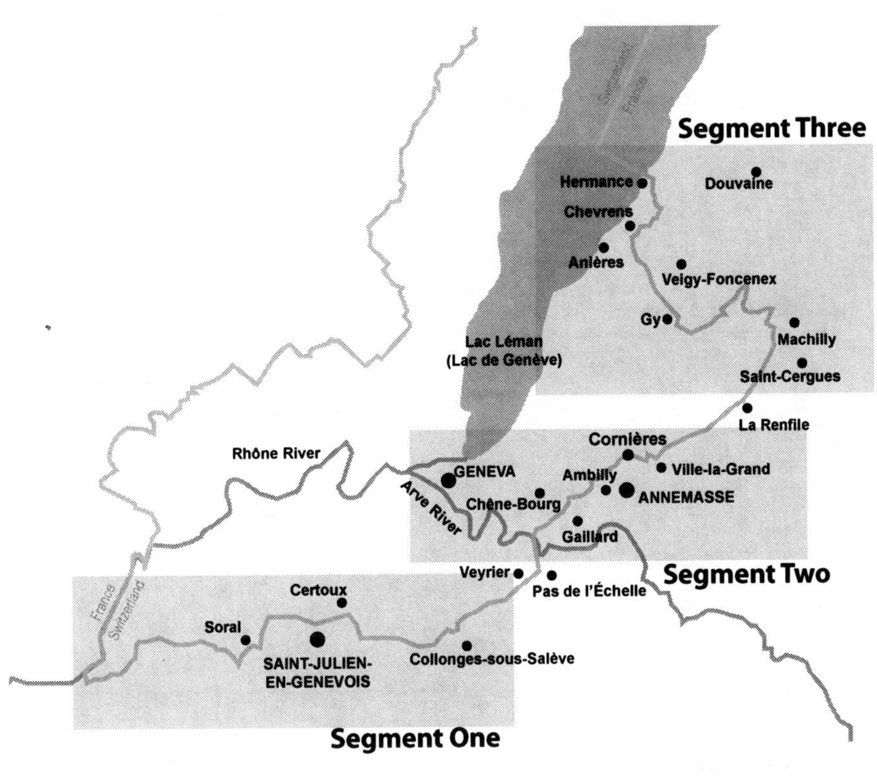

Segment One

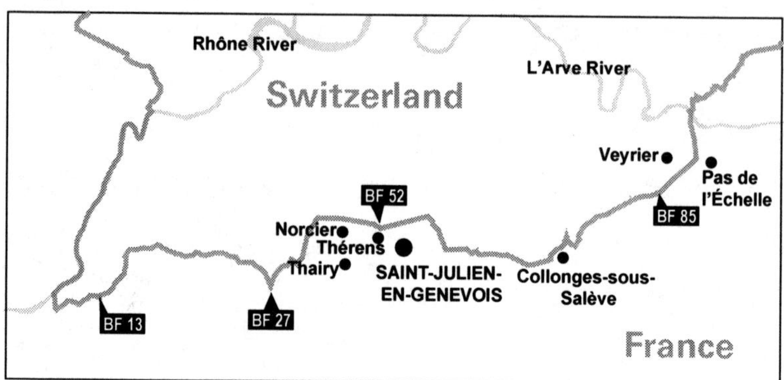

Segment Two

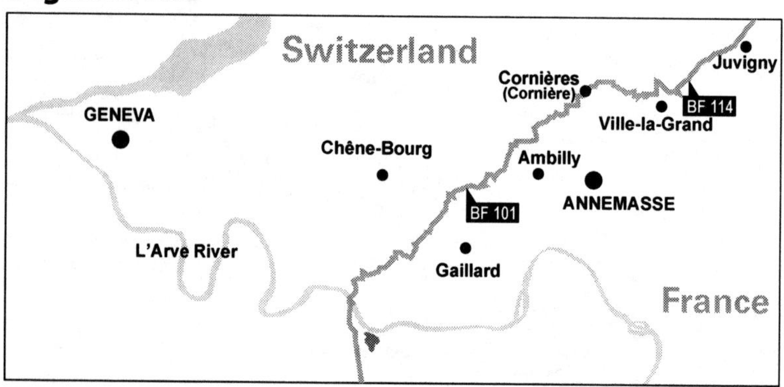

Segment Three

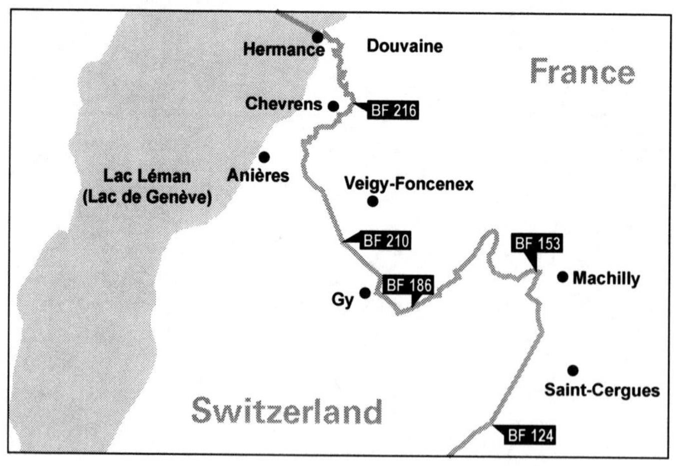

Foreword

Erev Pesach 5757—Monday, April 21, 1997. I had requested that each family member and friend attending our Passover seder bring something to share—a poem, a story, or simply a few thoughts. An article in the Sunday paper had featured three Holocaust survivors and their difficulties in obtaining reparations from Germany. I was especially moved by story of one individual—I will call her Lisette—and, that evening, I shared a short synopsis of it with family and friends.

In August 1942, when she was three years old, Lisette, her mother, and her sisters were imprisoned in an internment camp in the south of France. Shortly before being deported, Lisette's mother was given the choice of taking her daughters with her or leaving them behind, in the hands of persons whom she did not know. She chose to leave them behind. Lisette and her sisters were somehow smuggled into Switzerland. Her father was also deported from France, and both of her parents were murdered in Auschwitz. Lisette was a "child survivor"—a term not yet in my vocabulary but one that I would soon come to know.

In the article, Lisette spoke not only of her difficult past but also of many present-day challenges. It appeared she was going through a period of crisis. I contacted her through the newspaper and asked if there were some way I might help. She responded and, several weeks later, we met.

Lisette had undergone much psychological trauma at a young age. As an adult, she struggled to make a living and to deal with issues of anger, resentment, and depression. She had no memories of her parents—a fact that is not surprising given her young age in 1942. It was surprising, however, that she had no memory of events occurring prior to her emigration to the United States, when she was six years old. The lack of memories—or, one might say, inability to access memories—frustrated her. Moreover, she had little understanding of what had happened during the first six years of her life: her information was fragmentary and she could make little sense of it. Lacking a coherent narrative of her own childhood, she was plagued by questions. A researcher by profession and nature, I decided to see if I could help her reach back into the past and find some answers.

The German occupation of France was not a static condition that lasted for four years. It changed over time—sometimes in subtle ways and at other times dramatically. In order to understand what had happened to Lisette's family, I had to learn about the Occupation and how it had evolved. I also had to learn about the chronology of Jewish persecution enacted by German and French authorities. In the early months, I spent many hours in the United States Holocaust Memorial Museum and the Library of Congress delving into the general subject of Jews in Occupied France and the specific subject of the rescue of Jewish children from French internment camps. In regard to the latter, there was not much information available in English. There were many more French language texts with relevant passages, but my French reading skills were poor. I photocopied a great deal of material so that I could slowly and laboriously work my way through it at home. I also wrote to government offices in France to obtain copies of documents that would help establish the timeline of the family's whereabouts.

At a certain point, it became apparent to me that the child rescue organization known as OSE may have had a hand in the rescue of Lisette and her sisters. I found that the organization is still very much alive and prepared a letter of inquiry for Lisette to send to its headquarters in Paris. In response, she received copies of the several pages that comprised the contents of a dossier compiled on her and her sisters during the war. Among the documents were some that bore the signatures of Lisette's mother and father, signatures that she had never before seen. Eventually, she made the acquaintance of the female rescuer whose pseudonym her sisters had remembered.

I am an American Jew born in 1951. I am not a historian. Prior to 1997, I had no knowledge of what life had been like for Jews living in France under the German Occupation. I knew nothing of their day-to-day struggles to meet basic human needs—food and shelter—while evading arrest and deportation. I had no idea that hundreds of Jewish men and women had worked clandestinely—many in organized networks—to save others, especially children. I had no idea that so many of the Jewish men and women who took on the mantel of rescue were so young. No idea that Jewish rescue networks worked hand in hand, entirely in secret, with Catholics and Protestants. No idea that so many sacrificed their lives while trying to save others from the fate that the Nazis had prescribed for them.

Wanting to delve deeper into the subject of Jews who rescued Jews, I traveled to France in 1998. It was the first time that I had ever gone overseas. I spent two weeks studying archival documents and books in the Mémorial de la Shoah Musée/Centre de documentation juive contemporaine (CDJC), the preeminent contemporary French Jewish archive and library. I also consulted the archives of OSE. What affected me most profoundly was reading testimonies written by Jews, particularly Jewish women, about the rescue work they had carried out. It is unusual to hear about Jewish rescuers and even more unusual to hear about female Jewish rescuers. Women were, in fact, an integral part of rescue networks, often called upon to take on the most dangerous jobs. They have been more reticent than men in documenting their accomplishments. Few women rescuers published their memoirs. For a long time, modesty dampened any inclination to do so.

The nature of the peril to Jews living in France is difficult to understand because it cannot be reduced to generalities and because it changed as the military situation changed and as popular attitudes toward the German Occupation authorities shifted. Above ground (legal) and underground or clandestine (illegal) rescue activities carried out by Jewish organizations evolved in response to the changing situation. When I undertook this research, I relied heavily on Lucien Lazare's excellent book, *Rescue as Resistance: How Jewish Organizations Fought the Holocaust in France,* to understand this evolution. Over the past decade, it has been my bible on the subject. My copy is so worn that, when I open it, sections that have broken away from the spine fall out in clumps.

It was in that source that I first read the names of Mila Racine and Marianne Cohn, two young Jewish women who smuggled Jewish children from France into Switzerland. They were the best of friends. After Mila was arrested while trying to pass a convoy of children across the border, Marianne stepped in and continued the work. Lazare mentions them only briefly, but the reference was enough to make me want to know who they were, what they did, and what happened to them. I tracked down all that I could and identified, located, and interviewed several individuals who had been in Marianne's last convoy, which fell into German hands while attempting to cross the Swiss border on May 31, 1944. I found that, although various sources document the arrest and imprisonment of one or the other or both women, few speak to the extent of the rescue work they accomplished. As I became more familiar with the subject, it seemed logical to focus my research on Mila and the team that she helped establish and lead.

Mila was the first member of the Mouvement de jeunesse sioniste (MJS; Zionist Youth Movement) asked to smuggle a group of unaccompanied children into Switzerland. It was the middle of August 1943. The twenty-three-year-old was a member of a large Jewish refugee community living in forced residence in Saint-Gervais-les-Bains, at the foot of Mont Blanc. Saint-Gervais was part of the Italian Occupation Zone, which encompassed the southeastern corner of France. The summer had been a pleasant one; Italian soldiers had protected the Jews and treated them benevolently. But the political situation in Italy had changed in late July. By early August, it was becoming clear that the time of the Italian occupation was nearing an end. Mila was asked to take eleven children from Saint-Gervais to the area outside of Geneva, between Annemasse and Saint-Julien-en-Genevois, and get them through the barbed wire barrier that had been erected along the border. This first convoy was a test—there was much at stake. If it succeeded, the MJS would immediately establish a *réseau,* a network, to rescue other hunted children. On August 16, when she and the children arrived at the designated point, things did not go as planned and the crossing was thwarted. If she had decided to take the children back to Saint-Gervais, no one would have faulted her. She had done all that was expected of her; what had happened was beyond her control. But Mila refused to give up.

The first convoy succeeded, as did the second, third, fourth, fifth, and many more. The rescuers worked entirely in secret, their identities concealed. They were helped by members of an underground network comprised of Catholics and Protestants, clergy and lay people, men and women, young and old. Nearly seventy years later, almost none whom they rescued know the true identities of their rescuers. Almost none know what the mysterious initials "MJS" stand for.

The fact that such things are not known, even though decades have elapsed, should not surprise us. Anonymity was the essential element of rescue work during the Shoah. It was work carried out in shadows and darkness. Recordkeeping was dangerous, for it implicated rescuers in illegal acts punishable by deportation and death. German recordkeeping, on the other hand, was so extensive that I struggle to find words that might adequately describe it. Millions of documents, billions of pieces of data have occupied historical researchers since the end of the war. In 2008, the archive of documents administered by the International Tracing Service in Bad Arolsen, Germany—sixteen miles worth of records—was opened to the general public. It seems as if there is no end in sight to how much the world will know about the where, when, and how of the Nazi killing machine. If rescuers had been able to maintain such records, the world would know how they too went about their business and how many would-be victims were spared because of their actions.

I present here not only the names of the rescuers but also the names of the rescued, each name linked to a specific date and place. How is such a degree of specificity possible? When unaccompanied Jewish children entered Switzerland illegally in 1943–44, Swiss authorities did not turn them back, but they did place them under formal arrest and prepare detailed arrest reports. For nearly fifty years after the end of the war, arrest reports and accompanying documentation on refugees who entered Switzerland illegally remained untouched and in storage. In 1993, officials of Yad Vashem made a formal request to the Swiss government for information concerning Jewish refugees expelled after having entered the country illegally. This prompted the canton of Geneva to examine the collection of records that had been largely forgotten. For the first time, archivists realized the historical value of the documents in their possession. (Few of the cantons responded positively to Yad Vashem's request, as the pertinent records had already been destroyed.) I have made extensive use of the original arrest records in preparing this book.

Even if the names of the rescued are available by date and place of passage into Switzerland, why include such detail in this account? Verifiable details bear witness to the work of the rescuers. Some of the rescuers of whom I write received no proper burial. In lieu of placing stones on gravesites, I place the names of 274 children and adults whom they rescued into the written record to honor their courage and their deeds. May the memory of righteous rescuers be for a blessing.

Acknowledgments

I am deeply indebted to the many people who helped me research and document this true story of rescue and who provided advice and encouragement. Chief among them are Bernard and Thérèse Kott of Roanne, France, and Gabriel and Anne-Marie Grandjacques of Saint-Gervais-les-Bains, France. Bernard is the son of Joseph Kott, the organizer and leader of the Jewish refugee community in Saint-Gervais in 1943. Gabriel, a native son of Saint-Gervais who has lived there all his life, is a retired history teacher who has written extensively about the region. I first met Gabriel on a trip to France in 2003. Sometime earlier, I had inquired at the Hôtel de Ville in Saint-Gervais as to whether any information was available on the Jewish refugee community that lived there in forced residence in 1943. The mayor's office had no information and forwarded my inquiry to Gabriel. He was surprised to receive it, as he had no idea that the town had accommodated an influx of Jewish refugees during the war. The three of us—Gabriel, Bernard, and I—began corresponding with one another. We met on a hot September day in 2004, our respective documents covering the surface of a long table on the patio of the Val Joly, where many MJS members had lived in the summer of 1943. It was a meeting that none of us will ever forget. Two years later, I had the pleasure of meeting these dear people again in Saint-Gervais, this time to dedicate a commemorative plaque installed on the exterior of the former Hôtel Eden, the headquarters of Joseph Kott's Saint-Gervais Committee so long ago. Words are hardly sufficient to thank the Kott and Grandjacques families for their friendship and support.

I also owe a special measure of gratitude to Ruth Fivaz-Silbermann, presently completing her doctoral dissertation, *La fuite en Suisse,* at the University of Geneva. Ruth is the preeminent authority on the subject of attempts to enter Switzerland made by Jews fleeing France during the time of the German Occupation. I do not recall if it was Ruth who first made me aware of the existence of original arrest records and accompanying documentation preserved in the Geneva archives, but she certainly opened my eyes to the vastness and richness of the collection. A tireless worker, attentive to every detail, she has generously shared with me results of her work as well as her working hypotheses.

I also owe a special measure of gratitude to the Racine family. I was honored to be able to interview Mila Racine's brother, Emmanuel (Mola), of blessed memory, in Israel in 2000 and her sister, Sacha Maidenberg, in Paris the same year. Emmanuel Racine allowed me to photocopy a large number of archival documents in his possession, including correspondence to and from Mila. I also had the pleasure of meeting his two daughters—Lili Peyser, the niece whom Mila adored, and Daniella Wexler, whom Mila never met. Lili sent me photos of Mila that I had not previously seen, including the lovely portrait of the two of them that appears on the cover. Daniella, an accomplished artist, sent me images of her four wonderful paintings of Mila. The extended Racine family living in Paris during the twenties and thirties was large and close-knit. Three of Mila's cousins in the United States—Helen Mirkine (née Racine), Nadine Gill (née Racine), and Nelly Harris (née Chender)—related their recollections of Mila and her parents and siblings. They also shared their memories of the family's flight from Paris in June 1940 and their temporary stay in Toulouse.

I am grateful to the Gryn family and to Miriam Brinbaum. Tito Gryn, the son of Tony Gryn, provided me with information and copies of archival documents in his possession. Tony's sister, Alice Gliklich, was helpful as well. Miriam Brinbaum (née Wajntrob), the daughter of Léa and Jacques Wajntrob, furnished biographical information and copies of archival documents in her possession. Also, on my behalf, she queried her mother on several items and relayed information to me.

I had the very great honor of interviewing five other individuals who were engaged in the rescue of Jewish children in the department of the Haute-Savoie in 1943–44. Each kindly and generously shared their recollections. I express my heartfelt thanks to: Georges Loinger of the OSE; Jeanne Brousse, employed during the war in the Prefecture of Annecy; and Frida Wattenberg, Georges Schnek, and Renée Wiener (née Kurz) of the MJS.

I have been privileged to have had the opportunity to interview many child survivors of the Shoah. They shared family histories, anecdotes, copies of archival documents, and, above all, their cherished memories. In most cases, I interviewed them face to face. In this regard, I am indebted to Gerda Bikales (née Bierzonski), Jacques Charmatz, Sonia Constant (née Veissid), Claude Emerich, Dr. Maurice Glazman, Sarah Gostynski, Victor Grabsztok, Edgar Kleinberger, André Panczer, Myriam Pupier (née Charmatz), Eliane Suernick (née Neoussikhin), Wolf Wapniarz, Esther Weil (née Constant), and Lydie Weissberg. I would also like to thank the following: Marcel Chetret; Isidore and Madeleine Jacubowiez; Carlo Lasar; Joseph Sosnowski; Michael Traumann; Simon Zaidenband and Nicole Rotmensz, son and daughter of Rebecca Zaidenband; and several other child survivors who do not wish to be identified by name.

Five courageous women, survivors of Ravensbrück, wrote to me to share recollections of their friend and comrade Mila. I humbly express my sincere thanks to Marie-Claude Bonaldi (née Mion), Marie-Jo Chombart de Lauwe, Violette Maurice, Anise Postel-Vinay, and Denise Vernay (née Jacob; known to her comrades as "Miarka"). I also thank Madame Vernay for giving me the opportunity to speak with her face to face.

One of the great pleasures of working on this project was having the chance to conduct archival research in Switzerland, France, Austria, Israel, and the United States. In each archive, many people assisted me. I wish to thank: Catherine Santschi, former State Archivist, Pierre Flückiger, State Archivist, and their staff at the Archives d'État de Genève in Geneva; Karen Taieb, Director of the Archives, Lior LaLieu-Smadja, Director of the Photography Service, and other staff of the Mémorial de la Shoah Musée/Centre de documentation juive contemporaine in Paris; Dr. Christian Dürr and Ralf Lechner at the Archiv der KZ-Gedenkstätte Mauthausen in Vienna; and Ron Coleman and Vincent Slatt, Reference Librarians, and other staff at the United States Holocaust Memorial Museum in Washington, DC. Sara Halperyn, of blessed memory, former Chief Librarian of the Mémorial de la Shoah Musée/Centre de documentation juive contemporaine in Paris, helped me during my early years of research and encouraged me to tell Mila's story. I also wish to thank staff associated with: the Alliance israélite universelle, Paris; Fondation pour la mémoire de la déportation, Paris; Yad Vashem, Jerusalem; Oral History Division, Institute of Contemporary Jewry, Hebrew University, Jerusalem; American Jewish Joint Distribution Committee Archives, New York; YIVO, New York; and the Air Force Historical Research Agency, Maxwell Air Force Base, Alabama. In addition, I would like to thank Katy Hazan, Historian, OSE-France, Paris.

Other individuals in France helped me in ways too varied and numerous to cite. I wish to acknowledge the help received from: Jean and Germaine Cochet (Aix-les-Bains); Mercédès Brawand (Saint-Julien); Sara Grunberg and Gabrielle Jacoubovitch-Bouhana (Paris); Sabine Maciol (Annemasse); Hyacinthe Vulliez (Thonon-les-Bains); and Father François Mercier and Robert Moos (Annecy). In Amstetten, Austria, I was helped by Silvia and and Fritz Draxler, Elke Strauss, and Herbert Katzengruber. I would also like to thank Léa Grundman in Israel, Lilly Leuwenkroon in Belgium, and Eliane Strosberg in the United States.

I am deeply indebted to Patrick Henry, Cushing Eells Professor Emeritus of Philosophy and Literature at Whitman College, for reviewing the manuscript of this book and providing editorial assistance and general advice. I also wish to thank the following individuals for reading this work in various stages and offering advice and encouragement: Chana Arnon; Esther-Ann Asch; Richard Hoffman; and Mark Lefenfeld. Rachel Bodner, a child survivor from Belgium, has helped me tirelessly for a decade, advising me on French, Yiddish, and German translations. She always gave generously of her time and spirit, and I shall be forever indebted to her. I am also extremely grateful for Anne-Marie Lanz's careful review of material I have translated, including letters written by Mila Racine in 1943–44 and excerpts from Declarations contained in personal dossiers that have been preserved in the Geneva archives.

I wish to thank the Hadassah-Brandeis Institute for a research grant received in 2000. I am also grateful for financial support received from the FJC, a Foundation of Donor Advised Funds, the Esther-Ann and Morton Asch Fund at the FJC, and individual donors who contributed to the Last Convoy Fund at the FJC.

It would have been impossible for me to conduct this research and write this account without the love and support of my family. Thank you, Bob, Ben, and Jake.

1. *Prelude*

From November 1942 until September 1943, the Italian army occupied the southeastern corner of France. During these ten months, Italian soldiers protected Jews living under their jurisdiction. In fact, by early 1943, Italy had so amply demonstrated its willingness to protect Jews in France that thousands of the persecuted made their way to Nice, Cannes, Grenoble, Chambéry, and neighboring towns and villages. These statements will surprise most readers, and it is not difficult to understand why. After all, Italy was an Axis power, aligned with Nazi Germany. It had enacted its own racial laws in 1938 and interned its own Jewish citizens.

This story of rescue in the Haute-Savoie region of France would not have unfolded—at least in the way that it did—if the Italians had not provided Jews with a safe haven in this particular time and place. How did it come into existence and why was it so important? To answer these questions, we must briefly revisit France during the earlier days of *les années noires,* the dark years.

Benito Mussolini, the head of the Italian Fascist state who was known simply as il Duce (the Leader), had meant to play a part in France's defeat in 1940, but events had passed him by. On May 13, German soldiers crossed the French border and began their march toward Paris. Mussolini was in no rush to send troops into France; he decided to delay their deployment a few weeks. To his complete surprise, the conflict was all over in less than a month, too soon for Italy to even give the appearance of having made a substantial contribution. German troops occupied Paris on June 14. By then, two-thirds of the entire population of Paris, normally three million, had fled south by car, truck, train, bicycle, and on foot.

French Prime Minister Paul Reynaud and his Cabinet fled the capital on June 10 for Bordeaux. Reynaud argued that they should all leave immediately for North Africa so that they could continue the struggle alongside the British. Philippe Pétain, the eighty-four-year-old World War I hero known as le Maréchal (the Marshal), was not the only French leader advocating surrender, but it was his voice that proved decisive. On June 17, Pétain addressed the nation in a radio broadcast, announcing his appointment as Prime Minister and calling for an armistice. Not all capitulated, however. Under-Secretary of State for War Charles de Gaulle went to London, where he vowed to fight on as leader of what he called the Free French. A few others went to Casablanca. Those who stayed behind signed an armistice with Germany on June 22, declared themselves to be the true patriots, and prepared to set up government operations in the spa and casino resort of Vichy. Before doing that, however, they signed a separate armistice with Italy, ceding a toehold that included the town of Menton on the Mediterranean Coast, less than two miles from the Italian border. Although the territory ceded was of little consequence, it riled French ministers to make any concessions at all to this Johnny-come-lately.

For their own purposes and to achieve their own ends, the Germans occupied only part of France. As the writer-historian Ian Ousby neatly states, "France kept her empire, her fleet, and the illusion of her national sovereignty." The Occupied Zone encompassed the northern half of the country and the entire Atlantic coast. It was separated from the Unoccupied Zone by a line of demarcation that could not be crossed without authorization. Although the town of Vichy was in the Unoccupied Zone, the government in Vichy was, throughout the war, the government of all of France. The lines of authority between German and French officials were never clearly delineated, but impromptu working relationships developed. The collaboration benefited Germany enormously.

At an estimated 330,000, the Jewish population living in France on the eve of the German Occupation was large—five times the size of the Jewish population of Belgium and seven times that of Italy. Native-born Jews comprised roughly two-fifths of the total, and foreign-born Jews roughly three-fifths. Many of the foreign Jews had emigrated to the land of *liberté, égalité, fraternité* in the twenties and thirties to escape oppression in Russia, Poland, Germany, Austria, and elsewhere. In 1940, they were joined by Jewish refugees fleeing their homes in Belgium, the Netherlands, and Luxembourg. Approximately one in three foreign-born Jews had gained French citizenship through naturalization.

In terms of their appearance and language, many native-born Jews resembled their Christian neighbors more than they did their foreign-born co-religionists. Christians regarded the assimilated French Jew as either not really a Jew or as a different kind of Jew than the foreign Jew. In the popular idiom, the word *Israélite,* polite and respectful, was applied to the native-born Jew, whereas the word *juif* (Jew), a slur, was applied to the foreigner. In the dark years, hoping not to draw attention, members of the French Israelite community distanced themselves from the foreign Jews.

Immigrants comprised the great majority of the roughly two hundred thousand Jews living in Paris prior to the Occupation. The immigrant family typically included members of three generations occupying spare, cramped quarters. Fathers, mothers, and grown children worked long hours in the home or neighborhood workshop or on the factory floor. They often found help and support through an extensive network of Jewish charities, which operated popular soup kitchens, medical clinics, and clothing dispensaries and provided vocational training. In late May and early June 1940, tens of thousands of Jews fled the capital, and the leaders of many Jewish organizations transferred their headquarters from Paris to cities in the south.

Although the four years of the German Occupation are called the dark years, the truth of the matter is that, for most Jews living in France, the first two years were dark and the latter two were pitch black. From the very beginning of the Occupation, French authorities in Vichy and German authorities in Paris issued ordinances that explicitly or implicitly targeted Jews. Often, measures instigated by French and German bureaucrats rivaled one another, as each side maneuvered to exert its authority and/or gain control of Jewish-owned businesses and property. Measures implemented were numerous and complicated, but their purpose was clear: to single out Jews as comprising an inferior race, strip them of legal rights they had exercised since 1846, and expel them from French society and the national economy. Jews were prohibited from working in the professions and barred from all but the most menial jobs. They were subjected to special registrations and censuses. Their bank accounts were blocked. Their businesses and property were expropriated and placed in the hands of provisional administrators. They were subjected to special curfews and prohibited from setting foot in many types of public places. They were required to obtain government authorization before moving from one jurisdiction to another. They were expelled from colleges, universities, and professional schools. They were not allowed to own radios, telephones, or bicycles.

Most Jews in France managed to survive the privation and persecution to which they were subjected during the first two years of the Occupation. Those who fared the worst were the foreign-born Jews and their children. Many of the children had been born in France and were French citizens, but they suffered the same treatment as their parents. Foreign-born Jews were the particular targets of much anti-Jewish legislation enacted in Vichy. Some were interned in primitive camps where food was scarce, living conditions harsh, and mortality rates high. Others were ordered to leave their homes, relocate to remote towns and villages, and live under police surveillance in an arrangement called *résidence forcée* (forced residence) or *résidence assignée* (assigned residence). Many Jews were stripped of their French citizenship by a commission established in July 1940 to review naturalizations that the government had granted since 1927.

From the first days of the Occupation, the German High Command had pressured French authorities in Vichy to establish a council that it could point to as representing all Jews. At the end of November 1941, French officials announced the establishment of a new entity, the Union générale des Israélites de France (General Union of French Israelites), subordinate to Vichy's Commissariat général aux questions juives (CGQJ; General Commissariat for Jewish Questions). Henceforth, all Jewish organizations were required to relinquish their independence and operate under the umbrella of the UGIF (pronounced u-geef). Most Jewish organizations complied with this requirement.

In December 1941, a new phrase entered the lexicon: deportation to forced labor in the East. No one knew what it meant. Although many had been arrested and interned indefinitely, none had yet been deported. Three months later, on March 27, 1942, the first deportation train left Drancy, the unfinished housing complex on the outskirts of Paris that had been converted to a dismal internment camp and antechamber to Auschwitz. The wheels of the Nazi killing machine brought to France were beginning to turn.

In June 1942, Adolf Eichmann held what historians Michael Marrus and Robert Paxton call a "sort of Wannsee Conference in miniature" with top Nazi officials from France, Belgium, and the Netherlands. Eichmann relayed Himmler's order to begin deportations on a massive scale, setting quotas on the number of Jews to be handed over from each country: ten thousand from Belgium, fifteen thousand from the Netherlands, and one hundred thousand from France. Upon his return to Paris, Theodor Dannecker, Eichmann's right-hand man in France, informed the new French Prime Minister, Pierre Laval, that he was responsible for meeting half of the quota and delivering fifty thousand Jews from the Unoccupied Zone. He also stipulated that the majority of Jews deported be between the ages of sixteen and forty.

Dannecker's directive did not entirely please the French Prime Minister. He wanted to deport children as well as adults, and he requested permission from Dannecker to do just that. The request was forwarded to Eichmann, who, after a brief delay, answered in the affirmative: children and the elderly could be deported along with everyone else.

The number of German soldiers stationed in France was small; Nazi leaders had to rely upon French policemen to hunt down, arrest, intern, and deport Jews. Very early on the morning of Thursday, July 16, a force of several thousand Paris policemen fanned out across the city to execute an operation code-named Vent printanier (Spring Wind). Its purpose was to round up and place under arrest twenty-seven thousand foreign Jews. The policemen were armed with lists of names and addresses culled from a special census of the Jewish population. All day Thursday and Friday, police officers combed the city, seizing those whose names were on the lists. Earlier roundups had been conducted on a much smaller scale and targeted mainly able-bodied men. Now, all were taken—men and women, young and old, able-bodied and infirm—not brutally, with truncheons, in the manner of East European ghettos, but with civility and efficiency. Families were hurried out of their apartments, through hallways, down stairs, a few belongings in their arms. Neighbors witnessed these scenes of departure. Some endeavored to help—to send a letter, contact a city official, safeguard a set of keys or a family heirloom. In the street, the unwanted and uprooted were loaded onto city buses.

Thirteen thousand were arrested during the two-day operation, four thousand of whom were children. Adults without children were taken to Drancy; families with children were taken to the Vélodrome d'Hiver, the winter bicycling stadium. No preparations had been made at the stadium so that it might serve as an adequate holding center. Consequently, during the several days that families were locked up that venue, the level of misery, hardship, and degradation surpassed all that had come before in France. Many families endured further, almost unspeakable tragedy—French authorities separated parents and children; parents were deported days or weeks ahead of their children; and children, lost and frantic, were left to face deportation and death alone.

The number of Jews arrested was less than half the number targeted. Had some been warned of the impending action? Yes, although not to the extent that they could have been. In June, as the internment camps in the Occupied Zone were emptied to fill the deportation trains, Jewish leaders suspected that new roundups were imminent. On the first of July, UGIF officials were ordered by the Commissariat général aux questions juives to prepare blankets and clothing for seven thousand people. They knew then that a massive roundup was imminent, but they did not launch a concerted effort to disseminate the information. Members of two Jewish groups operating outside the umbrella of the UGIF did take action. The Comité de la rue Amelot (Rue Amelot Committee), operating semi-legally and semi-clandestinely at this time, circulated information by word of mouth. (The work of the Rue Amelot Committee is discussed further in Chapter 5.) The Jewish Communist organization Solidarité, operating illegally and clandestinely, prepared, printed, and distributed notices, in Yiddish, that sounded the alarm and provided instructions on what to do. Lack of enthusiasm on the part of some French policemen also helped many Jews evade arrest. Prior to the roundup, some let slip a word of warning to a neighbor, shopkeeper, or concierge. On July 16-17, some carried out their orders without full diligence or haste.

At the beginning of August 1942, the French government in Vichy began to make good on its promise to deliver Jews from the Unoccupied Zone. First, they emptied half a dozen internment camps—Gurs, Le Vernet, Récébédou, Noé, Rivesaltes, and Les Milles—and sent the prisoners to Drancy. Then, having freed up space in the camps, they organized a large-scale *rafle* (roundup) throughout the Unoccupied Zone. It began on the morning of August 26. Like the Paris police, local policemen had been furnished names and addresses of Jews living in their cities, towns, and villages. In some places, the policemen concluded their work in a day; in others, it continued much longer. Those seized were held in internment camps until they could be put on trains and sent north. By the end of October, the Vichy government had delivered approximately 10,600 people from the Unoccupied Zone.

The transport trains sent from the Unoccupied Zone contained very few children. What happened to them? The representatives of various aid organizations active in the camps were able to save many of the children through a combination of legal and illegal means. Prior to August 18, official Vichy policy with regard to the inclusion of children in the transport trains was lenient—parents were allowed to take their children with them or leave them behind; unaccompanied children were not included; and parents with children younger than five were themselves exempted. On that date, worried that results might fall short of expectations, Secretary General of the Vichy Police René Bousquet tightened up the policy. Henceforth, parents were no longer allowed to leave their children behind, unaccompanied children were to be included; and only parents with children younger than two were themselves exempted. For aid workers in the camps, saving the children became not only a matter of convincing parents to leave their children behind but also finding ways of circumventing official policies and smuggling children out of the camps. The children taken out were scattered far and wide. Some were placed in children's homes operated by Jewish organizations; others, in Catholic orphanages and boarding schools or with families on farms or in rural villages.

In large cities and small towns, thousands of French Christians witnessed aspects of the massive deportation program. They heard the policeman pound on the neighbor's door. They heard the neighbor's cries and pleas. Concealed behind drawn curtains or standing in plain view, they watched sad scenes unfold—parents and children, clutching bundles and suitcases, being hurried down the stairs, through the streets, and aboard waiting buses. From time to time, a bystander—friend, neighbor, employer, housekeeper, or concierge—was unexpectedly pulled into the drama, as if swept up in a riptide. *Take my child,* a Jewish mother begged. *Take the child to your mother's house in the countryside. Hide the child in the cellar. Take the child to the orphanage.* They witnessed spectacles that appeared to have risen from the pages of Dante's *Inferno.* Observing cattle cars stopped on a railroad siding or rolling through the center of the town or passing by at a railway crossing, they noticed sets of eyes peering out and fingers extended through small openings. They heard moans issuing from the cars and voices pleading for water. They found postcards dropped along the tracks, which they picked up and took to post offices to be mailed. Many thousands of others who did not witness such scenes learned of them from friends and neighbors and read about them in newspapers.

Troubled by the nature and scale of deportations, some French Christians voiced their disapproval to members of the clergy. Monsignor Jules-Géraud Saliège, the seventy-two-year-old, partly paralyzed archbishop of Toulouse, was the first Catholic priest to publicly speak out against the treatment of foreign Jews in France. He wrote a pastoral letter on the subject and had it read in all the churches of his diocese on August 23, 1942. Similarly, Monsignor Pierre-Marie Théas, the bishop of Montauban, penned a letter of protest that was read throughout his diocese on August 30. Other clergy, Catholic and Protestant, voiced their opposition in September.

Forty-two thousand Jews—the great majority foreign-born and children of foreign-born parents—were deported from France to Auschwitz between March and November 1942. Thousands more had been targeted for expulsion but had eluded capture. For them, the illusion of safety was gone and the risk of arrest ever-present. They had no choice but to live in the shadows. Those whose names had not yet appeared on police lists faced a different question—was it safer for them to live inside or outside the confines of the law?

In November, the fate of thousands of Jews in France was altered by a situation no one could have predicted. On the eighth day of the month, the Allies landed in French North Africa. To thwart an Allied invasion from the south, German troops occupied most of the Unoccupied Zone. Germany ceded the southeast part of France to their Axis partner Italy. The Italian Occupation Zone extended from the Côte d'Azur on the south to Switzerland on the north. Its western boundary originally followed the Rhône River, but it was pushed eastward in several places when the German High Command refused to cede control of Lyon, Marseille, and other key cities along the river. The territory placed in the hands of the Italians included all of seven departments (the Alpes-Maritimes, Var, Basses-Alpes, Haute-Alpes, Drôme, Savoie, and Haute-Savoie), most of two others (the Vaucluse and Isère), and a small part of the Ain.

French officials in Vichy were rankled by this latest development. Italy had longstanding claims on part of the French territory they now occupied, and they had sacrificed nothing to gain this advantage. From the beginning, communication between Italian and French authorities was poor. Instead of developing working relationships, the two sides became locked in a struggle to demonstrate their sovereignty over day-to-day matters. One such matter was the fate of Jews. In early December 1942, the French government in Vichy issued several new anti-Jewish measures. One instructed department prefects to remove all Jews who had entered the country after January 1, 1938, from areas within thirty kilometers (approximately nineteen miles) of the coast. This was deemed necessary for security reasons; years of anti-Semitic propaganda had implanted the notion that Jews were Communists, leftists, subversives, and enemy aliens who posed a major threat.

The presence of foreign-born Jews in the cities and towns along the Côte d'Azur had long irritated French and German officials. Nice in particular had attracted many recent émigrés as well as a cadre of prominent Jewish writers, journalists, and artists who had lived in Paris prior to the German Occupation. Some of the foreigners were East European Orthodox Jews whose appearance clearly marked them as outsiders. Zanvel Diamant, a Yiddish writer who lived in Nice during the war, noted the irony of the situation:

> While all over Europe Jews were subjected to terrible persecution and they had to conceal themselves under assumed Aryan papers, the French Riviéra, the very center of fascism and collaborationism, where all the new French antisemitic and fascist organizations had their general staffs and propaganda machinery, presented a peculiar spectacle. Here one could see rabbis in their traditional apparel walking through the streets, here one could listen to Talmudic discussions and hear the old tunes of Hebrew prayer and Talmudic study.

Marcel Ribière, the prefect of the Alpes-Maritimes Department, in which Nice is situated, was, in the words of historian Daniel Carpi, one of the "faithful followers of the Vichy regime." In December 1942, upon receiving the instructions sent from Vichy, Ribière promptly decreed that all foreign Jews prepare themselves for immediate evacuation. They were to be sent to two departments in the country's interior—the Ardèche, which was in German hands, and the Drôme, which was in Italian hands but directly bordered the German Occupation Zone. Italian officials quickly interceded, prohibiting Ribière from implementing his evacuation plan.

French officials in Vichy issued two other anti-Jewish orders that same month. One called for the conscription of foreign Jewish men between the ages of eighteen and fifty-five into special labor battalions. The other required that all Jews, including those of French nationality, report to their local police stations to have the word *juif* stamped on their identity cards and ration books. The Italians again intervened, contradicting these orders and asserting their exclusive right to determine what measures were to be applied to Jews. Strangely enough, in Vichy France, the fortunes of Jews and those of Fascist Italy had fallen into alignment.

What would have happened if this had not been the case, if the interests of the Italian government had diverged from those of the Jews? Would the Italians have allowed the French police to seize Jews living in the Italian Occupation Zone and hand them over to the Germans? Would they themselves have taken on the task? This is impossible to say. What can be said is that Italian officials, civilian and military, were relieved to have a pretext for not engaging in the dirty business of hunting down, arresting, interning, and deporting Jews. Eyewitness reports and diplomatic communiqués about the fate of Jews "resettled in the East" had crossed the desks of Italian officials. They alleged that the Nazis were conducting mass murder on an unprecedented scale. Although it was too early to confirm the accuracy of these accounts, it was also too late to dismiss them as rumor. The eyewitness accounts of deportations carried out by the French police during the previous summer and fall had been enough to turn the stomachs of Italian officials. Italy had interned some of its own Jewish citizens in camps, but conditions in those camps were generally tolerable and prisoners were not threatened with deportation. Unlike the French, the Italians did not yet have Jewish blood on their hands, and they preferred to keep it that way.

In the early months of 1943, French and German officials in Vichy, Paris, Berlin, and Rome were preoccupied with the subject of Jews living in the Italian Occupation Zone. Vichy officials complained to German officials in Paris; they, in turn, contacted their superiors in Berlin; Berlin dispatched its diplomats to Rome to confront officials in the Italian Foreign Ministry. Foreign ministry officials insisted that troops stationed in France had already begun the work of rounding up Jews and concentrating them in locations under surveillance. Italian military commanders corroborated these assertions. Numerous meetings and communiqués were exchanged, but, rather than clarifying the situation, they obfuscated it. The Germans did not know how much, if any, truth there was to the Italian claim that they were "concentrating" Jews.

As winter turned to spring, two facts became eminently clear and deeply troubling to the Germans: their ally was not helping them fill the deportation trains, and Jews from all over France were making their way to the Italian Occupation Zone. According to Renée Poznanski, a historian who has chronicled Jewish daily life under the Occupation, word that Jews would find safe haven in the Italian Occupation Zone "spread like wildfire." As Jews from all parts of France and beyond made their way to Nice, Cannes, Grenoble, and Chambéry, the Jewish population in the Italian Occupation Zone rose to somewhere in the neighborhood of 25,000 to 30,000. One Jewish leader called it the "new Land of Canaan." SS-Obersturmführer Heinz Röthke, chief of the Judenreferat in France, used the same metaphor, writing, "The Italian zone of influence, particularly the Côte d'Azur, has become the Promised Land for the Jews in France."

In March, Italian Foreign Ministry officials decided on a course of action intended to placate their ally, at least for the time being, and they convinced il Duce to go along with it. To satisfy German demands, jurisdiction over matters pertaining to Jews in the Italian Occupation Zone was transferred from the army to the Polizia Razziale, the Race Police. Under the direction of Inspector General Guido Lospinoso, the Race Police were to oversee the transfer of foreigners away from the French Riviera to places located at least one hundred kilometers inland.

The Inspector General arrived in Nice on March 20 and immediately met with representatives of a Jewish refugee aid organization called the Comité Dubouchage (Dubouchage Committee). (The name, informally adopted, derived from the fact that the committee met in a building at number 24 on the boulevard Dubouchage.) The committee counted among its members several of the most prominent Jewish leaders in France. Joseph Fischer, the chairman of the Keren Kayemeth Le-Israel (KKL; Jewish National Fund) in France, was in charge of the Dubouchage Committee's Political Commission, which worked in cooperation with the occupying authorities. (Joseph Fischer later went by the name Joseph Ariel.) Dr. Vidal Modiano, a prominent surgeon and Zionist leader, directed the Social Commission, responsible for assisting the refugees (e.g., locating accommodations, supplying needed funds, and procuring legal documents). The committee's membership also included Nahum Hermann, head of the Keren Hayesod (the Foundation Fund for Palestine, associated with the World Zionist Organization) and Jules (*aka* Dika) Jefroykin, one of two representatives of the "Joint," the American Jewish Joint Distribution Committee, in France. Several of the Committee's leaders were also active in the affairs of the Fédération des sociétés juives de France (FSJF; Federation of Jewish Societies of France), the main umbrella organization of Jewish immigrant societies in France.

The Fate of Others

By the time Inspector General Guido Lospinoso arrived in March, the Dubouchage Committee and Italian officials stationed in Nice had developed a close, cordial working relationship. Lospinoso sought the committee's help in transferring foreigners away from the coast. The committee took on the tasks of preparing lists of Jews to be relocated and of hiring buses to transport them. (The Italian army, beset by shortages of fuel and spare truck parts, was not in a position to provide transportation.) Lospinoso traveled outside of Nice to select towns that would receive Jews. He was predisposed to choose locations in the Haute-Savoie. That department, which borders Switzerland and Italy, was not easily accessible to German troops. Some of its towns were ski resorts whose lodgings were scarcely utilized during wartime conditions. Lospinoso designated Saint-Gervais-les-Bains and Megève, two neighboring towns at the foot of Mont Blanc, to be the principal centers of forced residence. Small numbers of people were also to be relocated to several towns much closer to Nice: Saint-Martin-Vésubie, Venanson, Castellane, Barcelonnette, Vence, and Moustiers-Sainte-Marie.

On April 8, Jews gathered on the busy boulevard Dubouchage in the center of Nice to board the first buses bound for Megève. The sidewalks were crowded with those preparing to depart and those who had come to see them off. The air was filled with apprehension and excitement. No one knew what lay in store. But it was the season of the Exodus—amidst the hubbub, vendors were busy selling *le pain azyme,* unleavened bread—and, as they prepared to make their own small exodus, they were hopeful.

2. *Little Tel Aviv*

By the first or second week of May 1943, les Saint-Gervolains, the people of Saint-Gervais, had become attuned to the sounds that heralded the arrival of new busloads of Jewish refugees. The long distance buses came from the south, through Megève. Along the avenue de Mont Arbois, which tilts toward the center of the town, the rumbling of diesel engines mingled with the torturous sounds of braking to dispel the silence of the evening. In second story bedrooms, children climbed out of their beds and pressed their faces to the windows, hoping to catch a glimpse. The braking crescendoed as the buses negotiated a hairpin turn. Like slow beasts, the vehicles hunkered down the hill that runs by the *Hôtel de ville,* the city hall. They stopped on the avenue du Mont Paccard, their motors left to grumble for a time before being cut. A moment of silence before the doors opened. Then a sort of distant commotion, sounds one could learn to ignore or to distinguish. A baby's cry. Voices speaking in unfamiliar tongues. Shouts of *Grazie! Grazie!* to the handsome, young Carabinieri—they had convoyed with them in their army jeeps, rifles ready, to ensure their safety—before they drove off.

The trip between Nice and Saint-Gervais was an all-day ordeal. Although it would have been easier to have taken the train, that mode of transportation would have been far too dangerous; the rail line passed through Lyon, a city filled with German troops. Instead, the buses carried them along the route Napoleon, a road not built for buses but for motorcars, preferably those with lots of horsepower to climb the mountains. In happier times, motoring along this road would have been "an extraordinary tourist experience."

The passengers filed off the bus on stiff legs, laden with bags and bundles, draped in children collapsed beneath the weight of sleep. The night air of Saint-Gervais was much colder than the sunny city they had left that morning. The men pulled the tarpaulin from the rooftop cargo, a heap of battered, bulging suitcases restrained by cords and belts. Each suitcase was filled with the remnants of lives once so ordinary that they now seemed unbelievable. Each was claimed by a pair of hands. The passengers waited, knee deep in baggage. To one watching the scene from a nearby window, it must have looked as if they were wading in a dark river.

The new arrivals were young and old. Some were in groups; some alone. Some were whole families that had managed to stay together despite long odds. Others

Mila Racine, Nice, 1943. Photo courtesy of Racine Family.

were bits of families that had been broken apart. Few had lived in France before the war; they were refugees from Poland, Austria, Germany, Hungary, Czechoslovakia, Greece, Belgium, Luxembourg, everywhere. Few were fluent in French. Few had their own means of financial support, their life savings having run out months or years earlier. Few were familiar with French life outside of the cities. The dark center of Saint-Gervais seemed like the middle of nowhere.

On one of those nights, a young woman descended from the bus and waded into the dark river. But for a younger sister, she had no family members in the crowd. She was stylishly dressed. Her dark brown hair was pulled back in a French braided bun. She spoke French without the trace of an accent. Her family had emigrated from Moscow to Paris when she was six years old, and she had lived most of her life in the City of Light. She had also spent many months in forced residence in Luchon, a small town in the Pyrenees. Stepping out of the bus and onto the pavement of Saint-Gervais, she felt perfectly at home. The air was cold and pure; the stillness, enveloping. As the stars twinkled high above, she spoke with the others to assuage their fears. They listened to her. She had a melodious voice and a heart-shaped face. The older ones looked upon her like a grown daughter, and the younger ones, like an older sister. Her given name was Myriam, but they called her Mila.

A man stood on something that raised him up out of the dark river so that all could see and hear. Clutching a list, he shouted out the name of a hotel, *pension* (boardinghouse), or chalet. It could have been the Hotel Victoria, Les Capucines, the Hotel Robinson, or the Chalet Savoyard. Then he shouted out names of those in the crowd. When he finished, everyone knew the name of the place they were to call home.

Carrying whatever baggage they had brought with them, Mila, her sister, Sacha, and a knot of several other young men and women trudged back up the avenue du Mont d'Arbois to the hairpin turn. Instead of veering to the right and following the road back to Megève, they stayed to the left and followed the sign that pointed to Les Pratz. Leaving the sleeping town behind, they walked along the crest of a lonely hill. Perhaps they sang. Mila liked to sing when she walked; walking and singing went hand in hand. Finally, they arrived at a hotel called the Val Joly, the Pretty Valley. Built in the style of a chalet, its steeply pitched roof and muscular eaves promised protection from winter snows. The sisters climbed the narrow staircase to a room on the top floor, just beneath the eaves.

~

Before the buses and the suitcases and the reading of the list, there was only Joseph Kott and his wife, Chava. They had left their home in Roanne and come to Saint-Gervais at the request of their friend Marc Jarblum, the head of the FSJF. The Federation oversaw Saint-Gervais and the other centers of forced residence set up in the Italian Occupation Zone. In their cryptic letters and reports, Jewish

Hôtel Val Joly, Saint-Gervais-les-Bains, October 2003. Photo by N. Lefenfeld.

leaders would often refer to the organization as "Tante Feder" ("Aunt Feder") or simply "Feder." From Switzerland, where he had taken refuge, Jarblum had contacted Joseph Kott and asked him if he would be willing to take charge of a new center of forced residence.

The Italian Army had requisitioned the Villa du Mont Joly, a house on the rue de la Comtesse, for their local headquarters. One day in April, Joseph went there to receive his instructions. Tall young men with rifles slung over their shoulders filled the dim interior. They belonged to an elite sharpshooter corps known as the Bersaglieri. Like giants, they strode in and out, towering over Joseph, who was short and muscular and had broad, square shoulders. The most distinctive thing about them was their gray-green hats, which sprouted thick plumes of shiny, black capercaillie feathers.

Joseph was forty years old. His hair, untouched by gray, was combed straight back from his forehead. His eyes were dark, his gaze intent. The instructions he received from the man in charge, Captain Tuglio, were simple: Joseph and his people were persons under surveillance, and they had to adhere to certain rules. They had to register at the Italian headquarters on the rue de la Comtesse each day. They also had to observe an evening curfew and remain within the commune of Saint-Gervais. Anyone wanting to venture outside of the commune

Rue de la Comtesse, Saint-Gervais-les-Bains, with Villa du Mont Joly (taller of two buildings shown), September 2004. Photo by N. Lefenfeld.

had to first obtain a permit. The captain had requisitioned the Hôtel Eden, on the rue du Berchat, for Monsieur Kott to use as a headquarters. If requested, he would requisition lodgings for all those due to arrive.

The Kotts settled into a room in the Eden. It was the middle of April. Spring was performing a slow magic act, and Joseph and Chava had balcony seats. Spread out far below, the foothills of the Arve River valley turned from muddy brown to luscious green. The white snow cover of the Aravis Mountains receded little by little to reveal a blue-gray limestone.

There was not much time to make decisions; the first buses would be arriving shortly. Joseph conversed with proprietors in the dim interiors of their hotels, vacant and shuttered. The eerie quiet seemed to amplify each sound. The ticking of a clock. The turning of a key in a lock. The enumeration of business losses suffered since the war began. He thought of his own business in Roanne, a knitwear factory, which Vichy officials had taken from him because he was Jewish and placed in the hands of a provisional administrator. He decided it would be best to pay rent to proprietors for the use of their lodgings instead of having them requisitioned. Hotel rooms in the bourg, the center of the town, would run 70 to 120 francs per day; those on the outskirts, a bit less. He scribbled notes, made

00636

Carte d'identité

Nom : Kott

Prénoms : Joseph

Profession : Industriel

Né le 28 Octobre 1903

SIGNALEMENT

Taille :

Cheveux :

Front :

Yeux :

Sourcils :

Signes particuliers :

Nez :

Bouche :

Barbe :

Visage :

Teint :

— 9 JUIN 1943

Empreintes digitales

Le Titulaire,

Kott

Les Témoins, certificateurs d'identité civile,

Vu pour la légalisation des signatures de M.M. Chambel et Béguin

Le Maire,

Le 9 Juin 1943

Identity card of Joseph Kott dated June 9, 1943. Photo courtesy of Kott Family.

lists of rooms available, and prepared a budget. He was to receive one thousand francs per month from the Federation to support each indigent adult.

The buses began arriving. By night, a dark river washed over the pavement. By day, one hotel and then another and another came to life, as if awakened from a long sleep. Windows and balcony doors were flung open to the May breezes. Walking down a street, one couldn't help but hear a door closing, a mother calling to a child, someone laughing. A variety of smaller lodgings, scattered across the nearby hills like alpine gentians, were also opened to the refugees. Their very names evoked the promise of a mountain refuge: La Villa des Glaciers, Les Rhododendrons, Fleurs des Alpes. Some were *pensions* that welcomed ten or twenty boarders. Others were chalets and villas given over to one or two or three families. Some of the Saint-Gervolains found space within their own homes for the newcomers. The Berlioz family, which lived in the bourg, made room for the Bratslawski family. The Orset family, in Les Champs on the route des Contamines, took in the Kalischmann family.

By the end of May, the Jewish refugee community in Saint-Gervais numbered approximately 850. Most were parents with children; the names of 350 children younger than eighteen would be recorded in a special card index. Some of the parents had aged parents or other relatives who depended on them. They had spent so much time running; now, they sat. They sat in canteens, on park benches, in hotel reception areas, and on the stately portico of the Hôtel Eden. They tried not to think about what had been left behind or what lay ahead. They thought about their shoes, which were worn and in need of repair. They thought about the bones of their young children. Had they suffered permanent damage from the days and weeks when they had no milk? What a relief it was to watch them drain their glasses of Ovaltine! They spoke of small, providential acts of kindness, the memory of which sometimes made their throats constrict and their eyes well up. The offer of a spare bed on a freezing winter night. A loaf of bread placed unexpectedly in their hands.

Hôtel Les Capucines (today Alpin-Capucines), Saint-Gervais-les-Bains, October 2003. Photo by N. Lefenfeld.

The canteen in the Hôtel Eden was one of several canteens organized to feed the refugees living in hotels and boardinghouses. Twice a day, they came to eat and talk, read a scrap of newspaper, or listen to someone translate what the paper said. They took turns working in the canteens: hauling crates of produce, sacks of flour, and heavy cans of oil; peeling potatoes and, on a lucky day, slicing carrots; mixing up great batches of cabbage soup; carefully lading out the steaming soup; washing dishes and cutlery, pots and pans; and clearing tables. The meals they ate were simple but nourishing. The tongues that spoke so many different languages all knew the language of hunger. As they shared their meals, they also shared recipes, stories, and memories of dishes savored—the best kreplach ever, Mother's noodle kugel, Bubbe's gefilte fish, stuffed kishkas, cheese blintzes, apple cake, meat knishes, kasha varnishkes.

Sometimes, when the refugees came to take their meals, they would see Joseph meeting with the members of the Saint-Gervais Committee. Comprised of representatives whom the refugees had elected, the committee oversaw the day-to-day affairs of the Jewish community and served as its liaison with Italian and French officials. Most committee members were middle-aged men dressed in dark suits with thinning hair. One had a little mustache that looked a bit like Hitler's and walked around with a pipe sticking out of his mouth. Years later, their faces and

Former Hôtel Eden (today the Home Savoyard), Saint-Gervais-les-Bains, September 2004. Photo by N. Lefenfeld.

torsos, some with their arms crossed over their chests, would be frozen in black and white photographs but their names would be lost.

On the opposite side of town, in the hotel designated the "youth center," the canteen was crowded and noisy. Young men and women ate, talked, laughed, argued, flirted, smoked cigarettes, played cards, wrote letters, and lingered over coffee. They were kids in their late teens and early twenties. Many of them lived here at the Val Joly. Others boarded in *pensions* and private homes, but it was here that they felt most at home and here that they came to take their meals.

They were like dust blown in from the four corners of Europe. Dress, appearance, and language clearly marked some as foreigners. Some spoke French but with a thick Polish or German accent. Others struggled with the rudiments of a new language. Some had been on their own for months or years, their parents having been arrested or deported or having sent them away toward what they hoped was safety. They grew up quickly, learned to manage, took on new names, tried to blend in, tried to do nothing that would let slip the fact that they were Jewish. In Saint-Gervais, they revealed to one another their real names and the names of the towns in which they had been born. They spoke of adventures they had had along the way and of anxieties about family members left behind.

They were off by themselves at the Val Joly, and, of course, they preferred it that way. It did not take long for them to organize work crews and develop a job roster. The hotel's kitchen was tiny; they set up a long table outdoors, and, each morning, fifteen or twenty people would gather to peel, clean, and chop.

~

In some of the centers of forced residence during the war, the Jewish outsiders encountered a chilly or even hostile reception. It is not difficult to find letters in the departmental archives that register complaints about them. Frequently, the letters contend that the Jews are trading on the black market. Sometimes, they complain about rich Jews who spend their days idly sitting in cafés and who bid up prices for scarce commodities. There are cases where hostility rose to such a level that the departmental authorities transferred them out.

It must have seemed to the Saint-Gervolains that their town was flooded with refugees. In 1943, their own number probably did not exceed three thousand. The arrival of refugees swelled that number by 25 or 30 percent. Numerically and proportionately, the influx was larger than that which occurred in most other centers of forced residence. Yet, it provoked no widespread hostility. The Saint-Gervolains and the Jewish refugees lived peaceably, side by side. The mayor, Alfred Conseil, was cordial to the newcomers. Did he manifest a basic goodness that prevailed among the native people of his town? Did he set an example that influenced the behavior of others?

The mayor helped Joseph and his Saint-Gervais Committee when he could. Some refugees had lost their identity or ration cards or had left them behind when they escaped internment camps. Mayor Conseil helped the committee replace the needed documents. In a report about Saint-Gervais authored at the time of the Liberation, one observer would state unequivocally: "The relations between the Jewish Committee and the French and Italian authorities were the best all the way to the end."

~

Summer in Saint-Gervais. Rising in the morning, throwing open the window and leaning out, into the cool air, you feel as if you are living in the clouds. The lush green valley stretches out far below, as far as the eye can see. Simple white chalets with dark roofs and shutters dot the gracefully undulating hills. Here and there, a tiny curl of smoke rises from a chimney and drifts off. The air is pure and clear. In the morning, the sun's rays feel luxurious. In the afternoon, they beat down mercilessly, driving you into the shade or the icy waters of a mountain stream. You stop and listen to the distant clanging of a cowbell. When the sun goes down, the clean scent of pine resin fills the air.

For the adults, that summer in Saint-Gervais was "a relief and a respite." For the children, "a sort of paradise, a marvelous vacation."

From the beginning, Joseph Kott had a vision for this new diaspora. It was not enough to think only of basic necessities—food, clothing, and shelter. There were other needs to be met. Some of the refugees had medical problems that required attention. The children needed to be educated. The young adults needed to learn useful skills and prepare themselves, physically and mentally, for whatever lay ahead. Some needed to organize and attend worship services. Some needed to have the chance to read a book, attend a concert or a play, dance, make new friends, or find some other way to reclaim a sense of joy and humanity. Some needed the opportunity to share their talents, skills, or knowledge. Joseph understood this, and he understood what it meant to build a *kehilla,* a community, to meet these diverse needs.

Joseph had been a boy of ten, growing up in Blaszki, a village located in the Kalisz region of Poland, when one of the earliest Zionist youth movements came into being. It was 1913; the new HaShomer HaTza'ir adopted principles of the scouting movement, which had been established in England several years earlier by Robert Baden-Powell and was becoming known around the world. HaShomer HaTza'ir sought to cultivate in young Jews a strong sense of self-reliance, a love of nature, and a desire to return to the land, to agricultural pursuits. The goal of the movement was to create young *chalutzim* (pioneers) who would establish farming communities in Palestine. Like many young Polish Jews, Joseph joined the new movement.

At the age of eighteen, Joseph left his family and made *aliyah* (immigrated to Israel), settling on the Kibbutz Tel Yosef in the Lower Galilee. Life on the early kibbutzim was difficult and dangerous. The land was mostly barren, arid, and rocky, and the process of improving the soil and growing food entailed tremendous effort. The settlers were threatened by disease, especially malaria, and by the bellicosity of some Arab neighbors. At times, the young Joseph, dressed in Arab garb, patrolled the perimeter of the kibbutz on horseback. In 1925, a woman named Chava Laja Wolkowicz, also from the Kalisz region and also a member of the HaShomer HaTza'ir, arrived on the kibbutz. Joseph and Chava soon married, and, the following year, Chava gave birth to a daughter, whom they named Sara. When the baby was just a year old, Joseph contracted malaria, and he and Chava decided they must leave Palestine and seek medical treatment. They went to Lyon, France's second largest city, where Chava's uncle lived.

The Kott family would become rooted in French soil, although not in Lyon. Chava's brother, Elie, lived fifty miles northwest of the city, in Roanne. He was one of several young, unmarried Jewish men, originally from Poland, who had been lucky enough to obtain work at the Gillet-Thaon textile factory, the town's largest employer. It was essential for an immigrant to obtain a work contract, for it enabled him to secure a *permis de séjour* (residence permit) and settle down. By 1926, the Polish Jews in Roanne had a minyan. Some of the men were joined by

Left to right—Hélène Gorgiel-Sercarz, Marie Grünberg, Marianne Hartann, Alex Derczanski, Sarah Grünberg, and Maurice Grünberg, Saint-Gervais-les-Bains, Summer 1943. © Mémorial de la Shoah/CDJC, MXII_5935.

sisters or other female relatives, whom they introduced to one another. Before the end of the decade, the young Jewish community had celebrated several marriages and births.

Hailed as the lace capital of the Russian empire and having elevated embroidery to the level of high art, Kalisz, Poland, was an important textile center. Elie had an expertise in embroidery and was skilled at operating the popular new Rachel knitting machines. He was also an entrepreneur, and, in 1927, he established his own atelier (workshop). His brother-in-law Joseph had also worked in the textile industry. In 1929, Elie proposed to Joseph that he move his family to Roanne and become his business partner. Joseph accepted.

Paradoxically, it was the Great Depression that helped the new enterprise grow. The Gillet-Thaon company went bankrupt in 1930. This created an opportunity and impetus for Polish Jews in Roanne to establish their own businesses and hire their *landsmen* (people who came from the same town or region) who had lost their jobs. A new industry was born, one that became known throughout France as *"bonneterie juive roannaise,"* Jewish knitwear of Roanne. Joseph's family settled into a comfortable life and expanded; in 1933, their son Bernard was born. In 1935, Elie and Joseph dissolved their business partnership, and Joseph established his own factory. Capable and hardworking, he built a successful enterprise.

As the business grew, so too did Joseph's commitment toward building the new Jewish community, one that was from the beginning "singular and original." Other Jewish communities organized themselves around the religious predilections of their rabbis. Not so in Roanne, according to Monique Lewi, the community's biographer. "Here, from the time of its creation, the '*Kehilla*' (Community) is organized without a rabbi, without a kosher butcher, without a ritual bath, drawing its power from Jewish traditions and the Zionist ideal." Lay members, educated in their hometown *chedarim* (traditional Jewish elementary schools) led the services in the synagogue and served as instructors in the religious school.

Joseph saw himself as an emissary to those seeking to emigrate to France and to newly-arrived immigrants. He helped with the practical difficulties of resettlement—finding employment, establishing legal residence, and securing housing—and worked to integrate newcomers into the Jewish community of Roanne. He extended his hand not only to fellow *landsmen* from Poland but also to German Jews who fled their homes after Hitler came to power. In 1936, he returned to Poland to help his parents, six brothers and a sister, and numerous other family members prepare to emigrate.

When the war came, Joseph served in the French army. Not long after he returned home, the Vichy government embarked on its far-reaching program to eliminate Jews and Jewish influence from the national economy. Joseph's factory was placed in the hands of a provisional administrator. Family legend has it that the local police, acting on orders from Vichy, reluctantly arrested Joseph, whom

MJS *gdoud*, Saint-Gervais-les-Bains, Summer 1943. Mila Racine appears in center of third row, wearing dark blouse open at collar. © Mémorial de la Shoah/CDJC, MXXXIIIa_46.

they knew and liked, on two occasions. Upon being sent to arrest him a third time, one of the gendarmes was so upset—in tears, according to the story—that Chava gave him a glass of cognac to steady his nerves so that he could carry out the task. In August 1942, when massive roundups of foreign Jews in the Unoccupied Zone began, Joseph and Chava placed Sara and Bernard with a Christian family by the name of Mazeau who lived in La Bourbole, in the Puy-de-Dôme Department in southcentral France.

Although Joseph was an observant Jew, he had no religious fervor and no inclination to engage in theological debate. His raison d'être was to bring people together, care for those in need, solve problems, foster lively conversation, enjoy the company of others, laugh, and live life to the fullest. This is what he set out to do in Saint-Gervais.

It was clear to Joseph that many of the older adults had a weariness that would take some time to dissipate but that the young men and women were strong and spirited. He was determined to put their energy to good use. To help him do this, he looked to the young woman with the heart-shaped face named Mila, and he was thankful to find in her an ally. Mila was a leader and activist in the Mouvement de jeunesse sioniste (MJS; Zionist Youth Movement). She had been sent to Saint-Gervais to recruit adolescents and young adults and establish a new MJS brigade. Her assignment dovetailed perfectly with Joseph's plan.

~

It is possible that, prior to his arrival in Saint-Gervais, Joseph had never heard of the Mouvement de jeunesse sioniste. It was a nascent organization, barely a year old, formed at a Zionist congress convened in May 1942 in Montpellier. It was also a successor of sorts to the HaShomer HaTza'ir. Prior to its formation, a dozen or so Zionist youth organizations, offshoots of movements that had flourished in Eastern Europe, existed in France and competed with one another for new recruits. Simon Lévitte, a national leader of the Éclaireurs israélites de France (Jewish Scouts of France) and an ardent Zionist, organized the Montpellier congress in order to appeal for unity. The fact that the Zionist youth movement was fractured into small, ineffective groups drove him to despair. He lectured the delegates on the new facts of life: powerful forces were bent on annihilating all of them, the time for division had long passed, and they must lay aside their differences and face their enemies together. His appeal succeeded—nearly all of the delegates voted to dissolve their existing organizations and form a single, new entity, which they called the Mouvement de jeunesse sioniste. They chose Lévitte to be their leader. It was an extraordinary moment; a prominent scholar of the period, Lucien Lazare, calls it "an unprecedented instance in the history of Zionism throughout Europe."

At the time that the MJS was founded, Jewish organizations in France were going through a period of profound crisis. In December 1941, leaders learned that, in order for their organizations to operate legally, they would have to relinquish their independence and become part of the UGIF, the Jewish council established by Vichy officials in response to German demands. When the MJS was established, delegates debated whether the new entity should place itself within the framework of the UGIF or operate illegally. They chose the latter.

The new MJS was structured in *gdoudim*, Hebrew for brigades. At first, the Montpellier *gdoud* served as the organization's headquarters. After the Italian Occupation Zone was established, Simon Lévitte moved the operation to Grenoble. By the spring of 1943, the Grenoble and Nice *gdoudim* were large and well-organized.

Some of the adolescents and young adults living in Saint-Gervais had had their first contact with the MJS in Nice. Arriving in the city alone or with family members, they had been directed to the refugee center at number 24 on the boulevard Dubouchage. The Centre Dubouchage was, in the words of Zanvel Diamant, a "beehive" of activity, not only the headquarters of the Dubouchage Committee but also the main gathering place for foreign Jews. It was here that they came looking for whatever they needed—financial assistance, the address of a room to rent or a canteen that served hot meals, news about a loved one. It was also here that they socialized, held cultural programs and events, and prayed. As the *juifs* conducted their worship services in the modest Synagogue Dubouchage, the *Israélites* worshipped three blocks away, in the Grande Synagogue on the rue Gustave Deloye.

The Dubouchage Committee had allocated some space in the center to the Nice *gdoud*. It was an arrangement that made sense—the young MJS members worked hand in hand with members of the Committee, helping refugees obtain financial assistance, find lodgings and meals, and "regularize their situation." (To "regularize one's situation" was a colloquial term used to mean that an immigrant had procured documentation needed to change his or her status from that of an illegal alien to a legal resident, if only temporarily. Practically speaking, for Jewish foreigners living in the Italian Occupation Zone, regularizing one's situation meant that they would not be subject to arbitrary arrest and internment by French police and that they could apply for ration cards.) A young man named Jacques Wajntrob greeted newcomers who ventured through the door that bore the mysterious letters "MJS." To the newcomers, this leader of the Nice *gdoud* seemed thoroughly French. It was only when he conversed with them, often in Yiddish or Polish, that they learned that Jacques was born "Jankiel" in Poland and that his family had arrived in France in the early thirties.

Jacques was only twenty-three years old in 1943, but he seemed older or, at least, more settled. His wife, Léa, worked alongside him, and their baby daughter, Miriam, crawled about on the floor, sat on her mother's lap, or slept in a make-shift bassinet. Some of the teenagers and young adults who came through the door had been adrift for months or years, and they felt disoriented, despondent, and alone. Jacques empathized with them; he had suffered his share of hardships since the German Occupation began and had experienced these same feelings. He understood that, although this one might need a place to sleep and that one might need a hot meal, each and every one of them needed a sense of purpose and a feeling of self-worth. He welcomed them as fellow Jews, and he made it clear that he saw them as a resource, not a burden. Above all, he recruited them to become members of the *gdoud*, and he gave them the chance to step forward and help others.

Newcomers might also make the acquaintance of Mila Racine, seated in a corner of the office, absorbed in typing a letter or report. She was an assistant to Jacques and Léa, ready to pitch in and do whatever needed to be done. She too empathized with those who needed help. Some of the older ones reminded her of her parents and aunts and uncles, many of whom still conversed in Russian and had difficulty expressing themselves in French.

The twenty-one-year-old Sarah Grunberg joined the MJS in Nice in early 1943 and met Mila in the *gdoud's* meeting room in the Centre Dubouchage. Mila was typing a document, completely absorbed in her work. "What struck me in the first place," Grunberg recalled in a letter written six decades later, "[was] her charm, her beauty, an aristocratic grace that emanated from her being."

When the exodus arrived, Mila found herself on a bus bound for Saint-Gervais. She immediately set about recruiting members and establishing a new *gdoud,* and her efforts were successful. By early June, nearly all of the adolescents and young adults living in Saint-Gervais identified themselves with the MJS. The Val Joly served as their de facto *gdoud* headquarters.

~

In late May or early June, Joseph Kott and the Saint-Gervais Committee "rounded up all the youths" and held a meeting "on a little hill off Main street." He called upon the young people to take a very active part in building the community. Their immediate priority was to organize and open a school. Almost without exception, the refugee children had had their schooling interrupted because their families had been constantly on the move. Mila had agreed to oversee this effort. Sarah Bomberg, a *jardinière diplomée* (certified kindergarten teacher), and Esther Veissid, a teaching assistant, took charge of the youngest children, those between 2 ½ and 7. Several other young women, including Hélène Gorgiel-Sercarz, volunteered to be teachers. The Saint-Gervais Committee was given the use of a wooden barracks adjacent to the *patinoire,* the winter skating rink. Before long, the dressing rooms normally used by the hockey players and "Sunday skaters" had been turned into classrooms.

Oeuvre de secours aux enfants (OSE, pronounced oh-zeh), a prominent child welfare organization, sent a twenty-two-year-old named Armand Rein to Saint-Gervais to establish what they called a medical-social center. He and the Saint-Gervais Committee found ways to supplement the meager diets of the children. They also enlisted the services of four refugees who were physicians, one of whom was a cardiologist and another a dermatologist. The refugee doctors could not legally practice in France. However, local doctors made it possible for them to circumvent this difficulty by authorizing what were referred to as visits of *dépistage*—the tracking down of illness—and by signing their prescriptions.

ORT, an international vocational training organization, opened a half dozen or so ateliers, and some of the teenagers and young adults worked as apprentices. The woodworkers built desks and chairs for the students to use in their makeshift classrooms. The shoemakers, dressmakers, and tailors recycled and repaired whatever they were brought. In this time of strict rationing, it was nearly impossible to obtain a new pair of shoes or a new article of clothing. Nothing could be wasted; every item had to be used to the end of its days. Some youths worked the fields owned by local farmers or attended to kitchen gardens, raising fruits and vegetables to feed the refugees.

Group dancing the hora, Saint-Gervais-les-Bains, Summer 1943. Mila Racine appears on the right, wearing a checked skirt. Photo courtesy of Strosberg Family. The young man to the left of Mila—whose waistband Mila has in her grip—is Isy Leuwenkroon, father of Eliane Strosberg.

For the adolescents and young adults, it was a time that was both intoxicating and sobering. Like the adults, they understood that these tranquil moments were transitory and that they must savor them. They also knew that this was their last chance to grow up and grow strong before the final trials and that they must take advantage of it. At the Val Joly, they took turns presenting lectures on diverse subjects—Jewish history, modern Zionism, the geography of Palestine, mathematics, chemistry, and philosophy. Sometimes, after the dinner dishes were cleared away, they would crowd into the dining room to see a skit or hear a musical program. Or they would go outside on the grass, where Mila would teach them Hebrew songs or a new variation on the hora. Late at night, on the balcony, some played chess or taught each other card games, such as blackjack. Some met their future husbands and wives. Some had their hearts broken. Always, there was discussion about the future. The road ahead forked, and they argued about which direction to take. Should they join one of the Resistance groups, take up arms against the Germans and their French collaborators, and work for the liberation of France? Or should they devote themselves to aiding and rescuing their fellow Jews?

By July, the little diaspora had firmly rooted itself in the rocky mountain soil. The situation for the refugees was far from ideal, but they made do with what they had. Each was safe and sound; each had a bed, enough food to get by, and, if needed, medical care. They had a leader, Joseph, whom they called "the king of Saint-Gervais." They had a committee responsible for resolving their disputes and establishing rules and regulations. They had a school for the children to attend and vocational workshops for the adolescents and young adults. They had even organized a synagogue. The Committee had rented the villa des Genêts, across from the Hôtel Eden, and, on Shabbat, the chanting of Hebrew prayers filled the narrow rue du Berchat. A report prepared for Marc Jarblum summed up the situation: "But what is the most comforting over there is the atmosphere. It is a veritable Kwutsa. [*Kwutsa* refers to a harmonious gathering and comes from the same Hebrew root as kibbutz.] The people have an air of contentment." The refugees shared Joseph's vision of a *kehilla,* and they called their community Little Tel Aviv.

It was no secret to anyone that it was a precarious existence. A contemporaneous report quotes an unidentified member of the refugee community summing up his or her impressions of life in Saint-Gervais.

> Survivors on the high sea. The sea is forever surging; an iceberg is reported to be nearby. The collision might happen in one instant or another but it also might be avoided. Uncertainty and anxiety. If the collision happens, it may be terrible. It will be every-man-for-himself or an organized rescue. That depends on many factors. But the captain on board and the crew have but one end: TO KEEP GOING! to assure until the final moments a little bit of orders [sic] and joy for the passengers.

3. *Pas de l'Échelle*

Late in the evening of July 25, 1943, Vittorio Emanuele III, the King of Italy, backed by the Fascist Grand Council and the Army, deposed and arrested Mussolini. The king called on Marshal Pietro Badoglio, a well-known army general, to form a new government. In Nice, Jewish refugees, French citizens, and even Italian soldiers greeted the news with wild jubilation. For twenty-four hours, they allowed themselves to indulge in the wishful thinking that the fall of Mussolini heralded the end of the war. They celebrated throughout the day and night, but, the next morning, many adopted a more sober view as they recognized the grave danger now present.

The situation in Italy had become destabilized and unpredictable. On July 10, the Allies had launched one of the largest operations of the war—the invasion of Sicily. Now, as the month drew to a close, they were engaged in a bloody battle for this rocky island just two and a half miles from the toe of Italy's boot. The strategic importance of the island was readily apparent: once Axis forces were driven out of Sicily, the Allies would use it to launch their invasion of the Italian peninsula.

No one knew how events would unfold or what would happen in the Italian Occupation Zone. It seemed likely that the Italian army would withdraw from all or part of the territory it now occupied in France, but no one knew when or how this would occur. Although the situation was unsettling for many who lived in the Italian Occupation Zone, it was particularly perilous for Jews. What would happen to them? Would they fall into the hands of German and French authorities, eager to arrest and deport them? Would they be allowed to retreat along with Italian soldiers and remain under their protection?

As August began, anxiety was high among Jews living in Saint-Gervais, Megève, and other centers of forced residence established by the Italian authorities. Joseph Kott and the members of his committee kept in close contact with the leaders of the Dubouchage Committee. They waited to receive instructions about when the refugees should evacuate Saint-Gervais and where they should go. Believing that their chances for survival were best if they remained in Italian hands, they sought assurances from Italian officials that they would not be left behind when their soldiers withdrew from all or part of the French territory they occupied.

By the third week in August, a plan was in place. In negotiations with its Axis partner, Italy had agreed to withdraw from most of its occupation zone. It would hold onto the eastern half of the Alpes-Maritimes, east of the Var and Tinée

Rivers. The area was small in size, but it included the city of Nice and Italian officials felt it to be of strategic and political importance. The fate of the Jews living under the protection of the Italian Army did not enter into the negotiations about troop withdrawal. Nevertheless, Italian officials did not want the Jews to fall into German hands, and the agreement that they negotiated seemed to offer a means of protecting them. Most of the Jews in the Italian Occupation Zone lived in Nice. Of the several centers of forced residence to which Jews had been sent, Saint-Gervais and Megève were of greatest concern: these two centers were far from the area slated to remain in Italian hands and they had become home to large numbers of Jews. In the ensuing days, members of the Dubouchage Committee would begin working with Guido Lospinoso and his staff to plan for the orderly transfer of the refugees to towns in what they called the new Italian zone. Jews living in Saint-Gervais were to be transferred to Saint-Martin-Vésubie and Venanson; those in Megève, to Peira Cava.

All along, there was discussion about Switzerland, the tiny nation with the long tradition of taking in the dispossessed, dislocated, and dispersed of Europe. It was so tantalizingly close to Saint-Gervais. Why didn't the Jews seek refuge there? The following discussion briefly addresses Swiss policies regarding acceptance or turning back of Jews who entered the country illegally during the war. For a fuller discussion of this complex subject, the reader is referred to Appendix 1.

Throughout the war, Jews had attempted to enter Switzerland by any means possible in order to escape Nazi persecution. Simply setting foot on Swiss soil was a difficult and dangerous undertaking. Where the terrain was flat, multiple rows of barbed wire impeded passage. One could avoid the barbed wire barrier by going on foot over the mountains, but, even for the able-bodied, mountain climbing was treacherous in the summer and all but impossible the rest of the year. If apprehended in France while trying to cross illegally, one ran the risk of arrest and deportation.

Did those who made it across the Swiss border find the refuge they had sought? Some did and some did not. Some were sent back across the border immediately or in the days, weeks, or months that followed, a practice that French speakers referred to as *refoulement* (driving back). During the first two years of the Occupation, it was nearly impossible to predict who would be sent back and who would be allowed to stay. Swiss cantonal authorities interpreted and enforced Swiss Federal directives as they saw fit. Consequently, the treatment of Jewish refugees varied from one canton to another and from one time period to another.

A turning point came in the middle of August 1942. Thousands of foreign Jews in France were being rounded up and deported. Desperate, without options, many tried to cross the Swiss border. Swiss Federal authorities issued a clear directive to all cantons that, henceforth, the border was closed to civilian refugees and asylum would be granted only to military personnel (deserters and escaped prisoners of war) and political refugees. It went so far as to say, "Those who only took flight because of their race—Jews, for example—should not be considered political refugees." The directive had, in fact, been issued for the express purpose of keeping Jews out.

The closure of the border shocked many Swiss citizens and elicited a storm of protest. Soon afterward, in response to public outcry, the policy was liberalized to grant exception to so-called hardship cases. The criteria for such cases were clearly defined: unaccompanied children younger than sixteen, parents with their own children younger than sixteen, the sick, pregnant women, elderly persons over sixty-five, those with immediate family members living in Switzerland, and those with other close ties to the country. Just a few months later, after public outcry had died down, the directive was modified yet again, this time tightening the criterion with respect to families with children. Now, only parents accompanying children younger than six years old were to be allowed to stay. Although the closure of the border was not a welcome development for Jews fleeing persecution, it did have one unintended, beneficial consequence: it made clear who would be allowed to remain in Switzerland and who would be sent back. The uncertainty that had existed up until this time was gone.

The criteria regarding acceptance and *refoulement* of refugees were still in effect in August 1943, when those responsible for Jewish refugees living in Saint-Gervais and Megève considered their options. (One slight change had been made in July 1943: the age limit for unaccompanied girls had been raised from sixteen to eighteen.) Jewish leaders were well-acquainted with the Swiss criteria. They knew that unaccompanied children and families with very young children would not be sent back to France. They also knew how dangerous it was to attempt a border crossing. By the middle of the month, Italian soldiers had already begun to pull back from the far reaches of their occupation zone, and German troops had been spotted in the Haute-Savoie.

One Jewish organization had a considerable amount of experience in smuggling Jewish children from France into Switzerland. OSE had first entered into this type of illegal activity in the fall of 1942. Its early efforts were small-scale and sporadic: once or twice each month, one or two or three children would be passed across the border. There were grave risks involved; the French troops who patrolled the border did not shrink from arresting and deporting children who fell into their hands.

In late December 1942 and early January 1943, Italian soldiers replaced the French troops along the border. This removed the risk involved in trying to cross illegally because the Italians would not arrest and deport the children. OSE directors decided to expand the smuggling operation. On February 22, 1943, the "first true OSE convoy," consisting of ten children, crossed the border. Between March 15 and May 7, seven more convoys, comprising seventy-three children, followed. May, June, and July 1943 would have been a propitious time to transfer Jewish children from France to Switzerland. However, for reasons that remain unknown, OSE shut down its smuggling operation after the first week in May.

Just what was this organization that called itself OSE, and how did it end up in this dangerous line of work? When the organization was founded in Russia in 1912, "OSE" stood for Obshchestvo sdravochraneniya evreev, Society for the Health of the Jewish Population. In the aftermath of the Russian Revolution, the organization relocated to Berlin. When Hitler came to power, it moved again—this time to Paris—keeping its acronym but adopting a new name, Oeuvre de secours aux enfants, loosely translated as Children's Rescue Network. (The French word *ose* means dare.)

Paris in the thirties was home to thousands of Jewish families who were recent immigrants. For many, life was extremely hard and poverty the general rule. Lacking residence and employment permits, they could not seek salaried jobs in factories or other enterprises but had to get by doing piecework in their homes and turning to soup kitchens and other forms of charity. OSE carved out a role for itself ministering to the health needs of immigrant children, dispensing medical care, and teaching proper hygiene, nutrition, and disease prevention.

In 1938, OSE significantly broadened its mission and expanded its operations. The organization began receiving Jewish children sent to Paris from parents in Germany and Austria. OSE leaders made the decision to house the children collectively. By August 1939, it had established four *maisons d'enfants* (children's homes) in and around Paris—Les Tourelles, La Villa Chesnaie, La Petite Colonie, and Villa Helvetia. The declaration of war on September 1, 1939, engendered fear among the population that Paris would be subjected to aerial bombardments. OSE leaders decided it would be more prudent to house children away from the capital. Between November 1939 and June 1940, it hurriedly opened six children's homes in the southcentral part of the country; three of the six—Le Masgelier, Chabannes, and Chaumont—were châteaux in the department of the Creuse. Even before the organization had a chance to transfer the refugee children out of Greater Paris to the newly established homes, some beds were filled by children orphaned, abandoned, or turned over by parents living in France.

The need for such facilities escalated once the German Occupation began and Jews were subjected to discrimination, persecution, and arbitrary arrest and internment. OSE moved quickly to open as many new children's homes as possible. By August 1942, it had fourteen children's homes under its direct control, and these homes sheltered approximately nine hundred children. Still, the need exceeded the supply, and some children were placed with foster families and in orphanages. During the first two years of the Occupation, OSE operated in the open and within the confines of the law.

The situation changed dramatically in the summer of 1942. During the massive Vel d'Hiv roundup in Paris in July, four thousand children were swept up and deported. In the Unoccupied Zone in August and September, children were also seized; some escaped deportation and some did not. OSE officials then initiated the creation of a secret, underground network responsible for making Jewish children "disappear" from sight by placing them, under Aryan identities, with Christian families and in institutions. Led by Georges Garel, a newcomer to rescue work and a man completely unknown to government officials, the network became known as the *réseau* Garel (Garel network).

In late 1942, some OSE leaders called for the immediate closure of the children's homes and dispersal of the children. It was, they believed, only a matter of time before German and French officials came after the wards in the homes. Other OSE leaders cautioned against taking such drastic action or indeed making any conspicuous changes. They feared drawing the attention of authorities, who might choose to investigate and consequently uncover the existence of the *réseau Garel*. Advocates of maintaining the status quo won out, and most of the children's homes continued to operate as before.

By the middle of 1943, the threat to all Jews living in France, regardless of nationality or age, had escalated. The distinction between *Israélite* and *juif* mattered little to German authorities; they were anxious to arrest and deport all Jews. Authorities had begun raiding children's homes operated by the UGIF in and around Paris. The number of Jewish children that needed to "disappear" from view kept growing; and, at the same time, it was becoming more difficult to locate new host families and institutions. Members of other Jewish organizations who had worked in cooperation with OSE to hide Jewish children—notably the Rue Amelot Committee—had been arrested in June 1943, increasing the burden on the shoulders of those who remained. The prospect of losing the safe haven that had existed in the Italian Occupation Zone threatened to compound these difficulties.

OSE leaders decided to resume smuggling children into Switzerland and to step up the pace, organizing larger convoys and passing them across the border in more rapid succession. On July 29, four days after the fall of Mussolini, OSE passed a convoy of twelve children across the Swiss border at the town of Hermance, on Lake Geneva. The organization sent three more convoys into Switzerland during the second week of August.

This is the point in time that the MJS entered the picture. Andrée Salomon, the head of the social service branch of OSE, was in communication with Simon Lévitte, the leader and soul of the MJS. The two agreed that the MJS would organize a second, separate network to smuggle children across the border. Their first order of business would be to evacuate children who were living in Saint-Gervais and whose parents agreed to relinquish them. At the same time, several young OSE workers would seek to accomplish the same thing in Megève. After having evacuated children from Saint-Gervais, the new (MJS) *réseau* would continue to work parallel to the older (OSE) *réseau*, smuggling Jewish children brought to it from other parts of France.

It is not known whether the idea to establish a second *réseau* originated with leaders of OSE or the MJS. By the middle of 1943, OSE bore a weighty responsibility: approximately four thousand children had been entrusted to it. The organization was using all possible means, legal and illegal, to maintain and safeguard their wards. Regardless of whether Salomon or Lévitte first suggested the establishment of a second *réseau*, OSE leaders would have welcomed the additional help.

~

MJS leaders and militants had demonstrated that they were willing to engage in illegal rescue activities and that they could do so admirably. One need not look further than the work of the Grenoble *gdoud* in manufacturing false papers to see how resourceful, reliable, and discreet they were. Toto Giniewski, an MJS leader and doctoral student in chemistry at the University of Grenoble, had experimented with a variety of forgery methods and documents. Essentially, false papers were of one of two types—so-called *bifs* or *synthés*. What distinguished the one category from the other was whether the forged document could be expected to withstand scrutiny. The *synthé* was fabricated utilizing data pertaining to an individual whose identity was verifiable and who was not sought by authorities. The *bif* was fabricated without reference to a real person. If a fastidious French gendarme or Gestapo agent placed a phone call to the city hall listed as having issued the document, the bearer of the *bif* would be exposed. In 1943, Giniewski developed an expertise in producing the more sophisticated *synthés* and trained fellow MJS member and chemistry student Georges Schnek to be his assistant.

In an address delivered at an international colloquium held in Grenoble in 1997, Schnek spoke of his life as a *faussaire* (forger).

> The young local leader of the MJS, Otto Giniewski, called Toto, quickly initiated me into the trade of a forger. With some of his associates, I have, I believe, along with my group, produced between 3,000 and 3,500 false identities, more or less perfectly but which, in 90 percent of the cases, made possible the rescue of so many of our threatened and hunted coreligionists. Thanks to the efficiency of our group, impelled by Toto, they came from all over begging us for these *synthés* . . . As for myself, I was enrolled under a false identity at the Chemistry Institute of Grenoble. Our group had this particularity: comprised of 20 young women and a dozen young men, it had a remarkable diversity of activity.

> The forgery specialists often traveled through the Grenoble region by bicycle, train bicycle, or bus bicycle [i.e. taking a bicycle along on a train or bus]. We all lived in the city or in the neighboring suburbs, in Seyssins, Eybens, la Tronche, Gières, etc. We had two or three meeting places; we often moved as a precaution. The building, bd [boulevard] Ed. Rey [Édouard-Rey], sheltered our forgery laboratories in two maids' rooms on the 9th *étage* [the tenth floor].
>
> For lack of time, I will spare you the details on the many *synthèses* that we realized or completed. Certain city halls in the region allowed us to work peaceably in their offices. We can never sufficiently render homage to these modest teachers or mayors' secretaries or often both. Thanks to them, hundreds of Jewish lives were spared.

Only a small cadre of MJS leaders and militants were directly involved in or had knowledge of the group's clandestine, illegal rescue work. Other MJS members may have been aware of the existence of such activity but knew little about it. From time to time, they may have heard someone mention Éducation physique (Physical Education), the cover name used to obliquely reference the organization's underground activity.

On summer weekends, MJS leaders and militants would gather at les Michalons, a rented chalet located high in the mountains west of Grenoble, in the commune of Saint-Nizier-du-Moucherotte. In his memoir, Rabbi René Kapel, the spiritual guide of the Grenoble *gdoud,* recalls the "business" that they did at les Michalons: "We used these weekend meetings to exchange ideas on what was happening, make decisions regarding our clandestine activities, give directions to our militants, or, quite simply, engage in physical and paramilitary exercises." Summer weekends were not all business, however. There were guest lecturers and colloquia on many different subjects—Judaism, Jewish history, Zionism, the history of Palestine. They sang the "Song of the Deportees," the Zionist anthem "HaTikvah," and other songs of Eretz Israël. They danced the hora under the stars. They felt a part of something larger than themselves. For Georges Schnek, weekends at les Michalons were especially important because "the long evenings allowed us to deepen our understanding of Judaism and, above all, imbued us with ideas and diverse visions leading to the realization in Israel of a state for the Jews."

All that summer, strange and horrifying news filtered into France about the fate of the deported. There was talk of trucks and shower chambers in which people were asphyxiated by poison gas. It was impossible for those who heard the news to make sense of it or to know how much of it was true. How could one believe that such senseless slaughter could occur? And yet, if it were not true, why were the Nazis taking those who were unfit for work—children, old people, and those ill and infirm? It made no sense. Uncertainty hung over all "like a dark cloud." At the same time, a different kind of news reached them. This news had the opposite effect; it was nothing short of exhilarating. On April 19, *erev Pesach* (eve of Passover, traditionally, the night of the first seder), Jews living in the ghetto in Warsaw had staged an uprising. They had held back the German and Polish forces that had come to liquidate the ghetto, not only for hours or days but for nearly a month! Hélène Gorgiel-Sercarz was a twenty-year-old MJS member who lived in Saint-Gervais in the summer of 1943. She later wrote that the courage of the ghetto fighters had a "fierce impact" on them. "It made our bond of belonging to our people even stronger and strengthened our dedication to struggling on for survival."

Saint-Gervais is ninety miles from les Michalons, but, despite the distance, Mila managed to spend some summer weekends there. She craved this time with her friends and comrades. She loved listening to the lectures and being part of the discussion and debate. She loved the singing and dancing. Upbeat and optimistic, she felt certain that they would get through the difficult days ahead and that, when the war was over, they would make their way to Palestine and build a Jewish state.

~

In the months preceding his execution in April 1947, Rudolf Höss, the Commandant of Auschwitz from May 1940 until November 1943, was encouraged by Jan Sehn, the prosecuting attorney for the Polish War Crimes Commission in Warsaw, to write about the founding, development, and operation of the Auschwitz-Birkenau complex and high-ranking SS officers with whom he had worked. After Höss had written about those subjects, "he remarked to Sehn one day that there was nothing to do in his jail cell in Cracow." The prosecutor then suggested that he write about himself. With the luxury of having plenty of peaceful days and a sufficient number of pencils and sheets of paper, and with others seeing to it that he was fed, clothed, and kept warm and safe, Höss wrote his autobiography. At one point, he states:

> On my seventh birthday, I was given Hans, a coal-black pony with flashing eyes and a long mane. I was exploding with joy. I had finally found my friend. [Lest this last statement elicit pity for Höss, the reader should know that, elsewhere in the autobiography, he states that he had two "devoted" parents, two "loving" and "affectionate" sisters, and "plenty of playmates" his own age.] Hans was so faithful that he followed me everywhere, just like a dog. When my parents were away, I would even take him up to my room. I got along well with the servants, and they looked the other way as far as my childish behavior was concerned, and they never told on me.

3. Pas de l'Échelle

The wistful, rambling reminiscences of the Commandant of Auschwitz, including the name and color of his childhood pony, have found their place in history. They have been preserved in their original, handwritten form, translated into multiple languages, and published numerous times. They may be located online, purchased in their entirety, and downloaded in less time than it takes to finish reading the words on this page.

Mila Racine was not given the opportunity to write her autobiography. She was not given the chance to fill so much as a file card with words that would be preserved and handed down to posterity. If she had been, she may well have written of the moment that changed her life, the moment when she was asked if she was willing to risk everything to save others from the fate that the Nazis had prescribed for them. As it is, the details of what transpired in that moment have been lost to history. One might say they lay buried in the wreckage of that terrible period.

There is little doubt that, in the middle of August 1943, Simon Lévitte personally met with Mila Racine and asked her if she would attempt to smuggle a group of children across the Swiss border, into the canton of Geneva. Where did the meeting take place? Was it at les Michalons, she having made the trip from Saint-Gervais in order to celebrate Shabbat with other MJS leaders and militants? Was it in Saint-Gervais, Lévitte having gone to see her? How much did he know then about what the smugglers might be getting themselves into? Why did he choose her for this assignment? What was it about Mila, just twenty-three years old, that made him feel she was up to the task? What information did he convey to her? Did he give her adequate time to think about the danger involved before making her decision? Did she hesitate at all before taking up the mantle of rescue work? Was she flattered in being asked to do something so dangerous and daring? Why did she accept the assignment? Was she out to prove something, either to herself to to someone else? Was she looking for adventure? Was she brash and reckless? Who was she and how had her life come to this?

~

She was born on September 14, 1919, in Moscow and, although her given name was Myriam, she was always known as Mila. To this day, younger cousins use the endearing form of her name that they used long ago, pronounced "*Mil*-ush-ka." In 1926, the family, along with their Russian housekeeper, emigrated from Moscow to Paris. They lived in an apartment at number 97, rue de Rome, in the Eighth Arrondissement, slightly north and west of the Gare Saint-Lazare and the Place de l'Europe.

Two translations of her Russian birth certificate were filed with agencies in Paris—one upon the family's arrival in France, in 1926, and the other in 1931.

The earlier translation lists her father's name as Hirsch and her mother's name as Bassia. In the later translation, the Russian names have become parenthetical: the father's name appears as "Georges (Hirsch)" and mother's name as "Berthe (Bassia)." In conversation with the author, family members referred to Mila's father as Hirsch, which they pronounced "*Gear*-shuh," and to her mother as Berthe, which they pronounced "*Beer*-tuh."

Recollections of Berthe summon up images of the traditional—or perhaps stereotypical—Jewish mother flecked with sparks of a *bonne vivante.* She was short but strong-willed, outspoken, opinionated, and energetic. She maintained a Jewish household, celebrating Shabbat and holidays, but she was not pious. When the family first arrived in Paris, Berthe was enthralled with the exotic profusion of the city markets and did not hestitate to sample new foods. (Seventy-five years later, Sacha still recoiled at the memory of her mother eating snails and oysters.) A cousin living in New York recalled the extended family gathered around the table in what she described as Berthe's tremendous dining room. "No matter who sat there, she [Berthe] started peeling apples and pears and putting them on your plate, and, whether or not you wanted to eat, you ate!" Music was Berthe's passion—according to Sacha, her mother had been an opera singer in Russia—and life in the apartment on the rue de Rome revolved around the piano. Berthe played the instrument, and taught Mila how to play. Gathered around the piano, the Racine clan sang songs in Russian, Yiddish, Hebrew, French, Italian, and Ladino (Judeo-Spanish).

Hirsch was quite the opposite of Berthe. Thirteen years older than his wife, Hirsch was forty-two when Mila was born. Tall and thin, gentle and mild-mannered, he was a man who loved the quiet of Shabbat. In the early 1920s, he had dreamed of moving his family to Palestine. He traveled there in 1925 and purchased land in what is now Tel Aviv. However, many members of his large and close-knit family had already emigrated to Paris, and it was hard for Hirsch and Berthe to resist being pulled in that direction. His experiences in Palestine and the Zionist dream lived on in the stories he told to the children. They loved most when he would tell them of the time he read a Russian newspaper while floating on his back in the Dead Sea.

In physical build and temperament, Mila resembled her father. She was a beautiful child, with wavy dark brown hair and blue eyes. Intelligent and thoughtful, she was imbued with a sense of calmness and poise. Growing up, she was closer to her brother, eight years her senior, than she was to her sister, four years her junior. Mila and her brother, Emmanuel, whom everyone called Mola, would often retreat to a quiet room in the apartment to read novels written by Victor Hugo or another favorite author, shutting out the infuriated Sacha. In one respect, Mila was very much like her mother: she had a passion for music and a magnificent voice. Although she loved to play the piano, nothing pleased her more than singing with others as part of a chorale.

Left to right—Mila, Emmanuel (Mola), and Sacha Racine, Paris, circa 1927. Photo courtesy of Racine Family.

When Mila was twelve or thirteen, she suffered from an infection of the mastoid bone, a honeycomb-like structure of small air cells located in the temporal lobe of the skull, just behind the ear. In that era before the advent of antibiotic drugs, the condition was life-threatening. It required surgery and entailed a long and painful period of hospitalization and recuperation. A nerve that controls facial muscles runs through the mastoid bone and can be injured as a result of infection or surgery. Mila suffered some nerve damage. After the surgery, she developed a facial tic that was, according to some who knew her, quite pronounced. Although she may have felt self-conscious about the tic, she neither gave voice to such feelings nor allowed them to interfere with her desire to sing or speak in front of an audience.

If one can honestly say that anything about Paris is ordinary, then Mila had an ordinary adolescence. Like Proust and Zola, she spent afternoons in the Parc Monceau, a short walk from her home on the rue de Rome. The park had been a favorite spot of Baron Haussmann, the man who oversaw the reconstruction of mid-nineteenth century Paris—he called it the city's most elegant promenade. As a student at the Lycée Racine, Mila excelled in her English language courses. She was easy to get along with and well-liked. She went with friends to the movies and on picnics at the Bois de Boulogne, the huge park at the city's western edge. Sometimes, she and Sacha spent summer vacations away from Paris, on a rustic farm that had no electricity and no running water.

After graduating from the Lycée Racine, on July 7, 1936, Mila took on two entirely unconventional challenges. First, hearkening to the dream of her father, she created a new branch of WIZO in Paris. The Women's International Zionist Organization had been founded in Great Britain in 1920 for the purpose of aiding women and children in Palestine. Most members of WIZO-Paris were women of Berthe's generation who, according to Sacha, "wore big hats, ate cake, and met with other women, not with men." Wanting a Zionist organization that was more with it, one that included men as well as women, Mila created Jeune WIZO (Young WIZO). Second, she left Paris and went to London to live on her own and become fluent in English. A document preserved in the private collection of Mola Racine indicates that, in March 1938, Mila was enrolled as a student at the City of London College on Ropemaker Street, near Margate Station, taking a course in "English for Foreigners."

It is not known whether either or both of the unconventional pursuits described above were part of some larger aspirations Mila had for her future. Neither is it known at what point in time she moved back to Paris, whether she had been able to complete the studies on which she had set her sights, or whether the cataclysmic events of 1938-39 caused her to change her plans. What is known is that she was again living with her family in their apartment on the rue de Rome in June 1940, as the German army, approaching from the north, prepared to occupy Paris. Along with Hirsch, Berthe, Sacha, and Mila, the Racine household included Mola's wife Sara (née Wexler) and their one-year-old daughter, Lili. Mola was serving in the French army; having been assigned to Vice Admiral Charles Dumesnil, he found himself in Bordeaux, arranging for members of French National Assembly to leave for Casablanca on the steamship Massila.

Nearly three-quarters of the population of Paris, which normally numbered three million, fled the capital in the weeks preceding the German Occupation. In an interview with the author, Sacha stated that the family fled in June, on a day when "we awoke and there were fires all around." The statement suggests that the family may have refrained from leaving their home until June 14, the very day that German soldiers entered the city. Before dawn that day, at the order of French officials, petroleum reserves around the city were set ablaze so that they would not fall into enemy hands. A cousin who owned a metals business, Alexander Racine, dispatched three trucks and two cars to pick up twenty-five members of the clan, including Hirsch, Berthe, Mila, Sacha, Sara, and Lili. The caravan traveled to Pau, a town in southwestern France near the Pyrenees. By late June or early July, they had settled in Toulouse.

In the summer of 1940, Toulouse was overrun by Parisians and by refugees from Belgium, the Netherlands, Luxembourg, Germany, Poland, Austria, and elsewhere. A Jewish émigré writer named David Knout wrote, "*La ville rose* [the pink city] is monstrously encumbered by all sorts of vehicles and by a heterogeneous, teeming humanity that, like a swarm of grasshoppers, flows endlessly through the congested streets of the city, pours out into the squares and the crammed cafés, overflows the entire width of the sidewalks, spills into the roadway." Although accommodations were hard to come by, the Racine family managed to rent two villas that were near one another. Hirsch, Berthe, Mila, Sacha, Sara, and Lili lived in a home on the rue Deodora; other family members occupied a villa on the allée des Demoiselles.

In the summer and fall of 1940, Mila spent much of her time caring for two cousins—the nine-year-old Helen Racine and her seven-year-old sister, Nadine. Their father, Michel, had died of tuberculosis the previous year. Struggling to cope with the loss, uprooted from all they knew, the girls craved warmth and affection, but their mother, Fanny, was cold and distant. Their lively, grown-up cousin Mila assumed the nurturing role: each day, she appeared at the villa, took Helen and Nadine by the hand, and set out on foot to explore the city they now called home—its neighborhoods of pinkish-orange brick, majestic parks and gardens, great green Garonne River, and narrow tree-lined canals. Along the way, they stopped to picnic, play games, and share confidences. Mila was a storyteller who had an affinity for trees; on their daily excursions, her imagination transported them to enchanted forests peopled by friendly, talkative elves whom Helen and Nadine would remember many decades after the war had ended.

Mila Racine with niece Lili, location unknown but likely Toulouse, circa 1941. Photo courtesy of Racine Family.

When I interviewed them in 2000, Nadine Gill and Helen Mirkine recalled those walks in Toulouse with special feelings of affection, appreciation, and wonder. Nadine is is a professional artist whose paintings and drawings have been widely exhibited in New York and elsewhere. She believes that Mila opened her eyes to the power of storytelling and imagining. "I tell stories in painting, and I think she [Mila] left me with that because she was such a storyteller." The young Nadine learned from Mila that "stories were also a help in moments of fright, where you can go into that zone of imagining." Many of the artist's works feature trees, a fact she attributes to days spent with Mila in Toulouse. Yet, the most important gift she received from Mila was, she felt, "an insight into people." She endeavored to explain, saying, "Because she was so calm and delicate and lovely and porcelain-like, and yet she must have been ravaged by insecurities and fears because of that horrific tic that she had." As young girls, both Nadine and Helen had been a bit puzzled and fascinated by the tic. It originated in the hand, they remembered, although neither could recall whether it was the left or right. Whoever happened to be holding Mila's hand would feel a spasm. The spasm would travel up the side of her body to her eyes. Despite the tic, Helen described Mila as "gorgeous," commenting, "I wanted to look like her in the worst way." The young Helen let her hair grow long so that she could put it in a braid like Mila's. "One of her [Mila's] pinkies was always red because she never put her lipstick directly on her lips," Helen remembered. "She put it on her pinky and applied it to her lips."

In November 1940, Alexander Racine moved Fanny, Helen, Nadine, and other family members to Lyon. Throughout the winter, he made frequent trips to the American consulate in Marseille and, quite miraculously, secured documentation that would permit fourteen people to emigrate to the United States. He, Fanny, Helen and Nadine were among the first group of seven that departed France. (The second group departed several months later.) They traveled through Spain to Portugal and, on the first day of April 1941, boarded a ship called the Guinea. According to Helen Mirkine, the number of passengers aboard the small vessel well exceeded its stated capacity, and the decks were filled with people who, having no assigned cabin or berth, slept on lounge chairs. All of the passengers were Jews fleeing Europe. The transatlantic crossing took fifteen days; Helen spent most of that time shut in the cabin, plagued by seasickness. On the eleventh of April, however, she allowed herself to be coaxed outside and into the midst of a crowd, where she was lifted up onto the top of a table. It was the first night of Passover: everyone on board had gathered for a communal seder. Being the youngest who knew how to chant the four questions, an integral part of the celebration, Helen performed her duty and then returned to the cabin to resume vomiting.

As soon as they arrived in New York, Helen and Nadine made a pleasant discovery—they could converse in English rather easily. On their walks through Toulouse and and in the garden of their villa on the allée des Demoiselles, Mila had made a point of teaching the girls how to speak, read, and write this language she had grown to love. After the girls had been moved to Lyon, Mila corresponded with the girls in English so that they might retain as much as possible.

The Racine family members living in the villa on the rue Deodora did not attempt to leave France. Mola, Sara, and Lili lived in Toulouse until January 1941; Hirsch, Berthe, Mila, and Sacha, until April. For Mila, the Toulouse period constituted a time of profound change. On the nineteenth of September 1940, she turned twenty-one, crossing the symbolic threshold of adulthood. Within several months, she had crossed a different, more significant threshold: having been what Sacha called a "dreamy and romantic" child and adolescent, Mila became an activist deeply committed to helping those in need.

Jewish men and women reaching adulthood in France in 1940 had no choice but to set aside their plans and aspirations for the future and face harsh new realities. However, it was not inevitable they choose the path that Mila chose—and, in fact, most did not. Mila chose that path because something in her personality compelled her to do so. What she saw and heard while living in Toulouse greatly influenced her thinking.

The Racine home on the rue Deodora was the setting for some of the earliest debates about the possibility of Jewish resistance in France. One of the family's first visitors was David Knout, the author who so colorfully described the "heterogeneous, teeming humanity" that had overrun Toulouse. He was accompanied by his wife, Ariane Knout-Fixman, who, being the daughter of composer Alexandre Scriabin and niece of Vyacheslav Molotov, must have been received as a minor celebrity. Like Mola, David had served in the French army and been demobilized just a few weeks earlier.

Nobody knew what to make of David Knout. Here was a man who was convinced that the Germans were going to come after all Jews in France, regardless of who they were, where they had been born, whether they held French citizenship, or any other consideration. He even dismissed the popular belief that Jews who had fought for France in the Great War or in the recent conflict would retain their special status and be protected.

In his unpublished, undated biographical notes, Mola recalled that meeting:

> My family and I were settled in Toulouse in a house situated near the Pont des Demoiselles, rue Deodora, and one of the first visits that we had was that of the writer Knut [sic], who came to see us with his wife (a niece of Molotov). Knut had developed the idea that the Germans were going to go after the Jews, who numbered 300,000 to 320,000 in France, of which many were foreign Jews. It was absolutely necessary, he was saying, to organize the defense of this population, which was in no way prepared to protect itself from the Nazis and the French administration.

How did Mola and other Racine family members react to Knout's dire predictions? Did they view them as extreme? Mola does not say. Neither does he say how they reacted to the idea that Jews in France must prepare for their own defense. He mentions the idea because it was radical. Knout could have focused his energies on doing what so many others were doing—attempting to leave France. He could have joined the crowds who "bustle about, lay siege to the consulates, battle bureaucratic complications, run to Marseille in a feverish hunt for visas—for America, Argentina, Brazil, El Salvador, Cuba, even China, anywhere . . ." He could have met with one of the "specialists" to arrange an illegal crossing, on foot, over the Pyrenees, into Spain. However, Knout was critical of those who took flight. Echoing the words of Leon Pinsker, a predecessor to Theodore Herzl and modern Zionism, he called flight "our eternal tactic." He lauded the aims of those who were fighting the British in Palestine—to force open the doors to legal Jewish emigration. However, he knew that they would not achieve victory overnight and that, by the time significant numbers of Jews were able to settle there, it would be too late for millions now trapped in Nazi-occupied Europe.

Within days of that initial meeting with the Racine family, David wrote, printed, and circulated copies of a slim pamphlet entitled *"Que Faire"* (*"What to Do"*). The pamphlet took issue with Jews who acted only in their own self-interest, without regard to the fate of their co-religionists. It argued that, in order to survive, Jews must unite and resist. "We are seventeen million. United, we are a force. Disunited, flesh to be massacred." Its "doctrine of Jewish Resistance" called upon Jews to prepare for defensive and offensive action. Defensive resistance meant aid and rescue. Offensive resistance meant taking up arms against the enemy.

Knout sought to discuss his ideas with Jewish leaders who had taken up residence in Toulouse, but his efforts were rebuffed. None wished to be associated with him or his views. Some dismissed his predictions as too extreme or his call to action impractical. Others felt it was simply too dangerous to engage in such discussion because they would be labeled by government authorities as unpatriotic or subversive.

The Racine family did not distance themselves from Knout. Instead, they opened their home to him and several others interested in his ideas. In his biographical notes, Mola writes:

> These meetings that we held with Knut at home led to the organization of a small committee formed by Knut, Weis (Strasbourg), who is now a professor at Hebrew University in Jerusalem and goes by another name, Mr. Mandel, Paul Roitman and a few others whose names escape me. We had given the name "Main Forte" ["Strong Hand"] to this committee, and, the following month, Lublin, Kowalsky, Polansky, etc. . . . [ellipsis points in original] in their turn joined in.

Mola Racine was a man of action rather than of words, and the brevity and casual tone of this passage belies the historical significance of those meetings. Main forte, whose first member swore allegiance on August 29, 1940, was the earliest Jewish resistance group organized in France and predecessor to the Armée juive (Jewish Army) and the Organisation juive de combat (Jewish Combat Organization). Sometimes referred to as Forteresse juive (Jewish Fortress), its mission was twofold: to create a Jewish state in Palestine and to defend Jews wherever they lived. Its mottos were "*Partout présent*" ("Present everywhere") and "*Faire face*" ("Confront").

Although David Knout's rhetoric and writings had set things in motion, he was but one of four individuals who established Main forte. His wife, Ariane, as much of a zealot as he, also played a key role. A convert to Judaism, she was, in the words of fellow *résistante* Anny Latour, "more Jewish than many Jews, more Zionist than most Zionists." Abraham and Génia Polonski were also instrumental. Like the Racines, the Polonskis had emigrated from Russia during the twenties. The couple was a study in contrasts: the taciturn Abraham preferred to remain behind the scenes; the colorful Génia was outspoken. Using the group's initials, Abraham adopted the *nom de guerre* Maurice Ferrer. Génia preferred to be called "'Bat Mattitiahu' or 'Mattathias' daughter,' thus linking herself to the tradition of the Macchabees."

The Knouts and the Polonskis regarded themselves as Revisionists. This right-wing Zionist faction was founded in 1925 by Ze'ev Jabotinsky, best known for his efforts to promote Hebrew rather than Yiddish as the official language of Jews in Palestine. The Revisionists were more extreme and militant than the socialist Zionists, the majority led by David Ben-Gurion and Chaim Weitzmann, representing the Jewish Agency and the World Zionist Organization, respectively. Over the years, there had been many areas of disagreement between the Revisionists and the Zionist mainstream. A key issue during the latter half of the thirties was the Jewish response to escalating Arab terrorism against Jews in Palestine. Revisionists advocated the use of force to counter terrorism, whereas the social Zionists adopted a policy of restraint. Compared to the socialist Zionists, the Revisionists were small in number. By the later 1930s, the Revisionist movement had fractured into three subgroups. The more militant members comprised Etzel (what the British called the Irgun) and Lehi (what they called the Stern gang).

There is no indication that Mila was directly involved in the birth or growth of Main forte. Nevertheless, she was a part of the milieu that gave rise to the group. At a minimum, she met the dynamic men and women who were its driving force, heard discussions about Jewish resistance in her home, and discussed the subject with family members.

Although few Jews in Toulouse were talking about Jewish resistance, many were participating in, and providing financial support to relief efforts aimed at helping those imprisoned in internment camps. This was partly an accident of geography: most of the large internment camps were located in southwest France, and Toulouse was the nearest city. In all of the camps, living conditions were harsh. In Gurs, one hundred fifty miles southwest of Toulouse, conditions were dire. The sprawling agglomeration of primitive wooden barracks had become the main detention center for foreign Jews arrested in or expelled to France. More than fifteen thousand men, women, and children were penned up in barbed wire enclosures. In addition to overcrowding, prisoners suffered from a severe lack of food, clothing, heat, and medical care. The mortality rate was high. Several Jewish, Christian, and nonsectarian aid organizations worked valiantly to alleviate suffering and save lives. Some, like the American Friends Service Committee (the Quakers), based their operations in Toulouse. There is reason to think that Mila may have participated in some type of relief work while living there, as she instituted her own ambitious effort in 1941, from Luchon.

Perhaps the greatest influence on Mila during this period took place fifty miles north of Toulouse, in the countryside outside of Moissac. After the fall of Paris, the national leadership of the Jewish Scouts had transferred the organization's headquarters to that small town on the Tarn River between Montauban and Agen. In September 1940, scout leaders held an intensive two-week leadership training camp in a place called Viarose. It was a rustic setting, nothing more than a clearing in the woods, a few abandoned sheds, some pitched tents, tables made of tree branches lashed together, and a flagpole. Each morning and evening, forty young Jewish men and women gathered around the blue and white Zionist flag to sing "HaTikvah" and other favorites—and Mila and Sacha were among them.

The leader of the camp had earned himself the nickname *l'homme-horaire,* the human-timetable. Dressed in traditional scouting attire, wristwatch and whistle at hand, the first to rise in the morning and the last to go to sleep at night, he directed the day's program of physical exercise, recreation, survival skills, and study sessions. He was aware that some of those in attendance had only the faintest idea of what it meant to be a Jew, and he was intent on introducing them to as many aspects of Judaism as possible. He packed the day's schedule with teaching and discussion about Jewish history and philosophy, religious customs, the Torah and the Talmud, the Hebrew language, Yiddish literature, Hasidism, Zionism, and other subjects. At twenty-eight, he was not much older than the men and women seated on the ground around him, but they looked to him unreservedly because he was a model of self-discipline and self-direction. His name was Simon Lévitte.

Lévitte was accomplished and experienced. In 1936, he had published a book on modern Zionism, a subject he felt was "very poorly known in France." Subsequently, he and his wife, Denise, made *aliyah,* settling on a kibbutz in the Upper Galilee. When he spoke of the strenuous physical effort required to clear

Simon Lévitte, location unknown, circa 1940. © Mémorial de la Shoah/CDJC, ARJF_MIX_35.

stones from the land so that fields could be planted, his listeners knew that he did not exaggerate—his body was lean and muscular, his face, hard and chiseled. On the eve of war, determined to contribute to the struggle against Facism in Europe, the Lévittes returned to France. Simon had been a leader of the Jewish Scouts in Metz, where his family had settled after emigrating from Yekaterinoslav, Russia (now Dnipropetrovsk, Ukraine). He was anxious to resume the work of leading Jewish youth.

Lévitte also spoke to the young leaders about the future. How would they meet the challenges ahead? Although they might not yet realize it, they had choices to make. Would they attempt to leave France or would they stay? If they stayed in France, what would they do? Would they take up arms against the enemy? Would they come to the aid of those in need? Regardless of which choices they made, regardless of what lay ahead, now was the time to begin preparing themselves physically, mentally, and spiritually.

During the two weeks that they spent at Viarose, Mila and Simon became well-acquainted. They discovered similarities in their backgrounds. Mila had been six years old when her family arrived in Paris; Simon had been five when his family arrived in Metz. Like other immigrant children, each had had to shoulder adult burdens. Both were serious, thoughtful, and reflective. She looked to him as a role model and inspiration. He was impressed by her uncommon poise and grace.

In April 1941, at the order of departmental authorities, Hirsch, Berthe, Mila, and Sacha moved from Toulouse to Bagnères-de-Luchon, in the foothills of the Pyrenees. (Mola, Sara, and Lili had left the city in January, going first to Narbonne and then to Marseille.) Luchon was a resort town, famous for its thermal baths and nearby ski slopes. Its main street was the Allées d'Étigny, a picturesque, tree-lined avenue whose broad sidewalks were filled with outdoor cafés. The Racine family settled into the Hôtel des Pyrénées, on the corner of the Allées d'Étigny and the rue Victor Hugo. The Spanish border was only three miles from Luchon, but reaching Bossòst, the nearest Spanish village, meant a journey of three times that length over rugged mountains.

The Racine family was part of a second wave of Jews who had appeared in Luchon since the war began. First, there were Jewish refugees from Belgium. For some of these early arrivals, it had been, quite literally, the end of the line. They had boarded trains in the north, ridden them as far south as they could, and found themselves deposited in Luchon, where the line ended. By July 1940, a Belgian Refugee Center was in full operation; its director had written to the Quakers in Toulouse that their needs were "numerous and urgent, particularly when it came to feeding the sick, the children—including newborns and nursing babies—pregnant women and nursing women." Many of the refugees were not only poor; they looked East European and they spoke little French. In early 1941, a few hundred of them were transferred from Luchon to Aulus-les-Bains, seventy miles away. Around the same time, other Jewish families—financially independent and largely assimilated—were sent to live in forced residence in Luchon. Later, these more affluent residents would draw criticism as well. They would be described as "idlers who 'pass their lives in the café' and who would be responsible for the rise in prices." It would be said that the town took on "an anti-Semitic climate."

Among the documents preserved in the private collection of Mola Racine is a program for a performance held on the evening of September 28, 1941, at the Théatre des Chimères in Luchon, a popular entertainment venue just a few steps away from the Hôtel des Pyrénées. The program states that the show was presented by the Scouts du Camp de la Flamme and "organized by Mlle [Mademoiselle] Mila Racine." It seems to have offered something for everyone—choral singing, duets, violin virtuosos, dramatic scenes from the Marquis de Priola, and "the Delicious Star" Danielle Nicolle. The scout choir sang an eclectic mix of scouting songs ("Soleil lève-toi"), popular tunes ("Dans la nuit"), and Beethoven's "Hymne à la Joie" ("Ode to Joy"). In addition to being the program's organizer and choir leader, Mila performed the lead role of Betty in the one-act

Allées d'Étigny (with Pyrenees in the background), Luchon, June 2010. Photo by N. Lefenfeld.

farce by Tristan Bernard "L'Anglais tel qu'on le parle" ("English as It is Spoken"). According to Sacha, a short time after the event, Mila resigned from the scout troop, her departure prompted by a member's anti-Semitic remark.

Mila's main preoccupation in Luchon was devising, implementing, and sustaining an emergency food relief program for internees confined to the nearby Gurs camp. Food rations there were below subsistence levels. Constant hunger and poor nutrition had weakened many and contributed to the high mortality rate. Mila made appeals to Jewish families in Luchon, and, according to Sacha, was able to collect donations without great difficulty. The greater challenge involved finding and purchasing food. With many items rationed and others simply not available, there was little choice in terms of what to buy. Further, one had to worry about the food's perishability and whether it could be adequately stored. Mila determined that the best choice would be beans, which she found she could purchase on the black market. Under normal circumstances, it would have been fine to send dried beans, but, during the previous winter, dried beans stored in Gurs had "rapidly deteriorated" because they were not properly protected from the elements. Mila decided to set up her own canning operation so that the beans would be protected from spoilage even if handled improperly. She found a metal worker who was willing and able to make tin cans and convinced the proprietor of a laundry service to allow her to use the laundry tubs as sterilization baths. Sacha worked alongside her; presumably, others did as well. They sent many food parcels to Gurs and, according to Sacha, received letters of appreciation from internees.

At the end of 1941, activists who had formed Main forte joined with mainstream Zionist leaders to form the Armée juive (AJ; Jewish Army). The AJ was dedicated to goals very similar to that of Main forte: to prepare Jews for self-defense and to work toward the establishment of a Jewish state in Palestine. The group's manifesto, drafted ten days before the Wannsee Conference, states "the extermination of the Jewish people is already being carried out."

Mila was one of the first sworn into the new group, sometimes referred to by its code name, Armand Jules. Like other recruits, she was blindfolded and taken to an unknown location. The blindfold removed, she found herself standing in a dark room. Suddenly, a spotlight was switched on, illuminating the blue and white flag and the Tanakh (Holy Scriptures). She recited an oath, swearing fidelity to the Jewish Army and loyalty to its leaders. "May my people live again! May Eretz Israel be born again! Liberty or death!"

The Racine family remained in Luchon until late 1942. Apparently, they were not bothered in the summer or fall, when Vichy authorities rounded up thousands of foreign Jews living in the Unoccupied Zone—this despite the fact that none of the four held French citizenship. (According to Sacha, Mola was the only one of the five family members who was a French citizen, having been naturalized in 1932.) The owner of the Hotel des Pyrénées offered to arrange for the Racine family to be taken over the mountains and smuggled into Spain, but they declined the offer, choosing to remain in France. After the Italians occupied the southeast part of France, the family left Luchon and made their way to Nice. There Mila and Sacha devoted themselves to the work of the MJS, and their lives revolved around the busy refugee center on the boulevard Dubouchage.

~

The fifteenth of August 1943 was a Sunday. The bells of Notre-Dame-des-Alpes, in the center of Saint Gervais, would have filled the morning air with their measured chimes. Mila sought out Lydie Weissberg and her mother to speak to them about an urgent matter. Lydie was a smart and spirited fifteen-year-old who shared a room with her mother and older sister at the Val Joly. Mila had been asked by Simon Lévitte to take a group of children from Saint-Gervais to the Swiss border the next day. She wanted to know if Lydie would join the group and if she would act as her first assistant.

Lydie had been born in Paris and had spent her childhood there. Her father was Léon Weissberg, well-known in Parisian art circles as a member of the Montparnasse colony of Jewish émigré artists. In June 1940, Lydie and her mother left Paris and went to Rodez, in the Unoccupied Zone (department of the Aveyron). Even though Léon was divorced from Lydie's mother, Marie, he took up residence nearby. They lived in relative peace until February 1943, when French gendarmes arrested Léon and sent him to Gurs. Two weeks later, he was transferred to Drancy and deported. After Léon's arrest, Lydie and her mother left Rodez for Nice. Along the way, they stopped in Marseille to see Wladimir Raykis, the director of the Galerie Zak, in order to collect money owed from the sale of several paintings. They arrived in Nice in April and, just a few days later, were sent to live in Saint-Gervais. Subsequently, they were joined by Oser Warszawski, a prominent Yiddish writer. Oser and Marie had married in 1942, but, for reasons unknown, he had not been able to join her in Rodez. Warszawski settled into a room in the Hotel Mont Blanc, in the bourg. He was one of the people who would gather around the long table set up outdoors at the Val Joly to peel and chop vegetables.

Mila recruited Lydie to join the convoy without her mother being present, for she was nowhere to be found. Lydie gave her assent right away—her family situation had changed and she was apprehensive about the future. Her older sister had recently left Saint-Gervais to join a Resistance group, and Lydie was worried that she might soon share close quarters with her mother and stepfather. She felt it was a good time to leave and do something important, dangerous, and heroic. She understood that this first convoy was "a test that could have important consequences for the future: if it succeeded, other groups would follow." She knew that Mila had asked her to be her first assistant because she regarded her as "reliable, determined, and quick." Lydie did not want to let her down. She was in awe of Mila, whom she regarded as "beautiful, lively, strong, and charismatic," "a luminous personality."

Late in the afternoon, Marie, accompanied by Oser, returned to the Val Joly. She was outraged to hear that Mila had not obtained her permission before recruiting Lydie. Oser kept silent at first, listening to mother and daughter argue over the matter. Finally, he spoke up, saying "Marie, if she wants to leave, let her leave." This put an end to the discussion.

Very early the next morning, eight families gathered in the dining room of the Val Joly. Eleven children were prepared to leave Saint-Gervais. Six were older kids: Cécile Gostynski (16), Marcus Hendler (15), Renée Perelmuter (14), Boris Szterenbarg (14), Jacques Veissid (16), and Lydie Weissberg (15). Cécile was responsible for her younger sister, Sarah (11). The same went for Marcus, whose kid brother, Henri, was 13, and for Jacques, whose younger sister, Sonia, was the same age. Two young children, Jacques Jakubowitz (9) and Sarah Revah (11), were alone, without older siblings. (Appendix 2 presents summary statistical data on MJS and OSE convoys smuggled into Switzerland between August 17 and October 21, 1943. It also presents a detailed profile of each MJS convoy, including the number of the dossier preserved in the Archives of the State of Geneva that pertains to each child or siblings and excerpts of statements appearing in documentation preserved therein.)

Mila went over all the instructions, including those she had given to each family the previous day. The children were not allowed to bring any belongings—no suitcases, backpacks, or packages. Neither were they to bring any mementoes of their families or their lives—no letters, papers, photographs, or addresses. They were not to bring food but could take along a handful of sugar cubes in a pocket. En route, they would present themselves as a youth group on an outing. They would refrain from calling Mila by her name but would instead call her Lili. Near Annemasse, a town situated on the border, outside of Geneva, they would attempt the crossing. If everything went well and they made it across, they would be arrested by Swiss officials and subsequently questioned. They were not to reveal that they had come from Saint-Gervais or that their parents were still living there. (The organizers of the convoy believed that there were Nazi spies or sympathizers in Switzerland and that such information might be used to track down family members still in France.) They were to stick to a cover story—that they were a group of lost children, Polish and orphaned, who had somehow made their way to Annemasse and who had found someone willing to take them to the border.

Parents and children said their goodbyes at the Val Joly. Mila and the children set off on foot in the direction of Le Fayet, the district, far below Saint-Gervais, where the train station is located. Perhaps they left the road and followed a path down the side of the mountain.

The canton of Geneva wraps around the southwestern end of the huge, crescent-shaped Lake Geneva. Its capital, the city of Geneva, is situated on the lakefront, at the point of the crescent. The boundary of the canton, which is also the boundary between France and Switzerland, forms a belt that encircles the land within two to eleven miles of the city.

There was a plan in place as to how the children's convoy would cross the border. Mila spoke privately of the plan with Lydie Weissberg and Renée Perelmuter, as each would have a role in executing it. Renée was not quick like Lydie, but she was unflappable. Mila explained that two barbed wire barriers ran along the border, one on the French side and one on the Swiss side. A narrow strip of land, called No Man's Land, lay between them. At a certain spot, cuts had been made in the barbed wire to allow the group to pass. When they reached this spot, Mila would lean down and tie her shoe. This was the signal for Lydie to run through the break as fast as she could. Renée was to stand bravely holding the barbed wire until the whole group had made it through.

The prearranged crossing point was between two French towns—Annemasse on the east and Saint-Julien-en-Genevois on the west. Differences exist in accounts as to how the group reached the area near the border. They may have taken the train from Saint-Gervais to Reignier and then traveled the rest of the way by car.

A country road linking Annemasse and Saint-Julien-en-Genevois runs directly alongside the border. The group walked along the side of the road in ranks, two by two, the barbed wire barriers on one side and the towering, striated cliffs of the Salève Mountains on the other. As they walked, they sang. When one song ended, Mila sang a few bars of another and the kids joined in. Their repertoire consisted mainly of well-worn scout songs and patriotic tunes, but, at one point, walking in a field, out of earshot, they sang the "Song of the Deportees."

Late in the afternoon, the group, still in ranks, passed a contingent of six or seven German soldiers standing by the barbed wire. After they had gone a little further, Mila told Lydie that the place at which the soldiers were standing was the prearranged crossing point. The soldiers had discovered the cuts in the barbed wire, even though they had been camouflaged. Mila assured Lydie that everything would be alright. Lydie felt confident that Mila would know what to do.

They walked a bit further, to a church in a nearby village. The *curé* (parish priest) was, in Lydie's words, as "as ice cold as the inside of the church," but he took them in and allowed them to stay for the night. The children were hungry and tired, having not eaten since early morning. They ate the sugar cubes that filled their pockets and drank water. Somehow, Mila was able to distract them from their hunger. The children knew Mila well enough to discern that, beneath her calm exterior, she was worried about the situation. When night fell, the children stretched out on the wooden pews and slept.

Striated cliffs of Salève Mountains with former SNCF train station (in center foreground), Pas de l'Échelle, France, July 2001. Photo by N. Lefenfeld.

In the morning, the priest brought the children something to drink. Mila had gone out to reconnoiter the border area; when she returned, she explained to Lydie that she would use the same signal that she had planned to use the day before. The group set out again, along the same road.

Around noon, they came to a hamlet called Pas de l'Échelle. A small building housing a *douane,* a customs house, sat directly on the border. Adjacent to the building was a break in the fencing where vehicles were allowed to pass after inspection. A group of German soldiers milled about, laughing and shouting at one another. Some of the soldiers, naked to the waist or with their shirts open, stood around a fountain, washing.

Just as they approached the soldiers, Mila leaned down as if to tie her shoe. For a split second, Lydie couldn't believe what was happening. Mila was signaling her to cross directly under the noses of German soldiers! Yet, she did as instructed, bolting through the opening toward the Swiss side of the border. One of the soldiers shouted, "Halt!" Shots rang out, but nobody stopped and nobody was hurt. Jacques Veissid ran so quickly that he overtook Lydie at the head of the line. Suddenly, Swiss border guards appeared in front of them, their rifles drawn. Stopped by the tip of a rifle poking his stomach, Jacques raised his hands and shouted, "Don't shoot! We are French children!" As they stood at gunpoint, Lydie glanced back, in the direction from which they came, to see if she could catch a glimpse of Mila. She had disappeared.

4. *Ville-la-Grand*

At the bottom of a wide, deep gorge traversing the town of Saint-Gervais, the Bonnant River rushes by in a torrent. The bridge over the gorge bears the name of the Devil, for legend has it that it was he who built the massive span after being tricked by the parish priest. Enraged, he promised to return one day and exact his revenge.

In the summer of 1943, the fourteen-year-old Maurice Glazman lived with his parents, Chaim and Sura, and his older sister, Gusta, in a house situated next to the Devil's Bridge. When they first moved into the house, at the beginning of June 1943, Maurice wondered how he would ever be able to fall asleep. His worry had nothing to do with the Devil's promise. Right outside his window, a waterfall cascaded into the gorge, filling the air with a tremendous roar. His fears were soon dispelled—the sibilant, monotonous *whooshing* became a part of those soft summer nights.

The Glazman family was like so many Jewish families in France. Chaim and Sura had been born in Poland. In the twenties, they had emigrated to Brussels, and it was there that Gusta and Maurice were born. In 1933, the family moved again, this time to Paris. Maurice's father, a tailor, worked hard. Although they had little in the way of material goods, Chaim and Sura did not regret having come to France. The immigrant Jews in Paris extended a hand to one another, and their community life was rich and satisfying. Moreover, they believed that the future was bright and that Gusta and Maurice would be able to achieve what they themselves could not. Even during the first two years of the Occupation, the family managed to scrape by.

Everything changed after the Vel d'Hiv roundup. The Glazman family evaded arrest, but henceforth they would have to live as fugitives. Right away, Chaim made arrangements for the family to leave Paris and attempt an illegal crossing into the Unoccupied Zone. As instructed, they took the train to Dax, in southwestern France, and met their contact. This man took them and others, twenty in all, by bus to the nearby town of Montfort-en-Chalosse. He placed them in the hands of a local farmer, who had agreed to smuggle them across the line of demarcation. As the farmer was leading the group through the town, he was stopped by a drunken man who had been his sergeant during the Great War. The sergeant was insulted because the farmer failed to salute him. He threatened to denounce him to the authorities. The farmer refused to salute, the sergeant refused to allow the group to go on, and the two argued. Amidst the commotion, two young children began to cry, and their mother offered money to the sergeant to allow the group to proceed. After half an hour, the farmer saluted the drunken sergeant, and the group was allowed to pass. They crossed a small river and arrived in the Unoccupied Zone. The very next day, the Glazman family learned that a group attempting to cross at the very same place had been seized. Based on the time of arrest, they concluded that, if not for the drunken sergeant who delayed them, they might have suffered the same fate.

A gendarme took the family into custody and sent them to live in forced residence in the nearby town of Grenade-sur-Adour. For a time, Chaim earned a small income repairing trousers belonging to the local policemen. After the work ran out, he obtained a permit to travel to Lourdes in order to look for a job. He was fortunate to find lodging and employment with a Jewish couple from Romania. The rest of the family joined him in early October.

In March 1943, Chaim and Sura decided that it would be better for them to leave Lourdes and seek refuge in the Italian Occupation Zone. As he had done previously, Chaim went to Nice by himself and then he sent for his wife and children. From time to time, Chaim went to the Centre Dubouchage to ask for help. He did this only when he judged it to be absolutely necessary, however. He suspected that, because Jews were always milling about outside the center, French authorities kept the building under surveillance.

The Glazman family arrived in Saint-Gervais on June 3, 1943. Much to their surprise, the winter snow had not yet entirely disappeared. To Maurice, Saint-Gervais was a sort of paradise, and he would have been happy to remain there until the war was over. In Nice, his stomach had often been empty, but in Saint-Gervais he ate his fill. His father managed to obtain the use of a sewing machine, and he repaired clothes for the local men who did manual labor and for the Italian soldiers. Maurice liked visiting the Val Joly because there was always something interesting going on and because he was sweet on a girl who lived there. The girl's name was Lydie Weissberg.

On the morning of August 26, Maurice and thirty-one other children left Saint-Gervais in order to attempt a border crossing. A few of the children had been living in Megève; the others, in Saint-Gervais. Maurice was happy because his good friend Hélène Waysbrot was also in the group. They all wore scout scarves around their necks and pretended to be scouts on an outing. Their mode of transportation was a bus powered by a wood-fired steam engine. Every sixty-five or seventy miles, they had to stop to stoke the engine.

Two MJS leaders—Mila Racine and Tony Gryn—had organized the convoy and were responsible for making sure that the children reached safety. Maurice knew Mila. He had heard her present a talk at the Val Joly on Jewish life in Palestine and the modern kibbutzim. He thought that she was beautiful but found it disturbing to see her body subjected to its occasional, wrenching spasm. He did not know the young man named Tony Gryn.

Their designated crossing point was near Collonges-sous-Salève, a village located a few miles southwest of Pas de l'Échelle. When they approached that point, they heard someone call out to them. Turning around, they spotted an Italian soldier standing on the top of a nearby hill. He ordered them to come up the hill, and they obeyed. Maurice noticed that Mila seemed worried. The soldier offered to sell them some cigarettes and instructed them to follow him. They made their way up the side of the mountain to the military post in Collonges. The soldier went inside and left them waiting by the front door. He returned with a few packs of cigarettes, sold them to Tony, and cautioned him to stay away from the border. "Ask the priest for lodging," the soldier advised; and Tony replied, "Yes, I know, I know."

Mila and Tony took the group to the Catholic church in Collonges, a small homely structure perched on the side of the mountain. In all likelihood, it was the same church in which the first convoy had sought shelter and spent the night. The priest who received Mila, Tony, and the children, Father Marius Jolivet, was, in all likelihood, the man whom Lydie Weissberg recalled as being "as ice cold as the inside of the church."

Church of Collonges-sous-Salève, September 2008. Photo by N. Lefenfeld.

Father Jolivet was part of an informal, ecclesiastical network in the Haute-Savoie region that rescued Jews. The network had originated in the fall of 1942. Many men and women—young and old, religious and lay, Catholic and Protestant—participated in the rescue network for short or extended periods of time. They lived in Annecy, Annemasse, Veigy-Foncenex, Douvaine, Thonon-les-Bains, and Evian as well as in many smaller villages. Particularly during the latter months of 1942, before the Italians took up positions in France, it was not uncommon for a Jewish individual or family to come to the Haute-Savoie from elsewhere in France, intent on crossing the border. Oftentimes, those in flight ended up on the doorstep of a church. The priest might call upon a parishioner whom he trusted to give temporary refuge to the person or persons in flight. He might arrange to have them taken to a parish church closer to the border. The clergyman of that parish might place the Jews in the hands of a "*passeur*," a person who would be responsible for effectuating the actual border crossing. The *passeur*, usually a local resident, made it his business to know the natural and manmade features along the border, the frequency and timing of patrols on both sides, and the means by which to avoid being spotted by patrols and get through the barbed wire barriers. Of course, all of these arrangements were conducted in strict secrecy.

Although the MJS leaders knew that Marius Jolivet was a person to whom they could turn for help, they would not have known the full extent of his underground activities. Despite what the historian Limore Yagil describes as his "precarious health and an emotional temperament," the thirty-six-year-old Jolivet played a crucial role in facilitating communication between the French Resistance and the Allies. From 1942 onward, his little church in Collonges was the "'mailbox'" for Allan Dulles, the key American intelligence officer in Europe. Critical information was funneled to and from the Office of Strategic Services in Berne, Switzerland, where Dulles was based. From time to time, Jolivet was also called upon to help smuggle members of the French Resistance across the border.

Mila, Tony, and the children stayed overnight at the church in Collonges. The following day, they made their way back down the side of the mountain to the road that runs along the border. They had been directed to a certain place where, they were told, the barbed wire had been cut. They could not find the cuts, however. At some point during the day or evening, the group was transported nearly twenty miles northeast, to a farm near the Swiss border in Veigy-Foncenex. They spent the night on the farm.

On August 28, two days after the group had left Saint-Gervais and Megève, they were given instructions to wait on the farm until evening, when two *passeurs* would come to take them to the border. In the evening, two men with guns appeared. Darkness fell, and the whole group set out. At some point, the group was divided in two. Although Maurice was not the oldest of those in his subgroup, he was asked to lead it. It is not known exactly how the crossing of the subgroups was coordinated—that is, whether they crossed in the same place but at different times or whether they crossed at different locations.

As Maurice and his subgroup set out, they had to traverse a broad field in the middle of which were two barracks about one hundred fifty meters apart. Between the two barracks, a line of white powder that looked like flour or plaster had been spread on the ground so that anyone venturing across would leave a trail of footprints. There was no barbed wire. As the children traversed the field, they saw Italian soldiers playing cards inside one of the barracks.

The *passeurs* had given Maurice the following instructions: "Go straight ahead. You will find the Hermance River. The first time you cross the Hermance, you will be in Switzerland; the second, back in France; the third, in Switzerland." He followed these instructions to the letter. They crossed the river once, twice, three times, covering a distance of about two hundred meters. After they had crossed the river the third time, they decided not to go any further but to stay right where they were. It was quiet all around, except, at one point, they heard a drunken man singing "L'Internationale," followed by the sound of gunfire. The shots seemed to come from Italian soldiers who were firing their weapons into the air. Shortly after sunrise, Maurice and the other children in his subgroup saw men dressed in green-grey uniforms. Mistaking them for German soldiers, they were frightened. It turned out that the men were Swiss customs officers. The children had reached their destination, and they were safe.

Documentation extant in the archives of Geneva indicates that nineteen children crossed the border that night and were arrested by Swiss officials in the vicinity of Chevran. Information preserved in the Archives départmentales de la Haute-Savoie (Departmental Archives of the Haute-Savoie) indicates that five others attempted to cross but were arrested on the French side of the border by Italian soldiers. The Italian soldiers turned them over to French authorities, who sent them back to the centers of assigned residence. The Swiss and French records account for twenty-four children altogether.

The nineteen children who succeeded in making it across the border were arrested at three different times and in three different locations. It is not known how this happened or how the three subgroups reflected in the Swiss data compare with the two subgroups cited by Maurice. A half an hour before midnight on August 28, ten children were arrested by Swiss soldiers very close to the border, at the Passerelle de la Cuillère. (A *passerelle* is a footbridge.) The children were Tibere Braunstein (10), Oscar Fleischer (14) and his siblings Jeanette (11) and Renée (9), Armand Halberthal (12), Fred Kempfner (14) and his brother Paul (11), Arny Lasar (12) and his brother Carlo (11), and David Milgram (15). Maurice Glazman and four others were arrested in the village of Chevran at 6:15 in the morning. The four others were Hélène Waysbrot (13), Rachele Linderman (15), and Simon Cymerman and his younger sister Anna (12). Finally, at 9:00 a.m. that same morning, four children were arrested a short distance south of Chevran, on the route de Vésenaz in Anières. The four consisted of two pairs of siblings: Sarah Goldstein (15) and her younger sister Berthe (13), and Ludwig Rosenbaum (15) and his sister Rosi (12).

No information is available on how the group reached Veigy-Foncenex, who arranged for the transfer to take place, or how Mila and Tony knew which farm in the Veigy countryside would provide them refuge for the night. Yet, I believe that anyone familiar with the ecclesiastical network in the Haute-Savoie region would reach the same conclusion that I reached: Mila and Tony made contact with the branch of the network known as the Douvaine filière—*filière* means "conduit" or "channel"—and the *filière* came to their aid.

Douvaine is a small town situated at the northern end of the French-Swiss border, three miles from Veigy-Foncenex. In the fall of 1942, its parish priest, Father Jean Rosay, vowed to do whatever he could to aid Jews fleeing persecution. Although he had served as the *curé* of Douvaine for only eighteen months, he knew how to relate to the people of this rural and predominantly agricultural area. He had grown up on a farm and studied at the little seminary in La Roche-sur-Foron. After being ordained in Annecy in 1926, he was assigned to one rural parish after another. Limore Yagil notes that, from the time he arrived in Douvaine, in 1941, Rosay "refused to adapt himself to the German occupants." When he made the decision to help save Jews, he knew that he had to find dependable and trustworthy accomplices who were willing to risk their own lives. He needed people to do all sorts of things—hide Jews until they could be smuggled across the border, take them from one place to another, devise plans for crossing the border, and effectuate the actual crossing.

Father Jean Rosay, date unknown. Photo courtesy of Paroisse Saint-Jean Baptiste en Chablais et Église Saint-Loup de Douvaine.

The forty-one-year-old priest with the boyish face and round, wire-rimmed *lunettes* (eyeglasses) was warm and genial. Many, particularly adolescents and young adults, were drawn to him. He assembled a loose agglomeration of activists who were willing to help, and they became known as the Douvaine *filière*. Some of the people were his own parishioners. Others were militant members of CIMADE and Amitié chrétienne (AC; Christian Friendship), two refugee aid organizations that functioned legally but also supported illegal rescue activities. CIMADE was a Protestant group, whereas the AC was a coalition of Catholics and Protestants.

The parish priest of Veigy-Foncenex, Father Michel Chevrier, may have been the most unlikely of those who heeded Rosay's call. During the early years of the Occupation, Father Chevrier was an ardent Pétainist and an active member of the Service d'Ordre Légionnaire, an ultra right-wing collaborationist militia. At the urging of Rosay, Chevrier recruited Joseph Lançon, a local farmer, to become part of the *filière*. The Lançon farm on the route Plantets is just a half a mile from the border. Lançon, a widower and father of seven, relied on the help of a young neighbor, François Périllat, to keep up with work on the farm. Joseph Lançon and François Périllat knew every feature of the terrain, every field and clump of trees and twist and turn of the shallow Hermance River that runs right along the border. Beginning in October or November 1942, Lançon and Périllat began receiving Jewish refugees whom Father Chevrier and others sent to them. They would shelter the refugees on the farm for brief periods of time, until the opportunity arose to pass them across the border.

During the course of the Occupation, the Douvaine *filière* helped hundreds of Jews reach safety. Many had made their way to the Haute-Savoie region entirely on their own. Detraining at Annemasse, Machilly, Thonon-les-Bains, or elsewhere, they would make discreet inquiries of local townspeople, eventually appearing on the steps of Father Rosay's church or finding themselves taken in hand by a member of the *filière*.

In May 1943, OSE began relying on the Douvaine *filière* to help them pass convoys of Jewish children across the border. Prior to that time, all of the OSE convoys had crossed the border in the immediate vicinity of Annemasse, and the children were arrested in the Swiss communities of Thônex, Moillesulaz, and Pierre-à-Bochet. After the middle of May, all of the OSE convoys except one crossed the border near Douvaine and Veigy-Foncenex, and the children were arrested in Chevran and Hermance.

~

Mila Racine, Tony Gryn, and Simon Lévitte must have done some soul searching at the end of August and beginning of September. Neither of the first two MJS convoys had gone as planned; they knew that they needed to find a safe and reliable way of getting the children across the border. They did not want to have to call upon the Douvaine *filière* on a regular basis. After all, the mission of the MJS team was to establish a *réseau* that operated entirely separate from and parallel to that of OSE. In the event that the OSE *réseau* was temporarily or permanently disabled, the second conduit must continue to function. Besides, the loose agglomeration of activists who comprised the Douvaine *filière* already had their hands full. Passing too many children into Switzerland along a particular length of the border would draw unwanted attention and jeopardize all of the smuggling operations.

The OSE–Douvaine *filière* collaboration could not be restructured to make a place for the MJS team, but it could serve as a model that could be duplicated. The model had an elegance to it, an elegance that derived from the fact that many people participated and responsibility was diffused. The diffusion of responsibility made it harder for German or Vichy authorities to pin down exactly what was happening or who was involved. The participants can be loosely grouped in four categories—Christian clergy and lay leaders; OSE leaders and activists; inhabitants of Douvaine and Veigy who assisted when called upon; and *passeurs* who executed the border crossings.

When the children were brought to the Haute-Savoie region in preparation for the border crossing, they did not stay in Jean Rosay's church in Douvaine. They were sheltered in various institutions, houses, farms, and other structures owned and/or under the control of individuals sympathetic to the cause. This was important because it helped keep everyone in the dark about who was responsible for the children and where they had stayed prior to the border crossing. Among those kept in the dark were the children themselves. This was intentional. Once the children had reached Switzerland and were placed under arrest, they were interrogated about how they reached the border and who had helped them along the way. Of course, if they were seized on the French side of the border and unable to make the crossing, they were also interrogated about such matters. It was important to the viability of the *réseau* that they not be able to clearly identify where they had stayed prior to making the crossing. It was best, therefore, if they stayed somewhere nondescript, such as an abandoned house or a barn. It was also important they not be able to identify any of the individuals involved in the smuggling operation—neither those who had sheltered or fed them nor those who had taken them from place to place or shown them where and how to cross the border.

Jean Rosay bore the singularly heavy burden of directing and coordinating the operation. His status as a member of the clergy gave him some measure of protection, making it less likely that French authorities would arrest him.

Was there a location where the MJS team could duplicate the model of the OSE–Douvaine *filière* collaboration?

Annemasse is the largest town on the French side of the border outside of the canton of Geneva, but it does not sit directly on the border. Three small villages—Gaillard, Ambilly, and Ville-la-Grand—are nestled between the border and Annemasse. One of the links in the ecclesiastical network that had developed in the region operated in Ville-la-Grand, at the Collège Saint-François de Sales, a Jesuit seminary that was also known as Le Juvénat.

It was an accident of geography that placed staff at Le Juvénat in a unique position to help others during the war. The school's property is triangular in shape, and two sides of the triangle coincide with the Swiss border. A request for help from the MJS team would have come as no surprise to the men at Le Juvénat. They had been helping people secretly cross the border since 1941. By August 1943, they had helped hundreds reach Switzerland, most, although not all of them, Jews. Two teachers—Fathers Louis Favre and Gilbert Pernoud—and the school's gardener, Brother Raymond Boccard, facilitated the passages. These activists could not have carried out their work without the complicity of the school's director, Father Pierre Frontin, and other members of the school's community, many of whom witnessed unusual comings and goings and chose to remain silent.

Father Favre was the indisputable driving force behind humanitarian resistance efforts carried out at the seminary. Born in Bellevaux-en-Chablais in 1910, he was ordained in 1936. For the next few years, he taught at the Institute Florimont, a school in Geneva established by the Missionaries of Saint-François de Sales. He was mobilized in 1939 and subsequently sent to teach at Le Juvénat. According to historian Limore Yagil, the young priest was a man of "fragile constitution, with an innate taste for the arts, [who] exercised an irresistable attraction on his entourage." He became the linchpin of resistance operations, motivated by "charity and patriotism."

Father Louis Favre, 1943. Photo courtesy of Louis Favre, nephew of Father Louis Favre and Mayor of Pers-Jussy, a commune in the Haute-Savoie.

The configuration of the property and location of buildings and other structures afforded two means of crossing the border clandestinely. In the rear of the main school building, there is a garden surrounded by a stone wall, six to ten feet high, that runs directly along the border. The building itself is two full stories in height plus an attic with dormer windows. Looking out from the dormer windows, one was able to observe the movement of patrols back and forth along the border.

One method of crossing the border involved using a ladder to scale the stone wall that surrounds the garden, making one's way through the rows of barbed wire positioned at the top of the wall, and dropping oneself down from the wall. This method was used from time to time when it was necessary that the crossing occur during the daytime. Brother Raymond Boccard would position himself in one of the dormer windows and observe the soldiers on patrol. From the garden, standing with those ready to scale the wall, Father Favre or Pernoud or Favrat would watch Brother Raymond Boccard and wait for him to give them the all-clear signal. When he raised his cap, they sent those who were waiting scrambling up the ladder and over the top of the wall.

The second method of crossing did not involve entering the garden or going over the stone wall. One could bypass the main building and walk two or three hundred yards to the west or northwest in order to reach the border directly. Barbed wire ran along the border, but, in at least one place, the rows of wire were distended enough so that people could make their way through. This second method of crossing was preferred over the first because it did not compromise the safety of the school's students, teachers, and staff to the extent that the first means did. If those in flight were seen scrambling over the garden wall, the authorities would presume that they had received some sort of assistance from someone at the school. This presumption did not hold for those who might be caught sneaking through the woods along the border. Additionally, it was simply safer to cross at night than during the day, and the second method lent itself to night crossings, whereas the first did not.

Although the literature speaks mainly about escapes that involved scaling the garden wall, it seems unlikely that this method would have been used much once the Germans took up positions in the Haute-Savoie in late August 1943 and the nature of the risk increased enormously. This supposition is consistent with another key fact known about the rescue work that went on at Le Juvénat. At various times, people waiting to cross the border were sheltered in buildings on the school property until they could cross. However, this practice was stopped because it posed an unacceptable danger to those in the school community.

Scholars credit the men of Le Juvénat and their accomplices in the surrounding area—let us call them the Ville-la-Grand *filière*—with effecting the passage of one to two thousand people, the great majority of whom were Jews. Very few of the rescued have been identified by name. In September and October 1943, many MJS children's convoys were arrested on Swiss soil in the immediate vicinity of Le Juvénat. This suggests to me that the Ville-la-Grand *filière* assisted the MJS team in smuggling children into Switzerland. More specifically, it is my hypothesis that, at the beginning of that September, the MJS and the Ville-la-Grand *filière* duplicated the OSE–Douvaine *filière* model and began working together, functioning as a second, separate *réseau*.

The Douvaine model lent itself to use in Ville-la-Grand. The children could be brought to Annemasse. They could be sheltered in safe houses in Ville-la-Grand,

Annemasse, Ambilly, and Gaillard rather than in buildings on the Juvénat property. Under cover of darkness, they could be taken to the western or north-western corner of the school property late in the evening, avoiding contact with members of the school community. There, at the edge of the property, a *passeur* could show them where and how to cross.

With this piece of the puzzle in place, Mila and Tony were able to move ahead. Their first priority was to finish organizing the small cadre of young men and women who would comprise the MJS team and take responsibility for the children's convoys. The second priority was to establish their base of operations in a new location more accessible to the border.

~

Tony Gryn was a tall, slim, and handsome twenty-two-year-old with a gentle-looking smile, high forehead, soft brown eyes, and wavy brown hair. Like Mila, he was a *juif,* not an *Israélite.* Like her, he had lived in Paris for a long time, spoke French fluently, and knew his way around. Tony was born in Lublin, Poland. His father, Icek (Isaac), had managed his father-in-law's textile export company. In the wake of the stock market crash of 1929 and its effects on commodity markets in Europe, the company went bankrupt. Isaac went to Paris in 1931 to build a new life for his family. Two years later, he sent for his wife, Rwyka, and their children, Nethanel (Tony) and Esther (Alice). Tony became fluent in French and enrolled in the Lycée Maimonide, the only Jewish secondary school in France. He received a classical education, learning Latin and Greek, and a Jewish education, learning modern and classical Hebrew, Mishnah, and Talmud. His curriculum also included physics, mathematics, and chemistry. Like Mila, he had a natural aptitude for learning languages; somewhere along the way, he became fluent in German.

Nethanel (Tony) Gryn, Paris, 1946. Photo courtesy of Gryn Family.

If the war had not intervened, Tony would have been on his way to becoming a physician. In the spring of 1940, he had completed his first year of medical school at the University of Paris. Up until that time, his life had followed a normal course, but, during that first summer of the German Occupation, things took an unexpected turn. At the beginning of August, he and a friend were sitting in a café in the town of Étréchy, south of Paris, when they happened to strike up a friendly conversation with two German pilots regarding the likelihood that the United States would enter the war. A Gestapo agent overheard the conversation and proceeded to arrest the two on charges of disseminating anti-German propaganda. The pilots came to their defense, but they could not sway the agent. Tony was locked up in the infamous Cherche-Midi prison in Paris for three months and then sent to the equally infamous Fresnes, south of the capital. He finally regained his freedom on August 17, 1941.

After his release, Tony returned to Paris and found that the situation had worsened considerably. Roundups of foreign Jewish men had begun in May 1941. Drancy was placed in operation as an internment camp four days after his release, on August 21, 1941. Tony had been granted French citizenship in January 1940, but, despite that fact, he ran the risk of being picked up and sent to Drancy. He was fortunate enough to obtain a German *laissez-passer*, a document that allowed him to circulate in public without being arrested. A French law enacted in June 1941 established a *numerus clausus* that limited Jewish representation in higher education to three percent of the total number of students. Because of the strict quota, Tony was unable to resume his medical studies. He was hired by the Consistoire central des Israélites de France (Central Consistory, the representative body of French Jewry in terms of religious affairs) to teach Hebrew to students.

At some point in 1942, Tony was warned that the Gestapo was looking for him. He left Paris and made his way across the line of demarcation to the Unoccupied Zone. Traveling from town to town, he helped Jewish refugees in whatever way he could—endeavoring to gain one's release from an internment camp, procuring false papers or a *permis de séjour* (permission to reside) for another. His resources spent, seeking work, he went to Marseille in July, where he happened to meet one of his teachers from the Lycée Maimonide. The teacher advised him to go to a farm in the department of the Ain where a number of young Alsatian Jews had established an agricultural community. (This may have been the farm at Saint-Germain, near Villemotier, established by the Oeuvre d'Entr'aide Française Israélite, which, according to Zosa Szajkowski, was organized to aid French Jews evacuated from the Occupied Zone to the Unoccupied Zone.) The chance meeting occurred at the same time that Tony learned that his mother had been seized by French police during the Vel d'Hiv roundup. He took the teacher's advice, went to the farm, and was soon joined by his father and sister, who had somehow managed to get out of Paris and make their way to the Unoccupied Zone. Most of the people living on the farm identified themselves as Israelites, and they gave

Isaac and Alice a chilly reception. The Gryns left and went to Lyon, where they found an apartment outside of the city, in the suburb of Villeurbanne.

In October 1942, Isaac was arrested for carrying a false identity card and was interned in Rivesaltes, a large camp near Perpignan. Tony later wrote, "It took me two months to succeed in getting him out of this camp that meant deportation and death." Obtaining the release of someone from Rivesaltes was a near-impossible task, and Tony makes no mention of how he was able do it. Once "miraculously free," his father went to live in Grenoble, in the new Italian Occupation Zone.

Through his father's association with members of the Poale Zion Hitachdut (Association of Zionist Workers), Tony met Lucien Lublin, one of the founders of the Armée juive. Lublin invited Tony to join the AJ and subsequently sent him to work with Simon Lévitte and the Grenoble *gdoud*. Lévitte was impressed with Tony's intelligence, maturity, reliability, and good judgment. At the end of August 1943, he sent the young man to Saint-Gervais to join Mila in organizing and leading the child rescue operation.

Did Tony and Mila know one another prior to the time they began working together? I cannot say. It's very likely they had spent time together at les Michalons. In any event, they quickly forged a good working relationship.

Toward the end of August and beginning of September 1943, groups of families who met the Swiss criteria for acceptance were being organized in Saint-Gervais and Megève and leaving for the border almost every day. Between August 26 and September 8, at least eight family convoys with 121 people crossed into Switzerland. Through consultation of dossiers preserved in the Archives of the State of Geneva (AEG), I identified the following family names of persons comprising the eight family convoys: Feldhandler, Levy, Garbownik, Zlotowicz, Probst, Hayum, Seckler, Frajermauer, Cige, Zylbersztein, Fenster, Szkolny, Ringort, Hops, Procel, Eilander, Merzer, Papo, Levi, Koch, Majufes, Goldschmidt, Sagalowitsch, Schoenbach, Rosenberg, Siemiatycki, Uboghi, Langszner, Szmulewicz, Schaechter, Roubanowicz, Kielmanowicz, Teitelbaum, Herz (or Hertz), Atzstein, and Kandel. Salient data on the family convoys, including date and time of crossing and place of arrest in Switzerland, are presented in the notes.

MJS activists and OSE workers living in the centers of assigned residence chaperoned family convoys to the border. The chaperones were sometimes assisted by capable young men and women who did not identify themselves with a specific group. Isy Leuwenkroon was one such individual. Originally from Poland, Isy and his wife, Lilly, were Belgian refugees. During the summer of 1943, the couple and their young son, Robert, occupied the first floor of a house on the outskirts of the Saint-Gervais. They regularly gathered and socialized with a large group of young adults—including many MJS members—at the Val Joly. (It was while living in Saint-Gervais that Lilly's brother, Arthur—"Thur"—

met Maurice Glazman's sister, Gusta—"Gus." They were married in 1946.) They became well-acquainted with Mila, who was "full of zip," taught them the hora, and spoke often of her Russian roots and her brother. The twenty-three-year-old Isy helped Mila organize and transport family convoys to the border. Jacques and Nicole Salon (née Weil) were young OSE workers stationed in Megève. Nicole played an active role in conveying families to the border, rising at 4:30 in the morning and returning shortly before midnight.

I did not include the family convoys in Appendix 2, which presents summary statistical data on MJS and OSE convoys between August 17 and October 21, 1943, as well as detailed profiles of MJS convoys. Existing archival data does not provide a sufficient basis for determining the precise role that MJS activists and OSE workers played in the rescue of the aforementioned families.

In some instances, organizers of family convoys created a certain number of "pseudo-families" in order to increase the number of adults who would be allowed into Switzerland. In his memoir, Jacques Salon describes the practice:

> When a mother of a child of five has no husband because he has disappeared or is a prisoner, we have her "married." Two of these marriages will last after the war and, upon their return to Paris in 1944, one of these couples will bring me from Switzerland an entire ham, which I will devour with great gusto; in 1944, our eyes were larger than what was stocked on the shopkeepers' shelves. In terms of couples having several children less than six years old, we leave only one and have his brothers or sisters "adopted" by parents without children.

The smuggling of families across the border proved to be an expensive undertaking. *Passeurs* hired to effectuate the actual border crossings charged what were, apparently, market rates—4,500 francs per person. (I estimate that this was equivalent to roughly €900 to €1,000 or $1,100 to $1,400 today.) It is not known exactly where convoy organizers in Saint-Gervais and Megève found these funds. Perhaps a portion of the monthly allocations that the Federation provided to the Saint-Gervais and Megève Committees to support the refugees was unspent and available for this use. Perhaps the Federation provided special funding to cover the costs of hiring *passeurs*. The relatively small number of Jews who had private funds at their disposal also contributed. Jacques Salon states in his memoir that convoy organizers required that "the rich pay for two." Despite the policy, a shortfall in funds in Megève threatened to halt the operation. The organizers turned to Joseph Kott for help. Somehow Kott managed to meet their request for 180,000 francs. Where did the money come from? From the Saint-Gervais Committee? From Joseph's own pocket? From others whom Joseph convinced to contribute? No one really knows.

What about the convoys of unaccompanied children? Did the MJS and OSE teams have to pay people to pass the children across the border and, if so, how much? The clergy who assisted in these passages acted altruistically, neither asking for, nor accepting payment for their help. The two *passeurs* in Veigy-Foncenex who assisted Father Rosay—Joseph Lançon and François Périllat—also refused payment. The MJS team typically hired a professional *passeur* to effectuate the border crossing. However, there is clear evidence that the amount that the MJS team paid was substantially below market rates. Thus, one must conclude that their actions were partially motivated by a sense of altruism.

Meanwhile, the majority of Jewish refugees who had spent the summer in Saint-Gervais and Megève were awaiting instructions concerning their evacuation. According to Armand Rein, the young OSE worker in Saint-Gervais, by the fourth of September, "all seemed to be falling into place." The refugees understood that they would be taken to Nice, which was supposed to remain in the hands of the Italian Army. Most of those to be evacuated were to travel in a convoy of trucks that would follow the Napoleon Road south. However, the organizers knew that this mode of travel would be very difficult for the elderly, pregnant women, the infirm, nursing mothers, and mothers with young children. They were able to requisition five rail cars to transport the most vulnerable people.

On September 6, the refugees awaiting evacuation were instructed to pack their bags and prepare for departure on the eighth. The battered suitcases stored beneath beds and in closets were pulled out, opened up, and aired out. The clothing was washed and left to dry in the sun. The remnants of lives once so ordinary were sifted through one more time to see if anything might be jettisoned without regret. The suitcases were repacked and secured with belts and cords. All the communal facilities of Little Tel Aviv—kitchens, workshops, classrooms, and synagogue—were hastily dismantled. Approximately 240 people were given permission to ride in the rail cars. In the midst of everything, the refugees learned that German soldiers had infiltrated the immediate area, and they became afraid. Some members of the MJS team were not in Saint-Gervais while these preparations were taking place. They had been called upon to take a third convoy of children, children whom they did not know, to the border.

~

Jacques Charmatz was eight years old in September 1943, when his father placed him in the hands of people whom he did not know, people who were going to take him to Switzerland. Beside him were his seven-year-old sister, Myriam, and three-year-old cousin, Claude Emerich. As the oldest, he felt he had to put up a brave front. He managed to do that, despite the fact that some aspects of the experience were frightening.

Jacques, Myriam, and Claude were French children, born in Nancy. David Charmatz, the father of Myriam and Jacques, was originally from Smorgon, Poland (now Belarus), located between the cities of Minsk and Vilnius. He distinguished himself as a bright and diligent student, but, because he was Jewish, there was no opportunity to enter a university. He left in pursuit of higher education. He lived in Berlin for a brief period of time, and it was there that he met a young woman from Frankfurt on the Oder named Rachel Gordon.

In 1927, David immigrated to Nancy, France. He studied agronomy, botany, and other natural sciences on the university level and received his degree in 1929. He was granted French citizenship that same year and spent the next two years in the French army. After his discharge from service, he returned to Nancy and found employment as an official translator and interpreter of Polish and German in the judicial courts. He also took a position as a cantor in one of the local synagogues. It is said that his voice was so beautiful that he was urged to devote himself entirely to the profession. In 1932, Rachel joined David in Nancy and the couple married. She, too, became a French citizen. Unlike David, however, she only really felt at home among German-speaking friends.

Nancy is in the Alsace-Lorraine region, the territory along the Franco-German border over which the two countries have historically quarreled and fought. After defeating the French in 1940, the Germans did not simply occupy the region, they annexed it. Rachel immediately took the children to Limoges and found temporary refuge with friends who had also left Nancy. David, mobilized when France went to war, was demobilized at the end of July, and he joined his family in Limoges. There he continued working as a translator and interpreter.

At the beginning of 1942, David was appointed director of La Roche, an ORT farm-school near the village of Penne-d'Agenais, in the Lot-et-Garonne department. He moved there immediately, and the rest of the family joined him at the end of March.

La Roche was one of several farm-schools that ORT had established in the south of France to receive Jewish refugees and to teach agricultural skills in preparation for emigration to Palestine. By the time the Charmatz family moved there, it had been designated a school for adolescent boys. Most of the *stagiaires* (trainees) were between the ages of fourteen and eighteen and were foreign-born. Many had come from Germany and Austria, had been interned in Gurs or Rivesaltes, and had been liberated by aid workers using whatever means available—legal procedures, illegal maneuvers, and semi-legal ruses. La Roche provided them with a rustic, peaceful refuge. They cultivated fields, tended fruit trees, kept dairy cows, raised rabbits, and established bee colonies. They received intensive instruction in French and in Jewish history and culture. The young Jacques and Myriam reveled in this new, bucolic world. When they were not attending school in Penne-d'Agenais, they were out chasing cats and dogs, taking care of cows and chickens, climbing trees, and roaming the fields and pastures.

The feeling of peace and security came to an end in late August 1942, when deportations from the Unoccupied Zone began. On August 25, David was warned by a local policeman that arrests were imminent and that older adolescents were in danger. Apparently, it was thought that the threat applied to individuals eighteen and over; consequently, boys of that age were sent into hiding while those who were younger stayed on the farm. However, on the twenty-sixth or twenty-seventh, local police arrested five sixteen- and seventeen-year-olds, detained them in a camp in nearby Casseneuil, and sent them to Drancy. They were all deported. An eighteen-year-old who had evaded arrest by going into hiding returned to La Roche, but, in December, he too was seized.

According to a letter that David wrote immediately after the Liberation, addressed to an official in the Prefecture of the Lot-et-Garonne, a Monsieur LaBonne "had particularly distinguished himself in hunting down hidden and camouflaged Jews, without distinction as to age, claiming to his credit that, of the 500 Jews levied for deportation from the department of the Lot-et-Garonne, he succeeded in furnishing the total number, carrying out montrous *rafles* in the streets of the city of Agen in order to meet the quota." Due to David's efforts, however, Labonne was able to seize only six students at La Roche. David believed that it was in retaliation for this that Labonne convinced the prefect of the department to issue a warrant for his arrest and internment, which was to take place on June 6, 1943. Warned the night before, he fled immediately to the Italian Occupation Zone. Rachel, Jacques, Myriam, and Claude Emerich, a three-year-old cousin who had joined them, remained at La Roche.

David first went to the regional ORT office in Voiron. The regional directors sent him to Megève to oversee the agricultural work that the Jewish refugees had begun there and in Saint-Gervais. In the middle of August, David requested a document—an *"ordre de mission"*—that would allow him to travel from Megève to La Roche and back to Megève without being subject to arrest. The purpose of the trip was to bring the three children to Megève. David had learned that OSE and the MJS were smuggling groups of unaccompanied children from France to Switzerland, and he wanted his son, daughter, and nephew to be included.

Along with ten others, Jacques and Myriam Charmatz and Claude Emerich crossed the border late in the evening of September 6. One of the other children in the convoy, the seven-year-old Suzette Kaatz, had also lived on a farm in the Lot-et-Garonne. The Charmatz family knew the Kaatz family; presumably, David helped in making the arrangements to have Suzette included in the convoy. All of the other nine children in the convoy had come to the Haute-Savoie from Paris. Prior to leaving Paris, they had been in the care of the Rue

Amelot Committee, a Jewish social assistance organization. (Their names appear on lists preserved in the Rue Amelot Committee archives, maintained at YIVO.) Unlike the previous convoys, this one included three very young children. Two of those very young children were traveling alone, without older siblings. When questioned by Swiss authorities, neither knew their date of birth. Officials guessed that Cécile Berasse must be four years and Monique Fischel, six. The other children in the group were David Bergman (13), Suzanne Harra (10), Bernard Jacob (12) and his sisters Ginette (9) and Marie-Claire (3), Emile Najdberger (9), and Michel Piekarski (11).

The crossing of the border lived on in Jacques' memory as a "terror and as an exploit."

> Being the oldest in my family, I had to play the big man, he who fears nothing and who is sure that, one day, he will conquer these *boches* [pejorative term for Germans]. But fright all the same, considering this journey through the darkness with children whose sobs we tried to stifle, with detonations of machine gun fire, with noises of the forest teeming with nocturnal animals. We were fugitives, potentially orphans, a patrol of children who had left parents, country, language, and culture but who swelled with pride resisting the enemy.

Jacques' sister, Myriam, remembers staying in "a house like a farm" and then:

> . . . it was night. We walked with other people and they helped us little children to climb over the barbed wire, and they promised that, on the other side, we will eat some chocolate, and, when we arrived, we drank some hot chocolate.

Neither Jacques nor Myriam nor Claude knew, either at the time of the crossing or afterwards, that the MJS had been the organization in charge. They were not able to discuss the subject with their father; David Charmatz died in a tragic accident in Lyon shortly after the Liberation, on September 29, 1944. Rachel Charmatz and Claude's parents simply knew that David was in contact with Jewish resisters and that he had managed to arrange for the children to be taken to safety.

Shortly before midnight, the thirteen children comprising the third MJS convoy were arrested and taken to the Swiss border guard post at Mon Idée, on the other side of the border from Ambilly and a short distance west of Ville-la-Grand. The crossing went without a hitch. Over the next several weeks, the MJS team would return to Ville-la-Grand, their preferred crossing point, again and again.

5. *Annecy*

On Wednesday, September 8, 1943, the refugees who had been living in Saint-Gervais and Megève were evacuated. The most vulnerable went to Le Fayet station to board the train. The others piled into big military trucks that had arrived during the night. At ten o'clock in the morning, the truck convoy, escorted by Italian soldiers, left. It followed the Napoleon Road back to Nice and arrived in the city without incident. Each truck driver had been given the name of a hotel at which to discharge his passengers, and all went according to plan. The rail cars were a different matter. At nightfall, they were still sitting on the tracks, just where they had been at sunrise.

At 6:30 that evening, General Dwight Eisenhower announced over United Nations Radio that Italy had unconditionally surrendered to the Allies. Historians have called the timing of the announcement premature, but this may not be a fair characterization given the way that events unfolded. On September 3, the Italian government had entered into an armistice. They agreed not only to surrender but also to render certain forms of assistance to the Allies in fighting the Germans. (British forces had landed at the tip of Calabria, on Italy's toe, the same day.) The signing of the agreement was kept entirely secret so that the American forces could make final preparations for carrying out Operation Giant II. The operation called for the 504th Parachute Infantry Division, part of the 82nd Airborne Division, to drop into airfields twenty-five miles northwest of Rome on September 8. These American forces were to help Italian forces secure the capital and keep it out of German hands. On September 7, General Maxwell Taylor, the commanding general of the paratroop division, made a secret mission to Rome to meet with Italian military commanders, review preparations that the Italians had been made, and finalize arrangements. To his astonishment and great dismay, he discovered that no preparations had been made. He insisted on meeting with the head of the government, Marshal Badoglio. It was already evening; the American paratroopers were due to begin landing in a matter of hours. Arriving at the Marshal's home, he found that Badoglio was asleep and had to be awakened. Badoglio confirmed that the Italian forces were not prepared and that the operation would have to be postponed. The operation was cancelled just hours before it was scheduled to begin. On September 9, American and British troops landed at Salerno and immediately encountered fierce resistance on the part of German troops. For those who regard the September 8 announcement of the armistice as premature, the question remains as to what the more appropriate date would have been.

Eisenhower's announcement caught many off-guard, but some were ready and waiting. The German High Command in France had been busy preparing to seize Jews who had been living under the protection of Italian soldiers as soon as the soldiers were gone. German troops had quietly taken up positions throughout the Italian Occupation Zone and were awaiting the order to pounce. On Saturday, September 4, SS-Obersturmführer Heinz Röthke, the head of the Judenreferat, had issued a directive to his sub-lieutenant, SS-Stürmbannführer Hagen, to arrest and deport all Jews, regardless of citizenship status.

The significance of what happened on September 4 is not to be overlooked. Heinz Röthke had spent a great deal of time pressuring Vichy officials to revoke the citizenship of Jews naturalized after August 10, 1927, in order to create a legal pretext for arresting and deporting them. In June 1943, when French Prime Minister Pierre Laval and Justice Minister Gabolde signed a draft of the legislation, Röthke assumed it was a done deal. In early August, he learned that Laval had withdrawn his support. Despite pressure exerted by Röthke and other high-ranking German officials, the Prime Minister refused to acquiesce. By the time Röthke issued the directive in early September, German officials responsible for executing the Final Solution in France had resolved that legality would no longer be an issue: all Jews in France—*Israélites* and *juifs*—would be arrested, sent to Drancy, and subject to deportation. This significant change in policy was to be inaugurated in the territory vacated by the Italian army.

In his directive, Röthke also briefed Hagen on various procedural matters: "to prevent the Jews from escaping the action will begin in the frontier areas and work inward . . . from east to west"; "[the Jews] may take with them essential clothing, and articles of daily use"; "the bureaus in Lyon and Marseille have prepared provisional assembly-points in these two towns"; and "when the capture of the Jews is completed, they will be transferred from the provisional camps in transports of 1.000 to 2.000 heads to the Jewish camp in Drancy, whence after thorough examination of their citizenship they will be immediately evacuated to the east . . ." Röthke further noted that two of their superiors—SS-Hauptsturmführer Brunner and SS-Hauptscharführer Brückler—were scheduled to arrive in Lyon and Marseille on the fifth or sixth of September. Complaining that the Italian authorities failed to take measures that would facilitate the identification of Jews—the stamping of identity papers and ration cards or preparation of lists of names—he directs Hagen to adopt a method that had not previously been used to any significant degree in France but that had proven its effectiveness elsewhere. "Consequently, it is necessary to appoint French antiSemites to spy out and denounce Jews who are camouflaged or hidden. Money should be no consideration (propose to pay 100 francs per Jew)."

With the benefit of hindsight, one registers the reference to Brunner and the suggestion that he was to involve himself personally in the operation as particularly alarming. Alöis Brunner was Adolf Eichmann's key deputy. The thirty-one-year-old Brunner had amply demonstrated his ideological zeal for the Nazi program of mass murder, his ability to marshal resources and overcome logistical obstacles, his fondness for psychological manipulation and inventive ruses, and his penchant for gratuitous brutality. Over a period of eight weeks—March 15 to May 9, 1943—he and Dieter Wisliceny had overseen the deportation of forty-eight thousand Jews from the city of Salonika, Greece, annihilating the largest Sephardic Jewish community in the world. Before that, Brunner had directed massive deportations of Jews from Vienna and Berlin.

In June, Eichmann sent Brunner to Paris. His first assignment was to transfer jurisdiction of the Drancy transit camp from French to German jurisdiction. This was done in early July, and, from then on, the fate of Jews imprisoned in the camp—selecting who would be sent to Auschwitz and who would be spared, at least temporarily—was in German hands. Secondly, he was charged with overseeing the organization of forces that could be relied upon to arrest native-born as well as foreign Jews. He sought to mobilize groups that would take orders directly from German authorities—"SEC [Sections d'Enquête et Contrôle], the Doriotists (supporters of the flagging fascist movement of prewar fame), the Francists of Marcel Bucard, and various other auxiliaries—but never the French police." Thirdly, he was given the task of "purging the region [of the former Italian Occupation Zone] of Jews."

~

At the same time that families from Saint-Gervais were settling into their hotel rooms in Nice, members of the MJS team were busy smuggling the fourth convoy of children across the border. Surviving Swiss documentation shows that thirteen children were arrested at 10:40 p.m. on the eighth of September and taken to the Swiss border guard post at Mon Idée. The names and ages of the children are as follows: Elie Chetret (11), his brothers Maurice (10) and Marcel (6), and his sister Yvette (4); Maurice Loberstein (16), his sisters Lisa (13) and Ginette (11), and his brothers Jules (8) and Nathan (5); François Lustman (7); Suzanne Plewa (14); Henri Wolkowski (14); and Mendel Zanger (15).

The names of eleven of the thirteen appear on lists of names preserved in the archives of the Rue Amelot Committee. I have not located the names of Henri Wolkowski or Mendel Zanger on the Rue Amelot lists. However, the surviving lists are far from complete, and it is possible that these two adolescents had been in the care of that organization. What was the Rue Amelot Committee, and how did children in its care end up in the hands of the MJS team?

The Rue Amelot Committee was among the most important social assistance organizations serving immigrant Jews in Paris during the Occupation. Its soup kitchens, medical clinics, and clothing dispensaries helped thousands of indigent families. It was also one of the first Jewish organizations to engage in humanitarian resistance—illegal and clandestine—while continuing to carry out its traditional (i.e., legal and above ground) relief work. After the Vel d'Hiv roundup, the Rue Amelot Committee took on the task of rescuing Jewish children who had been orphaned or whose parents could no longer care for them. It developed a special underground branch devoted to placing and maintaining the children in hiding with non-Jewish families who lived on the outskirts of Paris and in the countryside.

On June 1, 1943, the Gestapo raided the premises used by the Committee, shut down its operations, and arrested its director, David Rappoport. Committee members secretly transferred responsibility for some of the hidden children to OSE. It was OSE leaders who decided that it would be a good idea to transfer some children to Switzerland. They arranged to place them in the hands of the MJS team in the Haute-Savoie.

Jules Jacoubovitch was the Secretary of the Rue Amelot Committee and the group's second in command. In his memoir, he states that fifty-eight children who had been in the care of the Rue Amelot Committee were "evacuated" to Switzerland, and he credits "Simon Lévit [sic] and Madame Marcel" with achieving this feat in September 1943. (He does not provide any information as to the identity of Madame Marcel.) The archives of the Rue Amelot Committee, maintained at YIVO at the Center for Jewish History in New York, contain lists of names of some of the children who were in the organization's care. Through consultation of the surviving Rue Amelot lists I located in that collection, I identified the names of thirty-seven children whom I knew to have been smuggled into Switzerland by the MJS in the fall of 1943.

Like the children who comprised the third MJS convoy, those in the fourth had never heard of the MJS. They had no idea who was responsible for smuggling them into Switzerland. How is it possible that I am able to identify each child in each convoy by name? How do I know which convoys were taken to the border by members of the MJS and which by members of OSE or some other group? The answers to these questions are to be found in two different archives, in two different cities, in two different countries.

~

The Old City of Geneva is situated at the top of a steep hill. It doesn't matter which narrow cobblestone street you climb to reach the summit; eventually, you will find yourself in front of the Hôtel de Ville, emblazoned with the city's red, yellow, and black flags. The reading room of the archives is on the second floor of city hall. It is a peaceful place; when the weather is seasonable, its tall windows are flung open and the room is flooded with light. In the early afternoon, the chiming of church bells mixes with the clattering of dishes being cleared from nearby café tables.

When an unaccompanied child illegally entered the canton of Geneva in 1943, a member of the Corps des gardes-frontière (Border Guard Corps) placed him or her under arrest and prepared a formal arrest report. If siblings or other persons related to the child accompanied him or her, all of their names were recorded on a single arrest report. Covering the front and back of a single page, the report was organized to solicit information about the individual(s), his/her (their) background (date of birth, nationality, "race and religion," etc.), the circumstances surrounding the arrest, the motive for entering Switzerland illegally, and other subjects.

The child was then placed under the control of a military body known as the Arrondissement territorial Genève. The "Arr. ter. GE," as it was commonly abbreviated, was one of sixteen territorial arrondissements established in 1939 for the purpose of overseeing and protecting Switzerland's borders. A military official would question the child further, supplementing or modifying information contained on the arrest report. The official would record a few key pieces of data on an index card, to be filed alphabetically. He would also prepare a one-page document called a "*Déclaration*." As in the case of the arrest report, a single *Déclaration* covered all family members who had crossed the border together. In addition to summarizing salient data, the Declaration set forth a narrative statement, usually two or three paragraphs in length. Typically, the narrative statement mentioned where the child had been born, where he or she had attended school, when he or she had come to France, the names of the various places where the family had lived, and where and with whom the child had been living before making the border crossing. Often, the Declaration would include a brief statement explaining why the child had entered Switzerland illegally. In most instances, the statement would read something like, "I crossed the Swiss border to escape measures taken by the German authorities against the Israelites." The Declaration was written in the first person and bears the child's signature. This gives the reader the impression that the child wrote the Declaration, but that was not the case.

The arrest report and Declaration were placed in a dossier that was numbered and cross-referenced in the alphabetical card index. Other documents pertinent to the child's case, such as correspondence, might be subsequently placed in the child's dossier as well.

Academic researchers and those seeking clues to their own personal histories are able to peruse the original dossiers in the reading room of the Geneva archives. Each individual dossier consists of a single sheet of mustard-color construction paper, folded in half, stamped with the word "SECRET," in blue ink

2911

No. 251/ 237 B.S. 4301
Corps des gardes-frontière
VIème Arrondissement

B.C. VI No. 251/2. 2916
24.9.43

Cornières, le 24. 9. 1943.

Au poste de gardes-frontière
Cornières

Arrestation de réfugiés.

1. Etat-civil : Nom Wapniarz Prénom : Wolf
Date de naissance : [obscured] Nationalité : polonaise
Race et religion : juive Profession : —
2. Papiers : /
3. Situation militaire : /
4. Domicile avant la guerre : Metz
5. Itinéraire suivi : Paris Annemasse
6. Arrestation : Date : 24.9 heure : 20.40 lieu barrage
par 3. gfs
Comment, où et quand la frontière a-t-elle été franchie ?
clandestinement
passeur éventuel : oui
à quelles conditions ? ?
Le réfugié était isolé - faisait partie d'un groupe de 21 personnes
dont les membres de sa famille désignés ci-contre.
7. Motif de la fuite : échapper aux all.
8 Moyen d'existence en Suissé : non
9. Etat de santé (déclaration du réfugié) : bon
10. Proches parents en Suisse (père, mère, conjoint, enfants)
nom et adresse :
11. Relations étroites avec notre pays ?
Séjours antérieurs :
12. Observations diverses :

Exhibit 1: Front and back sides of Arrest Report Prepared for Wolf Wapniarz, with birthdate obscured by N. Lefenfeld. © Archives d'État de Genève. Reproduced with permission of Wolf Wapniarz.

13. Etat-civil des membres de la famille du prénommé arrêtés avec lui, pour lesquels il n'est pas fait de rapport spécial:

Nom	Prénom	Naissance	Profession	Lien de parenté

14. Liquidation du cas par:

Refoulement immédiat ______ (heure, lieu) ______

" p.c. de l'Of.Pol. " " ______

Remis à la gendarmerie de Ct. Bg. p. o. plt Gauthier

Signature de l'agent:

Transmis au Cdt. du Corps, Genève.

gi Duc...., Bg

L'Of. de sct.:

Transmis à:

Direction générale des douanes, Berne, par vds.

Of. de police Ar. ter. GE

Le Commandant du Corps:

Décision de l'Ar. ter.

Au poste de:

Exhibit 1, continued.

ARRONDISSEMENT TERRITORIAL
GENEVE

Genève, le 27-9-43.

4911

DECLARATION

Concernant :

WAPNIARZ Wolf, né le [obscured] à Metz, fils de Zureck et de Golda née Judess, Français, israel., écolier, cél., dernier dom. Paris, 21 rue Paul Albert.

Il déclare : Je suis resté à Metzé jusqu'en 1940. Dans cette ville j'ai commencé mes écoles puis je suis allé à Royon avec mes parents , puis à Angoulême puis je suis venu à Paris car mesé parents ont été déportés. A Paris j'ai été dans un centre d'enfant où je suis resté jusqu'à ces derniers jours.

C'est à ce centre qu'un monsieur est venu me chercher pour me conduire à la gare et de là avec 19 enfants nous avons été conduits par une personne jusqu'à Annecy et ensuite par des passeurs.

Nous avons passé la frontière le 24-9-43 vers les 2h30 dans la région de Chêne-Bourg . Dès notre passage nous avons été arrêt9s et conduits au poste de douane puis au centre d'acceuil des cropettes.

Visite sanitaire : effectuée

Moyens d'existence : aucun

Connaissances : aucune

Pièces d'identité : aucune

i/f. G.A. Geiger

Lu et confirmé :
Wapniarz Wolf

Exhibit 2: Sample of Declaration Prepared for Wolf Wapniarz, with birthdate obscured by N. Lefenfeld.

that has faded, along with the dossier number. The construction paper protects the fragile onionskin papers that contain the arrest report and Declaration. It may seem to be a small miracle that such documents have survived the passage of time. In fact, it is.

In 1984, the archives of the Arr. Ter. GE—consisting of thousands of index cards and dossiers—were turned over to the Archives d'État de Genève, the Geneva State Archives (AEG). The state archivist contacted the director of the Federal Archives, Oscar Gauye, about sending the collection on to Berne, the Swiss capital. This would have been a natural thing to do, as the documents originated within a branch of the army. Guaye advised the state not to send the collection to Berne but to hold onto it. Although this advice surprised Geneva officials, they followed it.

For nearly fifty years after the end of the war, the archives of the Arr. Ter. GE served little purpose beyond being used to furnish certificates to those residents of the border area who had been interned in Switzerland during the Second World War. In 1993, officials of Yad Vashem made a formal request to the Swiss government for information concerning Jewish refugees refused entry during the war. A review of Federal archives carried out under the direction of the Swiss historian Guido Koller revealed that much of the documentation pertaining to refugees who had been turned away during the war had been destroyed. Why and when the records were destroyed remains unknown. Federal authorities then forwarded the request from Yad Vashem to state archivists in the cantons along the country's borders. According to Catherine Santschi, Geneva state archivist in 2000, "Although most of the cantons responded negatively or maintained their silence, the response of the Archives of the State of Geneva was straightaway positive: the collection of the territorial arrondissement of Geneva was known but little exploited, because it contained personal data, sometimes sensitive, and therefore subject to legal restrictions and regulations, federal and cantonal, regarding the protection of personal data."

Yad Vashem's request came at a time when worldwide attention was focused on the conduct of Swiss banks during and after the war. Switzerland was in a defensive posture, undergoing a painful but necessary period of reexamination. No definitive analysis of the number of refugees turned away at the border—Jewish or otherwise—had ever been done, and historical estimates had often been inaccurate. Federal and cantonal officials recognized that the archival collection of the Arr. Ter. GE could shed light on the issue. For the first time, the uniqueness and value of the collection were revealed. State archivists embarked on the time-consuming job of documenting the nature of the collection and analyzing its contents.

The collection is extensive and rich in detail, but, for a visitor or visiting researcher, the process of locating records pertinent to one's area of inquiry can be slow and cumbersome. A computerized database of information contained in the dossiers has been developed, but its use is restricted. State archivists graciously accommodated my requests to query the database and extract informtion. I was not permitted to do this myself.

The researcher must also bear in mind the circumstances under which the information was collected and assembled and the limitations upon its accuracy. Information recorded by the Swiss border guards on date, time, and place of arrest constitute a reliable data source. To the best that can be determined, personal data pertaining to the child (e.g., name, date and place of birth, parents' names) are usually correct. One must be wary, however, of information contained in the Declaration regarding the circumstances leading up to the border crossing, as this information may or may not be accurate. Typically, before making the crossing, the children were given instructions as to what they should or should not say in response to questions posed by Swiss authorities. A careful reading of the children's Declarations suggests that the instructions varied from group to group. However, it is clear that, in general, children were instructed to avoid providing precise information on how they reached and crossed the border. In particular, they were to avoid furnishing information on the person or persons responsible for getting them to and/or across the border. Moreover, the child being questioned by Swiss authorities may or may not have known the actual identities of his or her rescuers or the name of the organization with which they were affiliated. In the case of convoys entrusted to the MJS team, the situation regarding what the children did or did not know seems clear and straightforward: those who made the crossing on August 17 and August 28 had some idea of how and by whom their rescue was effectuated (because their groups were organized in Saint-Gervais and Megève); those comprising other convoys did not. In other words, the great majority of children in MJS convoys neither learned the actual identities of their rescuers nor heard any reference whatsoever to an organization called MJS.

By itself, the collection of dossiers preserved in the Geneva State Archives provides a sufficient basis for reconstructing the convoys of unaccompanied children that were smuggled into Switzerland. However, how is one to ascertain with any degree of certainty which rescue organization bore the responsibility for each individual convoy? To find information useful in making this determination, it is necessary to visit an archive in Paris.

The OSE archives are now maintained in the Mémorial de la Shoah Musée/Centre de documentation juive contemporaine (Shoah Memorial Museum/Center of Contemporary Jewish Documentation), located in the Fourth Arrondissement, at the edge of the Marais, the historic Jewish quarter. Until recently, however, they were kept in the headquarters of the Alliance israélite universelle (AIU), at 45, rue La Bruyère in the Ninth Arrondissement. Unlike the AEG reading room, which sits at the top of the world, the AIU reading room, situated on the basement level, is as cool and sheltering as a cave and not a sound from the outside world intrudes. At that time, the OSE archives were loosely organized and filled several dozen boxes. The index to the archive provided a general description rather than a specific listing of the contents of each box. Consequently, until one sifted through the contents, one did not know precisely what documents one might find.

Buried in the wartime records of OSE was a twenty-seven-page list entitled *"Liste des enfants partis en Suisse en 1943-1944"* ("List of children who left for Switzerland in 1943-1944"). The typewritten compendium of 978 names is dated June 1, 1945. In addition to the child's first and last names, the list presents data on the child's date and place of birth and *"date du départ"* ("date of departure"; i.e., the date that the child crossed into Switzerland). In addition to these five columns, a sixth column entitled "observation" appears on twenty-one of the twenty-seven pages; it contains miscellaneous comments relating to a very small number of children listed.

The data contained in the list are fragmentary. In most cases, information is provided on the child's first and last names and his or her date and place of birth. However, in some cases, only the child's last name appears and the remainder of the row is blank. Overall, data on the date of passage are the least complete. Precise dates (day, month, and year) appear for about two-fifths (39 percent) of the children. Entries citing month and year appear for 25 percent, whereas, for the remaining 36 percent, no date is cited or only the year is cited. The list was obviously a working document—entries are checked off, crossed out, and annotated with handwritten words and numbers. Some entries are difficult or impossible to read. Yet, it is the only surviving list prepared by OSE of children in its care who were smuggled into Switzerland during the war, and, despite its limitations, it is a very useful document.

If the list had been entered into a computerized spreadsheet, it would have had a seventh column, and the column would have contained data for every child. Regardless of whether or not the date of passage is indicated, the column entitled *"date du départ"* contains the words *"par OSE"* or *"par Simon"* ("by OSE" or "by Simon"). In fact, this designation—"par OSE" and "par Simon"—dictates the quasi-alphabetical ordering of the list. Twenty-three children whose last names begin with the letter "A" and who are categorized as "par OSE" appear first, followed by ten names beginning with the letter "A" categorized as "par Simon." These are followed by twenty-seven names beginning with the letter "B" that are also designated as "par Simon." The list then switches back to "B" listings—forty-six in all—designated as "par OSE." It continues on through the alphabet in this back and forth manner.

The "Simon" to which the designation "par Simon" refers is Simon Lévitte. The earliest date of departure listed for a name appearing beneath the designation "par

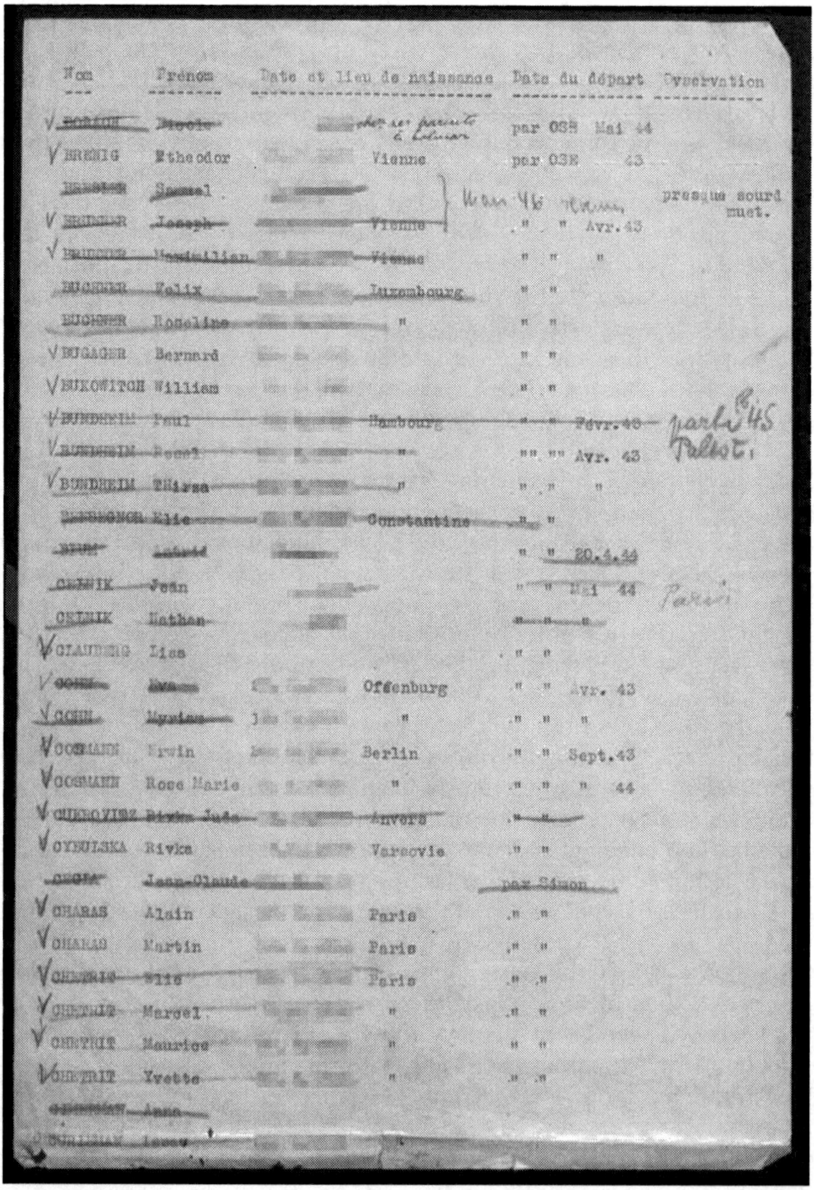

Nom	Prénom	Date et lieu de naissance	Date du départ	Observation
√ [illegible]	[illegible]	chez ses parents à Colmar	par OSE Mai 44	
√ BRENIG	Theodor	Vienne	par OSE 43	
[illegible]	Samuel			presque sourd muet.
√ BRUNNER	Joseph	Vienne	" " Avr. 43	
√ BRUNNER	Maximilian	Vienne	" " "	
BUCHNER	Felix	Luxembourg	" "	
BUCHNER	Roseline	"	" "	
√ BUGAGER	Bernard		" "	
√ BUKOWITCH	William		" "	
√ BUNDHEIM	Paul	Hambourg	" " Févr. 43	parti 45
√ BUNDHEIM	[illegible]	"	" " Avr. 43	
√ BUNDHEIM	Thirza	"	" " "	
[illegible]	Elie	Constantine	" "	
[illegible]	[illegible]		" " 20.4.44	
CZERNIK	Jean		" " Mai 44	Paris
CZERNIK	Nathan		" " "	
√ CLAUBERG	Lise		" "	
√ COHN	Eva	Offenburg	" " Avr. 43	
√ COHN	Myriam	"	" " "	
√ COSMANN	Erwin	Berlin	" " Sept. 43	
√ COSMANN	Rose Marie	"	" " " 44	
√ CUKROVICZ	[illegible]	Anvers	" "	
√ CYBULSKA	Rivka	Varsovie	" "	
[illegible]	Jean-Claude		par Simon	
√ CHARAS	Alain	Paris	" "	
√ CHARAS	Martin	Paris	" "	
√ CHERRIK	Elie	Paris	" "	
√ CHERRIT	Marcel	"	" "	
√ CHERRIT	Maurice	"	" "	
√ CHERRIT	Yvette	"	" "	
[illegible]	Anna			
[illegible]	[illegible]			

Exhibit 3: Sample pages (4 and 5) from *"Liste des enfants partis en Suisse en 1943-1944"* ("List of children who left for Switzerland in 1943-1944"), with column containing birthdates obscured by N. Lefenfeld. © Mémorial de la Shoah/CDJC, OSE (II)-307.

III

Liste des enfants partis en Suisse 1943-1944.

Nom	Prénom	Date et lieu de naissance	Date du départ	Observation
[illegible]	Albert	Sosnow	par Simon	
[illegible]LANG	Bernard	Paris	" "	
DIAMAND	Felix		" "	
DIEWALD	Heinz		" "	
DOBETSKY	Daniel		" "	
DRAZNIN	Léa		" "	
DREYFUS	Gérard		" "	
DZIERLATKA	Renate		" "	
DAISHEIM	Hans	Kaisersberg	par " "Ose Avr. 43	
DANAILOFF	Boris	Vienne	par Ose	
DAVID	Nicolas	Anvers	" "	
DAVID	Solange	"	" "	
DEUTSCH-STERN	Toni		" "	
DOERNBERG	Pierre-Jacques		" "	
DREYFUS	Edouard	Strasbourg	" "	
DREYFUS	Jacques		" " Mai 44	
DREYFUS	Michel-Simon		" " Mai 44	
DREYFUS	Berthe	Karlsruhe	" "	
DREYFUS	Léon	"	" " 44	
DRIMMER	Oscar	Toulouse	" " 44	
DYM	Béatrice	Anvers	" " Avr. 44	
DYM	Richard	Anvers	" " "	
DZIERLATKA	(garçon)			
DZIERLATKA	(garçon)			
EHRENREICH	Rachel		" " Avr. 44	
EHRENREICH	Paulette		" " "	
EHRLICH	Daniel	Strasbourg	" " Mars 44	
EHRLICH	Jacques	"	" " "	

Exhibit 3, continued.

Simon" is August 17, 1943, the date of the first MJS convoy. The existence of the OSE list makes it possible to distinguish between OSE convoys and MJS convoys.

The OSE list correlates extremely well with the information contained in dossiers preserved in the Geneva archives. Minor discrepancies in the spelling of last names exist. This is not surprising, however, given the fact that many of the last names are of East European origin and may be written by French speakers in any number of ways. Analysis of data contained in the children's dossiers preserved in the Geneva archives reveals errors and omissions on the OSE list. Yet, all in all, the OSE list is reasonably accurate and complete.

~

When the sun rose on the morning of September 9, the rail cars filled with the most vulnerable refugees were still sitting on the tracks at le Fayet station in Saint-Gervais. Finally, they were connected to a very slow-moving freight train. The train arrived in Chambéry eight hours later and remained there throughout the night. OSE was headquartered in Chambéry, and its personnel provided the refugees with additional provisions for the trip. The train would leave Chambéry the next morning; but, instead of being directed to Nice, it would be diverted at Saint-Michel-de-Maurienne toward Italy. It would arrive in Nice two days later, empty. It wasn't until March 1944 that OSE officials learned what had happened to the 240 people on the train. At that time, they received a report from Dr. Léon Silber, the physician who had accompanied the group in order to provide medical services. He informed them that, after a seven-day journey, the refugees had reached Rome.

Meanwhile, Nice was undergoing a sea change. In the hours following the announcement of the armistice, Wehrmacht troops began surrounding the city, seizing points of strategic importance, such as key roads and bridges. For ten months, the Italians had done their best to keep the Jews from falling into German hands. Throughout August, even as their own foothold on French soil slipped, they had promised Jewish refugees that they would protect them. However, once the armistice was announced, Italian soldiers faced the immediate threat of being shot or captured as *franc-tireurs,* guerilla fighters not entitled to prisoner of war status. To save themselves, they took flight.

Hélène Gorgiel-Sercarz recalls the morning of September 9:

> We didn't sleep much that night and when I woke up it still was dark outside. I saw my father standing at the window, and at the same time I noticed a faint noise of heavy rolling vehicles and when I joined my father at the window, I saw the unending stream of laden military trucks passing by. Our hotel was situated on a wide principal road which led to the mountains and seemingly to the Italian border. Father declared solemnly: "The Italians are leaving and they have left us behind!" I had no notions at hand to contradict him or to

> reassure him. We did not have much time left to plan what to do, when next we heard loud voices coming up from downstairs. We immediately made out that those voices were speaking German! I opened the door of our room and through the corridor I could clearly hear somebody shouting in German to the man at the reception desk that, by noon the same day, the hotel was to be cleared of all his lodgers and was requisitioned for the German officers. As dawn was coming upon us, we decided to leave the hotel at once. We understood that the requisition of the hotels was going on everywhere and that a hotel had become a dangerous place for us to stay in. And so, on the morning of the ninth of September 1943, just a year after we had arrived in France, we must have been among the first ones to notice that the Italian occupation of this small part of France had come to its end and that the German army was completing the occupation of the whole of France.

Alöis Brunner, his "inseparable adjutant" SS officer Ernst Brückler, and his hand-picked commando team arrived in Nice on September 10. They lost no time getting down to work. By the middle of the afternoon, SS police were combing hotels and apartment buildings room by room, streets, cafés, and public squares, indiscriminately arresting whomever they thought might be Jewish.

Unlike the situation in Paris during the Vel d'Hiv roundup, the Gestapo did not have lists of names and addresses of Jews living in Nice. This was not for lack of trying. In the months prior to the Italian capitulation, the Germans had been stymied in their efforts to lay their hands on lists of Jews living in the Italian Occupation Zone. Upon entering Nice, Brunner had members of his commando team search for any lists that might exist, before they could be destroyed or taken out of the country. They scoured the headquarters of the Italian Race Police and the residence of its commander, Inspector General Lospinoso. They did the same at the Italian Consulate. In a deposition given shortly after the end of the war, a member of the Consulate staff, Antonio Aniante, describes what happened.

> Immediately upon arriving in Nice, the Germans demanded of the Consulate the dossiers of Israelites from the Alpes-Maritimes. Monsieur Spejchel responded that the dossiers had already left for Rome and that that was done in order to avoid the identification and persecution of the Israelites. In reality, these dossiers have been partly burned, partly hidden and what remained is still in the archives of the Consulate. Accused of philosemitism, Consul Spejchel and the vice-consul Borromeo were deported two days later by the Gestapo. The S.S. rushed, revolvers drawn, into the Consulate, inspecting office after office to see if we were hiding Jews.

The commando team was unable to find any lists. What lists actually existed and what happened to them is far from clear.

~

On the same day that Alöis Brunner, Ernst Brückler, and the commando team began their work in Nice, the chief of the newly established German liaison headquarters in Annecy wrote a letter to the Prefect of the Haute-Savoie, Henri Trémeaud, requesting information about the internment of Jews and others in the department. In a letter written on the thirteenth, under the subject line "concentration camps," the Prefect responded to the request.

> In response to your letter dated the tenth, I have the honor of informing you that no concentration camp was established by the Italian authorities in the department. However, these authorities themselves established, without referring to the French administration, 700 Israelites and foreigners in forced residence at Megève and Saint-Gervais.
>
> These civilians were placed under the surveillance of the Italian Carabinieri. They were evacuated by them September 6 and directed, it appears, to Saint-Martin-Vésubie (Alpes-Maritimes).
>
> In addition, no French or foreign concentration camp exists or is envisioned in the department.

The succinct response must have disappointed the German commander, who had, apparently, hoped to find one or more concentration camps filled with Jews in the Haute-Savoie. One can imagine this man standing in his office in the Hôtel Splendid, at the edge of Lake Annecy, reflecting on the contents of the letter. Perhaps he has spent part of the war commanding troops on the Eastern Front or overseeing prisoners in a labor camp. Now he throws open the window and gazes out across the peaceful blue and green panorama. The weather is warm and inviting. A satisfying stillness fills the air. Sunlight glistens on the surface of the huge glacial lake. On the opposite shore, mountains rise to meet the heavens. Below the treeline, green foliage is flecked with tiny patches of red and orange signaling summer's end. The man thinks to himself that there are worse places—much worse places—to be stationed. What does it matter that he does not know the whereabouts of some Jews who have so craftily slipped through his fingers?

Some of them were, in fact, under the officer's nose. At the same time that the Germans were setting up their new liaison office, Tony Gryn and Mila Racine were establishing their base of operations in Annecy. From that time on, the town would serve as the staging point for the MJS convoys destined for Switzerland. The MJS team in Annecy was small: in addition to Tony, Mila, and Mila's sister, Sacha, it included Bella Wendling and Maurice Maidenberg. The twenty-two-year-old Bella, originally from Cologne, Germany, had, like Tony, been a member of the Grenoble *gdoud*. Mila and Bella probably knew one another from summer weekends spent at les Michalons. The young Maurice, only eighteen, had

Edge of Annecy Lake, September 2006. Photo by N. Lefenfeld.

been part of the refugee community in Saint-Gervais. Maurice identified with the Sixième, the underground branch of the Jewish Scouts.

On September 12, the fifth MJS convoy managed to make its way to Switzerland near Pas de l'Échelle, where the first MJS convoy had crossed. The arrest reports indicate that they were spotted by Swiss border guards around noon and taken to the post designated Veyrier I. How and why the group crossed the border in the middle of the day is a mystery. Perhaps a sympathetic customs officer facilitated the passage. Or perhaps Madame Baudet and her daughter, Violette Crotti, rendered assistance. Mother and daughter were the proprietors of café Chez la Marthe, situated very close to the border in Pas de l'Échelle. They are credited with helping many people—refugees as well as *résistants*—reach safety.

The convoy was comprised of fifteen children. Information contained in their Declarations states that, up until a few days earlier, all had been living in Paris. The names of eight children can be found on surviving lists of the Rue Amelot Committee: Bernard Berkowicz (4); Isaac Cukierman (11); Henri Galinsky (15) and his brothers Wolf (13), Jean (11), Joseph (9), and Charles (5);

and Isaac Kramache (13). Some or all of the other seven children might also have been in the care of the Rue Amelot Committee, although I did not locate their names on lists. The seven are Maurice Zysman (15), Edmond Rajchman (14), and Ida Zlotnitzky (13) and her sisters Odette (12), Ginette (10), Hélène (8), and Marguerite (7).

~

Annecy is an ancient city: archaeologists have dated human settlement on the shores of the lake to 4000 B.C.E. Each century has left its mark on this, the most dreamlike place in the French Alps, although none more distinctly than the seventeenth. It was then that the man who would be canonized as Saint François de Sales served as Bishop of the Catholic diocese seated in Annecy.

Although the product of an aristocratic Savoyard family educated in Paris and Padua, Italy, the young François was endowed with a natural humility and a plain way of speaking and writing. In 1593, the Bishop of Geneva ordained him a priest in his family's parish church in Thorens. At this time in history, Annecy was part of the Geneva diocese. Geneva was so firmly in the hands of Calvinists that the Catholic bishop was in permanent residence in Annecy. The inhabitants of the area known as the Chablais—that part of France directly adjacent to the canton of Geneva, along the southern shore of Lake Geneva—was historically Catholic. However, in the early 1500s, militant Protestants from Berne had taken over the Chablais and outlawed Catholicism. Those who clung to their faith were persecuted—priests were expelled, religious orders suppressed, worshipers fined, and churches destroyed.

The year after his ordination, Father François volunteered to serve as a missionary to the Chablais. It was a dangerous and difficult undertaking. By that time, most in the area had converted to Protestantism; few considered themselves Catholics; and those who did so dare not speak about it. Father François spent his nights in the Château des Allinges, a protected hilltop fortress outside of Thonon-les-Bains that was the sole Catholic presence in the area. He spent his days on the road, striving to welcome the people of the Chablais back into the faith of their ancestors and introduce them or re-introduce them to its religious practices, teachings, and fellowship. Catholic history holds that, after he had served as missionary for several years, nearly all the inhabitants of the Chablais had converted back to Catholicism.

François was only thirty-five years old when he was appointed bishop and took up residence in Annecy. In the history of the church, he is presented as an especially beloved figure. He treated those cast as outsiders, such as heretics and prisoners, with love and kindness. It is said that little children followed him around, seeking his blessing. People from all walks of life wrote to him seeking advice on spiritual and mundane matters, and he responded. He published many books during his lifetime; his *Introduction to the Devout Life* was wildly popular in his day and is still read today. In it, he counsels a young married woman on how to lead a devout and worthy life amid daily distractions, temptations, and difficulties.

The bishop preached that, although faith and hope may lead one toward salvation, it is charity that makes it possible to attain that state. Life presents each one of us with opportunities to practice charity. "Every moment comes to us pregnant with a command from God," he wrote, "only to pass on and plunge into eternity, there to remain forever what we have made of it."

The life and teachings of Saint François de Sales have left their mark on many inhabitants of the Haute-Savoie. Some are true spiritual successors to the saint.

Camille Folliet was thirty-two years old when the German Occupation began. Born in Annecy, he had been ordained priest in Annecy's cathedral in 1932 and then sent to serve as vicar in the nearby industrial town of Ugine. The town's major employer was a factory that produced equipment used to harness hydroelectric energy. Many of the men in the town were employed as steelworkers. Wages were low and working conditions dangerous; but, as the world was in the grip of a severe depression, employers had little incentive to ameliorate these conditions. L'abbé Cam, as he was known, worked with labor unions to help secure higher wages and better working conditions. He also organized a local chapter of a national youth movement, the Jeunesse Ouvrière Chrétienne (JOC; Christian Working Youth). His superior did not look kindly on his work with *les jocistes*, which, they believed, was outside the traditional sphere of ministerial duties. In 1939, Father Folliet was mobilized and served in the army.

After the armistice, Father Folliet was appointed chaplain of the JOC for the diocese, and he returned to Annecy to live and work. He was given the use of a building called la Maison du Peuple—the People's House—located in the heart of old Annecy on the passage de la Cathédrale. There, the *jocistes* socialized, held study circles, and met with new recruits. To assist those who were unemployed, Father Folliet organized a nearby vocational center.

For the first two years of the Occupation, most Catholic clergy in France supported Maréchal Pétain unreservedly. They had confidence that he and his regime would restore the Church to a central role in French society and reinstate traditional values, which, they believed, had been severely eroded under the liberal Third Republic. No French Catholic bishops publicly protested discrimination against, or persecution of Jews prior to August 1942.

Well before that date, a minority of Catholic clergy at lower levels of the Church hierarchy had begun calling upon Christians to resist collaboration and renounce anti-Semitism. Between November 1941 and August 1942, four issues of an underground journal entitled *Cahiers du Témoignage chrétien* (*Notebooks of the*

Christian Testimony) were published in Lyon. The number of copies of each issue produced was necessarily small, but each copy, passed from hand to hand, was read by many. The chief instigator of the journal was a teacher at the Jesuit school at La Fourvière, Father Pierre Chaillet. Shortly after the appearance of the first issue, an ecumenical organization aimed at helping Jews was organized in Lyon under the name Amitié chrétienne (Christian Friendship).

The Annecy diocese was, in the words of Hyacinthe Vulliez, Camille Folliet's biographer, the "picture of French Catholicism." But Folliet identified with underground Catholic dissenters. He was in close contact with activists in Lyon, and he discreetly circulated copies of the *Cahiers du Témoignage chrétien* among those he trusted. In response to the stepped-up persecution of Jews during the summer of 1942, Father Folliet progressed from dissenter to resister.

For a Jew living in France in the summer or fall of 1942, flight to Switzerland typically entailed clearing three hurdles. First, one had to make one's way across the line of demarcation to the Unoccupied Zone. Second, one had to reach the department of the Haute-Savoie. Third, one had to figure out where, when, and how to cross the physical barrier at the border. Annecy is the principal town in the Haute-Savoie and the seat of the prefecture. Many Jews first set foot in the Haute-Savoie when they stepped off the train in Annecy. It was, for many, a steppingstone on the way to the border.

Camille Folliet recognized the importance of Annecy's location to Jews in flight, and he resolved to play a key role in assisting them. He developed a support network of individuals willing to temporarily shelter and aid the hunted individuals. One was Père Alphonse Baud, *frère supérieur* (brother superior) of the Capuchin monastery on the avenue de Cran; a second was Père Pluot, the director of the private Collège Saint-Michel, on the Faubourg des Balmettes. The fact that the Capuchin monastery and the Collège Saint-Michel are within easy walking distance of the Annecy train station made them particularly valuable to the rescue effort. Occasionally, those in flight were sheltered in institutions located outside of the town, such as the Trappist monastery in Tamié and the Sisters of the Cross convent in Chavanod.

During the same time period, l'abbé Cam established and developed linkages between rescue efforts in Annecy and those in towns situated near the border. He worked closely with many of the priests in these towns, such as Simon Gallay in Évian-les-Bains, Jean Rosay in Douvaine, Philibert Bublens in Thonon-les-Bains, Marius Jolivet in Collonges-sous-Salève, and Louis Favre in Ville-la-Grand.

The Catholic rescuers did not work alone; Protestant clergy and lay people played essential roles. The head of the Protestant parish of Annecy, Pasteur Paul Chapel, and his wife, Odette, provided temporary shelter in the presbytery and elsewhere on the church property for Jews on their way to the border. Members of the Protestant CIMADE—notably Geneviève Priacel-Pittet (whose underground name was Tatchou), Suzanne Loiseau-Chevalley, and Mireille Philip—routinely received Jewish children and families at the train station in Annecy and accompanied them to safe houses near the border. This ecumenical effort was very active between September 1942 and February 1943.

Out of necessity, the rescue work was conducted in great secrecy, leaving virtually no written proof or explanation of how it originated or developed. Much of what is known today has been gleaned from post-war memoirs and interviews. However, many of the individuals who played crucial roles did not survive the war. Moreover, it wasn't until the 1980s that real interest in documenting these rescue efforts emerged. By then, some of the participants who had survived the war were no longer alive.

The enactment of the Service du Travail Obligatoire (STO)—compulsory labor service in Germany—in February 1943 caused major shifts in public attitudes and priorities that are worth noting. The Reich had been pressuring Vichy officials for some time to provide labor for munitions plants and related industries essential to the war effort. In the summer of 1942, France had begun recruiting volunteer workers under a lopsided arrangement known as the *relève* (relief shift), whereby Germany returned one French prisoner of war for every three skilled workers it received. The *relève* failed to meet the demands of the Reich in terms of manpower and was quickly discredited among the French population. The STO was a draconian measure that subjected an entire group of young Frenchmen—initially those born between January 1920 and December 1922—to two years of slave labor in Germany. More than any other single action, the institution of the STO turned French opinion against the Germans and gave rise to the Resistance.

At first, Vichy authorities referred to STO evaders as "*défaillants*" (defaulters) and "*insoumis*" (insubordinates). Soon, the term "*réfractaires*" (recalcitrants) entered common usage. By the spring of 1943, Vichy authorities knew that, in the Haute-Savoie and elsewhere, armed bands of *réfractaires* had set up camps in the mountains and woods and were preparing for combat. The Maquis scholar H. R. Kedward states: "But during April [1943], out of a period of both determined and tentative refusal [of the STO], there grew an aggressive movement, a combative discourse, and a romantic mystique of rural revolt. '*Prendre le maquis*,' '*le maquis*,' and '*le maquisard*' entered the history and language of Resistance with an effect which it is difficult to exaggerate." Kedward explains that "*maquis*" is a word used by Corsicans to describe woods and scrubland on the island and that, in France in 1943, it came to mean "a committed and voluntary fighter out in the woods," a "*combattant*."

Around the same time that the STO took effect, the immediate threat to the Jews in the Haute-Savoie diminished, as the Italian army demonstrated its willingness to protect them. At this point, Camille Folliet turned his attention to the needs of the *réfractaires*, many of whom were his young *jocistes*. Most of the leaders of the Catholic youth movements instructed their followers to obey the STO requirement, but Father Folliet urged them to resist. He insisted that the young French man or woman who willingly went to Germany to work was betraying his country. Folliet's voice was clear and forceful, and he attracted *réfractaires* from many parts of France. By the beginning of April, Folliet had put the *réfractaires* in contact with the Armée Secrète de Thônes, a *maquis* group based in the mountains east of Annecy.

On June 10, members of the secret Italian police organization known as the O.V.R.A. (Organizzazione per la Vigilanza e la Repressione dell'Antifascismo, meaning Organization for Vigilance and Repression of Anti-Facism) arrested Camille Folliet as he descended from the train at the station in Annecy. Charged with aiding armed insurgents, he was interned in prisons in Cuneo and Fossano, Italy. The arrest and deportation of Folliet dealt a psychological blow to activists and resisters throughout the Haute-Savoie. Nevertheless, the framework for rescue that he had helped establish remained firmly in place. It was the existence of this framework that made it possible for the rather inexperienced MJS team to establish a base of operations in Annecy and succeed in its smuggling efforts.

Two women who were, to some extent, disciples of l'abbé Cam stepped forward to help the Jewish rescuers. This proved to be of the utmost importance. Rolande Birgy and Colette Dufournet were the same age—thirty years old in 1943—and both were longtime members of the JOC. Birgy was known simply as Béret Bleu because of the blue beret that she habitually wore. Dufournet used the cover name Brigette Lambert. Each had played an active role in helping to smuggle Jews across the border during the earlier period of activity (September 1942 to February 1943). They knew who in Annecy would be sympathetic to their cause, offer assistance, and maintain strict secrecy. To the best that I can determine, Rolande and Colette worked with both the MJS and OSE teams in the fall of 1943.

Despite the fact that the Germans established a regional headquarters in Annecy, the town would prove to be a good staging point for the children's convoys destined for the border. Jewish children would arrive at the train station at various times of the day and night. Someone connected with the rescue operation would meet them and discreetly take them to a school, convent, home, or other safe house, where they would remain until it was time to leave for the border. Their stay in Annecy would be between a few hours and a few days. Many of the inhabitants of Annecy contributed to the rescue effort in large or small ways. Others caught wind of the fact that something was afoot, but they chose to betray neither their friends nor their neighbors nor the strangers in their midst.

~

Whether all five members of the MJS team blended in equally well among les Anneciens, the native people of Annecy, I cannot say. Each team member carried a good quality *synthé*. Mila's *synthé*, made to appear to have been issued by the Prefecture of the Isère, stated that she was Marie-Anne Richemond, a twenty-year-old student born in Grenoble whose place of residence was Saint-Pierre-d'Entremont (Savoie). Sacha's papers presented her as Suzanne Racine, an eighteen-year-old student also born in the Isère. Tony's papers were in the name of Victor Antoine Michault. Maurice Maidenberg used the nom de guerre François Fauron. Bella used the alias Jeanne, although it is not known exactly what name appeared on her false papers.

Like other Jewish resisters, the MJS team in Annecy had to maintain strict secrecy about every aspect of the work they were doing. Even when communicating with close family members or friends, they could not reveal the fact that they were engaged in a rescue operation or disclose any information about their activities. Similarly, they received from others instructions deemed essential to their carrying out the mission. They were not briefed on the larger subject of how their activities were being coordinated with those of other resisters working elsewhere in France. Limiting the individual's knowledge of the broader operation was a security measure routinely used by resistance groups; it limited the amount of compromising information that an individual could possibly disclose under torture or duress.

Only eighteen to twenty-four years old, the members of the MJS team bore a weighty responsibility and lived with the daily threat of being unmasked, arrested, and deported. While traveling with children or by themselves in the region or simply walking in Annecy, they had to be vigilant, always alert and aware of what was going on around them. They had to learn to trust their own instincts. They had to rely on one another, trust one another, and look to one another to solve problems. It is not surprising that they formed strong attachments to one another and that some fell in love.

The love story of Sacha Racine and Maurice Maidenberg began in August, in Saint-Gervais. The two volunteered to smuggle a group of children to Switzerland by going over the mountains east of Morzine. (This also had been a kind of test case, and, although it had succeeded, convoy organizers decided not to use this route, which was particularly arduous, on a regular basis.) They took the train to Morzine. When night fell, they began their climb up the side of the mountain. Sometime during the night, they reached the summit and began their descent. Depite the fact that it was still summer, the air was very cold. Shortly after sunrise, they arrived at a farm. The people on the farm were busy making cheese, but they received the strangers with kindess and hospitality. They assured the group that they had indeed reached Switzerland, built a fire so that they could warm themselves, and fed them bread and cheese. Then they invited them to lay down and rest in their barn. There, in the barn, Maurice kissed Sacha. It was the first time that she had ever been kissed. Later in the morning, the children continued on their adventure, and Maurice and Sacha returned to Saint-Gervais. After the MJS team had established its base of operations in Annecy, the pair, preferring to stick together, would routinely accompany groups of children to the border. Their feeilngs for one another continued to grow. The love story that began in August 1943 would last their entire lives.

Bella too had met her future husband and was head over heels in love. Asher Michaeli, whom everyone called Ado, was a member of the Grenoble *gdoud* engaged in the manufacture of false papers. His job was to seek out sympathetic administrative personnel in the towns and villages of the Isère and obtain information that could be used in preparing the *synthés*.

Maurice Maidenberg and Sacha Racine, location and date unknown. Photo courtesy of Racine Family.

Bella Wendling and Ado Michaeli, Grenoble, 1943 or 1944. © Mémorial de la Shoah/CDJC, ARJF_MLXXXIII_C_88.

And what about Mila? Did she have romantic feelings for anyone? In July 2000, I interviewed Sacha Maidenberg in her apartment in Paris, in the Sixteenth Arrondissement. A profusion of red, purple, and pink flowering plants filled the long balconies. On the mantel sat a tiny black and white photograph, the face of a newborn grandchild framed in an announcement. One of the questions that I asked Sacha was whether Mila had ever been in love. Her reply, half in English and half in French, was, "I don't know because, in that time, when we were young, *on ne couchait pas avec des garçons*" ("we did not sleep with boys"). I asked again, trying to clarify the original intent of my question: Did she have a special boyfriend? She replied, *"Elle n'avait pas rencontré son grand amour. Mais, elle n'était jamais seule. Elle avait toujours un amoureux."* ("She had not met the love of her life. But she was never alone. She always had a sweetheart.") The following year, I spoke with Denise Vernay, the woman who went by the name Miarka during the war and who had been a close friend and confidante of Mila's in the Ravensbrück and Mauthausen concentration camps. She asked me what I knew about "the boyfriend." Mila had spoken to her of her feelings for someone whom she had not identified by name. I was not able to answer her question. I suspected it might be Tony Gryn, as the two had worked as a pair throughout the period of time that the smuggling operation was underway. However, I had no confirmation of this until 2006, when I contacted Tito Gryn. At the outset of our first phone conversation, I introduced the subject of my research and mentioned my interest in the key roles played by his father and Mila Racine. He immediately interjected, "She was his girlfriend, you know." Was Sacha correct in saying that Mila had not met *son grand amour,* her great love? One will never know.

6. *Nice*

I think of the border between the Swiss canton of Geneva and the French department of the Haute-Savoie as consisting of three segments. Segment one, the westernmost segment, runs from west to east, beginning at the Rhône River and ending at the Arve River. The terrain is generally flat, and, apart from the small town of Saint-Julien-en-Genevois, development is sparse. Small residential enclaves are interspersed with fields and farmland. Segment two begins at the Arve River and extends in a northeast direction to La Renfile. The city of Annemasse and the adjoining towns of Gaillard, Ambilly, and Ville-la-Grand meet the neighborhoods on the eastern side of the canton of Geneva to form a continuous urbanized area. Segment three extends north from La Renfile to Lac Léman, also called Lac de Genève (Lake Geneva), at the Swiss commune of Hermance. This segment is hillier than the other two. There is little that one would describe as urban; woods, farmland, and fields predominate.

To the best that I can determine, in 1943 some parts of the border between the canton of Geneva and the department of the Haute-Savoie were divided by four barbed wire barriers (two on each side). Other parts were divided by two barriers (one on each side). Finally, in some places where the international boundary followed the course of a river whose banks were lined with trees and other vegetation, no barbed wire barrier existed.

The barbed wire barriers that existed during the war are not in place today. It seems likely to me that, apart from that fact, the general character of segments one and three has not changed dramatically over the past seven decades.

In the late eighteenth century, numbered *bornes* (boundary markers) were placed along the fifty-eight-kilometer border that separates the canton of Geneva from the department of the Haute-Savoie. *Borne* number one was set at the southwestern end of the boundary line, near the Rhône River; while *borne* 219 was set at the northeastern end, at Lake Geneva. The stone markers were not uniformly spaced; nor were they uniform in terms of height or appearance. Some were large and distinctive; others were short and squat. Some of the original markers have been replaced over time. Regardless of stature and age, they were engraved with an "S" on one side and a "G" on the other. The "S," which faces France, stands for Savoie; the "G," which faces Switzerland, stands for Genève. Some of the markers still exist and can be located with the help of a guidebook. One can also find maps of the border area that include *borne* numbers.

Many of the arrest reports prepared by the Swiss border guards cite a specific *borne* number in referring to the place of arrest. This is quite helpful because it tells us the precise location at which the arrest was made. Although some features of the landscape have changed over time, the *borne* numbers have not. In the arrest reports, "*borne*" is abbreviated "b." Thus, *borne* number 185, for example, would be written as b. 185.

It is because of the *borne* numbers appearing on the arrest reports that we know that a group of Jewish children crossed the border at Le Juvénat in Ville-le-Grand on September 14. The place of arrest cited on their arrest reports, b. 108, references the *borne* situated at the southwestern corner of the school property. This convoy, MJS convoy number 6, would be the largest to cross the border anytime during the fall of 1943. There were so many children in the group—twenty-nine in all—that the organizers divided it into two subgroups. The time of arrest indicated for children in the first subgroup was 9:45 p.m., whereas that of the second subgroup was 11:10 p.m. The children were taken to the border guard post at Cornières. (On the Swiss side of the border, the name usually appears as "Cornière," as in the "route de Cornière.")

A new member of the MJS team, Roland Epstein, helped smuggle the group across the border. The twenty-one-year-old, whose false papers bore the name Roland Estienne, was originally from Szczuczyn, Poland. He had been a member of the Grenoble *gdoud*.

All of the children in this convoy had been living in the Paris region prior to their departure for Switzerland. It appears that the group was assembled in Paris and taken directly to Annemasse. Many of the children were very young and were traveling without older siblings. The names of ten children appear on surviving lists of the Rue Amelot Committee: Victor Grabsztok (13); Madeleine Gwiazda (9) and her sister Jeannette (7); Henri Kamer (5); Raymond Kuperas (12); and Fradja Rosenfeld (16) and her sisters Berthe (12), Rachel (9), Marie (7), and Sarah (5). It is very possible that some of the other children were also in the care of the Rue Amelot Committee even though their names have not been located on surviving lists. The other children in the convoy were as follows: Esther Alamand (12); David Ejzenbaum (13); Jérémie Kantorowicz (12) and his brothers Bernard (10) and Maurice (6); Isaac Kotkowski (16) and his brother Max (8); Paulette Kuperhant (14) and her brother Max (14); Albert Madjora (13) and his sister Rose (9) and brothers Michel (8) and Maurice (6); Eliane Neoussikhin (9); Edwige Plaut (7 or 8); Esther Sidi (13) and her brother Elie (10); Dora Tovy (13); and Emile Waksman (9).

Eliane Neoussikhin was an only child, the daughter of two electrical engineers who had met while students at La Houille Blanche (IEG) of Grenoble, a prestigious engineering school. Her father, Anatole, was originally from Moscow, and her mother, Valentine, was from Ukraine. After finishing school, her mother found

Roland Epstein (on the right), Chambéry, Summer 1943. (Victor Sullaper, also a member of the MJS, appears in the center; the individual on the left is unidentified.) © Mémorial de la Shoah/CDJC ARJF_MLXXXIII_A_49.

employment in Paris with Thomson-Houston, a large electrical company. Her father was unable to find a job and so established an atelier in which he produced and assembled transformers. On the eve of war, Eliane's father enlisted in the French army in order to gain French citizenship. His outfit was taken prisoner and sent to a stalag in Neubrandenburg. He remained a German prisoner until the end of the war.

Eliane and her mother struggled through the dangers and privations of the Occupation as best they could. At some point, Thomson-Houston dismissed Valentine from her job because she was Jewish. She then found employment with the Jewish social service organization COJASOR (Comité juif d'action sociale et de reconstruction or Jewish Committee for Social Action and Professional Reorientation). In 1942, Valentine placed Eliane in a boarding school in Viroflay, outside of Paris. It had become increasingly difficult for her to support and care for her daughter. When her oldest sister, whose son was a student at the boarding school, offered to pay the costs of maintaining Eliane in the school, Valentine accepted. Each day, the students at the school would be assembled to sing the unofficial anthem of Vichy France, "Maréchal, Nous Voilà" ("Marshal, Here We Are").

In June 1942, Eliane left the boarding school and returned to her home on the rue Meilhac, in the Sixteenth Arrondissement, in order to spend a school holiday with her mother. One afternoon, finding herself home alone, she decided to visit her grandmother, who lived twenty minutes away. She wore, over her blouse, a little jacket on which the requisite six-pointed yellow star had been firmly sewn onto the left side. In accordance with the German ordinance that took effect in the Occupied Zone on June 7, 1942, the star was the size of a hand outspread, outlined in black, bearing the word *juive*. (*Juive* is the feminine form of *juif*.) The requirement to wear the distinctive star at all times applied to all persons six years of age or older whom the authorities regarded as being Jewish.

Eliane had a pleasant visit with her grandmother. Her *bubbe* wanted her to taste some fruit compote that she was cooking and to take some home to her mother. It was not ready, however, and Eliane had to wait until it was done. By the time she left for home, it was getting late. The weather was warm; instead of wearing the jacket, she folded it and draped it over her arm. Sometime after 8 p.m., she arrived home to find her mother sobbing and upset. Although Eliane was not aware of it, Jews were not permitted to be on the streets between eight in the evening and six in the morning; a curfew had gone into effect in February, and the Paris police were diligent in enforcing it. Because Eliane had failed to arrive home before the start of the curfew, her mother feared she had been arrested. The episode startled Eliane. She realized that, had she not happened to drape the jacket over her arm, she might very well have been seized. She began to comprehend the enormity of the danger that she faced simply because she was Jewish.

Shortly after this incident, a French policeman came to the house to warn Valentine that her name was on a list of people to be arrested. By this time, Eliane had returned to the boarding school in Viroflay. Valentine immediately left Paris and went to the suburb of Bagneux, where other family members were living. Apparently, the warning had come just before the Vel d'Hiv roundup. By coincidence, Valentine's twin sister was also saved from deportation at this time by the kindness of a French policeman. She and her five-month-old baby had been arrested and were being held in the Vélodrome. A French policeman took pity on them and allowed them to escape by unlocking an exit door.

It is not known exactly how Valentine arranged to place Eliane in the group of children leaving Paris, bound for Switzerland, in September 1943. However, Eliane was related to Simon Lévitte—Valentine and Simon were first cousins—and it seems that her mother made arrangements through family contacts.

As would be expected, Eliane's memories of the departure from Paris and trip to the border are fragmentary. She remembers that her mother, after saying good-bye, left her alone in some unknown place, on a street corner, waiting for a man who would come to meet her and take her to the train station. She has another memory of walking along a road once the group had reached the Haute-Savoie. She followed the leader's instruction to throw herself down upon the ground and remain completely still whenever they heard a car approaching. To help the younger children remain calm, each had been paired with an older child. Eliane had been paired with a thirteen-year-old boy named Victor. Her most vivid memory of the entire ordeal is that, throughout the frightful experience of crossing the border, she clung tightly to Victor's hand.

Victor Grabsztok was the only child of Yankiel and Syrla, Polish immigrants who had arrived in Paris in 1928. He had six half-brothers and sisters, children of his parents' previous marriages. (Three of the children had come to Paris with Yankiel and Syrla; three remained in Poland until 1936.) Like the father of Maurice Glazman, Yankiel Grabsztok worked as a tailor. The family occupied a two-room apartment, about 500 square feet of space. Two sewing machines and a large ironing table occupied one of the rooms. During the day, the room served as his father's workshop; at night, Victor and one of his half-brothers pulled out a folding bed and slept there. The apartment had no toilet. In the morning, they washed at the kitchen faucet, and they went down one flight of stairs or up one flight to use the W. C. (abbreviation for water closet, the compartment containing a toilet). On Saturdays, they paid a visit to the public showers. When Victor's half-sisters arrived in Paris in 1935, seven people occupied the small apartment. (By that time, a brother and a sister had each gotten married and moved out.) They were packed as tightly as sardines and had little in the way of material goods, but they did not particularly mind. Many immigrant families in Paris lived much the same way. Victor's family was happy to be together and to be part of a diverse, vibrant Jewish community that had come from all parts of Europe.

The situation changed drastically for the Grabstzok family in 1941. One of Victor's brothers, Léon, was arrested and imprisoned in a French internment camp. Two sisters and a brother left Paris and made their way across the line of demarcation to the Unoccupied Zone. In July 1942, during the Vel d'Hiv roundup, a sister and her seven-year-old son as well as a sister-in-law and her three-year-old son were arrested and deported. Victor, his parents, and his sister, Marie, were more fortunate. A policeman came to their home, instructed them to begin packing their bags, and informed them that he would return for them later. They fled and hid in hotels and with friends. They returned to their apartment in October.

On December 26, 1942, Syrla, only forty-seven years old, suffered a fatal heart attack. In mid-January, Yankiel entrusted Victor to La Mère et l'enfant, one of the constituent organizations of the Rue Amelot Committee. The organization placed Victor and another boy, Raymond Kuperas, with a family who lived eighty kilometers outside of Paris. They were not able to attend school, and they had little to do except to try to make themselves useful around the house. In September, a social worker came to take the boys back to Paris so that they could join the group leaving for Switzerland.

Many years later, Victor would remember that he held the hand of a little girl as they made their way toward the border at night. They had been warned "not to talk, not to cough, not to cry . . . in short, absolute silence." At some point, the leader of the group gave the children the order to throw all of their bags and backpacks over the top of the rows of barbed wire. Eliane had a backpack and a red handbag that her mother had given to her. The red handbag contained a piece of paper on which the name of her grandmother's uncle, Mendel Slatkine, had been written. Monsieur Slatkine lived in Geneva and was prepared to receive Eliane once she had crossed the border. Eliane threw the backpack and handbag over the top of the rows of barbed wire. The children then lay down on the ground and crawled beneath the wire. The items thrown over the top had landed in a place where the grass was very high. Eliane retrieved the backpack; but, as it was dark and everyone was scrambling, she was unable to find the red handbag.

After passing through the No Man's Land and the subsequent row or rows of barbed wire, Victor, Eliane, and the others comprising their subgroup were suddenly surprised when a soldier, wearing what appeared to be a German helmet, leapt out from behind a tree and yelled "Halt!" in German-accented French. The children were paralyzed with fear. When the soldier saw their fright, he assured them that they were in Switzerland and that they were not in danger.

~

Unable to find any lists of Jews, Alöis Brunner devised his own strategy for hunting down his prey. In a contemporaneous report on the situation in Nice, an unidentified member of the MJS described the "*procédés*," the methods, employed:

a) The Germans set forth as an absolute rule that circumcision was the equivalent of being Jewish. So all the papers, for the most part, were losing their value.

b) voiturettes [small, two-seater automobiles], mounted by "physiognomists" circulated, sweeping up everyone who looked Jewish, even if they had to release them had there been a mistake.
c) frequent roundups in hotels and furnished rooms.
d) an army of denunciators gets to work. Comprising real, organized bands, these denunciators, called "false Gestapo," systematically hunted down the rich Jews to plunder them, after which "real Gestapo" would come to arrest them . . . .
e) ferocious control of trains prevented the departure of Jews . . . .

Were any of these methods new? No. The presumption that circumcision was evidence or proof of being Jewish, the use of so-called "physiognomists" to identify Jews by their facial features, widespread roundups in hotels and apartment buildings, payments to informers, and surveillance of public transportation—all had been used in Nazi-occupied Europe, and all had been used in France. Yet, the situation in Nice in the fall of 1943 is generally described by those who lived through it and by those who have studied it as having been different from the rest of the time spent under the Occupation. The listing of *"procédés"* cited above is actually prefaced by the statement, *"And the persecution began in forms and with a frequency unknown up until then"* [emphasis added]. What set this manhunt apart from the others?

The first thing was the extent to which it was indiscriminate. Without lists of names and addresses, Brunner relied on what we today call racial profiling along with information supplied by collaborators and informers. Anyone was subject to arrest and interrogation on suspicion of being of a Jew. Poznanski describes it this way:

> . . . Brunner recruited paid informers, "physiognomists"—experts on the "specifically Judaic facial features"—who assisted the Gestapo's units as they went up and down the streets, going from hotel to hotel, building to building, casting their nets far and wide and arresting as many people as they could. Those arrested were made to drop their pants, and all who were circumcised were once and for all considered to be Jewish. It was an effective alternative to the identity card stamped with the word "Jew."

No distinction was made between *Israëlite* and *juif*; all were targeted for deportation. Also targeted were those who harbored Jews and persons engaged in any activities that the Nazis wished to characterize as sabotage or aiding the enemy. Maintaining a pretext of legality had been important to German and Vichy authorities up until this time, but this was impossible to do in an environment where terror rained down with little reason or cause.

The second distinguishing aspect was its ferocity. When the Paris police rounded up approximately thirteen thousand Jews on July 16–17, 1942, they did so largely without violence or brutality. Even Gestapo agents and Nazi soldiers in

France had been careful about where they brutalized their Jewish captives. They did not publicly torment or humiliate Jews in France as they routinely did in Eastern Europe and, at times, in other Western European countries. Particularly in the early years of the Occupation, they worried too much about French public opinion to engage in such activities. However, in Nice, in the fall of 1943, Brunner's commando team publicly maltreated and humiliated Jews and those whom they believed to be Jews to a degree that offended French sensibilities. Brunner did not rely on the French police to conduct the manhunt, as he worried that they would not carry out his orders. Some sources state that he used the French police to cordon off blocks or neighborhoods in preparation for an SS raid. Some suggest that, in executing raids, the SS was helped by the Milice française (French Militia), a paramilitary force, known simply as the Milice, created in January 1943 to fight the French Resistance.

The Niçois (native inhabitants of Nice) couldn't help but see and hear men, women, and children being driven through the hallways of their own apartment buildings and the streets beneath their windows. Klarsfeld quotes an "indignant" (his word) letter sent on September 23 from a Niçois to Monsignor Saliège, the Archbishop of Toulouse, which was intercepted and sent to the Gestapo. The quotation contains a description of the kinds of persecution inflicted on the Jews, and it concludes with the statement, "The population is outraged and appalled."

The third thing that accounted for the difference was the fact that the manhunt was long and relentless, continuing until Brunner's departure a few months later, on the fourteenth of December.

~

Some buildings requisitioned by the Gestapo during the Occupation are permanently cloaked in the gloom of those years. This is not true of the Hotel Excelsior in Nice. With its whitewashed interior and sparkling chandeliers, it couldn't be any lighter or airier. Lunching at a table beneath a palm tree in the sun-drenched courtyard, it would be hard to imagine that Brunner formally designated the Excelsior the annex to Drancy, which was itself the antechamber of Auschwitz. Jews—and those "accused" or "suspected" of being Jews—were brought to the hotel to be interrogated, tortured, and deported. Located at number 19 on the avenue Durante, the Excelsior is quite literally a stone's throw away from the central train station, a fact that may explain why it was selected to serve in such an ignominious capacity.

Dr. Abraham Drucker was a Jewish physician who was interned in Drancy in May 1943 and who worked in the camp's infirmary. On September 13, he and two comrades were sent from Drancy to Nice, where they arrived two days later. "We were directed to, and locked up in the Hotel Excelsior in Nice, and Captain Brunner gave me the order to organize an infirmary on the model of Drancy and to take care of my comrades who were interned, sick or wounded." His testimony provides one of the most vivid accounts of the period:

> During the three months that I was detained at the Excelsior, I have witnessed and been the victim of terror and frightening atrocities. The team, comprised of twelve to fourteen torturers, under the command of Brunner, carried out arrests of Jewish men, women, and children, for the most part done at night, all enduring endless interrogations, at gunpoint and often brutally beaten, in order that they confess their Jewish nature and that they reveal the addresses of parents, spouses, children, brothers, etc.
>
> Among those arrested, there were the sick, the handicapped, the old, infants, pregnant women, and all were subjected to violences and the tortures of these brutes; most had been plucked from their beds and taken in their nightclothes, shivering from fear and cold.
>
> Day and night, the majority of those arrested required medical care—dressing of wounds, by gunshot, to the thigh, leg, buttocks, cuts to the scalp, severing of an ear by the butt of a revolver, multiple hematomas and ecchymoses all over the body, broken teeth, split lips, scratches on the face, broken ribs, sprains, etc.

Dr. Drucker found himself trapped in a situation that may be a physician's worst nightmare: he was routinely called upon to treat patients so that they could be subjected to further torture and interrogation. Among several specific cases that the doctor describes in his testimony is that of a patient named Rosenbaum, whom they refer to as "Roz," brought into the infirmary covered in bruises, barely breathing, pulse barely perceptible, and in a state of shock:

> Doctress Spiegel and I were making desperate efforts to revive him (injections of caffeine, camphor oil, warm drinks, and hot water bottles). Nearly the whole night, this wounded comrade was between life and death. When he regained a little consciousness, he begged us desperately to give him shots in order to finish him off because he was afraid to be subjected again to these terrible interrogations and that the suffering would let slip a confession.

The doctor explains that, the next day, his patient was taken away for further interrogation. He was brought back to the Excelsior in the evening, locked in a room on the fifth floor, and prohibited from receiving any care whatsoever. Despite that, Doctors Drucker and Spiegel managed to enter his room. Once again, Roz begged them to give him an injection that would end his life. The doctors said what they could to encourage him to hold on and then left to attend to others. A short time later, they heard a cry, and they came to find that Roz had thrown himself out of the window. He lay in the courtyard unconscious and with multiple fractures. Dr. Drucker and two others carried him into a bedroom.

> . . . he was still breathing; his condition was extremely grave. The first thing that the butchers said to Doctress Spiegel and to me was: "Take care of him at any cost; he must live; we want him to talk"; we kept watch over our comrade part of the night, and towards morning, without having regained consciousness, he died.

In preparing his testimony, Dr. Drucker felt that it was important for him, as a witness to these events, to identify by name the Gestapo members at the Excelsior who committed atrocities. He cites the following: (1) Brunner, the commandant of the group; (2) Vogel; (3) Brückler, described as "particularly ferocious"; (4) Ullmann, the man who who tormented the patient Roz (Rosenbaum); (5) Bilartz, identified as *adjudant-chef* (master sergeant); (6) Zitter, identified as *oberscharführer* (senior squad leader) and described as "particularly ferocious, fanatical, having seen him strike many internees"; and (7) Gorbing, described as "elegant, speaking politely with the internees, but brutal in action, going as far as murder . . . pledging body and soul to Brunner . . ."

Once Wehrmacht troops took up their positions in and around Nice, the organizations that had hitherto placed themselves at the forefront of refugee assistance—the Dubouchage Committee and the Federation—disbanded. With just a few exceptions, the leaders of these organizations either went into hiding or left the city. This sudden turn of events left many Jewish refugees in desperate straits, without money, hiding places, or means of leaving the beseiged city. It is worth noting that the prominent scholars of the period concur on this point. Carpi states, "At the end of this meeting [on September 9], the Dubouchage Committee's activities were in fact over. Most of the active members dispersed, left Nice, or found shelter in some hiding place in the city." Lazare notes, "The almost complete disappearance of the FSJF staff in Nice, leaving thousands of Jewish refugees defenseless and without resources for their basic subsistence, could have been a brilliant victory for the Gestapo. But young people took up the battle." Poznanski makes the same point: "There had been increasingly urgent calls sent from Nice to Marc Jarblum in Switzerland, but all the offices that might have distributed such aid—which was vital for Jews to find lodging—had been mercilessly raided. The Rue Dubouchage committee no longer existed, nor did OSE, which had remained in operation for a time, nor did the UGIF."

Wolf Toronczyk, a member of the Dubouchage Committee, wrote about the last meeting of that group, on September 9: "The Political Commission then established a commission of camouflage and gave Jacques Weintraub [sic] the mission of taking care of hiding places and false cards; the terrible time of the reign of the Gestapo in Nice had begun."

Although it was extremely dangerous for Jews—especially men and boys—to be seen on the streets, it was also extremely difficult for them to find safe hiding places. They dared not return to the hotels or boardinghouses in which they had been staying for fear of being denounced or identified by others. Niçois who were not themselves hunted by the Nazis nevertheless feared for their own safety in the event that they knowingly or unknowingly rented lodgings to Jews.

Hélène Gorgiel-Sercarz speaks of the experiences of her family in finding shelter in a variety of living situations, each of which lasted for a brief period of time. After leaving their hotel on September 9, Hélène was fortunate enough to meet up with an acquaintance from Saint-Gervais, who had found shelter with a "company of theater artists" living in an "old, nearly collapsing house" in an old part of the city. Hélène and her parents were offered a room in the house, which they gladly accepted. One day, shortly after the family had moved in, the acquaintance burst into the house and told them they were in danger and had to leave immediately. They then went to a café, where a man overheard them asking the barman if he knew of a room available for rent. The man's sisters were away for two weeks on vacation, and he sublet their apartment to the Sercarz family. They stayed in the apartment for an unspecified number of days, but the sisters who lived there returned home early from their vacation. They were kind enough to allow the Sercarz family to stay in the apartment for one more night. The next day, Hélène and her parents again found themselves in a café trying to find a room to rent:

> . . . I asked around if somebody knew of a room to let. While sitting at the counter, father spotted, sitting next to us, an Italian looking man and he told me to ask him about a room. When I got a negative response the man went on explaining kindly that he himself, being on his own, was living in a rented room and he regretted not being of any help. When I translated this, father told me I should ask the man if he could not take us to his room for the night and we would pay him [for] a hotel room plus a sum of money. I was flabbergasted by this daring proposition on behalf of my father and said I could not possibly make such a proposition to a stranger. The man was listening to our fierce discussion and quarrel and asked me what it was all about. I don't know how I explained why "we" couldn't go to a hotel and deeply distressed I told him of my father's request. After some hesitation he said that he agreed to take us to his room for the night! The one night turned into a stay of several weeks and we became the sub-sub lodgers in the flat where we avoided meeting the other lodgers or the landlady. The following days, mother busied herself with repairing the huge heap of worn socks she had found in the wardrobe and sewing buttons onto the shirts of our miraculous "Italian." He came each day to enquire how we fared and each day he repeated his invitation to me to go with him to the movies and I steadfastly refused to accept. Mother and I went out to have a hot meal once a day

> because we couldn't use the kitchen for more than making a hot drink in the mornings on account of our precarious status in the flat. Our meals consisted mostly of pumpkin soup and pumpkin puree with sometimes some noodles and occasionally, on Sundays I gather, we had a treat of rabbit-meat. Each day we brought home grapes and bread for father and this was his only "menu" for quite a long time.

The Sercarz family was in a better position to evade arrest and secure hiding places than were many of the other Jewish refugee families trapped in Nice. They still had enough money to tide themselves over. They had at least one family member who was young and able-bodied and who spoke French. Able to blend in on the street, Hélène could serve as scout and lookout as well as translator. Perhaps most importantly, the family did not have young children. The presence of young children made it extremely difficult to find or keep hiding places. It also multiplied the difficulties involved in finding enough food.

Prior to the German occupation of Nice, OSE operated a local office at number 29 on the avenue Georges Clemenceau. The office was closed when the reign of terror began. (One source states that OSE officials continued their work underground, in liaison with MJS activists.) A few days after the Germans occupied Nice, two members of the Dubouchage Committee, Claude Kelman and Ignace Fink, forced open the door of the OSE office and quietly began receiving individuals seeking help. They kept the shutters drawn and the lights extinguished; their wives stood guard on the boulevard to alert them of any danger. Word passed from person to person; and, for two days, Kelman and Fink distributed money, food ration tickets, false papers, and advice on where to look for shelter and which neighborhoods to avoid. On the third day, the Gestapo arrived. The two distributing the help, alerted in time, managed to escape. They tried to warn others to stay away from the office, where Gestapo agents lay in wait; but, by the end of the day, seventy people had been arrested.

~

A copy of a photograph taken in July 1943 shows the young Jacques and Léa Wajntrob to be not simply beautiful but stunning. The twenty-three-year-old Jacques, squinting in the bright sunlight, has the slightest hint of a smile on his face. His hair brilliantined, dressed in vested suit and tie, he looks as if he is about to step into a court of law or the headquarters of a bank. His shoulders are broad and square. Léa, a year younger than her husband, has a soft radiance about the eyes and mouth. She looks at ease; he does not.

Jankiel Wajntrob grew up in Tarczyn, Poland, which today comprises part of the suburbs on the southwest side of Warsaw. Léa Eisenbaum grew up in Ostrowiec, ninety miles south of Warsaw. They met in Paris when they were teenagers, both enthusiastic members of the HaShomer HaTza'ïr. The Eisenbaum family had arrived in France in 1930; the Wajntrob family, in 1933.

The first mass arrest of Jews in France occurred in Paris on May 14, 1941; Jacques was one of approximately 3,700 foreign-born men seized on that date. He was sent to the internment camp of Pithiviers, approximately fifty miles south of Paris, where he worked as a carpenter. In July, he and Léa were married. He had been granted a twenty-four-hour furlough that permitted him to travel to Paris, and he dutifully returned to Pithiviers afterward. In December, however, making good use of his carpentry tools, he escaped.

In February 1942, Jacques and Léa set up their household at number 70 on the rue François Grosso in Nice. In the wake of the Zionist unification conference in May 1942, Jacques and Léa organized an MJS *gdoud* in Nice. They celebrated the birth of a daughter at the end of August, and, not long after, saw the entry of Italian troops, followed by an influx of Jewish refugees. The members of the *gdoud* placed themselves at the service of the Dubouchage Committee, doing whatever

Jacques and Léa Wajntrob, Nice, 1943. Photo courtesy of Brinbaum Family.

needed to be done to help care for the new arrivals. In December 1942, Léa approached the leaders of the Committee to request that they allocate some space in their building on the boulevard Dubouchage for the work of the *gdoud,* which they did. This was an important step; being in the center of this hive of activity gave the young MJS members opportunities to observe, learn, prove themselves, and, over time, assume greater responsibilities. It also raised the visibility of the organization and helped recruitment efforts.

When the reign of terror began, no one would have blamed Jacques and Léa if they had decided to hide or to leave Nice, just as the heads of most of the Jewish organizations had done. However, the Wajntrobs did not allow themselves to make that choice. The Dubouchage Committee had delegated to Jacques a responsibility that was too heavy for any one man, but he struggled to bear the weight of it. Using the alias Jacques Wister (some spelled it "Wyster"), he and members of the *gdoud* joined with members of the Sixième (Sixth), the clandestine arm of the Jewish Scouts, to form an underground rescue operation. Lazare is one of several scholars who emphasize this point, saying: "In Grenoble and Nice in particular, the two clandestine rescue organizations of the MJS and the EIF (the Jewish Scouts) remained intact during the Italian debacle. The Dubouchage Committee and the UGIF, including the OSE dispensary, had to close their doors during the general flight provoked by the reign of terror inflicted by Brunner's Gestapo, so the teams of Gutman (*Sixième*) and Weintrob (*Éducation physique*) remained the only recourse for a large part of these hunted Jews."

Members of the MJS and the Sixième worked together, twenty to twenty-five young men and women who "circulated among the hotels to unearth unfortunates." Some, like Claude Gutmann, alias Claude Duprat, went about the business of finding secure hiding places for those who were hunted. Others distributed financial assistance to those already in hiding. In early 1943, the Sixième had set up a laboratory for the fabrication of false papers. When the reign of terror began, they moved the lab to a new location. From a building situated at number 12 on the rue Guiglia, a group of several young men worked around the clock to churn out as many documents as they could. The group included activists who identified with three underground movements: Roger Appel and Jacques Marburger, who identified with the Sixième; Pierre Mouchenik, who identified with the Armée juive and the Sixième; Ernst Appenzeller and Maurice Loebenberg, with the Armée juive; and Serge Karwaser, with the Armée juive and the MJS.

The Wajntrobs quickly recognized that separating children from parents and getting the children out of the terror-stricken city held the greatest promise for saving children and parents alike. If the MJS could get the children to Annecy, the chances were good that they could make it across the border and find safe haven in Switzerland. Relieved of the responsibility of safeguarding their children, the parents would have an easier time finding hiding places and maintaining themselves in hiding.

Jacques and Léa took it upon themselves to begin organizing convoys of children and making arrangements for them to be taken out of Nice. Jacques handled the logistics, purchasing train tickets and arranging when and where the children would meet up with the chaperones. Léa found Jewish families in hiding, met with them, persuaded them to place their children in the convoys, and arranged for the transfer of the children at the appointed time. Who supplied the funds necessary to purchase train tickets and pay the other costs involved? The answer to this question is not known. Presumably, Jacques received funds from the Dubouchage Committee before or after it was disbanded and/or funds from the Federation.

In the middle of September, the MJS managed to take sixty-three children from Nice to Annecy so that they could be smuggled into Switzerland. This was no easy feat. Train travel was especially dangerous. German and Vichy authorities were constantly checking the identity papers of passengers in train stations and en route. The train ride itself was long and exhausting. Even today, the trip takes six-and-a-half hours on the high-speed TGV and nine hours on the conventional train. In the fall of 1943, the equipment was not what it is today and trains were often delayed due to sabotage along the tracks and the movement of soldiers and supplies. In terms of transferring the children to Annecy, however, there was, apparently, no alternative.

It is not known how many individuals were responsible for getting these children from Nice to Annecy or who they were. Declarations signed by a dozen children comprising the convoys of September 23 and 24 state that "Jeanne," "Thérèse," "Jeanne and Thérèse," "a girl," or "two girls" accompanied them. "Jeanne" probably refers to Bella Wendling of the MJS team in Annecy. "Thérèse" probably refers to Frida Wattenberg, a nineteen-year-old member of the Grenoble *gdoud*. Frida, whose alias was Thérèse Verdier, did, in fact, accompany children to Annecy from various places in France.

In a period of four days—September 21 to September 24—the MJS smuggled five convoys of children across the border. The five convoys comprised a total of seventy-two children; sixty-three had been brought to Annecy from Nice. In order to stage the convoys, it was necessary for some of the children to remain in Annecy for one, two, or three days. Some may have been sheltered in the Lycée Berthollet, a public secondary school, or in the Collège Saint-Michel, the Catholic secondary school on the Faubourg des Balmettes. Others may have been sheltered in private homes.

~

The eight-year old André Panczer was one of the youngest of twenty children who crossed the Swiss border on September 21 at Ville-la-Grand. The group was arrested at 10 p.m. and taken to the border guard post at Cornières. All of the children in the convoy had been brought to the Haute-Savoie from Nice.

The only child of Désiré and Thérèse Panczer, André was born in Paris and lived with his parents and Désiré's mother, Sarah, on the Faubourg Saint-Denis, in the Tenth Arrondissement. In 1925, after her husband died from typhus, Sarah and her sons and daughter had emigrated from Budapest to Paris. It was there that Désiré had met Thérèse, who was from Warsaw. The four lived in a two-room apartment that contained a tiny kitchen with sink, faucet, and two-burner stove. Thérèse used one of the rooms as her atelier; she sewed garments for some of the *haute couture* (high fashion) design houses. Désiré was a metalworker in a suburban factory that produced equipment for the army and private aviation. Sarah was a devoted grandmother to André, but her warm-heartedness extended far beyond their small apartment. In his exquisite memoir, André speaks of her as "the grandmother of every member of the family, near or far, of friends, of neighbors and of merchants in the neighborhood, of fruit and vegetable peddlers with their little bottle green carts, of shopkeepers perched on their doorsteps . . ." Sarah attended synagogue and observed Jewish holidays, but her children did not.

In June 1940, the Panczers left Paris as part of the *exode* (exodus), but they returned shortly after the armistice. As far as André was aware, life continued on much as it had done previously.

André was six years old when the German ordinance regarding the wearing of the yellow star took effect in the Occupied Zone, on June 7, 1942. He did not venture outside of his apartment building without wearing a garment on which his mother had sewn the distinctive star. One day, shortly after he began wearing the star, a "man in gabardine" came to the apartment to warn Désiré that he was going to be arrested. Indeed, the very next day, two police inspectors came looking for him. Désiré had already left Paris. He made his way across the line of demarcation and, reaching Prayssac, a village in the Lot River Valley, sent word to his wife of his whereabouts. She immediately made preparations to join him. Grandmother Sarah went to live with her son, Eugène, and his family in a Paris suburb. Thérèse and André left the city, and, with the help of a paid *passeur*, made their way across the line of demarcation and reached Prayssac.

"We were happy in Prayssac," writes André in his memoir. For the first time in his life, André experienced the simple delights of small town life. He attended the local school, got on well with the other students, and became good pals with a few. He spent most of his free time at a neighbor's farm, where he was given the chance to try his hand at everything—watering the oxen, gathering nettles for the geese, plowing the fields. He worked and celebrated alongside the farmhands during the *dépiquage* (threshing of grain) and the *vendange* (grape harvest).

André remembers the eight months that he spent in Prayssac as an idyll, but his accounting of events is sobering. After the family arrived in Prayssac, both parents found work; Désiré, in a sawmill, and Thérèse, with a local dressmaker. They experienced no discrimination or persecution. Many befriended them, and at least a few endeavored to help. The secretary of the mayor gave Désiré and Thérèse an unclaimed marriage contract. This enabled them to obtain identity papers in the name of Jacques and Louise Tanays. However, several weeks after they arrived, someone denounced Désiré, and French gendarmes arrested him. On September 1, 1942, he was registered in a foreign labor battalion, Groupement de travailleurs étrangers (GTE) n° 554, and sent to a work camp in the nearby village of Catus.

At the end of February 1943, shortly before he was to be deported, Désiré escaped from the camp and made his way to Nice. He managed to send word to Thérèse, and she and André joined him. After a short stay in Nice, the family was sent to live in assigned residence in Megève.

In that "paradisiacal place," the Panczers occupied a room in La Vallée Blanche, one of several hotels requisitioned by the Italian army. André attended classes until the summer vacation began. Thérèse taught sewing to young women in a workshop organized by ORT. The Jewish families living in the hotel "did not separate themselves from one another except to sleep." André and the other children enjoyed having the run of the place: "At certain times, the whole hotel became our playground; the corridors, the dining room, the reception, the kitchen—not a corner of the building was unknown to us." They played outside the hotel and ran wherever they liked. André loved what he saw all around him—picturesque chalets, fields of bright yellow buttercups, pine forests, the majestic Mont Blanc. It instilled in him a deep love of the mountains.

The paradise did not last very long, however. André suddenly found himself uprooted once again, at the beginning of September, when the family left Megève in the truck convoy and returned to Nice. The next thing he knew, they were living in a room on the rue Garibaldi, just opposite the Château de Nice, which housed the German Kommandantur (garrison headquarters). So that there would be no indication that anyone was occupying the room, they kept the shutters permanently closed and placed a thick covering over the window before turning on the light. Day by day, the danger increased. Désiré and Thérèse decided that it would be best if they separated from their son and placed him in the hands of people who would smuggle him to Switzerland.

The scene of their parting has remained fixed in André's memory. His father took him upon his knee and spoke to him solemnly about how he was to conduct himself. His mother, sad but maintaining her composure, filled a *musette,* a sort of single-strapped sac worn over one shoulder, with items that he would need—a shirt, a pair of pants, an extra pair of socks. Then each took him in their arms and, without saying a word, hugged him very tightly. Although he wanted to cry, he did not do so because his father had said to him, "At eight years old, you are a big boy, sensible and courageous." He and his father left the house. He knew that his mother was watching him from behind the closed shutters, but, so as not to betray her, he did not glance in her direction. He held his father's hand as they walked to the train station. They entered the waiting room and stopped in front of a glass case to look at the items on display. Suddenly, his father let go of his hand and disappeared into the crowd.

> I remained there, nose against the display case, my *musette* on my shoulder, fighting against the urge to turn around to look for papa somewhere in the throng and the duty to wait for something to happen. After awhile, which seemed like an eternity to me, someone took me by the hand and led me to the platform. I suspect that papa, hidden in the train station crowd, kept watch over the unfolding of the events. Someone had me board the train, someone settled me in a compartment in which there was already a couple, who paid no attention to us. The man and the woman did not raise their eyes from their reading. "Someone" descended from the train, and I found myself alone again with these people whom I did not know. The compartment filled little by little, and the train started up. Looking at the scenery or dozing, I traveled in this manner until, that evening, the train reached Annecy. It was there that the couple seated near me since Nice had me descend onto the platform, where they entrusted me to a young woman and disappeared surreptitiously.

In Annecy, André found himself in the company of six or seven children. After bathing and having something to eat, they slept on mattresses on the floor. The next day, someone took them to a café on the outskirts of Annemasse. There, in the back room of the café, they joined the other children who would comprise the convoy. Instructed not to make a sound, given something to eat and drink, they hid in the back room all day. Some of the children slept. Once darkness fell, four young people led the group out of the café through a rear door. They walked for a long time, stopping briefly when their guides signaled for them to do so. Although the children were frightened, they remained absolutely silent; not a complaint or sob issued forth from any of them. When they reached a river, one of the guides walked out into the middle of the current and helped the children across, one by one. The boys and girls had been told that, after crossing the river, they would encounter barbed wire, which marked the border, and that they must crawl beneath it. They did this, and, having cleared this last obstacle, found themselves in an orchard.

The oldest among them suggested that they begin to cry in order to indicate to anyone that might see them that they were children. They seated themselves at the foot of a tree, pressed tightly against one another. Suddenly, a soldier or border guard appeared; he was wearing what appeared to be a German helmet, and he spoke German. They needn't have been instructed to cry; frightened to death, it was their natural response. They followed this man to the border guard post. There, a French-speaking guard calmed them, assured them that they were safe, offered them each a banana, and invited them to lie down and sleep on a bed of straw until morning.

The convoy that entered Switzerland on the evening of September 21, the seventh MJS convoy, included nineteen children in addition to André. Their names are as follows: Lilianne Benadon (14); Isidor Brust (10); Isidore Eherlich (13); Estelle Goldfarb (14) and her sister Frida (14); Anna Granat (16) and her brothers Jacob (16), Simon, (13) and Joseph (10) and her sister Sarah (11); Hélène Karwasser (11) and her sister Génia (16); Arnold Katz (6); Léa Korzen (12); Renée Lipschitz (15); Léon Majerovicz (13); Joseph Sosnowski (12) and his brother Marcel (9); and Gertrude Zegel (14).

~

The MJS team began delivering convoys of children across the border in rapid-fire fashion. On September 23, a group of seven children was arrested in a place called the Plaine du Loup (Wolf's Plain) and taken to the border guard post at Sézenove. Arrest reports prepared for these children state that they had crossed the border between *bornes* 50 and 51. These markers are situated on the edge of the little farming community of Norcier, approximately one mile northwest of Saint-Julien-en-Genevois. This was the first time that the MJS team had crossed at Norcier.

All of the children in this, the eighth MJS convoy, had been brought to the Haute-Savoie from Nice. The Declaration signed by Albert Reisz, an eighteen-year-old born in Vienna, states, "I made the acquaintance of a certain Monsieur Wyster, Jacques, at the Café de Paris in Nice, Rue Pasteur Elie, who told me I could reach Switzerland with a convoy of children." In addition to Albert, the group included: Rosette Dolbert (14); Renata Dzierlatka (14); Harry Goldberg (14); Adolphe Herz (15); Henriné Hirschhorn (15); and Harry Walter (15).

The same evening, nineteen children, comprising MJS convoy number 9, crossed at the traditional crossing point in Ville-la-Grand. They were arrested at 10:45 p.m. and taken to the border guard post at Cornières. These children, too, had been brought from Nice. Their names were as follows: Cécile Axelrad (15), her sister Rosie (13), and her brother Simon (9); Hélène Feferman (15) and her sister Sarah (13); Victor Harif (8); Marcel Horowitz (15) and his brother Julien (14); Jacob Litman (15); Lore Mantel (12), her sister Cécile (7), and her brothers Jacques (13) and Maurice (10); Marie Meller (13); Blanche Perles (9) and her sister Léa (7); Gilles Segal (14); Betty Seiden (14); and Rudolph Unterman (14).

Twenty-four hours later, the pattern was repeated: a group of seven crossed at Norcier, and a group of nineteen crossed at Ville-la-Grand. Like those who had preceded them, the group of seven was arrested at *borne* 50 and taken to the border guard post at Sézenove. Five of the seven had been brought from Nice, the other two, from Grenoble. The names of the children in MJS convoy number 10 were Georges Kornfeld (15), Suzanne Marburger (15) and her brother Joseph (13), Jean Manasse (13), Jacques Polac (15) and his sister Rose (12), and Rosette Wolczak (15). The last of these individuals—the fifteen-year-old Rosette Wolczak—would not survive the war. On October 16, 1943, Swiss officials sent her back to France, having judged her to be "undeserving of Swiss hospitality." (As her dossier is not available to researchers for review, information is lacking on the events that resulted in expulsion.) Three days later, Rosette was arrested near Annemasse. She was deported to Auschwitz on November 20, 1943.

The twin of the convoy that had crossed at Ville-la-Grand the previous night was arrested at 8:40 p.m. and taken to the border guard post at Cornières. The names of the rescued comprising this, MJS convoy number 11, were Janine Antcher (13), Henriette Balez (13), Myrianne Berger (14), Lisa Glauberg (14), Jacques Halegua (13), Jacqueline Korinschtain (13), Louis Korn (10), Bella Leszkowitz (12) and her sister Rose (4), Marie Leviner (13) and her brother Maurice (10), Isidore Ménaché (12), Marcelle Refkolevsky (15) and her sister Mireille (14), Annette Rosenzweig (8), Nathan Torezynski (13) and his brother Henri (10), Michel Traumann (10), and Wolf Wapniarz (12). Seven of the children (Balez, Halegua, Korn, Ménaché, Torezynski, and Wapniarz) had been brought to the Haute-Savoie from Paris; the others had been brought from Nice.

The twelve-year-old Wolf Wapniarz was the oldest of five children born to Zureck and Golda, who were Polish immigrants. In addition to a sister, Régine, he had three brothers: Armand, Robert, and Josef. Wolfi and all of his siblings had been born in Metz, in Alsace-Lorraine. Like the Charmatz family living in nearby Nancy, the Wapniarz family fled the region when the war began. They went to Royan on the Atlantic coast, in the Charente-Maritime, and then to Châteaubriant, in the Loire-Atlantique. The departments of the Charente-Maritime and the Loire-Atlantique comprised part of the German Occupation Zone.

When I interviewed Wolfi in 2008, he spoke of a traumatic event that occurred while the family was living in Châteaubriant. He recalled that, in retaliation for the killing of a German officer, French police arrested Zureck and held him as one of a group of hostages threatened with execution. He was eventually released. Although Wolfi was not aware of it, Zureck may have been swept up in the aftermath of one of the earliest acts of resistance carried out in France. On October 20, 1941, three Communist resisters assassinated a high-ranking German officer, the Feldkommandant in Nantes. The assassination occurred just a month after the chief of the Wehrmacht high command had issued a policy calling for the execution of fifty to one hundred hostages in retaliation for each German soldier killed. Persons deemed to be Communists and anarchists were being held at a camp in Châteaubriant, about forty miles north of Nantes. On October 22, twenty-seven of the hostages were executed. Another fifty were threatened with execution but were eventually given a reprieve. Was Zureck seized by French police in the wake of the assassination and held along with other hostages? Possibly. French authorities commonly assumed that Jews were Communists, that Communists were Jews or worked in alliance with Jews, and that Jews and Communists were anarchists and agitators. In France and elsewhere, it was common for Jews to be rounded up and executed in retaliation for attacks against Nazi soldiers carried out by others. After Zureck regained his freedom, the family moved to the nearby town of Gardes-le-Pontaroux.

In the fall of 1942, French authorities arrested all of the members of the Wapniarz family and sent them to Drancy. Upon their arrival, on November 7, 1942, Wolfi was separated from the rest of his family. The reason for the separation is unknown. Somehow, his mother managed to come over to him. She saw that the group in which Wolfi had been placed was not heavily guarded. She took off the scarf that she was wearing and wrapped it around Wolfi's neck, and, as she did so, she whispered in his ear that he must try to escape immediately. Wolfi obeyed her; he fled before his name was even recorded in the camp records.

For days, Wolfi wandered the streets of Paris, hungry and cold. Eventually, a French policeman arrested him while he was asleep in a public garden. He was taken to a police station and then to an internment camp. Astonishingly, he managed to escape once again. A policeman stopped him and questioned him. Wolfi told him that he was lost and hungry. The policeman took him to the station, gave him some bread, and allowed him to sleep in one of the cells. The next morning, a police lorry took him to number 16 on the rue Lamarck, the address of one of several children's centers that the UGIF operated in and around Paris.

Wolfi lived in the Lamarck children's center for nine or ten months, during which time he attended school. At some point in 1943, the Paris police began conducting raids on Lamarck, arresting foreign-born Jewish children. Having been born in France, Wolfi held French citizenship, and he did not fear being taken away. One day, however, a man whom Wolfi did not know came to Lamarck and told him that his name was on a list of people who were going to be arrested and that he must leave immediately. The man instructed him to go to the end of the street, where another man would be waiting. He followed these instructions and met up with a man and three other boys. They joined another small group of children. Then, that group linked up with another group, "like a chain." A man took them to the train station, and all of them, including the man, boarded the train. The man instructed the children to destroy all of the personal papers and photographs that they had in their pockets. They had to tear them into pieces and throw them out of the windows of the train. Then he had the children disperse themselves throughout the train. During the journey, the man made several trips through the rail cars checking on the children. At one point, they all changed trains.

Eventually, the group reached Annecy. They remained there for two days, occupying an abandoned house on the outskirts of the town. Then they were taken from Annecy to Annemasse, where they stayed in a house for two or three days. They had permission to leave the house at night, but they had to remain inside during the day. On the night that they left the house to go to the border, they walked and walked. It was difficult for the smaller children; some fell down along the way. From time to time, one of the adults leading them told them to be quiet. They crossed a river and then some men cut the barbed wire that marked the border. All of a sudden, everything was illuminated, and the children heard men cry out in German. They were terrified. The men who had cried out assured the children that they were Swiss officials.

Wolfi remembered that the Swiss officials who received the children at the border also arrested the *passeurs* who had cut the barbed wire. His recollection proved to be correct. A document preserved in the archives of the Paul Grüninger Foundation, "Procès-verbal de l'audience du 2 décembre 1943, à Lausanne Palais de Justice de Montbenon," is a judgment against four French *passeurs* convicted of illegally passing Jewish children across the border on September 23 and 24, 1943, at Cornières. Each of those apprehended—Carlo Crivelli, Roger Pasteur, and Albert and André Pillet—was sentenced to seventy-five days in prison. More than sixty-five years later, on March 2, 2009, the Swiss government officially rehabilitated 137 men and women of various nationalities who had helped refugees flee Nazi persecution. Crivelli, Pasteur, and the Pillet brothers were among them.

~

On the afternoon of September 25, in the center of Nice, Jacques Wajntrob and Jacques Marburger left number 12 on the rue Guiglia, the building that housed their false papers laboratory, and mounted their bicycles in order to return to their respective homes. Suddenly, a black sedan veered in front of them, and Gestapo agents leapt out, ordering them to halt. Hoping to get away, Marburger began pedaling furiously. Immediately, the men threatened to shoot, and Marburger stopped. If the agents had suspected Wajntrob and Marburger of being Jewish, they would have taken them to the Hotel Excelsior. Apparently, they did not, for they delivered them to the Hotel l'Ermitage, where the Germans held and interrogated non-Jews whom they suspected of carrying out subversive or undesirable activities.

Wajntrob was carrying a briefcase filled with compromising materials. Upon entering l'Ermitage, he was able to discretely leave the briefcase in a cloakroom. He and Marburger were led to separate rooms to await interrogation. Marburger was not carrying a briefcase, but his pockets were filled with false papers that he had intended to deliver. He found himself seated in a big armchair, and, although he was kept under surveillance, he managed to empty his pockets and stuff the incriminating papers behind or beneath the cushions of the armchair.

Gestapo agents suspected Wajntrob and Marburger of being involved in the manufacture or distribution of false papers, but they had no proof. They questioned and beat Marburger, but he insisted that he was a student who had come to Nice to pursue his studies. His identity card, which claimed he was from a small village in the Isère, was a high quality forgery and withstood Gestapo scrutiny. Following the individual interrogations, Wajntrob and Marburger found themselves together again, placed in a room with an unidentified third detainee. In order to communicate to Wajntrob what he had told his interrogators, Marburger, feigning anger and indignation, ranted about his situation until Gestapo agents shut him up. A short time later, Marburger and Wajntrob were interrogated together.

Their cover stories corresponded well enough with one another to satisfy their questionners, and, around eight o'clock in the evening, Wajntrob, Marburger, and the unidentitifed detainee were informed that they were free to go but would be kept under surveillance. As he prepared to leave the building, Marburger heard Wajntrob say to someone that he had left his briefcase in the vestiary and would like to get it back. The briefcase contained information that placed others at risk, and Wajntrob felt compelled to try and retrieve it even though he placed himself in great danger by doing so. Upon hearing Wajntrob ask for the briefcase, Marburger hurried the third man out of the building and fled the scene as quickly as possible. He feared that the request could have catastrophic results, and it did. The briefcase was searched, and Wajntrob was promptly re-arrested.

The following day, the Gestapo seized Germaine Meyer, a member of the Nice *gdoud* who had served as the secretary to Angelo Donati. Donati was an influential Italian Jewish banker who had been president of the Italian Chamber of Commerce in Paris during the thirties. From the time that the Italians first took up their positions on French soil, he had played a unique role, serving as liaison between Italian authorities and the Dubouchage Committee. Even as he worked to improve the living conditions of Jewish refugees in the Italian Occupation Zone and ensure their safety, he pursued a bold course of action to avert future tragedy. In the spring of 1943, Donati developed a secret plan to evacuate thousands of Jews—the number most often cited is thirty thousand—from France into Italy. He made several trips to Rome to meet with government officials in an effort to gain approval of the plan. He also enlisted the help of Father Pierre-Marie Benoît, a Capuchin monk living in Marseille who had, since 1940, completely dedicated himself to rescue work. Father Benoît communicated the secret plan to Vatican officials in the hope that the Pope's tacit approval might influence Mussolini. After July 25, when the situation in Italy became destabilized, Donati modified his plan. He still tried to convince Italian authorities to allow the thousands of Jews living in the Italian Occupation Zone to enter Italy. Rather than remaining in Italy, however, they would be transported by ship to newly liberated parts of North Africa. With Father Benoît's help, Donati secretly entered Vatican City in order to meet with American and British representatives to the Holy See, present the evacuation plan, and seek the support of their governments. He also sought the financial support of Jewish organizations in the United States and elsewhere to underwrite the costs of the massive undertaking. By the end of August, the Italian government had consented to the plan and had agreed to place certain passenger ships at his disposal. The implementation of the plan came to an abrupt end in early September, when General Eisenhower announced the existence of an armistice. At the time of the announcement, Donati was in Italy, en route to Nice. Instead of returning to France, he went to Switzerland, where he was granted asylum. Germaine Meyer stayed in Nice and worked underground with other *gdoud* members to assist embattled refugees. While returning from Cannes with a cache of false papers, she was seized. Subjected to torture, she managed not to disclose information that would have placed others at risk.

The Gestapo delivered a third major blow to the child rescue effort in Nice on September 28, when it arrested the Jewish scout leader Claude Gutmann. Later, a telegram would be sent from the Gestapo commandant stationed in Marseille to Section IV-B of the Gestapo in Paris, the Judenreferat, to inform them that they had arrested Wajntrob, Meyer, and Gutmann. The Gestapo's own words attest to the importance of the work that they had accomplished. "WAJNTROB Jankiel, alias WISTER Jacques, Jew of Polish origin, head of the Jewish youth in Nice and organizer of transports of children to Switzerland" was reported to have organized three convoys of twenty-five children each destined for Switzerland. "GUTMANN Claude, alias DUPRAT Claude, charged by the UGIF with [delivering] Jewish social assistance to young people in the Southern zone" was reported to have been arrested at the Jesuit monastery located at number 8 on the rue Mirabeau, "where he was in the process of discussing the question of the assistance that the Catholic Church could bring to Jewish youth." It further notes, "According to the papers that we found on him, it follows that the Compagnons de France [Companions of France], the Comité National des Unions Chrétiennes des Jeunes Gens de France [National Committee of the Christian Unions of Young People of France], as well as the Mouvement des Éclaireurs Unionistes de France [Movement of Unionist Scouts of France] would have given him full support."

On September 28, the same day that the Gestapo arrested Claude Gutmann, Bella Wendling took seven children from Annecy to Norcier. None of the seven had been brought from Nice. Three had been brought from the region of Toulouse; three, from Challes-les-Eaux, southeast of Chambéry; and one, from Paris. The seven were passed across the border in two mini convoys. The first mini convoy (MJS convoy number 12) consisted of three young children—Boris Epstein (8) and his sister Renée (5) and Ilia Muszkatblat (8). The three crossed that same night (September 28), were arrested at *borne* 51 at 9:15 p.m., and were taken to the border guard post at Sézenove. The other four—Simon Grimberg (9) and Marcel Zauberman (12) and his sisters Mireille (9) and Hélène (7)—were held back and made to wait until the following night (MJS convoy number 13). I do not know who sheltered the children overnight and during the next day. On September 29, they crossed the border at around the same time and the same place as the preceding convoy, and they were taken to the same border guard post.

September had proved to be a good time for smuggling Jewish children across the border. The MJS team aided by the Ville-la-Grand *filière* had managed to smuggle eleven convoys containing 149 unaccompanied children across the border. Further north, the OSE team and the Douvaine *filière* had passed seven convoys with 107 people, eighty-nine of whom were unaccompanied children. Altogether, 256 people, including 238 unaccompanied children, had made it to safety.

September 30 was Rosh Hashanah. According to the Jewish calendar, a new year, 5704, had begun.

7. *The Wolf's Plain*

On the first day of October, one of the members of the MJS team in Annecy, Bella Wendling, was arrested in Saint-Julien and charged with carrying false identity papers. Contacted on behalf of the MJS, Mado Hérisson, a capable lawyer in Annecy, defended Bella in court. She received a light sentence—twelve days in an Annecy prison. Throughout September, Bella had played an extremely important role in the smuggling operation. However, it would have been too dangerous for her to attempt to continue this work. After serving her sentence, she returned to Grenoble, rejoining her boyfriend and future husband, Ado Michaeli.

If any of the members of the Annecy team regarded Bella's arrest as anything other than a stroke of bad luck, as a portent or warning of things to come, there is no indication of such. They were used to living and working in a world where they might be arrested, interrogated, and deported at any moment, for any reason at all or for no reason at all. The team had weathered other changes and shown itself to be resilient. Sometime in September, Maurice Maidenberg had left Annecy to be with his mother, who lay dying in a hospital in Lyon. After being released by the Gestapo in Nice, Jacques Marburger came to Annecy and joined Mila, Tony, and the others.

~

By the third week of September, the Gestapo had achieved enough success in Nice that it could begin sending trainloads of Jews to Drancy every other day. One such trainload, carrying eighty-five people, left Nice on October 2 and arrived in the Paris suburb on October 5. Jacques Wajntrob was among those on board. So was Tristan Bernard, the author of the one-act farce, "L'Anglais tel qu'on le parle," that Mila had staged in Luchon and in which she played the lead role of Betty. Also on board was Serge Klarsfeld's father, Arno.

Among Americans, Serge Klarsfeld and his wife, Beate, have the reputation of being famous French Nazi hunters. Few know the extent and importance of their scholarly research on the persecution of Jews in France under the Occupation. Their *Memorial de la déportation des juifs de France (Memorial of the Deportation of the Jews of France)*, published in 1978, was the first publication to comprehensively set forth the names, birth dates, and nationalities of each of the approximately seventy-six thousand Jews deported from France to killing centers, mainly

Auschwitz, by convoy number and date. This essential volume was followed by numerous other works that chronicled and analyzed aspects of the Shoah in France. Few know that Klarsfeld was a young boy hiding with his family in Nice in September 1943 or the supreme sacrifice that his father made to save his loved ones. The following account is presented in two of his publications.

> The author of this work had just turned eight years old when the Germans occupied Nice, where his father, his mother, his sister, and he had taken refuge in 1942 and were living at 15, rue d'Italie, in the immediate vicinity of the Hotel Excelsior.
>
> As it was impossible to flee the city, and under the threat of an impending sweep, Arno Klarsfeld installs a false back in a large cupboard, dividing the space with a fragile plywood partition, concealed by a wardrobe, the lower part of which opens and closes from the inside by a simple hook.
>
> On the night before the school year begins, September 30 around midnight, floodlights illuminate the building. Immediately, the children's beds are remade; the mother and children go into the hiding place, their clothes in their arms. The father does not join them; he has decided to open the door to the *gestapistes* [Gestapo members] to avoid, by sacrificing himself, their breaking down the door of the apartment and sounding out the walls and partitions with butt strokes, which would inevitably lead them to discover the false back . . . .
>
> The *gestapistes* proceed on their search, floor after floor, apartment after apartment. First, they enter the apartment adjoining that of the Klarsfelds, where the Goetz family lives, Alsatian Jews. With a butt stroke, they break the nose of the older daughter who dared to ask them for their papers, and, under the eyes of her parents, they rough up the little Marguerite to obtain the address of the son, housed at a different address. The father Goetz yells, "Help, French police, help! We are French! Save us, save us!" It is at that moment that they knock at the door. Arno Klarsfeld opens the door to them. Immediately, in French, with a German accent, a voice asks, "Where are your wife and your children?" Arno replied, "They are in the country because we just disinfected the apartment." The *gestapistes* undertake a search, without a doubt with less care than if no one had opened the door to them. One of them gets inside the cupboard, and the author still remembers today the noise of clothing being pushed back on the rod in order to see if someone was concealing himself behind. By some miracle, the *gestapiste* did not touch what he believes to be the wall at the back and is nothing but a thin layer of painted wood. Inside we can hear, "Get dressed and follow us."

Raïssa Klarfeld managed to take her children out of the city the next morning and find a room to let in a house in the suburbs. Serge Klarsfeld concludes his account of the tragic episode as follows: "Two days later, at the Nice train station, Raïssa

Klarsfeld will see her husband leave for Drancy among a group of eighty people, including the Goetz family and Tristan Bernard . . . [ellipsis points in original]"

On the same day that Jacques was sent from Nice, Léa Wajntrob, her daughter, Miriam, and her father, Moïse Eisenbaum, crossed illegally from France into Switzerland. They had fled Nice after Jacques's arrest. Although it is not known whether they stopped in Annecy or traveled directly to Saint-Julien, it is known that they crossed the border at *borne* 51, made their way across the Plaine du Loup, and were arrested at Lully. Thus, they quite literally followed in the footsteps of many of the children from Nice whom they had saved.

~

On the third of October, Joseph Lançon, the farmer in Veigy-Foncenex on whom Father Jean Rosay had placed great reliance, went into hiding. A friend had warned him that the Gestapo was coming to arrest him. As he was a widower and father of seven, it was left to his seventeen-year-old daughter, Thérèse, to manage the household. For Rosay and other members of the Douvaine filière, it was an ominous development, an indication that the Gestapo had some information on the child rescue operation.

OSE had already organized a convoy of thirteen people whom they planned to pass into Switzerland with the help of the Douvaine *filière*. The group consisted of four families and three unaccompanied children. The families were in desperate straits, all of them traveling with infants or toddlers. Three of the families—Kolodny, Szer, and Weinstein—had managed to elude capture in Nice. Incredibly, Henriette and Jankiel Kolodny had escaped with their daughter Rachel-Liliane, only seven weeks old. Boba Szer was traveling alone with her one-year-old daughter, Nicole. According to the Declaration she signed, the little girl's father had been deported in 1942. Esther Weinstein was also traveling alone with her seven-month-old son, Michael. Her Declaration indicates that her husband had been seized by the Gestapo in Nice. The fourth family—Mordka and Laja Grynsztejn and their two-year-old son Léon—had been living in Grenoble. The unaccompanied children in the convoy were Rebecca Zaidenband (15) and her brothers Léon (12) and Simon (7).

The convoy was assembled in Chambéry, where OSE had its headquarters. Apparently, the group arrived in Thonon-les-Bains on October 2 and remained there for two days. They crossed the Swiss border on October 4, were arrested at 6 p.m. at Les Glands, north of the Croix de Bailly, and taken to the Swiss border guard post at Hermance. The curious thing about the convoy is that, on the OSE list, the names of the Zaidenband children are notated as "par Simon." This leads me to believe that members of the MJS team were called upon to take responsibility for the group after the Douvaine *filière* was disrupted. Thus, I have included this convoy, which I believe to have been the fourteenth MJS convoy, in Appendix 2.

The Gestapo had established its regional headquarters in the Hôtel Pax in Annemasse, and they had converted the hotel annex, a three-story building located directly across the street, into a prison. On October 5, Gestapo agents arrested Thérèse Lançon at the family's farm in Veigy-Foncenex and imprisoned her in the Pax annex. She was held there for three weeks, subjected to repeated interrogations. Father Jean Rosay decided that he must shut down the Douvaine *filière*. This meant that the OSE team had no way to get the children across the border, and they too ceased their smuggling operations.

The MJS team continued its work much as it had done before. One change became evident, however: the large convoys with fifteen, twenty, twenty-five or more children were eliminated. After October 4, no convoys contained more than nine children.

On October 7, the fifteenth MJS convoy, comprising seven children, crossed the border at Ville-la-Grand. The children were arrested at 5:40 p.m. and taken to the border guard post at Cornières. Five of the seven had been living in Toulouse, and two in Nice. The names of the children are as follows: Myriam Czarny (14), her sister Jeannine (11), and her cousins Annette Krist (7) and Eveline Rosenkern (7); Elie Knout-Fixman (8); and Pia-Manon Russak (15) and her sister Ursula (7). Elie Knout-Fixman was the son of Ariane Knout-Fixman. He had been living with his mother in Toulouse up until the time that a young woman took him to Annecy in preparation for the border crossing. His Declaration states that he knew the person who took him to Annecy, although he did not know her name. Statements appearing in the Declaration in regard to his father are rather ambiguous. His name is listed as "Fixman Elie-Knout" and his signature appears simply as "Fixman." The statement "My father must be in Switzerland or on the Côte d'Azur" appears in the Declaration, but it is unclear if this is meant to refer to his father or stepfather. His stepfather, David Knout, targeted by authorities, had crossed into Switzerland in November 1942.

A lull of three days (October 8–10) followed, during which no border crossings occurred. Perhaps this was due to the fact that Yom Kippur fell on October 9. Immediately after this lull, the work of the MJS team increased noticeably. They organized convoys and passed them across the border day after day, without a break. Tony and Mila began to feel that their operation had become overextended. Tony would later write:

> The "transports" of children do not stop growing. Then it's the turn of Toulouse, Limoges, Paris. Our service is further extended. Entire families succeed, through our efforts, in reaching Switzerland. The occupation along the border by the Germans increases the risk but does not diminish our "traffic." Quite the contrary, we sometimes feel ourselves flooded with the new arrivals.

Over the next eleven-day period (October 11–21), the MJS team would be called upon to pass ten more convoys across the border. This was a much more rapid pace than either the MJS *réseau* or the OSE *réseau* had ever attempted. It was equivalent to an average daily rate of 0.91 convoys. By way of comparison, during the month of September, the OSE team achieved a rate of 0.33 (10 convoys over 30 days) and the MJS team achieved a rate of 0.37 (11 convoys over 30 days).

Who was responsible for sending so many convoys to the Annecy team in such a short period of time? Did Mila and Tony try and slow the flood of new arrivals? And, if so, why did no one listen to them?

~

The name Plaine du Loup (Wolf's Plain) routinely appears on the arrest reports that the Swiss border guards completed in the fall of 1943, although it does not appear on present-day maps. Even today, however, a remnant of the wolf's presence can be found: the road that cuts across the plain, beginning at the route de Thérens on the southeast and ending at the route de Laconnex on the northwest, is the chemin du Loup (the Wolf's Path). Along the border, three *bornes* mark the edge of the Plaine du Loup. *Bornes* 50 and 51 are closest to Norcier and *borne* 52 is near Thérens. The arrest reports indicate that the convoys of children who crossed here in September were arrested at *borne* 50, at *borne* 51, or between 50 and 51. Those who crossed in October were arrested between *bornes* 51 and 52.

Whether or not the Plaine du Loup looks exactly as it did in 1943, I cannot say. It is a patchwork of fields, some cultivated and some fallow, that stretches between the little farming enclaves of Norcier and Thérens in France and the towns of Sézenove and Lully in Switzerland. In October, looking across some of the fields, one sees bright orange pumpkins waiting to be picked. Nine MJS convoys first set foot on Swiss soil here, on the Plaine du Loup, and yet it remains a complete mystery as to why it was this place rather than some other. It is impossible for me to walk the area today without searching for clues.

What strikes one immediately about Norcier is that it looks like a jumble of walled compounds. The typical compound contains a house and adjoining courtyard, sheds, and haylofts where animals are kept and farm equipment and feed are stored. It is surrounded by a high stone wall, which would make it a perfect place in which to hide.

So often it was a sympathetic priest who helped facilitate the border crossings. Was there someone in the vicinity of Norcier and Thérens who did just that? A gray stone church with a tall steeple and clock tower sits on the crest of a nearby hill. Built at such a vantage point, it seems to keep watch over a broad swath of the countryside. It is the most distinctive feature of the landscape. Indeed, standing near the border, one would likely fail to notice the existence of the village of Thairy, just a half mile away, were it not for the Church of Saint-Brice. Standing in the church steeple, armed with a pair of binoculars, one

Typical Walled Compound, Norcier, September 2008. Photo by N. Lefenfeld.

could have observed patrols along the border. One could have sheltered people in the church or permitted them to hide in the nearby church cemetery, hidden from view behind a high stone wall. And, yet, I have not identified any clergy or lay persons in Thairy, Norcier, or Thérens who were involved in this rescue work.

At 10 p.m. on October 11, eight children crossed the border between *bornes* 51 and 52 and made their way across the Plaine du Loup. Little is known about the origins of the children in this group, MJS convoy number 16. Four of the children had been living in or near Grenoble; two had come from Lyon; and two from Aix-les-Bains. Their names were Gerda Bierzonski (12), Abraham Cymerman (14), Gérard Dreyfuss (14), Denise Rivet (9), Hélène Rubinstein (12) and her brother Georges (11), and Blanche Uklejska (14) and sister Esther (12).

In her memoir, Gerda Bikales (née Bierzonski), born and raised in Breslau, Germany, explains how she came to be included in the convoy. She, her mother, Bronia, and her mother's companion, Srulke Mandelman, were living in Grenoble. "Time was running out for us," she writes. The Germans were brutally rounding up as many Jews and French resisters as they could find.

View from Thairy, looking north, September 2008. (Town of Norcier, France, is on the left; Switzerland is in the background.) Photo by N. Lefenfeld.

> One group of young Jews, mostly recruited from the leadership ranks of the scout movement, operated a network to save a few Jewish children by smuggling them across the border from France to Switzerland. Their realistic appraisal was that many Jews still alive in France would not survive until the country's liberation, and they were hoping to salvage a small remnant of Europe's Jewry by smuggling a core of children into neutral Switzerland. Several social workers had approached my mother to plead that she allow me to be smuggled to Switzerland, a plan that she and I fiercely resisted. Mandelman, however, never one to believe in separation before, now insisted that I go because he shared the pervasive pessimism about our slim chances of survival.

Bronia was afraid to place Gerda in a convoy, as she understood the tremendous risks involved. A friend of Bronia's had sent her son to Switzerland, and, in early October, she received word that he had arrived safely. After this news arrived, Mandelman became even more insistent that Gerda should leave for Switzerland. Gerda was reluctant to leave her mother and Mandelman because she was worried about their safety. However, their landlord put them in touch with a Resistance leader living in the mountains outside of Grenoble, who promised to arrange a safe hiding place for Bronia and Mandelman. After the three of them met with this man, Gerda felt relieved, and she agreed to join the children's convoy.

The origins of the October 12 convoy (MJS convoy number 17) are less of a mystery. That group followed directly in the footsteps of the group that crossed the preceding evening and was arrested around 9:30 p.m. Two 15-year-old boys, David Hirsch and Heinz Diewald, had come from the Château de Chabannes, an OSE children's home located in Saint-Pierre-de-Fursac, in the department of the Creuse. French police had carried out periodic raids on the home since August 1942, arresting and deporting some of the children. OSE had dispersed children believed to be most at risk by hiding them in the countryside or smuggling them into Switzerland; but the home had not yet been closed and some children were still living there. The other six children in the convoy had come from Paris. The names of two of the children—Maurice Szwed (12) and his brother Marcel (9)—appear on surviving lists of the Rue Amelot Committee. The remaining four children were siblings belonging to the Rozenberg family: Madeleine (15), Suzanne (13), Bernard (9), and Rachèle (5). Although names of four Rozenberg children appear on the Rue Amelot lists, I do not know if they refer to the Rozenberg children in this convoy, as three of the four first names differ from those cited here. However, the Declaration signed by Madeleine Rozenberg states that their mother and older brother had been deported and that the four children had been living in a boardinghouse in the department of the Seine. This certainly leaves open the possibility that they were in the care of the Rue Amelot Committee.

The weather was turning colder, the German patrols were becoming more attuned to smuggling activity along the border, and yet Jewish children kept arriving in Annecy at an unprecedented pace. Moreover, some members of the Annecy team were making trips to Lyon and Nice in order to get the children and bring them to the Haute-Savoie. Declarations signed by the children in the October 13 convoy (MJS convoy number 18) state that it was a "Monsieur Roland" who accompanied the eight children from Lyon to Annecy. It is quite possible that this was a reference to Roland Epstein. All of children had been brought to Lyon from Paris. Although none of the names of the children appear on the surviving lists of the Rue Amelot Committee, it is nevertheless possible that they were in the Committee's care. The names of the children in the convoy are as follows: Charles Beinart (14) and his brother Maurice (9); Jacques Rosenberg (13) and his sister Jeanne (11) and brother Victor (5); and Fanny Zilberg (12) and her sisters Anette (11) and Lili (7). The group used the crossing point at Ville-la-Grand and was arrested at 5 p.m. How and why they would have crossed in broad daylight is unknown.

The MJS convoys that crossed the border during the first two weeks of October contained few children who had come from Nice. The arrest of Jacques Wajntrob, Claude Gutman, and Germaine Meyer in late September had temporarily decapitated the operation that had succeeded in bringing children from Nice to Annecy. It did not take long, however, for those who remained at large to reorganize and restart rescue efforts. They made contact with Jewish families in hiding and arranged to have unaccompanied children transferred to the Haute-Savoie. They also expanded the operation to include parents with children younger than six years of age.

Between October 14 and 21, thirty-five of forty-three children and adults who entered Switzerland in five MJS convoys came from Nice. It is known that Mila made at least two trips between Annecy and Nice in order to bring people out of that terrorized city. Making such trips was an exhausting business. One could count on being subjected to numerous identity checks, both on and off the train. Handing over one's identity papers, one had to maintain one's composure and appear nonchalant and at ease. Agitation or nervousness would only draw unwanted attention. A train delay might leave one unexpectedly stranded for some period of time. An anxious child, newly separated from his or her parents, might threaten to draw undue attention. One had to be ever vigilant. It was not a job for the fainthearted.

Two MJS convoys crossed the border on October 14; one (MJS convoy number 19) made the crossing at Ville-la-Grand, and the other (MJS convoy number 20) at Norcier. The convoy that crossed at Ville-la-Grand consisted of the following nine children: Louis Folbaum (11) and his brother Bernard (4); Alain Charas (7) and his sister Martine (7); Jacques Jungerman (12); Lucie Kuhn (15) and her sister Sonia (6); Edith Salik (15); and Fernande Valigora (12). The Folbaum brothers, the Kuhn sisters, and Jacques Jungerman had come from Nice. The Declarations signed by both Lucie Kuhn and Louis Folbaum state that a "Mademoiselle Mila" accompanied them from Nice to Annecy. Three of the children had come from locations in the vicinity of Grenoble, and one from Rodès, near Perpignan.

The convoy that crossed that same day at Norcier (MJS convoy number 20) consisted of a family of four and four unaccompanied children, all of whom had come from Nice. (None of the Declarations that they signed mentioned who had accompanied them from Nice.) The names of the eight are Hélène Junger (15) and her twin sister Berthe, Lydia Merwitzer (15), Marcel Morgenstern (4), and Louis Salomons (55), his wife Alice (44), his son Philippe (3), and his stepdaughter Anne Ischwall (13).

Families with young children now became a part of each assembled convoy. A group of nine that crossed in the vicinity of Norcier on October 18 (MJS convoy number 21) included a mother and baby. Everyone in the group had come from Nice. Their names are as follows: Dora Chimon (11); Sarah Kalmanowicz (39) and her daughter Paulette (9 months); Simon Rozen (13); Louise Tchoukran (16) and her brother Nisso (12); Henri Wander (14); and Berthe Weinstein (6) and her brother Robert (4). Two of the Declarations mention that a young woman had accompanied them to Annecy.

Still they kept coming. Two groups crossed on October 20, one at Cornières and one at Norcier. The group that crossed at Cornières (MJS convoy number 22) consisted of a family of three and six unaccompanied children. The family and one unaccompanied child had come from Nice. Three others had come from Vizille, near Grenoble, and one from Paris. Their names are as follows: Mylan Isaack (6); Dora Israel (37), her son Robert (14), and her daughter Fortunée (3); Lisette Palestrant (13); Liba Rosenberg (13) and her brother Paul (8); Suzanne Sobelman (7); and Jeanette Wahl (8).

The group that crossed the same evening at Norcier consisted of the Lubelski and Rapoport families and comprised eight people. The families had come directly from Chambéry, where OSE was headquartered, suggesting that they may have been sent by OSE to the MJS team. Three generations of the Lubelski family crossed together: Mager (65) and his wife, Hinda (61); and their son Maurice (23), daughter-in-law Nadia (22), and granddaughter Elly (almost 2). The Rapoport family included Adam (28), his wife Mirjam (25), and their daughter Sylvie (almost 2). The name Elly Lubelski does not appear on the OSE list entitled *"Liste des enfants partis en Suisse en 1943–1944."* Neither does does the name Sylvie Rapoport. Thus, in this respect, the group differs from all preceding MJS convoys. What basis is there for believing that the group comprised MJS convoy number 23? Arrest reports clearly indicate that the families were arrested by Swiss officials between *bornes* 51 and 52, on the Plaine du Loup. This was the very same location at which individuals comprising MJS convoys number 16 (October 11), 17 (October 12), 20 (October 14), and 21 (October 18) had been arrested.

~

Thursday, October 21, corresponded to the twenty-second day of Tishri in the Hebrew calendar, the Biblical Jewish holiday known as Shemini Atzeret. Immediately following the seven days of Sukkot, its name literally means the eighth day of assembly. It marks the beginning of the rainy season following the harvest in Israel, and the only ritual associated with the holiday is the recitation of the Tefilat Geshem, the prayer for rain.

Mila arrived in Annecy that morning with a group of people she had brought from Nice. They had traveled by train throughout the night. The MJS team had planned to smuggle two groups across the border that evening—one at Cornières during the early part of the evening and the other at Norcier a few hours later. Tony and Mila had been assigned to take the earlier group; Sacha and Roland were to take the later group. When Mila arrived in Annecy, Tony saw that she was exhausted, and he insisted that she rest for a few hours. He decided that he and Sacha should take the earlier group and that Mila and Roland should take the later one.

That afternoon, Tony and Sacha accompanied two families to their customary crossing point at Ville-la-Grand. One of the families was that of Zanvel Diamant, whose later writing would serve as a window onto the Jewish community in Nice during the Italian occupation. Zanvel (39) crossed along with his wife Rivka (34) and their sons Henri (10) and Paul (4). The other family in the convoy was that of Srul Engiel, his wife Léa, and their daughters Rachèle (14) and Yvonne (4). The Diamant and Engiel families had come from Nice; it is not known if they were among the people who had made the trip from Nice with Mila during the night. Neither the names of the Diamant children nor those of the Engiel children appear on the previously referenced OSE list. Nevertheless, one can say with near certainty that this group comprised MJS convoy number 24. The crossing occurred in the location long been favored by the MJS team. Moreover, Sacha Maidenberg and Tony Gryn have stated, in written accounts and during the course of interviews, that they successfully passed a group of people across the border at their traditional Ville-la-Grand—Cornières crossing point during the middle part of the day on October 21.

A few hours later, Mila and Roland stood with several people at the edge of the Plaine du Loup. The composition of the group was unusual: a couple in their late fifties; two mothers with babies; and an elderly woman believed to be the grandmother of one of the babies. They were accompanied by a *passeur,* who instructed them to stop and wait for a moment. "Wait for me a moment; I will return," he assured them, and then he left. They crouched on the ground, chilled in the night air of late October. A light rain was falling.

8. *Farewell to France*

Time and again, I have found that, in terms of its sheer volume and degree of specificity, documentation pertaining to the arrest, deportation, and death of a Jew who rescued other Jews during the Shoah outweighs documentation pertaining to the rescue work that he or she accomplished. This reality, although unfortunate, is understandable. The ever-present danger of being hunted down by or denounced to authorities dictated that rescue work be done in the near complete absence of recordkeeping. Nothing prevented German or French authorities from keeping records, however. On the contrary, recordkeeping was a high priority. Moreover, after the war had ended, surviving family members and comrades oftentimes recounted the specific events and circumstances surrounding the loss of a loved one or friend in an effort to come to terms with it.

What happened on the night of October 21, 1943, to the group that waited, crouched, in the wet grass of the Plaine du Loup? Various accounts have been published, although none constitutes eyewitness testimony per se. However, Jacques Lazarus' memoir, *Juifs au combat*, presents a stark, staccato statement made by Roland Epstein. "A light rain was falling on a dozen people, in the noise of the grass crushed and trampled underfoot. Suddenly, guttural calls, whistles blowing, dogs barking, spotlights, gunshots, groans, a dog having bitten me on the calf."

German soldiers had ambushed the group and fired upon them. The elderly woman believed to be the grandmother and the baby that she was holding lay dead. There was no sign of the *passeur.*

Roland's statement continues:

> I found myself at the Hôtel de France, in Saint-Julien, with my companions of the evening; an old woman and a baby were missing; both had been killed. I remember that Mila was seated facing me. We secretly exchanged a few words to get our story straight. I recall a compromising piece of paper that I chewed conscientiously, my interrogation in a room on the first floor, my return to the hall while a dressing on my face indicated the insistence with which they had questioned me.

The last part of the statement refers to the fact that he was beaten during the interrogation.

At the time of their arrest, Roland was carrying a large sum of money, intended as payment for the *passeur.* Apparently, the German soldiers who seized the group believed Roland and Mila to be professional child smugglers. They had no idea that they were Jews working on behalf of a Jewish rescue organization. Roland's false papers listed his last name as Estienne. Apparently, Mila was not carrying the false papers that she had used on some previous occasions, in the name of Marie-Anne Richemond. Her false papers were in the name of Marie-Anne Racine, a nineteen-year-old from the Paris suburb of Boulogne-sur-Seine. (Racine is a common French name, so using this name would not have posed a problem.) At the Hôtel de France, Roland was ordered to drop his trousers so that two German interrogators could see for themselves whether or not the young man was circumcised and, hence, in their view, Jewish. Inexplicably, one declared immediately that he was not. Questioned many years later about this, Epstein was at a loss to explain how or why this had happened.

Mila, Roland, and the five others with whom they were arrested were held at the Hôtel de France only until morning. They were then taken to the Pax prison in Annemasse. The original prison register used during those years has survived; in it, one can find the names and birth dates of seven people who were arrested at Saint-Julien and brought to the prison on October 22, 1943. The handwritten entries in the prison register list, in addition to Marie-Anne Racine and Roland Estienne, the following: twenty-six-year-old Erica Mauren; forty-year-old Olga Stiasny and her son, listed simply as "*kind*," German for "child"; and seventy-five-year-old Abraham Vengerowsky and his sixty-seven-year-old wife, Rachel. It seems likely that the baby shot at the time of the arrest belonged to Erica Mauren and that her mother or mother-in-law, who was perhaps holding the child, was the other casualty.

The Pax prison was generally used for incarceration on a short-term basis; most prisoners were transferred from Pax to other places within a matter of days or weeks. During their incarceration, many were subjected to torture, including the infamous "*baignoire*." ("*Baignoire*" means "bathtub." The Gestapo's use of the "*baignoire*" as a method of torture involved their repeatedly submerging their victim in a bathtub filled with freezing cold water and holding him or her underwater for long periods of time.) Pax was not built as a prison and was ill-equipped to serve as such. It lacked heat, blankets, and mattresses. Moreover, neither the German nor French authorities considered it their responsibility to feed the prisoners.

The mayor of Annemasse was Jean Deffaugt, forty-seven years old, a veteran of the Great War who had spent time in German prisoner of war camps. Photos taken in 1944 show a portly man with a receding hairline and the suggestion of a mustache. Jovial and self-assured, Deffaugt mingled, seemingly at ease, with German soldiers in and around the prison. He was a member of the underground resistance network known as the *réseau* Gilbert, which specialized in smuggling information out of France to liaison agents of the Allied forces in Geneva.

It was not usually within Jean Deffaugt's power to gain the release of prisoners held in Pax or to avert their transfer to more notorious venues. Nevertheless, he did what he could to care for them. He had the *chutzpah* to seek authorization

Lfd. Nr.	Name	Geburtsdatm	Geburtsort	Nationalität	Wohnort	Zelle Nr. Dat.	Wenn u. von wem eingel.	Akt. Zeich.	Wenn entl. oder an wen übergeben	Akt. Zeichen	
125	Telders, Florin	[illegible]	[illegible]	Holländer	in Haag	4	21/10.43/Toll Annem.	I/21	15/11.43/SD Lyon	3/21	+
126	Kahn, Alfred	[illegible]	[illegible]	Holländer	Haag, Josef Israel Laan 17	6	21/10.43/Toll	I/22	15/11.43/SD Lyon	3/21	+
127	Racine, Marie [illegible]	[illegible]	[illegible]	Französin	Grenoble, 8 Pl. Notre Dame	5	22/10.43/Toll St. Jul.	I/23	[illegible].43/SD Lyon	3/21	–
128	MAUREN, Lucie	[illegible]	Brüssel	Belg.	Nizza, Hotel Bristol	[illegible]	22/10.43/Toll	I/24	[illegible].43/Krankenh. überf.		–
129	STIASNY, Olga [illegible]	[illegible]	[illegible]	[illegible]	Nizza, 17 Rue [illegible]	[illegible]	22/10.43/Toll	I/25	[illegible].43/Krankenh. überf. / [illegible].43 nach Drancy	I/16	–
130	VENGEROWSKY, Rachel	[illegible]	[illegible]	[illegible]	Nizza, [illegible] Hotel [illegible]	10	22/10.43/Toll	I/26	25/10.43 nach Drancy	I/16	–
131	VENGEROWSKY, Abraham	[illegible]	[illegible]	[illegible]	" "	9	22/10.43/Toll	I/27	27/10.43 nach Drancy	I/16	–
132	ESTIENNE, Roland	[illegible]	Oran	Franz.	Annecy, [illegible] Hotel	[illegible]	22/10.43/Toll	I/28	[illegible].43/SD Lyon	3/21	–
133	BOURLON, Jean	[illegible]	[illegible]	Franz.	Chatlons [illegible]	[illegible]	22/10.43/Toll		[illegible].43/Ort. Annecy	3/18	+
134	PAPADOPOULOS, [illegible]	[illegible]	[illegible]	[illegible]	Morner	[illegible]	22/10.43/SD Annem.		25/10.43/entl. d. SD.		+
135	ROSMOWICK, [illegible]	[illegible]	[illegible]	[illegible]	[illegible] Jura	[illegible]	23/10.43/Toll Annem.	I/29	[illegible] 25/10.43 Drancy	I/16	–
136	TUCHT, [illegible] (2 Kinder)	[illegible]	[illegible]	[illegible]	[illegible]	4	23/10.43/Toll	I/30	[illegible] 25/10.43 Drancy	I/16	–
137	BLOCH, David (2 Kinder)	[illegible]	Straßburg	Franz.	Monte Carlo	9	23/10.43/Toll	I/31	" " 25/10.43 Drancy	I/16	–
138	BLOCH, geb. [illegible]	[illegible]	[illegible]	Franz.	Monte Carlo	[illegible]	23/10.43/Toll	I/32	25/10.43 nach Drancy	I/16	–
139	KARGHALI, [illegible]	[illegible]	[illegible]	[illegible]	[illegible]	9	[illegible]	[illegible]	[illegible]		

Exhibit 4: Excerpt from Pax Prison Register. © Municipal archives, Ville d'Annemasse.

Former Pax Prison, Annemasse, July 1999. Photo by N. Lefenfeld.

from the head of the Gestapo in Annemasse, a Captain Einsohn, to enter the prison in order to bring food and necessities to the prisoners. Authorization was granted but with a key proviso: that he not speak to anyone outside of the prison of that which he saw or heard inside.

The very fact that he entered into an agreement with the Germans and visited the prisoners each day placed Deffaugt at great risk. Yet, he knowingly multiplied the risk. "In this prison, I functioned as the 'mailbox,'" he states in written testimony. "My wife had sewn a pocket beneath the fly of my pants, and I passed all the mail. Needless to say that when the Germans signaled for me to come up, I had a horrible fear of being searched."

Deffaugt smuggled out of the prison at least five letters that Mila wrote, four of which are reproduced in translation here. (In the first letter reproduced here, Mila states that she wrote to her parents; to the best of my knowledge, that letter no longer exists.) The first two surviving letters are addressed to the post office box that Mila shared with Sacha in Annecy. The letters appear to have been written hurriedly. Some words or phrases are difficult or impossible to read, perhaps because they were written in such haste. Others have faded over time and are too faint to decipher. Mila used the type of cryptic wording that resisters typically used to protect both themselves as well as intended recipients. In some cases, the true meaning of coded references is clear; in other case, it is not.

The first two surviving letters both appear to be dated October 25. Based on the contents of the letters, one can speculate that Jean Deffaugt visited Mila in prison on the twenty-fifth, delivered a parcel to her that day, and smuggled out of the prison two letters she had written—one prior to his arrival and the other during his visit.

The first surviving letter was written on stationery that bears the professional letterhead of Docteur Georges Périnel, an Annemasse physician. It requests that responses be directed to F. Chapelier, 17, rue du Jura, Ambilly, which is the address of the Annemasse Hospital. Mademoiselle Françoise Chapelier was a nurse in the hospital. Deffaugt mentions both Docteur Périnel and Mademoiselle Chapelier in his written testimony, and it is clear that they assisted him in his rescue work.

Mlle S. Racine
Post Office Box - Annecy
October 25, 1943

My dear friends,

I am very well. Neither my appetite nor my sleep suffers because of my health. As to morale, it is flourishing more than ever. Did you go to Grenoble to give the message to my landlord? I have here detective novels, which have a magical effect to put me to sleep after reading the 10th line.

You can get news of my health from the doctor as well as from the nurse.

I hope to soon receive the requested clothing, because, if I have to leave to convalesce in the mountains, I would like to have good footwear and be well dressed. I wrote to the parents to warn them that I will probably go to Marc and pray Suzanne to write them the same thing. Write to them everyday, my little darling, so that they will not worry.

My dear friends, I think of you, of each one in particular. And you will believe me without a doubt if I assure you that I would rather be with you at this moment.

[Sentence too faint to read.]

From time to time, I see Roland, who is fine, and we sing together often.

Marie is very angry with Fanny and no longer wants to see her.

I kiss you on both cheeks and hope very fervently to see you soon.

My little Suzanne, I kiss you tenderly.

Be courageous.

M-Anne

You can write to
F. Chapelier
17, rue du Jura
Ambilly (Hte. Savoie)

The "landlord" of whom she speaks most likely refers to Simon Lévitte and the MJS *gdoud* in Grenoble. The doctor and nurse are Doctor Périnel and Nurse

Chapelier, the mayor's contacts at the hospital. In this first surviving letter as well as succeeding ones, Mila equates the fact of her arrest with a malady ("You can get news of my health . . ."). "Marc" was a code name for the infamous Fort Montluc prison in Lyon, run by Klaus Barbie. Mila expects that she is going to be sent there. She requests warm clothing and footwear so that she may be better equipped to "convalesce in the mountains," a reference to incarceration. Worried about the effect that her imprisonment may be having on her parents, she implores Sacha, whose alias was Suzanne, to do whatever she can to lessen their anxiety.

Two sentences in the letter are puzzling: "From time to time, I see Roland; he is well and we sing together often. Marie is very angry with Fanny and no longer wants to see her." One can only speculate as to what these sentences mean. My guess is that they are intended as a warning: *some compromising information has been disclosed and the operation should be shut down*. Perhaps "Marie is very angry with Fanny" was a coded message prearranged for this type of eventuality. In any event, the MJS smuggling operation was shut down immediately after the tragic night of October 21.

The second surviving letter was not written on Doctor Périnel's stationery but on a blank sheet of paper. Mila's writing is followed by a dark line, drawn by hand, and a series of cryptic notes penned by Mola Racine.

Racine
Post Office Box – Annecy
Annemasse, the 25 10-43 [October 25, 1943]

My darlings,

I just received your parcel, which gave me great pleasure. I just had a very nice conversation with my innkeepers. As I am looking for work, they advised me to leave for Germany as a free worker on the assurance that I will be fine there. But, as I told them I was not keen on leaving my beautiful country, they understood, being themselves patriots. They scolded me amicably to take better care of my health. It is possible that I will be with you soon. Of course, I will have to follow the medical prescriptions, and my treatment may last some weeks. But I am really pleased to be here. I have a dainty room with a big sofabed. There is a small courtyard where we walk several times a day.

I just played a game of chess with one of the boarders who is very kind. My innkeepers are anti-Semitic and sent back all the Jews today, which leaves just a few of us here.

I hope you are all well and my only pain is the thought that you are worried about me.

I kiss you tenderly,
Marie-Anne

Saw D: Mila says only spectator Nurse Mila says sac story. Then story I. Told us ND Boulogne – Woman wants to leave – Deceive nurse also – Saw Def – says sac hands Ger

St Ju – accus – pass I fr money Choice free Ger or pris. France – Refuses Germany – says if must will but not voluntarily – Def advises to leave rather than 3 months Lyon horrible – Food excellent – do not be too fearful – 3 Mila – 3 Rola – France all – story Ham brandy – cheese etc . . . leave vegetables – reading and smoking – etc. More diff. than Roland – See C.Ac. fr Roland and letter less constrained – his easier less closely watched Def says shoes received Monday?? Impossible to say no because he is unaware of letters received – interrogation Ger proposes to leave Roland Mila together possib marry etc. Atmosphere very relaxed since depart Jews. Give food to Ger – Are extreme well – all stroll hallway

It is impossible to decipher the meaning of all of Mola's notes. However, based on the contents of the letter and the notes, certain facts are incontrovertible. Mila and Roland were offered the choice of going to Germany to work or serving prison sentences in France. Because of the horrible conditions at Montluc prison in Lyon, where they would undoubtably be sent, Deffaugt advised them to go to Germany. Mila and Roland both rejected that option.

Mila writes that her innkeepers "sent away all the Jews today." Indeed, entries in the Pax prison register indicate that Olga Stiasny and her son and Abraham and Rachel Vengerowsky were sent to Drancy on October 25. Rosette Wolczak, the fifteen-year-old who had been sent back to France after having been judged undeserving of Swiss hospitality, was also among the group of Jews sent from Annemasse to Drancy on October 25. (After her arrest on October 19, she too had been imprisoned in Pax.) Erica Mauren, the mother of the baby believed to have been shot, was not identified as Jewish and was not sent to Drancy.

Roland was beaten during interrogations at the Gestapo headquarters in the Pax Hôtel. It is not known if Mila was beaten or abused. On one occasion, Roland was taken from the prison across the street to Gestapo headquarters for what he refers to as a "new interrogation, without brutality." He was asked to describe the *passeur* who had taken them to the border on the night of the arrest. Intending to mislead the interrogator, he gave a description that did not match the actual person at all. He was then shown a photo of the actual *passeur* and asked if it were he. Roland protested emphatically that it was not. According to the account, the SS officer, who spoke only German, then turned to the woman serving as his translator and, referring to Roland, said, "He is a Jew, isn't he?" "No," she responded. "He [the SS officer] does not insist, and the interrogation stops there. Roland did not understand the reason for this peremptory assertion, but luck appears to smile on him one more time."

What happened next was truly astonishing. One day, Simon Lévitte and Mola Racine appeared inside the prison, accompanying the mayor on one of his visits. Deffaugt had smuggled them in under false identities so that they could make contact with Mila and Roland. In an emotional meeting, the visitors tried to comfort the prisoners, reminding them that the war had taken a new turn, that the Nazis were being beaten back on all fronts, and that the Allies could not continue to delay their landing in France for very long.

~

At 10:30 in the morning on October 28, a deportation train left the Bobigny station, in the northeast suburb of Paris, destined for Auschwitz. Locked within its forty cattle cars were one thousand Jewish prisoners who had been interned at Drancy. Jacques Wajntrob and Arno Klarsfeld were among them. The deportation train was the sixty-first such convoy to leave France.

During the approximately three weeks that he had been at Drancy, Jacques managed to organize an impromptu *gdoud*. He speaks of this in the first of two undated letters smuggled out of the camp. (To the best of my knowledge, ellipsis points contained in letter reproduced below appear in original.)

> My Dear *Haverim* [Friends],
> Up until now, I had no possibility of writing to you. Now, E. [possibly Ernest Appenzeller] has informed me of your work, and I cannot but congratulate you.
> We have already formed a *Gdoud*, and we hope to be able to do good work . . .
> Our morale is good. Every evening, we gather and evoke the memory of the *Gdoud*, accompanied by songs, Hebrew naturally. Now, to you: continue on to the end, but be careful, very careful; be suspicious of new acquaintances . . .
> We think of you as if we had continued to work . . .
> *Hasak veemats Chalom* [Strength courage Peace].
> Jacques

In the second, more somber letter, Jacques bids farewell to his comrades:

> My Dear *Haverim* [Friends],
> A few words before my departure. I leave Drancy tomorrow for an unknown destination. I am feeling very well, and I have much hope. Soon, we will all see one another again. In any case, I hope that in your hands the work continues as before. Ernest remains here and will be able to maintain contact with you.
> I address this letter to all my *Haverim* in France. Those of you who receive it initially will want to pass it on to Simon.
> I have maintained very good morale, and I wish you good work and a cordial *Chalom* [Peace].
> *Hasak veemats lehitraoth baaretz* [Strength courage; see you again in the Land, i.e. Palestine].
> Jacques
> (Regional Head M.J.S. Deported)

The story of Jacques Wajntrob—at least what is known—ends in the medieval town of Bar-le-Duc, in the Lorraine region of northeast France. Around 6:30 in the evening, the deportation train stopped at the Bar-le-Duc station. A police report included by Serge Klarsfeld in *Le Calendrier* describes what happened next:

> During the stop, having ascertained that the floorboard of a wagon at the front had been knocked out, the soldiers on watch climbed up into the car and made all the occupants, which numbered about 30, undress.
>
> Leaving each one either a pair of shorts or a shirt but never both, they made all these men step down onto the platform dressed in that manner. They directed them to another car towards the end of the convoy.
>
> All of the clothing that had just been taken off was left in the first car.
>
> This incident, as soon as it became known in the town, caused a profound unease among the population, who criticizes it severely.

Below the report, Klarsfeld notes, "Similar escape attempts were punished, upon arrival at Auschwitz, by immediately putting to death the deportees who were undressed."

Léa Wajntrob believes that Jacques was among those who attempted to escape the deportation train. The case is compelling: he was an experienced carpenter who, two years earlier, had escaped the internment camp at Pithiviers. After the war was over, comrades who were with Jacques in Drancy told his widow that he had smuggled carpenter's tools onto the deportation train. Léa also wonders if Jacques and others were murdered in Bar-le-Duc in reprisal for the attempted escape. Some persons who arrived at Auschwitz in Deportation Convoy 61 later reported to Léa that they never saw Jacques enter the camp. This is a mystery not likely to be solved. It is possible that Jacques and others were killed at Bar-le-Duc, their bodies buried in an unknown, unmarked grave. It is also possible that a group of men, marked for immediate death by their state of partial undress, were murdered upon arrival at Auschwitz apart from the remainder of the convoy.

~

In early November, Mila sent two additional letters from Pax prison; one is dated the fifth and the other the eighth. The November 5 letter begins with the statement, "I arrived at Marc just fine and feel wonderful." This would suggest that she had been transferred to Fort Montluc prison in Lyon on or just prior to November 5. However, data contained in the Pax prison register indicate that the transfer did not place until November 15. Apparently, Mila intended the statement to convey the message that she has managed to avoid being sent to work in Germany and will instead be allowed to remain in France.

Throughout most of the two letters, she adopts a tone that is jovially sarcastic. However, as in the first surviving letter, she expresses concern about the effect that her imprisonment may be having on her parents. She worries that their anxiety in regard to her situation may take a toll on their physical well-being. (It is possible that Mila's father was suffering from poor health prior to the time of her arrest; he died of cancer before the war was over.)

November 5, 1943

My darlings,

I took advantage of an opportunity to give you some news.

I arrived at Marc just fine and feel wonderful. Frankly, it is not at all as good as we thought. The children are in good health and well taken care of; the others are not.

Everybody is very kind to me and they don't want to let me go. In any case, I will have benefited greatly from my stay here. It is a good internship, and I learn a bunch of new things.

What I miss most is your news. Especially that of Ma Pa [Mom and Dad]. I think of them non-stop. How is their health. I very much wish that we could finally be reunited. Send them my letter so that they will not worry about me.

I do not yet know how long I will stay at the camp. Maybe 1 or 2 months. I will try to give you news from time to time.

I kiss you on both cheeks.

Your Marie-Anne

November 8, 1943

All my darlings,

What a beautiful vacation I am having here. I am getting fatter, and it is beginning to worry me. Everybody spoils me (my guards, to begin with), and it's frightening. This afternoon, I organized some games. All were convulsed with laughter. We have a great stove around which we all gather. At this moment, they are really generous with us. Every day I eat chicken or duck because, as soon as one receives a parcel, I have to accept a share.

There will be a departure on Wednesday. I do not know if I am in it. I almost prefer to be in it because otherwise I do not know the surprise they have in store for me. Well, I don't worry too much about it.

I would like to have a few tickets. You never know, if I want to make a short stop during the trip, that could help me.

I played chess with the secretary this morning and beat him soundly after a fierce battle.

I have to finish my letter speedily. (It is as if we are in middle school, where we do things in secret.)

A thousand kisses. To my Lili the best.

Marie-Anne

In the fall of 1943, Mola's wife, Sara, suffered a miscarriage and was cared for in a hospital in Aix-les-Bains, a spa town not far from Annecy. The head of the maternity section, Dr. Germaine Cochet, became aware of the fact that Sara was Jewish. She and her husband, Jean, took on the role of helping and supporting the family in whatever way they could. They provided Mola, Sara, and Lili with living quarters in their spacious home on the rue des Bains. (Subsequently, in May 1944, when Sara was again pregnant, Germaine Cochet would arrange for her and Lili to be smuggled into Switzerland.) After Mila was arrested, Mola, fearing for Sacha's safety, insisted that she come to Aix-les-Bains and stay with him and his family.

On November 15, Mila and Roland were transferred, by train, from Annemasse to Lyon. In the letter reproduced in translation below, dated November 24, Mila expresses her delight at seeing Mola and Sacha standing on the platform of the station when the train stopped in Aix-les-Bains. How did they happen to appear on the station platform at that moment and for what purpose? Shortly before the transfer took place, Mola had been alerted by a contact in Annemasse. Not only did Mola and Sacha see Mila when the train pulled into the station but Mola also boarded the train and rode it to Lyon in the hope of snatching Mila from the hands of her German guards. As if that were not surprising enough, a second would-be rescuer did the same thing. Emmanuel Haymann states that Tony, "armed with a small revolver," boarded the train that carried Mila and Roland from Annemasse to Lyon. (Haymann does not specify the station at which Gryn boarded the train. He does state that he boarded "a few stations" before it reached Aix-les-Bains.) Haymann writes, "Tony and Emmanuel [Mola Racine] do not know one another; they make the journey without knowing that they are two Jewish *Résistants* [Resistance fighters] carrying similar suffering in their hearts." The prisoners were heavily guarded, and no occasion arose to free Mila.

Mila and Roland arrived at the Perrache train station in Lyon and were taken to Fort Montluc. Roland spoke of the "brutal change in climate" that the two experienced upon their arrival in Lyon:

> A welcoming committee is waiting for them at Fort Montluc, the fortress prison ruled by the sadly famous Klaus Barbie. It is with blows of a bludgeon and raucous cries that they are pulled from their vehicle and pushed towards the portal. Mila is immediately led to the women's quarters.

Ten thousand victims of the Nazi regime were imprisoned in Montluc during the Occupation. Seven thousand prisoners died there, subjected to unimaginable tortures and extreme deprivation. How did so many prisoners end up in this one place? The Gestapo office in Lyon exercised authority not only over that city but also over much of the region. In November 1942, when the twenty-nine-year-old Barbie arrived, Lyon had already emerged as the capital of the Resistance. Jean Moulin, De Gaulle's chief envoy in France, was Montluc's most famous prisoner during the war, but many other heroes of the Resistance spent weeks or months in Fort Montluc.

Mila, designated prisoner number F826482 (the F standing for female), was incarcerated in Fort Montluc for approximately two months. Mola Racine's private collection contains only one piece of correspondence from the period—a postcard on which Mila had crammed as many words as possible. Communication to and from prisoners was made possible through the involvement of the French Red Cross, and prisoners knew that their exchanges were read by prison authorities.

In contrast to letters she wrote from Pax prison, the postcard from Fort Montluc is written in a tone that is quietly reflective and a bit nostalgic.

> Sender
> No. 826482
> French Red Cross
> 11, Place Antonin-Poncet, Lyon

> Addressee
> Mr. and Mrs. E. Racine
> Post Office Box
> Aix-les-Bains

> Lyon 11/24/43 [November 24, 1943]
> P. S. 1 hairbrush please
> & a large barrette
> the comb for hairwashing

> My loved ones! I finally have the pleasure of writing to you to give you some news. My morale and my health are excellent. Naturally, I think of Annemasse with regret, but I'm holding up pretty well. Sometimes, in the evening, I tell myself, when I open my eyes, I will be near you with my little Lili on my lap. Perhaps this will happen soon! In any case, I don't stop hoping. But, in general, I am strict with myself and push aside all sentimental thoughts; sing all day and take everything with a smile. What troubles me above all is the health of Pa. Hoping that he and Ma are feeling well and are not worried in any way about me; for that, I depend on you. And my little Suzanne! How I miss her. When I dream of the day when we will all be together again! My God, I think that will be the most beautiful in my life! My ski pants are really a treasure. I have enough blankets. I am neither cold nor hungry. I will ask you to send me by the Red Cross: a hand towel, a bar of soap, a spoon, two handkerchiefs, a dark blouse – because it is difficult to wash – a bra (if Simone found mine,

> I can mend it here), a piece of material to use in mending, a full length slip. We can receive medications; so send me the Nestrovit [a multivitamin and mineral supplement manufactured by Nestlé] and the boxes of granules that Lili crunched. I hope that she works well at school and is well-behaved. My dear little Suzanne, how happy I was to see you at the station, you and Mola both smiling. This is the image that I see again and again. I hug you tenderly, also my Lili, mom, and Good Papa. See you soon, I hope, your Marie-Anne.
>
> My dear little Suzanne, I would like to be with you already and squabble as in the past, it's crazy how much I miss you but darn cannot get carried away. Take good care of mapa. I kiss you on both cheeks and kiss you again. Hello to all the friends.

The only other communication dating from the period in Mola's collection is a preprinted form distributed to, and completed by prisoners to request needed clothing and toiletries from persons outside the prison. It reads "I would like to receive:" followed by a listing of twelve items, including apparel (e.g., "2 shirts," "1 pair of shoes") and toiletries (e.g., "1 bar of soap," "1 comb"). The form instructs the prisoner to cross out the items not requested. It further directs individuals filling the request to bring items to Fort Montluc, Monday through Friday, between the hours of nine and eleven in the morning, except from December 24 to 26, 1943. Packages were to be accompanied by a listing of their contents. The instructions end with this warning: "It is strictly forbidden to add food products or letters. In the event that letters or provisions are found in the package, I would be severely punished." Mila appears to have printed her name—written as "Racine, Marie-Anne"—and prisoner number at the bottom of the form and signed "M. A. Racine" beneath the list. Except for "1 tube of toothpaste," all of the items listed have been crossed off. Although no date appears on the request form, the reference to the Christmas holiday suggests that it was sent in December.

Mola received three additional communications from Mila during the first half of 1944. They confirmed that she was alive, revealed where she was interned, and provided a basis for hope that she would return; and, in this respect, they were precious beyond measure. However, they were brief and revealed scant information about her or the difficult conditions under which she lived. Her months in German captivity would be largely unknowable were it not for various accounts written by fellow prisoners after the end of the war. Of these accounts—which include not only published books and articles but also unpublished letters and speeches—the one that holds a singular importance is the memoir *Journal de Ravensbrück*, written by Nelly Gorce.

Nelly was thirty-three years old and a mother of two young children in October 1943, when she was arrested and interned in Montluc. As its name suggests, her *Journal* mainly chronicles the months that she spent imprisoned in Ravensbrück, the largest Nazi concentration camp built specifically for women. In accordance with her wishes, the publication of her book was delayed until twenty years had elapsed after her death, appearing in print in 1995. In the *avant-propos*, the foreword, Lucien Neuwirth attributes the delay in publication to "*une sorte de pudeur,*" a sort of modesty, noting, "*Dans son esprit, trop de cicatrices n'étaient pas encore refermées*" ("In her mind, too many scars had still not healed").

Many Holocaust scholars have written of the nature of friendship and support networks in concentration camps. Some have specifically addressed the subject of how women formed small groups whose members helped one another survive the daily violence, trauma, and deprivation. At Ravensbrück, women prisoners formed camp "families"—groups of between two and eight but generally consisting of three to five persons—to sustain close friendships and support one another. Nelly and Mila first befriended one another in Montluc, and, despite the difficulty and danger involved in communicating with one another, they formed a group of five. Nelly writes:

> Feeling drawn to one another, small groups have been formed. Ours is ideal. We are five, all very young, myself the only one married. It is in going round in a circle in the courtyard at Montluc, during the quarter hour of walking that we were sometimes granted, that we got to know one another. Menaced by blows—our guard, a brute with spectacles riding on his nose, not a tender-hearted person—we exchanged our first words. Blows rained down heavily on the talkative one who allowed herself to get caught. In the rare instances when he turned his back, we whispered our identity or our story, at least that which we could confess. So, word by word, at the end of four months, we had expressed the maximum about ourselves and had become friends.

In a four-page handwritten letter that she wrote to Mola immediately after the end of the war, Nelly also speaks of her nascent friendship with Mila:

> I had known Mila in going around Montluc, and we immediately got on well together. In the lavatory, we schemed to be near one another and to exchange a few words. She must have told you briefly that she had not been tortured and that she had some good cellmates. An older woman of Macon . . . and the wife of the Director of the Institution of Deaf-Mutes in Villeurbanne, whose name escapes me. They had ordered their days, doing a lot of exercising, while making time for conversation and songs.

The woman whose name had escaped Nelly was Marguerite (Mag) Pellet (née Baud). Mag and her husband, René, had been in charge of the Institut des sourds-muets-aveugles et déficients (Institute of Deaf-Mutes, Blind, and Deficients) in Villeurbanne. They had also become important members of the *réseau* Marco

Polo, an underground resistance group that specialized in gathering intelligence on Germany's secret weapons, particularly the V-1 and V-2 rockets. The Pellets "had readily agreed that the school buildings should serve as the centre of the group's activity, the place where the post was collected and prepared, where the archives were kept and so on—in short, that their school should be the headquarters and centre of the network." In October 1943, René was secretly flown to London to confer with British intelligence officers. He sought to impress upon them the fact that the German rocket program was still moving forward despite the losses they had suffered at Pennemünde. (On the night of August 17-18, 1943, British bombers had attacked the German military test site at Pennemünde, on the Baltic Sea, where the V rockets were being developed.) Secretly flying into or out of Occupied France was not an easy matter—René's return to Lyon was delayed until December 10. During his extended absence, Mag directed the school administration and soldiered on in the Resistance. On November 23, 1943, Gestapo agents raided the Institute, arresting the thirty-nine-year-old Mag and several others.

As an aside, I should mention that OSE had also been using the Institute as a "transfer point, where children were sometimes lodged before being dispersed into homes, religious institutions, or more generally into Switzerland." Within hours of the raid, Gestapo agents who had camped out in the school seized an OSE worker named Madeleine Dreyfus. Having telephoned the school to inquire about the welfare of a Jewish child in hiding, Dreyfus had been instructed to "come by the school right away." She did not know that the individual with whom she spoke was being held at gunpoint.

Although Nelly speaks of "Mila" in her letter, it was only after the end of the war that she learned that this was her name. From the time of her arrest onward, Mila maintained her assumed identity as Marie-Anne Racine, the twenty-year-old Catholic student from Boulogne-sur-Seine. She did not reveal her true identity—neither the name Mila nor the fact that she was Jewish—even to her closest friends. She most certainly knew that revealing the fact that she was Jewish would significantly diminish her chances of survival. While imprisoned in Montluc, she may have witnessed or heard about the fact that Jews were separated from other prisoners and confined to what was called the Baraque aux Juifs (Jews' Hut), a wooden shed erected in the prison courtyard. Documenting the experiences of André Frossard, imprisoned in the Baraque aux Juifs in 1943, Ted Morgan states, "The world in Montluc Prison, according to Frossard, was like the world outside—it was divided between those who were and those who were not Jews. Those who were, were not treated as enemies. They were not even treated as an inferior race. They were treated as a completely different species. They were not even given the respect one gives an enemy."

Mila's fellow prisoners apparently pronounced her name Marie-Anne as one word; in their memoirs, they write of "Marianne" or "Mariane." In the *Journal de Ra-*

vensbrück, Nelly refers to Mila as "Miane." Presumably, Nelly used this diminutive form of the name as a term of endearment. She describes her friend Miane this way:

> Miane is more reserved [than others in their group]. Behind her pure forehead and her classic features of an Italian virgin is a soul of incredible depth. She is interested in all of the sciences, all of the arts. Her mind constantly on watch, her critical sense allowing her to judge human beings and things would make her our elder if a certain naiveté did not render her a very young girl.
>
> She ignores deviousness and believes only in noble virtues. She has a great passion, her family, and, above all, her brother.

In addition to Nelly and Mila, their group of five included nineteen-year-old twins Marie-Claude and Hélène Mion and a woman named Michou. Speaking of the twins, Nelly says: "They look like two dolls, chubby-cheeked and pink. They have the limpid eyes of a child and hair flooded with light." The circumstances that led to the arrest and imprisonment of the Mion twins are unknown. What is known is that Hélène's fiancé, André, was also imprisoned in Montluc, that he was tortured "three days and two nights," and that, on the eighth of January 1944, he was executed. I have not been able to determine the actual identity of the woman whom Nelly refers to as Michou, said to be the first of the five to arrive at Montluc. The prisoners were prohibited from speaking to one another, but, standing at the sink in the lavatory one day soon after her arrival, Nelly dared to speak to Michou. She believed she would not get caught because the sound of the running water would drown out the sound of her voice. The guard saw her lips moving, however, and gave Nelly her first beating.

The last time that Mila, Mola, and Sacha saw one another was on or around January 26, 1944. Mola and Sacha happened to have traveled from Aix-les-Bains to Lyon in order to take a parcel to Mila. As they arrived at the Perrache train station, they noticed a train, filled with women, waiting to depart. They determined that the women on the train were prisoners. According to Sacha, she and Mola were able to board the train, give Mila the parcel that they had brought to her, and remain with her for a few minutes. Sacha and Mola were the ones who couldn't hold back the tears. "Mila consoled us; she was laughing," Sacha wrote shortly after the Liberation. "The last thing that she said to me: I am leaving for the grand adventure!"

~

Despite the significance of Fort Montluc in the collective memory of Lyon and, indeed, France, it takes some doing to find the place. The map distributed by the city's tourism office in 2000 showed Montluc to be located on the south side of the avenue Félix Faure, directly east of the rue Général Mouton Duvernet. That location, I found, consisted of nothing more than a vacant lot surrounded by a perimeter wall covered in graffiti. Arriving there, I concluded that the former prison had been demolished. Later that day, someone informed me that the prison still existed; and so, the next morning, lacking precise directions but determined to find it, I went back to the Sans Souci neighborhood in which it is located. If there were any signs pointing to the prison posted on the principal streets—the avenue Félix Faure, the boulevard Marius Vivier-Merle, cours Albert Thomas—I did not see them. After hunting for an hour and making several inquiries, I stumbled upon it, directly north of the rue Jeanne Hachette and west of the Square Alban Vistel. The neighborhood is mostly occupied by nondescript apartment buildings, several stories in height. The Université Jean Moulin Lyon 3 is nearby.

It was impossible to see the buildings that comprise the prison, as the whole complex is surrounded by a high concrete wall. A few red tile roofs were visible above the top of the wall. What appears to have been the main entrance, a large stone arch, was completely sealed off so that one could not see inside at all. Although that entrance did not appear to be used, it was still a place of memory: beneath the *tricolores* (French flags) and plaques installed on either side of the arch were fresh bouquets of red and white roses. Resistance fighters liberated the prison, with 950 surviving prisoners, on August 24, 1944.

It seems that, in Lyon, many things are, if not exactly hidden, at least inconspicuous. On my visit in 2000, I was not aware of the significance of the Hôtel Terminus, the hotel in which Klaus Barbie installed his Gestapo team when the Germans occupied Lyon in November 1942. (This hotel, located at number 12 on the cours de Verdun-Rambaud, across from the Perrache train station, is now the Grand Hôtel Mercure Château Perrache.) Tom Bower states in his biography of Barbie that fifty members of the SS team moved into sixty rooms on the second and third floors of the hotel. Their living and sleeping quarters were on the second floor; they interrogated their victims on the third. The interrogation rooms were not specially equipped with torture apparatus, however. "That would only come in June 1943," Bower notes, "when the Gestapo, clearly suffering [sic] from an increased work load and insufficient space, moved into the vast École de Santé Militaire on the Avenue Berthelot." That former medical school now houses the city's Centre d'Histoire de la Résistance et de la Déportation (CHRD), whose exhibits of archives, artifacts, and videotaped testimony provide an engaging overview of the Occupation, the French government in Vichy, the deportations, and the Resistance. I toured the entire museum in 2000 and did not realize that the Terminus is just a few blocks away, across the nearby bridge called the Pont Galliéni.

Inconspicuous also is the Grande Synagogue of Lyon, the preeminent synagogue in the region, located on the right bank of the Saône at number 13, quai Tilsitt. It is unlikely that you will notice the synagogue at all as you stroll along the water's edge, for it is hidden behind a façade that blends in with those of its neighbors. If you stand on the red metal footbridge called the Passerelle Saint-Georges, just a half a block away, you may notice the large Magen David that fills a circular window high above the street level. The Bulgarian *shames* explained that, in order to obtain permission to build the structure, the Jewish community had to agree to the stipulation, set forth by the Archbishop of Lyon, that the synagogue building be concealed behind an outer wall and hence not identifiable from the exterior. More precisely, the *shames* said that the Archbishop did not want the synagogue to be within the view of the Basilica de Notre Dame, which crowns the nearby Fourvière Hill. I do not know the source of this explanation nor have I attempted to verify its accuracy. The Grande Synagogue (completed in 1863 or 1864) predates the present basilica (built between the early 1870s and the late 1890s). The basilica, a massive, fortresslike structure, would have been in the planning stages at the time that the synagogue was being built. (A church already stood at the top of Fourvière Hill, having been built two hundred years earlier.) Did the Archbishop actually stipulate that the synagogue be concealed, and, if so, was it because of the vista viewed by Catholics atop Fourvière? Or was it perhaps because of the proximity of Saint-Georges Church, located directly across the river from the synagogue? This church, which is quite old—documents refer to it having been restored in the ninth century—was reconstructed in the 1840s. Or did leaders of the Jewish community choose to conceal the true nature of the building for their own reasons? That would not have been unusual; many synagogues in France were designed and built so as to conceal their identity.

Despite its name, the synagogue is *haimish* (homey). Beneath the cornflower blue dome of the sanctuary, worshippers sit on simple wooden pews, well burnished from years of use. During the war, the building was ransacked and the Torah scrolls desecrated. Judaism forbids the discarding of any texts or documents containing the name of God. Torah scrolls, prayerbooks, and even mundane materials containing God's name are required to be stored in a repository called a *genizah* until they can receive proper burial in a Jewish cemetery. The *shames* opened the doors of a cabinet—a small *genizah*—beneath the ark. There rested the desecrated scrolls. For some reason—perhaps to bear witness—the Torah scrolls had never been buried.

~

There was a time when the name Compiègne was best known for the forest that served as a royal hunting ground of French monarchs, but I doubt that this is still the case. Compiègne is a small city located about fifty miles northeast of Paris. The forest of Compiègne was selected as the place to execute the armistice ending the Great War. What recommended it for this distinction was the fact that the rail configuration could accommodate two trains stopped in close proximity to one another and hidden from plain view. On November 7, 1918, two trains arrived, one carrying Marshall Foch and French and British officers, and the other a delegation sent by the German government. They met at a place called Rethondes, six miles east of the city, where, early on the morning of November 11, the armistice agreement was signed. It did not take long for the French to establish what is called the Clairière de l'Armistice, the Armistice Clearing, a memorial built on the exact spot where the meeting took place and which embodied, in the minds of many Germans, the complete humiliation they had suffered in defeat. Dedicated on November 11, 1922, it featured a large granite slab that read, "Here, on the eleventh of November 1918, the criminal pride of the German Empire succumbed, vanquished by the free people it intended to enslave." A monument to the fallen of Alsace and Lorraine depicted a German eagle immolated by a sword. In 1927, the railway carriage used by Marshall Foch, a *wagon-lit* (sleeping car) that had been converted to an office, was brought from Paris to Rethondes and exhibited in a small museum built for that purpose. A decade later, a statue of Marshall Foch was erected.

On June 19, 1940, according to Hitler's instructions, German engineers carefully demolished a wall of the small museum building, removed the *wagon-lit,* and set it down upon the railroad tracks in the exact same spot on which it had stood on the morning of November 11, 1918. Two days later, just before the arrival of the French delegation, Hitler installed himself in the carriage, in the same chair used by Marshall Foch when the first armistice was signed. According to William Shirer, who was covering the historic event for CBS Radio, "They [the French delegation] had not been told that they would be led to this proud French shrine to undergo such a humiliation, and the shock was no doubt just what Hitler had calculated."

Immediately after the armistice was signed, the *wagon-lit* was packed up and taken to Berlin, where it was put on display. The monument to the fallen of Alsace and Lorraine was destroyed. The granite slab marking the Allied victory was broken into several large pieces and hauled off to Berlin. In accordance with Hitler's instructions, the statue of Marshall Foch was left unharmed to oversee a pile of rubble.

There was a prison camp in Compiègne; its formal name was Frontstalag 122. Towards the end of January 1944, Mila and her friends from Montluc—Nelly, Hélène, Marie-Claude, and Michou—arrived at this camp. Compared to the terrifying days that they had passed at Montluc, their brief stay seemed "paradisiacal":

> The open air, the varied companionship of comrades, the decent food offered by the Red Cross had replaced the narrow cell of one and eight-tenths meters across, where four of us languished, without air and with almost no light, constrained, by lack of space, to immobility. Above all, we no longer feared those interrogations, the sole thought of which haunted our nights and days . . . .
>
> Alas! This marvelous haven lasted only three days.

On January 30, the women in the camp learned that their deportation was imminent. They were not told the name of the camp to which they were being deported. Even if they had been told its name, it would have meant nothing to them.

The size of the group—957—was unusual for a transport comprised entirely of women. In fact, it would prove to be the single largest transport of women deported from France during the war. Prior to departure, the prisoners had been assigned the new numbers that they would use when they arrived. Their numbers ranged between 27030 and 27988; Mila's number was 27918. The substitution of numbers for names was a standard element of the Nazi program to dehumanize prisoners. In the case of this particular group of women, however, the numbering process had an unintended effect. The use of consecutive numbers, while submerging the individual identities of these women, offered them a group identity. They seized upon that group identity and never let it go. From that first day on, the women of the transport proudly identified themselves as the twenty-seven thousands.

They were a diverse and illustrious group. Denise Dufournier, prisoner number 27389, notes in her memoir that they came from all parts of France.

> At that departing roll call, which brought us all together (we were close to one thousand) in the large courtyard of Compiègne, no province of France was missing. The names carried within them their natal villages, as if each region was anxious to be represented in the symbolic sacrifice which was, from now on, going to unite these lives, so diverse, hurled by a single ideal into a common and monstrous adventure.

They were of all ages—Nelly notes that the women in their cattle car ranged in age from eighteen to sixty-six. Some had been active members of the Resistance; others had come to the aid of a husband, son, brother, fiancé, or boyfriend. Nelly specifically refers to women who provided a loved one a few moments to escape. In the simple act of delaying or misleading those in pursuit, they had sacrificed themselves to the cause. They were keenly aware of the fact that, although their acts of resistance may seem small, they carried their weight in the "courageous revolt of a people." Yet, she muses, "We will never know the heroism of our women, the simplicity of their consent."

Reputable sources differ as to whether the transport left Compiègne on January 30 or 31. After reviewing various sources, it seems likely to me that the women prisoners boarded the train on January 30 but that the train was delayed in leaving Compiègne until sometime after midnight. Thus, it would not be surprising that survivors would remember that they left on the thirtieth, whereas official documentation recorded the departure as having occurred on the thirty-first.

After leaving Compiègne, the transport traveled east through Soissons and Reims in northeast France, proceeding at what must have been an achingly slow pace. The prisoners were given no food or water. Particularly at night, they suffered from the cold. Before dawn on February 2, the train stopped. Renée Euvrard, prisoner number 27682, describes what happened next:

> A stop, a stop that drags on for one hour, maybe two . . . . [ellipsis points in original] We are numbed by the terrible cold, by hunger, by thirst. We hear frightening noises. They have just unsealed our wagons, and a big sergeant appears before us. He has, in one hand, a riding whip of inordinate length, and, in the other, a large field lantern. With his whip, he puts all of the prisoners on one side, then sends them back to the other, counting them one by one.

In Nelly's wagon, the officer, wielding what was described as a "*badine*"—a switch or cane—delivered a sharp blow to each woman as she passed in front of him to be counted. It was their official welcome to Germany, the stop having taken place immediately after they crossed the border. Of the ordeal, Nelly observes sardonically, "Germany had just officially taken possession of the daughters of France."

By the time the train crossed the German border, Mola and Sacha Racine had probably received the two postcards that Mila had been allowed to send from Compiègne on January 30. One card was preprinted with a message that read: "I will be transferred to another camp. Do not send any more packages. Wait for my new address." Underneath the message, Mila had written "*Baisers*"—"Kisses"—and "Marie Anne." The second was handwritten.

> Absender [Sender]:
> Marie Anne Racine
> Gefangenennummer [Prisoner number]: 26620
> Lager-Bezeichnung [Camp name]: Compiègne
>
> Empfangsort [Receiver]:
> Poste Restante
> Aix-les-Bains
> France
>
> Compiègne
> January 30, 1944
>
> My darlings,
>
> We leave today for Germany. The morale is excellent. Good humor prevails in the camp. I am happy, so happy to have seen Mo[la] and Sa[cha]. and to have some news of MaPa. We will see each other again soon. Be of good courage. With all my love,
>
> Marie-Anne

9. *Borders*

Shortly after crossing the border from France into Germany, the train stopped again. This time, the women were allowed to exit the cars and relieve themselves in a ditch that had been dug by the side of the tracks. Then, "an organization of the Red Cross" served them some type of soup or porridge in paper cartons.

As dawn broke, a light drizzle fell. "And the train keeps on rolling," Nelly writes. "We are thirsty; our sick are exhausted. Fear, anxiety make the women tense; they quarrel without the least reason. One thinks of a ghost ship without its mast in the middle of the ocean." A third stop, this time in Berlin.

Soon the train reached its destination, Fürstenberg/Havel, sixty miles north of Berlin. The small Fürstenberg station was dark, illuminated only by moonlight. The women were immediately routed from the cattle cars—they had barely a moment to gather their belongings. They were lined up in rows of five and led off in a procession. The landscape was pleasant. Denise Dufournier writes:

> The soil was sandy, and, all around us, we could make out pine trees. A healthy scent of resin, of air that left a salty taste on our lips, made us hope that we were not far from the sea, who knows? maybe even along a coast, which one? probably the Baltic.

The walk was short—about one mile—but difficult. Weighed down by their belongings, their feet sank in the soft sand. They passed a lake whose tranquil surface reflected the moon. As they approached the camp, they saw a word on a signpost, written in Gothic letters: Ravensbrück. It was Thursday, February 3, 1944.

~

On the very same day that the twenty-seven thousands arrived at Ravensbrück, German soldiers raided Le Juvénat and arrested Fathers Favre and Favrat. The director of the school, Father Frontin, was in Annecy when the raid took place. Upon his return, he went immediately to the commandant's office to demand an explanation. He too was arrested. The three priests were taken to the

Pax prison. The commandant requisitioned the school, evicted the teachers and students, and bivouaced his soldiers in the student dormitories.

One week later, the Germans struck the Douvaine *filière*. On February 10, at nine o'clock in the evening, they arrested Joseph Lançon and his young farmhand and accomplice, François Périllat. Several hours later, they went to the presbytery and seized Father Rosay; then, to the local orphanage, where they seized the director, Father Figuet. They, too, were taken to Pax.

~

Although the twenty-seven thousands had traveled north from Berlin, in the direction of the Baltic Sea, they were far from the coast. They had arrived in the Mecklenberg Lake District. Approaching Ravensbrück, they had walked around the northern perimeter of a lake named Schwedtsee. The camp was on the east side of the lake, directly across the lake from the picturesque town of Fürstenberg/Havel.

Ravensbrück was the only concentration camp that the Nazis built specifically for women prisoners. Constructed in 1938 using the slave labor of male prisoners from the nearby Sachsenhausen camp, the facility began operation in May 1939. Its physical plant originally consisted of sixteen wooden barracks, a central kitchen, a shower building, a roll call square, and a cell block, all of which were surrounded by a thirteen-foot high brick wall topped with electrified barbed wire. The commandant's headquarters and homes for Nazi officers and guards were built adjacent to the camp, outside the wall. Fourteen of the sixteen barracks were utilized as sleeping quarters, and two were used as an infirmary, the *Revier*. Barracks were referred to as "blocks," and each block was designed to house two hundred prisoners. The initial capacity of the camp was approximately three thousand.

In the early years (1939–41), the prisoners were "primarily German women arrested for resistance work, religious beliefs, or political activities in opposition to Nazi ideology, or as so-called asocials—criminals (often accused of 'crimes' such as having physical contact with men considered enemies or 'racial inferiors') and prostitutes." Life in the camp was "organized and orderly, even though slave labor, brutality, and torture were routine." The women received clean uniforms and towels; meals, although meager, were distributed on a regular basis; and facilities—sleeping quarters, washrooms and lavatories, and the *Revier*—were adequate to accommodate the number of inmates. The death rate was relatively low, and a small number of prisoners were actually released.

The Ravensbrück that received the twenty-seven thousands in early February 1944 scarcely resembled the Ravensbrück of 1939–41. The number of prisoners recorded during roll call in January 1944 was over seventeen thousand, six times the number of prisoners in early 1940. Germaine Tillion, an experienced ethnologist and member of the Resistance who was deported to Ravensbrück, observed:

> . . . during the three years from May 1939 to May 1942, the camp received about 10,000 prisoners. Then from August 1942 to August 1943, there were about 9,000 arrivals—the rate had almost tripled; from August 1943 to August 1944 there were 36,000—more than ten times the rate of the first three years. At that point, the rate of arrivals leaped to about 10,000 a month.

There is a difference between the number of prisoners living in the camp at a particular point in time (i.e., the number recorded during roll call) and the number of prisoners who had entered the camp prior to that point in time (i.e. registered and numbered as of a particular date). Thus, although Tillion states that seventeen thousand women were counted during roll call in January 1944, the new arrivals received numbers in the twenty-seven thousands. This is not a discrepancy, nor does it indicate that ten thousand prisoners had already perished. Although some of the ten thousand were already dead, some were still alive, working in one of Ravensbrück's approximately seventy subcamps. The historian Jack Morrison speaks of a "mini-empire" of subcamps, some quite distant from the main camp, that had been established to provide slave labor to factories crucial to the Nazi war machine, mainly munitions and aircraft manufacturers.

Ravensbrück passed through three phases during its six years of existence. Between 1939 and 1942, it functioned as a detention center for women deemed criminals, enemies of the state, and undesirables. Although working conditions were harsh, food was adequate to sustain prisoners. From mid 1942 to late 1944, Ravensbrück was a concentration camp, analogous to Dachau and Bergen-Belsen. Its purpose was twofold: labor and murder (or, one might say, murder by means of forced labor). Prisoners, like food and energy, were consumable goods, to be consumed during production. As the war passed its midpoint in 1942, this particular input of production (i.e., forced labor) became more readily available relative to other inputs of production (food and energy). Thus, in Ravensbrück as in other concentration camps, conditions faced by prisoners became more difficult to endure, and, consequently, death rates increased. Beginning in late 1944, Ravensbrück was in the process of being transformed from a concentration camp to a death camp. The camp administration was actively engaged in the process of killing prisoners, mainly the sick, weak, and elderly. (Those over fifty years of age were considered to be elderly.)

The original camp had been continually enlarged over the years. By the time the twenty-seven thousands arrived on February 3, 1944, it resembled a small, crowded, macabre city. In order to take advantage of the slave labor available, the SS had built textile factories on the site. Three thousand prisoners labored in its workshops, producing uniforms and other articles of clothing for soldiers as well as items sold to civilians. Nearly as many prisoners were employed in the Siemens plant built in 1942 immediately adjacent to the camp, which produced specialized electrical components for armaments.

Those prisoners not assigned to work in the SS-owned textile factories or rented out to private firms nearby and in the subcamps performed the work necessary to keep the camp in operation. Organized in *Kolonnen* (work crews), they did every kind of work imaginable—drained swamps, moved things from place to place, painted barracks, repaired washrooms, collected garbage, cut down trees and chopped wood, built streets, unloaded and hauled coal, moved piles of sand and gravel, staffed the kitchens, performed the secretarial work in the offices of camp administrators, attended to the sick and dying, and hauled away the bodies of the dead.

Even though new and larger barracks had been added to those originally built in 1939, by early 1944 facilities had become severely overcrowded. Sleeping quarters were infested with lice and fleas. Incoming prisoners no longer received clean uniforms but rather soiled, often bloody, garments, some of them not at all suited to the work and weather conditions. The camp became "the perfect incubator for typhus: thousands of undernourished women living in overcrowded conditions, surrounded by filth and unable to practice even minimal hygiene." Tuberculosis, acute and highly communicable, was also prevalent. Inmates suffering from these diseases were not expected to recover. They were isolated in separate blocks so that they would not contaminate the rest of the population, but they were not provided with medical care. The problem of dysentery was epidemic and, given the conditions in which the women lived, hardly surprising. What made the situation especially dire, however, was the lack of adequate toilet and washroom facilities and prohibition on using sanitary facilities except at certain times of the day.

Each prisoner was assigned to one of five categories and required to wear the color-coded triangle of the group: Criminals (green); Asocials (black); Jehovah's Witnesses (purple); Jews (yellow); and Politicals (red). Prisoners typically used the badge color rather than the category name when they wished to identify the group to which an individual belonged—for example, the "green badge *Stubowa*." (*Stubowa*, sometimes written as *Stubova*, is a Polish term that was commonly used to refer to the woman assigned to oversee one half of a block. In English texts, this term is generally translated as room senior. The formal German term was *Stubenälteste*.) Apart from the Criminals, the majority of prisoners comprising the other groups had never been accused or convicted of a crime. They were deemed enemies of the state or undesirables because of the circumstances in which they found themselves or their unconventional behavior

(Asocials), their religious convictions (Jehovah's Witnesses), their imputed racial characteristics (Jews), or their divergent political beliefs and/or resistance to the Nazi regime (Politicals).

Although one can draw generalizations about the backgrounds of prisoners comprising one group or another, in actuality, the process of assigning incoming prisoners to groups was far from rigorous. Most of those designated Criminals (green triangles) were, apparently, German. Particularly during the early years, the SS enlisted green triangle prisoners to help oversee—and at times terrorize—the prisoner population.

The Asocials (black triangles) group was extremely diverse; anyone whose behavior was unconventional and therefore suspect and who had the ill fortune to attract the attention of Nazi authorities could find herself in Ravensbrück wearing a black triangle. Some Asocials were women who had engaged in prostitution or were accused of having done so. Others had simply had a liaison deemed illegal under Nazi rule. Gypsies (Sinti and Roma) were also classified as Asocials.

From the beginning, the Third Reich outlawed Jehovah's Witnesses because, in accordance with their strong religious convictions, they refused to say, answer, or acknowledge the official Nazi greeting, *"Heil Hitler."* The Jehovah Witnesses looked upon the Nazi regime as a work of Satan; many vowed that they would not accommodate it or compromise with it in any way, thereby choosing a path of martyrdom. Some ended up in concentration camps; others lost their jobs, pensions, and, in some cases, their children, who were taken to foster homes or orphanages so that they would receive a proper Nazi upbringing. The Jehovah's Witnesses in Ravensbrück (purple triangles) very deliberately engaged in certain forms of passive resistance. They refused to do any type of work that they believed helped German soldiers or benefited the Reich, and they refused to demonstrate the degree of respect demanded of them during roll call and at certain other times. Prior to 1943, the camp administrators sought to break their will, subjecting them to beatings, solitary confinement in the Bunker (the camp prison), long periods of standing outside in the cold, and other tortures devised especially for the purpose. These efforts proved unsuccessful, and they were apparently abandoned in later years.

Prior to 1942, Jewish women in Ravensbrück were treated much the same as other prisoners. Unlike others, however, they wore two triangles. Some wore two yellow triangles, one placed on top of the other to form a yellow star. Others were categorized as Criminals, Asocials, or Politicals in addition to being Jews and bore a green, black, or red triangle sewn over a yellow triangle. Once the Final Solution was formally implemented in January 1942, steps were taken to remove all Jewish women from Ravensbrück and send them to Auschwitz and other extermination centers. By June 1943, Ravensbrück was effectively, if not completely, *Judenrein*. (The German word *rein* means clean, pure, or unadulterated. Under the Third Reich, the Germans used the word *Judenrein* to denote an area "cleansed" of Jews.) Beginning in the fall of 1944, large numbers of Jewish women and some children were brought from camps and ghettos in the east to Ravensbrück. They were subjected to conditions worse than those endured by other prisoners at the time and worse than those that I have described so far.

At first, the Politicals (red triangles) were mainly German citizens persecuted for their anti-Fascist views. Most were Communists; some were Socialists. The most charitable view of these women advanced by Nazi Party officials was that they needed to be "re-educated"; the least charitable was that they were simply traitors. As time went on, large numbers of women of other nationalities—mainly Russian and Polish—were brought to the camp, and they were also designated Politicals.

Nationality was a determinant of survival. Some nationalities had considerably more influence in the camp than did others. Prisoners self-identified by nationality, not by category, and there was fierce loyalty within national groups and rivalry among them. Most Politicals were allowed to indicate their country of origin by placing a letter inside the red triangle that they wore. Women from France and Germany were prohibited from doing this, and this prohibition was deeply resented and, for a time, rebelled against by the French women.

By 1942, the Poles had become the largest nationality and had managed to install themselves in key positions. Many of the *Blockowas* (or *Blockovas;* block seniors) and *Stubowas* (room seniors) were Polish. As noted above, the word *Stubowa* is Polish. *Blockowa* is also Polish; it was used instead of the German word *Blockälteste*. The fact that the Polish rather than German names were used is revealing in itself. *Blockowas* and *Stubowas* wielded great power over other prisoners. Moreover, they did not wage the same daily battle for survival that others did. They had better sleeping quarters, clothing, and food, and they were not subjected to the heavy—at times, backbreaking—labor or the beatings that other prisoners had to endure. Most of the kitchen crew was also Polish, an obvious benefit in a world dominated by constant, unfathomable hunger. As has been well documented in other camps, food—bread and soup rations—functioned as the medium of exchange for goods and services. Food smuggled out of the kitchen could be used to purchase whatever else might be available and could be given to friends, enhancing their chances of survival.

The French women at Ravensbrück did not occupy positions of authority or privilege. They were not present in the camp in significant numbers until rather late in the war, the first sizable group (219 people) having arrived at the end of April 1943. Even if they had arrived earlier, it is doubtful that they would have filled the ranks of the prisoner administration to any significant degree. The

SS, fearing that the French women would organize passive or active resistance, did everything they could to keep them "divided and powerless." Many of the French women were fervent patriots who had made the supreme sacrifice for France, and they were not about to seek or accept positions of authority or work in close cooperation with the SS. Such activities represented, in their minds, a form of collaboration with the enemy.

As I read the memoirs of Nelly Gorce and Denise Dufournier, it occurred to me that the French women developed coping mechanisms uniquely their own and, in a sense, uniquely French. First and most importantly, those who had actively participated in resistance activities at home or had come to the aid of resisters looked upon deportation and imprisonment in the camp as part of the overall struggle to free France. Second, a French chauvinism prevailed, and it helped many of the French women, including those who had not engaged in any sort of resistance efforts, psychologically distance themselves from the squalidness in which they lived. Third, although the use of humor seems far-fetched under the circumstances, joking, banter, and ridicule were common, and this restored a sense of solidarity and humanity. Fourth, despite the inherent danger, some women engaged in small acts of psychological resistance. (At times, humor and psychological resistance were used in tandem.) Finally, some were able at times to summon up a mindfulness of the historical nature of what was unfolding before their eyes. They well understood that they were witnesses to historical events and that whoever survived would be called upon to testify on behalf of themselves and their comrades who had perished.

~

The twenty-seven thousands arrived at Ravensbrück on February 3, 1944, at 3:30 in the morning, just as the siren sounded to signal the start of the camp day. As they entered the camp proper, they saw "strange creatures" who, two by two, struggled to carry what appeared to be large vats. (They would learn later that these prisoners were carrying vats of *ersatz* coffee from the kitchen to the blocks.) Their first glimpse of this macabre city was completely disorienting. Dufournier asks, "Had we suddenly gone mad? Was it day or night?" Although it was the middle of the night, there was a great deal of activity inside the camp. On every side, the human beings they saw were emaciated, clothed in striped garments and head coverings, and collapsing under the heavy weight they bore. Dufournier felt a terror rise within her. Three or four of these bizarre creatures stealthily approached their line, asked them if they were French, informed them that they themselves were also French, and urged them to eat all the food that they had brought because otherwise it would be confiscated.

The group was crammed into an empty room in Block 26, which, although large, was barely able to hold the nearly one thousand women. According to

Nelly, "A wisecracking voice announces: 'The principle of the box of sardines.'" As had been the case in the cattle cars, there was not enough space to lie down or stretch out and the women slept curled up or draped over one another. There was one washroom and a lavatory with four toilets. Some of the women were seriously ill. Using the means at hand, a woman named Marcelle set up an impromptu infirmary in the washroom. She summoned the physicians in the group to attend to the ill, and she called on all of the women to proffer their medicines. Mila took it upon herself to organize an orderly procedure for using the lavatory.

They were introduced to the rutabaga soup that would become a staple of their diets. Some refused it, too repulsed by its smell or the fact that it was served in dirty bowls that had to be used by one woman after another without being rinsed. Some joked over this first meal: "Girls, we are going to feast! If it is the same thing at each meal, we are going to gain weight!" "You said it. I am never returning to France; I've had enough of rationing. We are going to guzzle the provisions of Adolf."

Confined to the holding block for four days, the new arrivals tried to assure themselves that they were not destined to become part of the gruesome spectacle they had witnessed upon arrival. Dufournier writes, "The most optimistic rumors began to circulate; it was obvious that they were not counting on us, that we were in a disciplinary camp while waiting to be transferred to a concentration camp, that said concentration camp had certainly been bombarded."

Finally, they were informed that they were going to be taken, in groups of fifty, to the showers. The thought of streams of warm water washing over their bodies lifted their spirits. However, in Ravensbrück as in other concentration camps, the initial shower was part of a sinister intake process meant to completely dehumanize prisoners. The women surrendered all of their possessions. They were subjected to humiliating body cavity searches and long periods of forced nudity. Most had their heads shaved, although a few, including Mila, were spared.

The intake process was shocking and humiliating. Both Gorce and Dufournier identify it as a turning point, the moment when they were forced to shed their former lives. Each attempted to counter the feelings of dehumanization in her own particular way.

Gorce tried to convince the Polish women in charge not to shave her head, but she was unsuccessful. She then used humor to hide her pain and humiliation.

> Above all, these she-animals must not see my misery. I laugh as if it were a good joke and demand a mirror. Dumbfounded, the woman . . . grants my request, and with my most angelic smile, I look at my little boy's face while proclaiming forcefully that I find myself ravishing. I believe that they take me for a madwoman.

Dufournier had an astounding capacity to step outside of herself and view the situation from a historical perspective.

> The moment had come, I thought, for us to abandon the role of spectator in order to take up, with the uniform, a role in this drama, of which the denouement would be our defeat or our victory, our death or our life. But, at the same time that the surrounding hideousness wrote itself on my spirit, the certainty of another danger—one just as formidable, one that threatened our individualities, our intelligences, the very essence of our personality—infused itself in me in a persistent way.
>
> What good would it do to fight to save our lives if we were not strong enough to safeguard our souls? Certainly, it is not because you are suddenly clothed in a dress sewn like a bag; it is not because your hair is shaved that you betray in an instant the principles that have, for many years, been built up in you. But I did not doubt for a moment that it had to do with the application of the first article of a system meticulously developed so as to lead us by stages to decline . . . [ellipsis points in original] The future would, alas! justify my fears.

Like other groups of new arrivals, the twenty-seven thousands were placed in quarantine due to fear of epidemic. The transport was split into at least two parts, housed in at least two different blocks. Nelly, Mila, Marie-Claude, Hélène, and Michou were all assigned to Block 13. "*Le club des Cinq*," the club of Five, was reunited. Marie-Claude, Hélène, and Michou occupied one bed on the third level; Nelly and Mila occupied a bed on the second level. Dufournier was part of a group quarantined in Block 22.

In light of the above, it would not be correct to assume that, from this point on, all of the twenty-seven thousands shared a common experience as they had done up until that time. Nevertheless, the accounts of the months spent in quarantine written by Gorce and Dufournier are similar in many respects. They reveal that, although some physical distance separated the two memoirists, the conditions to which the groups were subjected and the experiences that they underwent were very similar.

During the period of quarantine, the newcomers enjoyed the indisputable luxury of not having to work. They did, however, have to adhere to the camp's routine. At 3:30 in the morning, their green-triangle German *Blockowa* woke them with screams of *Aufstehen!* (Get up!) They were given thirty minutes to get dressed, make their beds, and, if possible, use the lavatory or washroom. The latter was not easy to do, as there were few toilets in the lavatory and few basins in the washroom, and it was necessary to stand in a long queue to reach one or the other. They then had to line up in front of the block for *Appel* (roll call). Roll call would last at least one hour and sometimes two or three, until any and all discrepancies in the count had been resolved. All of the women except those who had received permission to go to the *Revier* were required to be at roll call, regardless of their age or physical condition. The women were not allowed to move or to talk; the slightest infraction could subject one to a beating. Winter mornings were frigid: "In winter, the thermometer regularly drops to −10° C [14° F], often to −30° [−22° F], sometimes to −33°C [−27° F], without our tormentors being at all moved." The proximity of the camp to the Baltic also subjected them to violent winds and torrential rains.

Between morning and evening roll call, the women in quarantine were confined to the block. Around ten, the morning soup was served. According to Gorce, some were "loathe to swallow the vile soup of dehydrated rutabagas," and they went hungry. "We, the Five, never had enough of it, and, when the serving ended, we dove into the vats to scrape the edges. At the beginning, our companions made fun of us with a dash of contempt, but soon, to our great misfortune, we had many imitators."

This time spent in quarantine, relatively calm, reinforced the feelings of solidarity that already existed among the French women. Despite the fact that their uniforms and shaved heads were supposed to render them anonymous, their personalities, abilities, and accomplishments distinguished one from the other. Dufournier writes that the group included journalists, professors, students, physicians, *paysannes* (women from the countryside), workers, businesswomen. They presented lectures and engaged in discussion on all sorts of subjects.

> Travelogues, philosophical essays, descriptions of our folklore alternated with analysis of a work of Shakespeare, explanation of tragedies of juvenile delinquency, visits to world capitals, study of ancient Chinese civilization as well as the way to raise rabbits or tame lions. Certain talks were very interesting; others horribly boring. The reactions that they received lacked neither spontaneity nor enthusiasm. Sometimes, the unruliness was such that the speaker was obligated to withdraw, confused. No matter! That was part of the risk; what was necessary above all was to strive to go on living.

The women pursued all sorts of artistic endeavors, staging original plays, reciting original poetry, and presenting concerts. Speaking of Mila, Nelly remarks:

> Miane has an amazing choral group that she directs with talent; exceptionally talented in music, she has succeeded in bringing together a dozen girls that she has rehearse all day long; but, as it is necessary to hide, we hear these vocalizations in all the recesses of the block . . .

Another friend, Violette Maurice, was moved by the experience of hearing Mila's choral group. Writing in the third person, she relates the story of a prisoner named Catherine, who, passing by a group of children, overhears them squabbling with one another over who will get to play SS officers in the game of SS and prisoner. (In 1944, there were several hundred children at Ravensbrück. Some had been brought into the camp from the outside; others had been born in the camp.) Feeling completely disheartened by the spectacle, she approaches Block 13, the quarantine block, and stops for a moment to look in the window.

> Suddenly, an unexpected sweetness comes to pull her out of her sorrow, like so many kind hands seeking to free her. A few notes rise up, then a song, taken up again by tens of voices, that increases, rises, and bursts forth, supreme: it is Beethoven's "Hymn to Joy." The silhouette of Marianne, with her long, shining hair, becomes visible to her, while she [Marianne] beats time with her long hands, pale and expressive. Grouped around her, twenty faces, young and not so young, raise themselves towards her, as if transcended by the music.
>
> Catherine, too, feels transcended in that moment.

Although they were not assigned to regular work details during the period of quarantine, they were, at times, marched out from the camp to labor at what was called *Planierungmachen* (leveling detail), which consisted of shoveling sand from one place to another all day long. The guards who oversaw the work would sic their dogs on any woman who shoveled too slowly or dared to stop momentarily. Both memoirists describe this useless work, whose sole purpose was to subjugate and exhaust. Marching back to their block after their first day of shoveling sand, Dufournier's group, although dead tired, lustily sang "Quand Madelon," a popular French drinking song from the Great War. They were promptly warned not to sing any more songs in French; only songs sung in German were permitted. The next day, on their return to the block, they raised their voices again, this time using the tune of "Quand Madelon" but substituting *"ja, ja, ja"* for the song's lyrics. They were then given a list of permissible songs, with accompanying music, that they were instructed to learn.

Occasionally, the prisoners were allowed to write letters home and receive letters and packages. Two letters that Mila wrote to her family while at Ravensbrück have survived. In accordance with camp regulations, letters were limited in terms of their length and they had to be written in German. (Responses also had to be written in German.) All letters were subjected to the scrutiny of the camp censor. Although Mila's message was not censored, the letter nevertheless bears the bold red slashes of the censor's marker, which obscures the date on which it was written. The letter was sent to Mola in care of Mado Hérisson, the attorney in Annecy who had represented Bella Wendling after her arrest at the beginning of October 1943.

Racine, Marie-Anne
Block 13
N° 27918
Ravensbrück
Fürstenberg i) Meckl[enberg]
Deutschland

Me M. Hérisson, Attorney
(for M. E. Racine)
Annecy
(Haute-Savoie)
France

April 1944

My Dears,

I am doing very well. I hope to get an answer from you soon, [and] send me, as often as possible, packages of food and, above all, a piece of soap. I think about you alot, and I hope that you are well and that we will see each other soon.

With best regards, your Marie-Anne

My dear Lili is already a big girl. I have you in my thoughts every day. How are Mapa, Mola, Simone, Suzanne (my best wishes for your birthday). (Please answer in German.)

Around this time, the twenty-seventh thousands were subjected to the first of many selections for work transports. The women were made to stand, nude, against a wall while a male civilian, accompanied by the head of the work bureau in the camp, looked them over and chose those who seemed most fit for work. No information was offered as to where the work transport was going to be sent or how many weeks or months the prisoners might be away. However, they had reason to believe that those selected were going to be sent to work in a munitions factory. Dufournier says, "The words transport, factory, munitions circulate . . . [ellipsis points in original], the greatest consternation reigned." The whole experience was frightening. The thought of being separated from friends and comrades and thrust into a new and unknown situation was bad enough; but the idea of contributing to the manufacture of shells and other ammunition that would be used against their families, their countrymen, their *patrie* (homeland) was sickening.

Nelly was selected and faced the dreadful prospect of being separated from the Five. Immediately, Mila took her aside and advised her: "Miane steered me into a corner and counsels me mysteriously: 'You are going to pass in front of the *Arbeitseinsatz* [person overseeing the Nazi program of slave labor]. You will tell him that you do not see well. It is because of my eyes that the doctor sent me back.'"

Nelly followed Mila's advice. She told the *Arbeitseinsatz* that her eyesight was not good. "You have glasses," he said, to which she responded that they belonged to a comrade who had lent them to her. In this way, she managed to avoid being sent out from the camp on a transport.

After Dufournier escaped the first selection, she looked at the useless work of moving sand in a completely new way: "The next day, I flung, tossed back, and scattered myriad grains of sand twinkling in the sun like stars. I applied myself to this marvelously useless and perfectly stupid work." She escaped a second selection but was chosen during a third. Immediately afterward, a nurse approached her and spoke to her in French with an accent that she recognized as Belgian. Without explanation, the nurse offered to strike Dufournier's number from the list, which was to be in her possession for a short period of time. Dufournier was grateful to her, of course. She was also dumbfounded, struck by the realization that her conception of the power structure within the camp was faulty. Up until that time, she had perceived it in overly simplistic terms: "There was, on the one hand, the enemy that commanded, personified by the SS and the various [female] guards; on the other hand, the mass of prisoners who obeyed." The nurse's offer to strike her name from the transport list was the event—she calls it a "providential intervention"—that made her aware that *"le schéma"*—"the diagram"—is much more complex. "If this nurse, a simple prisoner like me, could succeed in having me escape departure for a factory by a single stroke of a pencil, what should be the power of all those who were occupying important posts!" She resolved to learn the subtleties of the system so that she could determine ways to circumvent it.

~

In April 1944, Father Rosay, Joseph Lançon, and François Périllat were imprisoned in Frontstalag 122, in Compiègne, awaiting deportation. They had been sent there from the Pax prison in Annemasse in March. Father Rosay was one of a dozen priests in the camp. He found solace in the fact that they were allowed to celebrate Mass each day and that they had organized a solemn procession on Easter Sunday. He placed himself entirely at the service of his comrades. Nothing mattered more to him than what he called their "spiritual progress."

On April 27, 1,670 male prisoners were crammed into cattle cars—Rosay, Lançon, and Périllat among them. They traveled for three days in suffocating heat, tortured by thirst. The transport arrived in Auschwitz on April 30, in the evening. It was only the third transport of non-Jews that German and French authorities had sent to Auschwitz. Upon their arrival, 1,655 men were registered; fifteen men had died along the way. Installed in two barracks in what was known as Camp Canada, in Birkenau, near Crematorium IV, the men were tatooed on their left forearms with numbers between 184936 and 186590. The men comprising the transport would later become known as the *tatoués*, the tatooed. I suspect that this was because it was rare for non-Jews who had been Nazi prisoners to bear tattooed numbers. (Only Auschwitz slave laborers were tattooed, and the great majority of them were Jews.)

Most of the men in the transport were sent to Buchenwald on May 12. Ninety-two *malades* (sick) remained behind; Jean Rosay was one of them. (Some of the ninety-two *malades* were transferred to Buchenwald later, although Rosay was not.) In a letter dated May 22, 1944, he wrote home, "I am in the same state [of poor health] as in 1932 at Thorenc but without being sick." What did he mean by this? When he was a young priest serving in Megèvette, he spent several months, from October 1932 to May 1933, at a sanatorium for clergy in Thorenc, near Nice. The source material does not identify the condition or malady that necessitated his being sent to the sanatorium. It does state that, even after Father Rosay had completed his convalescence, his health remained fragile. It is very possible that the priest suffered from tuberculosis and that the statement appearing in the letter alluded to an earlier time when the illness had seriously weakened him. In any event, it is clear that Father Rosay did not have the physical constitution to withstand the hardships and privation to which prisoners were subjected.

Many of the *tatoués* sent to Buchenwald, including Joseph Lançon and François Périllat, were sent on to a different camp, Flossenbürg, on May 24. Then, shortly afterward, Lançon, Périllat, and others were sent to the subcamp Hersbruck. The prisoners held in this subcamp, twenty-two miles east of Nuremberg, provided slave labor for a vast underground factory called Doggerwerk, built into the side of a mountain. The factory, consisting of eight interconnected tunnels used for the production of aircraft engines, was operated by BMW.

~

On June 6, 1944, word of the Allied landing at Normandy spread throughout Ravensbrück. At first, Nelly would not permit herself to believe the news; she feared it would prove to be a false rumor, like so many others. "However, this time, it has such an air of truth that we allow ourselves to be invaded by a sweet madness." They celebrated by singing "La Marseillaise" and allowed themselves the momentary indulgence of daydreaming about their return home.

Shortly afterward, a work transport was selected. At the time, Mila and Hélène were in the *Revier*, recuperating from scarlet fever. Although Nelly avoided selection, Hélène's twin sister, Marie-Claude, was selected and sent away. In the ensuing months of captivity, Hélène would become Mila's closest friend and confidante. They shared what little they had in their daily struggle to survive.

Mila's family received a final letter from her, written sometime in June.

Racine, Marie-Anne
Block 13
N° 27918
Frauen – Konzentrationslager
Ravensbrück bei Furstemberg
Mecklenburg
Deutschland

Monsieur E. Racine
c/o Dr. Cochet
2, rue des Bains
Aix-les-Bains
(Savoie)
France

June 1944

My darlings! I have indeed received your package, and just now I received your letter, dear Mola. I can scarcely describe my joy! Pa's health worries me a lot. Does he know that Mila is with Max? Do you have any news from Simone and my little Lili? Where is Suzanne? Give me some news about Lola and her family, our cousins from Toulouse. My morale and health are excellent, and I hope that our family will be together soon. Do send me packages often: food, toiletries – anything. I need neither money nor underwear. Dear Ma, don't worry about me. I think about you and Pa all the time and want to find you beautiful and healthy and Pa too. Many kisses to you all. Your Marie-Anne.

~

On July 16, 1944, German soldiers executed Father Louis Favre and seven other resisters and dumped their bodies in a makeshift grave in Vieugy, near Annecy. During the five months of his incarceration, the priest had been transferred from one German prison in Annecy to another. Interrogated and tortured on numerous occasions, he had refused to talk. His sister visited him regularly, and he managed to slip notes to her that chronicled what was happening to him and others in the prisons. At some point, members of the *réseau* Gilbert had devised a plan to wrest Father Favre from prison, but he refused to go along with it. The Germans had released Father Favrat, but Father Frontin was still in their hands. He feared that, if he escaped, the Germans would take revenge on his fellow priest, fellow prisoners, and/or family members and friends. On April 8, the day before Easter, he carved a message into a piece of wood in his prison cell: "The real Prison? Society. Within these walls, I have known Liberty. (April 8, 1944)"

~

With more than twenty nationalities represented, Ravensbrück, like most other concentration camps, was a virtual Tower of Babel. Few of the French prisoners spoke German or Polish. Because German- and Polish-speaking women occupied most positions of power and authority, one's inability to understand commands or to communicate with them could be life-threatening. Mila had a natural affinity for languages, and, according to Nelly Gorce, she often served as an interpreter. Gorce does not indicate Mila's level of fluency in either German or Polish; however, she does make clear that Mila was able to communicate with their German overseers as well as with their Polish block chiefs.

At the end of July, Gorce came down with the measles and was allowed to spend two weeks in the *Revier*. When discharged, she found that her group had been reassigned from Block 13 to Block 15. The new block was crowded; she had difficulty locating the members of her "family." Mila and Hélène had been lucky enough to find a bed that they could share, and Michou had found a place for herself. Having no place to go and no one with whom to share a bed, Nelly felt bereft and disoriented. Eventually, she managed to find some sort of accommodation in what had been the day room.

At this point, the *travail de sable*—the exhausting make-work that consisted of shoveling sand—ceased and the prisoners entered into the regular work life of the camp. Some were assigned to work in the SS factories that operated within the confines of the camp and in private enterprises near the camp. Others were assigned to the crews that performed the work required to keep the camp going. Still others were unassigned; they were called *Verfügbaren*, German for "available." (*Verfügbaren* is the plural form; the singular is *Verfügbar*.) The French referred to the *Verfügbaren* as *"disponibles."* Each morning, the *Aufseherin*, the female overseer, would draft *Verfügbaren* prisoners to round out their work crews. Being a *Verfügbar* was like playing a daily game of Russian roulette: one might avoid work altogether or one might be drafted to do the most backbreaking or noxious work in the camp. Although a prisoner entering the camp in 1944 might spend some time as a *Verfügbar*, she was usually eager to receive a permanent assignment. Some of the French prisoners, however, made the conscious decision to remain *disponibles*. At the root of this decision was a fierce opposition toward contributing to German productivity in any form. It is also worth noting that the French women rarely had the opportunity to join a work crew that would be regarded as desirable. Desirable jobs were filled by those with power or influence. Some work crews were completely off limits to the French.

~

In 1944, Ravensbrück became severely overcrowded. Data compiled and analyzed by Tillion indicates that the prisoner population rose from approximately

17,300 in January to 43,700 in December. Morrison estimates the camp was designed to hold between eight thousand and ten thousand persons. (His estimate reflects the fact that the camp had been enlarged since it first opened in 1939 and that many newer, larger blocks had been added to the sixteen originally built.) How then is it possible that the actual prisoner population was four to five times the capacity of the camp as constructed? Women were crammed into the three-tiered bunk beds, three to a bed. They slept on the floor and in the lavatories and day rooms on each side of the block. Some prisoners were never assigned to a barracks at all but were confined to a large tent.

Who were the new arrivals and where were they coming from? They had been deported to Ravensbrück from many places throughout Europe. In the spring and summer of 1944, Gypsy (Sinti and Roma) women and children who had been in Auschwitz were brought to Ravensbrück. (The Gypsy camp at Auschwitz II-Birkenau was being liquidated; during the first week in August, those who had not yet been sent out to other camps were gassed.) Late summer saw the arrival of thousands of Polish women and children. The Warsaw Uprising had begun, and these arrivals had had the bad luck of being implicated in it. (This should not be confused with the Warsaw Ghetto Uprising carried out by Jewish resisters in April and May 1943. The Warsaw Uprising was carried out by Poles in August and September 1944.) As there was no block space available, these prisoners—whom the SS referred to as evacuees from Warsaw—were confined to a large tent erected between Blocks 24 and 26. (What was to have been Block 25 had never been built.) The Polish women and children remained in the tent for a relatively short period of time before being moved to conventional blocks.

In October and November 1944, a large group of Jewish women and children who had been deported from Budapest arrived in Ravensbrück. They too were confined to the tent, and the conditions under which they struggled to survive defined a new level of misery and affliction within the camp. Although some received work assignments and were sent away to subcamps, many remained in the tent as the weather grew frigid. One may wonder how it was that these women and children were sent to Ravensbrück rather than to Auschwitz, as was the case with many other Hungarian Jews. In November 1944, Auschwitz ceased to function as the extermination center that it had been. The last transport of Jews and last gassing of new arrivals occurred in early November. During October and November, the gas chambers and crematoria were destroyed. In fact, during the winter of 1944–45, many Jewish prisoners from Auschwitz were brought to Ravensbrück. They were also forced to stay in the tent. Despite the fact that the tent lacked heat, electricity, and plumbing, it would continue to be used throughout the fall and much of the winter, until February 1945.

Denise Dufournier was living in Block 31, directly next to the tent, at the time that Hungarian Jews arrived. She speaks at length of the horrible conditions that existed in the tent and the shame that she felt at not being able to help those who were suffering:

> When we lay down in the evening, on our half bunks, hearing the wailing coming from the tent all night long, we were overcome by an unspeakable shame at the thought that we could not come to the aid of these poor beings living, if you can call it that, very close to us, in a destitution and a misery after which our own block, our bed, our blankets were a supreme luxury.

Dufournier observed that the Jews confined to the tent were not given the type of clothing that would normally be given to arriving prisoners; they were given *"robes d'été"* and *"robes du soir"*—summer dresses and evening dresses. Why on earth would this type of clothing be given to prisoners confined to an unheated tent exposed to the cold weather? Was there a shortage of warmer clothing? Not at all. The immense *Bekleidungswerk* (clothing warehouse) at Ravensbrück was packed with clothing and shoes, along with an assortment of other items that the Nazis had plundered. There was no interest on the part of camp administrators to prolong the lives of Jews; they were, in fact, intent on just the opposite. Dufournier notes that the prisoners in the tent died at the rate of about fifty per night.

As conditions in the camp devolved and the cold weather set in, the difficulty of avoiding temporary work assignments increased. So, too, did the nature of the risk faced by the *Verfügbar* who managed to avoid work. If one remained inside the block during the work day, one was subject to being selected for a work transport. The situation prompted many of the French women to seek permanent work assignments.

Mila and Hélène joined the team of *charbonnières*, the coal women. Nelly tells us of the work that they did:

> ... their work consists of taking the coal brought to the quay by the barges and bringing it into the rooms of the SS and the *Aufseherinnen* [female overseers]. Each day, they arrive at noon and pull six briquettes from their dresses. I am thus able to give them a little extra soup and make them accept my supplement; I have much less need of it than they! Aren't they twenty years old? And my physical expenditure is less. I suffer when I see my young friends arrive at noon, my friends whose limbs are so chilled they can hardly make them move. I am especially pained by the poor, eager look assessing the thin dole that I pour in their tins; and, in spite of myself, I must definitely confess, I fill the ladle a little more. I would like to have a large, full vat to see the desperate anguish extinguish itself from their eyes, to make them smile.

Even when prisoners are emaciated, exhausted, and ill, death may not arrive swiftly or easily. A sick prisoner might die in her sleep after having worked the previous day, or she might remain ill for some period of time. Camp administrators regarded a sick prisoner as a drain on resources. They dealt with her in any number of ways, depending on the nature and severity of her illness, conditions prevailing at the time she was ill, and happenstance. She might have been admitted to the *Revier*, received a little medical attention and care, and given the chance to recuperate. Or she might have been denied access to the *Revier* and sent back to her block and to her work assignment in order to hasten death.

Camp administrators also periodically purged the camp of the sick and dying, sending them to euthanasia centers and extermination camps in what were called black transports. (The French referred to them as *transports noirs*.) Those considered elderly and those who had gone mad or were suffering from other mental disorders were also sent out on these transports. Some were directed to the euthanasia centers in Bernburg, Germany, and at Hartheim Castle near Linz, Austria. Others were sent to Auschwitz and Majdanek. Although efforts were made to suppress information about the black transports, the prisoners knew well the fate of those selected even if they did not know their final destination. Survivor memoirs speak of the feelings of terror that rose up when these selections were being made.

There came a point in 1944 when a decision was made to develop methods of killing prisoners on site rather than sending them away. The prisoner population had doubled between January and July 1944, and it was continuing to rise, creating not only a strain on existing resources but also a labor surplus. Meanwhile, the number of weakened, sick, and dying prisoners had increased tremendously. These circumstances devalued the life of the individual prisoner to the point that it was barely worth the camp administrator's daily expenditure of thirty-five pfennigs. There was no incentive at all to prolong the lives of those who were ill or weak; efficient production dictated that they simply be disposed of, replaced by more able-bodied workers.

In November and December 1944, camp leaders began developing the means to kill prisoners on site, and Ravensbrück began the transition from a concentration camp to a death camp. A preliminary step involved converting a former *Jugendlager* (youth camp) named Uckermark, located outside of but near the main camp, into a sort of isolation center. Uckermark had been built in 1942 as a detention center for adolescent girls identified as troublemakers or asocials. It had operated as such until early 1944, when it was closed. In December, the camp—which many still called the *Jugendlager*—was reopened to receive the least able-bodied prisoners—the sick, weak, old, dying, and impaired.

Prisoners in the main camp were told that Uckermark was a convalescent camp, where they would not be subjected to roll calls and would receive better food rations and bed rest. Many of the prisoners confined to the Typhus and Tuberculosis Blocks were sent to Uckermark. Camp administrators also directed

Blockowas to draw up lists of prisoners deemed unfit for work. From the beginning, many of the prisoners distrusted what they were being told by camp administrators about Uckermark. Although administrators made every effort to maintain a veil of secrecy, it did not take long for information on the true nature of Uckermark to circulate.

At Uckermark, outside of the main camp and out of the view of all but a small number of people, camp leaders tested various methods of killing prisoners. The basic method used was extreme deprivation and hardship. Upon their arrival at Uckermark, prisoners' undergarments, woolens, and any warm clothing they had accumulated were taken away from them. They were made to stand outside in the frigid cold and snow for five, six, or more hours per day. The food ration was reduced to half of the meager amount normally doled out. The barracks to which they were confined were bare, lacking blankets, beds, and other accommodations.

Extreme deprivation and hardship accelerated the death rate, but it did not reach the level targeted by camp administrators. Two other methods readily available—poisoning and shooting—were used on what seems to have been a sporadic basis. A more effective means of murder would be placed in service in January 1945.

~

After the Allied landing at Normandy, Nelly and some of the other French prisoners had allowed themselves to hope that they would be back home for *les vendanges,* the fall grape harvest. The fall came and went, and, as Christmas approached, their disappointment at not having been liberated was compounded by the despair that arose from the worsening day-to-day conditions. They struggled to support one another physically and psychologically.

Mila continued to rehearse her choral group whenever possible. Her dear friend Hélène, to whom she was devoted, was a member of the chorus. Another close friend, who went by the name Miarka, acted as the group's lookout. In a speech delivered in 1981, Miarka, whose real name was Denise Vernay (née Jacob), presents a description of Mila that she wrote in 1945:

> I will always remember her hand, thin but very white, that expresses, as do her deep blue eyes also, her sensibility to beauty. It is this hand that beats time as we sing: about ten who, at times, assemble to create something pure in that infernal atmosphere. Rehearsals of songs always more difficult to do because we are more and more hounded for work, and, for me who keeps watch—I sang too off-key to be of any other use—nothing exists but a horizon of backs striped and crossed. From there, I am afraid to see emerge a green uniform or a too elegant *"lager polize"* ["camp police"], a stick in her hand, but a horizon from which suddenly rises a real human miracle, as one forgotten, a song that dares to spring up, grows larger, explodes victoriously, "Dona nobis pacem," a canon of Beethoven or of Mozart.

Marie-Jo Chombart de Lauwe was one of the French prisoners in Ravensbrück who found some solace and purpose in becoming a member of the chorus. She had been deported to Ravensbrück in August 1943, when she was only nineteen years old, after having been arrested in Rennes for her involvement in resistance activities along the northern coast of Brittany. She met Mila in the fall of 1944; a friend had invited her to attend a study group that Mila had organized. In her memoir, published in 1998, Chombart de Lauwe spoke of the impression that Mila made upon her and the nature of the study group:

> Her manner and especially her voice draw me extraordinarily towards her. Her light eyes beneath her black eyebrows probe mine. What a calm and radiant force emanates from her. Her whole being seems to have attained a calm fullness. All the force and authority of ripe age were, in her, accompanied by the dynamic enthusiasm of youth. From her came the initiative to form this group and also to form a chorus.
>
> Our meetings begin with some song, march, or such. Then, we study a question, be it from the news, be it philosophical, or be it a general idea—for example, responsibility, "honor."

Mila's French chorus was one of several groups that received permission to present a special program to sick prisoners on Christmas Day. The event was important—both to those who performed the program and those who heard it. Preparations and rehearsals in the weeks leading up to the performances gave the members of the chorus and their helpers a sense of purpose. The sick prisoners and others who managed to crowd into the barracks where the performances took place found some moments of temporary deliverance from the feelings of despair that threatened to overwhelm them on that holy day. Miarka and Marie-Jo Chombart de Lauwe are among the survivors who wrote about the musical program presented by the French chorus. Miarka describes it this way:

> I remember the exhausting tour that our little group undertook the day of Christmas 1944; in all of the sick rooms, it brings the voice of France to our isolated comrades and makes the tears flow, tears that bring relief despite all. We had established the program carefully: create an ambiance dignified and cheery but not too sentimental. "Knights of the Round Table" to begin and with some heart—I will never be able to hear it sung with indifference—then "À Saint Michel en grève," some canons, some Christmas songs. Not without sorrow were we able to sing that day for the pleasure of all.

Like Miarka, Marie-Jo Chombart de Lauwe not only remembered the event but also recalled songs they had sung.

> In the afternoon, it's my turn to rejoin Marianne and the group, and we sing to [Block] 32 the sad and sweet tune "Saint Michel en grève," "La Ravine," and our usual chorals, scout songs, songs of life and joy . . . . Already Marianne hurries us away; in the neighboring block, they are waiting for us. All nationalities are there, especially Russians and Czechs. We sing to give them a little of the French soul that they revere.

In the weeks leading up to Christmas, friends had prepared small gifts for one another, using whatever scraps of fabric, paper, or other materials they could find. A poem neatly printed on a card surrounded by a decorative border, an embroidered handkerchief, a cross of Lorraine fabricated out of a scrap of metal—these were the types of items exchanged and treasured.

Alhough grateful for the tokens of love and friendship she received, Nelly felt a darkness enveloping her. Many in the block were dying from dysentery; beds were vacated and then filled again by new occupants. "Death hastens its work," she writes. Christmas Day was filled with the cries of officers and guards celebrating recent victories that Germany had achieved in the Ardennes (i.e. the Battle of the Bulge).

~

François Périllat had been born in Viegy-Foncenex on January 5, 1920. He died of pneumonia at the Hersbruck subcamp on December 18, 1944, eighteen days shy of his twenty-fourth birthday.

~

Nelly's journal entry of January 14, 1945, is the first to bear a specific date, and it is the first to reflect on the act of recording the events that she was witnessing. "I write. Why?" she asks herself. "What will be the fate of these pages?" From this date onward, all entries are dated. It is not known to what extent or in what form, if any, Nelly had recorded journal entries prior to this time. It does appear, however, that she made a very deliberate decision at the beginning of 1945 to keep a careful written record. The act of keeping a written record placed Nelly in danger—if discovered, she would almost certainly have faced severe punishment or even death. Simply finding the opportunity to write and sufficient writing materials must have been difficult.

In January, Dufournier and her compatriots were moved from Block 31 to Block 15, the block in which Nelly, Mila, Hélène, and Michou also lived. Block 15 was one of the blocks built in 1939, comprising part of what was referred to as the old camp. These original blocks were smaller than, and considered preferable to, the new blocks. Dufournier found Block 15 cleaner and more orderly than the block from which they came. Within a few days of their transfer, however, all of the women living in Block 15 were evicted. They were made to stand outdoors in the bitter cold during the entire day. Finally, late in the evening, they were allowed to enter Block 27. According to Nelly's journal entries, the date of the move from Block 15 to 27 was January 14.

Filth, stench, noise, and death defined this new, overcrowded circle of hell. Nelly writes that in the *Waschraum* (lavatory) "the living are mixed with the dead." The lavatory is used as a temporary morgue; corpses remain until carted off by the *croque-mort colonne*—the undertaking work detail. At the sinks, the living—half-nude women with shrunken breasts and extended bellies, their bony frames jutting out—sing and wash their clothes. It occurs to Nelly that the scene is so bizarre that it would terrify Dante.

On January 26, Mila and Hélène returned from the *Revier*. "They are doing better," Nelly notes. The four friends are happy to be reunited, although Nelly complains that "their bed is far from ours [apparently, that belonging to her and Michou]." There does not seem to be any mention of when they were admitted to the infirmary or what illness they had contracted.

By the end of January, a gas chamber was operating at Ravensbrück. Camp administrators had used inmates from the men's camp at Ravensbrück to construct the gas chamber in the outer section of the camp, near the crematorium. SS-Hauptscharführer Otto Moll, who had supervised the operation of gas chambers and crematoria at Birkenau, oversaw its operation. Moll used male inmates to operate it; no women prisoners were involved in its operation.

German guards who selected women to be sent to the gas chamber told them that they were being transferred to a camp that went by the name Mittwerda. In reality, no such camp existed. Groups of approximately one hundred fifty women were sent on a regular basis from Uckermark to the gas chamber. After being killed, their bodies were cremated, and their ashes were dumped in the lake. The number of prisoners gassed at Ravensbrück is not known but is estimated to have been in the range of four thousand five hundred to six thousand.

Although few women prisoners knew with certainty that a gas chamber had been placed in operation, many suspected it. What they saw and heard in the ensuing weeks confirmed their suspicions. For example, soon after their friends were selected, items of clothing that they recognized were brought back into the main camp. This was also the time that a new administrator, a man by the name of Dr. Winkelmann, appeared upon the scene. One might say that he served as the Dr. Mengele of Ravensbrück, conducting daily selections of women to be killed. Most of the women selected were taken to Uckermark, although some were taken directly to the gas chamber.

By early February, the situation in the camp was spiraling completely out of control. Food rations, which had already been reduced, began arriving late, and the women found themselves plagued by hunger more extreme than that which they had known. Periodically, because of enemy bombing raids in the region, the Germans cut off electrical power to the camp, plunging it into darkness. One morning, they were awakened to find that the entire sewage system in the camp had stopped working. The cellar used to hold corpses was no longer large enough to hold all of the dead; piles of dead bodies were stacked outdoors, blanketed by snow. The two ovens in the crematorium burned twenty-four hours a day—the prisoners saw the flames leaping from the tall chimneys and smelled the burning flesh—but they were unable to keep pace.

In the second week of February, Nelly fell ill. She remained in the barracks as long as she could, for she knew that, if she went to the *Revier*, she ran the risk of being selected and sent to Uckermark. Michou, Mila, and Hélène attended to her diligently. They managed to steal a few potatoes for her from the kitchen, but she was unable to eat. This distressed the three of them. They spoke to her of things that they hoped would fortify her and buoy her spirits. On February 10, she was too weak to stand at roll call, but Mila and Michou supported her. On the eleventh, she was not able to get out of bed in the morning. She had resigned herself to going to the *Revier*, but a woman whom she refers to as "our doctor" dissuaded her. Her next journal entry, dated February 16, was written after she had been taken to the *Revier*. She explains that their *Blockowa*, Maya, had decided that she could no longer remain in the barracks. Before leaving, Nelly had the opportunity to speak with Michou of her last wishes. "My affairs in order, I feel perfectly calm. The future no longer frightens me." She did, however, have one regret: she had not had a chance to say goodbye to Mila and Hélène because they were with their work crew at the time she was taken to the infirmary.

Gravely ill with typhus, Nelly was tempted to succumb to death. Yet, she felt that she could not yield to this temptation because her failure to return home would be too painful for her loved ones. On February 22, she learned, in a letter from Hélène, that Michou had been sent away on a work transport. Hélène and Mila knew how difficult the separation would be for Nelly, and it is clear that they felt obligated to break this sad news to her themselves.

With the help and care of one of the nurses, Nelly miraculously survived her bout of typhus and was discharged from the *Revier* on Thursday, March 1. She was sent to Block 23 rather than to 27, the block from which she had come. She knew no one in the block—none of her French compatriots were there—and she was unable to communicate with anyone because no one spoke French. She found herself utterly alone, weak, and overcome by anguish and despair.

~

When I study the photographs I took in July 2001 of the Mahn- und Gedenkstätte Ravensbrück, I notice that not one of them contains a living soul. I did not manage to capture a single person in any of the ten panoramic views or thirty normal size snapshots taken. Did I make a conscious effort to exclude people? I don't remember doing so. July is the height of the tourist season in the Mecklenberg Lake District, but Ravensbrück is not on the list of must-see sights. There couldn't have been more than a couple dozen visitors to the memorial on either of the two days that I spent there. Recalling my visit summons up a sense of emptiness or, perhaps more precisely, hollowness.

Few Westerners had the chance to visit Ravensbrück prior to the mid-1990s because of its location in East Germany. Immediately after the war ended, the Soviet Army established a military post that occupied most of the concentration camp site. More specifically, it occupied all of the area contained within the perimeter wall, including the area comprising the camp square (roll call area), Lager Street I, blocks, and industry yard (SS workshops). For clarity's sake, I refer to this area as the inner section of the former camp. A small portion of the former camp, located outside of the perimeter wall, was not occupied by the army. This outer section includes the area occupied by the former SS headquarters, camp prison, gas chamber, crematorium, waterworks/garages, and SS garage wing. The outer section was not generally accessible to Ravensbrück prisoners.

The Soviet military post remained in operation for nearly fifty years. It was finally dismantled in 1994. The large segment of the former concentration camp site that the army had occupied was turned over to the Stiftung Brandenbrugische Gedenkstätten (Brandenburg Memorials Foundation). Most of the inner section of the camp had already been cleared. In particular, all the blocks in which the prisoners had lived—the vermin-infested, wooden dormitories in which the women had slept, eaten, and, in many cases, died—had been demolished.

The visitor today approaches the memorial along the same road that the prisoners themselves used when entering and leaving the camp. The villas that line the road, which housed the SS officers and guards and their families, have been restored; they now serve to provide accommodations and conference center space for groups visiting the camp. When Ravensbrück was operating, the gardening work crew would tend to the gardens surrounding the villas. From time to time, Dufournier would catch a glimpse.

> From these little houses, a bit separated one from the other, a flash of civilized life sometimes appeared: it was a child being walked by an impeccably dressed nanny or even a civilian dressed for sports, a tennis racquet in hand. From time to time, we stole a glance towards these frightful rooms, bare and impersonal, but where, one could imagine, human beings lived lives similar to those we had known, in a world defined neither by sirens, nor roll calls, nor work.

Right outside the main entrance—the opening in the stone wall through which one passes from the outer section to the inner section—is a building that housed the waterworks and some of the SS garages. After passing through the camp entrance, you find yourself looking out across a vast field covered in gray gravel. It is almost completely empty; mature trees rise up out of the gravel in one particular area. Also, the gravel is not uniform; it is raised in places to define broad rectangular areas. I learned that the trees have been planted along what was Lager Street I, the street that ran between the two rows of the original blocks. The rectangles formed by the raised gravel mark the footprints of those blocks. At the edges of the gray field are scattered one-story buildings, some of which were part of the camp and some of which were built by the army after 1945.

In contrast, most of the structures comprising the outer section of the camp have been preserved and maintained. The Ravensbrück National Memorial Museum, inaugurated in 1959, incorporated the crematorium, Bunker (camp prison), site of the former gas chamber, and a section of the thirteen-foot high wall. The Bunker has been used to house commemorative exhibits prepared by representatives of the various nations whose citizens were imprisoned here. In the 1990s, commemorative exhibits pertaining to Jewish prisoners and to Sinti and Roma prisoners were added. In 1984, the former SS headquarters was incorporated as part of the memorial. It now houses administrative offices, a library/archive, and exhibits. The SS headquarters is a pleasant-looking building, partly shaded under a canopy of trees and flanked by a curving cobblestone drive. If you were shown a photograph of this building out of context, you would guess that it was a classroom building on a college campus. The library/archive contains survivor memoirs, oral histories, and other forms of eyewitness accounts. However, it does not contain any of the original camp records, as those were destroyed shortly before the camp was liberated.

Just a short walk from the former SS headquarters, a bronze sculpture stands atop a granite pedestal that rises approximately twenty feet in the air at the edge of the lake, the Schwedtsee. The sculpture depicts a tall, gaunt woman carrying the body of another in her arms. She holds her head erect, casting her gaze forever outward, across the surface of the lake. The name of the work, one of several at Ravensbrück by German sculptor Will Lammert, is "Tragende" ("Woman Carrying"). This is a sacred spot—the brackish water of the lake holds the ashes of thousands of women whose bodies were cremated in the nearby ovens. I tried to peer beneath the surface of the water—as if something of the nature of heaven might be revealed—but the surface was a mirror, and all I could see were trees, clouds, and my own reflection.

~

In the lexicon of the Third Reich, "NN" signified a special iniquity. The letters stood for *Nacht und Nebel,* Night and Fog (or, in French, *Nuit et Brouillard*). The term originated in a decree issued by Hitler on December 7, 1941. The *Nacht und Nebel Erlass* (Night and Fog Decree) and accompanying directives stipulated that, within the occupied territories, the only adequate punishment for offenses committed that endangered German security or its state of readiness was the death penalty. It further stipulated that offenders not immediately executed were to be taken to Germany and that no information whatsoever was to be provided to anyone about such individuals. In other words, the NN prisoner was to disappear, without a trace, into the night and fog. Hitler issued the decree because he believed that disappearance and uncertainty regarding the fate of a resister would act as a deterrent to future resistance, whereas death and martyrdom would have the opposite effect.

Many of the French prisoners in Ravensbrück were classified as *Nacht und Nebel*. Beginning in February 1944, NN prisoners were confined to Block 32. They were not allowed to receive packages, nor were they allowed to send or receive letters. They were also prohibited from working in any commandos that would take them outside of the camp. Germaine Tillion was an NN prisoner. She writes:

> Our block was one of those which never saw the delivery of outside packages; thus one which experienced more hunger than most of the others. But it was the only block where a crust of bread could be left around without disappearing instantly; and it was relatively clean—and free of lice. Resistance to the Germans was always a common goal, and a woman trying to hide for one reason or another could always find accomplices. It was the only block where the *troc*—the camp's infamous black market—had been banished and replaced by a system of fraternal sharing; the only one with a regular system of helping the sick with small portions of extra food—hungry women would give up a potato or a spoon of ersatz jam they received once a week to help a tubercular live a little longer.

On Thursday, March 1, the SS surrounded Block 32, and the NN prisoners were informed that they were going to be sent away on a transport the next day. According to Marie-Jo Chombart de Lauwe, they did not know what sort of transport this was or where they were going. (She does note that, on Friday, rumors circulated that this was a "bad transport.") Some NN prisoners managed to evade the transport by hiding. Some French prisoners who were not NN but who had friends in the NN group voluntarily joined the transport. The group was taken to the *Strafblock*, the punishment cellblock, where they were held overnight.

As they prepared to leave the next morning, a few more prisoners were brought to the Strafblock.

> In the morning, the N. N. who were at work the day before join us. Some others have slipped in among them: Marianne Racine, Miarka, the group of young people who had formed the choral group in which I often participated. They want to accompany their friends; they hide.

Mila, Hélène, and Miarka were among the 1,980 women loaded into cattle cars on Friday, March 2, 1945. In addition to French prisoners (the NN prisoners and those who had slipped in among them), the transport included Belgian prisoners also designated NN as well as Gypsy women and children.

On the day the transport departed, Nelly learned that Mila and Hélène had slipped in among the NN prisoners. Mila and Hélène did not know that Nelly had been discharged from the *Revier*. They never had the chance to say goodbye.

~

Having struggled to survive despite dysentery and other serious medical conditions, Joseph Lançon succumbed to death at Hersbruck subcamp on March 5, 1945. He was fifty years old.

10. *The Final Crossing*

Twenty-five years after the end of the war, Miarka wrote of the strong friendships that had prompted her along with Mila and Hélène to join the departing transport:

> We had left Ravensbrück on the second of March 1945 in a mixed convoy, and we did not know for what destination, but we were together, determined to remain together come what may. Seven who had promised one another to return home together, and, in this "family," we went a bit by pairs: Mariane and Hélène, Mag, Violette and Micheline, Frédérique and me. Cautious about the present, we were making plans for the future. The "afterward" was supposed to keep us together.

How well did the seven members of the "family" know of one another's backgrounds and/or the resistance activities in which they had engaged? It is impossible for me to answer this question. It was dangerous for prisoners to speak to one another about such things; the possibility that one might be subjected to torture and consequently disclose information about one's compatriots was ever-present.

Mag, Violette, and Micheline were NN prisoners, destined to disappear into the night and fog. Mag was none other than Mag Pellet, Mila's cellmate in Montluc prison whose Institut des sourds-muets-aveugles et déficients in Villeurbanne had served as the center of the *réseau* Marco Polo. Violette was the twenty-five-year-old Violette Maurice, who had been a member of the Mithridate resistance group in Lyon and was arrested in October 1943. The third NN prisoner in the group was Micheline Gravillon. Thirty-nine years old, Gravillon, whose first name was actually Eugénie, was from Amplepuis, a town in the department of the Rhône. Did she belong to a resistance group? Did she help a family member or friend who was engaged in resistance? I cannot say.

Of the group of seven, Hélène and Miarka (Denise Vernay, née Jacob) were the youngest, both having been born in 1924. Hélène and Mila were deeply devoted to one another. So too were Miarka and Mila. Miarka had been part of the Resistance, working first as a member of Franc-Tireur in Lyon and subsequently as a MUR agent in the Haute-Savoie. (Franc-Tireur merged with two other resistance movements, Combat and Libération, to form MUR, Mouvements unis de la Résistance or United Movements of the Resistance.) In June 1944, Miarka was seized by the Gestapo as she was tranferring materiel, dropped by parachute, from a location in the department of the Saône-et-Loire to Aix-les-Bains. Imprisoned in Montluc and subjected to the infamous *bagnoire*, she was sent to Ravensbrück in July. Like Mila, Miarka hid from her captors the fact that she was Jewish. All of the members of her family had been arrested in Nice at the end of March 1944. Among the very few bits of information I have about the woman known as Frédérique are these: she was an American, born in New York in 1902; her actual name was Raymonde Thibouville; and her maiden name was Dreyfus. Presumably, she too was Jewish.

~

Soon after leaving Fürstenberg/Havel, the train carrying the 1,980 Ravensbrück prisoners made its way through Berlin, and the women witnessed the fact that Allied bombs had inflicted heavy damage on the city. Outside the city, in the countryside, they were able to catch a glimpse of a place name now and then. Locating place names on a map—given to them by a friend who stayed behind—they determined that they were heading south. At some point, they became aware of the fact that they had left Germany and were traveling through Czechoslovakia. The mountainous landscape through which they traveled was silent, covered by a deep layer of snow.

For five days, they traveled toward an unknown destination. Weak and emaciated, they struggled against starvation and freezing cold. The prisoners were packed so tightly—eighty to a car—that they could not all sit down. They had no straw, no blankets, and, of course, no heat. They had been given a little black bread and margarine before leaving Ravensbrück. Once the train had departed, they received no more food and were provided with water only once.

Writing soon after the end of the war, Violette Maurice recalled those five days in which they found themselves "doomed to total darkness and rectilinear movement."

> Forever rolling along, we get to the point of no longer knowing in which direction we are going. Is it to the right? Is it to the left? Are we falling down a vertical chute? It matters little. For a moment, the jerking and pawing of the machine tells us that we are going through a town; then the long beast calms down and recovers its regular gait. From time to time we doze off for a few minutes; then we are awakened by a whistle or a curse or even the animal groan of an old woman who is dying next to us . . . [ellipsis points in original] Finally, a stop! We ask for water for the dying woman, who never stops saying, in the persistent tone of a litany, "I'm thirsty!" "Let her croak," says the man, and the train sets off again . . . [ellipsis points in original]

On March 7, they arrived at the town of Mauthausen, Austria, twenty kilometers (twelve miles) east of Linz. As they left the cattle cars and assembled in the cold night air, snow was falling. They learned that some of the Gypsy children had died along the way and that one woman had given birth. It was seven kilometers to their destination. A vehicle was waiting to take those who felt they would not be able to walk the distance. Few stepped forward, certain of the consequences. They walked through the little town that bordered the railway, picturesque in the moonlight. Then they began an uphill climb.

> All at once a gunshot. Then again this oppressive silence. The endless uphill climb. A hundred meters further, along the edge of the road, we pass a body sprawled out, dark against the snow: they finished off a comrade. We press against one another more closely, arms linked at times, but the legs tremble with weakness, the heart beats wildly, the breathing is short. A woman falls to her knees; quickly, quickly, we lift her up and drag her along.

All along the route, women continued to fall and were shot by the SS, their bodies left by the side of the road.

Finally, after following a turn in the road, the prisoners reached the camp, a massive stone structure set on the top of a hill, fully illuminated at night. They passed through the main gate into an enclosed courtyard, went up a flight of steps, and entered the camp proper. They were forced to line up and wait there, at attention, all through the night, "unreal silhouettes under the moon." Finally, they were taken to an underground shower room, where they were forced to undress in front of joking male guards and subjected to humiliating physical examinations. Leaving the showers, having relinquished all of their clothes and belongings, with only canvas shirts to wear, the women were led to the Gypsy blocks at the rear of the camp, surrounded by a stone wall. The seven friends who had promised themselves that they would return home together were assigned to Block 17. The women from Ravensbrück remained in their blocks, in quarantine, for nearly two weeks.

~

It is impossible to describe the appearance of Mauthausen as anything other than a fortress. Approaching the camp, one sees only massive stone walls, tall and long, without openings of any sort. The walls are built of grayish granite mined at the Wienergraben quarry that is part of the camp. The quarry was here long before the camp. Owned by the city of Vienna, its granite was used to pave that city's streets. In 1938, the concentration camp was built next to the quarry—Hitler planned to use the stone to rebuild his hometown of Linz.

The quarry was the centerpiece of a large and brutal enterprise that included not only the main camp but also fifty permanent subcamps, most notably Gusen, Melk, and Ebensee. A crudely fashioned stairway, appropriately named the Stairway of Death, leads from the top of the quarry to the floor below. It consists of 186 steps, uneven and of varying widths and heights. Clad in wooden clogs, the prisoners were forced to haul large blocks of granite, positioned on their backs, up the treacherous stairs.

~

In my mind's eye, I had pictured the archives of the Mauthausen concentration camp housed in a somber room with a long counter—dark wood, smooth and polished, gleaming. I pictured visitors standing at the long counter, speaking in subdued tones to . . . to whom? A middle-aged woman, perhaps. One of the archivists—who knew if they were men or women, as they signed their letters with a first initial and last name—who had answered my inquiries precisely, in detail, and in perfect English.

When I visited Vienna in 2002, the camp archives were housed at number 5 Braunerstrasse, a five-story, gray stone building that looked as if it could house the somber room with the polished counter that I had imagined. The brass plaque on the front of the building read Bundesministerium Für Inneres, Federal Ministry of the Interior. Instead of a front door, I found a passageway and, on the right, a window set at eye level. A large, round face rose, moonlike, in the window and peered down at me. I opened the door next to the window and entered a small room painted mint green. The man with the large round face spoke to me very quickly in German. I do not speak German. "*Sprechen Sie Englisch?*" I ventured. He shook his head. "*Nein.*" He looked away. It seemed as if the conversation was over. "Mauthausen archive," I ventured, and then added, "*bitte,*" meaning "please." He didn't look back at me. He seemed to pretend that I was no longer there. I stood and waited. After a while, he picked up the telephone receiver and called someone somewhere.

Its proper name is Archiv der KZ-Gedenkstätte Mauthausen. The somber room with the smooth and polished counter did not exist. In terms of size and contents, the third floor room in which I found myself was very much like a college dorm room. No beds, of course, but the usual sorts of items that one would expect: two desks and two computers, a dorm-size refrigerator, an electric fan, a clock radio, a CD player, a hot plate, a bottle of Tabasco sauce, an automatic coffee maker with brown paper towels hanging over the edge of the filter basket. The wastebasket beneath one of the desks overflowed with pizza boxes.

At first, I didn't realize that the young man sitting across from me was one of the individuals with whom I had corresponded. His face was framed with heavy dark hair and heavy dark glasses, and his eyes were large and dark. His skin was smooth and boyish-looking, with just a few dark hairs on the upper lip. When he introduced himself, I had difficulty catching his name. It was only when I glanced down at the stack of papers in front of me that I realized that it was he who had responded to my recent email.

I took an immediate liking to this young man, whose name is Ralf. He was earnest and intense, gentle and soft-spoken. As we conversed, the smoke from his cigarette wound slowly around his fingers. It seemed to me that he must be in his late twenties.

Although the archive lacked the somber room with the polished counter, it did not disappoint. Ralf and his young colleagues have developed an extraordinarily detailed, computerized database pertaining to Mauthausen prisoners. A good collection of archival documents has also survived. One of the surviving documents is a two-page list of numbers entitled *"Arbeitskommando Bahnbau II (Amstetten),"* meaning "Work commando—Track construction (Amstetten)." The numbers are those of five hundred women prisoners who were informed on the afternoon of March 19, 1945, that, early the next morning, they would be taken by train to the nearby town of Amstetten. Mila's number (2414) and the numbers belonging to Hélène, Miarka, Violette, Mag, Micheline, and Frédérique appear on the list.

~

March 20, 1945. A Tuesday. At four in the morning, five hundred female prisoners were called to the esplanade to line up in rows of five and count off in groups of one hundred. Mila, Hélène, Mag, Micheline, and Frédérique were the last five in a group of one hundred, cut off from Violette and Miarka. They tried desperately to arrange for a swap, to exchange two in the one group for two in another or a line of five in one group for a line of five in the other. None of the other prisoners were willing to swap, fearing it would be bad luck to try and change the hand that they had been dealt.

Packed one hundred to a car, in the dark and cold, they made the short trip to Amstetten. They disembarked and were given shovels and pickaxes. Then they were herded away from the train station, into the marshalling yards, where the railroad tracks had been heavily damaged by Allied bombing raids. Male prisoners, overseen by guards, were already at work clearing the rubble, filling in craters, and repairing the damaged rail lines so that trains could get through. Weak and emaciated, the women took up the heavy tools and set themselves to the task.

The sun rose in the sky. The air began to warm. Some of the prisoners felt hopeful. "The weather was fine, it was the twentieth of March 1945, we were awaiting the rout of the Germans . . . ," Miarka wrote many years later.

An eyewitness report written by a male prisoner echoes the same sentiment.

> It was about 9 o'clock. Then we heard the call: "Attention! Attention!" Shortly thereafter we noticed a slight trembling of the tracks; then we saw the locomotive and, behind it, 10 to 15 passenger cars. The train was moving very slowly. The cars were filled with civilians; people were also on the roof and on the steps of each car. These were, in fact, cars of an older type that had steps on the outside. Our guard repeated the order: "Attention! Attention! The train is coming. Step back from the tracks." As soon as we had stepped back from the tracks, the locomotive was already passing by.
>
> On the steps of one of the cars, desperately clinging to the handles, young men were standing. One of the Poles asked, "Where is this train going?" The strangers answered in flawless Polish: "Compatriots! Chin up! Another three or four more weeks and the war is over!"

The women worked throughout the morning. Miarka and Violette were still worried about their separation from Mila, Hélène, Mag, Micheline, and Frédérique. Around midday, the air raid siren sounded. "The alert is received by the women with joy," Miarka later wrote. Many of the male prisoners hurried toward a stand of trees off in the distance, the only place away from the tracks that appeared to offer cover. The women followed them, but, according to Miarka, this was done "more for the pleasure of the woods and the flowers than for fear." The woods were near the top of a rise; it must have taken some effort to reach them. Once their eyes had adjusted to the deep shade of the forest, they noticed tiny bursts of white and yellow, the first flowers of spring. They picked dandelions and ate them, trying to assuage their hunger pangs. Somewhere nearby, there was singing. Miarka remembered, "We heard them sing, led by Mariane, whose voice was so beautiful, so clear."

~

Until recently, I never thought much about the fact that the laws of relativity govern our concept of home just as they govern our concept of time. Returning from a trip abroad, I feel that I am home when the plane touches down on American soil. I may have landed in New York and have another half a day's travel ahead of me, and yet I am relieved because *I am home.* When I am in New York for business or pleasure, not having flown in from overseas, I do not feel that I am home. Indeed, it does not seem that I am truly home until the Amtrak train has pulled into Baltimore's Penn Station. But my home is thirty minutes outside of Baltimore. When I visit Baltimore for some reason or another, I do not consider myself home. You get the idea.

For a time, the Apulia region of Italy, along the boot-shaped peninsula's heel, was home to the airmen of the American Fifteenth Air Force. They lived in canvas tents erected on makeshift airfields in places whose names sound romantic today—Lucera, Celone, Spinazzola, Pantanella, and Grottaglie. It was not a romantic life. It was difficult and dangerous. The men of the Fifteenth were responsible for strikes on many oil refineries and aircraft manufacturing plants supplying the Third Reich.

Very early on the morning of March 20, 1945, airmen of the Fifteenth rose and began preparations for a bombing mission. They ate what they called their last meal—a hearty breakfast, probably bacon and eggs. Many received last rites. They assembled and were briefed on their targets. The airmen comprised five wings: the 55th, 49th, 47th, and 304th Wings had four bomb groups each; the 5th Wing had six bomb groups. Each bomb group had four squadrons. Each squadron had ten planes. Most of the planes were heavy bombers—B-17 Flying Fortresses and B-24 Liberators. Each bomber carried a crew of ten. At 8 a.m., the first of approximately 840 aircraft began taking off. A short time later, eight thousand men were airborne, heading north.

The primary targets to which they had been assigned lay in Hungary and Austria. The primary targets of the 5th Wing were oil refineries located on the outskirts of Vienna—Kagran, northeast of the city; Korneuburg, to the northwest; and Vosendorf, to the south. The 47th Wing was assigned the Saint Valentin tank works, between Amstetten and Linz; and the 304th Wing, the Kralupy oil refinery in Germany. The 49th Wing was directed to the marshalling yards in Gyor, Hungary, between Bratslavia and Budapest. I have not been able to determine the primary target assigned to the 55th Wing.

Each wing was assigned alternate targets in case it was impossible, because of cloud cover or other circumstances, to strike the primary target. The Amstetten marshalling yards is listed among other alternates. In reading the 370-page mission report preserved on microfilm—370 pages of narrative explanation, charts, diagrams, photographs and maps—I was not able to determine with any degree of certainty if or how the alternates were ranked in terms of priority.

It was 1 p.m. when the prisoners working in the marshalling yards in Amstetten heard the air raid siren go off. They could see planes in the distance, an aerial formation visible but barely decipherable, like a line of fine print held at arm's length.

The 464th and 465th Bomb Groups of the 55th Wing arrived at Amstetten first, followed several minutes later by the 460th and the 485th. The mission summary prepared for the 55th Wing states that weather conditions had prevented them from bombing their primary target. This was why they dropped their bombs on Amstetten, an alternate target. The squadrons of the 55th Wing came in one after another, like waves breaking on the shore. By 1:30 p.m., all of the squadrons had finished their bombing runs, and they headed home.

Part of the 5th Wing came in on the heels of the 55th. Four of the six bomb groups had found their primary targets obscured by poor weather conditions, and they attacked Amstetten, referred to later in their mission summary as the number one alternate. They bombed Amstetten for forty-five minutes, from 1:35 to 2:20 p.m.

By two-thirty in the afternoon, three hundred heavy bombers had dropped their payload of nearly seven hundred tons on Amstetten. The marshalling yards, train station, and nearby industrial area were heavily damaged. Parts of the town, including the Herz Jesu-Kirche (Heart Jesus Church), had also been hit. Thick black smoke hung over much of the area. Most of the townspeople survived the attack by taking refuge in a large bomb shelter beneath the New Cemetery.

It was around this time that twelve of the sixteen squadrons comprising the 47th Wing approached Amstetten, having been unable to bomb their primary targets because of cloud cover. They could see nothing of the marshalling yards because of the smoke. Two excerpts from the mission report convey the difficulty the American flyers encountered.

> All four squadrons of the 450th [Bomb Group] attacked AMSTETTEN M/Y [marshalling yard]. The Yard was completely covered by smoke from previous bombs and none of the Yard was visible, so all bombardiers were considerably handicapped in synchronization.
>
> All the units of the 98th [Bomb Group] attacked the AMSTETTEN M/Y. This group was also considerably handicapped by smoke from previous bombs. After being squared away at the target by the PFF operator, Bombardier BEARD of the 343rd [squadron] took over and turned in a fine job, leading his squadron in to score SUPERIOR results on the assigned aiming point. The second Squadron, the 344th, could not pick up the target so they made a 360 and came in again. This time smoke again covered the aiming point and the lead bombardier intended to go around again but the deputy dropped and all the other ships in the squadron toggled—with bombs going into the smoke. The 345th [squadron] (after making a 360) and the 415 [squadron] were unable to pick up the aiming point so each synchronized on check points and then displaced into the smoke. Results in each case, however, were unsatisfactory.

Throughout the bombardment, Miarka and Violette Maurice experienced feelings of joy rather than of terror. Miarka writes:

> The first bombs did not impinge upon our good humor. They were coming from our friends, helping to liberate all. We try to calm the terror of a few Ukrainians traumatized by recent ordeals of bombardments, and we lay down next to them under the trees, still gray, all along the ground, still cold. Five waves of planes released their loads very near, on the town, on the railroad station, on the same track where we were a few minutes earlier. With the last wave, the bombs burst closer still . . . . [ellipsis points in original]

> At one o'clock, all was finished. We met up with all the women and wait for the news. Two o'clock, three o'clock, we are still waiting for some news and the soup that would have been buried beneath the bombs. For more than twelve hours, we have been up with nothing to eat. Rumors circulate: there would be some victims among the women, some wounded, some dead. The last wave of planes would have released its bombs onto the part of the woods where we happened to be, the shininess of the guns of our guards having made them believe, because they flew very low, that some troops had found shelter in the woods.

Violette Maurice's description of the bombing is much more graphic than that of Miarka. She speaks of the planes dive-bombing over their heads, bombs whistling, tanks exploding on the track, the ground beneath them vibrating. "To tell the truth, we have almost no fear . . ." She later concludes: "The bombardment lasted four hours. The earth is toasted because of it; the smoke suffocates us."

It is difficult for one in the midst of an aerial attack to judge the passage of time. Miarka thought it lasted for about one hour. Maurice stated that it went on for four hours. In actuality, it lasted approximately two hours. According to the mission report, the first plane reached the target at 12:59 p.m., and the last plane, at 3:07 p.m.

The stand of trees beneath which the prisoners took cover is located slightly northeast of the town of Amstetten, in a hamlet known as Preinsbach. On the target chart used by the Fifteenth Air Force, the trees appear, within a patchwork quilt of angular shapes, as a round smudge, slightly smaller than a thumbprint.

Around three p.m., a few bombs were dropped into the stand of trees. They may have been the payload of one plane. The plane may have belonged to the 98th Bomb Group of the 47th Wing, which dropped its bombs between 2:54 and 3:07. However, it is also possible that they belonged to the 97th Bomb Group of the 5th Wing. Although most of the bomb groups comprising the 5th Wing had finished their bombing runs by 2:20, it seems that the 97th Bomb Group had become separated from the rest of the wing. It dropped its payload at 2:53.

I will never know for certain why the bombs fell upon the stand of trees. It could have been purely accidental, a result of bombs dropped prematurely or in the wrong location because of poor visibility. Or it could have been intentional. Miarka believed that it was the shininess of the guards' guns that drew the attention and fire of the attackers. Another explanation later offered was that the women prisoners had placed the black pots they carried for soup on their heads in order to protect themselves during the bombing and that the pots were mistaken for soldiers' helmets. An historian who lives in Amstetten believes that the airmen were able to see that the people in and near the stand of trees were wearing striped uniforms and that they bombed them in full knowledge of the fact that they were prisoners. At eighteen thousand feet—the altitude at which the bombing was carried out—it seems unlikely that shiny guns, black soup pots, or striped uniforms would have been visible to the bomber crews. If the bombing was intentional, the real explanation may simply be this: the marshalling yards were completely ablaze, there was movement of some kind along the edges of the trees, and, in an effort to subdue the enemy and bring the war to an end, anything that moved was targeted.

Thirty-six female prisoners from Mauthausen were killed. Mila, Hélène, Mag, Micheline, and Frédérique were among them. The youngest of the dead was seventeen; the oldest, fifty-three. According to information in the Mauthausen database, the number of dead by nationality was as follows: French, 13; Belgian, 10; Russian, 6; Hungarian, 2; German, 2; Dutch, 1; Polish, 1; and American, 1 (Frédérique).

All of the women who were killed in the Preinsbach woods on March 20, 1945, are listed in Mauthausen records as "*vermisst*" (missing). Many of the bodies were blown apart, their limbs and other body parts left hanging in the trees. Local residents gathered the remains and loaded them into several carts. In response to my inquiry, the eighty-year-old Frau Augustine remembered that the carts were taken to the *Totenkammer*, the morgue, at the Old Cemetery. Were they buried there? This seems unlikely. Cemetery records maintained in the mayor's office do not have any record of such a burial in either the Old Cemetery or the New Cemetery. Were they buried in an unmarked mass grave?

~

Thirteen days after Mila was killed in the Allied aerial bombardment, Father Jean Rosay died in Bergen-Belsen. His had been a long and terrible journey. On January 18, 1945, he and thousands of others from Auschwitz-Birkenau were forced to embark on a two-day death march. They were then loaded onto rail cars normally used to carry coal and completely open to the elements. The train reached its destination, the Gross-Rosen concentration camp, four days later. By then, many of the prisoners were dead, having succumbed to the cold and starved to death.

Miraculously, Father Rosay survived the terrifying conditions at Gross-Rosen for nearly three weeks. On February 20, he was evacuated to Nordhausen; then, a short time later, to Bergen-Belsen. Each evacuation entailed the same trials: the men covered part of the distance by forced death march and part in rail cars open to the freezing cold, without food or water. A few days after his arrival in Bergen-Belsen, the priest knew that the end was near. He told a comrade, a Doctor Sephar, that he had only one final wish: to survive until Easter. Then he entered the infirmary. Those who have addressed the question most carefully believe that Jean Rosay finally succumbed to death on April 2, 1945, one day after Easter.

Postscript: The Angel of History

The stand of trees beneath which the women prisoners took cover in the little hamlet known as Preinsbach is still there today, although it is impossible for me to say whether it is smaller or larger than it was in 1945. It follows the rise of a hill that begins near Preinsbacherstrasse on the south and extends a little beyond Eichenhangstrasse on the north. I do not know how many acres it covers. Being an American, however, I tend to fall back on the football field as a convenient unit of measurement, and I would say that the stand of trees is the size of one football field, more or less.

Eichenhangstrasse is not so much a road as a country lane, unpaved, with short tufts of grass sticking up in the middle. When you stand on Eichenhangstrasse, you can look north across the broad green meadow that leads to the crest of the hill. Or you can look south into the woods. The sunlight drenches the foliage along the woods' edge, and so it is difficult to see into the dim interior. Peering into the shadows will not help very much, as the pupil, still registering sunlight, refuses to open very wide. The trees, both deciduous and evergreen, several stories in height, form a thick canopy. I do not know if there are footpaths; I never found any. Stickers from the tangled undergrowth catch on your socks and the legs of your pants. No sound is audible except the sound of your own shoes on dried leaves. You will come to the edge of a deep, wide crater, partially filled with dirt and old branches. It looks like the ground simply gave way.

Standing at the northeast edge of the woods, near Schabfeldstrasse, you can look down over the roofs of the houses in Preinsbach, across flat fields that are planted or not planted, green or ochre, to the railroad line, the Westbahn, that runs straight as an arrow, east to west, as far as the eye can see. The distance from the woods in Preinsbach to the Westbahn is not very far—eight-tenths of a kilometer or half a mile.

Trains come through often, as the Westbahn is the lifeline of the region. When a train approaches Preinsbach from the east, you will hear the whistle blow because the town of Amstetten is just up ahead. The sound is nothing like the high-pitched, piercing blast of German trains captured in World War II movies. It is low and harmonic, smooth and soothing. Once, when I visited Amstetten, I stayed in an apartment on Mozartstrasse, just around the corner from the train station. When I lay down to go to sleep at night, I listened to the trains go by. It seemed that they came by at regular intervals and that they sped through the town without stopping or even slowing down. They must have been freight trains on their way to or from the big cities—Vienna, Linz, Salzburg. Each sent forth its long, low whistle into the night, and each whistle was a like a wave that washed over me, engulfed me, carried me along for a moment, and then left me behind.

~

Two weeks before Mauthausen was liberated by American soldiers on May 5, 1945, a delegation of the International Committee of the Red Cross took most of the French, Belgian, and Dutch women prisoners out of the camp. They left in a convoy of trucks on April 22 and traveled across Austria for three days. When they reached the Swiss border, German soldiers barred them from leaving the country. They remained on the Austrian side of the border throughout the night, while the heads of the delegation sought the needed authorization. The next morning, they were allowed to cross. They stayed in Switzerland for a few days, undergoing disinfection and medical examination.

On May 2, the French women returning from Mauthausen set foot on French soil once again. Despite the poor state of their health, Miarka (Denise Jacob) and Violette Maurice felt that they had the duty to go immediately to the family of each of the dear friends that they had lost at Amstetten in order to personally deliver the sad news and return personal effects. Miarka set out to visit the Mion, Thibouville, and Racine families. In Lyon, she sought out the apartment of Hélène's family. Madame Mion was not at home, and so Miarka waited in the stairwell for her to return. When the mother learned of her daughter's death, she tried to throw herself out of the window, and Miarka had to enlist the help of neighbors to restrain her. Frédérique Thibouville was divorced from her husband and had two children, a teenage boy and girl. Miarka sought out and spoke with the children. Finally, she met with Mola Racine. Hirsch had died of cancer just a short time earlier, and Berthe was overcome with grief upon learning of Mila's death. According to Sacha, her mother wanted to kill herself. She threw herself against the walls, and the children were forced to restrain her. Finally, in order that she might go on living, she resolved to pretend that Mila had gone back to Russia. She steadfastly refused to speak to or meet with Miarka because it would force her to acknowledge what had really happened. Berthe never spoke of Mila again. Out of loyalty to Berthe, not wanting to inflict pain, family members did not speak of her either.

~

On or around March 7, 1945, a prisoner working in the administrative offices at Mauthausen took a blank index card, fed it vertically into the carriage of a typewriter, and tapped out, in abbreviated fashion, what the Nazis believed to be key bits of information about female prisoner number 2414. Her name was Marie Anne

Racine. She was a French political prisoner (the abbreviation *Franz. Sch.* stands for *französischer Schutzhäftling*) who had been transferred from Ravensbrück (*KL Rav* is the abbreviated form of *Konzentrationlager Ravensbrück*). She was born on September 14, 1923, in Boulogne-sur-Seine. She was a student, a Roman Catholic (*RKath* stands for *römisch Katholisch*), and unmarried (*ledig*).

A few weeks later, the index card was retrieved from the file. Someone drew a V, encircled by a thick line. To Americans, V stands for victory, but, to the camp administrators, it stood for *Vermisst*, which means missing. Someone scrolled the card into a typewriter whose worn ribbon was incapable of imprinting letters as dark as those of the original entries. Like anyone who has fed an index card through a manual typewriter, the Mauthausen typist must have known that typing in the bottom right-hand corner was risky business. The rollers can no longer grip the card properly. The pounding of the keys lifts it out of the carriage. This is what happened with the last entry made on the card of Marie Anne Racine. "*Vermisst beim Fliegerangriff am 20.3.45 (Amstetten*" means "missing in an aerial attack 20.3.45 (Amstetten." The closing parenthesis, meant to close the book on female prisoner number 2414, was jettisoned into the rolling night, a tiny black crescent, invisible to the naked eye.

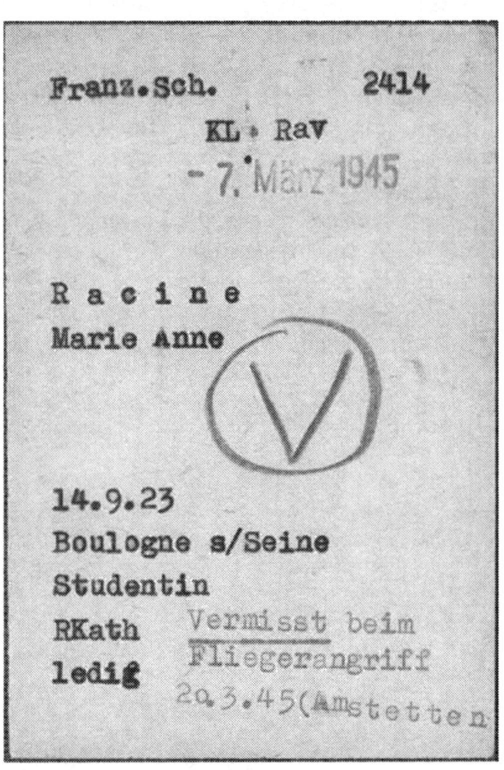

Franz.Sch. 2414
KL Rav
- 7. März 1945

R a c i n e
Marie Anne

V

14.9.23
Boulogne s/Seine
Studentin
RKath Vermisst beim
ledig Fliegerangriff
20.3.45(Amstetten

Exhibit 5: File card of Marie Anne Racine, Mauthausen Female Prisoner 2414. © Archiv der KZ-Gedenkstätte Mauthausen E5/13.]

Most of the index cards pertaining to the women prisoners in Mauthausen were destroyed. A handful have survived and are preserved in the Archiv der KZ-Gedenkstätte Mauthausen. I do not know whose hand pulled them from the wreckage. The index card that bears the name of Marie Anne Racine is reproduced on page 177 of the definitive work on women prisoners in Mauthausen, *Die vergessenen Frauen von Mauthausen* (*The Forgotten Women of Mauthausen*).

Marie Anne Racine was a victim of Nazi persecution. Her name or prisoner number appears on various records that the Nazis so meticulously maintained. But Mila Racine is a different story. The Nazis knew nothing of her. They knew nothing of the Jewish baby named Myriam, the six-year-old who came to Paris from Moscow, the twelve-year-old who acquired the Zionist dream from her father, the twenty-two-year-old who swore allegiance to the Jewish Army, the twenty-four-year-old who slipped past German patrols in Nice. In every sense of the word, she is the one who is *"vermisst."* The "V" belongs to her.

~

In 1965, Yad Vashem formally bestowed the title of Righteous Among the Nations upon Jean Deffaugt. In the ensuing decades, many other men and women whose names appear in this book have been similarly honored: Eugène Balthazar (2006), Madeleine Barot (1988), Father Pierre-Marie Benoît (1966), Rolande Birgy (1983), Brother Raymond Boccard (1987), Father Philibert Bublens (2000), Father Pierre Chaillet (1981), Father Louis Favre (1986), Father Camille Folliet (1991), Father Pierre Frontin (2011), Father Simon Gallay (1989), Father Marius Jolivet (1986), Joseph Lançon (1989), Thérèse Neury-Lançon (1989), Suzanne Loiseau-Chevalley (2007), François Périllat (1989), Father Gilbert Pernoud (1987), Mireille Philip (1976), Geneviève Priacel-Pittet (1993), Father Jean Rosay (1987), Monseigneur Jules-Géraud Saliège (1969), and Monseigneur Pierre-Marie Théas (1969).

The program of recognizing and honoring the Righteous Among the Nation was instituted fifty years ago, in 1963. The purpose of the program was to honor Gentiles who rescued Jews during the Holocaust. Consequently, Jewish rescuers have been excluded. Neither Yad Vashem nor any other remembrance authority or memorial has instituted a comparable program that focuses on Jewish rescuers.

Notes

"A Klee painting named 'Angelus Novus'": Walter Benjamin's "Theses on the Philiosphy of History" was written in 1940 and first published, in German, in 1950. The translation that appears here is from *Illuminations,* edited and with an introduction by Hannah Arendt, translated by Harry Zohn, 257–258. New York: Schocken Books, 1988.

1. Prelude

Page

2 "her empire, her fleet, and the illusion of her national sovereignty": Ousby, *Occupation,* 67.

2 The Occupied Zone encompassed the northern half of the country: At first, the French referred to the Unoccupied Zone as the *zone libre,* the Free Zone. In December 1940, the Germans prohibited the use of that term, requiring that it be called the *zone nonoccupée.*

2 the word *Israélite*: Ousby, *Occupation,* 180: "The popular idiom of the day distinguished between the two groups by calling native-born Jews *Israélites* and foreign-born Jews, naturalized or not, *Juifs*. The first term was polite; the second was not. The *Israélites* were 'assimilated.' . . . Until special attention was drawn to them, many *Israélites* could pass almost unnoticed by their neighbors or, when noticed, be regarded as not really Jewish. The *Juifs,* on the other hand, were 'unassimilated.' At least in the popular imagination, they were distinctive in their religion and their culture, perhaps even their language and their physical appearance." It is important to emphasize that many Jews themselves thought in these terms.

3 placed in the hands of provisional administrators: The provisional administrator was charged with determining whether the expropriated business was important to the national economy. If the business was judged to be important, it would be sold to an Aryan owner who would continue to operate it. If judged to be not important, it was liquidated and its assets auctioned off. Marrus and Paxton, *Vichy France and the Jews,* 152–160, provides an excellent discussion of the subject.

4 "sort of Wannsee Conference in miniature": Marrus and Paxton, *Vichy France and the Jews*, 228.

4 Eichmann, who, after a brief delay, answered: See Marrus and Paxton, *Vichy France and the Jews*, 263, for a discussion. The authors state that Laval made the request to Dannecker "just after Eichmann's visit on July 1." Dannecker forwarded the request to Berlin on July 6 and pressed repeatedly for a reply. "Finally, on 20 July, Eichmann telephoned his answer. Jewish children and old people could be deported as well as those capable of work." Note 180 on page 403 accompanies this statement. It is not clear from the body of the text or the note if it was Eichmann himself or someone else who approved the request. Also, the reader may take note of the fact that, even before the answer had been received (July 20), Paris police had already rounded up whole families, including children and old people, on July 16 and 17 (i.e. the Vel d'Hiv roundup). What had they intended to do with them if not deport them 'to the East'? The answer to that question is not clear.

5 UGIF officials were ordered by the Commissariat: Cohen, *The Burden of Conscience*, 74–80, provides a lengthy discussion of communications between UGIF and CGQJ officials during the first two weeks of July 1942. He concludes that, "During the preparations for the deportations, UGIF exhibited little foresight and ingenuity" and that they "acted passively."

7 it was pushed eastward in several places: Carpi, *Between Mussolini and Hitler*, 80.

7 Basses-Alpes: This is the former name of the department known today as the Alpes-de-Haute-Provence. The name was changed in 1970.

7 Nice in particular had attracted: Among the circumstances that had given rise to this situation was the collapse of the tourist industry. With thousands of hotel rooms, tourist houses, and villas left vacant, hotelkeepers were willing, if not eager, to rent rooms to Jews.

7 "While all over Europe Jews were subjected": Diamant, *"Jewish Refugees on the French Riviera,"* 265.

8 one of the "faithful followers of the Vichy regime": Carpi, *Between Mussolini and Hitler*, 276 – 277, note 19.

8 In the early months of 1943: Carpi, *Between Mussolini and Hitler*, provides a fascinating, detailed account of the communication and miscommunication among the Germans, French, and Italians.

9 "spread like wildfire": Poznanski, *Jews in France*, 387.

9 in the neighborhood of 25,000 to 30,000: Carpi, *Between Mussolini and Hitler*, 294, note 13. This is Carpi's estimate, which is based on the fact that, when Inspector General Lospinoso assumed his post in March 1943, "he was informed by sources at the Armistice Commission in Nice that the number of Jews in the city and its surroundings at that time had been estimated at approximately 22,000 souls" (pages 142 and 294, note 12). Reflecting the realities of conditions under which Jews lived in France during the war, no definitive data on the number of Jews living in the Italian Occupation Zone exist. Nor are there data on how many Jews moved into the zone from other parts of France or beyond the country's borders. In a document dated July 21, 1943, and whose subject line reads "Present State of the Jewish Question in France," SS-Obersturmführer Heinz Röethke, chief of the Judenreferat in France, reviewed the "numerical situation." He cited a figure of fifty thousand Jews in the Italian Occupation Zone, although no indication of its source was provided. Poliakov and Sabille, *Jews Under the Italian Occupation*, 104.

9 "new Land of Canaan": Poznanski, *Jews in France*, 387. The quotation is attributed to Albert Manuel, then secretary-general of the Central Consistory, the representative body of French Jewry in terms of religious affairs. (Its formal name is the Consistoire central des Israélites de France.)

9 "The Italian zone of influence, particularly the Côte d'Azur": Poliakov and Sabille, *Jews Under the Italian Occupation*, 106.

9 a Jewish refugee aid organization called the Comité Dubouchage: I have found no source that provides a full discussion of the Dubouchage Committee. Nor have I found documentation on the precise nature of the relationship between the Dubouchage Committee and the Federation. Fragmentary information is contained in various texts, such as: Carpi, *Between Mussolini and Hitler*; Lazare, *Rescue as Resistance*; Najman and Haymann, *Claude Kelman*; Rayski, *The Choice of the Jews Under Vichy*; and Rutkowski, *La lutte des juifs en France*.

10 On April 8, Jews gathered: Dupraz, *Bientôt, la liberté*, 85, states that Jewish refugees first arrived in the centers of assigned residence in the Haute-Savoie on this date. Grandjacques, *La montagne refuge*, 103-105, explains that the earliest groups were sent to and settled in Megève.

10 *le pain azyme*, unleavened bread: Rochlitz, *The Righteous Enemy: Document Collection*, 78. A document dated April 14, 1943, and signed by Ignace

Fink mentions that vendors were selling *le pain azyme*—unleavened bread (matzah)—to Jews gathered in front of the Synagogue Dubouchage. It notes that this is the location where "all the unfortunate Jews" come to obtain the subsidies they have been allocated while awaiting their departure for a place of forced residence.

2. *Little Tel Aviv*

Prefatory remarks: In writing this account of everyday life for the Jewish refugees living in the center of forced residence at Saint-Gervais, I relied heavily on two documents. One is the unpublished memoir of Hélène Gorgiel-Sercarz, *Memoirs of a Jewish Daughter.* The second is CDJC, OSE(II)-134, *"Rapport sur les événements de 1943 en France occupée par les troupes italiennes: les centres de résidence assignée en Savoie (mars-septembre 1943)"* or "Report on the events of 1943 in France occupied by the Italian troops: the centers of assigned residence in Savoie (March-September 1943)." (The reference to "Savoie" rather than "Haute-Savoie" is a error; in the CDJC database, it has been corrected to read "Haute-Savoie".) This 15-page report, dated August 1944, was written by Armand Rein, Director of the OSE Medical-Social Center in Saint-Gervais in the summer of 1943. (The acronym OSE stands for Oeuvre de secours aux enfants, generally translated as Children's Rescue Network.) I also utilized various reports written by members of the Féderation des sociétés juives de France (FSJF). The Federation oversaw the centers of forced residence created in the Italian Occupation Zone in the spring of 1943. It was originally founded in 1913 to serve the needs of immigrant Jews. According to Lazare, *Rescue as Resistance,* 14, by 1938 the Federation represented nearly ninety constituent organizations, mostly *landsmanshaften,* fraternal organizations comprised of immigrants of the same region. A general note about wartime reports, memoranda, and letters is in order. The heads of Jewish social assistance organizations operating in France during the Occupation were acutely aware of the dangers inherent in written communication and documentation. Reflecting this fact, many reports are unsigned and undated. Often, authors made use of code words so that unintended recipients of the documents would not decipher their true meaning. Many of the code words were rooted in Biblical, Hebraic, or Yiddish words and references.

Page

11 By the first or second week of May 1943: Gorgiel-Sercarz, *Memoirs of a Jewish Daughter,* 93, and CDJC, CCXIV-21, *unsigned and undated FSJF report concerning the refugee community in Saint-Gervais, 1.* It is unclear whether the first buses of refugees arrived in Saint-Gervais toward the end of April or the beginning of May. Gorgiel-Servarz states that her family arrived at the end of April and that theirs was the "second or third bus to arrive." CCXIV-21 states that the first car destined for Saint-Gervais departed Nice on May 6.

11 the *route Napoleon*: This commemorative road, opened in 1932, follows the route that Napoleon I took when he returned to France from his exile on

the island of Elba. The Emperor and his troops landed at Golfe Juan on March 1, 1815. He immediately set off for Paris, intent on overthrowing Louis VIII. Anticipating that they would encounter hostile forces in the Rhône Valley, they made their way across the southern Alps to Grenoble. Today, the 325-kilometer road, part of N85, is marked by the symbol of a flying eagle.

11 "an extraordinary tourist experience": Gorgiel-Sercarz, *Memoirs of a Jewish Daughter*, 93.

13 Clutching a list: Gorgiel-Sercarz, *Memoirs of a Jewish Daughter*, 93.

13 It could have been the Hotel Victoria: Grandjacques, *La montagne-refuge*, 143–160, provides a detailed discussion of where the Jewish refugees lived. Many of the hotels used by the refugee community, including the Val Joly, are still in operation.

14 the Villa du Mont Joly: the address of the house is 292, rue de la Comtesse.

16 The Berlioz family: Grandjacques, *La montagne-refuge*, 152. The reference to the Orset family taking in the Kalischmann family is from the same source, 153.

16 the Jewish refugee community in Saint-Gervais numbered approximately 850: JDC NY archives, Saly Mayer Collection, 1939-50, Folder 32, unsigned, undated report *"Travail de Feder à St. Gervais" ("Work of Feder in St. Gervais"), 1.* Report is attached to letter from Marc Jarblum to Saly Mayer dated August 30, 1943.

16 the names of 350 children: CDJC, OSE(II)-134, *"Rapport sur les événements de 1943,"* written by Armand Rein, August 1944, 6.

17 drain their glasses of Ovaltine: CDJC, OSE(II)-134, *"Rapport sur les événements de 1943,"* written by Armand Rein, August 1944, 7. Armand Rein states, "Our Central Directorate in Chambéry sent us large quantities of Ovaltine that our friends in Switzerland had sent to us." To whom does the phrase "our friends in Switzerland" refer? The report does not say. Possibly, it refers to the Secours suisse aux enfants (Swiss Aid to Children), a part of the Swiss Croix-rouge (Red Cross) that provided a variety of kinds of aid to Jewish children in France during the war. Or it could have been OSE's world headquarters in Geneva (i.e. the World Union-OSE), another organization, or individuals not affiliated with an organization.

17 The canteen in the Hôtel Eden was one of several: At least three documents speak to the organization of the refugee community in

Saint-Gervais, paying particular attention to the system set in place to purchase food and prepare and serve meals on a collective basis. One is CDJC, OSE(II)-134, *"Rapport sur les événements de 1943,"* written by Armand Rein, August 1944. The second is the previously cited report from the JDC NY archives, Saly Mayer Collection, 1939-50, Folder 32, unsigned, undated report *"Travail de Feder à St. Gervais."* Page 1 of that report states: "To avoid having everyone spread out across the town, looking for provisions, we prohibit direct purchasing except for rationed commodities, such as bread, cheese, sugar, etc. All of the purchases are made by a central bureau, which has the advantages of collectivity, buying in bulk, and then dividing the commodities acquired among the various canteens and mess halls." The third is a document entitled *"Memorandum: St. Gervais mai – août 1943,"* written by Gerson Epstein and dated January 1954. The memorandum was preserved in the personal papers of Joseph Kott. Joseph's son, Bernard, kindly provided a copy of the document to the author. It is not known why or for whom Epstein wrote the memorandum in 1954.

17 the Saint Gervais Committee: CDJC, OSE(II)-134, *"Rapport sur les événements de 1943,"* written by Armand Rein, August 1944, 5, uses the term "local committee," but most called it (and remember it as) the *Comité de Saint-Gervais.* In the summer of 1943, a song about the *Comité de Saint-Gervais* was written. It was, apparently, quite a hit: Sacha Maidenberg (née Racine), Esther Weil (née Veissid) and Lydie Weissberg all remembered the song lyrics decades later. Esther Weil set forth the lyrics to the first verse in the *Enfants Cachés Bulletin* of June 1996 (Number 15). There was a second committee responsible for administering the refugee community. Rein, 5, refers to it as the Comité UGIF and also as the Comité de la Fédération. It consisted of representatives of Jewish organizations that had established a presence in the community. The two committees worked together. Quite possibly, some in the community used the name Comité de Saint-Gervais when referring to either group.

18 the "youth center,": CDJC, OSE(II)-134, *"Rapport sur les événements de 1943,"* written by Armand Rein, August 1944, 4, refers to it as *"le Centre de la Jeunesse." Memorandum: St. Gervais,* written by Gerson Epstein, January 1954, 2, refers to the *"foyer de jeunesse."*

19 they set up a long table outdoors: Lydie Weissberg interview. Lydie Weissberg and her mother lived in the Val Joly in the summer of 1943. On September 11, 2006, I interviewed Lydie Weissberg in Paris and recorded the interview on audiotape. I subsequently transcribed the audiotape

and submitted the transcription to Lydie for her review, corrections, and changes. Reflecting the nature of the process, I have placed excerpted portions of the transcription in quotation marks.

19 In some of the centers of forced residence during the war: I know of no comprehensive study of how Jewish refugees were received in the various places of forced residence during the war. Various books and articles mention hostile reactions exhibited by the local population and/or cite or reproduce letters of complaint preserved in the departmental archives.

19 their own number probably did not exceed three thousand: No data are available on the actual number of persons living in the town just prior to the arrival of foreign Jews in the spring of 1943. The statement that the number of Saint-Gervolains probably did not exceed three thousand is my own judgment, which took into account data from the mayor's office indicating that the town's population was 2,775 in 1936 and 3,574 in 1946.

19 "The relations between the Jewish Committee and the French and Italian authorities": CDJC, OSE(II)-134, *"Rapport sur les événements de 1943,"* written by Armand Rein, August 1944, 5–6.

19 "a relief and a respite": Lydie Weissberg interview.

19 "a sort of paradise, a marvelous vacation": Lydie Weissberg interview.

20 Joseph had been a boy of ten: Biographical information on the Kott family was obtained from: interviews, discussions, and correspondence with Bernard Kott between 2004 and 2012; and a book authored by Jacques Kott (Joseph Kott's nephew) and his wife, Aline, entitled *Roanne: Enquête sur les origines d'une communauté juive atypique . . .*

22 As the business grew, so too did Joseph's commitment: Joseph was fortunate to find a capable factory manager, a Russian immigrant named Samuel Resnick, to oversee the new factory. This allowed him to devote much of his time and energy to the communal and political activities toward which his passions ran. He served as president of the Association Culturelle Israélite de Roanne (ACIR), the only officially sanctioned Jewish organization in the city. He was active in Zionist and Socialist organizations, such as the Poale Zion (Workers of Zion) and the S.F. I. O., the Section Française de l'International Ouvrière (French Section of the Workers' International). He also supported the Yiddish language press.

22 "singular and original": Lewi, *Histoire d'une communauté juive,* 32.

22 "Here, from the time of its creation": Lewi, *Histoire d'une communauté juive*, 32.

24 "an unprecedented instance in the history of Zionism": Lazare, *Rescue as Resistance*, 68.

24 a "beehive" of activity: Diamant, "*Jewish Refugees on the French Riviera*," 272.

25 The Dubouchage Committee had allocated some space: Biographical information on Jacques and Léa Wajntrob is from the following: the author's interview of their daughter, Miriam Brinbaum, on September 14, 2006, in Paris; from correspondence conducted with Miriam; and from a three-page biographical summary received from Miriam entitled "Jacques Wajntrob." As far as I know, the summary is unpublished. At my request, Miriam kindly posed several questions to her mother about the operation of the Nice *gdoud*, including its relationship to the Dubouchage Committee prior to September 1943 and its work in aiding hunted Jews once the reign of terror had begun.

25 A young man named Jacques Wajntrob: The family name typically appears in published materials as "Weintrob." The spelling used here is the spelling used by Jacques and Léa's daughter, Myriam Brinbaum.

25 Jacques Wajntrob greeted newcomers: Gorgiel-Sercarz, *Memoirs of a Jewish Daughter*, 89.

26 "What struck me in the first place,": Letter from Sarah Grunberg to N. Lefenfeld, November 2004. I interviewed Sarah Grunberg by phone on November 6, 2004. I subsequently received a letter from her. (The undated letter was postmarked November 18, 2004.)

26 "rounded up all the youths": Gorgiel-Sercarz, *Memoirs of a Jewish Daughter*, 94. There is a photograph of some fifty people, some seated and some standing, on the side of a hill, squinting in bright sunlight. At the bottom, nearest to the photographer, Joseph is seated with members of the Saint-Gervais Committee, several middle-age men dressed in dark suits and ties. Behind them, young men and women are loosely assembled. Most of them are smiling and appear to be at ease, their shirt sleeves rolled up, shirt collars open. The assembly captured on film is, quite possibly, Joseph's organizational meeting. I received a copy of this photograph from Bernard Kott, who received it from Esther Weil (née Veissid). The photo is reproduced in the *Enfants Cachés Bulletin* of June 1996 (Number 15).

26 to take a very active part in building the community: CDJC, OSE(II)-134, *"Rapport sur les événements de 1943,"* written by Armand Rein, August 1944, 8, states that everyone fourteen years of age and over was expected to perform some type of work, learn a trade, or study.

26 Their immediate priority: Gorgiel-Sercarz, *Memoirs of a Jewish Daughter,* 94.

26 Mila had agreed to oversee this effort: Several women who lived in Saint-Gervais in the summer of 1943 spoke and/or wrote to me about the school and Mila's supervisory role: Sonia Constant (née Veissid), who was one of the children in the first MJS convoy; Sonia's sister, Esther Weil (née Veissid), who was the *"jardinière adjointe,"* assistant kindergarten teacher; Mila's sister, Sacha Maidenberg; and Sara Grunberg. Photos of the teachers and kindergarten pupils are reproduced in Grandjacques, *La montagne-refuge.* I interviewed Sonia Constant on August 5, 2001, in Lyon and corresponded with her prior to and after that date.

26 the dressing rooms: Grandjacques, *La montagne-refuge,* 174. The term "Sunday skaters" (*patineurs du dimanche*) is his.

26 four refugees who were physicians: CDJC, OSE(II)-134, *"Rapport sur les événements de 1943,"* written by Armand Rein, August 1944, 7.

26 ORT: This organization originated in Russia in 1880 as a fund established to promote economic development among Russian Jews through assistance to existing trade and agricultural schools and agricultural colonies, establishment of new schools and colonies, and assistance to artisans. The acronym "ORT" was derived from the Russian name: *Obschestvo Remeslenovo i zemledelcheskovo Trouda* (Society for the Promotion of Handicrafts, Industry and Agriculture Among Jews). After the end of World War I, ORT became an international organization. Today, the organization, headquartered in Geneva, has vocational training and education programs in fifty countries.

27 they took turns presenting lectures: Gorgiel-Sercarz, *Memoirs of a Jewish Daughter,* 95; and recollections of Sara Grunberg conveyed in a phone interview and subsequent letter.

27 mathematics, chemistry, and philosophy: Grandjacques, *La montagne-refuge,* 174, notes that Jacques Wajntrob sent two MJS members, Gérard Halberthal and Alex Derczanski, to Saint-Gervais to initiate the establishment of a collège-lycée. Halberthal taught mathematics and chemistry, and Derczanski taught philosophy.

27 Mila would teach them Hebrew songs: Lydie Weissberg interview; Sonia Constant (née Veissid) interview.

27 Late at night, on the balcony: Lydie Weissberg interview.

28 "the king of Saint-Gervais": Lewi, *Histoire d'une communauté juive*, 53.

28 They had even organized a synagogue: Grandjacques, *La montagne-refuge*, 184.

28 "But what is the most comforting over there": JDC NY archives, Previously cited report entitled *"Travail de Feder à St. Gervais," 1, from Saly Mayer Collection, 1939-50, Folder 32.*

28 they called their community Little Tel Aviv: Gorgiel-Sercarz, *Memoirs of a Jewish Daughter*, 96.

28 "Survivors on the high sea": CDJC, CCXIV-21, unsigned and undated FSJF report concerning the refugee community in Saint-Gervais, 5.

3. *Pas de l'Échelle*

Page

29 They celebrated throughout the day and night: Carpi, *Between Mussolini and Hitler,* 166.

29 By the third week in August: On August 15, commanders of the Axis armies met in Bologna and negotiated the agreement mentioned here.

29 a plan was in place: The plan described here was not the only one pursued during the summer of 1943 in an effort to save the Jews who had found refuge in the Italian Occupation Zone. Two other efforts warrant mention. The more audacious was a plan developed by Angelo Donati to evacuate thirty thousand Jews from France to Italy (see Chapter 6, Nice). The other effort that warrants mention was initiated by two Italian government officials in early August. Augusto Spechel, who succeeded Alberto Calisse as Italian Consul General in Nice in May 1943, worked with his friend, Count Luigi Vidau, the head of the Political Department in the Italian Foreign Ministry, to obtain the approvals needed in order to allow Jewish refugees fleeing France to enter Italy. See Carpi, *Between Mussolini and Hitler,* 169. I should mention that Count Vidau had, on at least two previous occasions, taken the initiative to protect Jews. In response to German pressures exerted on the Italian Foreign Ministry in early February 1943, he unequivocally communicated to the German Embassy in Rome that the Italians had sole authority over the Jews living in their occupation zone. He not only stated that Jews would not be turned over to the French authorities, but he also stated the reason for this—namely, that they would end up in German hands and then be deported to Poland. Later that same month, upon learning that the German Foreign Minister, von Ribbentrop, was going to meet with Mussolini, the Count had his staff assemble information regarding atrocities being committed against deported Jews. He had a detailed memorandum prepared on the subject, which he gave to il Duce in advance of the meeting. Carpi, *Between Mussolini and Hitler,* 105, 112, 116.

30 Jews living in Saint-Gervais were to be transferred: Rochlitz, *The Righteous Enemy: Document Collection,* F-25 – F-27, 94–97.

31 "Those who only took flight": ICE, *Bergier Report,* Section 3.2, 90.

31 the policy was liberalized to grant exception to so-called hardship cases: ICE, *Bergier Report,* Section 4.2.2, 122, and Section 4.3.1, 133; and Fivaz-Silbermann, *Le Refoulement de réfugiés civils juifs,* 5–6.

31 "first true OSE convoy": Fivaz-Silbermann, Doctoral dissertation in progress, *La fuite en Suisse*. The scholar used this term in an unpublished list of convoys that she prepared and that she kindly shared with me. As noted in the text, prior to this date, some children in the care of OSE had been taken into Switzerland individually, with siblings, or in very small groups.

31 Between March 15 and May 7: Fivaz-Silbermann, Doctoral dissertation in progress, *La fuite en Suisse*.

32 When the organization was founded in Russia in 1912: On the history of OSE, see: Archives et histoire de l'OSE, *Une mémoire pour le futur: L'Oeuvre de secours aux enfants, 90 ans d'histoire; A Legacy for the Future: 90 Years of History* (Paris: Somogy éditions d'art and Association Oeuvre de secours aux enfants, 2003); Lemalet, ed. and author, *Au secours des enfants du siècle: Regards croisés sur l'OSE* (Nil Éditions, 1993); and Dr. L. Wulman, ed., *In ḳamf farn gezunṭ fun Idishn folḳ (50 yor "Oze"); In Fight for the Health of the Jewish People (50 Years of OSE)* (New York: World Union OSE and The American Committee of OSE, 1968).

32 these homes sheltered approximately nine hundred children: Zeitoun, *L'Oeuvre de secours aux enfants (O.S.E.) sous l'occupation*, 124.

33 Led by Georges Garel: The transcript of an oral history provided by Georges Garel in October 1963, ICJ-OH Number (1) 64, provides interesting reading on the origin and growth of the network.

33 On July 29, four days after the fall of Mussolini, OSE passed a convoy of twelve children: Fivaz-Silbermann, Doctoral dissertation in progress, *La fuite en Suisse*.

33 The organization sent three more convoys into Switzerland: Fivaz-Silbermann, Doctoral dissertation in progress, *La fuite en Suisse*.

33 Andrée Salomon, the head of the social service branch of OSE: CDJC, DLXI-35, Tony Gryn testimony, August 1975. Of the origins of the collaboration between OSE and the MJS, Gryn states: "My work began in the summer of '43. I was in Grenoble. I was designated by Simon Lévitte to organize in Annecy the passage of the children into Switzerland." (Page numbering of the testimony is a bit difficult to understand; the quotation cited appears in the first section, on the first page.) He adds (first section, third page): "Mila was my associate." He subsequently states (first section, fourth page): "It was at the time when we began to fear for this Italian zone that Simon Lévitte sent me to Saint-Gervais and

to Megève to organize the evacuation of the children. From everywhere, people brought children to us in Annecy; I was in contact with Andrée Salomon in particular."

33 soul of the MJS: I have borrowed this term from Latour, who, in *The Jewish Resistance in France*, 88, speaks of Simon Lévitte as the "soul of the movement."

34 "The young local leader of the MJS, Otto Giniewski": On March 16, 2001, in Great Neck, New York, I interviewed Georges Schnek, who provided me with a copy of a four-page address that he delivered at an international colloquium in Grenoble in 1997. I have quoted from page 2 of that address. The address appears, with very minor changes, in Dereymez, *Être jeune en France (1939–1945)*, 60–61.

35 "We used these weekend meetings": Kapel, *Un rabbin dans la tourmente*, 102.

35 the "Song of the Deportees,": The "Chant des déportés" ("Song of the Deportees"), also called the "Chant des marais" ("Song of the Marshes") was composed in the mid-thirties by two inmates of the Borgermoor concentration camp in Germany, Rudi Goguel and Herbert Kirmse. A song of hope and courage as well as anguish, it spread throughout Europe and became a well-known song of resistance. The original name of the song was *"Die Moorsoldaten"* ("The Peat Bog Soldiers"). Kapel, *Un rabbin dans la tourmente*, 167, writes that the song "had become with Hatikvah, during the years of occupation, the favorite song of the Zionist Youth Movement of France."

35 "the long evenings allowed us to deepen": Schnek, page 4 of four-page address provided to the author.

35 why were the Nazis taking those who were unfit for work: Gorgiel-Sercarz, *Memoirs of a Jewish Daughter*, 97. Gorgiel-Sercarz writes: "Our anxiety about the destiny of the deported people grew steadily. We could not understand the purpose of deporting young and old from all over Europe and no normal human mind could foresee or fathom the enormity of the slaughter and the manner in which it was performed. All this uncertainty weighed like a dark cloud on our seemingly serene life and activity in beautiful Saint-Gervais."

35-36 Uncertainty hung over all "like a dark cloud": Gorgiel-Sercarz, *Memoirs of a Jewish Daughter*, 97. (See preceding note.)

36 "fierce impact": Gorgiel-Sercarz, *Memoirs of a Jewish Daughter*, 97.

36 "It made our bond of belonging to our people": Gorgiel-Sercarz, *Memoirs of a Jewish Daughter*, 97.

36 Mila managed to spend some summer weekends: During our interview, Georges Schnek stated that he often saw Mila at les Michalons.

36 "he remarked to Sehn one day": Höss, *Death Dealer*, 20.

36 "On my seventh birthday": Höss, *Death Dealer*, 49.

37 She was born on September 14, 1919: Biographical information on the Racine family was obtained from interviews conducted by the author with the following family members: Mila's brother, Emmanuel (Mola) Racine, during the week of March 13–17, 2000, in Tel Aviv; Mila's sister, Sacha Maidenberg (née Racine) on July 18 and July 30, 2000, in Paris; Mila's cousin Helen Mirkine (née Racine) on August 22, 2000, in Manhattan; and Mila's cousins Helen Mirkine, Nadine Gill (née Racine), and Nelly Harris (née Chender) on October 20, 2000, in Manhattan. Information was also obtained from copies of documents that these individuals kindly shared with me, particularly documents in Mola's private collection. As far as I know, Mola Racine left no detailed testimony or memoir about his experiences during the war. However, when I interviewed him in Tel Aviv, he provided me with a copy of a five-page untitled and undated account that covers the period of time from 1939 to 1944 and that addresses the movements and activities of Racine family members and others. To the best of my knowledge, this account has not been published. I refer to this document as his unpublished, undated biographical notes.

38 "No matter who sat there, she [Berthe] started peeling apples": Nelly Harris (née Chender) interview.

40 The Women's International Zionist Organization had been founded in Great Britain: The founders were Rebecca Sieff, Dr. Vera Weizmann, Edith Eder, Romana Goodman, and Henrietta Irwell.

40 Mila created Jeune WIZO (Young WIZO): A lengthy retrospective published on the occasion of the WIZO's fiftienth anniversary mentions Mila and the Jeune WIZO group she formed. Grove-Pollak (ed.), *The Saga of a Movement*, 61–62.

41 "*La ville rose* [the pink city] is monstrously encumbered": Knout, *Contribution à l'histoire de la Résistance juive en France*, 141.

44 "My family and I were settled in Toulouse": Private collection of Emmanuel (Mola) Racine, Emmanuel Racine, unpublished, undated biographical notes, 2.

45 "bustle about, lay siege to the consulates": Knout, *Contribution à l'histoire de la Résistance juive en France,* 141–142.

45 one of the "specialists": Knout, *Contribution à l'histoire de la Résistance juive en France,* 142. Toulouse is only sixty miles north of the Spanish border. During the war, some came to Toulouse in order to arrange for an illegal crossing into Spain. Even for the able-bodied, crossing the Pyrenees Mountains on foot was a difficult and dangerous undertaking.

45 "our eternal tactic": Knout, *Contribution à l'histoire de la Résistance juive en France,* 142. He references Pinsker's work entitled *Auto-Emancipation.*

45 to force open the doors to legal Jewish emigration: In issuing the White Paper of May 1939, the British had severely curtailed legal Jewish emigration to Palestine. Only seventy-five thousand Jews were to be admitted to the country over the next five years (ten thousand immigrants per year plus twenty-five thousand refugees).

45 a slim pamphlet entitled "*Que Faire*": Knout, *Contribution à l'histoire de la Résistance juive en France,* 142–143.

45 "We are seventeen million": Knout, *Contribution à l'histoire de la Résistance juive en France,* 143.

45 "doctrine of Jewish Resistance": Knout, *Contribution à l'histoire de la Résistance juive en France,* 143.

45 "These meetings that we held with Knut": Private collection of Emmanuel (Mola) Racine, Emmanuel Racine, unpublished, undated biographical notes, 2–3.

46 Main forte, whose first member swore allegiance: Latour, *The Jewish Resistance in France,* 96. Latour notes, on page 95, that the name "Main Forte" is the French equivalent of the Hebrew "Yad Hazaka," the title of a work written by the twelfth-century Jewish philosopher Maimonides.

46 Its mottos were "*Partout présent*": Knout, *Contribution à l'histoire de la Résistance juive en France,* 143.

46 "more Jewish than many Jews": Latour, *The Jewish Resistance in France,* 94. Latour, a member of the Sixième and the Armée juive knew Ariane

Knout-Fixman, who used the alias Régine. She paints a vivid picture of this heroine of the Jewish resistance.

46 "'Bat Mattitiahu' or 'Mattathias' daughter'": Poznanski, *Jews in France*, 156.

46 The more militant members comprised Etzel: Etzel is an acronym formed of the initials of the group's full name—HaIrgun HaTzva'i HaLe'umi BeEretz Yisra'el (National Military Organization in the Land of Israel). Sacher, *A History of Israel*, 265, speaks of the origin of Etzel in 1931 and its subsequent development.

47 Several Jewish, Christian, and nonsectarian aid organizations worked valiantly: The literature on the subject recognizes the work carried out by OSE, ORT, CIMADE, Secours suisse aux enfants, YMCA, and the Quakers. Madeleine Barot, one of the founders of CIMADE (Comité inter-mouvements auprès des évacués; Inter-Movement Committee in the Service of Evacuees), described the origin of the organization this way: "It had been created by the Protestant youth movements, the Boy Scouts and Girl Scouts, the YWCA and YMCA, and the Federation of Student Christian Movements to help the displaced persons from Alsace and Lorraine, who had been 'evacuated' from the Border Zone in September 1939, toward the departments of the Haute-Vienne and the Dordogne." This quote is from Fabre (ed.), *God's Underground*, 27. That book provides an overview of the various kinds of work that CIMADE did throughout the war to aid and rescue Jews in France. The Secours suisse aux enfants (Swiss Aid to Children) was an organization connected with the Swiss Red Cross.

47 leadership training camp: Information on the camp was obtained from various sources, including: my interview with Sacha Maidenberg (née Racine); Gamzon, *Les Eaux Claires*, 17–18; and www.le-scoutisme-francais-en-franche-comte.org/rgchp7.html. The webpage, on the website of the Collège de Franche-Comté du Scoutisme Français, is one of a fifteen-part series featuring Robert Gamzon, the founder of the EIF and its national commissioner during the war. The author of the series is Isaac Pougatch, a close associate of Gamzon's during the war.

47 the blue and white Zionist flag: The flag of the Zionist movement became the flag of the State of Israel.

47 *l'homme-horaire*: www.le-scoutisme-francais-en-franche-comte.org/rgchp7.html

47 "very poorly known in France": Lévitte, *Le Sionisme*, 5.

49 First, there were Jewish refugees from Belgium: The Jewish refugees from Belgium included many Germans and Austrians who had moved to Antwerp and Brussels during the thirties.

49 For some of these early arrivals, it had been, quite literally, the end of the line: Zuccotti, *Holocaust Odysseys*, 33: "The trains from Belgium headed for southern France with no apparent destination. Nearly all the passengers stayed on board for several days, hoping to get as far from the war as possible." Zuccotti also notes on page 33: "Although it seemed haphazard to the refugees from Belgium, the trains usually left them in French towns especially designated by harassed authorities." The discussion suggests that the prefects in the various departments through which these trains filled with refugees passed determined how many and/or who would disembark at each stop along the way. The only citation that appears with respect to this point is Kapel, *Un rabbin dans la tourmente*, 89. Kapel simply makes reference to Belgians who had fled to France in June 1940, first settled in and around Toulouse, and were subsequently directed by "prefectorial decision" to live in assigned residence in Luchon. To what extent did the prefects of departments in the Unoccupied Zone direct the disembarkation of refugees from trains in May and/or June 1940? This is an interesting question, one that I cannot answer.

49 "numerous and urgent": USHMM, AFSC Records Relating to Humanitarian Work in France, 1933–1950 (Şeries I Perpignan Office, Sub-series: Correspondence Box 11, Folder 27 of 134), Letter from Centre des Réfugiés de Luchon (P. Lambot, Director) to Helga Holbek of the Delegation in Toulouse, July 7, 1940.

49 In early 1941, a few hundred of them: René Kapel was a rabbi who, in 1941, ministered to a Jewish refugee community living in forced residence in Aulus-les-Bains. In his memoir, *Un rabbin dans la tourmente*, 89, he notes that most of the 375 Jews who comprised the Aulus-les-Bains community in 1941 had been sent there from Luchon. (As referenced in a previous note, they were Belgian Jews who had fled to France in June 1940, first settled in and around Toulouse, were subsequently directed by "prefectorial decision" to live in forced residence in Luchon, and were later transferred to Aulus-les-Bains.) He also notes on page 89: "They hoped to be able to stay there [in Luchon] until the end of hostilities, but, for an unknown reason (they sometimes referred to the black market), they had been subsequently transferred to Aulus-les-Bains." He further

notes, on page 90, "Having just arrived at their new place of residence, the refugees rented a wooden barracks that they transformed into a synagogue. In effect, a good number of them were strictly observant Jews, originally from Antwerp." The "black marketeer" accusation was often slapped on Jews and served as a pretext for arrest, internment, or forced change of residence. France during the war was bled dry by the Germans, and the vast majority of the French population dealt with hunger and shortages of basic necessities as best as they could. Ousby, *Occupation,* 128: "The inadequacy of official rations and the need for *débrouillardise* [resourcefulness] meant that sooner or later everyone broke the law, in however minor or innocent fashion. Le *système D* merged inevitably with the *marché gris* [grey market], and the grey market shaded inevitably into the black market, the *marché noir*. But where exactly did such distinctions lie? And, besides, did they matter any more?"

49 "idlers who 'pass their lives in the café'": Estèbe, *Les Juifs à Toulouse,* 53.

49 "an anti-Semitic climate": Estèbe, *Les Juifs à Toulouse,* 53.

49 "organized by Mlle [Mademoiselle] Mila Racine": Private collection of Emmanuel (Mola) Racine, Programme, Théatre des Chimères, Luchon, Soirée du 28 Septembre 1941.

51 "L'Anglais tel qu'on le parle": The young Englishwoman Betty and her French fiancé, having eloped to Paris, are pursued by Betty's irate father and "helped" by an interpreter who speaks no English. This work was first performed in 1899.

51 dried beans stored in Gurs had "rapidly deteriorated": Marrus and Paxton, *Vichy France and the Jews,* 172.

51 Mila decided to set up her own canning operation: Interview with Sacha Maidenberg (née Racine).

51 joined with mainstream Zionist leaders to form the Armée juive: Abraham Polonski and Aron-Lucien Lublin were the key individuals who forged this union. Polonski, a Revisionist, and Lublin, a socialist Zionist, were friends. Like many of the other activists in Toulouse, Lublin was originally from Russia. Polonski introduced Lublin to Knout and other members of Main forte.

51 "the extermination of the Jewish people": Lazare, *Rescue as Resistance,* 101. Vigée, *La lune d'hiver,* Appendix 4, 403–412, reproduces part of the manifesto. The statement cited appears on page 404.

51 Mila was one of the first: Lazarus, *Juifs au combat*, 60. Jacques Lazarus was one of the leaders of the AJ in 1943–44. During the Italian Occupation, he was based in Grenoble, and he provided military training to young people living in that zone, particularly those of the MJS. (See Les Anciens de la Résistance juive en France, *Organisation juive de combat*, 81.) In *Juifs au combat*, his memoir, Lazarus, known as Capitaine Jacquel, states, on page 60, that Mila had been "one of the first" to join the ranks of the AJ, in Luchon in 1941. Also, when I interviewed her in 2000, Sacha Maidenberg stated that Mila was initiated into the Armée juive in a secret ceremony around this time.

51 Like other recruits, she was blindfolded: Several sources describe the secret initiation ceremony that new recruits to Main forte and the Armée juive underwent, including: Poznanski, *Jews in France*, 158; Latour, *The Jewish Resistance in France*, 93; and Vigée, *La lune d'hiver*, 88. The oath cited here appears in Poznanski and Latour. Apparently, this was not the first oath used by Main forte. In *The Jewish Resistance in France*, 95, Latour writes of Arnold Mandel, a founding member of Main forte: "According to Mandel, the first oath required of members of the Main Forte was a word-for-word translation of the oath taken by the members of the Irgun: 'To fight against England, consider Palestine our Homeland, and to work toward returning to Palestine, and defeating the occupying enemy forces.'"

52 Mila sought out Lydie Weissberg: My account of the events of August 15, 16, and 17 is based on interviews that I held with Lydie Weissberg in 2006 and with Sonia Constant (née Veissid) in 2001 and on correspondence with them. I also utilized correspondence that I received from Sonia Constant's sister, Esther Weil (née Veissid).

52 Lydie was a smart and spirited fifteen-year-old: Biographical information on the Weissberg family is from my interview with Lydie Weissberg.

52 "a test that could have important consequences": Lydie Weissberg interview.

53 "reliable, determined, and quick": Lydie Weissberg interview.

53 "beautiful, lively, strong, and charismatic": Lydie Weissberg interview.

53 "a luminous personality": Lydie Weissberg interview.

53 Jacques Veissid (16): Normally, a sixteen-year-old boy would be turned back at the border. According to Jacques' sister, Sonia Constant, Jacques was small for his age, and convoy organizers decided that he could pass

as younger. I should note that, on the Declaration that he signed, his age is given as sixteen. Apparently, even though Swiss officials learned of his true age sometime after he entered the country, they did not send him back to France. Archives d'État de Genève, Justice et Police, dossier #4250.

53 They were not to reveal: They were instructed not to mention Saint-Gervais for two reasons. As noted in the text, it was believed that information provided to Swiss authorities might fall into the hands of Nazi spies and endanger family members still in France. Also, it was felt that, if Swiss authorities knew that the children's parents were living so close by, in Saint-Gervais, they might be tempted to turn them back at the border.

53 Nazi spies or sympathizers in Switzerland: Lydie Weissberg interview.

53 a cover story: Lydie Weissberg interview.

54 There was a plan in place: Lydie Weissberg interview. The description of the plan's various elements is from Lydie Weissberg. Although I have enclosed only a couple of phrases in quotation marks, many used to describe the plan are Lydie's.

54 A country road linking Annemasse: Today, this road is designated route N206.

54 to a church in a nearby village: It is very likely that this was the church of Abbé Marius Jolivet in Collonges-sous-Salève. As discussed further in Chapter 4, Father Jolivet was part of an ecclesiastical network that had, on numerous occasions, helped Jewish refugees cross the Swiss border.

54 "as ice cold as the inside of the church": Lydie Weissberg interview.

54 Mila was able to distract them: Sonia Constant interview.

54 The children knew Mila well enough: Sonia Constant interview.

4. Ville-la-Grand

Page

57 Maurice Glazman lived with his parents: Biographical information on the Glazman family is from an interview with Dr. Maurice Glazman on September 11, 2008, in Paris, and from correspondence.

58 On the morning of August 26, Maurice and thirty-one other children: My account of the events of August 26, 27, and 28 are based on the interview that I held with Dr. Maurice Glazman and on correspondence.

59 and Tony replied, "Yes, I know, I know": Maurice Glazman interview. In his testimony dated August 1975, CDJC, DLXI-35, first section, fourth page, Tony Gryn states: "It was she [Rolande Birgy] who put me in touch with the old priest of Collonges, abbé Jolivet, who helped us during the first crossing that I organized." As noted earlier in the text, it appears very likely that it was Father Jolivet who helped Mila and the children (i.e., the first convoy) on August 16. Based on information gleaned from the Lydie Weissberg and Sonia Constant interviews, it seems to me that Father Jolivet may have been surprised on the evening of August 16 by the sudden appearance of the group seeking refuge is his church. Consequently, what may have transpired is that, at her own iniative or at the request of someone else, Rolande Birgy intervened, formally introducing the young MJS leaders to Father Jolivet and soliciting his help.

60 "precarious health and an emotional temperament": Yagil, *Chrétiens et Juifs sous Vichy*, 189.

61 Documentation extant in the archives of Geneva: I have identified the dossiers of the nineteen children whose names are cited here. As discussed in Chapter 5, Annecy, these dossiers have been preserved in the Archives of the State of Geneva, in the section referred to as "Justice et Police."

61 Information preserved in the Archives départmentales de la Haute-Savoie (Departmental Archives of the Haute-Savoie): Fivaz-Silbermann, Doctoral dissertation in progress, *La fuite en Suisse*.

61 The Swiss and French records account for twenty-four children altogether: Maurice Glazman remembered quite distinctly that thirty-two children were in the convoy. I do not know what could account for the discrepancy between his recollection and the group sizes reflected in the archival data. It is possible that, when the group set out from Saint-

Gervais, it numbered thirty-two but that some returned to Saint-Gervais and/or Megève before or after the attempted crossing and thus were not accounted for in the arrest records.

62 "refused to adapt himself": Yagil, *Chrétiens et Juifs sous Vichy,* 187.

63 an ardent Pétainist and an active member of the Service d'Ordre Légionnaire: Croquet, *Chemins de passage,* 33. At the beginning of 1943, the Service d'Ordre Légionnaire (SOL) became the Milice. It is not known how long Father Chevrier supported Maréchal Pétain or the SOL.

63 In May 1943, OSE began relying on the Douvaine *filière*: General discussion of the collaboration between OSE and the Douvaine *filière* appears in Croquet, *Chemins de passage,* 33; and Curé de Douvaine, *Resistance non violente,* 31–33.

63 all of the OSE convoys except one: The exception was one convoy of nine children that crossed into Switzerland on August 8, 1943, in the vicinity of Ambilly.

65 They had been helping people secretly cross: Yagil, *Chrétiens et Juifs sous Vichy,* 183: "From the end of 1941, there were young people, especially those from Holland, who, after having clandestinely crossed one or two borders already, in addition to the line of demarcation, came in small groups to ask the Juvénat for a way to clear the last obstacle before joining their consulate in Geneva, and, from there, free forces to continue the struggle against the invaders of their countries."

65 "fragile constitution, with an innate taste": Yagil, *Chrétiens et Juifs sous Vichy,* 183.

65 "charity and patriotism": Yagil, *Chrétiens et Juifs sous Vichy,* 183.

66 Brother Raymond Boccard would position himself: Lazare, *Le livre des Justes,* 94–95.

66 in at least one place, the rows of wire were distended: Croquet, *Chemins de passage,* 83. An excerpt from testimony of A. Muller states: "We were a very short distance from the barbed wire at the border, which at this place was a little distended. My husband crossed first, Father Pernoud passed our daughters to him, and I crossed last."

66 sheltered in buildings on the school property: Lazare, *Le livre des Justes,* 94.

66 However, this practice was stopped: Munos-du Peloux, *Passer en Suisse,* 59. In 1982, Munos-du Peloux interviewed Father Frontin. She writes:

"Father Frontin, now retired to the house of missionaries of Saint-François-de-Sales in Annecy, told me that he himself and a few of the seven professors who were then teaching had helped the illegals. The latter [the illegals] were not sheltered in the college but were passed as rapidly as possible."

66 effecting the passage of one to two thousand people: Croquet, *Chemins de passage*, 83; Lazare, *Le livre des Justes*, 94; and Yagil, *Chrétiens et Juifs sous Vichy*, 182.

67 Tony was born in Lublin, Poland: Biographical information presented here about the Gryn family is from the following: an interview with Tony's son, Tito Gryn, held on June 27, 2006, in Roslyn, New York; phone convervsations and correspondence with Tito; and copies of numerous documents that Tito furnished to me from his private collection. Of those various documents, a nine-page autobiographical account written by Tony shortly after the end of the war proved particularly helpful, as it contains a great deal of information about his family, education, and wartime experiences. Tony refers to this account as a curriculum vitae. Additional information was obtained from correspondence with Tito Gryn and Alice Gliklich (née Gryn) and from a website prepared by Tito Gryn, *The Story of Tony Gryn*, appearing on titogryn.com/titogryn/Tony%20Gryn-EN.pdf

67 he became fluent in German: The website prepared by Tito Gryn, *The Story of Tony Gryn*, presents a statement made by Tony regarding his trial in 1940: "Speaking fluent German, I was monitoring the proceedings of various Court Marshals that took place before ours and noticed that every time the judge asked a condemned if he had anything to say, and the condemned stated his innocence, the judge doubled his sentence. When it was our turn to be asked by the judge if we had anything to say, I told him that we do accept the punishment as just and that we respect the German military court and its laws, and then proceeded and asked the judge to consider the four weeks of incarceration we endured prior to our court date as part of our twelve-month sentence. The judge, surprised by my comments, immediately agreed and we both were sentenced to eleven months' imprisonment."

68 infamous Cherche-Midi: Alfred Dreyfus is among the well-known prisoners of Cherche-Midi. Fresnes was routinely used by the Germans to house members of the French Resistance and captured foreign agents.

68 despite that fact, he ran the risk of being picked up: The earliest piece of legislation enacted by the Vichy government, passed on July 22, 1940, established a commission to review all naturalizations granted since August 10, 1927, and to revoke the citizenship of all those deemed undesirable. Like similar laws passed in 1940 that revoked certain rights of naturalized citizens, the legislation was not explicitly anti-Semitic but it was generally understood that it could have a profound effect upon Jews. The significance of the cut-off date—August 10, 1927—lay in the fact that, as of that date, the residency requirement for gaining citizenship had been reduced from ten to three years.

68 He was fortunate enough to obtain: Private collection of Tito Gryn, undated Curriculum Vitae written by Nésanel (Tony) Gryn, 2. Commenting on the *laissez-passer,* he states, "That was my first step into the 'False Papers,' at which I was going to become a specialist some time later."

68 established a *numerus clausus*: The law itself did not specify exactly how the quota was to be applied. Marrus and Paxton, *Vichy France and the Jews,* 125, addresses the subject.

68 This may have been the farm at Saint-Germain: Szajkowski, *Analytical Franco-Jewish Gazetteer,* 44, 151.

68 identified themselves as Israelites: Private collection of Tito Gryn, undated Curriculum Vitae written by Nésanel (Tony) Gryn, 4. Tony Gryn states: "On the farm, dominated by 'French Israelite' elements, a very chilly reception is given to my loved ones, who are 'foreigners' (in effect, only I was naturalized)." This suggests that the French Israelites on the farm were willing to accept Tony as part of the community but were unwilling to accept his father and sister. One wonders whether the fact that Tony was naturalized and the other family members were not accounted entirely for the prejudice exhibited. Perhaps Isaac's appearance and/or speech marked him as an outsider, whereas Tony (and perhaps his sister, Alice) were more assimilated in terms of appearance and/or speech.

69 "It took me two months to succeed": Private collection of Tito Gryn, undated Curriculum Vitae written by Nésanel (Tony) Gryn, 4.

69 "miraculously free": Private collection of Tito Gryn, undated Curriculum Vitae written by Nésanel (Tony) Gryn, 4.

69 at least eight family convoys: Through consultation of dossiers preserved in the Archives of the State of Geneva (AEG), I identified eight family convoys, with 121 people, that originated in Saint-Gervais and Megève. Because of procedures used to access data from the Geneva archives, I cannot be certain that I identified all of the family convoys that originated in these centers of assigned residence. Nor can I be certain that I identified all of the families comprising the eight convoys. The convoys and families identified are listed below. The numbers appearing in parentheses refer to AEG dossier numbers. The reference letters are mine.

Family convoy A – On August 27, at 1:10 a.m., a group of three families (fifteen people altogether) from Saint-Gervais was arrested at Les Chenaillettes and taken to the Swiss border guard post at Hermance. The families were: Feldhandler (4335), Levy (4339), and Garbownik (4340).

Family convoy B – On August 27, at 6:45 a.m, five families (nineteen people) from Megève and Saint-Gervais were arrested at the "old bridge" in Hermance and taken to the Swiss border guard post at Hermance. The families from Megève were: Zlotowicz (4338), Probst/Hayum/Seckler (4346), Frajermauer (4348), and Cige (4350). The family from Saint-Gervais was Zylbersztein (4336). Although the Zylberszteins were arrested one hour earlier than the others, the itineraries cited in the arrest reports suggest that all five traveled together by train as far as La Roche-sur-Foron, at which point they split up. Two notes in regard to this convoy are warranted. First, it would not have been at all surprising for families from Saint-Gervais and Megève to have traveled together. There were close connections between families living in Saint-Gervais and Megève (i.e., some living in one town had relatives and/or friends in the other). By train, Megève and Saint-Gervais are just several minutes apart. Second, it is possible that the convoy included a sixth family. One of the questions included in the arrest reports is whether the refugee was by himself/herself or whether he/she comprised part of a group. Further, if he/she comprised part of a group, the size of the group was to be indicated. It appeared to me that data on group size were usually, although not always, verifiable. The arrest report for the Zylbersztein family, consisting of a mother and her two daughters, indicates that the group size was five persons—this suggests that they crossed with another family. I have not yet identified the missing family, however. In cases such as this, I have not included the two "missing" persons in the data presented regarding the total number of persons in the convoy.

Family convoy C – On August 28, at 10:00 p.m., three families (nine people) from Saint-Gervais were arrested at b. 185 and taken to the Swiss border guard post at Gy. The three families were: Fenster (4353), Szkolny (4354), and Ringort (4393).

Family convoy D – On September 2, at 7:00 a.m., three families from Megève (eleven people) were arrested on the Chemin des Etôles and taken to the Swiss border guard post at Jussy. The families were: Hops (4415), Procel (4420), and Eilander (4421).

Family convoy E – On September 4, at 11:20 a.m., two families (seven people) were arrested near Chevran and taken to the Swiss border guard post at Chevran. One of the two families was from Saint-Gervais; it consisted of the sculptor Arieh Merzer and his wife and two children (4466). The other, the Papo family (4451), was not from Saint-Gervais. The group size indicated in the arrest reports is ten persons, indicating that there may have been a third family. However, I have not identified such.

Family convoy F – On September 4, at 6:00 p.m., five families (twenty people) from Megève were arrested at b. 185 and taken to the Swiss border guard post at Gy. The families were: Levi (4447), Koch (4448), Majufes (4468), Goldschmidt (4469), and Sagalowitsch (4476).

Family convoy G – On September 5, at 3:30 p.m., seven families (nineteen people) were arrested at b. 171 and taken to the Swiss border guard post at Gy. Six of the families had been in Megève. They were: Schoenbach (4481), Rosenberg (4482), Siemiatycki (4485), Uboghi (4490), Langszner (4492), and Szmulewicz (4493). The seventh, Schaechter (4491), had been living in Marseille.

Family convoy H – On September 6, at 6:50 p.m., six families (twenty-one people) were arrested at b. 169 and taken to the Swiss border guard post at Gy. Four of the six families had been living in Megève: Roubanowicz (4507), Kielmanowicz (4531), Teitelbaum (4535), and Herz (or Hertz) (4537). The other two families, who had not been living in Megève, were Atzstein (4536) and Kandel (4514).

69 Isy Leuwenkroon was one: Biographical information on the Leuwenkroon family is from a telephone interview with Lilly Leuwenkroon on May 10, 2010, and from conversations and correspondence with Eliane Strosberg, daughter of Lilly and Isy Leuwenkroon. Eliane kindly provided me with

copies of many group photographs taken in Saint-Gervais in the summer of 1943 and of other photos and documents from the period. She also kindly shared with me a lengthy biographical summary she prepared entitled "Isy and Lilly, 1943."

70 Mila, who was "full of zip,": In the biographical summary entitled "Isy and Lilly, 1943," (see preceding note), Eliane Strosberg uses the term in conveying her mother's recollections of Mila.

70 Nicole played an active role in conveying families: Salon, *Trois mois dura notre bonheur,* 101.

70 a certain number of "pseudo-families": The term pseudo-families appears in Lazare, *Rescue as Resistance,* 202. In terms of my own research, I have found no evidence that the practice of creating pseudo-families was used in the region of the Haute-Savoie in the fall of 1943 other than during the evacuation of Megève during the first week of September. Cross-referencing names of children on the OSE list (*Liste des enfants partis en Suisse en 1943–1944*), discussed in Chapter 5, with the names of children appearing in the dossiers of families who entered Switzerland, I noted a curious fact. With respect to the convoy from Megève that entered Switzerland on September 4 (family convoy F), names of nine of the ten children appear on the OSE list as "par OSE." Similarly, the names of all eight children who were part of the family convoy from Megève that crossed on September 5 (reference letter G) appear on the OSE list as "par OSE." This is similarly the case with respect to four of the nine children who were in the family convoy from Megève that crossed on September 6 (reference letter H). What does this mean? Were the children whose names appear on the OSE list wards of the organization? Did OSE place these children with adults who had been living in Megève and thereby create the pseudo-families of whom the literature speaks? And, more generally, in creating pseudo-families, whose names were actually used? If the "parents" entered Switzerland using their actual names (or the actual name of one of them), then the child's name appearing on the OSE list would be false. Alternatively, if the "parents" entered Switzerland using the child's last name (and, presumably, bearing false papers that created this new identity), then the child's name appearing on the OSE list would be correct. Examination of information contained in personal dossiers developed and maintained by OSE would probably yield insights into this question. Such dossiers have not been made available for review by researchers or other outside parties. I should also note that the earliest group of families that I identified as including children

listed as "par OSE" on the OSE list was arrested on September 4, in the morning. It consisted of three families and eleven people altogether. None of the families had come from Saint-Gervais or Megève. Names of three of the seven children in the group appear on the OSE list. The practice of creating pseudo-families may only partly explain why the names of children who crossed the border as part of families appear on the OSE list. It is possible that some of these children made the crossing in the company of their own parents. However, I have no explanation as to why the names of children who crossed with their parents would appear on the list. As to the question of whether the practice was also used in Saint-Gervais, I must mention that Eliane Strosberg states on page 5 of her biographical summary, "Isy and Lilly, 1943," that Isy Leuwenkroon, who helped Mila organize and transport family convoys, "fabricated families" in order to maximize the number of adults who would be allowed to remain in Switzerland. The statement does not contradict what I have set forth above. I do not claim to have identified every family convoy that left Saint-Gervais and Megève for Switzerland in August and September 1943. And, indeed, there may very well have been others. Also, it is very possible that individuals living in Saint-Gervais may have helped organize, transport, and/or chaperone family convoys consisting of people who had been living in Megève and vice-versa (i.e., that organizers from Megève may have helped organize, transport, and/or chaperone family convoys consisting of people who had been living in Saint-Gervais).

70 "When a mother of a child of five": Salon, *Trois mois dura notre bonheur*, 99.

70 I estimate that this was equivalent to: www.insee.fr/fr/indicateur/pouvoir_achat.pdf indicates that the purchasing power of a French franc in 1943 was equivalent to about 0.212 Euros in 2008.

70 "the rich pay for two": Salon, *Trois mois dura notre bonheur*, 100. On pages 99–100, Salon states: ". . . we need money: per person, 4,500 francs at the time. Where to find it? Most of the refugees are impoverished; we provide them with allocations. We try to measure out our convoys: the rich pay for two. We will also set priorities: pregnant women (we have five of them seven months or further), households with very young children, then the old people. Our first convoy, fourteen people, is planned for August 21, but those paying slip away and cause it to be aborted. Moreover, this will not be the only time: the poor have nothing to lose, the rich risk fortune and comfort. These setbacks plunge us into disarray; no one can do anything for us. Fortunately—we will never be

able to repeat this often enough—Monsieur Kott, to whom we explain our difficulties, states that he is ready to help us. He already had twenty people leave Saint-Gervais; a team at his side is looking for less costly *passeurs*; they will take some able-bodied young people on foot over the mountain."

70 their request for 180,000 francs: Salon, *Trois mois dura notre bonheur,* 101.

71 the amount that the MJS team paid was substantially below market rates: Paul Grüninger Foundation, "Procès-verbal de l'audience du 2 décembre 1943, à Lausanne Palais de Justice de Montbenon." This document is a judgment against four *passeurs* convicted of illegally passing Jewish children across the border on September 23 and 24, 1943, at Cornières. For each convoy passed, the group of *passeurs* received 5,000 francs. As noted in the text, it appears that the "market rate" was on the order of 4,500 francs per person. An examination of Declarations suggests that it was not uncommon for a family to pay 15,000 to 20,000 francs to a *passeur.*

71 "all seemed to be falling into place": CDJC, OSE(II)-134, "*Rapport sur les événements de 1943,*" written by Armand Rein, August 1944, 11.

71 On September 6, the refugees awaiting evacuation: CDJC, OSE(II)-134, "*Rapport sur les événements de 1943,*" written by Armand Rein, August 1944, 12.

71 In the midst of everything, the refugees learned: CDJC, OSE(II)-134, "*Rapport sur les événements de 1943,*" written by Armand Rein, August 1944, 12.

71 Jacques Charmatz was eight years old: Biographical information on the Charmatz and Emerich families is from the following: an interview held with Jacques Charmatz on September 20, 2008, on the west shore of the Lac du Bourget, near Chambéry; an interview held with Myriam Pupier (née Charmatz) on October 6, 2009, in Saignon, France; and correspondence with Jacques Charmatz, Myriam Pupier, and Claude Emerich. Myriam also furnished me with copies of numerous archival documents, including letters and postcards written by and to her father during the war.

72 They cultivated fields, tended fruit trees: Vielcazat-Petitcol, *Lot-et-Garonne: Terre d'exil,* 335. Chapter III (pages 329–350) gives an excellent overview of La Roche and other ORT farm-schools in the Lot-et-Garonne.

73 On August 25, David was warned by a local policeman: Doulut and Labeau, *Les 473 déportés Juifs de Lot-et-Garonne*, 400.

73 However, on the twenty-sixth or twenty-seventh, local police arrested five: *Les 473 déportés Juifs de Lot-et-Garonne*, 67, 233, 275, 369, 400–401, 429. This work provides profiles of the six boys who were arrested at La Roche in 1942. One of those seized, Moszech (Maurice) Szmidt, was from Poland; the other five (Jacques Bursztyn, Norbert Winter, Erich Mayer, Emmanuel Sigall, and Hans Last) were from Germany. All were deported. Bursztyn, Szmidt, and Last survived; Winter, Mayer, and Sigall perished.

73 "had particularly distinguished himself in hunting down": Private collection of Myriam Pupier, letter written by David Charmartz, dated September 6, 1944, to the Commissaire de la République à Toulouse.

73 David had learned that OSE and the MJS: Of various photographs from the period that have survived, two place David, Jacques, Myriam, and Claude in les Pratz, near the Hôtel Val Joly. One cannot help but wonder if the photos were taken on a day when David met with Mila, Tony, and/or other members of the MJS team who would be responsible for the convoy.

74 "terror and as an exploit": Correspondence with Jacques Charmatz.

74 "Being the oldest in my family": Correspondence with Jacques Charmatz.

74 "a house like a farm": Correspondence with Myriam Pupier.

74 ". . . it was night. We walked with other people": Correspondence with Myriam Pupier.

5. Annecy

Page

75 military trucks: Gorgiel-Secarz, *Memoirs of a Jewish Daughter,* 100.

75 Each truck driver: Gorgiel-Sercarz, *Memoirs of a Jewish Daughter,* 100–101. Hélène Gorgiel-Secarz had managed to place her parents in the "big tourist car" that was at the head of the convoy. When the convoy arrived in Nice and the vehicles went to their assigned hotels, she did not know where or how to find her parents. She writes: "Another fellow was in the same position as myself and together we ran to the center of 'Dubouchage' street and there we got some names of hotels where maybe we could find the travelers on the bus. After asking at several hotels, we finally found our respective parents in a big luxurious hotel . . ."

75 The rail cars were a different matter: Exactly why the train was delayed is not known. CDJC, OSE(II)-134, "*Rapport sur les événements de 1943,*" written by Armand Rein in August 1944, maintains a journalistic style and dispassionate tone. In only one instance does the author criticize the actions of an individual (page 13): "Before ending this report, I will yet mention the fate reserved for 240 people, pregnant women, old people, the sick, and children who left with the rail convoy that was put at their disposal. I emphasize first of all the malevolence of the Station Master of Fayet, who found all excuses possible to delay the departure of the train. He did not give the order to leave until the next day, even though the armistice had already been disclosed. As he had had it connected to a freight train, the convoy took eight hours to arrive in Chambéry."

75 Historians have called the timing of the announcement premature: Marrus and Paxton are one example. See *Vichy France and the Jews,* 320.

75 given the way that events unfolded: Agarossi, *A Nation Collapses: The Italian Surrender of September 1943,* provides an excellent account of events.

76 Heinz Röthke, the head of the Judenreferat, had issued a directive: An English translation of the full text of this communication is reproduced in Poliakov and Sabille, *Jews Under the Italian Occupation,* 119–122.

76 had spent a great deal of time pressuring Vichy officials: A law that went into effect on August 10, 1927, reduced the residency requirement from ten years to three years.

76 legality would no longer be an issue: Marrus and Paxton, *Vichy France and the Jews*, 321–329, presents an excellent discussion of the denaturalization issue in France. Of Laval's refusal to sign and enact the legislation, the authors state (page 325), "For the first time in the history of the Final Solution in France, Laval had said No." They attribute the about-face mainly to the "changed texture in Vichy's relationship to the Germans," resulting from the fact that it began to seem less certain that Germany would win the war (page 326). What is interesting about the subject of denaturalization is that, until the fall of 1943, the Nazis more or less adhered to the distinction that French officials maintained between Jews who held French citizenship and those who did not, and they refrained from targeting the former for arrest and deportation. Of course, although this distinction provided a measure of protection for those who held citizenship, it was far from absolute. Whomever the authorities decided met their racial criteria could be swept away in a roundup and sent to Drancy; and it was extremely difficult to gain the release of one ensnared in the machinery of deportation. Nevertheless, this distinction does not seem to have existed in other countries where the Final Solution was carried out. It existed in France because, up until the fall of 1943, the Germans relied on the French police to carry out the arrest and deportation of Jews. German officials worried that they would provoke widespread adverse reaction on the part of the police and the French public in general were they to order the seizure of those regarded as "*Israëlites*" rather than "*juifs*." This was why the Germans began using manpower resources under their direct control rather than the French police to arrest and deport all Jews, regardless of citizenship status.

76 "to prevent the Jews from escaping": Poliakov and Sabille, *Jews Under the Italian Occupation*, 120–121.

77 his fondness for psychological manipulation and inventive ruses: In *Nice: Hotel Excelsior*, 55, Klarsfeld writes: ". . . Brunner goes to Berlin, where he takes an active part in the massive deportation to the East of the Berlinese Jews. Accustomed to working with the Central Organization of Austrian Jews, he introduces to Berlin the method of individual summons ordering Jews to go to such and such assembly point before being deported to the East, supposedly to work there; in the same way does he break new ground with members of the Jewish 'command service,' who assist in the organization of transports and eventually accompany the Jews as far as their assembly point in order to avoid panic and disorder. Brunner looks to send off the deportees with the least amount of problems possible for

the Gestapo. As a ruse, he assures them by giving them back detailed receipts for their suitcases and the conversion of their German money to Polish zlotys."

77 annihilating the largest Sephardic Jewish community in the world: Various sources chronicle the swift, tragic destruction of the Jewish community of Salonika. Mazower, *Salonica*, 399–411, provides a succinct and excellent account.

77 His first assignment was to transfer jurisdiction of the Drancy transit camp: Of the transfer, Marrus and Paxton, *Vichy France and the Jews*, 330, states: "Vichy thereby lost control of the key point in the administrative network of deportation. Thereafter, the French police and bureaucracy were excluded from any influence on the composition of convoys to the east." Poznanski, *Jews in France*, 314–321, also provides an extensive discussion of changes implemented in Drancy under Brunner's command.

77 "SEC [Sections d'Enquête et Contrôle], the Doriotists": Marrus and Paxton, *Vichy France and the Jews*, 330. The authors refer to the SEC as the "anti-Jewish police squad" (page 268) and as the "the para-police organization of the CGQJ [Commissariat général aux questions juives]" (296).

77 "purging the region [of the former Italian Occupation Zone] of Jews": Carpi, *Between Mussolini and Hitler*, 188.

78 The Rue Amelot Committee was among the most important: Few English language sources discuss the work of the Rue Amelot Committee at length. An exception is Adler, *The Jews of Paris and the Final Solution*. French language books written specifically on the subject include: Jacoubovitch, *Rue Amelot: Aide et résistance*; and Baldran and Bochurberg, *David Rapoport: "La Mère et l'enfant", 36 rue Amelot*.

78 fifty-eight children who had been in the care of the Rue Amelot Committee were "evacuated" to Switzerland: Jacoubovitch, *Rue Amelot: Aide et résistance*, 95.

78 he credits "Simon Lévit [sic] and Madame Marcel": Jacoubovitch, *Rue Amelot: Aide et résistance*, 95.

79 Corps des gardes-frontière: The Swiss border guards comprise part of the Administration fédérale des douanes, the Federal Customs Administration, itself a part of the Federal Department of Finance.

79 the report was organized to solicit information: The actual data fields are as follows: (1) civil status: last name, first name, date of birth, nationality, "race and religion," profession, domicile; (2) papers; (3) military situation; (4) domicile before the war; (5) itinerary followed; (6) arrest: date, hour, place, by whom, how and where the crossing occurred, whether a *passeur* was used, under what conditions the crossing occurred, whether the individual was alone or part of a group, and, if part of a group, the number of persons in the group; (7) cause of flight; (8) means of support in Switzerland; (9) health status; (10) immediate family members in Switzerland, including name and address; (11) close relations with Switzerland, including former stays; (12) miscellaneous observations; (13) data on other family members arrested along with the forenamed individual: first and last name, date of birth, profession, relationship; and (14) decision made regarding the immediate disposition of the case.

79 cross-referenced in the alphabetical card index: The numerical classification system was used between July 1942 and December 1945. Between the end of 1939 and 1942, an alphabetical classification system was used.

83 served little purpose: Flückiger and Bagnoud, *Les réfugiés civils et la frontière genevoise*, 9.

83 "Although most of the cantons responded negatively": Flückiger and Bagnoud, *Les réfugiés civils et la frontière genevoise*, 9.

83 No definitive analysis: For a brief overview of this issue, see the Preface by Serge Klarsfeld to Fivaz-Silbermann, *La refoulement de réfugiés civils juifs*.

83 documenting the nature of the collection: In addition to the report cited above (Flückiger and Bagnoud, *Les réfugiés civils et la frontière genevoise*), Archives d'État de Genève, *Le passage de la frontière durant la Seconde Guerre mondiale: Sources et méthodes* provides a wealth of information on the subject.

84 Alliance israélite universelle: The Alliance, as it is generally called, is a prominent French Jewish educational and cultural institution, founded one hundred fifty years ago in the liberal tradition. It operates schools in France, Spain, Belgium, Israel, and Morocco. Its library, established in 1860 and now one of the largest Jewish libraries in Europe, is dedicated to preserving documentation on the Jewish presence in France. The Alliance website did, at one time, contain this interesting historical

note: "In 1940, shortly after the fall of Paris, the Nazis laid siege to the building, moving several hundred cases of books, archives, manuscripts, and periodicals to the Research Institute on the Jewish Question in Frankfurt. At this location, a fantastic collection of Jewish books stolen from all over Europe was assembled while the Nazis implemented their systematic massacres. During the Liberation, in Offenbach, American troops gathered all the books, precious objects, and documents stolen by the Nazis while European libraries tried to recuperate their stolen goods. Among the books that came back from Germany, many had the indelible mark of the German institute." twenty-seven-page list entitled *"Liste des enfants partis en Suisse en 1943–1944"*: CDJC, OSE (II)-307, dated June 1, 1945.

88 errors and omissions: The convoy of August 17 provides a good example of this. When I interviewed Sonia Constant (née Veissid), she was quite certain that the group with whom she had crossed the border on August 17 was comprised of eleven children, although only ten could be identified on the OSE list. Data contained in the Geneva archives confirmed that the convoy did, in fact, contain eleven children. Although the name of Cécile Gostynski appears on the OSE list, the name of her sister, Sarah, does not.

88 When the sun rose on the morning of September 9: The account of events cited here is from CDJC, OSE(II)-134, *"Rapport sur les événements de 1943,"* written by Armand Rein, August 1944, 13–14. Grandjacques, *La montagne refuge,* 246–248, provides further information on what happened to the refugees once they left Saint-Gervais. He states that, once they reached Rome, they received asistance from the Jewish aid organization DELASEM (Delegazione per l'Assistenza degli Emigranti Ebrei, meaning Delegation for the Assistance of Jewish Emigrants).

88 "We didn't sleep much that night": Gorgiel-Sercarz, *Memoirs of a Jewish Daughter,* 101.

89 "inseparable adjutant": Rayski, *The Choice of the Jews Under Vichy,* 201.

89 By the middle of the afternoon: CDJC, CCCLXVI-64, unsigned report entitled *"Nice,"* dated December 20, 1943, 1. The author pinpoints the time that it began: "15h 30." Poznanski, *Jews in France,* 561, note 206, states that the report "was obviously written by a young member of the AJ, probably Henri Pohorylès."

89 "Immediately upon arriving in Nice": CDJC, CCXVIII-88G, deposition given by Antonio Aniante on July 11, 1945, 1. In the deposition, Aniante describes the scene at the Italian Consulate as refugees frantically tried to obtain documents that would permit them to enter Italy: "The same evening that the Germans arrived, the Hotel Continental, the headquarters of the consulate, was literally taken by storm by an Israelite crowd that, seized with panic, was asking for any document that would enable them to go to Italy through unauthorized border crossings. To this crowd of Israelites had joined many other co-religionists who, having no documents, needed to regularize their situation toward the French authorities at the border posts. The employees of the consulate worked late into the night in order to place visas on hundreds of passports and to distribute certificates with Italian names to those who, not having papers, would have been able to try their luck in [finding a *planche de*] *salut* in Badoglio's Italy." (A "*planche de salut*" is a plank thrown to a shipwrecked person to cling to so as not to drown.)

89 what happened to them is far from clear: Marrus and Paxton, *Vichy France and the Jews*, 320, states that Jean Chaigneau, appointed Prefect of the Alpes-Maritimes in May 1943 to replace the ardent Pétainist Marcel Ribière, was sympathetic to the Jews and "destroyed the lists of Jews at his prefecture." Carpi, *Between Hitler and Mussolini*, 188, states, "Chaigneau had made certain of burning the lists in good time, and Spechel claimed he had long since transferred all the documentary material of the consulate to Rome (which in fact had been done)." In regard to the former part of the statement, he cites Marrus and Paxton, and, in regard to the latter part (i.e. the transfer of documentary material to Rome), he cites Klarsfeld, *Vichy-Auschwitz: Le rôle de Vichy*, 116–119. (Those pages correspond to *Vichy-Auschwitz: La "solution finale,"* 302-305.) On 116, Klarsfeld quotes excerpts of the statement made by Antonio Aniante cited here. However, he omits the sentence that reads, "In reality, these dossiers were already partly burned, partly hidden and those remaining were still in the archives of the Consulate." Carpi also claims that one would assume that the Italian Consulate only kept lists of Jews with Italian citizenship and that lists of other Jews should have been at the headquarters of the Race Police (188). He says that Angelo Donati stated in a written declaration made in 1946 that Lospinoso had taken care to burn all the lists and records he had before leaving France. As Carpi explains on page 304, note 58, Donati made the declaration in defense of Lospinoso, who appealed his conviction of having collaborated with the Fascist Republican government and having sworn allegiance to it.

He also remarks that Donati would not have seen Lospinoso destroy any lists, as he (Donati) had left Nice prior to the time that the lists were supposedly burned. Poznanski, *Jews in France*, 391, states, "Prefect Chaigneau claimed he had turned all such lists over to the Italians, while Lospinoso, before clearing out of his offices, had burned the ones he had drawn up." No source is cited. None of the sources I have consulted have referred to the reappearance of any such lists after the end of the war, a fact that would suggest that whatever existed was probably destroyed.

90 "In response to your letter dated the tenth": USHMM, Record Group 43.084M, Selected Records of the Departmental Archives of the Haute-Savoie, 1940–1961," Reel 4, 1490. Letter from S. Trémeaud, Prefect of the Haute-Savoie, to Monsieur le Chef de l'État-Major allemand de liaison (Chief of the German liaison headquarters) in Annecy, dated September 13, 1943. The German officer's letter does not refer to concentration camps but to internment camps. The Prefect's letter does not refer to internment camps but highlights the term concentration camps by putting it in the subject line and subsequently repeating it.

90 Bella Wendling: Scant biographical information is available about Bella Wendling. Some information appears in ARJF, *Organisation juive de combat*, 153–154. In 1943, Bella was not married, and Wendling was her maiden name. She later married Ado Michaeli, also a member of the MJS. In the literature, she is referred to as either Bella Michaeli or Bella Wendling. To the best that I can determine, she left behind no written or oral testimony or memoir.

91 Madame Baudet and her daughter, Violette Crotti: Croquet, *Chemins de passage*, 42.

93 a nearby vocational center: Vulliez, *Camille Folliet*, 52. Vulliez notes that this was located at number 12 on the rue Filaterie.

94 "picture of French Catholicism": Vulliez, *Camille Folliet*, 69.

94 He developed a support network of individuals: In addition to the institutions cited in the text, Yagil, *Chrétiens et Juifs sous Vichy*, 174, note 3, mentions that girls were sometimes housed in the Orphanage Sacré-Coeur on the rue Berthollet, run by the Sisters of Charity. The name of the individual who was in charge of the orphanage is unknown.

94–95 Members of the Protestant CIMADE: Fabre (ed.), *God's Underground*, is an excellent source on the work of CIMADE during the war and contains accounts written by Geneviève Priacel-Pittet and Suzanne Loiseau-Chevalley.

95 Vichy authorities knew: Kedward, *In Search of the Maquis*, 26.

95 "But during April [1943], out of a period of": Kedward, *In Search of the Maquis*, 29.

95 Kedward explains that "*maquis*": Kedward, *In Search of the Maquis*, 29–30.

97 The love story of Sacha Racine and Maurice Maidenberg: Interview with Sacha Maidenberg (née Racine).

6. Nice

Page

101 with the help of a guidebook: For example, Bodénès, *Promenades sur la frontière Franco-Genevoise.*

101 One can also find maps of the border area: Maps showing *borne* numbers include: the series Carte Nationale de la Suisse, 1:25000 scale, published by the Office fédéral de topographie (Sections 1281, 1300, and 1301); and Genève, Annemasse, Le Léman, 1:25000, published by the Institut géographique national (3429 OT).

102 It appears that the group was assembled: There is a high degree of consistency in the information cited in Declarations signed by children in this convoy regarding the circumstances of the convoy—that is, that the children had been living in Paris and that they were assembled as a group in Paris and then brought to the border. As noted previously, one cannot assume that information contained in the Declarations is entirely accurate. The recollections of Eliane Suerinck (née Neoussikhin) and Victor Graimont (formerly Grabsztok) conform with the key pieces of information cited here about the convoy.

102 Eliane Neoussikhin was an only child: Biographical information on the Neoussikhin family contained here is from an interview held with Eliane Suerinck (née Neoussikhin) on September 20, 2008, in Lyon and from correspondence.

103 He remained a German prisoner: Eliane's father was liberated by the Russian army and returned to France at the end of 1945.

105 Victor Grabsztok was the only child: Information presented here is from my correspondence with Victor Graimont (Grabsztok), in particular a two-page letter received November 11, 2008, and a three-page memoir received January 26, 2009.

106 "not to talk, not to cough,": Letter from Victor Graimont (Grabsztok) to N. Lefenfeld, received November 11, 2008.

106 In a contemporaneous report on the situation in Nice: CDJC, CCCLXVI-64, unsigned report entitled *"Nice,"* dated December 20, 1943, 1. My reading of primary and secondary sources suggests that, despite its brevity, this listing is accurate and essentially complete. There are many eyewitness accounts (contemporaneous reports and letters as well as testimonies

prepared after the events) that speak of how the Germans, aided by local collaborators, carried out raids in Nice, arresting, brutalizing, and torturing Jews, resisters, and others deemed undesirable. Excerpts from some have been reproduced in several of the texts cited here.

107 "systematically hunted down the rich Jews": The term used here is *"dépouiller,"* which means to strip or skin. The author of this summary report does not explain precisely how the so-called "false Gestapo" operated. The report does say that some of these individuals were executed for not having respected the *"clause financière"* (the financial clause). Denunciators were paid by the Gestapo to hunt down and identify Jews. The implication in this report is that the "financial clause" was part of the agreement entered into between the "real Gestapo" and denunciators, prohibiting the latter from from despoiling their prey. The report seems to lump together all denunciators under the heading of "false Gestapo." It seems likely to me that the author simply did not take the time to clarify the actual use of this term. The term itself suggests that some denunciators posed as members of the Gestapo who promised to release Jews that they captured in exchange for money, jewelry, etc.

107 *"And the persecution began in forms"*: CDJC, CCCLXVI-64, unsigned report entitled *"Nice,"* dated December 20, 1943, 1.

107 information supplied by collaborators and informers: It is important to stress that, although Brunner's commando team relied heavily on information supplied by collaborators and informers, the majority of the population in Nice did not actively assist the Germans as they conducted the manhunt. Indeed, many actively aided Jews, helping them to secure hiding places or to leave the city. The literature indicates that many of the collaborators and informers were associated with the Milice or the Parti populaire français (PPF; French Populist Party). Some informers were lured by the promise of bounty money, which was initially set at 100 francs per Jew but was subsequently raised. Zuccotti, *The Holocaust, the French, and the Jews,* 183, states, "That reward increased to 1,000—and occasionally 5,000—francs." I have not come across references as to whether the Germans made good on their bounty promises.

107 ". . . Brunner recruited paid informers": Pozanaski, *Jews in France,* 391.

108 "indignant" (his word) letter: Klarsfeld, *Vichy-Auschwitz, La "solution finale,"* 304.

108 "The population is outraged": Klarsfeld, *Vichy-Auschwitz, La "solution finale,"* 305.

108 annex to Drancy: Brunner formally designated the Excelsior the *"camp de recensement des Juifs arrêtés, dépendant du camp du Drancy"* ("camp for the census of arrested Jews, under the control of Drancy"). This designation is quoted in various texts, including, for example, Klarsfeld, *Le calendrier,* 885. I have not been able to identify its origins, however.

108 "We were directed to, and locked up in the Hotel Excelsior": CDJC, CCXVI-66, testimony of Dr. A. Drucker, February 2, 1946, 8.

109 "During the three months that I was detained": CDJC, CCXVI-66, testimony of Dr. A. Drucker, February 2, 1946, 8.

109 "Doctress Spiegel and I were making desperate efforts": CDJC, CCXVI-66, testimony of Dr. A. Drucker, February 2, 1946, 9.

110 ". . . he was still breathing": CDJC, CCXVI-66, testimony of Dr. A. Drucker, February 2, 1946, 9.

110 Brückler, described as "particularly ferocious": CDJC, CCXVI-66, testimony of Dr. A. Drucker, February 2, 1946, 11.

110 "particularly ferocious, fanatical, having seen him strike": CDJC, CCXVI-66, testimony of Dr. A. Drucker, February 2, 1946, 11.

110 Gorbing, described as "elegant, speaking politely": CDJC, CCXVI-66, testimony of Dr. A. Drucker, February 2, 1946, 11.

110 "At the end of this meeting [on September 9]": Carpi, *Between Mussolini and Hitler,* 191.

110 "The almost complete disappearance of the FSJF staff": Lazare, *Rescue as Resistance,* 232.

110 "There had been increasingly urgent calls": Poznanski, *Jews in France,* 391.

110 "The Political Commission then established": Rutkowski, *La lutte des Juifs,* 317. This is document number 217, an extract and translation of CDJC CCXVI-61, testimony of Wolf Toronczyk, in German, dated "end of 1944 or beginning of 1945."

111 "company of theater artists": The efforts of Hélène Gorgiel-Sercarz to find lodging that are recounted here are from *Memoirs of a Jewish Daughter,* 102–106.

112 One source states that OSE officials: Rayski, *The Choice of the Jews under Vichy*, 204.

112 Claude Kelman and Ignace Fink, forced opened the door: Najman and Haymann, *Claude Kelman*, 61. This tragic episode is also briefly described in CDJC, CCCLXVI-64.

113 The Eisenbaum family had arrived: Léa's mother had died when she was six years old, and she came to Paris with her father and brother.

113 The first mass arrest of Jews in France: On May 13, 1941, "green notes," signed by the police chief, were delivered to approximately 6,700 adult males requiring them to report to various locations, bearing their identity papers, for a review of their legal status. Approximately 3,700 persons responded to the summons. All or nearly all were arrested and interned in Pithiviers and Beaune-la-Rolande, two internment camps located near one another in the department of the Loiret. By the end of the year, approximately nine thousand Jews had been brought there. Poznanski, *Jews in France*, 56–61, provides a particularly good discussion of the first roundup and the conditions in these two camps in 1941.

114 the young MJS members: It is sometimes hard to remember how just how young the members of the MJS were. ARJF, *Organisation juive de combat*, 117–167, presents brief synopses pertaining to seventy-four MJS members of various *gdoudim* who were actively engaged in rescue activities during the war. (In addition to the seventy-four listed, the organization had members who did not participate in rescue activities.) In most (82%) of the cases, data are included on the rescuer's date of birth. Birth date information is included for twenty-nine of the thirty-two men profiled, and it indicates that the average age was 22. Eight of the twenty-nine (28%) were between the ages of 15 and 19, and twenty-four (83%) were below the age of 25. Overall, the women were even younger. Age data presented for thirty-two of forty-one women profiled indicate that the average age was 21 years. Astonishingly, twenty-two (69%) were between the ages of 15 and 19. All but three of the women (91%) were below the age of 25.

114 helped recruitment efforts: ARJF, *Organisation juive de combat*, 118, states that "the Nice *gdoud*, under the direction of Jacques Weintrob (also a member of the AJ), brought together more than 150 members." The statement appears in the introduction to the section on the MJS prepared by Tsilla Hersco with the concurrence of MJS leaders Otto Giniewski (today, Eytan Guinat) and Georges Schnek.

114 "In Grenoble and Nice in particular": Lazare, *Rescue as Resistance,* 233. Carpi, *Between Mussolini and Hitler,* 191, makes the point as well: "The main activities within the Jewish community from then on were conducted by active members of the Jewish underground." Carpi adds, on page 306, note 75: "The operation was first directed by Claude Gutmann and Jacques Weintraub . . ."

114 "circulated among the hotels to unearth unfortunates": Lazare, *Rescue as Resistance,* 233.

114 In early 1943, the Sixième had set up a laboratory: I do not know when this laboratory was first put into operation. ARJF, *Organisation juive de combat,* 302, mentions that, between May and September 1943, Raymond Heymann assisted Maurice Loebenberg in the laboratory.

114 The group included activists who identified: Information cited here on group identity by individual corresponds to that contained in the database of *résistants* maintained by Mémorial de la Shoah Musée/ Centre de documentation juive contemporaine, which can be accessed at www.memorialdelashoah.org Also see Anciens de la Résistance juive en France (ARJF), *Organisation juive de combat: Résistance/sauvetage France 1940–1945.*

114 Maurice Loebenberg: He is often referred to by his alias, Maurice Cachoud.

115 Léa found Jewish families in hiding, met with them: This information was provided to me by Jacques and Léa's daughter, Miriam Brinbaum, who, in 2006, kindly queried her mother on my behalf on the subject of the children's convoys. Léa recalled that one of the families with whom she met accused her of being worse than the Nazis because, they argued, at least the Nazis kept parents and children together.

115 Who supplied the funds necessary: Lazare, *Rescue as Resistance,* 233, refers to "funds provided by the FSJF and the UGIF and money raised by Raymond Heymann from individuals (more than 380,000 francs in three months)." This reference is not specific to funds that would have been required for the smuggling of children into Switzerland. Rather, it refers to the various underground rescue activities carried out by members of the MJS and the Sixième. Heymann was a member of the Sixième. Further, Lazare notes, "Of the FSJF, only Claude Kelman and four young social workers remained" (232). And, he later adds that Kelman was "[S] hort of personnel but able to use the FSJF assistance funds . . ." (233).

115 Frida Wattenberg: Wattenberg, born in Paris in 1924, had remained there until the summer of 1943, when her underground activities rendered her "*recherchée*" (sought after). She left Paris in July and went to Megève. A few days after arriving in Megève, walking by the open window of a villa, she heard a group of children singing a familiar refrain: "*Hee-nay ma-tov u-ma nah-yeem, Sheh-vet achim gam yah-chad.*" (The lyrics of this popular Jewish song are from the opening of Psalm 133, as follows: "Behold, how good and how pleasant it is for brethren to dwell together in unity!") She introduced herself to Sacha Racine and Maurice Maidenberg, who were leading the group in song. Sacha immediately recruited Frida for the MJS. Frida joined the Grenoble *gdoud*. She was soon called upon to accompany groups of children from place to place. At times, she was also asked to smuggle sums of money from one Jewish rescue organization to another. Frida Wattenberg is one of the authors of ARJF, *Organisation juive de combat*. The information about her cited here is from an interview that I held with her on July 20, 2000, in Paris.

115 sheltered in the Lycée Berthollet: Some Declarations signed by children in the convoys specifically mention the Lycée Berthollet. This does not necessarily mean that the children actually stayed there. It is possible that the children were specifically given this name, in lieu of the actual name, so as to mislead authorities. Munos-du Peloux, *Passer en Suisse*, contains an interesting notation on this. On page 44, she quotes a statement in the Gryn testimony, which she mistakenly cites as CDJC, DLXI-16 and is actually CDJC, DLXI-35: "Because of her [Rolande Birgy], I was able to transform the refectory of the *lycée* [secondary school] of Annecy into a reception center: we often had thirty kids who were sleeping there." (Page numbering of the testimony is a bit difficult to understand; the quotation cited appears in the first section, on the fourth page.) Based on her interview with Rolande Birgy in 1983, Munos-du Peloux follows the Gryn statement with her own: "Rolande Birgy specifically stated to me that this lycée was, in fact, the private college of Saint-Michel where Father Pluot is in collusion with them."

116 André was born in Paris: Biographical information regarding the Panczer family is mainly from his memoir, *Je suis né dans l'faubourg Saint-Denis. . .* I also relied on information obtained in an interview with André held on September 12, 2008, in Paris, and from discussions and correspondence held between 2008 and 2012.

116 "the grandmother of every member of the family": Panczer, *Je suis né dans l'faubourg Saint-Denis. . .*, 13.

116 "man in gabardine": Panczer, *Je suis né dans l'faubourg Saint-Denis. . .*, 24.

116 "We were happy in Prayssac," Panczer, *Je suis né dans l'faubourg Saint-Denis. . .*, 34.

116 at a neighbor's farm: the farm belonged to the family of Maurice and Fernande Bouges. Panczer, *Je suis né dans l'faubourg Saint-Denis. . .*, 28.

117 The secretary of the mayor: Panczer, *Je suis né dans l'faubourg Saint-Denis. . .*, 34–35.

117 foreign labor battalion: The law of September 27, 1940, authorized the departmental prefects to assign to forced labor units (Groupements de travailleurs étrangers) able-bodied male foreigners between fifteen and fifty-five years old who were deemed "superfluous to the national economy." Zuccotti, *The Holocaust, the French, and the Jews*, 76: "Estimated at as many as 60,000 at the end of July, 1941, these workers at first were primarily refugees from the Spanish Civil War, demobilized foreign volunteers in the French army and the Foreign Legion, and male enemy nationals arrested in the autumn of 1939 and May 1940. Their ranks were later swollen by foreigners, both Jewish and non-Jewish, arrested by Vichy police in late 1940 and 1941 . . ." Marrus and Paxton, *Vichy France and the Jews*, 171, states that a CGQJ note written in 1941 estimates that twenty thousand of sixty thousand GTE workers were Jews and most of the rest were Spanish refugees. Zucotti notes that each forced labor unit consisted of about two hundred fifty men. "Companies were initially organized on the basis of nationality, but the separation of 'Aryans' and 'non-Aryans' within units became increasingly formal and rigid until actual 'Palestinian companies' appeared." The units performed a variety of types of manual labor, performing construction work, agricultural work, mining, and industrial production. Living conditions were extremely harsh and discipline severe.

117 "paradisiacal place,": Panczer, *Je suis né dans l'faubourg Saint-Denis. . .*, 38.

117 "did not separate themselves from one another": Panczer, *Je suis né dans l'faubourg Saint-Denis. . .*, 36.

117 "At certain times, the whole hotel": Panczer, *Je suis né dans l'faubourg Saint-Denis. . .*, 37.

117 "At eight years old, you are a big boy": Panczer, *Je suis né dans l'faubourg Saint-Denis. . .*, 39.

118 "I remained there, nose against the display case": Panczer, *Je suis né dans l'faubourg Saint-Denis. . .*, 40.

119 The Declaration signed by Albert Reisz: Archives d'État de Genève, Justice et Police, dossier #4947. As noted earlier, the age limit for boys was sixteen and for girls, eighteen. Although eighteen, Albert Reisz was not turned back. From time to time, the children convoys would include a boy or girl who surpassed the age limit provided they appeared to be younger. To the best that I can determine, if a child appeared to the Swiss border guards to be beneath the age limit and thus was not turned back immediately (i.e., at the border), he or she would typically be allowed to remain in Switzerland even if his or her actual age were later revealed.

120 "undeserving of Swiss hospitality": Fivaz-Silbermann, *Le refoulement de réfugiés civils juifs*, 97. In this source, the phrase appears in quotation marks, indicating that Fivaz-Silbermann is citing the term that appears in a disciplinary measure prepared by Swiss authorities at the time of Wolczak's explusion. As noted in the text, the dossier of Rosette Wolczak (Archives d'État de Genève, Justice et Police, #4928) is not available for review. All information cited here about this tragic case is from the Fivaz-Silbermann text, 97–98.

120 Wolf Wapniarz was the oldest of five children: Biographical information on the Wapniarz family is from an interview held by the author with Wolfi on September 12, 2008, in Paris, and from correspondence.

120 three Communist resisters: The three were: Gilbert Brustlein, Marcel Bourdarias, and Spartaco Guisco. See Gildea, *Marianne in Chains*, 229–245, for an excellent discussion of the topic.

120 Feldkommandant in Nantes: His name was Lieutenant Colonel Karl Hotz.

121 "like a chain": This was Wolfi's description.

122 More than sixty-five years later, on March 2, 2009: Rapport de la Commission de réhabilitation sur son activité pendant les années 2004 à 2008, *Réhabilitation de personnes ayant aidé des fugitifs à fuir les persécutions nazis*. Crivelli is mentioned on page 2925; Pasteur and the Pillet brothers are mentioned on page 2928.

122 On the afternoon of September 25: The account presented here concerning the arrest and detainment of Jacques Wajntrob and Jacques Marburger on September 25, 1943, is a summary of a very detailed account given

by Jacques Marburger in a videotaped oral history interview conducted by Yvette Wirtschafter on December 15, 1993. USHMM, Record Group 50.146*0008, received from the Association Mémoire et Documents on October 25, 1995.

123 Donati developed a secret plan: Excellent discussions of the Donati plan are presented by Carpi in *Between Mussolini and Hitler* and by Zuccotti in *Under His Very Windows.*

124 "WAJNTROB Jankeil, alias WISTER": CDJC, XXXVII-9, Translation (from German to French) of a telegram dated November 18, 1943, signed by SS-Sturmbannführer Muehler, Détachement de la Police de Sûreté de Marseille (Detachment of the Security Police of Marseille) to Section IV, Paris. It is not known why the telegram was not sent until November 18. Also reproduced in Poliakov and Sabille, *Jews Under the Italian Occupation,* 127–128 (Document 37).

7. The Wolf's Plain

Page

127 sending trainloads of Jews to Drancy: Klarsfeld, *Nice: Hotel Excelsior,* 66–108, presents lists of the names of individuals sent from Nice to Drancy between September 17, 1943, and July 30, 1944. Organized chronologically by date of departure from Nice, the lists include the following fields of data: number of convoy in which the individual left Nice, maiden name, date and place of birth, and last known address. By the end of September 1943, 602 people had been sent from Nice to Drancy.

128 The following account is presented in two of his publications: Klarsfeld, *Nice: Hotel Excelsior,* 57–59, and *Vichy – Auschwitz: La "solution finale,"* 305–306.

128 "Two days later, at the Nice train station": Klarsfeld, *Vichy – Auschwitz: La "solution finale,"* 306.

129 Léa Wajntrob, her daughter, Miriam, and her father, Moïse Eisenbaum, crossed illegally: Archives d'État de Genève, Justice et Police, dossier #5041.

129 Incredibly, Henriette and Jankiel Kolodny: Archives d'État de Genève, Justice et Police, dossier #5049.

129 Boba Szer was traveling alone with her one-year-old daughter: Archives d'État de Genève, Justice et Police, dossier #5050.

129 Esther Weinstein was also traveling alone with her seven-month-old son: Archives d'État de Genève, Justice et Police, dossier #5051.

130 On October 5, Gestapo agents arrested Thérèse Lançon: Curé de Douvaine, *Résistance non violente,* 28.

130 Elie Knout-Fixman was the son of Ariane Knout-Fixman: Archives d'État de Genève, Justice et Police, dossier #5074.

130 "The 'transports' of children do not stop growing": Private collection of Tito Gryn, undated Curriculum Vitae written by Nésanel (Tony) Gryn, 5.

132 "Time was running out for us": Bikales (née Bierzonski), *Through the Valley of the Shadow of Death,* 121.

133 "One group of young Jews": Bikales (née Bierzonski), *Through the Valley of the Shadow of Death,* 121–122.

133 A friend of Bronia's had sent her son: Bikales (née Bierzonski) identifies the child as Raymond Finkel. Raymond Finkel entered Switzerland on September 19, 1943, and was taken to the border guard post at Chevran. The archival data indicates that he crossed the border with one other child. Archives d'État de Genève, Justice et Police, dossier #4819.

134 a Resistance leader: The author identifies this man as Henri Confignon. Bikales (née Bierzonski), *Through the Valley of the Shadow of Death*, 123.

134 three of the four first names differ from those cited here: The names of the Rozenberg children appearing on the surviving Rue Amelot lists are Claude, Esther, Jeannette, and Suzanne.

135 his stepdaughter Anne Ischwall: The Declaration states that Anne is Alice's daughter from a previous marriage. Archives d'État de Genève, Justice et Police, dossier #5174.

137 Srul Engiel: In their Declaration, Archives d'État de Genève, Justice et Police, dossier #5257, the family's name is spelled "Engel."

137 "Wait for me a moment; I will return": Lapidus, *Étoiles jaunes dans la France*, 20.

8. Farewell to France

Page

139 Various accounts have been published: For example, Haymann, *Le camp du bout du monde,* 202, and Lapidus, *Étoiles jaunes dans la France,* 20–21.

139 "A light rain was falling on a dozen people": Lazarus, *Juifs au combat,* 59.

139 "I found myself at the Hôtel de France": Lazarus, *Juifs au combat,* 60. The Hôtel de France sits right in the heart of Saint-Julien, at number 6, rue Fernand David, approximately two miles from the place where the convoy was arrested. Today, it has no stars and, in fact, operates as a boardinghouse rather than as a hotel. Nevertheless, I suspect that it looks much the same as it did during the war. In Chapter 6, Nice, I made reference to the fact that some buildings requisitioned by the Gestapo during the Occupation seem permanently cloaked in the gloom of those years. The Hôtel de France in Saint-Julien is one such example. In the middle of the afternoon, its restaurant, the Grand Café de France, is empty except for several men leaning against the bar nursing beers, smoking, and following sports events on the overhead television. On one of my visits, I asked the proprietor if I might see the upper floors of the building. She denied my request; and, moreover, she assured me that there is no truth to the rumor that the Wehrmacht requisitioned the building in 1943.

140 Questioned many years later about this: Lapidus, *Étoiles jaunes dans la France,* 21.

140 The original prison register: Archives of the Ville d'Annemasse. In addition to name and birthdate, the Pax prison register contains other information pertaining to the background of each individual arrested (e.g. place of birth, nationality, last known address) as well as information on place of arrest and place to which he or she was transferred.

140 The Pax prison was generally used for incarceration on a short-term basis: This square, three-story building with a mansard roof exists today and is easily recognizable from old black and white photographs. (See, for example, Croquet, *Chemins de passage,* 76.) I have visited this building several times since 1999. Each time, it has appeared that, except for a retail store on the first floor, the structure was completely vacant and in disrepair. The upper two floors of the building were dark and shuttered; the small dormer protruding from the roof was boarded up. A courtyard in the rear was empty except for some weeds and broken glass. Two windows that would have looked out onto the courtyard were boarded

over. Large double wooden doors were shut tight; they had no handles or knobs. On the right-hand side of the front facade, a small brown plaque with gold letters pays homage to the fifteen hundred persons imprisoned there between January 3, 1943, and August 18, 1944, and lists the names and ages of six of the region's own who are distinguished as martyrs.

140 The mayor of Annemasse was Jean Deffaugt: Two sources of written testimony prepared by Jean Deffaugt exist. The more extensive testimony is CDJC, DLXI-9, dated 1972. Additionally, the Annemasse Archives contains an undated statement entitled *"Comment Furent Sauvés 28 Enfants Israelites de la Deportation et Certainement de la Mort."* Deffaugt endeavored to save Jews whenever he could, although his opportunities were limited and his efforts were not always successful. On May 31, 1944, a convoy of Jewish children led by Marianne Cohn was arrested by German soldiers at the Swiss border. Deffaugt managed to persuade the Gestapo chief in Annemasse at that time, a man by the name of Mayer, to allow the seventeen younger children to be placed in a *colonie de vacances* (children's camp) in Bonne-sur-Menoge. Cohn was taken from the prison and brutally murdered in early July. Shortly thereafter, as the Allies advanced through France, Mayer told Deffaugt that he was preparing to deport the older children. Deffaugt convinced Mayer to turn the children over to him instead of deporting them, and he took them out of Annemasse to a safe location, where they stayed until the Liberation. *"Comment Furent Sauvés . . ."* speaks specifically of what happened to the convoy of May 31, 1944. The more extensive testimony, DLXI-9, speaks of that as well as two other instances where Deffaugt was able to rescue Jews. During Easter Week, 1944, a German border guard brought Deffaugt a little boy (pages 7–8): "Here is a little Jew, he says to me. He had found him near the border, crying for I don't know how long. Without a doubt, the *passeurs* had let him fall behind. This German had brought him to me instead of taking him to the office of the commandant. But he wanted to take him back from me after a few hours. 'Leave him with me,' I said. 'I am going to take care of him.'" The other instance refers to the family "L," arrested at the border and imprisoned in Pax (9). Deffaugt managed to find out that the head of the prison, Broski, was an avid philatelist. Monsieur L. had a collection of stamps from the principality of Monoco, which Deffaugt managed to barter for the family's freedom. Finally, the testimony recounts the instance where Deffaugt tried, unsuccessfully, to save a baby that had been imprisoned along with his mother (8–9). Deffaugt managed to have the baby transferred to the Annemasse Hospital for treatment of a hernia. However, he was unable to convince

Mayer to leave the boy behind at the time that his mother was being deported.

140 resistance network known as the *réseau* Gilbert: Croquet, *Chemins de passage*, 55–59, provides a discussion of the *réseau* Gilbert.

142 in order to bring food and necessities: On his daily visits, he brought food prepared under the auspices of the Centre d'accueil SNCF, the Reception Center of the SNCF, the national railway. The director of the center, Eugène Balthazar, often accompanied Deffaugt inside the prison. Annemassians, passing Deffaugt or Balthazar on the street, would slip them donations to help keep the center going.

142 "In this prison, I functioned as the 'mailbox'": CDJC, DLXI-9, testimony of Jean Deffaugt, dated April 1972, 5.

143 they assisted him in his rescue work: As mentioned in an earlier footnote, Deffaugt saved a very young boy who had apparently been abandoned at the border and who was brought to him by a German border guard. "I took him on my bicycle to the hospital of Annemasse, where I entrusted him to a nurse, Mlle Chapelier." CDJC, DLXI-9, testimony of Jean Deffaugt, dated April 1972, 8.

143 "My dear friends, I am very well": Private collection of Emmanuel (Mola) Racine, letter written by Mila Racine to Sacha Racine, dated October 25, 1943.

144 "My darlings, I just received your parcel": Private collection of Emmanuel (Mola) Racine, letter written by Mila Racine to the Racine family, dated October 25, 1943.

145 a "new interrogation": Lapidus, *Étoiles jaunes dans la France*, 21.

145 "He is a Jew, isn't he?": Lapidus, *Étoiles jaunes dans la France*, 22. About this incident, Haymann, *Le camp du bout du monde*, 203–204, quotes Roland as follows: "They told me afterwards that the *passeur* may have denounced us. The fact is that he himself was not arrested. Curious thing: during the course of one of the interrogations in Annemasse, they showed us his photo, asking us if that was our *passeur*. I responded in the negative, but two days later he arrived. He was arrested, then quickly released. At the time of the arrest at the border, he had apparently taken flight."

145 Simon Lévitte and Mola Racine appeared inside the prison: Lapidus, *Étoiles jaunes dans la France*, 22.

146 Jacques Wajntrob and Arno Klarsfeld: Klarsfeld, *Le mémorial de la déportation.* Jacques Wajntrob's name appears on page 455; Arno Klarsfeld's name appears on page 452. In addition to providing the lists of names of persons deported in each convoy that originated in France during the war, *Le mémorial* provides summaries of available information on such subjects as the following: how and when the convoy was authorized by German officials; departure time; number of cars; total number of persons; number of persons selected for work and number gassed upon arrival at Auschwitz.

146 "My Dear *Haverim* [Friends], Up until now": Private collection of Miriam Brinbaum, letter written by Jacques Wajntrob, undated.

146 "My Dear *Haverim* [Friends], A few words before my departure": Private collection of Miriam Brinbaum, letter written by Jacques Wajntrob, undated.

147 the medieval town of Bar-le-Duc: The town occupies a special place in French history because of the importance of the Bar-le Duc Road during the First World War. The road connected Bar-le-Duc with Verdun. It was impossible for Marshall Pétain, holding back the Germans at Verdun, to use the existing rail lines. He brought troops, munitions, and supplies by truck along the Bar-le-Duc Road. Motorized vehicles had not been relied upon for this purpose prior to that time. After the end of the war, the writer Georges Bernanos called it "La Voie Sacrée," "the Sacred Road," a name still used today.

147 "During the stop, having ascertained": Klarsfeld, *Le calendrier,* 904. Letter dated October 30, 1943, from the Police Commissioner, Office of General Information of Bar-le-Duc, to the Director of General Information at Vichy.

147 "Similar escape attempts": Klarsfeld, *Le calendrier,* 904. Although little has been written on the subject and despite the fact that it seems incredible, prisoners did from time to time manage to escape deportation trains sent from Drancy to Auschwitz. See, for example, Rutkowski, "Les évasions de Juifs de trains" in *Le Monde Juif,* No. 73 (1974): 10–29.

148 "My darlings, I took advantage of an opportunity": Private collection of Emmanuel (Mola) Racine, letter written by Mila Racine to the Racine family, dated November 5, 1943.

148 "All my darlings, What a beautiful vacation I am having here": Private collection of Emmanuel (Mola) Racine, letter written by Mila Racine to the Racine family, dated November 8, 1943.

149 On November 15, Mila and Roland were transferred: Archives of the Ville d'Annemasse, Pax prison register.

149 Tony, "armed with a small revolver": Haymann, *Le camp du bout du monde*, 203.

149 "Tony and Emmanuel [Mola Racine] do not know one another": Haymann, *Le camp du bout du monde*, 203. When I first read this statement years ago, it completely baffled me. Various secondary sources speak of Mola Racine as the head of the *Education physique* network, responsible for overseeing the smuggling of children into Switzerland. They fail to make clear that, although he served in this capacity during the spring of 1944, he was not involved in this network during the summer or fall of 1943. Therefore, he and Tony Gryn would not have known one another when they both boarded the train in November 1943.

149 "brutal change in climate": Lapidus, *Étoiles jaunes dans la France*, 22.

149 "A welcoming committee is waiting for them": Lapidus, *Étoiles jaunes dans la France*, 22.

150 Jean Moulin, De Gaulle's chief envoy: In 1942–43, Moulin had struggled to unite the nascent and fractured Resistance.

150 "My loved ones! I finally have the pleasure of writing to you": Private collection of Emmanuel (Mola) Racine, postcard written by Mila Racine to "Mr & Mme E. Racine," dated November 24, 1943.

151 preprinted form distributed to, and completed by prisoners: Private collection of Emmanuel (Mola) Racine, undated request for items of apparel and toiletries, signed by Mila Racine ("Marie-Anne Racine").

152 *"une sorte de pudeur"*: Gorce, *Journal de Ravensbrück*, 7.

152 *"Dans son esprit, trop de cicatrices"*: Gorce, *Journal de Ravensbrück*, 7.

152 Some have specifically addressed the subject: See, for example, articles contained in: Ofer and Weitzman, eds., *Women in the Holocaust*; Rittner and Roth, eds., *Different Voices*; and Gurewitsch, ed., *Mothers, Sisters, Resisters*.

152 At Ravensbrück, women prisoners formed: Morrison, *Ravensbrück: Everyday Life*, 125.

152 "Feeling drawn to one another": Gorce, *Journal de Ravensbrück,* 11.

152 "I had known Mila in going around Montluc": Private collection of Emmanuel (Mola) Racine, letter written by Nelly Gorce to Emmanuel Racine, dated July 3, 1945.

153 "had readily agreed that the school buildings should serve": Bergier, *Secret Weapons – Secret Agents,* 61.

153 "transfer point, where children were sometimes lodged": Henry, *We Only Know Men,* 72.

153 "come by the school right away": Henry, *We Only Know Men,* 72.

153 "The world in Montluc Prison, according to Frossard": Morgan, *An Uncertain Hour,* 247.

154 "Miane is more reserved": Gorce, *Journal de Ravensbrück,* 12.

154 a woman named Michou: I have not been able to confirm the actual identity of the woman referred to as Michou. I assume that Michou was a nickname, perhaps a diminutive form of Micheline, a popular French name. The woman whom Nelly refers to as Michou was in transport number 287 that departed Compiègne, France, for Ravensbrück on January 30, 1944. A listing of names of prisoners comprising that transport, obtained from the Fondation pour la mémoire de la déportation, includes several named Micheline.

154 "They look like two dolls": Gorce, *Journal de Ravensbrück,* 12.

154 "three days and two nights": Gorce, *Journal de Ravensbrück,* 15.

154 on or around January 26, 1944: On page 10 of the *Journal de Ravensbrück,* Gorce states that the group of five comrades spent only three days at the prison camp in Compiègne. They were deported on January 30 or 31. Working backward, this suggests that the train left the Perrache station in Lyon on or around January 26.

154 "Mila consoled us; she was laughing": Haymann, *Le camp du bout du monde,* 206. The quote is from a letter that Sacha sent to a friend in the United States. The excerpt from the letter begins on page 204. It is difficult to imagine what fortuitous circumstances allowed Sacha and Mola to board the prisoner train and visit with Mila. The excerpt of the letter written by Sacha and presented in *Camp du bout du monde* is consistent with the verbal account that Sacha shared with me in 2000.

155 fifty members of the SS team: Bower, *Klaus Barbie: The Butcher of Lyons,* 39.

155 "That would only come in June 1943": Bower, *Klaus Barbie: The Butcher of Lyons*, 39.

157 "They [the French delegation] had not been told": Shirer, *The Rise and Fall of the Third Reich*, 978. Shirer provides a vivid account of what transpired at Rethondes during the latter part of June 1940, particularly Hitler's reactions as he first observes the memorial.

157 left, unharmed, to oversee a pile of rubble: The *Clairière* was rebuilt after the end of the World War II. The *wagon-lit* was destroyed during an Allied air attack on Berlin; a reproduction was placed at the memorial. The broken pieces of the granite slab were recovered and reinstalled.

157 There was a prison camp in Compiègne: Compiègne was actually subdivided into three sections: one held prisoners of war; a second, French men and women deemed undesirable; and a third, Jews awaiting deportation.

157 its formal name was Frontstalag 122: The term *"frontstalag"* seems to refer to a prisoner of war camp not within the heart of the Reich but at or near the front.

157 "paradisiacal": Gorce, *Journal de Ravensbrück*, 9.

157 "The open air, the varied companionship": Gorce, *Journal de Ravensbrück*, 9–10.

158 it would have meant nothing to them: Survivor testimonies indicate that, when they first approached the camp on foot on the day of their arrival, they saw the name Ravensbrück on a signpost and it meant nothing to them. Gorce, *Journal de Ravensbrück*, 18, and Marzac and Rey Jouenne, *Irma Jouenne*, 41.

158 The size of the group—957: The range of numbers used—27030 to 27988—would suggest that the group comprised 959 women, but the figure of 957 is cited in Fondation pour la mémoire de la déportation, *Livre-mémorial des déportés de France, Volume 1*, various pages.

158 "At that departing roll call": Dufournet, *La maison des mortes*, 20.

158 "courageous revolt of a people": Gorce, *Journal de Ravensbrück*, 11.

158 "We will never know the heroism of our women": Gorce, *Journal de Ravensbrück*, 11. One wonders whether this prognostication reflects what Nelly was actually thinking at the time or what she concluded years later, aware of the role that history accorded—or failed to accord—these

women. It could, of course, reflect both, her early presentiment having been borne out by the passage of time.

159 "A stop, a stop that drags on for one hour": Marzac and Rey Jouenne, *Irma Jouenne,* 41. The accounts of the trip presented in the three memoirs (Gorce, *Journal de Ravensbrück;* Dufournier, *La maison des mortes;* and Marzac and Rey Jouenne, *Irma Jouenne*) correspond with one another quite well. Marzac and Rey Jouenne, *Irma Jouenne,* 42–43, refers to Trier and Aachen by their French names, Trèves and Aix-la-Chapelle.

159 "Germany had just officially taken possession": Gorce, *Journal de Ravensbrück,* 14.

159 "I will be transferred to another camp": Private collection of Emmanuel (Mola) Racine, postcard written by Mila Racine to the Racine family, dated January 30, 1944.

159 "My darlings, We leave today for Germany": Private collection of Emmanuel (Mola) Racine, postcard written by Mila Racine to the Racine family, dated January 30, 1944.

9. Borders

Page

161 "an organization of the Red Cross": Dufournier, *La maison des mortes*, 23.

161 "And the train keeps on rolling": Gorce, *Journal de Ravensbrück*, 16.

161 The landscape was pleasant: Gorce, *Journal de Ravensbrück*, 18, refers to it as the "*paysage de rêve*" ("landscape of a dream").

161 "The soil was sandy": Dufournier, *La maison des mortes*, 24.

162 the northern perimeter of a lake named Schwedtsee: The Schwedtsee is one of three lakes on which the town of Fürstenberg is situated, the other two being the Röblinsee and the Baalensee. The whole region is dotted with lakes, interconnected via rivers and canals. Whereas one would have likely seen coal barges navigating the waterways during the war, yachts and luxury touring barges are more likely sights today.

162 male prisoners from the nearby Sachsenhausen camp: Construction work did not end after the camp was opened in 1939. For a time, the SS relied on men brought in from Sachsenhausen to carry out the work. In 1941, seeing as there was no end in sight to the construction projects to be undertaken, it was decided that a permanent men's camp would be built adjacent to the women's camp. Twenty thousand prisoners would pass through this men's camp between 1941 and 1945.

162 The initial capacity of the camp: Saidel, *The Jewish Women of Ravensbrück*, 17, and Herbermann, *The Blessed Abyss*, 28. A good description of the layout of the block is presented in Morrison, *Ravensbrück: Everyday Life*, 17. A small drawing of the layout and elevation of the block from Audoul, *Ravensbrück: 15,000 Femmes en Enfer* is reproduced there. Morrison's figures on the number of blocks and the initial capacity of the camp differ somewhat from that stated by Saidel and implied by Elizabeth and Hester Baer in their introduction to the Herbermann memoir. On page 16, Morrison refers to twenty barracks having been built at the outset, each designed to accommodate two hundred prisoners, yielding an initial capacity of about four thousand. Regardless of this seeming discrepancy, sources concur on key facts: from the time that the camp opened, the inmate population grew at an unrelenting pace; construction projects were continually carried out to expand the capacity of the camp and exploit the available slave labor; and the overcrowding of camp facilities was clearly evidenced by early 1942 and became much more acute until early 1945.

162 "primarily German women": Herbermann, *The Blessed Abyss,* 28.

162 "organized and orderly": Saidel, *The Jewish Women of Ravensbrück,* 16.

162 The death rate was relatively low: Margarete Buber-Neumann was brought to Ravensbrück in August 1940. Her first husband was the son of Martin Buber; her second was Heinz Neumann, a leader of the German Communist party. In her memoir, *Under Two Dictators,* 211, Buber-Neumann states that forty-seven prisoners died in Ravensbrück in 1940. In that year, the number of inmates was approximately four thousand, and thus the death rate was slightly more than 1 percent.

162 The number of prisoners recorded during roll call: Tillion, *Ravensbrück: Eyewitness Account,* English translation of Second Edition, 244. This work is a meticulously detailed eyewitness account that also presents detailed investigation and analysis conducted after the end of the war. Tillion arrived at Ravensbrück at the end of October 1943. She made it her business to observe and analyze the structure and operation of the camp as completely as possible. She also surreptitiously recorded key pieces of information, despite the fact that such practice was dangerous. She notes that the number of prisoners recorded during roll call in January 1944 was 17,300. The section entitled "Chronology" (240–245) provides a good overview of the evolution of the camp between 1939 and 1945. Tillion also had a special interest in the convoy of the twenty-seven thousands—her mother, Madame Émilie Tillion, was one of them. Each of the three editions of *Ravensbruck* includes an analysis that she conducted of that particular convoy.

163 ". . . during the three years from May 1939 to May 1942": Tillion, *Ravensbrück, Eyewitness Account,* English translation of Second Edition, 17.

163 a "mini-empire" of subcamps: Morrison, *Ravensbrück: Everyday Life,* 206–222, provides an excellent discussion of the "mini-empire" of subcamps that "stretched from Königsberg to Hamburg and from the Baltic to Bavaria" (page 207). Factory overseers regularly came to Ravensbrück to select prisoners whom they judged to be the healthiest and best suited for the work. These groups of women were sent to work at the subcamps for varying lengths of time. In some, conditions were better than those at the main camp; in others, worse.

164 Organized in *Kolonnen*: The singular form of the word is "*Kolonne.*" In memoirs written by French survivors, the word "*colonne*" is used.

164 "the perfect incubator for typhus": Morrison, *Ravensbrück: Everyday Life,* 249. Typhus is an acute, infectious disease characterized by headache, high fever, and skin rash. It can be fatal to people with weakened immune systems. The disease is transmitted to humans by lice, fleas, and mites that carry any of several species of the bacteria Rickettsia.

164 Tuberculosis, acute and highly communicable: Tuberculosis is an acute, infectious disease caused by a bacterium (*Mycobacterium tuberculosis*). It is characterized by small lesions, called tubercles, on the lungs and others parts of the body; and its outward symptoms are cough, fever, shortness of breath, weight loss, and chest pain. "TB," also called "consumption," was a dreaded and deadly disease.

164 The problem of dysentery: Dysentery is an inflammatory disorder of the lower intestinal tract characterized by pain, fever, and diarrhea and often accompanied by the passage of blood and mucus. It is caused by a bacterial, parasitic, or protozoan infection.

165 The Asocials (black triangles) group was extremely diverse: Morrison, *Ravensbrück: Everyday Life,* 43–46, provides a good discussion about the women to whom this ignoble label was applied. He states (pages 43–44): "The National Socialist state never legally nor clearly defined what was meant by 'Asocial,' although a decree of 14 October 1937 approached the issue in a general way by noting: 'Asocials are those who do not fit into the community, even if they are not criminally inclined . . . . '" He further makes the point (pages 40–41) that some women who had engaged in activities clearly defined as criminal in nature were categorized as Asocials rather than as Criminals. This was typically the case in terms of prostitutes. It was also the case in terms of Aryan women who had obtained or sought abortions. Abortion was illegal in Germany before 1933, but enforcement of laws governing it had been lax. Immediately after coming to power, the Nazis cracked down on Aryan women seeking abortions. As Gisela Bocks explains, "Nazi pronatalism for desirable births and its antinatalism for undesirable ones were tightly connected." See her essay "Racism and Sexism in Nazi Germany: Motherhood, Compulsory Sterilization, and the State," in Rittner and Roth (eds.), *Different Voices,* 166.

165 The Jehovah's Witnesses in Ravensbrück: Morrison, *Ravensbrück: Everyday Life,* 57–59, and Saidel, *The Jewish Women of Ravensbrück,* 35.

165 Prior to 1942, Jewish women in Ravensbrück: Morrison, *Ravensbrück: Everyday Life,* 69.

165 they wore two triangles: Morrison, *Ravensbrück: Everyday Life,* 38.

166 Nationality was a determinant of survival: No definitive data are available on the distribution of prisoners by nationality. Morrison, *Ravensbrück: Everyday Life,* 86, presents statistical information that shows the following distribution: Poles, 25 percent; Germans 20 percent; Jews, 15 percent; Russians 15, percent; French, 7 percent; Gypsies, 5 percent; Ukrainians, 4 percent; Belgians, 3 percent; and other, 5 percent. (I have rounded the figures to the nearest percent.) Upon arrival, Jews and Gypsies were identified as such, not by nationality, and this fact is reflected in the statistical analysis. The distribution was derived from a study conducted by a Polish survivor, Wanda Kiedrzynska, using surviving entrance lists, which are incomplete. There is no indication as to the period of time covered by the lists. The distribution of new arrivals by nationality changed over time. Thus, I do not know if the percentage distribution by nationality for the twenty-five thousand records comprising the analysis bears any relationship to the actual percentage by nationality for the overall prisoner population.

167 "divided and powerless": Morrison, *Ravensbrück: Everyday Life,* 95.

167 it occurred to me that the French women developed: In some parts of this discussion, I refer to "the French women" as a group. Of course, not all individuals used all of these mechanisms, nor did they use them equally or in the same manner.

167 "strange creatures": Dufournier, *La maison des mortes,* 26.

167 "Had we suddenly gone mad": Dufournier, *La maison des mortes,* 26.

168 "A wisecracking voice announces": Gorce, *Journal de Ravensbrück,* 19.

168 Mila took it upon herself: Gorce, *Journal de Ravensbrück,* 21.

168 "Girls, we are going to feast": Gorce, *Journal de Ravensbrück,* 23.

168 "The most optimistic rumors": Dufournier, *La maison des mortes,* 30.

168 "Above all, these she-animals must not see": Gorce, *Journal de Ravensbrück,* 28–29.

169 "The moment had come, I thought": Dufournier, *La maison des mortes,* 36–37.

169 assigned to Block 13: Gorce, *Journal de Ravensbrück,* 61. Gorce does not identify the number of the block to which they were assigned at the beginning of the quarantine period. However, she mentions that, when

the quarantine ended, they were transferred from Block 13 to 15. The two surviving letters authored by Mila also indicate that they spent the quarantine period in Block 13.

169 *Appel* (roll call): There were several types of Appel. Amicale de Ravensbrück and ADIR, *Les Françaises à Ravensbrück,* 93–96, provides a good discussion of the various types of roll call. This book presents information contained in numerous survivor testimonies and other documents, compiled and edited by eighteen prominent French women who were survivors of Ravensbrück.

169 Roll call would last at least one hour: Morrison, *Ravensbrück: Everyday Life,* 111.

170 "In winter, the thermometer regularly drops": Amicale de Ravensbrück and ADIR, *Les Françaises à Ravensbrück,* 97.

170 "loathe to swallow the vile soup": Gorce, *Journal de Ravensbrück,* 33.

170 "We, the Five, never had enough": Gorce, *Journal de Ravensbrück,* 33.

170 "Travelogues, philosophical essays": Dufournier, *La maison des mortes,* 46.

170 "Miane has an amazing choral group": Gorce, *Journal de Ravensbrück,* 46.

171 In 1944, there were several hundred children at Ravensbrück: Morrison, *Ravensbrück: Everyday Life,* 262–274, provides an excellent discussion of the subject of children in the camp, including births to women prisoners.

171 "Suddenly, an unexpected sweetness": Maurice, *Les murs éclatés,* 99.

171 Both memoirists describe this useless work: Dufournier, *La maison des mortes,* 56–59, and Gorce, *Journal de Ravensbrück,* 50–52.

171 They were then given a list of permissible songs: Dufournier, *La maison des mortes,* 58–59.

172 *"My Dears, I am doing very well"*: Private collection of Emmanuel (Mola) Racine, letter written by Mila Racine to M. Hérisson for E. Racine, dated April 1944.

172 "The words transport, factory, munitions": Dufournier, *La maison des mortes,* 60.

172 "Miane steered me into a corner": Gorce, *Journal de Ravensbrück,* 41.

173 "You have glasses," Gorce, *Journal de Ravensbrück,* 41.

173 "The next day, I flung, tossed back, and scattered": Dufournier, *La maison des mortes*, 61–62.

173 "There was, on the one hand, the enemy that commanded": Dufournier, *La maison des mortes*, 64.

173 "providential intervention": Dufournier, *La maison des mortes*, 64.

173 "*le schéma*": Dufournier, *La maison des mortes*, 64.

173 "If this nurse, a simple prisoner like me": Dufournier, *La maison des mortes*, 64.

173 In April 1944, Father Rosay: Curé de Douvaine, *Résistance non violente*, 13, states that Father Rosay was sent from Annemasse to Compiègne on March 12, 1944. The same source (30) states that Joseph Lançon and François Périllat were sent from Annemasse to Compiègne on March 19, 1944.

173 Father Rosay was one of a dozen priests: Curé de Douvaine, *Résistance non violente*, 14.

173 "spiritual progress": Curé de Douvaine, *Résistance non violente*, 14.

173 On April 27, 1,670 male prisoners: Information cited here about the transport that departed Compiègne on April 27, 1944, comes mainly from www.bddm.org/liv/details.php?id=I.206.

174 "I am in the same state": Curé de Douvaine, *Résistance non violente*, 14.

174 Many of the *tatoués* sent to Buchenwald, including Joseph Lançon and François Périllat: A few letters written by Lançon and Périllat from Flossenbürg and Hersbruck are reproduced in Croquet, *Chemins de passage*, 37–39.

174 "However, this time, it has such an air of truth": Gorce, *Journal de Ravensbrück*, 53.

175 "My darlings! I have indeed received your package": Private collection of Emmanuel (Mola) Racine, Letter written by Mila Racine to E. Racine, dated June 1944.

175 Aix-les-Bains, (Savoie): I do not know why she would have written "Savoie" instead of "Haute-Savoie."

175 the priest had beem transferred from one German prison: Croquet, *Chemins de passage*, 85, states that Louis Favre "came to know most of the German prisons of the Haute-Savoie: the 'Pax' prison, then, in Annecy,

the prison of the Saint Francis school, the old château prison and the departmental prison . . ." (Ellipsis points appear in original.) Germain, *Mémorial de la déportation,* includes photographs of each of these prisons. Apparently, "la vieille prison du château" ("the old château prison") is the small stone structure known today as the Palais de l'Ile, situated in the middle of the canal Le Thiou, in the center of Annecy.

175 "The real Prison? Society.": Croquet, *Chemins de passage,* 86. I could find no information on when Father Favre was transferred from one prison to another or the name of the prison in which he carved the inscription cited.

176 one's inability to understand commands: Despite this, some French women resisted learning or speaking German because they viewed it as a form of collaboration. Morrison, *Ravensbrück: Everyday Life,* 96, and Amicale de Ravensbrück and ADIR, *Les Françaises à Ravensbrück,* 238–239.

176 she does make clear that Mila was able to communicate: Private collection of Emmanuel (Mola) Racine, Letter written by Nelly Gorce to Mola Racine, dated July 3, 1945.

176 Data compiled and analyzed by Tillion: Tillion, *Ravensbrück: Eyewitness Account,* English translation of Second Edition, 244–245, and Third edition, 491–494. Both the second and third editions contain very useful chronologies. The chronology presented in the second edition is tabular in form, whereas that in the third edition is a narrative that contains much more detail.

177 from many places throughout Europe: Saidel, *The Jewish Women of Ravensbrück,* 18, mentions Poland, Austria, France, Belgium, Holland, Norway, Yugoslavia, and Hungary.

177 confined to a large tent erected between Blocks 24 and 26: Dufournier, *La maison des mortes,* 93–94, and Tillion, *Ravensbrück,* Third Edition, 493. Dufournier indicates that the tent was standing by mid-August and that women and children from Warsaw were the first to occupy it. Tillion refers to a group of fourteen thousand from Warsaw brought into the camp in September and housed in the tent. I do not know how many different groups of prisoners from Warsaw entered the camp around this time or their actual dates of entry. The chronology presented by Tillion in Annexe 7, 488–495, is very detailed, but, of course, it does not purport to list every event that occurred during the camp's operation. It is possible that prisoners from Warsaw could have arrived in August.

178 "When we lay down in the evening, on our half bunks": Dufournier, *La maison des mortes,* 117.

178 "*robes d'été*" and "*robes du soir*": Dufournier, *La maison des mortes,* 117.

178 ". . . their work consists of taking the coal": Gorce, *Journal de Ravensbrück,* 85–86.

179 received a little medical attention and care: Even in the *Revier,* prisoners received little or nothing in the way of medical care. They were, however, excused from roll call and work and granted bed rest.

179 The prisoner population had doubled: Tillion, *Ravensbrück: Eyewitness Account,* English translation of Second Edition, 244.

179 daily expenditure of thirty-five pfennigs: Tillion, *Ravensbrück,* Third Edition, 218.

180 "I will always remember her hand": From the private collection of Emmanuel (Mola) Racine, Vernay (née Jacob) ("Miarka"), Speech delivered November 20, 1981, 2. This speech also appeared under the title "J'ai le Devoir, l'Obligation Douloureuse de Témoigner sur Mila," in *Revue de la WIZO,* November – Décember 1981.

181 "Her manner and especially her voice": Chombart de Lauwe, *Toute une vie de résistance,* 105.

181 among the survivors who wrote about: Gorce also makes note of the event. See *Journal de Ravensbrück,* 88–89.

181 "I remember the exhausting tour": From the private collection of Emmanuel (Mola) Racine, Denise Vernay (née Jacob) ("Miarka"), Speech delivered November 20, 1981, 3.

182 "In the afternoon, it's my turn to rejoin Marianne": Chombart de Lauwe, *Toute une vie de résistance,* 120.

182 cross of Lorraine: The Cross of Lorraine, consisting of a single vertical line crossed by two smaller horizontal bars and originally held to be a symbol of Joan of Arc, was a symbol of French patriotism. During World War II, it was the official symbol of the Forces Françaises Libres (FFL), the Free French forces, under Charles de Gaulle.

182 "Death hastens its work": Gorce, *Journal de Ravensbrück,* 88.

182 He died of pneumonia: Curé de Douvaine, *Résistance non violente,* 30, and Croquet, *Chemins de passage,* 35.

182 the first to bear a specific date: Although entries prior to January 1945, were not dated, a variety of references in the narrative provide a timeline that is, at times, approximate and, at other times, precise.

182 "I write. Why?": Gorce, *Journal de Ravensbrück*, 94.

182 cleaner and more orderly: Dufournier, *La maison des mortes*, 122–123.

183 "the living are mixed with the dead": Gorce, *Journal de Ravensbrück*, 99.

183 "They are doing better": Gorce, *Journal de Ravensbrück*, 109.

183 "their bed is far from ours": Gorce, *Journal de Ravensbrück*, 109.

183 By the end of January, a gas chamber: The actual date on which it began operation is not known. Some sources indicate that it began operation in December 1944; others, in January 1945.

183 in the range of four thousand five hundred to six thousand: Morrison, *Ravensbrück: Everyday Life*, 291.

183 many suspected it: See, for example, Dufournier, *La maison des mortes*, 127–128. The author mentions that her suspicions were heightened as a result of an incident that happened in mid-January. She and other members of the *colonne de peinture*—the painting work detail—were attempting to take some boards to the wood yard that adjoined their painting workshop. Normally, in order to reach it, they would use a road that ran beside the crematorium. On this occasion, they were barred from using the road.

183 Dr. Winkelmann: Dufournier, *La Maison des Mortes*, 140, states that he had come from Auschwitz and that he appeared to be a doctor of medicine. I have found no information to corroborate this statement. Adolf Winkelmann died in a Hamburg prison in February 1947, while awaiting trial for his part in war crimes carried out at Ravensbrück.

184 "our doctor": Gorce, *Journal de Ravensbrück*, 115. The reference suggests that one of the women in the block was a doctor who worked in the *Revier*.

184 "My affairs in order, I feel perfectly calm": Gorce, *Journal de Ravensbrück*, 117.

184 tempted to succumb to death: Gorce, *Journal de Ravensbrück*, 120, with ellipsis points as they appear in the original: "*Mourir . . . Ce serait presque doux . . .*" ("To die . . . That would be almost sweet . . .")

185 "From these little houses, a bit separated one from the other": Dufournier, *La maison des mortes*, 74–75.

186 The *Nacht und Nebel Erlass* (Night and Fog Decree): www.yale.edu/lawweb/avalon/imt/nightfog.htm contains an English translation of the text of the decree. Shirer, *The Rise and Fall of the Third Reich*, 1247–1248, addresses the subject.

187 Many of the French prisoners in Ravensbrück were classified as *Nacht und Nebel*: Tillion, *Ravensbrück: Eyewitness Account*, English translation of Second Edition, 91–92, states that the Gestapo stopped using the NN designation around July 1943. Nevertheless, some French men and women deported from France to Germany after that time were classified as NN, having received that designation earlier. (One NN transport sent from Paris arrived at Ravensbrück on January 24, 1945.) See Fondation pour la mémoire de la déportation, *Livre-mémorial des déportés de France, Volume 1*.

187 "Our block was one of those": Tillion, *Ravensbrück: Eyewitness Account*, English translation of Second Edition, 34.

187 they did not know what sort of transport: Tillion, *Ravensbrück*, Third Edition, 279, states that they knew that the transport was going to Mauthausen. She adds that, although they were quite knowledgeable about Auschwitz, they knew almost nothing about Mauthausen.

187 this was a "bad transport": Chombart de Lauwe, *Toute une vie de résistance*, 132.

187 Some NN prisoners managed to evade the transport: Tillion, *Ravensbrück*, Third Edition, 279, relates the story of what happened to the author and her mother. Thanks to the help of her friend Grete Buber-Neumann, Germaine Tillion managed to evade inclusion in the transport. Her mother tried to evade but she was taken.

187 "In the morning, the N. N. who were at work": Chombart de Lauwe, *Toute une vie de résistance*, 131–132.

10. The Final Crossing

Page

189 "We had left Ravensbrück on the second of March": Private collection of Emmanuel (Mola) Racine, Vernay (née Jacob) ("Miarka"), Unpublished testimony, 1970, 1.

190 In June 1944, Miarka was seized by the Gestapo: Roby, "Dans les mains de la police allemande sous l'occupation."

190 Soon after leaving Fürstenberg/Havel: Germaine Tillion makes the wry observation that, on March 2, 1945, in the middle of the German debacle, the SS commandant of Ravensbrück succeeded in requisitioning an entire train for the purpose of having it traverse the length of Germany filled with people whom the Nazis were in the habit of massacring with the greatest zeal. *Ravensbrück,* Third edition, 181–182.

190 made its way through Berlin: The description of the trip is from Chombart de Lauwe, *Toute une vie de résistance,* 134–135.

190 "doomed to total darkness": Maurice, *N. N.,* 65.

190 "Forever rolling along, we get to the point of no longer knowing": Maurice, *N. N.,* 65.

191 "All at once a gunshot": Chombart de Lauwe, *Toute une vie de résistance,* 136.

191 "unreal silhouettes under the moon": Maurice, *N. N.,* 66.

191 his hometown of Linz: Hitler was not born in Linz, but he considered it to be his hometown, having spent part of his childhood in one of its suburbs and having attended high school there.

193 March 20, 1945. A Tuesday: My description of what happened on this day is based on three sources: (1) private collection of Emmanuel (Mola) Racine, Denise Vernay (née Jacob) ("Miarka"), Unpublished testimony, 1970; (2) Maurice, *N. N.;* and (3) Mission Report, March 20, 1945, Air Force Historical Research Agency, Microfilm roll #A6508.

193 five hundred female prisoners were called to the esplanade: MAU, K/4a/1, K. L. Mauthausen Schutzhaftlager, *Arbeitskommando Bahnbau II (Amstetten),* dated March 20, 1945.

193 heavily damaged by Allied bombing raids: According to Zellinger, *Amstetten, 1938–1945,* 79–81, Amstetten had been bombed twice during the previous month, on Feburary 25 and March 16.

193 Male prisoners, overseen by guards: It is not clear whether some or all of the male prisoners had been brought from Mauthausen to Amstetten on the same train as the women prisoners.

193 Weak and emaciated, the women: Private collection of Emmanuel (Mola) Racine, Denise Vernay (née Jacob) ("Miarka"), Unpublished testimony, 1970, 2, states: ". . . this was ridiculous, indeed amusing, this marching off of a thousand women without strength, without color, in front of the devastation of the landscape."

193 "The weather was fine": Private collection of Emmanuel (Mola) Racine, Denise Vernay (née Jacob) ("Miarka"), Unpublished testimony, 1970, 2.

194 "It was about 9 o'clock": Freihammer, *Heimat Amstetten VI*, 71. Testimony written by a former Mauthausen prisoner by the name of Starowie is included in this book on pages 67–75. The excerpt presented here, a translation from German, is from the Starowie testimony.

194 "The alert is received by the women": Private collection of Emmanuel (Mola) Racine, Denise Vernay (née Jacob) ("Miarka"), Unpublished testimony, 1970, 2.

194 "more for the pleasure of the woods": Private collection of Emmanuel (Mola) Racine, Denise Vernay (née Jacob) ("Miarka"), Unpublished testimony, 1970, 2.

194 "We heard them sing, led by Mariane": Private collection of Emmanuel (Mola) Racine, Denise Vernay (née Jacob) ("Miarka"), Unpublished testimony, 1970, 3.

195 the primary target assigned to the 55th Wing: In the Operations Order issued for the mission at 18:00h on March 19 (No. 138), the 55th Wing had also been directed to the marshalling yards in Gyor. Their primary target was changed either later that evening or early the next morning. However, the new primary target does not seem to be identified by name or location in the mission report. Mission Report, March 20, 1945, Air Force Historical Research Agency, Microfilm roll #A6508.

195 Four of the six bomb groups had found their primary targets: Bomb Groups 97 and 99 of the 5th Wing hit their primary target, the oil refinery at Korneuburg. The other four—the 2nd, 301st, 463rd, and 483rd—bombed Amstetten. Mission Report, March 20, 1945, Air Force Historical Research Agency, Microfilm roll #A6508.

196 their payload of nearly seven hundred tons: All of the planes carried one thousand-pound bombs. It appears that the B-17 payload consisted of

four bombs and that the B-24 payload consisted of five bombs. Mission Report, March 20, 1945, Air Force Historical Research Agency, Microfilm roll #A6508.

196 "All four squadrons of the 450th": L. A. Cooper, Confidential Report of Headquarters of 47th Wing dated 25 March 1945, to the attention of the Commanding Officers of the 98th, 376th, 449th, and 450th Bomb Groups of APO 520. Subject line reads: "Tactical Analysis of the Mission of 20 March 1945." Quotation appears on page 2. Mission Report, March 20, 1945, Air Force Historical Research Agency, Microfilm roll #A6508, frame number 916.

196 "All the units of the 98th [Bomb Group] attacked": L. A. Cooper, Confidential Report of Headquarters of 47th Wing dated 25 March 1945, to the attention of the Commanding Officers of the 98th, 376th, 449th, and 450th Bomb Groups of APO 520. Subject line reads: "Tactical Analysis of the Mission of 20 March 1945." Quotation appears on page 2. Mission Report, March 20, 1945, Air Force Historical Research Agency, Microfilm roll #A6508, frame number 916.

196 "The first bombs did not impinge": Private collection of Emmanuel (Mola) Racine, Denise Vernay (née Jacob) ("Miarka"), Unpublished testimony, 1970, 3.

197 "To tell the truth, we have almost no fear": Maurice, *N. N.*, 68.

197 "The bombardment lasted four hours": Maurice, *N. N.*, 69.

198 Thirty-six female prisoners from Mauthausen were killed: MAU, Letter and attachment from i. A. Mag. Baumgartner to the author, July 18, 2001. Attachment contains list of female prisoners killed during the course of an aerial bombardment on Amstetten, March 20, 1945. The archivist prepared this list, in response to my written request, through a query of the Archiv der KZ-Gedenkstätte Mauthausen database.

198 Father Jean Rosay died in Bergen-Belsen: The events concerning his death are from Curé de Douvaine, *Résistance non violente*, 19 and 27.

Appendix 1: Acceptance and Expulsion at the Swiss Border

The Swiss tradition of granting asylum to the persecuted goes back at least four centuries, when, in 1562, Huguenots fleeing France after the Saint Bartholomew's Day massacre found refuge. At times, the number of asylum-seekers has swelled in response to specific religious and political events—the revocation of the Edict of Nantes by Louis XIV in 1685, the French Revolution in 1789, the failed revolutions in the German states in 1848, the repression of religious groups and political factions under Otto von Bismarck in the 1870s. Contending with waves of refugees has never been easy for the small country. It has often triggered internal debate and discord. To their credit, the Swiss people have struggled with these difficulties because, like the policy of neutrality and commitment to humanitarianism, the tradition of asylum is a defining element of their national character.

Four hundred years of dealing with the dispossessed, dislocated, and dispersed of Europe did not prepare the Swiss Confederation for managing the refugee crisis created by Nazi racial policies. Whether the Swiss handled the crisis adequately or not remains a subject of contentious debate, both within and outside of the country. Even before the war had ended, as the dimensions of the human tragedy began to emerge, questions arose as to what had or had not been done as well as what could have or should have been done.

Hundreds of thousands of pages have been written by Swiss government officials and ex-officials, politicians, historians, legal experts, and others examining the refugee policies enacted by Swiss Federal authorities and practices employed by cantonal authorities vis-à-vis wartime refugees seeking asylum. In 1954, the Swiss Federal Council commissioned Carl Ludwig, a law professor and former head of the Basel-Stadt Canton Police Department, to prepare an investigation and report on Swiss government policy in relation to refugees fleeing Nazism. Completed in 1955 but not presented to the Parliament until 1957, the Ludwig report—*La politique pratiquée par la Suisse à l'égard des réfugiés au cours des années 1933 à 1955*—is still highly regarded and extensively cited. In 1996, the Federal Council mandated that an International Commission of Experts (ICE) established by the Parliament examine the issue of Switzerland and refugees as an adjunct to its investigation of the movement of assets—gold, currency, securities, artwork and other cultural treasures—into Switzerland before, during, and immediately after the war. The commission was presided over by Jean-François Bergier, a historian and professor of economic history at the ETH (Eidgenössische Technische Hochschule; Swiss Federal Institute of Technology) in Zurich. Of twenty volumes issued by the ICE, Volume 17, *Switzerland and Refugees in the Nazi Era*, published in 1999, is the volume referred to as the *Bergier Report*. Apart from these extensive government-commissioned reports, many other studies, books, and articles have been published.

Although a voluminous amount of narrative analysis exists, complete and reliable statistical data are generally lacking. The *Bergier Report* contains two statistical tables that, taken together, barely fill one of its 343 pages. The first presents data on the number of civilian refugees granted asylum, by month, from September 1939 to May 1945. The second presents data on the nationality and religion of civilian refugees given refuge during the war on an aggregate basis (i.e., with no breakdown by time period). More importantly, no data are presented on the number of civilian refugees who sought but were not granted asylum in the years leading up to or during the war. Data on the practice of *refoulement*—the turning back of refugees at the border—are fragmentary. Many persons were turned back at the border informally, leaving behind no written record of their attempt or attempts to gain entry.

Despite the country's tradition of asylum, no specific law governing the practice existed prior to 1931, when the Federal Law on the Residence and Settlement of Foreigners (known as ANAG) was enacted.[1] ANAG set forth three types of residence permits that could be issued to foreigners: (1) a permanent residence permit, allowing for a stay of unlimited duration based on bilateral residence agreements with the country of origin, issued to those with valid identity papers; (2) a temporary residence permit, allowing for a stay of one to two years, also issued to those with valid identity papers; and (3) a tolerance permit, allowing for a stay of three to six months and requiring the payment of collateral. The tolerance permit was the only type of permit available to those without valid identity papers. The Police Division of the EJPD (Federal Department of Justice and Police) oversaw national refugee policy, issuing decrees and instructions to the twenty-two cantons, whose police forces controlled the border and issued permits to foreigners.[2]

Apart from the provisions set forth in ANAG, the Federal Council itself could grant asylum to politically persecuted refugees. In the words of the ICE report, federal officials "used great restraint" in exercising this option: between 1933 and 1945, it recognized only 644 persons as political refugees.[3]

[1] ANAG stands for Bundesgesetz über Aufenthalt und Niederlassung der Ausländer.

[2] EJPD stands for Eidgenössisches Justiz- und Polizeidepartment.

[3] ICE, Bergier Report, Section 1.4, 22.

The Federal law of 1931 was a response to rising concerns in Switzerland over what was called *Überfremdung*—a term whose literal meaning is foreign influence or foreign infiltration and whose broader connotation is foreign overpopulation and domination. It was often associated with, and sometimes used as a polite substitute for the word *Verjundung*, which means excessive Jewish influence and is usually translated as Jewification or Judaization.

The concerns about *Überfremdung* and *Verjundung* increased during the 1930s as the country was forced to contend with German Jews fleeing Nazism. A month after the Reichstag went up in flames, the EJPD issued a directive making it clear that Switzerland did not regard Jews trying to escape racial persecution to be political refugees and that they were to be granted only temporary residence while awaiting emigration to other countries.[4] As such, they were banned from employment and all other types of remunerative activity. Despite the restrictions, up until 1938 the situation seemed more or less manageable. The Swiss Jewish community bore the costs of supporting the newcomers, and they also helped to arrange for their emigration.[5] Most German Jews were able to leave Switzerland after a brief stay.[6]

The first turning point came in 1938, when, immediately after the *Anschluss*, Austrian Jews sought to escape Nazi persecution. Restricting unwanted visitors to temporary stays no longer seemed adequate, and steps were taken to prevent refugees from entering the country. The authors of the *Bergier Report*, speaking of 1938, state, "The desire to prevent Jewish immigration by any means possible motivated Swiss decision-makers."[7]

Two weeks after the *Anschluss*, the Swiss government required that an Austrian passport holder seeking to enter the country must have a consular visa. Consular officials were instructed not to issue a visa unless there was an assurance that the person intended to return to Austria or to leave Switzerland

---

[4] Hitler became Chancellor of Germany on January 30, 1933; the Reichstag building was set on fire on February 27; the Reichstag Fire Decree that rescinded habeas corpus and civil liberties was enacted on February 28; and the Reichstag passed the Enabling Act, which gave Hitler dictatorial powers, on March 23. The EJPD issued its directive on March 31.

[5] Two organizations—SIG (Schweizerischer Israelitischer Gemeindebund; Federation of Jewish Communities of Switzerland) and VSJF (Verband Schweizerischer Jüdischer Fürsorgen; Association of Swiss-Jewish Welfare Organizations)—apparently worked together to raise funds within Switzerland and abroad. The American Joint Distribution Committee contributed significantly. See Picard, Jacques, *On the Ambivalence of Being Neutral*. Chapter 5 of the *Bergier Report* discusses the subject also and presents statistical data on the amount of funds contributed by source.

[6] The extent to which Jews who sought refuge prior to 1938 were denied entry to Switzerland or expelled at some point after having entered the country is unknown. The literature suggests that the great majority of these refugees were granted temporary stays.

[7] ICE, *Bergier Report*, Section 3.1, 84.

and continue on to another country. Moreover, they were specifically instructed not to give visas to Jews fleeing Nazism.[8]

The visa requirement proved to be an ineffective and short-lived tool. In the summer of 1938, the Reich began to replace Austrian passports with German ones, and this rendered the visa requirement useless. Since the ratification of a bilateral accord in 1926, German and Swiss passport holders had not needed visas in order to travel back and forth between the two countries. Swiss officials were reluctant to rescind the accord unilaterally and reintroduce a generalized visa requirement because they did not want to antagonize their brutish neighbor or impede commerce. Johannes Baumann, the President of the Confederation, and Heinrich Rothmund, the Director of the Police Division of the EJPD, working through the Swiss legation in Berlin, tried to prod Nazi officials into helping them find an alternative way to prevent Jewish refugees holding German passports from entering Switzerland. Discussions dragged on throughout the summer of 1938, but nothing was resolved. Finally, on August 19, the Swiss Federal Council moved to force a resolution. It reinstated a general visa requirement that would become effective after the requisite thirty-day waiting period and was subject to revocation if an alternative were found. An alternative was found rather quickly. The German-Swiss Protocol of September 29, 1938, stipulated that passports issued to Jews by the Reich were to be prominently stamped with a red letter "J."[9] Holders of passports bearing the discriminatory sign were required to have visas in order to enter Switzerland.[10] The *Bergier Report* sums up the Catch-22: "In other words, anyone who wanted to flee to Switzerland had to

---

[8] This point is clearly stated in the *Bergier Report*. In regard to Austrian Jews, the authors state, "When the Swiss Federal council introduced visa requirements for holders of Austrian passports in the spring of 1938, they were really aiming at Jewish refugees." Moreover, the report notes that the Swiss General consulate in Vienna demanded proof of Aryan ancestry in issuing visas. ICE, *Bergier Report*, Section 4.1.2, 106.

[9] "If the documents do not allow us to be absolutely certain about who—German or Swiss—proposed a distinctive 'J'-stamp marking for Jews in German passports, they do clearly show that the initiative and energy that ended up leading to the discriminatory marking came from the Swiss side. It was Switzerland that was looking for a way of identifying and controlling a specific population: German and Austrian Jews, whose persecution marked them out for emigration and whom Nazi policies pushed to leave the Reich." ICE, *Bergier Report*, Section 3.1, 82.

[10] The Protocol provided a measure of reciprocity. German authorities would have the right to require Swiss Jews seeking entry into the Reich to produce authorization papers analogous to those required of German Jews seeking entry into the Confederation.

apply for a visa and be recognized as a refugee, even though that by doing so, he or she forfeited nearly all chances of receiving the visa."[11]

When war broke out, the Swiss Federal Council took additional measures to restrict illegal immigration. On September 5, 1939, it instituted a general visa requirement for all persons seeking to enter the country. On October 17, it issued a decree requiring that all foreigners who had entered the country illegally except deserters and political refugees were to be expelled to the country from which they came. The decree did not end illegal immigration, but it formed the legal basis for interning illegal refugees and requiring them to pay taxes to defer costs of their care.[12]

Between August 1938 and August 1942, the enforcement of Federal directives governing immigration was variable and erratic. Cantonal, not Federal, authorities were responsible for border surveillance, and they determined the fate of refugees. Some cantons sought to implement Federal directives to the letter; others did not. In a few instances, cantonal police officials actively aided persecuted individuals seeking entry.[13] For this reason, it was impossible to predict whether or not a Jew arrested at the border would be allowed to enter the country. An individual denied entry might be discreetly turned back and left to his own devices or seized and turned over to the very authorities from which he had fled. Similarly, it was impossible to predict whether or not a Jew who had managed to make his way to the interior of the country (i.e. beyond the border area) would be expelled or allowed to remain.

The second turning point came in August 1942. Massive deportation of Jewish refugees from France had begun during the summer. Desperate, without options, individuals and families sought refuge in Switzerland. With the consent of the Swiss Federal Council, Heinrich Rothmund, the Director of the Police Division of the EJPD, ordered that, effective August 13, the border

---

[11] ICE, *Bergier Report*, Section 4.1.2, 107. The report also notes that holding a visa did not guarantee that one would be able to cross the border.

[12] Until the end of the war, most illegal refugees were interned in civilian-run facilities. Family members were separated from one another. Able-bodied men were sent to labor camps; women and the elderly lived and worked in communal settings, i.e. "homes." Children were either placed in foster homes or children's homes.

[13] One such individual was Paul Grüninger, the police commander in Saint Gall, a canton that borders Austria and Germany. In August 1938, Grüninger decided to disobey Federal directives and to aid Austrian and German Jews seeking refuge. He used various tactics, including falsifying documents. He was suspended from his job in 1939, subsequently dismissed, convicted of crimes, and fined. Shortly before his death in 1972, Yad Vashem recognized him as one of the Righteous Among the Nations. It was not until 1996, however, after many efforts were made on his behalf, that the Saint Gallen government officially rehabilitated him.

be closed to civilian refugees seeking asylum. The closure was specifically aimed at keeping Jewish refugees out. Only political refugees and military personnel were to be granted asylum.[14] The directive clearly states, "Those who only took flight because of their race—Jews, for example—should not be considered political refugees."[15] It also stipulates that, the first time an illegal alien was apprehended, he or she was to be turned back but not placed in the hands of military or civilian authorities patrolling the other side of the border. However, any repeat offenders would be turned over to such authorities.

Although the situation bore some similarities to what had happened in 1938, there were essential differences. By August 1942, many Swiss citizens were fully aware of the fact that German and French officials were deporting tens of thousands of Jews from France. They had read accounts in Swiss newspapers of the roundups that had taken place in Paris in July and in the Unoccupied Zone in August. They were shocked not only by the sheer number of persons, including children, being deported but also by the wantonly inhumane way in which the arrests and deportations had been carried out. Many Swiss politicians, humanitarian workers, and clergy had heard or read accounts of massacres and systematic extermination of Jews "deported to the East."[16] If it was too soon to confirm the accuracy of the accounts, it was also too late to dismiss them as rumor.

The decision to close the border was met with enormous protest. Less than two weeks after being issued, the directive was modified to authorize the entry of hardship cases. Such cases were broadly defined and included: unaccompanied children less than 16 years of age; parents with their own children less than 6 years of age; the sick; pregnant women; elderly persons over 65; those with immediate family members living in Switzerland; and those with other close ties to the country.[17]

In a speech delivered at the end of August, Eduard von Steiger, a member of the Federal Council and the head of the EJPD, vigorously defended his department's efforts to keep illegal aliens out:

---

[14] Military personnel granted asylum included, for the most part, deserters and escaped prisoners of war.

[15] ICE, *Bergier Report*, Section 3.2, 90.

[16] The following three are among many sources that address this point: Laqueur, *The First News of the Holocaust*; Häsler, *The Lifeboat is Full*; and ICE, *Bergier Report*.

[17] ICE, *Bergier Report*, Section 4.3.1, 133; and Fivaz-Silbermann, *Le Refoulement de réfugiés civils juifs*, 5–6.

> When one has the responsibility of commanding a tightly crowded lifeboat with limited accommodations and equally limited provisions, while thousands of victims of a shipwreck are clamoring for rescue, one must seem cruel if one does not embark them all. And yet one is thoroughly human if at the same time one warns against false hopes and tries at least to save those already aboard.[18]

Clear and compelling, the crowded lifeboat metaphor framed the debate. Members of the National Council, bitterly divided on this issue, debated on September 22 and 23. Dr. Albert Oeri, a member of the Liberal Party and editor-in-chief of *Die Basler-Nachrichten,* accepted the legitimacy of von Steiger's metaphor but not its accuracy:

> This is a very impressive image. We should like to develop it and add to it: our lifeboat is not yet overloaded, it is not even full, and, as long as there is room aboard, we will take on everyone for whom there is space; otherwise we commit a sin. The terrible moment can come when we are threatened with an overload . . . [ellipsis points in original] But, to stick to the image: That moment has not yet arrived for us, and, God willing, it will not arrive. Therefore we do not wish to behave as if it had already come. May we never have to face the choice of offending against the duty of self-preservation or the obligation of help to our fellow-men![19]

The major parties holding seats in the National Council voted to stand by the Federal Council, and the directive remained in force. Yet, the debate raged on in public discourse and in the press.[20]

---

[18] Häsler, *The Lifeboat is Full,* 116. The quotation is from Ludwig, *La politique pratiquée par la Suisse,* 393–394.

[19] Häsler, *The Lifeboat is Full,* 165. In the same speech, Dr. Oeri introduced his own metaphor (page 164): "Assuredly I have no desire to ridicule the dangers that Federal councilor von Steiger has described to us with statistics, but all this that he has put before us is merely a future contingency, not a certainty. So I ask: Must we be inhuman in the present for the sake of a contingent future danger—must we, so to speak, 'stockpile inhumanity?'"

[20] In an article published on September 24 in *Die Tat,* Felix Moeschlin, also a member of the National Council, disputed the metaphor's legitimacy: "The comparison of Switzerland with a lifeboat . . . is gaining further interpretation today. I take no joy in this comparison, because it is false. The structure of Switzerland has not even the slightest resemblance to the structure of a lifeboat. If it is essential to draw a comparison from that oceanic world that nature has denied to us, then let it be that of a thoroughly organized, flawless, fully equipped ocean liner. We do not have to disclose its tonnage, but in any case it is no nutshell but rather, as I have said, a first-class ocean liner that is far from sinking even if it takes aboard a few more shipwreck victims in addition to its regular passenger list." Häsler, *The Lifeboat is Full,* 179.

In October 1942, Swiss Federal authorities took additional measures to secure the border. The army was called upon to reinforce customs officials and local police officials patrolling the cantons of Geneva and Valais (Wallis).[21] In places that had proved to be popular crossing points, rows of barbed wire were added or fortified. On December 29, 1942, further instructions regarding *refoulement* were issued to the border forces. The hardship provision that had permitted families with children younger than 16 years of age to enter the country was tightened considerably; henceforth, only those with children younger than 6 were to be admitted.[22]

The regulations issued between August and December 1942 regarding the acceptance or *refoulement* of refugees would remain in effect, largely unchanged, until July 1944.[23]

---

[21] The canton of Geneva borders France, and the canton of Valais (Wallis) borders Italy.

[22] Fivaz-Silbermann, *Le Refoulement de réfugiés civils juifs*, 6; and ICE, *Bergier Report*, Section 4.2.2, 122. In reference to the Police Division directive of December 29, 1942, the *Bergier Report* cites the German version of the Ludwig report, 231.

[23] In July 1943, the age limit for unaccompanied girls was raised from sixteen to eighteen.

Appendix 2: Statistical Summary Data and Profiles of Convoys, Fall of 1943

Table 1

Salient Data on MJS Convoys Smuggled into Switzerland, August 17 to October 21, 1943

Date of Crossing	Date of Arrest	Ref. Number	Border Guard Post	Place of Arrest	Time of Arrest	Place of Crossing	Number	
							Total	U/A Children*
08/17/43	08/17/43	1	Veyrier I	transformer at the marsh	12:05	near the transformer at the marsh	11	11
08/28/43	08/28/43	2a	Chevran	Passerelle de la Cuillere	23:30	Passerelle de la Cuillere	10	10
08/28/43	08/29/43	2b	Chevran	Village of Chevran	06:15	below Couty	5	5
08/28/43	08/29/43	2c	None	on the route to Vésenaz	09:00	Region of Anieres	4	4
09/06/43	09/06/43	3	Mon Idee	behind the customs house Ambilly II	21:00	behind the customs house Ambilly II	13	13
09/08/43	09/08/43	4	Mon Idee	upstream from the mill	22:40	upstream from the mill	13	13
09/12/43	09/12/43	5	Veyrier I	Veyrier marsh	Noon	Veyrier marsh	15	15
09/14/43	09/14/43	6	Cornieres	b. 108	21:45/23:10	b. 108	29	29
09/21/43	09/21/43	7	Cornieres	Chemin des Vignes	22:00	Not available	20	20
09/23/43	09/23/43	8	Sezenove	Plaine du Loup	21:00	between b. 50 and b. 51	7	7
09/24/43	09/23/43	9	Cornieres	at the toll bar	22:45	Not available	19	19
09/24/43	09/24/43	10	Sezenove	b. 50	21:00	b. 50	7	7
09/24/43	09/24/43	11	Cornieres	at the toll bar	20:00	Not available	19	19
09/28/43	09/28/43	12	Sezenove	b. 51	21:15	b. 51	3	3

(Continued)

Table 1 (*Continued*)

Salient Data on MJS Convoys Smuggled into Switzerland, August 17 to October 21, 1943

Date of Crossing	Date of Arrest	Ref. Number	Border Guard Post	Place of Arrest	Time of Arrest	Place of Crossing	Number	
							Total	U/A Children*
09/29/43	09/29/43	13	Sezenove	Lully	21:00	between b. 50 and b. 51	4	4
10/04/43	10/04/43	14	Hermance	Les Glands	18:00	Les Glands	13	3
10/07/43	10/07/43	15	Cornieres	Les Huteaux	17:40	Not available	7	7
10/11/43	10/11/43	16	Certoux	Plaine du Loup	22:00	between b. 51 and b. 52	8	8
10/12/43	10/12/43	17	Certoux	Plaine du Loup	21:25	between b. 51 and b. 52	8	8
10/13/43	10/13/43	18	Cornieres	Vignes de Bran	17:00	Not available	8	8
10/14/43	10/14/43	19	Cornieres	Chemin des Vignes	19:15	Not available	9	9
10/14/43	10/14/43	20	Certoux	Plaine du Loup	22:30	between b. 51 and b. 52	8	4
10/18/43	10/18/43	21	Certoux	Plaine du Loup	21:00	between b. 51 and b. 52	9	7
10/20/43	10/20/43	22	Cornieres	Les Huteaux	20:00	Les Huteaux	9	6
10/20/43	10/20/43	23	Certoux	Plaine du Loup	22:30	between b. 51 and b. 52	8	0
10/21/43	10/21/43	24	Cornieres	Les Huteaux	19:15	Not available	8	0
		24 convoys		Total			274	239

*"U/A" stands for "unaccompanied children."

Note: In addition to the above, the MJS smuggled convoys of families into Switzerland during the last week of August and first week of September.

Source: Archives of the State of Geneva; research and analysis by Nancy Lefenfeld.

Table 2

Salient Data on OSE Convoys Smuggled into Switzerland, August 17 to October 21, 1943

Date of Crossing	Date of Arrest	Ref. Letter	Border Guard Post	Place of Arrest	Time of Arrest	Place of Crossing	Number	
							Total	U/A Children*
08/21/43	08/21/43	A	Hermance	Les Chenaillettes	23:15	Les Chenaillettes	25	18
08/31/43	08/31/43	B	Hermance	Croix de Bailly	23:00	Les Coutils	13	13
09/08/43	09/08/43	C	Hermance	Croix de Bailly	23:00	Les Coutils	22	15
09/10/43	09/10/43	D	Jussy	Les Etoles	14:45	Les Etoles	28	27
09/13/43	09/13/43	E	Jussy	b. 157	13:30	b. 157	11	11
09/15/43	09/15/43	F	Jussy	route des Etoles	16:00	b. 156	3	3
09/17/43	09/17/43	G	Gy	b. 185	16:00	b. 157	13	10
09/22/43	09/22/43	H	Gy	b. 187	16:50	near b. 157	15	13
09/29/43	09/29/43	I	Hermance	Les Coutils	18:30	Les Coutils	15	10
10/01/43	10/01/43	J	Hermance	Croix de Bailly	22:15	Les Glands	18	14
10/18/43	10/18/43	K	La Renfile	b. 121	19:15	b. 121	3	3
		11 convoys		Total			166	137

Note 1: In addition to the above, OSE smuggled convoys of families into Switzerland during the last week of August and first week of September.

Note 2: The last OSE convoy shown here included two adults, OSE teachers, who were turned back to France. They are not included in the totals.

*"U/A" stands for "unaccompanied children."

Source: Archives of the State of Geneva; research and analysis by Nancy Lefenfeld.

Notes on the Translation of Excerpts from the Declarations

Appendix 2 presents a profile of each of the twenty-four MJS convoys. Each profile provides summary information on the convoy, followed by excerpts from the Declarations. Generally speaking, the excerpts include the portion of the narrative statement that pertains to the individual's life and itinerary up to and including the moment of time that he or she entered Switzerland.

The excerpts are presented in French as well as in English. English translations of excerpts were prepared by the author in consultation with a native French-speaker, born and raised in Lausanne, Switzerland. Translation, being an art rather than a science, is highly variable; therefore, I offer some explanatory notes as to my approach.

As explained in the text, the Declaration was prepared by a military official belonging to the Arrondissement territorial Genève (Arr. ter. GE) and read and signed by the child or adult to whom it referred. Many Declarations exhibit errors in spelling, grammar, punctuation, and/or verb tenses. In some cases, sentence construction is poor and/or sentences are run on or poorly punctuated. Also, at times, there are inconsistencies or lack of clarity in terms of information presented. It appears likely that some preparers were not native French-speakers. I have not corrected deficiencies in the French language excerpts shown in this appendix. That is, the French language excerpts presented here constitute a typed reproduction of that which appears in the original documents.

I have sought to translate the excerpts in a near-literal form. I have not sought to eliminate awkwardness of language that appears in the originals; nor have I sought to exaggerate it. I have used semi-colons to separate run-on sentences so that the material is more easily readable. Additionally, I have made the following changes:

1. In cases where it appears that place names have been misspelled, I have offered what I believe to be the correct spelling in brackets.
2. Border crossing dates, numerically abbreviated in the originals, have been fully written out.
3. Commonly used abbreviations appearing in the originals (e.g., "M." for "Monsieur") have been fully written out.
4. Names of departments, abbreviated in the originals, have been fully written out.

Profile of the Convoy of August 17, 1943
MJS Convoy Number 1

Summary Information:

Border Guard Post: Veyrier I
Place where Arrest was made: "the transformer at the Marais [marsh]"

Time of Arrest: 1205 (12:05 p.m.)
Place and Time of Crossing: "near the old transformer at the Marais"
Number of Persons: 11
Composition of convoy: 11 unaccompanied children
Correspondence with OSE list: 10 of 11 names appear on list as "par Simon"; 11th name is that of a sibling of a "par Simon" child

List of Children Comprising the Convoy and Excerpts from Declarations:

4241 **Lydie Weissberg**, 15, female, Paris, "par Simon":

> "I left Paris in 1939, and I went to Auvergne. I began my studies in Paris, and I continued them in the resorts where I went since. I stayed 3 years in Auvergne, and then I went to Saint-Gervais, passing through Grenoble, where I stayed recently. My father being deported and my mother at Saint-Gervais, she sent me to Switzerland for fear that I would suffer the same fate as my father."

> "J'ai quitté Paris en 1939 et je me suis rendue en Auvergne. J'ai commencé mes études à Paris et je les ai continuées dans les stations où je me suis rendue depuis. Je suis restée 3 ans en Auvergne et je me suis ensuite rendue à St. Gervais, en passant par Grenoble, où je suis restée jusqu'à ces derniers temps. Mon père étant déporté et ma mère à St. Gervais, elle m'a envoyée en Suisse de crainte que je subisse le même sort que mon père."

4242 **Jacques Jakubowitz**, 9, male, Valenciennes (France), "par Simon":

> "I was born in Valencienne and lived there until the war. At that moment, I went to Paris, where I stayed one month, after which I went from town to town, finally coming to Saint-Gervais. I had been living there about 3 months when they told us that the Germans were going to come into the region. We then left, 11 young children, led by a young lady. We wanted to come to Switzerland. We took the train as far as Reignier; then we continued by car and on foot to cross the border on August 17, 1943, in the region of VEYRIER around 1230 h."

> "Je suis né à Valencienne et y ai vécu jusqu'à la guerre. A ce moment je suis allé à Paris où je suis resté un mois après quoi je suis allé de ville en ville pour venir enfin à St. Gervais. J'y vivais depuis 3 mois environ lorsque on nous a annoncé que les Allemands allait venir dans la region. Nous sommes donc partis 11 petits enfants, conduita par une demoiselle. Nous voulions venire en Suisse. Nous avons pis le train jusqu'à Reignier puis nous avons continué en voiture et à pied pour franchir la frontière le 17.8.43 dans la région de VEYRIER vers 12.30 h."

4243 **Boris Szterenbarg**, 14, male, Rowno (Poland), "par Simon":

"I left, with my parents, Rowno to go to France. We were first in Grenoble and then in Paris, where I did all my studies, as well as in Lourdes (Haute-Pyrénées). I left Paris in 1940, and I was in Lourdes, where I stayed for 3 years. I then headed to Saint-Gervais, where I stayed until a few days ago. My parents, who are presently in Saint-Gervais, sent me to Switzerland because they feared that I would be deported. They themselves are being sought, and they told me that they will manage better alone than with me."

"J'ai quitté, avec mes parents, Rowno pour nous rendre en France. Nous avons abord été à Grenoble et ensuite à paris où j'ai fait toutes mes etudes ainsi qu'à Lourdes (H-Pyrénées). J'ai quitté Paris en 1940 et j'ai été à Lourdes où je suis resté 3 ans. Je me suis ensuite dirrigé sur St. Gervais où je suis resté jusqu'à ces derniers jours. Mes parents qui sont actuellement à St. Gervais m'ont envoyé en Suisse car ils craignaient que je sois déporté. Eux-même sont recherché et ils m'ont dit que seul ils se débrouilleront mieux qu'avec moi."

4245 **Marcus Hendler**, 15, male, Leipzig, "par Simon":

"I was born in Leipzig and lived there until 1939. During that year, I went to Belgium, to Antwerp. In May 1940, we were driven from there because of the war. We then took refuge in France, in Bordeaux and then near Pau for one year. Then we were locked up in a camp in the Basses-Pyrénées. I changed camps, then was liberated. I went to Nice, then to Saint-Gervais. Recently, the Germans have come to replace the Italians, so that one had to flee the Haute-Savoie. We left, 11 Jewish children, under the supervision of a young lady who led us from Saint-Gervais as far as the border near Veyrier." In addition to the Declaration, the dossier for Marcus and Henri Hendler contains a document dated August 18, 1943, entitled "Procès-verbal d'audition," which contains a longer and more detailed statement signed by Marcus Hendler.

"Je suis né à Leipzig et y ai habité jusqu'en 1939. Durant cette année je suis allé en Belgique à Anvers. En mai 1940 nous en avons été chasse à cause de la guerre. Nous nous sommes alors réfugiés en France à Bordeaux puis dans les environs de Pau pendant 1, an. Ensuite nous avons été enfermés dans un camp dans les Basses Pyrénées. J'ai change de camp puis ai été libéré. Je suis allé à Nice puis à St. Gervais. Ces derniers temps les Allemands viennent remplacer les Italiens de sorte qu'il a fal lu fuir de la Haute Savoie. Nous sommes partis 11 enfants juifs sous la direction d'une demoiselle qui nous a conduit de St Gervais jusqu'à la frontière près de Veyrier."

4245 **Henri Hendler**, 13, male, Leipzig. He is Marcus's brother. "par Simon"

4246 **Renée Perelmuter**, 14, female, Paris, "par Simon":

"I was born and I did all my studies in Paris before the declaration of war. I left Paris in 1939 with the school, and we were in Grasset (Cher). From there, I returned to Paris, where I stayed about 3 months. I then went to St. Raphaël, where I stayed one year, and I again came to Paris. After a stay of 5 months in Paris, I went to Saint-Gervais, passing through the Souterraine and Nice, where I stayed for awhile. I then stayed in Saint-Gervais until my departure for Switzerland. I came to Switzerland because I feared being deported like my father. My mother stayed in Saint-Gervais, and she's the one who sent me to Switzerland."

"Je suis née et j'ai fait toutes mes études à Paris jusqu'à la déclaration de la guerre. J'ai quitté Paris en 1939 avec l'école et nous avons été à Grasset (Cher) de là je suis retournée à Paris où je suis restée env. 3 mois. Je suis allé ensuite à St. Raphaël où je suis restée 1 année et je suis à nouveau venue à Paris. Après un séjour de 5 mois à Paris je suis allé à St. Gervais en passant par la Souterraine et Nice où je suis restée quelque temps. Je suis ensuite restée à St. Gervais jusqu'à mon depart pour la Suisse. Je suis venue en Suisse car je craignais la déportation comme mon père. Ma mère est restée à St. Gervais et c'est elle qui m'a envoyée en Suisse."

4247 **Cécile Gostynski**, 16, female, Lodz (Poland), "par Simon":

"At the age of 4, I left my place of birth to go to Noisy-le-Sec with my parents, where we stayed until April. In that suburb of Paris, I did all my studies, and, in 1932, my sister was born in Paris. My parents were deported in 1941, and, since then, I have stayed with my sister at my aunt's house. Afraid of being deported like our parents, we left our aunt and we were at Nimes—Nice; and there we were sent into forced residence in Saint-Gervais (Haute-Savoie), where we stayed until a few days ago. We left France because for some time rumors of deportation are circulating. And, as we do not wish to suffer the same fate as our parents, we crossed into Switzerland."

"A l'age de 4 ans j'ai quitté mon lieu de naissance pour me rendre à Noisy-le Sec avec mes parents où nous sommes restés jusqu'au mois d'avril. Dans cette banlieue de Paris j'ai fait toutes mes études et en 1932 ma soeur est née à Paris. Mes parents ont été déportés en 1941 et depuis je suis restée avec ma soeur chez ma tante. De crainte d'être déportées comme nos parents nous avons quitté notre tante et nous avons été à Nimes-Nice et là nous avons été envoyées en residence forcée à St. Gervais (H-S) ou nous sommes restées jusqu'à ces derniers jours. Nous avons quitté la france car depuis quelque temps des bruit de déportation courent. Et comme nous ne voulons pas subir le même sort que nos parents nous avons passé en Suisse."

4247 **Sarah Gostynski**, 10, female, Paris. She is Cécile's sister.

4248 **Sarah Revah**, 11, female, Salonika (Greece), "par Simon":

"I was born in Salonika, but, in 1932, I came to live in France, in Paris, where I stayed until 1940. At the time of the Occupation, I went to seek refuge in Corrèze, then in Nice, from where I was sent into forced residence in Saint-Gervais. Recently, as the Germans are coming, we were led into Switzerland by a young lady. We left Saint-Gervais and took the train as far as Reignier. From there, we reached the Swiss border by car and on foot. We were 11. We were let go by this young lady about 100 meters from the barbed wire in front of Veyrier . . ."

"Je suis née à Salonique, mais en 1932 je suis venu habiter en France, à Paris où je suis resté jusqu'en 1940. Lors de l'occupation je suis allé me réfugier en Corrèze puis à Nice d'où j'ai été envoyée en residence forcée à St. Gervais. Ces derniers temps comme les Allemands venaient, nous avons été emmenés en Suisse par une demoiselle. Nous sommes partis de St. gervais et avons pris le train jusqu'à Reignier. De là nous avons gagné la frontière Suisse en voitire et à pieds. Nous étions11. Nous avons été lâchés par cette demoiselle à 100 m. environs des barbelés devant Veyrier . . ."

4250 **Jacques Veissid**, 16, male, Paris, "par Simon":

"I was born in Paris and lived there up until the Occupation. Then I went to live in the Alpes-Maritimes and in the Haute-Savoie. I was able to live somewhat normally in the Haute-Savoie as long as the Italians were there; but, for some time, the Germans have been replacing them and I ran the risk of being deported within a short time. I therefore decided to come to Switzerland. I had been living in Saint-Gervais for one month. I therefore took the train as far as Reignier. From there, I traveled half by car, half on foot, passing through Annemasse, Etrembières, to finally arrive at Veyrier, where I crossed the border."

"Je suis né à Paris et y ai toujours habité jusqu'à l'occupation. Ensuite je suis allé vivre dans les Alpes Maritimes, et en Haute Savoie. J'ai pu vivre à peu près normalement en Haute Savoie tant qu'il y a eu les Italiens, mais depuis quelques temps, les Allemands les remplacent et je risquais d'être déporté dans un délai assez bref. J'ai donc décidé de venir en Suisse. Il y a un mois que j'habitais à St. Gervais. J'ai donc pris le train jusqu'à Reignier. De là, j'ai voyage moitié en voiture, moitié à pied en traversant Annemasse, Etrembières pour arriver enfin à Veyrier où j'ai franchi la frontière."

4250 **Sonia Veissid**, 13, female, Paris. She is Jacques' sister. "par Simon"

Profile of the Convoy of August 28(a), 1943
MJS Convoy Number 2a

Summary Information:

Border Guard Post: Chevran
Place where Arrest was made: Passerelle de la Cuillère
Time of Arrest: 2330 (11:30 p.m.)
Place and Time of Crossing: "on foot, Passerelle [footbridge] de la Cuillère"
Number of Persons: 10
Composition of convoy: 10 unaccompanied children
Correspondence with OSE list: 8 of 10 names appear on OSE list as "par Simon" and 2 appear as "par OSE"

List of Children Comprising the Convoy and Excerpts from Declarations:

4364 **David Milgram**, 15, male, Lodz (Poland), "par Simon":

"I stayed in Lodz until 1937. In that city, I began my schooling. I then came, with my parents, to Strasbourg, where I stayed until 1939. We then went to Paris, where I stayed until April; then I was in Limoges and in Nay. I came to Switzerland because I have had no more news of my parents since April, and I am afraid they have been deported. It is the people in whose home I was in Nay who sent me to Switzerland. A young man from Nay accompanied me right up close to the border area."

"Je suis resté à lodz jusqu'en 1937. Dans cette ville j'ai commencé mes écoles. Je suis ensuite venu, avec mes parents, à Strasbourg., où je suis resté jusqu'en 1939, nous sommes ensuite allés à Paris où je suis resté jusqu'au mois d'avril puis j'ai été à Limoges et à Nay. Je suis venu en Suisse car je n'ai plus de nouvelles de mes parents depuis le mois d'avril et je crains qu'ils aient été déportés. Ce sont les personnes chez qui j'étais à Nay qui m'ont envoyé en Suisse. Un jeune homme de Nay m'a accompagné jusque près de la frontière."

4371 **Armand Halberthal**, 12, Thionville (France), "par Simon":

"I left Thionville in 1939 and went to Poitiers because we had to evacuate Thionville. Until 41, I lived with my parents, who had a knitwear business.

My parents were taken and deported in a roundup in July 1942. I was taken in by friends of my parents until a few days ago. Upon learning that one could go to Switzerland, they sent me by train as far as Thonon on August 27, 1943. At Thonon, an unknown man came towards me and took me by bus to a small village that I do not know. Then we walked a little, and he had us wait until nightfall. Already, in Lyon, I had met some other children in the same situation as I, and a man had told me to go with them. The man who took us to Thonon came with us and helped us to get through the barbed wire." The notation "2300.28.8.43" appears in the left margin, adjacent to the phrase "à aidé à traverser les barbelés."

"J'ai quitté Thionville en 1939 et suis allé à Poitiers car nous dû évacuer Thionville. Jusqu'en 41 j'ai vévu chez mes parents qui avaient un commerce de bonneterie. Mes parents ont été pris et déportés dans une rafle en juillet 42. J'ai été reccueilli par des amis de mes parents jusqu'à ces derniers jours. Ayant appris que l'on pouvait aller en Suisse, ils m'ont envyé en train jusqu'à Thonon le le 27.8.43. A Thonon un monsieur inconnu est venu vers moi et m'en emmené dans un car jusque dans un petit village que je ne connais pas. Ensuite on a marché un peu, et il nous a fait attendre la nuit. A Lyon déjà j'ai rencontré d'autre enfants dans le même cas que moi, et un monsieur m'a m'a dit d'aller avec eux. Le monsieur qui nous avait pris à Thonon est venu avec nous et nous à aidé traverser les barbelés."

4373 **Oscar Fleischer**, 14, male, Karlsruhe (Germany), "par Simon":

"After two years I left my place of birth with my parents for Mulhouse, where were stayed a few months before leaving for Sedan [France]. We stayed 6 years in Sedan, and there I began my schooling. My two sisters were born in that town. In 1938, we left Sedan to go to Lens (Pas-de-Calais). We stayed there two years and we went to Lasbordes (Aude), then to the Bastide D'Angou and Paris, where we stayed until recently. My parents were deported in July, and, since then, we have been living in camps. I believe it is the Red Cross that brought us out of the camp. They put us on a train with a ticket for Thonon. There, someone was waiting for us at the station and we went by bus right up close to the border. A person waited for us at the way out of the village, and she led us up to the barbed wire."

"Après deux ans j'ai quitté mon lieu de naissance avec mes parents en destination de Mulhouse où nous sommes restés quelques mois pour partir à Sedan. Nous sommes restés 6 ans à Sedan et là j'ai commencé mes classes. Mes deux soeurs sont née dans cette ville. En 1938 nous avons quitté Sedan pour aller à Lens (Pas-de-Calias). Nous sommes restés deux ans et nous nous sommes rendus à Lasbordes (Aude) puis la Bastide D'Angou et Paris où nous sommes restés jusqu'à ces derniers jours. Mes parents ont été déportés au mois de juillet et depuis nous vivons dans des camps. Je crois que c'est la Croix-Rouge qui nous a fait sortir du Camp. On nous a mis en train avec un billet en destination de Thonon. Là nous étions attendu à la gare et en car nous avons été jusque près de la frontière. Une personne nous a attendue à la sortie du village et elle nous a conduit jusqu'aux barbelés."

4373 **Jeanette Fleischer**, 11, female, Sedan (France). She is Oscar's sister. "par Simon"

4373 **Renée Fleischer**, 9, female, Sedan. She is Oscar's sister. "par Simon"

4374 **Arny Lasar**, 12, male, Echternach (Luxembourg), "par Simon":

"My mother came to Echternach only to give birth, but I always lived in Luxembourg. At the time of the invasion, we left to go to Lodève [France] and always stayed there and went to school. My parents have been deported since the beginning of spring 43. One [woman] took me to her house with my brother, and and we stayed until the middle of August 43. The woman with whom we were in Lodève handed us over to a *passeur*, in order that he bring us to Switzerland. From Lodève, I came by train and bus right up very close to the border."

"Ma mére est venue à Echternach seulement pour l'accouchement mais j'ai toujours habité Luxembourg. A l'invasion nous sommes parti à Lodéve et y suis toujours resté et allais à l'école. Mes parents sont déportés depuis le début du printemps 1943. Une m'a pris chez elle avec mon frére et nous sommes restés jusqu'au milieur d'aout 43. La dame ou nous étions à Lodève nous a remis à un passeur, pour qu'il nous mène en Suisse. De Lodève je suis venu en train et en car jusque tout prés de la frontière."

4374 **Carlo Lasar**, 11, male, place of birth not indicated. He is Arny's brother. "par Simon"

4375 **Tibere Braunstein**, 10, male, Paris, "par Simon":

"I was born in Paris. I no longer have my parents because they were deported this year. Since then, I was in a woman's home. Another woman came looking for me, and she led me to the Gare de Lyon in Paris. She entrusted me to someone named FLEISCHER Oscar, whom I did not know but who was part of the Mouvement Sioniste [Zionist Movement] of Paris, who took me to Switzerland. (see declaration under the name Fleischer, also interrogated this day. Braunstein being very timid, it is impossible to draw out anything."

"Je suis né à Paris, je n'ai plus mes parents car ils ont été déportés cette année. Depuis j'ai été chez une dame. Une autre dame est venue me chercher, et elle m'a mené à la gare de Lyon à Paris. Elle m'a confié a un nommé FLEISCHER Oscar, que je ne connaissait pas, mais qui faisait partie du Mouvement Sioniste de Paris, qui m'a emmené en Suisse. (voir déclaration dunommé Fleischer interrogé également ce jour Braunstein étant très timide il est impossible d'en tirer quelque chose."

4376 **Fred Kempfner**, 14, male, Vienna, "par OSE":

"I stayed in Vienna until 1938. In that city, I began attending school. We then came in 1939 to Paris after having tried to get into Belgium but we were turned back. Since 1939 we have always stayed in Paris. My parents were deported one month ago, and, since then, I have been living with friends. These acquaintances with whom I was living sent me to Switzerland for fear that that I would suffer the same fate as my parents. In addition to that, I have acquaintances in Switzerland."

"Je suis resté à Vienne jusqu'en 1938. Dans cette ville j'ai commencé mes écoles. Nous sommes ensuite venu en 1939 à Paris après avoir essayé de passer en Belgique mais nous avons été refoulé. Depuis 1939 nous sommes toujours restés à Paris. Mes parents ont été déportés depuis un mois et depuis je vis chez des amis. Les connaissances ou je logeais m'ont envoyé en Suisse de crainte que je subisse le même sort que mes parents. En plus de cela j'ai des connaissances en Suisse."

4376 **Paul Kempfner**, 11, male, Vienna. He is Fred's brother. "par OSE"

Profile of the Convoy of August 28(b), 1943
MJS Convoy Number 2b

Summary Information:

Border Guard Post: Chevran
Place where Arrest was made: Village of Chevran
Time of Arrest: 0615 (6:15 a.m.) on August 29
Place and Time of Crossing: "on foot, below Couty" on August 28
Number of Persons: 5
Composition of convoy: 5 unaccompanied children
Correspondence with OSE list: 2 of 5 names appear on OSE list as "par Simon"; third name is that of a sibling of a "par Simon" child

List of Children Comprising the Convoy and Excerpts from Declarations:

4360 Hélène Waysbrot, 13, female, Warsaw:

"I left Warsaw with my parents at the age of 7 months. We came to France, to Paris, where I stayed until recently. In that city, I began attending school. I came to Switzerland because my parents have been deported since July. Since then, I am living with acquaintances; and, as I no longer have relatives in France and as they fear I would suffer the same fate as my parents, they sent me to Switzerland. I left Paris by train and I came as far as Annemasse. There, a woman was waiting for me, and she put me into the hands of a gentleman who led me, in the company of several people, right up close to the border."

"J'ai quitté Varsovie avec mes parents à l'âge de 7 mois. Nous sommes venus en France à Paris où je suis restée jusqu'à ces derniers jours. Dans cette ville j'ai commencé mes écoles. Je suis venue en Suisse car mes parents ont été déportés depuis le mois de juillet. Depuis je vis chez des connaissances et comme je n'ai plus de parents en France et que l'on craint que je subisse le même sort que mes parents l'on m'a envoyé en Suisse. Je suis parti de Paris en train et je suis venue jusqu'à Annemasse. Là une dame m'attendait et elle m'a remise entre les mains d'un Monsieur qui m'a conduite en compagnie de quelques personnes jusque près de la frontière."

4361 Rachele Linderman, 15, Paris, "par Simon":

"I was born and have always lived in Paris. In that city, I did all my studies and I stayed until my departure for Switzerland. My mother was deported one month ago, and my father is a military internee in Switzerland. I was alone in France, and I was living with some friends. Unable to continue this life, and in addition fearing that I would suffer the same fate as my mother, I came to Switzerland with the intention of seeing my dad, who is in Tessin. A woman, an acquaintance of my friends in Paris, came looking for me and took me as far as Annemasse. We took the bus and in the area she took me into a barn where there were already 20 people. From there, two gentlemen accompanied us, as we were nearly 30 people, close to the border. And from there we crossed the border. I crossed the border, with these people, on August 28, 1943, around 2330 in the region of Hermance. After our crossing, we arrived in a forest; and, as it was very dark, we lay down until morning. We followed a road and arrived in a village [and] we asked where the customs house was."

"Je suis née et je suis toujours restée à Paris. Dans cette ville j'ai fait toutes mes études et je suis restée jusqu'à mon départ pour la Suisse. Ma mére été déportée depuis un mois, et mon père est interné Militaire en Suisse, Je me trouvais seule en France et je logeais chez des amis. Ne pouvant pas continuer cette vie d'autant plus que je craignais de subir le même sort que ma mère je suis venue en Suisse avec l'intention de revoir mon papa qui est dans le Tessin. Une dame, connaissance de mes amis à Paris, est venue me chercher et m'a conduit jusqu'à Annemasse. Nous avons pris le car et dans la région elle m'a conduit dans une grange où se trouvait déjà 20 personnes. De là deux messieurs nous ont accompagnés, car nous étions près de 30 personnes, près de la frontière. Et de là nous avons passé la frontière. J'ai passé la frontière, avec ces personnes, le 28-8-43 vers les 2330 dans la région d'Hermance. Après notre passage nous sommes arrivés dans un bois et comme il faisait très nuit nous nous sommes couchés jusqu'au matin. Nous avons suivit une route et arrivé dans un village nous avons demandé où se trouvait le poste de douane."

4363 **Maurice Glazman**, 14, Brussels:

"I left Brussels in May 33 to go to Paris. I did all my schooling in that city. My parents are deported–my dad since 1942 and my Mom since January 1943–and I have had no further news. Alone, I was taken in by a friend of my parents, and he sent me to Switzerland; and, in order to do this, he had his son accompany me by train as far as Dijon; then either by train or bus; I no longer remember exactly the names of the towns."

"J'ai quitté Bruxelles en mai 33 pour aller à Paris. J'ai fait dans cette ville toutes mes écoles. Mes parents sont déportés, mon papa depuis 1942 et ma Maman depuis janvier 1943, et je n'ai plus eu de nouvelles. Seul, j'ai été recueilli par un ami de mes parents et il m'a envoyé en Suisse et pour ceci, il m'a fait accompagner par son fils en train jusqu'à Dijon puis et ensuite soit en train soit en car, je ne me rappelle plus exactement les noms de villes."

4370 **Simon Cymerman**, 15, male, Warsaw:

"I stayed with my parents in Warsaw until 1929. In that same year, we came to Courbevoie [France], and we stayed until recently. In that city, I did all my schooling. My parents were deported, and since then we no longer have parents. We have been lodging with some friends until a few days ago. It is the Israelite community that sends us to Switzerland, and we must ask to go to Sierre, where somebody is waiting. We crossed the border on August 28, 1943, around 2330 in the region of Hermance. After our crossing, we walked but, as it was very dark, we slept in the woods. The next morning around 06:00 we were arrested by a soldier . . ."

"Je suis resté avec mes parents en Varsovie jusqu'en 1929. Dans cette même année nous sommes venus à Courbevoie et nous sommes restés jusqu'à ces derniers jours. Dans cette ville j'ai fait toutes mes écoles. Mes parents ont été déportés et depuis nous n'avons plus de parents. Nous avons été hébergés chez des amis jusqu'à ces derniers jours. C'est la comunauté israelite qui nous envoie en Suisse et nous devons demander à aller à Sierre où l'on est attendus. Nous avons passé la frontière le 28-8-43. vers les 2330 dans la région de Hermance. Dès notre passage nous avons marché mais comme il faisait très nuit nous avons coucher dans un bois. Le lendemain matin vers les 0600 nous avons été arrêtés par un Sdt . . ."

4370 **Anna Cymerman**, 12, female, Warsaw. She is Simon's sister. "par Simon"

Profile of the Convoy of August 28(c), 1943
MJS Convoy Number 2c

Summary Information:

Border Guard Post: None
Place where Arrest was made: "on the route to Vésenaz"
Time of Arrest: 0900 (9:00 a.m.) on August 29
Place and Time of Crossing: Region of Anières; 22:00 on August 28
Number of Persons: 4
Composition of convoy: 4 unaccompanied children
Correspondence with OSE list: 2 of 4 names appear on OSE list as "par Simon"

List of Children Comprising the Convoy and Excerpts from Declarations:

4368 **Sarah Goldstein**, 15, female, Paris, "par Simon":

"We were born in Paris and we have always lived in that city. We did all of our studies, without finishing them, and we have always chosen to live in that city until our departure for Switzerland. Our parents were deported along with a little sister and since then we are living with some friends. No longer able to continue this life, these acquaintances send us to Switzerland, to the home of acquaintances in Sierre. We were afraid of suffering the same fate as our parents. We crossed the border on August 28, 1943, around 2200 in the region of Anières. It is a *passeur* who accompanied us right up close to the border. After our crossing, we were lost in the woods, and we waited until daylight to orient ourselves. We then followed the tramway and arrived in Geneva. While we are resting near the beach, a gendarme arrested us and took us to the gendarmerie post of Eaux-Vives and then to the Cropettes reception center."

"Nous sommes née à Paris et nous avons toujours vécu dans cette ville. Nous avons fait toutes nos études qui ne sont pas terminées et nous avons toujours élu domicile dans cette ville jusqu'à notre départ pour la Suisse. Nos parents ont été déportés avec une petite soeur et depuis nous vivons chez des amis. Ne pouvant pas continuer cette vie, ces connaissances nous envoient en Suisse où chez des connaissances à Sierre. Nous craignions de subir le même sort que nos parents, Nous avons passé la frontière le 28-8-43 vers les 2200 dans la région de Anières. C'est un passeur qui nous a accompagnée jusque près la frontière. Après notre passage nous nous sommes perdues dans un bois et nous avons attendu le jour pour nous diriger. Nous avons alors suivit la voie du tram et bous sommes arrivés jusqu'à Genève. Alors que nous nous reposons vers la plage un gendarme nous a arrêtées et nous a conduites au poste de gendarmerie des Eaux-Vives et ensuite au centre d'acceuil des cropettes."

4368 **Berthe Goldstein**, 13, female, Paris. She is Sarah's sister. "par Simon"

4369 **Ludwig Rosenbaum**, 15, male, Frankfurt (Germany):

"I stayed in Frankfurt until 1933. In that city, I did my school classes, which I finished in Paris. In 1933, we came to Strasbourg, where we stayed until 1934; then we were in St.-Dié (Vosges) for 3 years, then in Paris, where we stayed until recently. Our parents were deported; and, as we have no more family in France, we could not stay in France, all the more so because we feared suffering the same fate as our parents. We have relatives in Switzerland. We crossed the border on August 28, 1943, around 2300 in the region of Hermance. A *passeur* accompanied us right up close to the border. After our crossing, we spent the night in the woods waiting for daylight to orient ourselves. We followed the line of the tram and we got all the way to Geneva. While we are resting near the beach, a gendarme came to arrest us and took us to the post at Eaux-Vives and then from there, to the Cropettes reception center."

"Je suis resté à Francfort jusqu'en 1933. Dans cette ville j'ai fait mes classes scolaires que j'ai terminées à Paris. En 1933 nous sommes venues à Strasbourg où nous sommes restés jusqu'en 1934 puis nous avons été à St.-Dié (Voges) pendant 3 ans puis à Paris où nous sommes restés jusqu'à ces derniers jours. Nos parents ont été déportés et comme nous n'avons plus de famille en France, nous ne pouvions pas rester en France d'autant plus que nous craignions de subir le même sort que nos parents. Nous avons de la parenté en Suisse. Nous avons passé la frontière le 28-8-43 vers les 2300 dans la région d'Hermance. Un passeur nous a accompagné jusqe près de la frontière. Après notre passage nous avons passé la nuit dans un bois en attendant le jour pour nous diriger. Nous avons suivit la ligne du tram et nous sommes arrivés jusqu'à Genève. Alors que nous nous reposons vers la plage un gendarme est venu nous arrêtér et nous a conduits au poste des Eaux-Vives puis de là au centre d-acceuil des cropettes."

4369 **Rosi Rosenbaum**, 12, female, Frankfurt (Germany). She is Ludwig's sister.

Profile of the Convoy of September 6, 1943
MJS Convoy Number 3

Summary Information:

Border Guard Post: Mon Idée
Place where Arrest was made: "behind the customs house at Ambilly II"
Time of Arrest: 2100 (9:00 p.m.)
Place and Time of Crossing: "on foot, just behind the customs house at Ambilly II"
Number of Persons: 13
Composition of convoy: 13 unaccompanied children
Correspondence with OSE list: 11 of 13 names appear on OSE list as "par Simon"; 12th and 13th names (Charmatz) do not appear on list but Declarations state that they are cousins of "par Simon" child Emerich (incorrectly spelled Emeriche).

List of Children Comprising the Convoy and Excerpts from Declarations:

4515 **Emile Najdberger**, 9, male, Paris, "par Simon" "rue Amelot":

"My father died, and I know my mother but I do not know her name. I was living with someone else up until the age of 8 years at La Varenne (Seine) and then in an institution. Lastly, I was in Aviegneux [Vigneux]. I came to Switzerland because a woman told me that the Germans are picking us up."

"Mon père est décédé et ma mère je la connais mais je ne sais pas son nom. J'ai été en pension jusqu'à l'âge de 8 ans à la Varenne (Seine) et ensuite dans un hospice. Dernièrement j'étais à Aviegneux. Je suis venu en Suisse parce qu'une dame m'a dit que les Allemands nous ramasseraient."

4516 **Bernard Jacob**, 12, male, Paris, "par Simon" "rue Amelot":

"Born in 1930 in Paris, I lived there continually until the end of 1942, as did my sisters. I started primary school. At the end of 1942, my parents were deported, and I left with my sisters for the outskirts of Paris, to a woman's home in Vigneux. At the beginning of September 1943, a woman belonging to a rescue organization and whose name I do not know brought us as far as Lyon; then a gentleman, as far as the Swiss border. It was likewise for my comrades who crossed the border the same time as I did. We made our way to Switzerland to evade the measures taken by the German authorities against the Israelites. We got over the Swiss border on September 6, 1943, at 2300 in the region of Mon Idée. We were helped in crossing the border by some men whom we do not know."

"Né en 1930 à Paris, je suis resté constamment à Paris jusqu'à 1942 (fin), ainsi que mes soeurs. J'ai commencé mes écoles primaires. En fin 1942, mes parents ont été déportés et je suis parti avec mes soeurs dans les environs de Paris, à Vigneux chez une dame. Au début de septembre 1943, une dame faisant partie d'une organisation de secours et dont je ne connais pas le nom qui nous amené jusqu'à Lyon, puis un monsieur jusqu'à la frontière suisse. Il en est de même pour mes camardes qui ont passé la frontière en même temps que moi. Nous avons gagné la Suisse pour éviter les mesures prises par les autorités allemandes contre les israelites. Nous avons franci la frontière suisse le 6.9.43 à 2300 dans la région de Mon Idee. Nous avons été aidés pour passer la frontière par des messieurs que nous ne connaissons pas."

4516 **Ginette Jacob**, 9, female, Paris. She is Bernard's sister. "par Simon" "rue Amelot"

4516 **Marie-Claire Jacob**, age 3, female, Paris. She is Bernard's sister. "par Simon" "rue Amelot"

4517 **Jacques Charmatz**, 8, male, Nancy:

"I was born in Nancy, and it has been 4 years since I left that city with my parents and my sister. My father is the director of the ORT agricultural school in la Roche (Lot-et-Garonne). In Nancy, he was a lawyer in the court of Nancy. My mother and my father are still in France, and they are going to come to Switzerland soon. My uncle and my aunt, the parents of Claude EMERICHE, are also in France. We crossed the border on September 6, 1943, near Chêne; it was two men who showed us the border . . ."

"Je suis né à Nancy et il y a 4 ans que je ai quitté cette ville avec mes parents et ma soeur. Mon père est directeur de l'école d'agriculture de l'ORT, la Roche (Lot et Garonne). A Nancy il était avocat au Tribunal de Nancy. Ma mère et mon père sont toujours en France et ils vont bientôt venir en Suisse. Mon oncle et ma tante, les parents de EMERICHE Claude sont aussi en France. Nous avons passé la frontière le 6.9.43 près de Chêne, c'est deux hommes qui nous ont montré la frontière . . ."

4517 **Myriam Charmatz**, 7, female, Nancy. She is Jacques' sister.

4517 **Claude Emeriche**, 3, male, Nancy. He is Jacques' cousin. "par Simon"

4518 **Monique Fischel**. This little girl did not know her date of birth. Swiss authorities estimated that she was six years old. Her place of birth is not stated. "par Simon" "rue Amelot"

"I always lived in Paris. My mother has been deported, and my father is a prisoner in Germany. Since 1942, I have been in a foster home in La Varenne. Two women took me into Switzerland. That's all that I know."

"J'ai toujours habité Paris. Ma mère est déportée et mon père est prisonnier en Allemagne. Depuis 1942 je suis en nourrice à La Varenne. Deux dames m'ont conduit en Suisse. C'est tout ce que je sais."

4519 **Cécile Berasse**. No information was provided on Cécile Berasse. A handwritten note reads *"doit avoir 4 ans"* ("must be 4 years old"). In place of a narrative statement explaining her situation, her Declaration reads: *"Ne peut donner aucune explication. Trop petite."* ("Can't give any explanation. Too small.") "par Simon" "rue Amelot"

4520 **Suzette Kaatz**, 7, female, Mulhouse (France), "par Simon":

"I was born in 1935 in Mulhouse; then I lived in Dijon up until the war. Beginning in 1940, I was in the Lot-et-Garonne on a farm. A woman took care of me and took me as far as Lyon; then a gentleman, as far as the border."

"Je suis née en 1935 à Mulhouse, puis j'ai habité Dijon jusqu'à la guerre. Dès 1940, je suis dans le Loth et Garonne dans une ferme. Une dame s'est occupée de moi et m'a conduit jusqu'à Lyon, puis un monsieur jusqu'à la frontière."

4521 **David Bergman**, 13, male, Paris, "par Simon" "rue Amelot":

"Born in 1930 in Paris, I lived there continually until 1942. I started primary school. My mother was deported in 1942. My father went missing in 1939. From 1942 until now, I have been in a foster home, first in Vigneux, then in Monjeron [Montgeron]. It was a woman who took care of me. She was part of a rescue organization. I do not know her. She took me and my comrades as far as Lyon, and then two gentlemen accompanied us as far as the border. I made my way to Switzerland to evade the measures taken by the German authorities against the Israelites."

"Né en 1930 à Paris, j'y suis resté constamment jusqu'en 1942. J'ai commencé mes écoles primaires. Ma mère a été déporté en 1942. Mon père a été porté disparu en 1939. De 1942 à ce jour, j'ai été en nourrice d'abord à Vigneux puis à Monjeron. C'est une dame qui s'est occupé de moi. Elle fait partie d'une organisation de secours. Je ne la connais pas. Elle m'a conduit ainsi que mes camardes jusqu'à Lyon et puis deux meisseurs nous ont accompagnés jusqu'à la frontière. J'ai gagné la Suisse pour éviter les mesures prises par les autorités allemandes contre les israelites."

4859 Michel Piekarski, 11, male, Paris, "par Simon" "rue Amelot":

Note: In the Declaration, the last name appears as "Piekrski." The child's signature clearly indicates that the correct spelling is "Piekarski."

"I stayed in Paris until 1942. In that city, I began my schooling. My parents were deported, and since then I am in foster homes, placed by the Israelite community. I went to Champigny—Montjeron [Montgeron]—Avignieux [Vigneux]—Paris and from there, to Switzerland. It is the Israelite committee that organized this convoy. We were 13 children who were taken as far as Annecy, then Annemasse; and from there 3 *passeurs* led us up to the barbed wire."

"Je suis resté à Paris jusqu'en 1942. Dans cette ville j'ai commencé mes écoles. Mes parents ont été dépor és et depuis je vis chez des nourrices placé par un comité israelite Je suis allé à Champigny-Montjeron-Avignieux-Paris et delà en Suisse. C'est la comité israelite qui a organisé ce convoi nous étions 13 enfants qui avons été conduits jusqu'à Annecy, puis Anne,asse et de là 3 passeurs nous conduits jusqu'à barbelés."

4931 Suzanne Harra, 10, female, Paris, "par Simon" "rue Amelot":

[Note: The crossing date stated on the Declaration appears to be incorrect, as it does not correspond with the crossing date stated on the arrest report.]

"I always lived in Paris, and, in that city, I began my schooling. My mom has been dead for 6 years, and my dad has been deported since three years. From that time on, I have been in an orphanage, where I stayed until recently. Some people came looking for me in La Varenne to take me to Paris; and from there I took the train with a convoy of 13 children. We went as far as Lyon; and from there two gentlemen led us up to the border."

"Je suis toujours restée à Paris et dans cette ville j'ai commencé mes écoles. Ma maman est morte depuis 6 ans et mon papa est déporté depuis trois ans. De cette date j'ai été dans un orphelinat où je suis restée jusqu'à ces derniers jours. C'es t des personnes qui sont venues me chercher à la Varenne pour me conduire à Paris et de là j'ai pris le train avec un convoi de 13 enfants. Nous avons été jusqu'à Lyon et de là deux messieurs nous ont conduit jusqu'à la frontière."

Profile of the Convoy of September 8, 1943
MJS Convoy Number 4

Summary Information:

Border Guard Post: Mon Idée
Place where Arrest was made: "upstream from the mill"

Time of Arrest: 2240 (10:40 p.m.)
Place and Time of Crossing: "on foot just upstream from the mill"
Number of Persons: 13
Composition of convoy: 13 unaccompanied children
Correspondence with OSE list: All names appear on OSE list as "par Simon"

List of Children Comprising the Convoy and Excerpts from Declarations:

4550 **Henri Wolkowski**, 14, male, Brzezin (Poland), "par Simon":

"After I was born, my parents left Poland to come to Paris. In that city, my sister was born, and we stayed until recently in Paris. Our parents were deported 1 ½ [years] ago; and, since then, we have stayed with an acquaintance; then we came to the free zone, and a woman took us in. We came from Paris accompanied by unknown persons and we were 14 children."

"Dès ma naissance mes parents ont quitté la Pologne pour venir à Paris. Dans cette ville ma soeur est née et depuis nous sommes restés jusqu'à ces derniers jours à Paris. Depuis 1 ½ nos parents ont été déportés et depuis nous sommes restés une connaissance puis nous sommes venus en zone libre et une dame nous a receuillis. Nous sommes venus de Paris accompagnés par des personnes inconues et nous étions 14 enfants."

4551 **François Lustman**, 7, male, Paris, "par Simon" "rue Amelot":

"Since my birth, I have always lived in Paris until recently. My parents were deported two years ago; and since then, I am in the home of a friend of my parents. It was unknown persons who accompanied us because we were 14 children. They accompanied us to the border."

"Depuis ma naissance j'ai toujours habité Paris jusqu'à ces derniers jours. Mes parents ont été déportés depuis 2 ans et depuis je suis chez un ami de mes parents. C'est des personnes inconues qui nous ont accompagnés car nous étions 14 enfants. Elle nous ont accompagnés jusqu'à la frontière."

4552 **Suzanne Plewa**, 14, female, Siedlce (Poland), "par Simon" "rue Amelot":

"I came to France at the age of two with my parents; we came to Paris. In that city, I began began my schooling and I stayed until recently. I came to Switzerland because I no longer have parents in France. They were deported; and, since then, I have been raised by a foster mother, where I stayed until recently. It was persons unknown to me who took us to Switzerland because were we 5 children."

"Je suis venue en France à l'âge de 2 ans avec mes parents, nous sommes venus à Paris. Dans cette ville j'ai commencé mes écoles et je suis restés jusqu'à ces derniers jours. Je suis venue en Suisse car je n'ai plus de parents en France. Ils ont été déportés et depuis j'ai été élevé par une nourrice où je suis restée jusqu'à ces derniers jours. C'est des personnes inconues pour moi qui nous ont conduites en Suisse car nous étions 5 enfants."

4553 **Elie Chetret**, 11, male, Paris, "par Simon" "rue Amelot" :

"We were born in Paris, and we stayed in that city until recently. Those of us who were old enough attended primary school in Paris. We have not seen our parents for 2 ½ years; and, since that day, we have stayed with a foster mother, who raised us until recently. We came to Switzerland accompanied by people whose names I do not know. They took us because the foster mother who raised us no longer had the means to provide for our needs. We crossed the border on September 8, 1943, around 2115 in the region of Cornières. We were 14 children accompanied by a woman and a gentleman who led us up to the barbed wire."

"Nous sommes nés à Paris et dans cette ville nous sommes restés jusqu'à ces derniers jours. Ceux qui étaient en âge ont fait leurs premières classes à Paris. Nous n'avons pas revu nos parents depuis 2 ½ ans et de ce jour nous sommes restés chez une nourrice qui nous a élevés jusqu'à ces derniers jours. Nous sommes venus en Suisse accompagné de personnes dont je ne sais pas le nom. Ils nous ont pris car la nourrice qui nous a élevé n'avais plus les moyens de subvenir à nos besoins. Nous avons passé la frontière le 8-9-43 vers les 2115 dans la région de Cornières. Nous étions 14 enfants accompagnés par une dame et un monsieur qui nous ont conduit jusqu'au barbelé."

4553 **Maurice Chetret**, 10, male, Paris. He is Elie's brother. "par Simon" "rue Amelot"

4553 **Marcel Chetret**, 6, male, Paris. He is Elie's brother. "par Simon" "rue Amelot"

4533 **Yvette Chetret**, 4, female, Paris. She is Elie's sister. "par Simon" "rue Amelot"

4560 **Maurice Loberstein**, 16, male, Warsaw, "par Simon" "rue Amelot":

"Shortly after my sister was born, we came to Paris with our parents. We came to Paris, and, in that city, we began our schooling. Our parents were deported two years ago, and since then we went to the home of acquaintances. It was unknown persons who took us to Switzerland. We were 14 children on the train, and they led us up to the border. They told us to ask to go to the Sierre Camp (Valais), where friends would take care of us."

"Peu après la naissance de ma soeur nous sommes venus à Paris avec nos parents. Nous sommes venus à Paris et dans cette ville nous avons commenés nos écoles. Nos parents ont été déportés depuis 2 ans et depuis nous sommes allés chez des connaissances. C'est des personnes inconues qui nous ont conduites en Suisse. Nous nous sommes trouvés 14 enfants dans le train et l'on nous a conduits jusqu'à la Fronrière. Ils nous ont dis de demander à aller au Camp de Sierre (VS) où des amis s'occuperaient de nous."

4560 **Lisa Loberstein**, 13, female, Warsaw. She is Maurice's sister. "par Simon" "rue Amelot"

4560 **Ginette Loberstein**, 11, female, Paris. She is Maurice's sister. "par Simon" "rue Amelot"

4560 **Jules Loberstein**, 8, male, Paris. He is Maurice's brother. "par Simon" "rue Amelot"

4560 **Nathan Loberstein**, 5, male, Paris. He is Maurice's brother. "par Simon" "rue Amelot"

4565 **Mendel Zanger**, 15, male, The Hague (Holland), "par Simon":

"I lived in The Hague until 1930 and then in Antwerp until May 1940; then 1 month in France and again in Antwerp until August 1942. My father was a diamond cutter. My parents have been deported since October 1942. I come to Switzerland to avoid deportation, being Jewish."

"J'ai habité la Haye jusqu'en 1930 et ensuite Anvers jusqu'en mai 1940, puis 1 mois en France et de nouveau à Anvers jusqu'en août 1942. Mon père était diamantaire. Mes parents sont déportés depuis octobre 1942. Je me rends en Suiss e pour éviter la déportation étant juif."

Profile of the Convoy of September 12, 1943
MJS Convoy Number 5

Summary Information:

Border Guard Post: Veyrier I
Place where Arrest was made: "Marais of Veyrier [Veyrier marsh]"
Time of Arrest: Noon

Place and Time of Crossing: "Marais de Veyrier," noon
Number of Persons: 15
Composition of convoy: 15 unaccompanied children
Correspondence with OSE list: All names appear on OSE list as "par Simon"

List of Children Comprising the Convoy and Excerpts from Declarations:

4709 **Isaac Cukierman**, 11, male, Paris, "par Simon" "rue Amelot":

"I was born in Paris, and in 1934 my dad died. My mother remarried Maurice Bas in a religious ceremony; they had a son, my brother, whose last name is my mother's [maiden] name. We stayed in Paris until recently, and, in that city, I began my schooling. Our parents were deported; and, since then, we have been living in the countryside [in the home of] some people. As I no longer had relatives in France and these people had difficulty keeping us fed, we decided to come to Switzerland. We crossed the border with 13 other children on September 12, 1943, around 1100 in the region of Veyrier. We were accompanied by 3 young girls, and after our crossing we were arrested . . ."

"Je suis né à Paris et en 1934 mon papa est mort. Ma mère s'est remariée religieusement avec Maurice Bas; de ce mariage est né mon frère qui lui porte le nom de ma mère. Nous sommes restés à Paris jusqu'à ces derniers jours et dans cette ville j'ai commencé mes écoles. Nos parents ont été déportés et depuis nous vivons à la campagne des personnes. Comme je n'a vais plus de parents en France et que ces personnes avaient de la peine de nous nourir nous avons décidés de venir en Suisse. Nous avons été passé la frontières avec 13 autres enfants le 12-9-43 vers les 1100 dans la région de Veyrier. Nous avons été accompagnés par 3 jeunes filles et dès notre passage nous avons été arrêtée . . ."

4709 **Bernard Berkowicz**, 4, male, Paris. He is Isaac Cukierman's half-brother. "par Simon" "rue Amelot"

4710 **Maurice Zysman**, 15, male, Chimialiki (Poland), "par Simon":

"I left the city of my birth in 1931 to come to Paris with my parents. In that city, I did all my schooling and I began my apprenticeship as a metal worker. I stayed in Paris until recently. I came to Switzerland because my dad has been deported and my mom is in hiding for fear of suffering the same fate. I myself came to take refuge in Switzerland so as not to be deported. I crossed the border on September 12, 1943, around 1100 in the region of Veyrier. We were accompanied, 15 children that we were, by 3 young girls."

"J'ai quitté la ville de ma naissance en 1931 pour venir à Paris avec mes parents. Dans cette ville j'ai fait toutes mes écoles et j'ai commencé mon apprentissage d'ajusteur. Je suis resté à Paris jusqu'à ces derniers jours. Je suis venu en Suisse car mon papa est déporté et ma maman se cahce dans la crainte de subir le même sort. Moi-même je suis venu me réfugié en Suisse pour ne pas être déporté. J'ai passé la frontière le 12-9-43 vers les 1100 dans la région de Veyrier. Nous avons été accompagnés les 15 enfants que nous étions par 3 jeunes filles."

4712 **Isaac Kramache**, 13, male, Paris, "par Simon" "rue Amelot":

"I was born and have always lived in Paris. In that city, I began my schooling. And from there I came to to Switzerland. I came to Switzerland because I no longer have relatives in France and, as I am of the Jewish race, I fear being deported like my parents. I have an uncle in Switzerland. I crossed the border on September 12, 1943, around 1100 in the region of Veyrier. We were 15 children, and 3 young girls accompanied us as far as the border."

"Je suis né et j'ai toujours habité à Paris. Dans cette ville j'ai commencé mes écoles. Et de là je suis venu en Suisse. Je suis venue en Suisse car je n'ai plus de parents en France et comme je suis de race juive j'ai craint d'être déporté comme mes parents. J'ai un oncle en Suisse, J'ai passé la frontière le 12-9-43 vers les 1100 dans la région de Veyrier. Nous étion s 15 enfants et 3 jeunes filles nous ont accompagnés jusqu'à la frontière."

4713 **Henri Galinsky**, 15, male, Paris, "par Simon" "rue Amelot":

"We were born in Paris, and, in that city, we began our schooling. We always lived in Paris until recently. We came to Switzerland because our father was deported and our mom is very ill and she is unable to take care of us. We were sheltered with an aunt, who inflicted every possible misery on us so as not to keep us. So we came to Switzerland because we feared suffering the same fate as our dad. We crossed the border with a group of 15 children on September 12, 1943, around 1100 in the region of Veyrier. We were accompanied by 3 young girls."

"Nous sommes nés à Paris et dans cette ville nous avons commencés nos écoles. Nous avons toujours habités Paris jusqu'à ces derniers jours. Nous sommes venus en Suisse car notre père à été déporté et notre maman est très malade et elle ne peux pas s'occuper de nous. Nous étions réfugiés chez une tante qui nous faissait toutes les misères possibles pour ne pas nous garder. C'est alors que nous sommes venus en Suisse car nous craignions de subir le même sort que notre papa. Nous avons passé la frontière avec un groupe de 15 enfants le 12-9-43 vers les 1100 dans la région de Veyrier. Nous avons été accompagnés par 3 jeunes filles."

4713 **Wolf Galinsky**, 13, male, Paris. He is Henri's brother. "par Simon" "rue Amelot"

4713 **Jean Galinsky**, 11, male, Paris. He is Henri's brother. "par Simon" "rue Amelot"

4713 **Joseph Galinsky**, 9, male, Paris. He is Henri's brother. "par Simon" "rue Amelot"

4713 **Charles Galinsky**, 5, male, Paris. He is Henri's brother. "par Simon" "rue Amelot"

4716 **Edmond Rajchman**, 14, male, Paris, "par Simon":

"I have always lived in Paris, and, in that city, I began my schooling; I stayed until recently in Paris. I came to Switzerland because my parents are deported since 1941, and I no longer have relatives in France. Since the deportation of my parents, I am living with a woman in our building who took me in and cared for me until recently. I came to Switzerland for fear of being deported and so as not to cause trouble for this woman, as people who hide Israelite children are pursued just as fiercely. I came to Switzerland with a group of 15 children, and we came as far as Saint-Julien with a gentlemen; and from there 3 young girls accompanied us. We crossed on September 12, 1943, around 1030 in the region of Veyrier."

"J'ai toujours habité à Paris et dans cette ville j'ai commencé mes écoles; je suis resté jusqu'à des derners jours à Paris. Je suis venue en Suisse car mes parents sont déporté depuis 1941 et je n'ai plus de parents en France. Depuis la déportation de mes parents je vis chez une dame de la maison qui m'a receuilli et gardé jusqu'à ce jour. Je suis venu en Suisse dans la crainte d'être déporté et pour ne pas causer des ennuis à cette dame car les personnes qui cache des enfants israel. sont poursuivis avec autant d'apreté. Je suis venue en Suisse avec un groupe de 15 enfants et nous sommes venus jusqu'à St. Julien avec un monsieur et de là 3 jeunes filles nous ont accompagnés. Nous avons passé le 12-9-43 vers les 1030 dans la région de Veyrier."

4718 **Ida Zlotnitzky**, 13, female, Paris, "par Simon":

"We stayed in Paris until recently. In that city, we started school. Our dad was deported in 1942; then our mom, about four months ago. Since then, we are living at home with a big sister who takes care of us. Lately, our means were cut back; and, with the agreement of our big sister, we left with some friends to cross the Swiss border. We came to Switzerland because our means of support declined and we feared deportation. We crossed the border on September 12, 1943, around 1045 in the region of Veyrier. We came alone from Paris as far as Saint-Julien, and from there 3 young girls accompanied us as far as the border."

"Nous sommes restés à Paris jusqu'à ces derniers jours. Dans cette ville nous avons commencé l'école. Notre papa à été déporté en 1942 puis notre maman il y env. 4 mois. Depuis nous vivons à la maison avec une grande soeur qui s'occupait de nous. Ces derniers temps nos moyens étaient restreint et avec l'assentiment de notre grande soeur nous sommes partis avec des amis pour passer la frontière Suisse. Nous sommes venus en Suisse car nos moyens d'existence baissaient et nous craignions la déportation. Nous avons passé la frontière le 12-9-43 vers les 1045 dans la région de Veyrier. Nous sommes venus seul de Paris jusqu'à St. Julien et de là 3 jeunes filles nous ont accompagnés jusqu'à la frontière."

4718 **Odette Zlotnitzky**, 12, female, Paris. She is Ida's sister. "par Simon"

4718 **Ginette Zlotnitzky**, 10, female, Paris. She is Ida's sister. "par Simon"

4718 **Hélène Zlotnitzky**, 8, female, Paris. She is Ida's sister. "par Simon"

4718 **Marguerite Zlotnitzky**, 7, female, Paris. She is Ida's sister. "par Simon"

Profile of the Convoy of September 14, 1943
MJS Convoy Number 6

Summary Information:

Border Guard Post: Cornières
Place where Arrest was made: b. 108
Time of Arrest: 2145 (9:45 p.m.) and 23:10 (11:10 p.m.)
Place and Time of Crossing: b. 108, 21:45 (9:45 p.m.) and 23:10 (11:10 p.m.)
Number of Persons: 29
Composition of convoy: 29 unaccompanied children
Correspondence with OSE list: All names appear on OSE list as "par Simon"

List of Children Comprising the Convoy and Excerpts from Declarations:

4735 **David Ejzenbaum**, 13, male, Paris, "par Simon":

"I have always stayed in Paris, and in this city I did all my schooling. I stayed in Paris until recently except for a stay with a foster mother since the deportation of my parents. My parents were deported, and, subsequently, the

Israelite committee placed me in foster homes in the countryside. From there, a woman came to tell me to go to Paris because there was a convoy of children leaving for Switzerland. We left Paris, accompanied by some young people as far as the border. We crossed the border on September 14, 1943, around 2230 in the region of Cornières."

"Je suis toujours resté à Paris et dans cette ville j'ai fait toutes mes écoles. Je suis resté à Paris jusqu'à ces derniers temps à part un séjour chez une nourrice depuis la déportation de mes parents. Mes parents ont été déportés et depuis c'est le comité israelite qui m'a placé chez des nourrice à la campagne. De là une dame est venue me dire de me rendre à Paris car il y avait un convoi d'enfants pour la Suisse. De Paris nous sommes partis accompagnés par des jeunes gens jusqu'à la frontière. Nous avons passaé la frontière le 14-9-43 vers les 2230 dans la région de Cornières."

4736 **Victor Grabsztok**, 13, male, Paris, "par Simon" "rue Amelot":

"I have always stayed in Paris until recently. In this city I did all my studies. I came to Switzerland because my mother is dead and my dad was deported. It was the Israelite committee that organized my departure for Switzerland. I came with a group of 29 children, and we were accompanied as far as the border by some young people. We crossed the border on September 14, 1943, around 2230 in the region of Cornières."

"Je suis toujours resté à Paris jusqu'à ces derniers jours. Dans cette ville j'ai fait toutes mes études. Je suis venu en Suisse car ma mère est morte et mon papa a été déporté. C'est le comité israelite qui a organisé mon départ pour la Suisse. Je suis venu avec un groupe de 29 enfants et nous avons été accompagnés jusqu'à la frontière par des jeunes gens. Nous avons passé la frontière le 14-9-43 vers les 2230 dans la région de Cornières."

4737 **Raymond Kuperas**, 12, male, Paris, "par Simon" "rue Amelot":

"I always lived in Paris and until recently. I was always in secondary schools or colonies. Since my relatives were deported my dad is a prisoner [sic], I was placed by the Israelite committee in the home of some people. It was the Israelite committee that did what was necessary for my crossing into Switzerland, I left with a group of 29 children, and we were accompanied by some young people as far as the border. We crossed the border on September 14, 1943, around 2230 in the region of Cornières."

"J'ai toujours habité à Paris et jusqu'à ces derniers jours. J'ai toujours été dans des lycées où des colonies. Depuis que mes parents ont été déportés mon papa est prisonnier, j'ai été placé par le comité israelite chez des personnes. C'est le comité israelite qui a fait le nécessaire pour mon passage en Suisse, Je suis parti avec un groupe de 29 enfants et nous avons été accompagnés par des jeunes gens jusqu'à la frontière. Nous avons passé la frontière le 14-9-43 vers les 2230 dans la région de Cornières."

4738 **Fradja Rosenfeld**, 16, female, Lodz (Poland), "par Simon" "rue Amelot":

"I left Lodz at the age of three years with my parents, headed for France. We settled in Paris, and in this city all of my sisters were born. We began our studies in this city, and we lived there until recently. My dad was deported, and our mother, no longer able to provide for our needs, allowed the Israelite committee to send us to Switzerland. This committee, which had defrayed some of our everyday living expenses, completely ceased its allocations and recommended to our mother that we be sent to Switzerland. Our mother remained in France with my brother. It was the Israelite committee that organized this transport; we were 29 children coming from Paris. We were accompanied as far as the border by several young people. We crossed the border on September 14, 1943, around 2230 in the region of Cornières."

"J'ai quitté Lodz à l'âge de trois ans avec mes parents en direction de la France. Nous nous sommes instalés à Paris et dans cette ville toutes mes soeurs sont nées. Nous avons commencé nos études dans cette ville et nous avons élu domicile jusqu'à ces derniers jours. Mon papa a été déporté et notre mère ne pouvant plus subvenir à nos besoins a toléré que le comité israelite nous envoye en Suisse. Ce comité qui subvenait en partie à nos frais courants a cessé complétement ses alocations et a commendé à notre mère de nous envoyés en Suisse. Notre mère est restée en France avec mon frère. C'est le comité israelite qui à organisé ce transport nous étions 29 enfants venant de Paris. Nous avons été accompagnés jusqu'à la frontière par plusieurs jeunes gens. Nous avons passé la frontière le 14-9-43 vers les 2230 dans la région de Cornières."

4738 **Berthe Rosenfeld**, 12, female, Paris. She is Fradja's sister. "par Simon" "rue Amelot"

4738 **Rachel Rosenfeld**, 9, female, Paris. She is Fradja's sister. "par Simon" "rue Amelot"

4738 **Marie Rosenfeld**, 7, female, Paris. She is Fradja's sister. "par Simon" "rue Amelot"

4738 **Sarah Rosenfeld**, 5, female, Paris. She is Fradja's sister. "par Simon" "rue Amelot"

4739 **Albert Madjora**, 13, male, Paris, "par Simon":

"We have always lived in Paris, and in this city we began our schooling. From Paris, we came to Switzerland. It was our mom who sent us to Switzerland because she feared for us the bombardments and because the Germans are going to conduct new roundups of Jews. It was a gentleman of the Israelite committee who came to submit to our mom a possible departure for Switzerland; as my dad had been deported and my mom had difficulty supporting us, she accepted. We left Paris with a convoy of 29 children and were led up to the border by some young people."

"Nous avons toujours habités à Paris et dans cette ville nous avons commencé nos écoles. De Paris nous sommes venus en Suisse. C'est notre maman qui nous a envoyé en Suisse car elle craignait pour nous les bombardements et les Allemands vont faire de nouvelles rafles contre les juifs. C'est un monsieur du Comité israelite qui est venu soumettre à notre maman un départ éventuel pour la Suisse, comme mon papa a été déporté et que ma maman avait de la peine a nous entretenir elle a accepté. Nous sommes partis de Paris avec un convoide 29 enfants et conduits jusqu'à la frontière pq r des jeunes gens."

4739 **Rose Madjora**, 9, female, Paris. She is Albert's sister. "par Simon"

4739 **Michel Madjora**, 8, male, Paris. He is Albert's brother. "par Simon"

4739 **Maurice Madjora**, 6, male, Paris. He is Albert's brother. "par Simon"

4740 **Eliane Neoussikhin**, 9, female, Paris, "par Simon":

"I always stayed in Paris apart from 2 years spent in a boarding school in Viroflay. I did my classes in a secondary school in Paris. I came to Switzerland sent by my mom, who feared for me [deportation] to Germany and the bombardments because I was in a secondary school near a factory. My dad is a prisoner in Germany, and my mom is still in Paris. I came to Switzerland with a group of 29 children. Convoy organized by the Israelite committee, and we were accompanied as far as the border by some young people. We crossed on September 14, 1943, around 2230 in the region of Cornières . . ."

"Je suis toujours restée à Paris à part 2 ans passés dans une pension à Viroflay. J'ai fait mes classes dans un lycée à Paris. Je suis venue en Suisse ebvoyée par ma maman qui craignait pour mois le déportement en Allemagne et les bombardements car j'étais dans un lycée près d'une usine. Mon papa est prisonnier en Allemagne et ma maman est restée à Paris. Je suis venue en Suisse avec un groupe de 29 enfants. Convoi organisé par le comité israel. et nous avons été accompagné jusqu'à la frontière per des jeunes gens. Nous avons passé le 14-9-43 vers les 2230 dans la région de Cornières . . ."

4741 **Esther Alamand**, 12, female, Paris, "par Simon":

"I was born in Paris, and I always stayed in that city until recently. I began my studies. I came to Switzerland because I feared being deported by the Germans. My mother stayed in France, and I came to Switzerland in the hope of seeing my dad again, who is in Leysin. I came to Switzerland with a group of 29 children, and this transport was organized by the Israelite committee. We came from Paris, accompanied by some people as far as the border. We crossed on September 14, 1943, around 2230 in the region of Cornières . . ."

"Je suis née à Paris et dans cette ville je suis toujours restée jusqu'à ces derniers jours. J'ai commencé mes études. Je suis venue en Suisse car je craignais d'être déportée par Les Allemands, ma maman est restée en France et je suis venue en Suisse dans l'espoir de revoir mon papa qui est à Leysin. Je suis venue en Suisse avec un groupe de 29 enfants et ce transport à été organisé par le comité israelite. Nous sommes venus de Paris accompagnés par des personnes jusqu'à la frontière. Nous avons passé le 14-9-43 vers les 2230 dans la région de Cornières . . ."

4742 **Paulette Kuperhant**, 14, female, Minzk (Poland) (This is the place name as it appears in the Declaration. Perhaps it refers to Minsk Mazowiecki, Poland.) "par Simon":

"We came to Paris in 1930 with our parents. We went to Paris, and in this city we began our studies. We stayed in Paris until recently, except each year we would go on vacation in the countryside. Our parents have been deported since July, and since then we have been placed by the Israelite committee in the homes of various people. To escape the German roundups, the Israelite committee organized our departure for Switzerland. We left Paris, 29 children accompanied by some people as far as the border. We crossed the border on September 14, 1943, around 2230 in the region of Cornières."

"Nous sommes venus à Paris en 1930 avec nos parents. Nous sommes allés à Paris et dans cette ville nous avons commencé mos études. Nous sommes restés à Paris jusqu'à ces derniers jours à part chaque année nous allions en vacance à la campagne. Nos parents sont déportés depuis le mois de juillet et depuis nous avons été placés par le comité israel. chez divers personnes. Pour nous soustraire aux rafles Allemandes le comité israel. a organisé notre départ pour la Suisse. Nous sommes partis de Paris 29 enfants accompagnés par des personnes jusqu'à la frontière. Nous avons passé la frontière le 14-9-43 vers les 2230 dans la région de Cornières."

4742 **Max Kuperhant**, 14, male, Minzk (Poland). He is Paulette's brother. "par Simon"

4753 **Isaac Kotkowski**, 16, male, Metz, "par Simon":

"We stayed in Metz until 1939. In this city we began our studies, which we continued in Paris, where we were subsequently. We stayed in Paris until recently. Our parents have been deported since 41 and 42. And, since then, it is the Israelite committee that has taken care of us and placed us in the countryside. We were bad off in the homes of people with whom we had been placed, and we requested a change. It was then when we arrived in Paris that we were taken to the train station; and we left with a convoy of 29 children. We were accompanied by some young people as far as the border. We crossed on September 14, 1943, around 2230 in the region of Cornières . . ."

"Nous sommes restés à Metz jusqu'en 1939. Dans cette ville nous avons commencé nos études que nous avons continuées à Paris où nous avons été ensuite. Nous sommes restés à Paris jusqu'à ces derniers jours. Nos parenst ont été déportés depuis 41 et 42. Et depuis c 'est le comité israelite qui s'est occupé de nous et nous a placés à la campagne. Nous étions mal chez les personnes où nous étions placés et nous avons fait une demande de changer, C'est là quant nous sommes arrivés à Paris que nous avons été conduits à la gare et nous sommes partis avec un convoide 29 enfants. Nous avons été accompagnés par des jeunes gens jusqu'à la frontière. N ous avons passé le 14-9-43 vers les 2230 dans la région de Cornières . . ."

4753 **Max Kotkowski**, 8, male, Metz. He is Isaac's brother. "par Simon"

4755 **Esther Sidi**, 13, female, Paris, "par Simon":

"I stayed with my brother in the home of our parents until recently. We had begun our schooling in Paris. We came to Switzerland, sent by our parents and on the instructions of a gentleman who is part of an Israelite committee. This man came to our house and said that it was advisable to send the children into Switzerland for fear of the bombardments to come. My parents agreed, and we had to show up at the Gare de Lyon in Paris, where a convoy of children was organized. There, some young people were waiting for us, and they took us by train to Annemasse, passing through Dijon—Aix-les-Bains—Annecy—Annemasse; and here, two young girls led us—the same ones who took us at the Gare de Lyon—in a house not far from Annemasse; and from this house 4 young people led us up to the border. We were 29 children. We crossed the border on September 14, 1943, around 2230 in the region of Cornières."

"Je suis restée avec mon frère chez nos parents jusqu'à ces derniers jours. Nous avons commencé écoles à Paris. Nous sommes venus en Suisse envoyé par nos parents et sur les indications d'un monsieur qui fait partie d'un comité israelite. Ce monsieur est venu à la maison et indicat qu'il était préférable d'envoyer les enfants en Suisse de crainte des bombardements à venir. Mes parent s ont accépté et nous devons nous présenter à la gare de Lyon à Paris où un convoi d'enfants était organisé. Là des jeunes gens nous attendaent et en train nous ont conduits à Annemasse et passant par Dijon-Aix-les-Bains-Annecy-Annemasse etvlà deux jeunes filles nous ont conduits, les même qui nous ont pris à la gare de Lyon, dans une maison nom loin d'Annemasse et de cette maison 4 jeunes gens nous ont conduits jusqu'à la frontière. Nous étions 29 enfants. Nous avons passé la frontière le 14.9.43 vers les 2230 dans la région de Cornières."

4755 **Elie Sidi**, 10, male, Paris. He is Esther's brother. "par Simon"

4756 **Madeleine Gwiazda**, 9, female, Warsaw, "par Simon" "rue Amelot":

"We stayed until 1938 in Warsaw; then we came with our parents into France, to Paris. In this city I began my schooling. Our parents were deported, and since then it was the Jewish committee who took care of us [and] placed [us] in a foster home in Vigneux (Seine-et-Oise). Last Friday, a woman came looking for us and took us to Paris; and there we joined a convoy of children who were leaving for Switzerland. We were 29, and two young girls accompanied us as far as the border. We crossed the border on September 14, 1943, around 2230 in the region of Cornières."

"Nous somes restées jusqu'en 1938 à Varsovie puis nous sommes venues avec nos parents en France à Paris. Dans cette ville j'ai commencé mes écoles. Nos parents ont été déportés et depuis c'est le comité juif qui s'est occupé de nous a placés chez une nourrice à Vigneux (Seine et Oise) vendre di dernier une dame est venue nous chercher et nous a conduit à Paris et de là nous avons rejoint un convoi d"enfant qui pqrtai pour la Suisse. Nous étions 29 et deux jeunes filles nous ont accompagnés jusqu'à la frontière. Nous avons passé la frontière le 14.9.43 vers les 2230 dans la région de Cornières."

4756 **Jeannette Gwiazda**, 7, female, Warsaw. She is Madeleine's sister. "par Simon" "rue Amelot"

4757 **Jérémie Kantorowicz**, 12, male, Warsaw, "par Simon":

"We left Warsaw in 1933 with our parents to come to Paris. In that city, we began our schooling. My mother was deported, and my dad is hiding in France. Since the departure of our parents, the Israelite committee placed us in a private home in the countryside. A woman belonging to the committee came looking for us to take us to Paris; and from there we left with a convoy of children that they had organized, headed for Switzerland. We were 29 children, and we were led up to the border by some young girls belonging to the committee. We crossed on September 14, 1943, around 2230 in the region of Cornières."

"Nous avons quittés Varsovie en 1933 avec mes parents pour venir à Paris. dans cette ville nous avons commencé nos écoles. Ma mère a été déportée et mon papa se cache en France. Depuis le départ de nos parents le comité israelite nous a placés chez des particuliers à la campagne. Une dame du comité est venue nous chercher pour nous conduire à Paris et de la nous sommes partis avec un convoi d'enfant,organisé par eux,en direction de la Suisse. Nous étions 29 enfants et nous avons été conduits jusqu'à la frontière par des jeunes f lles du comité. Nous avons passé la 14-9-43 vers les 2230 dans la région de Cornières."

4757 **Bernard Kantorowicz**, 10, male, Warsaw. He is Jérémie's brother. "par Simon"

4757 **Maurice Kantorowicz**, 6, male, Paris. He is Jérémie's brother. "par Simon"

4758 **Emile Waksman**, 9, male, Paris, "par Simon":

"I have always stayed in Paris apart from a stay of 1 year in Hérisy [possibly Chérisy]. In that city, I began my studies. From Hérisy I returned to Paris to join a convoy of children who were leaving for Switzerland, organized by the Israelite committee. My dad died four years ago, and my mom was deported by the Germans. I crossed the border on September 14, 1943, around 2230 in the region of Cornieres. I crossed with a group of 29 children, and we were accompanied by some young people."

"Je suis toujours resté à,Paris à part un séjour de 1 an à Hérisy. Dans cette ville j'ai commencé mes études. De Hérisy je suis retourné à Paris pour rejoindre le convoi d'enfant qui partait pour la Suisse organisé par le comité israelite. Mon papa est mort depuis 4 ans et ma maman a été déportée par les Allemands, J'ai passé la frontière le 14-9-43 vers les 2230 dans la région de Cornières. J'ai passé avec un groupe de 29 enfants et nous étio s accompagnés par des jeunes gens."

4779 **Edwige Plaut**, 7 or 8 (as only year of birth, not month or day, is indicated), female, Paris, "par Simon":

"I have not seen my parents since the age of three years. My parents were deported, and since then I have not had any further news of them. I then went to my grandfather's house; then he too was deported. Then I was put in a children's home in La Varenne; then I was in an orphanage in Paris; then I was in a woman's home in Paris and another one in Michellet. [It is unclear to me what place name is being cited here.] It was a young boy who came looking for me in Michelet and took me to Paris. From there, I was taken with 29 children, and we were accompanied by some young people near the border. We crossed the border on September 14, 1943, around 2330 in the region of Cornières."

"Je n'ai pas revu mes parents depuis l'âge de trois ans. Mes parents ont été déportés et depuis je n'ai plus eu de nouvelles d'eux. Je suis enuiste allé chez mon grand-père, puis il a été déporté aussi. Puis j'ai été mise dans une colonie d'enfant à la Varenne, puis j'ai été dans un horphelina à Paris, puis j'ai été chez une dame à Paris et une autre a Michellet. C'est un jeune garçon qui est venu me cherchervà Michelet et m'a conduit à Paris. De là j'ai été conduite avec 29 enfants et nous étions accompagnés par des jeunes gens du côte de la frontière. Nous avons passé la frontière le 14-9-43 vers les 2330 dans la région Cornière."

4785 **Dora Tovy**, 13, female, Paris, "par Simon":

"I always stayed in Paris until recently. In that city, I did all my studies until now. My dad has been deported since June 42, and my mom is still in Paris. It was a man belonging to the Israelite committee who came to the house and spoke with my mother about a departure for Switzerland because there would soon be bombardments in France and also because my mother would be better able to hide herself from the German roundups against the Jews. I came with a convoy of children, 29, and we were accompanied by some young people right up close to the border, and from there two *passeurs* accompanied us. We crossed the border on September 14, 1943, around 2230 in the region of Cornières."

"Je suis toujours restée à Paris jusqu'à ces derniers jours. Dans cette ville j'ai fait toutes mes études jusqu'à cemoment. Mon papa est déporté depuis le mois de juin 42 et ma maman est restée à Paris. C'est un monsieur de comité israelite qui est venu à la maison et a parlé avec ma mère pour un départ en Suisse car il y aurait des prochain bombardements en France et que ma maman pourrait mieux se cacher des rafles Allemandes contre les juifs. Je suis venue avec un convoi d'enfants, 29, et nous avons été accompagnés par des jeunes gens jusque près de la frontière de là deux passeurs nous ont accompagnés. Nous avons passé la frontière 14.9.43 vers les 2223 0 dans la région de Cornières."

4786 **Henri Kamer**, 5, male. Place of birth not indicated. No Declaration was available for this child. An arrest report indicates that Henri is the cousin of Madeleine and Jeannette Gwiazda, also in this convoy. It also states that his parents had been deported, that he was living in a private home in Gagny (Seine-et-Oise), and that he was subsequently sent to La Varenne. "par Simon" "rue Amelot"

Profile of the Convoy of September 21, 1943 MJS Convoy Number 7

Summary Information:

Border Guard Post: Cornières
Place where Arrest was made: Chemin des Vignes
Time of Arrest: 2200 (10:00 p.m.)
Place and Time of Crossing: "through the barbed wire"
Number of Persons: 20
Composition of convoy: 20 unaccompanied children
Correspondence with OSE list: All names appear on OSE list as "par Simon"

List of Children Comprising the Convoy and Excerpts from Declarations:

4847 **Léa Korzen**, 12, female, Paris, "par Simon":

"I was born and I left Paris in 1942 to go to St. Antonin with my parents and to Nice. I began my schooling in Paris, and I stayed in Nice until recently. My parents are in Nice and are hiding from the Germans. They sent me to Switzerland for fear of German reprisals against the Jews. I came to Switzerland with a convoy of 20 children, and we were taken as far as Annemasse by [female] French scouts; then they placed us in the [hands] of *passeurs*. [The adjective and pronoun used to refer to scouts are both in the feminine form, indicating that the scouts were female.] We crossed the border on September 21, 1943, around 2300 in the region of Cornières."

"Je suis née et j ' ai quitté Paris en 1942 pour me rendre à St. Antonin avec mes parents et à Nice. J'ai commencé mes écoles à Paris. et je suis restée à Nice jusqu'à ces derniers jours. Mes parents sont à Nice et se cachent des

Allemands. Ils m'ont envoyée en Suisse de crainte des représailles Allemandes contre les juifs. Je suis venue en Suisse avec un convoi de 20 enfants et nous avons été conduits jusqu'à Annemasse par des scouts française, puis elles nous ont remis entre les de passeurs. Nous avons passé la frontière le 21-9-43 vers les 2300 dans la région de Cornières."

4848 **Lilianne Benadon**, 14, female, Salonika (Greece), "par Simon":

"I left Salonika at the age of two years with my parents to go to Paris, where we stayed until 1942. In that city, I began my schooling. We then went to Juan-les-Pins, and from there, Nice, where we stayed until recently. My father is deceased, and my mom stayed in Nice, where she is hiding. She sent me to Switzerland fearing that I would suffer reprisals of Germans against the Jews. I came to Switzerland with the convoy of children of 20, and we were accompanied by [female?] French scouts as far as Annamasse [Annemasse]; from there, they placed us in the hands of a *passeur.* [The adjective describing scouts is in the masculine form, while the pronoun used is in the feminine form.] We crossed the border on September 21, 1943, around 2300 in the region of Cornières."

"J'ai quitté Salonique à l'âge de deux ans avec mes parents pour nous rendre à Paris où nous sommes restés jusqu'en 1942. Dans cette ville j'ai commencé mes classes. Nous sommes ensuite allés à Juan-les-Pins et de là Nice où nous sommes restés jusqu'à ces derniers jours. Mon père est décédé et ma maman est restée à Nice où elle se cache- Elle m'a envoyée en Suisse de crainte que je subisse les représailles des Allemands envers les juifs. Je suis v enus en Suisse avec le convoi d'enfants de 2 0 et nous étions accompagnés de scouts français, jusqu'à Annamasse de là elles nous ont remis entre les mains de passeur. Nous avons passé la frontière le 21-9-43 vers les 2300 dans l a région de Cornières."

4849 **Hélène Karwasser**, 11, female, Berlin, "par Simon":

"My sister was born in Paris, where my parents had lived for many years. Then they came to Berlin, where I was born. Since Berlin, we went to Belgium, then to France, to Paris, where we stayed until 1940; then we went to Amélie-les-Bains, then to Nice, where we stayed until recently. My parents are hiding in Nice, and they sent us to Switzerland for fear of reprisals by Germans against the Jews. We came with a convoy of children accompanied by some [female] scouts as far as Annemasse; from there, they placed us in the hands of *passeurs.* [The pronoun used to refer to scouts is in the feminine form, indicating that the scouts were female.] We crossed the border on Setpember 21, 1943, around 2300 in the region of Cornières . . ."

"Ma soeur est née à Paris où mes parents ont habités de longues ans née puis ils sont venus à Berlin où je suis née. Depuis Berlin, nous sommes allée en Belgique puis en France à Paris où nous sommes restés jusqu'en 1940 puis nous sommes allés à Amélie-les-Bains puis à Nice où nous sommes restés jusqu'à ces derniers jours. Mes parents se cachent à Nice et ils nous ont envoyées en Suisse de crainte des représailles des Allemands contre les Juifs. Nous sommes venues avec un convoi d'enfants accompagnés par des scouts jusqu'à Annemasse, de là elles nous ont remis entre les mains de passeurs. N ous avons passé la frontière le 21-9-43 vers les 2300 dans la région de Cornières . . ."

4849 **Génia Karwasser**, 16, female, Paris. She is Hélène's sister. "par Simon"

4850 **Isidore Eherlich**, 13, male, Antwerp, "par Simon":

"I left Antwerp after my birth, and I was with my parents in Strasbourg; then we were in Nice, and, in that city, I began my schooling. I stayed in Nice until recently. My parents are hiding in Nice, and they sent me to Switzerland to evade the measures taken by the Germans against the Jews. We crossed the border on September 21, 1943, around 2300 in the region of Cornières."

"Je suis aprti d'Anvers dès ma naissance et j'ai été avec mes parents à Strasbourg puis nous avons été à,Nice et dans cette ville j'ai commencé mes écoles. Je suis resté à Nice jusqu'à ces derniers jours. Mes parents sont cachés à Nice et m'ont envoyé en Suisse pour éviter les mesures prise par les Allemands contre les juifs. N ous avons passé la frontière le 21-9-43 vers les 2300 dans la région de Cornières."

4851 **Léon Majerovicz**, 13, male, Melawa (Poland), "par Simon":

"I stayed until the age of 5 years in Melawa; then I came with my parents to Paris, where we stayed until 40; then I was in Nice, where I stayed until recently. My father is in Nice, and my mother was deported. I came to Switzerland to evade the measures taken by the Germans against the Jews. I came with a convoy of 20 children accompanied by [female?] French scouts as far as Annemasse; then they placed us in the hands of *passeurs*. [The adjective describing scouts is in the masculine form, while the pronoun used is in the feminine form.] We crossed the border on September 21, 1943, around 2300 in the region of Cornières."

"Je siis resté jusqu'à l'âge de 5 ans à Melawa puis je suis venu avec mes paremts à Paris où nous smmes restés jusqu'en 40 puis j'ai été à Nice, où je suis resté jusq 'à ces derniers jours. Mon père est a nice et ma mère à été déportée. Je suis venu en Suisse pour éviter les mesures prise par les Allemands contre les juijs. Je suis venu avec un convoi de 20 enfants accompagnés apr scouts français jusqu'à Annemasse puis elles nous ont remis entre les mains de passeurs. N ous a vons passé la frontière le 21-9-43 vesr les 2300 dans la région de Cornières."

4852 **André-Jacques Panczer**, 8, male, Paris, "par Simon":

"I stayed in Paris until 1942. In that city, I began my schooling; then I went with my parents to Pressac—Megève [Prayssac—Megève] and Nice, where I stayed until recently. My parents were placed in a sanatorium at St. Clair de la Tour, and they sent me to Switzerland to evade the measures taken by the Germans against the Jews. I came to Switzerland with a convoy of 20 children. We were accompanied by some French scouts as far as Annemasse; and from there they placed us in the hands of *passeurs*. We crossed the border on September 21, 1943, around 2300 in the region of Cornières . . ."

"Je suis resté à Paris jusqu'en 1942. Dans cette ville j'ai commencé mes écoles puis je suis allé avec mes parents à Pressac-Mégève et Nice où je suis resté jusqu'à ces dernier sjours. Mes parents ont été mis dans un sanatorium à St. Clair de la Tour et il m'ont envoyé en Suisse pour éviter les mesures prise par les Allemands contre les juifs. Je suis venu en Suisse avec un convoi de 20 enfants. Nous avons été accompagnés par des scouts fRançais jusqu'à Annemasse et de là ils nous ont remis entre les mains de passeurs. Nous avons passé la frontière le 21-9-43 vers les 2300 dans la région de Cornières . . ."

4853 **Gertrude Zegel**, age 14, female, Saarbrück (Germany), "par Simon":

"I stayed in Saarbrück until 1935. In that city, I began my schooling; then I came to Italy with my parents. We went to Merano; then we came to France, to Nice. My father is a prisoner in Germany, and my mother and my sister are hiding in Nice. They sent me to Switzerland to evade the reprisals taken by the Germans against the Jews. I came to Switzerland with a convoy of 20 children organized by the an Israelite committee. We were accompanied by some [female] scouts as far as Annemasse; and from there they placed us in the hands of *passeurs*. [The pronoun used to refer to scouts is in the feminine form, indicating that the scouts were female.]

We crossed the border on September 21, 1943, around 2300 in the region of Cornières . . ."

"Je suis restée à Sarbruck jusqu'en 1935. Dans cette ville j'ai commencé mes écoles puis je suis venue en Italie avec mes parents. Nous sommes allés à Mérano puis nous sommes venus en France à Nice. Mon père est prisonnier en Allemagne et ma mère et ma soeur se cachent à Nice, Elles m'ont envoyé en Suisse pour éviter les représailles prise par les Allemands contre les Juifs. Je suis venue en Suisse avec un convoi de 20 enfants organisé par un comité israelite. Nous avons été accompagnés par des scouts jusqu'à Annemasse et delà elles nous ont remis entre les mains de passeurs. Nous avons passé la frontière le 21-9-43 vers les 2300 dans la région de Cornières . . ."

4854 **Arnold Katz**, 6, male, Volklingen (Germany), "par Simon":

"I came to France with my parents, and we settled in Nice. My parents are hiding in Nice, and they sent me to Switzerland for fear of German reprisals against the Jews. I came to Switzerland with a convoy of children organized by an Israelite committee, and we were accompanied as ar as Annemasse by some French scouts. There, they placed us in the hands of a *passeur.* We crossed the border on September 21, 1943, around 2300 in the region of Cornières . . ."

"Je suis venu en France avec mes parents et nous nous sommes instalés à Nice. Mes parents sont cachés à Nice et m'ont envoyé en Suisse de crainte des représailles Allemandes contre les juifs. Je suis venu en Suisse avec un convoi d'enfant organisé par un comité israelite et nous avons été accompagnée jusqu'à Annemasse par des scouts Français. Là ils nous ont remis entre les mains d'un passeur . Nous avons passé la frontière le 21-9-43 vers les 2300 dans la région de Cornières . . ."

4855 **Anna Granat**, 16, female, Aubervilliers (France), "par Simon":

"We lived in Aubervilliers until 1940. Aubervilliers is in a suburb of Paris. We began our schooling in Paris; then we went to Nice, where we stayed until recently. My parents are hiding in the city of Nice; and, for fear that we would suffer the German reprisals against the Jews, they sent us to Switzerland. We came with a convoy of children organized by an Israelite committee, and we were accompanied as far as Annemasse by some scouts. From there, we were placed in the hands of *passeurs,* who led us up to the barbed wire. We crossed the border on September 21, 1943, around 2300 in the region of Cornières."

"Nous sommes restés à Aubervilliers jusqu'en 1940, Aubervilliers se trouve dans la banlieue de Paris. Nous avons commencé nos écoles à Paris puis nous sommes allés à Nice où nous sommes restés jusqu'à ces derniers jours. Mes parents sont cachés dans la ville de Nice et de crainte que nous subissions les représailles Allemandes contre les juifs ils nous ont envoyés en Suisse. Nous sommes venus avec un convoi d'enfant organisé par un comité israelite et nous avons été accompagnés jusqu'à Anne,asse par des scouts. De là Nous avons été remis en tre les mains de passeurs qui nous ont conduits jusqu'au barbelés. Nous avons passé la frontière le 21-9-43 vers les 2300 dans la région de Cornières."

4855 **Jacob Granat**, 16, male, Aubervilliers (France). He is Anna's twin brother. "par Simon"

4855 **Simon Granat**, 13, male, Paris. He is Anna's brother. "par Simon"

4855 **Sarah Granat**, 11, female, Paris. She is Anna's sister. "par Simon"

4855 **Joseph Granat**, 10, male, Paris. He is Anna's brother. "par Simon"

4856 **Joseph Sosnowski**, 12, male, Lens (France), "par Simon":

"I left Lens at the age of one year with my parents to go to Nice. In that city, we began our studies with my brother, and we stayed until recently. My parents are living hidden in Nice and sent us to Switzerland to evade the measures taken by the Germans against the Jews. We came to Switzerland with a convoy of children accompanied by [female] French scouts. From Annemasse, they placed us in the hands of *passeurs,* who led us up to the barbed wire. [The adjective describing scouts that appears in the previous sentence and the pronoun used in this sentence are feminine, indicating that the scouts were female.] We crossed on September 21, 1943, around 2300 in the region of Cornières."

"J'ai quitté Lens à l'âge d'une année avec mes parents pour aller à Nice. Dans cette ville nous avons commencé nos études avec mon frère et nous sommes restés jusqu'à ces derniers jours. Mes parents vivent cachés à Nice et nous ont envoyés en Suisse pour éviter les mesures prise par les Allemands contre les jui fs. Nous sommes venus en Suisse avec un convoi d'enfant accompagné par des scouts Française. De Annemasse elles nous ont remis en tre les mains de passeurs qui nous ont conduits jusqu'au barbelés. Nous avons passé le 21-9-43 vers les 2300 dans la région de Cornières."

4856 **Marcel Sosnowski**, 9, male, Nice. He is Joseph's brother. "par Simon"

4857 **Renée Lipschitz**, 15, female, Antwerp, "par Simon":

"I stayed in Antwerp until 1940. In that city, I began my schooling; then I came to Béziers with my parents. After a period of three years, we came to Grenoble, where we stayed for six months before going to Nice. My parents are hiding in Nice and sent me to Switzerland for fear that I would suffer persecutions of Germans against the Jews. I crossed the border on September 21, 1943, around 2300 in the region of Cornières. We were accompanied by young scouts as far as Annemasse and, from there, by *passeurs*."

"Je suis restée à Anvers jusqu'en 1940. Dans cette ville j'ai commencé mes écoles puis je suis venue à Béziers avec mes parents. Après un stage de trois ans nous sommes venues à Grenoble où nous sommes restés 6 mois, then going to Nice. Mes parents se cachent à Nice et m'ont envoyée en Suisse de crainte que je subisse les persécutions de Allemands contre les juifs. J'ai passé la frontière le 21-9-43 vers les 2300 dans la région de Cornières. Nous étions accompagnés de jeunes scouts jusqu'à Annemasse et de là par des passeurs."

4858 **Estelle Goldfarb**, 14, female, Warsaw, "par Simon":

"We stayed in Warsaw until 1930. From that city we came to Paris with our parents. We stayed in Paris until July 1942; then we went to Toulouse and Nice and from there, to Switzerland. Our parents are hiding in the city of Nice and sent us to Switzerland so that it would be easier for them to hide. In addition to that, they feared for us the reprisals of the Germans against people of the Jewish race. We crossed the border on September 21, 1943, around 2230 in the region of Cornières. We came with a convoy of 20 children accompanied by French scouts. They accompanied us as far as Annemasse and from there, placed us in the hands of *passeurs*." [The adjective describing scouts that appears in the previous sentence and the pronoun used in this sentence are feminine, indicating that the scouts were female.]

"Nous sommes restées à Varsovie jusqu'en 1930. De cette ville nous sommes venues à Paris avec nos parents. N ous sommes restées à Paris jusqu'au mois de juillet 42 puis nous sommes allés à Toulouse et N ice. et de là en Suisse. Nos parents sont cachés dans la ville de Nice et nous envoyées en Suisse pour qu'il aient plus de facilité de se cacher. En plus de cela ils craignaient pour nous les représailles des Allemands contre les personnes de ra ce juive. Nous avons passé la frontière le 21-9-43 vers les 2230 dans la région de Cornières. Nous sommes venues avec un convode 20 enfants accompagné par des scoutes Française. Elles nous ont accompagés jusqu'à Annemasse et de là nous ont remis en tre les mains de passeurs."

4858 **Frida Goldfarb**, 14, female, Warsaw. She is Estelle's twin sister. "par Simon"

4868 **Isidor Brust**, 10, male, Luxembourg, "par Simon":

"Born in 1932 in Luxembourg, I stayed there until the age of eight, that being May 1940. I began my primary schooling there. I came with my parents to the

Bas-Languedoc until 1943. In the spring of 1943, I was 4 months in Megève and then in Nice with my parents. I made my way to Switzerland to evade the measures taken by the German authorities against the Israelites and my parents are no longer able to continue to hide me. I crossed the border on September 22, 1943, at 0030 in the region of Cornières. I left Nice with a convoy of Israelite children. This convoy was put together by the Israelite committee of Nice. It was scouts who led us up to the border."

"Né en 1932 à Luxembourg, j'y suis resté jusqu'à l'âge de huit ans, soit jusqu'en mai 1940. J'y ai commencé mes écoles primaires. Je suis venu avec mes parents dans le Bas-Languedoc jusqu'en 1943, Au printemps 1943, j'ai été 4 mois à Mégève et ensuite à Nice avec mes parents. J'ai gagné la Suisse pour éviter les mesures prises par les autorités allemandes contre les israelites et mes parents ne pouvant plus continuer à me cacher. J'ai franchi la frontière le 22.9.43 à 0030 dans la région de Cornières. Je suis parti de Nice avec un convoi d'enfants israelites. Ce convoi était formé par le Comité Israelite de Nice. Ce sont des scouts qui nous ont conduits jusqu'à la frontière."

Profile of the Convoy of September 23 (1), 1943
MJS Convoy Number 8

Summary Information:

Border Guard Post: Sézenove
Place where Arrest was made: Plaine du Loup
Time of Arrest: 2100 (9:00 p.m.)
Place and Time of Crossing: between *bornes* 50 and 51 at 20:30 (8:30 p.m).; "crossed over top of the barbed wire"
Number of Persons: 7
Composition of convoy: 7 unaccompanied children
Correspondence with OSE list: 5 of 7 names appear on OSE list as "par Simon"

List of Children Comprising the Convoy and Excerpts from Declarations:

4947 **Albert Reisz**, 18, male, Vienna, "par Simon":

"Born in 1925 in Vienna, I stayed there until 1938. I did my primary schooling there. From 1938 to 1940, in Brussels. From 1940, I took refuge in France, first in Toulouse from May 1940 to October 40, then at Montélimar until February 1941, then in the Camp of Rivesaltes until June 1941; and I was liberated and put in forced residence in Vence (Alpes-Maritimes), where I worked as an office employee. This was my last place of residence in France. My mother is dead and my father is hiding in France. I doubt that he will come to Switzerland. I made my way to Switzerland to evade the measures taken by the German authorities against the Israelites. I crossed the Swiss border on September 23, 1943, at 2100 in the region of Saint-Julien. I had made the acquaintance in Nice of a certain Monsieur WYSTER, Jacques, at the Café de Paris in Nice, Rue Pasteur Elie, who told me I could reach Switzerland with a convoy of children. Since Nice, we went by train as far as Annecy accompanied by a young woman Thérèse. Then, in Annecy, we stayed for three days at the Lycée BERTHOLET; then we left by bus for Saint-Julien with Monsieur Roland and Mademoiselles Mila, Jeanne, and Théa. From Saint-Julien with M. Rolland and Mademoiselles Mila, Jeanne, and Théa. From Saint-Julien and to the border, we were accompanied by Monsieur ROLAND and Mademoiselle JEANNE."

"Né en 1925 à Vienne, j'y suis resté jusqu'en 1938- J'y ai fait mes écoles primaires. De 1938 à 1940, à Bruxelles. Dès 1940, je me suis réfugié en France, d'abord à Toulouse de mai 1940 à octobre 40, puis à Montélimar jusqu'en février 1941, puis au Camp de Riversalt jusqu'en juin 1941 et j'ai été libéré et mis enrésidence forcée à Vence (Alpes Maritimes) où j'ai travaillé comme employé de bureau- Ce fut mon dernier domicile en France. Ma mère est morte et mon père est caché en France. Je ne pense pas qu'il vienne en Suisse. J'ai gagné la suisse pour éviter les mesures prises par les autorités allemandes contre les israelites. J'ai franchi la frontière suisse le 23.9.43 à 2100 dans la région de St. Julien. J'ai fait la connaissance à Nice d'un certain Monsieur WYSTER Jacques au Café de Paris à Nice, Rue Pasteur Elie, qui m'a dit que je pourrais gagner la Suisse avec un convoi d'enfants. Depuis Nice nous sommes allés en train jusqu'à Annecy accompagnés par une demoiselle Thérèse . Puis à Annecy, nous sommes restés trois jours au Lycée BERTHOLET, puis nous sommes partis en autocar pour St.Julien avec M. Rolland et Mlles Mila, Jeanne et Théa. De St.Julien et à la frontière, nous étions accompagnés de M. ROLAND et Mlle JEANNE."

5019 Henriné Hirschhorn, 15, male, Metz, "par Simon":

[Note: The crossing date stated on the Declaration appears to be incorrect, as it does not correspond with the crossing date stated on the arrest report.]

"Born in 1928, I left at the age of 2 years with my parents to go to Luxembourg. I stayed 12 years in that city, and I did all my schooling. In 1941, I came with my mother to Marseille, where we stayed until February 1943; then we went to Nice—Megève—Nice; from that city, I came to Switzerland. My father is dead, and my mother stayed in Nice, where she is hiding. We learned from a Monsieur Jacques that you could come to Switzerland with a convoy. We were

17 children at the train station in Nice, and we left for Annecy with a young woman; there a young woman Jeanne took us to a secondary school, where we stayed for two days; then we left, accompanied by Mademoiselle Jeanne, by bus as far as Saint-Julien; then she placed us in the hands of *passeurs*. We crossed the border on September 24, 1943, around 2100 in the region of la Feuillée. We went to a farm, and we asked that he telephone the customs officer, who came looking for us and took us to the customs house . . ."

"Né en 1928 je suis parti à l'âge de 2 ans avec mes parents pour aller à Luxembourg. Je suis resté 12 ans dans cette ville et j'ai fait toutes mes écoles. En 1941 je suis venu avec ma mère à Marseille où nous sommes restés jusqu'au mois de février 1943 puis nous sommes allées à Nice-Mègève-Nice de cette ville je suis venu en Suisse. Mon père est mort et ma maman est restée à Nice où elle se cache. Nous avons appris par un Monsieur Jacques que l'on pouvait venir en Suisse avec un convoi. Nous étions 17 enfants à la gare de Nice et nous sommes partis pour Annecy avec une demoiselle, là une demoiselle Jeanne nous a conduits dans un lycée où nous sommes restés 2 jours puis nous sommes partis accompagnés de Melle Jeanne en car jusqu'à Saint-Julien puis elle nous a remis entre les mains de passeurs. Nous avons passé la frontière le 24.9.43 vers les 2100 dans la région de la Feuillée. Nous sommes allés dans une ferme et nous avons demandé qu'il tél. au douanier qui est venu nous chercher et nous a conduit au poste de douane . . ."

5020 Renata Dzierlatka, 14, female, Antwerp:

"Born in 1929 in Antwerp, I stayed there until 1940. I did my primary schooling there. From 1940 to 1942, in Marseille with my parents. From 1942 to June 1943, in Vence. Then, I was fifteen days in Nice, which is where my mother still is. Then finally, in Draguignan. My father was deported in December 1942. My mother also plans to have two brothers younger than I passed [into Switzerland]. I made my way to Switzerland to evade the measures taken by the German authorities against the Israelites. I crossed the border on September 23, 1943, at 2100 in the region of la Feuillée. The organization O.S.E. organized a convoy of children in Nice for Switzerland. A young woman JEANNE took us from Nice to Annecy and from Annecy to Saint-Julien by bus accompanied by Monsieur ROLAND and from Saint-Julien with a *passeur* whom I do not know. After the crossing, we went into a house, and the people who lived there called customs, who came looking for us and took us to the customs house . . ."

"Née en 1929 à Anvers, j'y suis restée jusqu'en 1940. J'y fait mes écoles primaires. De 1940 à 1942 à Marseille avec mes parents. de 1942 à juin 1943, à Vence,. Puis j'ai été quinze jours à Nice où se trouve encore ma mère. Puis enfin à Draguignan. Mon père a été déporté en décembre 1942. Ma mère compte faire aussi passer deux frères plus jeunes que moi. J'ai gagné la Suisse pour éviter les mesures prises par les autorités allemandes contre les israelites. J'ai franchi la frontière le 23.9.43 à 2100 dans la région de la Feuillée. L'organisation O.S.E. a organisé un convoi d'enfants de Nice pour la Suisse. Une demoiselle JEANNE nous a conduits depuis Nice à Annecy et de Annecy à St. Julien en autocar accompagné de M. ROLAND et de St.Julien avec un passeur que je ne connais pas. Après le passage, nous nous sommes rendus dans une maison et les gens qui y habient ont appelé la Douane qui est venue nous chercher et nous conduire au Poste de Douane . . ."

5025 **Adolphe Herz**, 15, male, Antwerp, "par Simon":

[Note: In the Declaration, the first name appears as "Adilf." The child's signature clearly indicates that the correct spelling is "Adolphe."]

"I lived in Brussels until March 1943 with my parents. My father was a theater artist. My parents have been deported since about 1 year. I am in Nice since March 1943 until recently. I came to Switzerland to evade the measures taken by the Germans against the Jews. A young woman took me as far as Annecy, then as far as the border, a young man whose name I do not know led us up to the barbed wire; we were 7 children. We crossed the border on September 23, 1943, at 0900 in the area of la Feuillée . . ."

"J'ai habité Bruxelle jusqu'en mars 1943 avec mesparents. Mon père était artiste de théâtre. Mesparents sont déportés depuis 1 an environ. Je suis à Nice depuis mars 1943 jusqu'à ces derniers jours. Je suis venu en Suisse pour éviter lesmesures prises par les Allemands contre les juifs. Une demoiselle m'a conduit jusqu'à Annecy, puis jusqu'à la frontière un jeune homme dont je ne sais pas le nom nous a conduit jusqu'aux barbelés, on étais 7 enfants. Nous avons passé la frontière le 23.9.43 à 0900 dans la région de La Feuillée . . ."

5027 **Rosette Dolberg**, 14, female, Liège (France):

"Born in 1928 in Liège, I stayed there until 1940. I did my primary schooling there. We took refuge in Nice with my parents, where we stayed constantly. My parents stayed in Nice. I made my way to Switzerland to evade the measures taken by the German authorities against the Israelites. I crossed the Swiss border on September 23, 1943, at 2100 in the region of la Feuillée. It was the organization O.S.E. that took care of our crossing into Switzerland. A young woman JEANNE accompanied us as far as Annecy; then, from Annecy to Saint-Julien, by bus with Mademoiselle JEANNE and Monsieur ROLAND,

and from Saint-Julien to the border with a *passeur* whom I do not know. In Switzerland, we arrived at a house that called the customs officers and these last took us to the customs house . . ."

"Née en 1928 à Liège, j'y suis restée jusqu'en 1940. J'y fait mes écoles primaires . Nous nous ommes réfugiés à Nice avec mes parents où nus sommes restés contamment. Mes parents sont restés à Nice. J'aigagné la Suisse pour éviter les mesures prises par les autorités allemandes contre les israelites. J'ai franchi la frontière suisse le 23.9.43 à 2100 dans la région de la Feuillée. C'est l 'organisation O.S.E. qui s'est occupé de notre passage en Suisse. Une demoiselle JEANNE nous accompagnés jusqu'à Annecy, puis de Annecy à St-Julien en autocar avec Mlle JEANNE et M. ROLAND et depuis St.Julien à la frontière avec un passeur que je ne connais pas. En Suisse, nous sommes arrivés dans une maison qui a appelé les douaniers et ces derniers nous ont conduits au Postede Douane . . ."

5038 **Harry Goldberg**, 14, male, Berlin, "par Simon":

"I lived in Germany until 1933; then I was in Paris, in Palestine and in Italy, [and] lastly in Nice. My father is a lawyer; he has been in the United States since 1939; my mother is in Nice; she is hiding. I came to Switzerland to escape being deported by the Germans. I crossed the border on September 23, 1943, at la Feuillée in the company of 6 children led by two men whom I do not know."

"J'ai habité l'Allemagne jusqu'en 1933, ensuite j'ai été à Paris, en Palestine et en Italie, dernièrement à Nice. Mon père est avocat, il est aux Etats-Unis depuis 1939, ma mère est à Nice, elle se cache. Je suis venu en Suisse pour éviter d'être déporté par les Allemands. J'ai franchi la frontière le 23.9.43 à La Feuillée en compagnie de 6 enfants conduits par deux hommes que je ne connais pas."

5071 **Harry Walter**, 15, male, Frankfurt (Germany), "par Simon":

"Born in 1929 in Germany, I stayed in this country for only 4 years, that being until June 6, 1932. From 1932 until 1943, the month of March, in Paris, where I did my primary schooling and the École Centrale de T.S.F. In March 1943, I left for Moissac, where there is the camp of the Israelite Scouts, to which I belong. The Germans were coming; I left for the home of my parents in Nice, from which I left for Switzerland. I made my way to Switzerland to evade the measures taken by the German authorities against the Israelites. I crossed the Swiss border September 23, 1943, at 2100 in the region of la Feuillée. It was the organization of Israelite scouts who took care of our crossing, with 7 comrades. From Nice to Annecy, we were accompanied by Mademoiselle JEANNE; and from Annecy to Saint-Julien, by bus, still accompanied by Mademoiselle and Monsieur ROLAND; and, from Saint-Julien, by two *passeurs* whom I do not know."

"Né en 1928 en Allemagne, je suis resté dans ce pays que 4 ans, soit jusqu'au 6 juin 1932.Le 1932 à 1943 au mois de mars, à Paris où j-ai fait mes écoles primaires et l-Ecole Centrale de T.S.F. En mars 1943, je suis parti pour Moissac où se trouve le Camp des Scouts israelites et dont je fais partie. Les allemands étant venus, je suis parti chez mes parents à Nice d-où je suis parti pour la Suisse. J'ai gagné la Suisse pour éviter les mesures prises par les autorités allemandes contre les israelites. J'ai franchi la frontière suisse le 23.9.43 à 2100 dans la région de la Feuillée. C'est l'organisation des scouts israelites qui s-est occupée de notre passage avec 7 camardes. De nice à Annecy, nous avons été accompagnés par Mlle JEANNE et de Annecy à St .Julien en car toujours accompagnés de Mlle JEANNE et de M. ROLAND et dès St.Julien par deux passeurs que je ne connais pas."

Profile of the Convoy of September 23 (2), 1943
MJS Convoy Number 9

Summary Information:

Border Guard Post: Cornières
Place where Arrest was made: "barrage" (meaning "barrier" or "toll bar")
Time of Arrest: 2245 (10:45 p.m.)
Place and Time of Crossing: "over the barbed wire"
Number of Persons: 19
Composition of convoy: 19 unaccompanied children (Note: Arrest reports indicate group size as 23, although I identified 19.)
Correspondence with OSE list: All names appear on OSE list as "par Simon"

List of Children Comprising the Convoy and Excerpts from Declarations:

5021 **Rudolph Unterman**, 14, male, Antwerp, "par Simon":

"I lived in Antwerp until 1942, Antwerp (Belgium), with my parents. My father is a shopkeeper. My parents are now in Nice. I have two brothers older than I; one is in Nice, the other in England. I came to Switzerland to escape deportation. A young woman accompanied me as far as Annecy; the group was comprised of 17 children. Then we came as far as Annemasse; three young people led us up to the barbed wire. We crossed the border on September 23, 1943, in the region of Cornières, and we were arrested shortly afterwards . . ."

"J'ai habité Anvers jusqu'en 1942 Anvers (Belgique) avec mes parents. Mon père est commerçant. Mes parents sont actuellement à Nice. J'ai deux frères plus âgés que moi, un est à Nice, l'autre en Angleterre. Je suis venu en Suisse pour éviter la déportation. Une demoiselle m'a accompagné jusqu'à Annecy, le groupe était composé de 17 enfants. Ensuite on est venu jusqu'à Annemasse, trois jeunes gens nous conduisirent jusqu'aux barbelés. Nous avons franchi la frontière le 23.9.43 dans la région de Cornières et nous avons été arrêtés peu après . . ."

5026 **Cecile Axelrad**, 15, female, Frankfurt (Germany), "par Simon":

"We stayed in Frankfurt until 1933. I began my primary schooling in Frankfurt, and I continued in the various cities in which we lived afterwards. We came to France, to Paris, in 1933 with our parents, where we stayed until 1942. We left Paris to go to the Free Zone, to Culan (Cher); and, after two months, we were taken and put into a camp, where we stayed for eight months. We fled this camp to go to Saint-Gervais; and from there we went to Nice, where we stayed until recently. My parents are hiding in Nice, and we came to Switzerland to evade the measures taken by the Germans against the Jews. We came to Switzerland with a convoy of children organized by the committee "OSE"; and, from the Nice train station, we were accompanied as far as Annecy by two young girls, Mademoiselles Jeanne and Thérèse. We were then alone as far as Annemasse, and there three gentlemen were waiting for us and led us up to the border. We crossed the border on September 23, 1943, around 2100 in the region of Cornières."

"Nous sommes restées à Francfort jusqu'en 1933. J'ai commencé mes écoles primaires à Francfort et je les ai continuées dans les différentes villes où nous avons habités par la suite. Nous sommes venues en France à Paris en 1933 avec nos parents où nous sommes restés jusqu'en 1942. Nous sommes partis de Paris pour aller en zone libre à Culan (Cher) et après deux mois nous avons été pris et mis dans un camp où nous sommes restés 8 mois. Nous nous sommes enfuis de ce camp pour aller à St. Gervais et de là nous sommes allés à Nice où nous sommes restés jusqu'à ces derniers jours. Mes parents se cachent à Nice et nous sommes venus en Suisse pour éviter les mesures prise par les Allemands contre les juifs. Nous sommes venus en Suisse avec un convoi d'enfants organisé par le comité "OSE" et de la gare de Nice nous avons été accompagnés jusqu'à Annecy par deux jeunes filles Melles. Jeanne et Thérése. Nous avons été ensuite seuls jusqu'à Annemasse et là trois Monsieurs nous attendaient et nous ont conduits jusqu'à la frontière. Nous avons passé la frontière le 23.9.43 vers les 2100 dans la région de Cornières."

5026 **Rosie Axelrad**, 13, female, Frankfurt (Germany). She is Cecile's sister. "par Simon"

5026 **Simon Axelrad**, 9, male, Paris. He is Cecile's brother. "par Simon"

5032 Lore Mantel, 12, female, Duibourg (Germany), "par Simon":

"Born in Duibourg in 1931, I left that city with my parents at the age of two to come to France, to Lille. In that city, my sister was born, and we began our primary schooling. We went to Brittany in 1940, to La Hisse—Clermont-Ferrand—Pont Gibeau—Nice—Megève—Nice and, from that city, to Switzerland. My cousins were born in Lille and stayed in that city until 1941. In that city, they began their studies and came to Nice in 1941 and stayed in that city until recently. Our parents are hiding in Nice and did not come with us because they were told that parents are not accepted in Switzerland with children older than six. We came to Switzerland to evade the measures taken by the Germans against the Jews. We crossed the border with a convoy of children organized by the Zionist movement of Nice. We crossed the border on September 23, 1943, around 2100 in the region of Cornières . . ."

"Née à Duibourg en 1931 j'ai quitté cette ville avec mes parents à l'âge de deux ans pour venir en France à Lille. Dans cette ville ma soeur est née et nous avons commencé nos écolesprimaires. Nous sommes allés en Bretagne en 1940 à La Hisse-Clermnot Ferrant-Pont Gibeau-Nice-Mègève-Nice et de cette ville en Suisse. Mes cousins sont nés à Lille et sont restés dans cette ville jusqu'en 1941. Dans cette ville ils ont commencés leurs études et sont venus à Nice en 1941 et sont restés dans cette ville jusqu'à ces derniers jours. N os parents sont cachés à Nice et ne sont pas venus avec nous car on leur a dit que les parents ne sont pas acceptés en Suisse avec des enfants âgés de plus de 6 ans. Nous sommes venus en Suisse pour éviter les mesures prise par les Allemands conre les juifs. Nous avons passé la frontière avec un convoi d'enfants organisé pa r le mouvement sioniste de Nice . Nous avons passé le 23.9.43 vers les 2100 dans la région de Cornièes . . ."

5032 Cecile Mantel, 7, female, Lille (France). She is Lore's sister. "par Simon"

5032 Jacques Mantel, 13, male, Lille (France). He is Lore's cousin. "par Simon"

5032 Maurice Mantel, 10, Lille (France). He is Lore's cousin. "par Simon"

5033 Marie Meller, 13, female, Metz, "par Simon":

"Born in Metz, I left that city immediately after my birth to go with my parents to Lens, where we stayed until 1939. I began my schooling in that city; and, subsequently, we went to Béziers—Lyon—Nice, and from there I came to Switzerland. I came to Switzerland to evade the measures taken by the Germans against the Jews. I came with a convoy of children organized by the

Zionist movement of Nice. We left Nice accompanied by two young girls, who accompanied us as far as Annecy. There we were taken to a school, where we stayed for two days. We were then put on a train in the direction of Annemasse; and, when we arrived, a young man was waiting for us and led us up to the border. I crossed the border on September 23, 1943 around 2100 in the region of Cornières."

"Né à Metz j'ai quitté cette ville de suite après ma naissance pour aller avec mes parents à Lens où nous sommes restés jusqu'en 1939. J'ai commencé mes écoles dans cette ville et depuis nous sommes allés à Beziers-Lyon-Nice et de là je suis venue en Suisse. Je suis venue en Suisse pour éviter les mesures prise par les Allemands contre les juifs. Je suis venue avec un convoi d'enfants organisé par le mouvement sioniste de Nice. Nous sommes partis de Nice accompagnés par deux jeunes filles qui nous ont accompagnés jusqu'à Annecy là nous avons été conduits dans une école où nous sommes restés deux jours. Nous avons été ensuite mis dans le train en direction d-Annemasse et à notre arrivée un Jeune homme nous attendait et nous a conduits jusqu'à la frontière. J'ai passé la frontière le 23.9.43 vers les 2100 dans la région de Cornières."

5034 **Betty Seiden**, 14, female, Berlin, "par Simon":

"Born in Berlin in 1928, I left that city in 1934 to go to Paris. In that city, I began my primary schooling, which I continued in the various cities where I was afterwards. I left Paris in 1939 to go on vacation in a children's colony in Brittany, at Dinard; from there, I went to Limoges and to Nice, where I rejoined my parents. I stayed in Nice until recently. My parents were deported; and since then without support, I came to Switzerland with a Zionist movement that organized a convoy. We came as far as Annecy, and, after having spent two days in that city, we went to Annemasse; and from there a young man accompanied us as far as the border. We crossed the border on September 23, 1943, around 2100 in the region of Cornières."

"Né à Berlin en 1928 j'ai quitté cette ville en 1934 pour aller à Pa ris. Dans cette ville j'ai commencé mes classes primaires que j'ai continuées dans les différentes villes où j'ai été par la suite. Je suis partie de Paris en 1939 pour aller en vacance dans une colonie d'enfants en Bretagne à Dinard de là je suis allée à Limoges-et à Nice où j'ai rejoint mes parents. Je s uis restée jusqu'à ces derniers jours à Nice. Mes parents ont été déportés et depuis sans appuis je suis venue en Suisse avec un mouvement sioniste qui a organisé un convoi. Nous sommes venus jusqu'à Annecy et après avoir passé deux jours dans cette ville nous sommes allés à Annemasse et de là un jeune homme nous a accompagné jusqu'à la frontière. Nous avons passé la frontière le 23.9.43 vers les 2100 dans la région de Cornières."

5035 Gilles Segal, 14, male, Folticeni (Romania), "par Simon":

"Born in Folticeni in 1929, I left that city to go to Bucarest, then to Paris. In that city, I did my schooling. At the end of 1942, we were arrested, the whole family, and taken to a camp. From this camp, my parents were deported; and I myself I was taken to a shelter for Jewish children, where I stayed for a few months; then I was in the home of acquaintances in Donzenac; then I came to Nice with some people. And from there I came to Switzerland. As my parents had been deported, these people sent me with a convoy of children organized by the Zionist movement. We were taken as far as Annecy; and, after spending two days in a school, we went to Annemasse, where a young man was waiting for us at the station and led us up to the border. We crossed the border on September 23, 1943, around 2100 in the region of Cornières . . ."

"Né à Folticeni en 1929 j'ai quitte cette ville pour aller à Bucarest puis ensuite à Paris. Dans cette ville j'ai fait mes écoles. En fin 1942 nous avons été arrêtés toute la famille,et conduits dans un camp. De ce camp mes parents ont été déportés et moi j'ai été conduit dans un asile d'enfants juifs où je suis resté quelques mois puis j'ai été chez des connaissances à Donzenac puis je suis venu à Nice avec ces personnes. Et de là je suis venu en Suisse. Comme mes parents ontété déportés ces personnes m'ont envoyé avec le convoi d'enfant organisé,par le mouvement sioniste . Nous avons été conduits jusqu'à Annecy et après avoir passé deux jours dans une école nous sommes allés jusqu'à Annemasse où un jeune homme nous attendait à la gare et nous a conduits jusqu'à la frontière. N ous avons passé la frontière le 23.9.43 vers les 2100 dans la région de Cornières . . ."

5036 Hélène Feferman, 15, female, Paris, "par Simon":

"Born in Paris, we stayed in that city until 1942. In that city, I did all my schooling and my secretarial apprenticeship, whereas my sister began her classes in Paris and continued them in Nice. We then came to Nice with my parents, and from there we came to Switzerland. Our parents are hiding in Nice, and we were sent to Switzerland to evade the measures taken by the Germans against the Jews. We crossed the border on September 23, 1943, around 2100 in the region of Cornières. We came with a convoy of children organized by the Zionist movement, and we were accompanied as far as Annecy; and, after having spent two days in that city, we left for Annemasse, where we were met by a young man who led us up to the border."

"Nées à Paris nous sommes restées dans cette ville jusqu'en 1942. Dans cette ville j'ai fait toutes mes écoles et mon apprentissage de secrétaire tandis que ma soeur a commencé ses écoles à Paris et les a continuées à Nice. Nous sommes ensuite venues à Nice avec mes parents et de là nous sommes venues en Suisse. Nos parents sont cachés à Nice et nous ont envoyées en Suisse pour éviter les mesures prises par les Allemands contre les juifs, Nous a vons passé la frontière le 23.9.43 vers les 2100 dans la région de Cornières. Nous sommes venues avec un convoi d'enfants organisé par le mouvement sioniste et nous avons été accompagnées jusqu'à Annecy; et après avoir passé deux jours dans cette ville nous sommes parties pour Annemasse où nous étions attendues par un jeune homme qui nous a conduits jusqu'à la frontière."

5036 **Sarah Feferman**, 13, female, Paris. She is Hélène's sister. "par Simon"

5037 **Marcel Horowitz**, 15, male, Antwerp, "par Simon":

"We were born in Antwerp, and stayed in that city until September 1942. We then went to Nice with our parents. We began our classes in Antwerp and continued them in Nice. From Nice, we came to Switzerland. Our parents are hiding in Nice, and we came to Switzerland to evade the measures taken by the Germans against the Jews. We came to Switzerland with a convoy of children organized by the Zionist movement of Nice. We were accompanied by two young girls as far as Annecy; and there, after having spent two days, we left for Annemasse, where a young man was waiting at the station to take us as far as the border. We crossed the border on September 23, 1943, around 2100 in the region of Cornières . . ."

"Nous sommes nés à Anvers et dans cette ville nous soummes restés jusqu'en septembre 1942. Nous sommes ensuite venus à Nice avec nos parents. Nous avons commencés nos écoles à Anvers et nous les avons contunuées à Nice. De Nice nous sommes venus en suisse. Nos parents sont cachés à Nice et nous sommes venus en Suisse pour éviter les mesures prise par les Allem nds contre les juifs. Nous sommes venue en Suisse avec un convoi d'enfants organisé par le mouvement sioniste de Nice. Nous sommes venus accompagnés par deux jeunes filles jusqu'à Annecy et là après avoir passé deux jours nous sommes partis pour Annemasse où un jeune homme nous attendait à la gare pour nous conduire jusqu'à la frontière. Nous avons passé la frontière le 23.9.43 vers les 2100 dans la région de Cornières . . ."

5037 **Julien Horowitz,** 14, male, Antwerp. He is Marcel's brother. "par Simon"

5043 **Victor Harif**, 8, male, Paris, "par Simon":

"Up until the war, I lived in Paris with my parents. My father was an accountant. Since 1941, I am living in Nice; my parents are there now, and I do not know if they will come to Switzerland. I came with a group of 23 children;

I crossed the border on September 23, 1943, with the aide of *passeurs;* there were three, but I do not know their names. We crossed near Cornières and were arrested soon after . . ."

"Jusqu'à la guerre j'ai habité Paris avec mesparents; mon père était comptable. Depuis 1941 je suis à Nice, mes parents y sont actuellement et je ne sais pas s'ils viendront en Suisse. Je suis venu avec un groupe de 23 enfants, j'ai franchi la frontière le 23,9.43 avec l'aide de passeurs, ils étaient trois, mais je ne sais pas leur nom. Nous avons passé près de cornières et avons été arrêté peu après . . ."

5044 **Blanche Perles**, 9, female, Lille (France), "par Simon":

"I lived in Lens until 1940; then I traveled a lot; recently, I was in Nice. My father was a shopkeeper who sold fabrics. My parents are now in Nice, as are a sister and a brother, age 3 and 2 years. My parents are going to come to Switzerland soon. We crossed the border, about 20 children altogether, and a man led us up to the barbed wire. It was September 23, 1943, in the evening in the region of Cornières . . ."

"J'ai habité Lens jusqu'en 1940, ensuite j'ai beaucoup voyagé, ces dernier temps j'étais à Nice. Mon père était commerçant en tissus. Mes parents se trouvant à Nice actuellement ainsi qu'une soeur et un frère agé de 3 et 2 ans. Mes parents vont bientôt venir en Suisse. Nous avons franchi la frontière une vingtaine d'enfants ensemble et un homme nous a conduit jusqu'aux barbelés. C'était 23.9.43 au soir dans la région de Cornières . . ."

5044 **Léa Perles**, 7, female, Lille (France). She is Blanche's sister. "par Simon"

5045 **Jacob Litman**, 15, male, Lodz (Poland), "par Simon":

[Note: The Declaration states that he crossed on "23.10.43," which would be October 23, 1943. All other documentation clearly indicates that this was an error and that the child was part of this convoy that crossed on September 23.]

"I lived [in Poland] until the age of 11, then 5 months in Italy, and since then in Nice. My father was a shopkeeper who sold fabrics; he is now in Nice, as is my mother. I came to Switzerland to escape being deported by the Germans. I came to Switzerland with a group of 23 children. The people who helped us cross the border are unknown to me; this was the first time that I had seen them. I crossed the border clandestinely on October 23, 1943, [sic] in the evening at Cornières; I was arrested soon after along with the other children in the group."

"J'ai habité jusqu'à l'âge de 11 ans, ensuite 5 mois en Italie et dès lors à Nice. Mon père était commerçant en tissus, actuellement il est à Nice, ainsi que ma mère. Je suis venu en Suisse pour éviter d'être déporté par les Allemands. Je suis venu en Suisse avec un groupe de 23 enfants. Les personnes qui nous ont aid é à passer la frontière étaient inconnues de moi, c'était la première fois que je les voyais. J'ai franchi clandestinement la frontière le 23.10.43 au soir à Cornières, j'ai été arrêté peu après ainsi que les autres enfants du groupe."

Profile of the Convoy of September 24 (1), 1943
MJS Convoy Number 10

Summary Information:

Border Guard Post: Sézenove
Place where Arrest was made: b. 50
Time of Arrest: 2100 (9:00 p.m.)
Place and Time of Crossing: b. 50, "underneath the barbed wire"
Number of Persons: 7
Composition of convoy: 7 unaccompanied children
Correspondence with OSE list: 6 of 7 names appear on OSE list as "par Simon"

List of Children Comprising the Convoy and Excerpts from Declarations:

4908 **Georges Kornfeld**, 15, male, Paris, "par Simon":

"Born in 1928 in Paris, I stayed there until 1941. I did my primary schooling there. From 1941 to 194[cannot tell if this is a 2 or 3], I took refuge with my parents in the Cher. From September 1943, in Nice with my parents. I worked there, doing stockroom work. My parents stayed in Nice. I made my way to Switzerland to evade the measures taken by the German authorities against the Israelites. I crossed the Swiss border on September 24, 1943, at 2100 in the area of la Feuillée. In Nice, my parents had made contact with a person whom I do not know. I went to the train station, where a young woman accompanied us as far as Annecy. This woman was named Thérèse. In Annecy, another young woman by the name of Jeanne took us to the Lycée BERTHOLET, [where we stayed] for three days. For the trip from Annecy to Saint-Julien, by bus, we were accompanied by Monsieur ROLAND and Mademoiselle JEANNE. At Saint-Julien we walked to the border that we crossed. We were arrested by a customs officer in a house that telephoned to alert the customs house . . ."

"Né en 1928 à Paris, j'y suis resté jusqu'en 1941. J'y ai fait mes écoles primaires. De 1941 à 194[3], jeme suis réfugié avec mes parents dans le Cher. Dès septembre 1943 à Nice avec mes parents. J'y travaillé du métier de magasinier. Mes parents sont restés à Nice. J'ai gagné la suisse pour éviter les mesures prises par les autorités allemandes contre les israelites. J'ai franchi la frontière suisse le 24-9-43 à 2100 dans la région de la Feuillée. A Nice, mes parents ont pris contact avec une personne que je ne connais pas . Je suis allé à la Gare où une jeune demoiselle nous accompagné jusqu'à Annecy. Cette demoiselle s'appelle Thérèse. A Annecy, une autre demoiselle du nom de Jeanne et qui nous conduisit au Lycée BERTHOLET pendant trois jours. Pour le voyage de Annecy à St.Julien en autocar nous étions accompagnés de M. ROLAND et de Mlle JEANNE. A St. Julien nous avons marché jusqu'à la frontière que nous avons traversé. Nous avons été arrêtés par un douanier dans une maison qui avait téléphoné pour avertir le Poste de Douane . . ."

4909 **Jacques Polac**, 15, male, Paris, "par Simon":

"We stayed in Paris until 1942. In that city, we began our schooling. We then went with our parents to Toulouse—Marseille—Nice and from there, to Switzerland. My parents are still in Nice, and sent us to Switzerland to evade the measures taken by the Germans against the Jews. It was a young man who came to tell our parents that the children could leave by convoy for Switzerland. We were at the train station; and from there a young girl, Thérèse, approximately 20 years old, accompanied us as far as Annecy; we were 19 children. And from there a young woman named Jeanne led us right up close to the border. We crossed on September 24, 1943, around 2130 in the region of Chêne-Bourg."

"Nous sommes restés à Paris jusqu'en 1942. Dans cette ville nous avons commencé nos écoles. Nous sommes ensuite allés avec nos parents à Toulouse-Marseille-Nice et delà en Suisse. Mes parents sont restés à Nice et nous ont envoyés en Suisse pour éviter les mesures prise, par les Allemands contre les juifs. C'est un jeune homme qui est venu dire à nos parents que les enfants pouvaient partir en convoi pour la Suisse. Nous avons été à la gare et de là une jeune fille, Thérése ap-20 ans, nous a accompagnés jusqu'à Annecy, nous étions 19 enfants. Et de là une demoiselle Jeanne nos a conduits jusque près de la frontière. Nous avons passé le 24-9-43 vers les 2130 dans la région de Chene-Bourg."

4909 **Rose Polac**, 12, female, Paris. She is Jacques' sister. "par Simon"

4917 **Jean Manasse**, 13, male, Berlin, "par Simon":

"I was born in Berlin, but, from 1932 and until the war, I lived in Paris. Then I went to the Aveyron, in an evacuation camp of the scouts. Then I moved continually from place to place because the Germans were becoming more of a threat. I finally arrived in Grenoble, where I lived until recently. Then a scout organization arranged my departure. I went as far as Annecy by train, and from there, by bus as far as a small village whose name I do not know. We were 7 children led by a young girl named Jeanne. This [person] took care of us and led us 200 or 300 meters from the border; then she went away. My parents intended to come but they were told that people older than 16 would be turned back. But I think that they will come in spite of everything. I crossed the border on September 24, 1943, around 2030 in the vicinity of la Feuillée."

"Je suis né à Berlin, mais dès 1932 et jusqu'à la guerre j'ai habité Paris. Ensuite je suis allé dans l'A veyron, dans un camp d'évacuation d'éclaireur. Puis j'ai changé continuellement de place car les Allemands devenaient plus pressants. Je suis arrivé enfin à Grenoble où j'ai vécu jusqu'à ces derniers jours. Ensuite une organisation scoute a arrangé mon départ. Je suis parti jusqu'à Annecy en train et de là, en autocar jusqu'à un petit village dont j'ignore le nom. Nous étions 7 enfats guidés par une jeune fille appelés Jeanne. Cette s'est occupée de nous et nous a conduit jusqu'à 200 ou 300 mètres de la frontière puis elle est repartie. Mes parents avaient l'intention de venir mais on leur a dit que les personnes en dessus de 16 ans seraient refoulées. Mais je pense qu'ils viendront malgré tout. J'ai franchi la frontière le 24.9.43 vers 20.30 dans les environs de la Feuillée."

4920 **Suzanne Marburger**, 15, female, Paris, "par Simon":

"Born in 1928 in Paris, I stayed there until 1940. I did my primary schooling there, as did my brother. From 1940, we took refuge in Toulouse, then at Albi, and finally in Nice, where my parents still are. We made our way to Switzerland to evade the measures taken by the German military authorities against the Israelites. We crossed the Swiss border on September 24 at 2030 in the region of la Feuillée. My parents contacted the Israelite Committee of Nice, who placed us in a convoy of 10 children and we left Nice for Annecy. In Annecy, a young woman JEANNE took care of us; and we left, a group of 7 children, by bus for the border. Mademoiselle JEANNE showed us the way to the barbed wire but did not come to the border."

"Née en 1928 à Paris, j'y suis restée jusqu'en 1940. J'y ai fait mes écoles primaires ainsi que mon frère. De 1940, nous nous sommes réfugiés à Toulouse, ensuite à Albi et enfin à Nice où se trouentencore nos parents. Nous avons gagné la Suisse pour éviter les mesures prises par les autorités militaires allemandes contre les israelites. Nous avons franci la frontière suisse le 24.9.43 à 2030 dans la région de la Feuillée. Mes parents se sont adressés au Comité Israelite de Nice qui nous a mis dans un convoi de 10 enfants et npus sommes partis de Nice pour Annecy. À Annecy, une demoiselle JEANNE s'est occupée de nous et nous sommes partis un groupe de 7 enfants en autocar pour la frontière. Mlle JEANNE nous amontré le chemin des barbelés, mais n'est pas venue à la frontière."

4920 **Joseph Marburger**, 13, male, Paris. He is Suzanne's brother. "par Simon"

4928 **Rosette Wolczak**, 15, female, Paris. Her dossier is not available for review. She was sent back to France on October 16, 1943, accused of immoral conduct. German officials arrested her in France, near Annemasse, on October 19. After being held in Pax prison, she was sent to Drancy on October 25. On November 20, 1943, she was deported to Auschwitz (Auschwitz convoy 62), and she did not survive.*

Profile of the Convoy of September 24 (2), 1943
MJS Convoy Number 11

Summary Information:

Border Guard Post: Cornières
Place where Arrest was made: "barrage" (meaning "barrier" or "toll bar")
Time of Arrest: 2040 (8:40 p.m.)
Place and Time of Crossing: "under the barbed wire"
Number of Persons: 19
Composition of convoy: 19 unaccompanied children
Correspondence with OSE list: 18 of 19 names appear on OSE list as "par Simon"

List of Children Comprising the Convoy and Excerpts from Declarations:

4899 **Louis Korn**, 10, male, Paris:

[Note: The crossing date stated on the Declaration appears to be incorrect, as it does not correspond with the crossing date stated on the arrest report.]

"Born in Paris in 1933, I stayed there for some time; then I was in Belgium with my parents. I returned to Paris in 1938, where I stayed until my departure for Switzerland. I did my primary schooling there and was lately in secondary school. My parents were deported in August 1942. I made my way to

* Fivaz-Silbermann, Ruth, La *Refoulement de réfugiés civils juifs*, 97-98.

Switzerland to evade the measures taken by the German authorities against the Israelites. I crossed the Swiss border on September 22, 1943, at 2330 in the area of Chêne-Bourg. A woman from the Israelite Committee of Paris organized my trip. I do not know her, as it was my grandfather who took care of it. A woman accompanied me as far as Annecy; then from there a man whom I also do not know took me to the border."

"Né en 1933 à Paris, j-y suis resté quelquestemps, puis j'ai été en Belgique avec mes parents. Je suis revenu à Paris en 1938 où je suis resté jusqu'à mon départ pour la Suisse. J'y fait mes écoles primaires et était ces derniers temps au lycée. Mes parents ont été déportés en aout 1942. J'ai gagné la Suisse pour éviter les mesures prisespar les autorités allemandes contre les israelites. J'ai franchi la frontière suisse le 22.9.43 à 2330 dans la région de Chêne.bourg. Une dame du Comité Israelite de Paris a organisé mon voyage. Je ne las connais pas, car c-est mon grand-père qui s'en est occupé. Une dame m'a acompagné jusqu-à Annecy puis delà un homme, que je ne connais pas non plus jusqu'à la frontière."

4900 **Jacqueline Korinschtain**, 13, female, Paris, "par Simon":

"Born in 1930 in Paris, I stayed there until 1942. I did my primary schooling there. In 1942, I went to take refuge with my parents 6 months in Marseille, then 6 months in 1943 in Nice, where one can still find my parents, who will maybe intend to follow me to Switzerland. I made my way to Switzerland to evade the measures taken by the German authorities against the Israelites. I crossed the Swiss border on September 24, 1943, at 2030 in the region of la Feuillère [presumably la Feuillasse]. My parents contacted the Israelite Committee of Nice, which was in charge of organizing a convoy of children to Switzerland. I boarded the train in Nice; and, upon my arrival in Annecy, a young woman took care of me. I do not know her name. We then took the train to Annemasse, where two men led us to the border and passed us across. I do not know the names of these gentlemen."

"Né en 1930 à Paris, j-y suis restée jusqu-en 1942. J-y ai fait mes écoles primaires. En 1942, je suis allée me réfugier avec mes parents 6 mois à Marseille, puis 6 mois en 1943 à Nice où se trouvant encore mes parents, qui auront peut-être l'intention de me suivre en Suisse. J'ai gagné la Suisse pour éviter les mesures prises par les autorités allamendes contre les israelites. J'ai franchi la frontière suisse le 24.9.4 à 2030 dans la région de la Feuillère. Mes parents se sont adressés au Comité Israelite de Nice qui se chargeait de faire un convoi d'enfants pour la suisse. Je suis montée dans le train à Nice et à l'arrivée à Annecy, une demoiselle s-est occupé de moi. Je ne connais pas son nom. Nous avons ensuite pris letrain pour Annemasse ou deux hommes nous ont conduits à la frontière et nous l-ont faite passer. Je ne connais pas le nom de ces messieurs."

4910 Annette Rosenzweig, 8, female, Colmar (France), "par Simon":

[Note: The crossing date stated on the Declaration appears to be incorrect, as it does not correspond with the crossing date stated on the arrest report.]

"I left Colmar with my parents a few months after I was born, and we went to Paris. I left Paris at the age of 4 to go to Limoges, then to Nice. I began my schooling in Limoges. From Nice, I came to Switzerland. A gentleman came to our home looking for me and took me to the train station; from there, a young girl took us, as we were 19 children, and took us as far as Annecy; from there, *passeurs* led us up to the border. We crossed on September 27, 1943, around 2130 in the region of Chêne-Bourg . . ."

"J'ai quitté Colmar avec mes parents quelques mois après ma naissance et nous sommes allée à Paris. J'ai quitté Paris à l'âge de 4 ans pour a ller à Limoges puis à Nice. J'ai commencé mes écoles à Limoges. Depuis nice je suis venue en Suisse. Un monsoieur est venu me chercher à la maison et m'a conduite à la gare de là une jeune fille nous a conduits,car nous étions 19 enfants, et nous a conduits jusqu'à Annecy de là des passeurs nous ont conduits jusqu'à la frontière. Nous avons passé le 27-9-43 vers les 2130 dans la région de Chêne-Bourg . . ."

4911 Wolf Wapniarz, 12, male, Metz, "par Simon":

"I stayed in Metz until 1940. In that city, I began my schooling; then I went to Royon with my parents, then to Angoulême, then I came to Paris because my parents were deported. In Paris, I was in a children's center, where I stayed until recently. It was at this center that a gentleman came looking for me to take me to the train station; and from there, with 19 children, we were taken by someone as far as Annecy and then by some *passeurs*. We crossed the border on September 24, 1943, around 2130 in the region of Chêne-Bourg."

"Je suis resté à Metz jusqu'en 1940. Dans cette ville j'ai commencé mes écoles puis je suis allé à Royon avec mes parents, puis à Angoulême puis je suis venu à Paris car mes parents ont été déportés. A Paris j'ai été dans un centre d'enfant où je suis resté jusqu'à ces derniers jours. C'est à ce centre qu'un monsieur est venu me chercher pour me conduire à la gare et de là avec 19 enfants nous avons été sonduits par une personne jusqu'à Annecy et ensuite par des passeurs. Nous avons passé la frontière le 24-9-43 vers les 2130 dans la région de Chêne-Bourg."

4912 **Isidore Ménaché**, 12, male, Paris, "par Simon":

"I always stayed in in Paris, and, in that city, I began my schooling. My mom died 11 years ago, and, as for my father, I do not know where he is. I was raised by a woman until the age of 9; then I was in an orphanage in Paris. Then I spent some time in the countryside; and then I returned again to Paris, where I was in a children's center. From this center I was sent to Switzerland. A gentleman came looking for me and took me to the train station; then there another man took charge of us, 19 children, and took us Annecy; from there, some *passeurs* led us up to the border. We crossed the border on September 24, 1943, around 2130 in the region of Chêne-Bourg."

"Je suis toujours resté à Paris et dans cette ville j'ai commencé mes écoles. Mamaman est morte depuis 11 ans et mon papa je ne sais pas où il se trouve. J'ai été élevé par une dame jusqu'à l'âge de 9 ans puis j'ai été dans un orphelinat à Paris . J'ai été ensuite quelques temps à la campagne et depuis je suis rentré à nouveau à Paris où je me trouvais dans un centre d'anfants. C'est de ce centre que l'on m'a envoyé en Suisse. Un Mr. est venu me chercher et m'a conduit à la gare puis là un monsieur nous a pris avec 19 enfants et nous a conduits à Annecy de là des passeurs nous ont conduits jusqu'à la frontière. Nous avons passé la frontière le 24-9-43 vers les 2130 dans la région de Chêne-Bourg."

4913 **Nathan Torezynski**, 13, male, Radom (Poland), "par Simon":

"I was born in Poland, but I have lived in Paris from the time I was two until recently. I leave France because of the Germans. I came in a convoy organized by the Israelite Community of France. I left Paris about a week ago; then I stopped in Annecy; and I came in a convoy, whose *passeurs* were arrested, on September 24, 1943, around 2200 hours."

"Je suis né à Pologne mais ai habité Paris depuis l'âge de deux ans et ce jusqu'à ces derniers jours. Je quittela France à cause des Allemands. Je suis venu en convoi organisé par la Communauté israélite de France. Je suis parti de Paris il y a une semaine environ, ensuite je me suis arrêté à Annecy et je suis venu par un convoi dont les passeurs ont été arrêtés le 24.9 43 vers 22.00 h."

4913 **Henri Torezynski**, 10, male, Paris. He is Nathan's brother. "par Simon"

4915 **Marcelle Refkolevsky**, 15, female, Paris, "par Simon":

"We stayed in Paris until 1942. In that city, we began our primary schooling. We then went to Nice, where we stayed until recently. My parents are still in Nice, but they are hiding from the Germans and sent us to Switzerland to evade the measures taken by the Germans against the Jews. It was my parents who took us to the train station in Nice, and there we were placed into the hands of a young girl, Mademoiselle Thérèse, who accompanied us as far as Annecy; we were 19 children. Since Annecy, it was a young man and a young girl, Mademoiselle Mila, who took us as far as Annemasse and from there, placed us in the hands of *passeurs*. We crossed the border on September 24, 1943, around 2030 in the region of Chêne-Bourg."

"Nous sommes restées à Paris jusqu'en 1942 Dans cette ville nous avons commencé nos écoles primaires. Nous sommes ensuite allés à Nice où nous sommes restées jusqu'à ces derniers jours. Mes parents sont encore à Nice mais ils se cachent des Allemands et nous ont envoyées en Suisse pour éviter les mesures prise par les Allemands contre les juifs. C'est mes parents qui nous ont conduites à la gare de Nice et là nous avons été mises entre les mains d'une jeune fille, Melle Thérèse, qui nous a accompagnées jusqu'à Annecy, nous étions 19 enfants. Depuis Annecy c'est un jeune homme et une jeune fille, Melle Mila, qui nous ont conduits jusqu'à Annemasse et de là nous ont remis entre les mains de passeurs. Nous avons passé la frontière le 24-9-43 vers les 2030 dans la région de Chêne-Bourg."

4915 **Mireille Refkolevsky**, 14, female, Paris. She is Marcelle's sister. "par Simon"

4916 **Myrianne Berger**, 14, female, Brussels (Belgium) "par Simon":

"Born in 1929 in Brussels, I stayed there until 1940. I did my primary schooling there. In 1940, I took refuge with my parents in Toulouse and then in Nice. My mother was deported in 1942, and my father is still in Nice. I made my way to Switzerland to evade the measures taken by the German authorities against the Israelites. I crossed the Swiss border on September 24, 1943, [at] 2000 in the region of Annemasse. My father had made contact – of this I am not sure – with the Israelite Committee of Nice to pass me into Switzerland. At the train station in Nice, I met a few comrades, and a young man whom I do not know had us board the train. In Annecy, a young woman whom I do not know took care of us and we took a bus. This young woman did not come with us but showed us the way to the border."

"Née en 1929 à Bruxelles, j'y suis restée jusqu'en 1940. J'y fait mes écoles primaires. En 1940, je me suis réfugiée avec mes parents à Toulouse et ensuite à

Nice. Ma mère a été déportée en 1942 et mon père se trouve toujours à Nice. J'ai gagné la Suisse pour éviter les mesures prises par les autorités alledmandes contre les israelites. J'ai franchi la frontière suisse le 24.9.43 2000 dans la région d'Annemasse. Mon père a pris contact, je n'en suis pas sûre, avec le Comité Israelite de Nice pour me faire passer en Suisse. A la Gare de Nice, j'ai rencontré quelques camarades et un jeune homme que ne connais pas nous a fait montés dans le train. A Annecy, une demoiselle que je ne connais pas s'est occupé de nous et nous avons pris un autocar . Cette demoiselle n'est pas venue avec nous, mais nous a montré le chemin de la frontière."

4919 **Marie Leviner**, 13, female, Paris, "par Simon":

"We stayed in Paris until 1939. In that city, I began my schooling. We then went to Châstel-Nouvel (Lozère), then to Nice—Megève—Nice, then from there, to Switzerland; we have always stayed with our parents. In Nice, we were in a boarding school, and our parents came looking for us and took us to the train station, where a young girl was waiting for us; we were 19 children, and she accompanied us as far as Annecy; there another young girl accompanied us as far as Annemasse and placed us in the hands of *passeurs*. We crossed the border on September 24, 1943, around 2130 in the region of Chêne-Bourg."

"Nous sommes restés à Paris jusqu'en 1939 . Dans cette ville j'ai commencé mes écoles. Nous sommes ensuite allés à Châstel-Nouvel (Lozère) puis à Nice-Mègève-Nice puis de là en Suisse, nous sommes toujours restés avec nos parents. À Nice nous étions dans une pension et là nos parents sont venus nous chercher et nous nous sommes rendues à la gare où une jeune fille nous attendait, nous étions 19 enfants, et elle nous a accompagnés jusqu'à Annecy, là une autre jeune fille nous a accompagné jusqu'à Annemasse et nous a remis entre les mains de passeurs. Nous avons passé la frontière 24-9-43 vers les 2130 dans la région de Chêne-Bourg."

4919 **Maurice Leviner**, 10, male, Paris. He is Marie's brother. "par Simon"

4921 **Janine Antcher**, 13, female, Paris, "par Simon":

"Born in 1930 in Paris, I stayed in that city until 1930 [sic],* where I did my primary schooling. From 1940, I took refuge with my parents in Montpellier, then in Rodèze, Megève, and Nice, which was my last place of residence. My parents are still in Nice. I made my way to Switzerland to evade the measures

* It is apparent that this is supposed to read "1940."

taken by the German authorities against the Israelites. I crossed the Swiss border on September 24, 1943, at 2000 in the area of la Feuillère [presumably la Feuillasse]. In Nice, I was not living with my parents; I was in hiding. A few hours before the train was leaving, my parents came looking for me and took me to the train station, where I found some other children leaving for Switzerland. In Annecy, a young woman took care of us; I do not know the name of this young woman. From Annecy, by train as far as Annemasse. From there, some *passeurs* whom I do not know led us up to the border."

"Née en 1930 à Paris, je suis resté dans cette ville jusqu'en 1930. où j'ai fait mes écoles primaires. De 1940, je me suis réfugié avec mes parents à Montpelier, puis à Rodèze, à Mégève et Nice, qui fut mon dernier domicile. Mes parents sont toujours à Nice. J'ai gagné la suisse pour éviter les mesures prises par les autorités allemandes contre les israelites. J'ai franchi la frontière suisse le 24.9.43 à 2000 dans la région de la Feuillère. A Nice je ne vivais pas avec mes parents, je me cachais. Quelques heures avant le départ du train, mes parents sont venus me chercher et me conduite à la Gare où j'ai trouvé d'autres enfants en partance pour la Suisse. A Annecy, une demoiselle s'est occupée de nous, je ne connais pas le nom de cette demoiselle. Depuis Annecy en train jq. Annemasse. De là des passeurs que je ne connais pas nous ont conduits à la frontière."

4924 **Jacques Halegua**, 13, male, Salonika (Greece), "par Simon":

"I was born in Greece and lived there until the age of 4 and a half, after which I came to France, to Paris. My parents are now in Palestine, and I was raised by my grandparents, presently deported to Germany. I come to Switzerland to escape the Germans. I was taken away from Paris about a week ago by a person of the Israelite Committee of France, who took me as far as Annecy, where I had to wait the formation of a convoy to Switzerland. I was put up at the Lycée BERTHOLET. Friday, September 24, I left by train, in which I joined some other children and a young woman named Jeanne. We got off at Annemasse; and from there we went by foot as far as the border, which we crossed the same evening around 2200 hours. During that time, the *passeurs* were arrested at the same time as we."

"Je suis né en Grèce et y ai vécu jusqu'à l'âge de 4 ans et demi après quoi je suis venu en France, à Paris. Mes parents sont actuellement en Palestine et j'ai été élevé par mes Gds parents, actuellement déportés en Allemagne. Je viens en Suisse pour fuir les Allemands. J'ai été emmené de Paris il y a une semaine environ par une personne du comité israélite de France, qui m'a guidé jusqu'à Annecy où je devais attendre la formation d'un convoi pour la Suisse. J'ai été logé au Lycée BERTHOLET Le vendredi 24 septembre je suis parti en train dans lequel j'ai rejoint d'autres enfants et une demoiselle appelés Jeanne. Nous sommes descendus à Annemasse et de là, nous sommes allés à pied jusqu'à la frontière que nous avons franchi le même soir vers 22.00 h. Pendant ce temps, les passeurs ont été arrêtés en même temps que nous."

4925 **Michel Traumann**, 10, male, Saint Quentin (France), "par Simon":

"I was born in St. Quentin and lived there until the arrival of the Germans. I left with my parents for Tarbes, where I lived for 3 years. Last March, we fled to Nice. From there, I went for four months to Megève, after which I returned to Nice. Not long ago, the Commission of Israelites of France made it known to my parents that it was still possible to have children passed into Switzerland. Therefore, my mother signed me up, and I left Wednesday evening, September 22, 1943, by train. We were around 20, and we stayed on the train as far as Annemasse. From there, we made our way to the border guided by four men, who were arrested."

"Je suis né à St Quentin et y ai vécu jusqu'à l'arrivés des Allemands. Je suis parti avec mes parents jusqu'à Tarbes où j'ai vécu 3 ans. En mars dernier nous nous sommes enfuis à Nice. De là, je suis allé pendant 4 mois à Megève, après quoi je suis r venu à Nice. Dernièrement la Commission des Israélites de France a fait savoir à mes parents qu'il était encore possible de faire passer quelques enfants en Suisse. Ma mère m'y a donc inscrit et je suis parti le mercredi soir 22.9.43 par le train. Nous étions environ 20 et nous sommes restés dans le train jusqu'à Annemasse. De là nous avons gagné la frontière guidés par 4 hommes qui ont été arrêtés."

4926 **Henriette Balez**, 13, female, Paris, "par Simon":

"I always stayed in Paris, and, in that city, I began my schooling. I left Paris recently to come to Switzerland. My parents are in the St. Étienne prison, and after [their arrest], I was put into a camp and then in a boarding school. I came to Switzerland to evade the measures taken by the Germans against the Jews. It was my brother who sent me to Switzerland. He contacted a Monsieur Roland to have me evacuated to the countryside, and this gentleman told him that he would be able to pass me into Switzerland. My brother accompanied me to the train station and there placed me into the hands of a gentleman, and, with 11 comrades, [he] accompanied us as far as Annecy; from there, a gentleman accompanied us as far as the border. We crossed on September 24, 1943, around 2130 in the region of Chêne-Bourg."

"Je suis toujours restée à Paris et dans cette vile j'ai commencé mes écoles.j'ai quitté Paris ces derniers jours pour venir en Suisse. Mes parents sont à la prison de St. Etienne et depuis j'ai été mise dans un camp et ensuite dans un pensionat. Je suis venue en Suisse pour éviter les mesures prise par les Allemands contre les juifs. C-Est mon frère qui m'a envoyée en Suisse. Il s'est adressé à un Mr. Roland pour me faire évacuer à la campagne et ce Mr. lui a répondu qu'il pouvait me faire passer en Suisse. Mon frère m'a accompagnée jusqu'à la gare et là m'a remise entre les mains d'un monsieur et avec 11 camarades nous a accompagné jusqu-à Annecy de là un monsieur nous a accompagné jusqu'à la frontière. Nous avons passé le 24-9-43 vers les 2130 dans la région de Chêne-Bourg."

4927 **Lisa Glauberg**, 14, female, Frankfurt (Germany), "par Simon":

"I stayed in Frankfurt until 1935. I then went to Paris with my parents, and, in that city, we stayed until 1942. We went to Lyon—Marseille—Nice, and from there I came to Switzerland. My parents remain hidden in Nice and sent me to Switzerland to evade the measures taken by the Germans against the Jews. They sent me to the home of my uncle, Mr. Glauberg, who lives in Lausanne. I crossed the border with a convoy of children that was organized by a Jewish committee in Nice. We came to Annemasse accompanied by some young people; and from there they placed us into the hands of *passeurs*. We crossed the border on September 24, 1943, around 2030 in the region of Chêne-Bourg."

"Je suis restée à Francfort jusqu'en 1935. Je suis ensuite allée à Paris avec mes parents et dans cette ville nous sommes restés jusqu'à 1942. Nous sommes allés à Lyon-Marseille-Nice et de là je suis venue en Suisse. Mes parents sont restés cachés à Nice et m'ont envoyée en Suisse pour éviter les mesures prise par les Allemands contre les juifs. Ils m'ont envoyée chez mon oncle Mr. Glauberg, qui habite Lausanne. J'ai passé la frontière avec un convoi d'enfants qui à été organisé par un comité juif à Nice. Nous sommes venus accompagnés Annemasse par des jeunes gens et de là ils nous ont remis entre les mains de passeurs. Nous avons passé la frontière le 24-9-43 vers les 2030 dans la région de Chêne-Bourg."

4929 **Bella Leszkowitz**, 12, female, Strasbourg (France), "par Simon":

"I was born in Strasbourg and lived there until the beginning of the war. At that time, I went to Dordogne with my parents. We stayed there about 3 years, after which we went to live in Nice, where we stayed until recently. We come to Switzerland to flee the Germans. We left Nice, my sister and I, September 22, 1943, by train. We were 19 children who traveled together to Switzerland. Along the way, there were a few more children who joined us. We got off the train at Annemasse and crossed the border about one hour later in the area of Chêne-Bourg. We had been led by 3 men and 2 Italians [sic], who were arrested by Swiss customs officers, on September 24, 1943, around 2200 hours."

"Je suis née à Strasbourg et y ai vécu jusqu'au début de la g[uer]re. A ce moment je suis allée en Dordogne avec mes parents. Nous y sommes restés 3 ans environ après quoi nous sommes allés vivre à Nice où nous sommes restés jusqu'à ces derniers temps. Nous venons en Suisse pour fuir les Allemands. Nous avons quittés Nice, ma soeur et moi le 22 septembre 1943 par le train. Nous étions 19 enfants qui avons voyagés ensemble jusqu'en Suisse. En cours de route il y a eu encore quelques enfants qui se sont joints à nous. Nous sommes descendus du train à Annemasse et avons franchi la frontière environ 1 h. plus tard dans la région de Chêne-Bourg. Nous avions été conduits par 3 hommes et 2 Italiens qui se sont faits arrêter par les douaniers suisses, le 24.9.43 vers 22.00 h."

4929 **Rose Leszkowitz**, 4, female, Strasbourg (France). She is Bella's sister. "par Simon"

Profile of the Convoy of September 28, 1943
MJS Convoy Number 12

Summary Information:

Border Guard Post: Sézenove
Place where Arrest was made: b. 51
Time of Arrest: 2115 (9:15 p.m.)
Place and Time of Crossing: b. 51, 21:15 (9:15 p.m.)
Number of Persons: 3
Composition of convoy: 3 unaccompanied children
Correspondence with OSE list: All names appear on OSE list as "par Simon"

List of Children Comprising the Convoy and Excerpts from Declarations:

4980 **Ilia Muszkatblat**, 8, female, Paris, "par Simon":

"I always lived in Paris with my parents. My father is a leather craftsman; presently, he has been deported since August 1943 and my mother, since 1942. A young woman Jeanne took me as far as Saint-Julien in the company of 6 other children; then afterwards a man led us to the barbed wire. I crossed the border on September 28, 1943, in the region of Bernex, and we were arrested by a customs officer. Until a few days ago, I was living with my aunt, Madame Jenny LEVENBERG, Fontaine (Isère), the one who told me that things were good in Switzerland and that I must go to a children's colony at Sierre."

"J'ai toujours habité Paris avec mes parents. Mon père est maroquinier, actuellement il est déporté depuis août 1943 et ma mère depuis 1942. Une demoiselle Jeanne m'a conduit jusqu'à St-Julien en compagnie de 6 autres enfants, puis ensuite un homme nous a amenés jusqu'au barbelés. J'ai franchi la frontière le 28.9.43 dans la région de Bernex et nous avons été arrêtés par un douanier. Ces derniers temps j'habitais avec ma tante M. Jenny LEVENBERG, Fontaine (Isère), celle-ci m'a dit que l'on était très bien en Suisse et que je devais m'y rendre pour aller dans une colonie d'enfants à Sierre."

4985 **Boris Epstein**, 8, male, Roanne (France), "par Simon":

[Note: In the Declaration, the last name appears as "Epsten." The child's signature clearly indicates that the correct spelling is "Epstein." Also, the crossing date stated on the Declaration appears to be incorrect, as it does not correspond with the crossing date stated on the arrest report.]

"Born in Roanne, we left that city in 1940. We went to Clisson—Toulouse—Aussonne, and from there we came to Switzerland. Our parents are hiding in Aussonne and sent us to Switzerland for fear of measures taken by the Germans against the Jews. It was a gentleman who came looking for us in Aussonne and who took us from Toulouse as far as the border. We crossed the border on September 29, 1943, around 2030 in the region of la Feuillée."

"Nés à Roanne nous avons quitté cette ville en 1940. Nous sommes allés à Clisson-Toulouse-Aussonne et de là nous sommes venus en Suisse. Nos parents se cachent à Aussonne et nous ont envoyé en Suissse de crainte des mesures prise par les Allemands contre les juifs. C'est un monsieur qui est venu nous chercher à Aussonne et nous a conduits depuis Toulouse et jusqu'à la frontière. Nous avons passé la frontière le 29-9-43 vers les 203 0 dans la région de la Feuillée."

4985 **Renée Epstein**, 5, female, Roanne (France). She is Boris' sister. "par Simon"

Profile of the Convoy of September 29, 1943
MJS Convoy Number 13

Summary Information:

Border Guard Post: Sézenove
Place where Arrest was made: Lully
Time of Arrest: 2100 (9:00 p.m.)
Place and Time of Crossing: "through the barbed wire" between b. 50 and b. 51, 20:30 (8:30 p.m.)

Number of Persons: 4
Composition of convoy: 4 unaccompanied children
Correspondence with OSE list: All names appear on OSE list as "par Simon"

List of Children Comprising the Convoy and Excerpts from Declarations:

4977 **Simon Grimberg,** 9, male, Brussels (Belgium), "par Simon":

"I lived in Brussels until May 1940 with my parents. From then on, I took refuge in France. My father is a watchmaker-jeweler; presently, my father left by way of Portugal for the Belgian Congo; my mother will surely join him. I came to Switzerland so as not to remain in France, seeing as how my mother is going to leave for Portugal and she has not been able to take me with her. I crossed the border on September 29, 1943, during the night in the area of Bernex in the company of 3 other children. The *passeur* that passed us across was named Michel, age 23 to 25."

"J'ai habité Bruxelle jusqu'en mai 1940 avec mesparents. Dès lors je me suis réfugié en France. Mon père est horloger – bijoutier, actuellement mon père est parti par le Portugal pour le Congo belge, ma mère ira sûrement le rejoindre. Je suis venu en Suisse pour ne pas rester en France, vu que ma mère va partir au Portugal et qu'elle ne pouvait pas me prendre avec elle. J'ai franchi la frontière le 29.9.43 durant la nuit dans la région de Bernex en compagnie de 3 autres enfants. Le passeur qui nous a fait passés s'appelait Michel âgé de 23 à 25 ans."

4978 **Marcel Zauberman,** 12, male, Paris, "par Simon":

"Born 1931 in Paris, I stayed there for a very short time. I left immediately for LENS with my parents. We stayed in Lens until 1942. I did my primary schooling there. Then we went to the Cantal to take refuge until spring 1943, still with my parents. Lately, we were in Challes-les-Eaux, still with my parents. We made our way to Switzerland to evade the measures taken by the German authorities against the Israelites. We crossed the Swiss border on September 29, 1943, at 2230 in the region of la Feuillée. From Challes-les-Eaux, a certain Monsieur ROLAND took care of us and led us to Saint-Julien, where a Monsieur MICHEL had us cross the border. I did not pay anything. It was my parents who took care of everything."

"Né en 1931 à Paris, je n'y suis resté que très peu de temps. Je suis parti immédiatement pour LENS avec mes parents. Je suis resté à Lens jusqu'en 1942. J'y ai fait mes écoles primaires. Puis nous sommes allés dans le Cantal jusqu'au printemps 1943 pour nous réfugier, toujours avec mes parents. Dernièrement nous nous trouvions à Châles les Eaux où se truvent encore mes parents. Nous avons gagné la suisse pour éviter les mesures prises par les autorités allemandes contre lesisraelites. Nous avons franchi la frontière suisse le 29.9.43 à 2230 dans la région de la Feuillée. Depuis Châles les Eaux, un certain M. ROLAND s'est occupé de nous et nous a conduit à St.Julien où un Monsieur MICHEL nous a fait franchir la fronrière. Je n'ai rien payé du tout. C'est mes parents qui se sont occupés de tout."

4978 **Mireille Zauberman**, 9, female, Lens (France). She is Marcel's sister. "par Simon"

4978 **Hélène Zauberman**, 7, female, Lens (France). She is Marcel's sister. "par Simon"

Profile of the Convoy of October 4, 1943 MJS Convoy Number 14

Summary Information:

Border Guard Post: Hermance
Place where Arrest was made: Les Glands
Time of Arrest: 1800 (6 p.m.)
Place and Time of Crossing: Les Glands, 18:00 (6:00 p.m.)
Number of Persons: 13
Composition of convoy: 3 unaccompanied children and 4 families (6 adults and 4 children)
Correspondence with OSE list: Names of all unaccompanied children appear on OSE as "par Simon." No names of accompanied children (i.e. children with parents) appear on OSE list.

List of Children Comprising the Convoy and Excerpts from Declarations:

5047 **Mordka Grynsztejn**, 32, male, Kozienice (Poland):

"Born in 1911 in Poland, I stayed there until 1932. I did my primary schooling there and my apprenticeship as a shoemaker. From 1932 to 1942, in Paris, where I likewise practiced my trade as a shoemaker. I was married in 1928 in Paris. Since 1942, we have taken refuge in the Lot-et-Garonne at Bon-Encontre, where we were in forced residence. We made our way to Switzerland to escape the measures taken by the German authorities against the Israelites. We crossed the Swiss border on October 4, 1943, at 1800 in the region of Hermance. We crossed on our own."

"Né en 1911 en Pologne, j'y suis resté jusqu'en 1932. J'y fait mes écoles primaires et mon apprentissage de cordonnier. De 1932 à 1942 à Paris où j'ai également exercé mon métier de cordonnier. Je me suis marié en 1928 à Paris. Depuis 1942, nous nous sommes réfugiés dans le Loth et Garonne à Bon Encontre où nous étions enrésidence forcée. Nous avons gagné la Suise pour éviter les mesures prises par les autorités allemandes contre les israelites. Nous avons franci la frontière suisse le 4.10.43 à 1800 dans la région d'Hermance. Nous avons passé par nos propres moyens."

5047 **Laja Grynsztejn**, 23, female, Warsaw. She is Mordka's wife.

5047 **Léon Grynsztejn**, 2, male, Paris. He is Mordka's son.

5048 **Rebecca Zaidenband**, 15, female, Brussels (Belgium), "par Simon":

"Born in Brussels, we stayed in that city until 1940. We began our primary schooling that we continued in the various cities where we went afterwards. We left Brussels in 1940 for Toulouse; we lived in Gripiac [Grépiac], near Toulouse, and until recently. My parents stayed in Gripiac because we have a brother who is ill; they will come to join us as soon as he has recovered. We came by the intermediary of the committee OSE; we took the train from Toulouse to Thonon; and there two people were waiting for us. We spent two days; then they came in taxis looking for us and took us to the edge of a forest. There we were with 14 people, and we headed towards the border. We crossed the border on October 4, 1943, around 1800 in the region of Hermance."

"Nés à Bruxelles nous sommes restés dans cette ville jusqu'en 1940. Nous avons commencé nos écoles primaires que nous avons continuées dans les diverses villes où nous sommes allés par la suite. Nous sommes partis de Bruxelles en 1940 pour Toulouse, nous habitons à Gripiac, près de Toulouse, et jusqu'à ces dreniers jours. Mes parents sojt restés à Gripiac car nous avons un frère qui est malade ils viendrons nous rejoindre dés qu'il sera guéri. Nous sommes venus par lIntermédiaire du comité "OSE" nous avons pris le train à Toulouse et jusqu'à Thonon et là deux personnes nous attendaient. Nous avons passé 2 jours puis on est venu nous chercher en taxis et l'on nous a conduits jusqu'à la lisière d'un bois. Là nous nous sommes trouvé avec 14 personnes et nous nous sommes dirigés sur la frontière. Nous avons passé la frontière le 4.10.43 vers les 1800 dans la région de Hermance."

5048 **Léon Zaidenband**, 12, male, Brussels (Belgium). He is Rebecca's brother. "par Simon"

5048 **Simon Zaidenband**, 7, male, Brussels (Belgium). He is Rebecca's brother. "par Simon"

5049 **Jankiel Kolodny**, 39, male, Horodec (Poland):

"Born in 1904 in Poland, I stayed there until 1923. I did my primary schooling there and began my studies, which I finished in Paris, where I stayed until 1940. I practiced my profession as a teacher at the Consistoire Israélite. I was married in 1931 in Paris. Mobilized in the middle of 1940 in the Polish Army, I only stayed there a very short time, the exodus having followed soon afterwards. We took refuge in Montpellier until 1942; then were placed in forced residence in Nice until recently. We made our way to Switzerland to evade the measures taken by the German authorities against the Israelites. We crossed the Swiss border on October 4, 1943, around 1900 in the region of Hermance. We crossed by our own means."

"Né en 1904 en Pologne, j'y suis resté jusqu'en 1923. J'y fait mes écoles primaires et le commencement de mes études que je suis venu finir à Paris où je suis resté jusqu'en 1940. J'y ai exercé ma profession de professeur au consitoire Israelite. Je me suis marié en 1931 à Paris. Mobilisé au milieu de 1940 dans l'Armée Polonaise, je n'y suis resté que très peu de temps, l'exode ayant suivi tòt après. Nous nous sommes réfugiés à Montpellier jusqu'en 1942, puis mis en résidence forcée à Nice jusqu'à ces derniers temps. Nous avons gagné la Suisse pour éviter les mesures prises par les autorités allemandes contre les israelites. Nous avons franchi la frontière suisse le 4.10.43 à 1900 dans la région d'Hermance. Nous avons passé par nos propres moyens."

5049 **Henriette Kolodny,** 41, female, Phlippopoli [Philippopolis] (Bulgaria). She is Jankiel's wife.

5049 **Rachel-Lilianne Kolodny**, 7 weeks, female, Nice. She is Jankiel's daughter.

5050 **Boba Szer**, 39, female, Krasnik (Poland):

"Born in Krasnik in 1904, I stayed in that city until 1929. I did all my primary classes, and I was married in 1927. We went to live in Lublin for 2 years; then we came to Paris, where we stayed until the month of August. My husband was deported in 1942. Since then, I have lived alone, and recently I came to Nice with my child. From that city, I came to Switzerland. I came to Switzerland to evade the measures taken by the Germans against the Jews. I crossed the border on October 4, 1943, around 1800 in the region of Hermance."

"Née à Krasnik en 1904, je suis restée dans cette ville jusqu'en 1929. J'ai fait toutes mes classes primaires et je me suis mariée en 1927. Nous avons été ha biter à Lublin 2 ans puis nous sommes venus à Paris où nous sommes resté jusqu'à u mois août. Mon mari a été déporté en 1942. Depuis j'ai vécu seule et ces derniers temps je suis venue à Ni ce avec mon enfant. De cette ville je suis venue en Suisse. Je suis venue en Suisse pour éviter les mesures prises par les Allemands contre les juifs. J'ai passé la frontière le 4.10.43 vers les 1800 dans la région d'Hermance."

5050 **Nicole Szer**, 1, female, Paris. She is Boba's daughter.

5051 **Esther Weinstein,** 43, female, Usky (Czechoslovakia):

"Born in Czechoslovakia in 1900, I stayed there until 1928. I did some schooling there. From 1928 to 1940, I am in Antwerp with my husband. I was married in Czechoslovakia in 1922. In 1940, I took refuge in France with my husband in Saint-Gervais; then put in forced residence in Nice. My husband was deported just a few weeks ago. We made our way to Switzerland to escape the measures taken by the German authorities against the Israelites. We crossed the Swiss border on October 4, 1943, around 1900 in the region of Hermance. We crossed by our own means."

"Née en Tchécoslovaquie en 1900, j'y suis resté jusqu'en 1928. J'y ai fait quelques écoles. de 1928 à 1940, je suis à Anvers avec mon mari. Je me suis mariée en Tchécoslovaquie en 1922. En 1940, je me suis réfugié en France avec mon mari à St.Gervais, puis mis en résidence forcée à Nice. Mon mari a été déporté il y a seulement quelques semaines. Nous avons gagné la Suisse pour éviter les mesures prises par les autorités allemandes contre les israelites. Nous avons franci la frontière suisse le 4.10.43 à 1900 dans la région de Hermance. Nous avons passé par nos propres moyens."

5051 **Michel Weinstein**, 7 months, male, Rodez (France). He is Esther's son.

Profile of the Convoy of October 7, 1943 MJS Convoy Number 15

Summary Information:

Border Guard Post: Cornières
Place where Arrest was made: Les Huteaux
Time of Arrest: 1740 (5:40 p.m.)
Place and Time of Crossing: "through the barbed wire"
Number of Persons: 7
Composition of convoy: 7 unaccompanied children
Correspondence with OSE list: 3 of 7 children's names appear on OSE list as "par Simon"

List of Children Comprising the Convoy and Excerpts from Declarations:

5074 **Elie Knout-Fixman**, 8, male, Paris, "par Simon":

"I lived in Paris until the bombardments, and I have been in a boarding school since then. My father was a French officer in Paris. My father must be in Switzerland or on the Côte d'Azur. A woman accompanied me to Annecy; I know her but I do not know her name. In Toulouse, I was with my mom, Madame Arianne Fixman.?? There is no way that my father is in Germany. I come to Switzerland to be more at ease. I crossed the border on October 7, 1943, in the company of 6 children."

"J'ai habité Paris jusqu'au bombardements et j'ai été en pension depuis. Mon père était officier français à Paris. Mon père doit d'être en Suisse où à la côte d'Azur. Une demoiselle m'a accompagné jusqu'à Annecy, je la connais mais je ne sais pas son nom. A Toulouse j'étais avec ma maman Mme Arianne FIXMAN.?? Mon père n'est en tout cas pas en Allemagne. Je viens en Suisse pour être plus tranquille. J'ai passé la frontière le 7.10.43 en compagnie de 6 enfants."

5076 **Pia-Manon Russak**, 15, female, Plauen (Germany), "par Simon":

"I lived in Germany until April 19, 1939, with my parents. My father was a dentist in Germany. My parents have been deported since August 31, 1942, and I have had no news since then. In France, we were first in Paris, then in Blois (Loir-et-Cher), Châteauroux (Indre), and, finally, in Nice. I came to take refuge in Switzerland to escape deportation because of my Jewish race. We were 7 children in Annecy to cross the border. A *passeur* whose name I do not know led us up to the barbed wire. I crossed the border on October 7, 1943 around 1800 . . ."

"J'ai habité l'Allemagne jusqu'au 19.4.39 avec mes parents. Mon père était dentiste en Allemagne. Mes parents sont déportés depuis le 31.8.42 et je n'ai pas de nouvelle depuis. En France nous avonsété tout d'abord à Paris, puis à Blois (Loire et Cher), Châteauroux (Indre), et enfin à Nice. Je suis venue me réfugiés en Suisse pour éviter la déportation à cause de ma race juive. Nous nous sommes trouvés 7 enfants à Annecy pour passer la frontière. Un passeur dont je ne connais pas le nom nous a conduit jusqu'aux barbelés. J'ai passé la frontière le 7.10.43 à 1800 environ . . ."

5076 **Ursula Russak**, 7, female, Plauen (Germany). She is Pia-Manon's sister. "par Simon"

5079 Myriam Czarny, 14, female, Biala (Poland):

"Born in Biala in 1929, I left that city with my parents in 31. We came to Paris; and in that city my sister was born; we began our schooling that we continued in Toulouse, where we went after Paris, in 1940. We stayed in that city until recently. We came to Switzerland because my father has been deported and our mom is hiding in Toulouse; we came to evade the measures taken by the Germans against the Jews. KRIST Annette [cousin; see below] was born in Paris in 1936 and stayed in that city until 1941, then came to Toulouse, where she stayed until recently. Her parents are hiding in that city and and sent her to Switzerland to evade the measures taken by the Germans against the Jews. Eveline Rosenkern [cousin] was born in Paris in 1936 and stayed in that city until 1940; then she came to Toulouse with her mother, who is still there now, where she is hiding, her father having been deported; and she came to Switzerland to evade the measures taken by the Germans against the Jews. We left Toulouse accompanied by a young girl as far as Annecy; from that city, we went to Annemasse; and there a farmer was waiting for us and led us up to the border. We crossed the border on October 7, 1943, around 1730 in the region of Cornières."

"Née à Biala en 1929 j'ai quitté cette ville avec mes parents en 31. Nous sommes venus à Paris et dans cette ville ma soeur est née, nous avons commencés mes écoles que nous avons continuées à Toulouse où nous sommes venues après Paris en 1940. Dans cette ville nous sommes restées jusqu'à ces derniers jours. Nous sommes venues en Suisse car mon père est déporté et notre maman se cache à Toulouse, nous sommes venues pour éviter les mesures prises par les Allemands contre les juifs. KRIST Annette est née à Paris en 1936 et est restée dans cette ville jusqu'en 194i pour venir ensuite à Toulouse où elle est restée jusqu'à ces derniers jours. Ses parents sont cachés dans cette ville est l'ont envoyée en Suisse pour éviter les mesures prises par les allemands contre les juifs. Rosenkorn Eveline est née à Paris en 1936 et est restée dans cette ville jusqu'en 1940 puis elle est venue à Toulouse avec sa maman, qui y est encore actuellement où elle se cache, son père a été déporté et elle est venue en Suisse pour éviter les mesures prises par les Allemands contre les juifs. Nous sommes parties de Toulouse accompagnées d'une jeune fille jusqu'à Annecy de cette ville nous sommes allées jusqu'à Annemasse et là un paysan nous attendait et nous a conduites jsuqu'à la frontière. Nous avons passé la frontière le 7.10.43 vers les 1730 dans la région de Cornières."

5079 Jeannine Czarny, 11, female, Paris. She is Myriam's sister.

5079 Annette Krist, 7, female, Paris. She is Myriam's cousin.

5079 Eveline Rosenkern, 7, female, Paris. She is Myriam's cousin.

Profile of the Convoy of October 11, 1943
MJS Convoy Number 16

Summary Information:

Border Guard Post: Certoux
Place where Arrest was made: Plaine du Loup
Time of Arrest: 2200 (10:00 p.m.)
Place and Time of Crossing: "beneath the barbed wire between *bornes* 51 and 52"
Number of Persons: 8
Composition of convoy: 8 unaccompanied children
Correspondence with OSE list: 7 of 8 children's names appear on OSE list as "par Simon"

List of Children Comprising the Convoy and Excerpts from Declarations:

5122 **Blanche Uklejska**, 14, female, Lipno (Poland), "par Simon":

"We left Poland in 1934 and, since then, in France, in Paris. My father is a tailor. My parents are now in Vizille, and I do not know if they will come to Switzerland. We come to Switzerland to escape measures taken by the Germans concerning the Jews. We clandestinely crossed the border on October 11, 1943, in the area of Bernex, along with 8 children. A gentleman led us up to the barbed wire; we do not know his name; he was around 50 years old and must live in Saint-Julien. On Swiss [soil], we were arrested right away . . ."

"Nous avons quitté la Pologne en 1934 et dès lors en France, à Paris. Mon père est tailleur. Mes parents se trouvent actuellement à Vizille et je ne sais pas s'ils viendront en Suisse. Nous venons en Suisse pour échapper aux mesures prises par les Allemands concernant les juifs. Nous a vons passé clandestinement la frontière le 11.10.43 dans la région de Bernex en compagnie de 8 enfants. Un Monsieur nous a conduit jusqu'àux barbelés nous ne savons pas le non, il est âgé d'une cinquantaine d'années et doit habiter St-Julien. Sur Suisse on a été arrêtées tout de suite . . ."

5122 **Esther Uklejska**, 12, female, Lipna (Poland). She is Blanche's sister. "par Simon"

5142 **Gérard Dreyfuss**, 14, male, Rueil (France), "par Simon":

"Born in 1929 in Rueil in the Seine-et-Oise, I stayed there until 1939. I did part of my schooling and studies there. In 1939, we headed towards the Pyrenees, near Biarritz, then to Issoire (Puy-de-Dôme), where my father had established his factory. My mother, my sister, and my brother were taken by the occupation troops as hostages in reprisal of an attack, and my father escaped and I myself came to Switzerland. I came to Switzerland to evade the measures taken by the German authorities against the Israelites. I crossed the Swiss border on October 11, 1943, at 2230 in the region of Certoux. I was at my aunt's home in Lyon, and she entrusted me to a young woman whom I do not know who took me to Saint-Julien (having come by bus from Annecy). From Saint-Julien a *passeur* led me up to the border. I did not know this *passeur*."

"Né en 1929 à Rueil dans la Seine et Oise, j'y suis resté jusqu'en 1939. J'y ai fait une partie de mes écoles et écoles. En 1939, nous nous sommes dirigés sur Les Pyhrénées, près de Biarritz, puis à Issoire(Puy de Dôme) où mon père avai t établi son usine. Ma mère, ma soeur et mon frère ont été pris par les troupes d'occupation comme otages en représailles à un attentat et mon père s'est sauvé et moi'même est passé en Suisse. J'ai gagné la Suisse pour éviter les mesures prises par les autorités allemandes contre les israelites. J'ai franchi la frontière suisse le 11.10.43 à 2230 dans la région de Certoux. J'ai été chez une tante à Lyon et cette dernière m'a confié à une jeune dame que je ne connais pas qui m'a conduit jusqu'à St.Julien(en car depuis Annecy) et de St. Julien un passeur m'a conduit à la frontière. Je ne connais pas ce passeur."

5144 **Gerda Bierzonski**, 12, female, Breslau (Germany), "par Simon":

"I lived in Germany until 1939 with my parents; then, until November 1941, in Belgium, then in France, Lyon, Saint-Hilaire-le-Château, and Grenoble. My father is a shopkeeper dealing in fabrics. My parents are now in France, and I do not know if they want to come to Switzerland. I come to Switzerland to evade deportation; in Poland I have a relative who has been deported. I crossed the border on October 11, 1943, at 2230 in the region of Bernex; we were 8 children. Two people led us up to the barbed wire . . ."

"J'ai habité l'Allemagne jusqu'en 1939 avec mes parents, ensuite jusqu'en novembre 1941 en Belgique, puis en France, Lyon, St-Hilaire le château et Grenoble. Mon père est commerçant en tissus. Mes parents sont actuellement en France et je ne sais pas s'ils veulent venir en Suisse. Je viens en Suisse pour éviter la déportation, en Pologne j'ai de la parenté qui a été déportée. J'ai franchi la frontière 11.10.43 à 2230 dans la région de Bernex, nous étions 8 enfants. Deux personnes nous conduisirent jusqu'aux barbelés . . ."

5147 **Hélène Rubinstein**, 12, female, Brussels-Uccle (Belgium), "par Simon":

"Born in 1931 in Brussels-Uccle, I stayed there until the declaration of war, that is until 1940. I did the beginning of my primary schooling there, as did my brother. In 1940, we took refuge with my parents in Paris, Marseille, in Nice, and finally Aix-les-Bains. Our parents are still in Aix-les-Bains. We made our way to Switzerland to evade the measures taken by the German authorities against the Israelites. We crossed the Swiss border on October 11, 1943, at 2230 in the region of Certoux. It was a relief organization that organized the crossing. We were 8. A young woman took us from Aix-les-Bains as far as Annecy, then from Annecy to Saint-Julien. Her name is Mademoiselle ROLANDE. From Saint-Julien, we had two *passeurs* whom we do not know."

"Née en 1931 à Bruxelles-Uccle, j'y suis restée jusqu'à la déclaration de la guerre soit jusqu'en 1940. J'y ai fait le commencement des mes écoles primaires, ainsi que mon frère. En 1940, nous nous sommes réfugiés avec mes parents à Paris, Marseille, à Nice et enfin à Aix-les-Bains. Nos parents se-trouvent encore à Aix-les-Bains. Nous avons gagné la Suisse pour éviter les mesures prises par les autorités allemandes contre les israelites. Nous avons franchi la frontière suisse le 11.10.43 à 2230 dans la région de Certoux. C'est une organisation de secours qui a organisé le passage. Nous étions 8. Une jeune femme nous a conduit d'Aix-les-Bains jusqu'à Annecy, puis d'Annecy à St.Julien. Elle s'appelait Mlle ROLANDE. Dès St. Julien nous avons eu deux passeurs que nous ne connaissons pas."

5147 **Georges Rubinstein**, 11, male, Brussels-Uccle (Belgium). He is Hélène's brother. "par Simon"

5148 **Denise Rivet**, 9, female, Annecy:

"Born in 1933 in Annecy, I left that city in 1938 to go to Lyon with my parents. I stayed in that city until a few days ago, and I began my schooling. It was my parents who sent me to Switzerland to come and join my grandmother. My mom was Swiss before her marriage, and she sent me to Switzerland for fear of bombardments. I crossed the border with a convoy of children organized by the committee "OSE," and we were accompanied as far as Annecy by a young woman. My mom came with me as far as Annecy; and from there I left with this young woman and went to Saint-Julien; then a gentleman accompanied us as far as the border. We crossed on October 11, 1943, around 2230 in the region of Certoux."

"Née en 1933 à Annecy je suis partie de cette ville en 1938 pour aller à Lyon avec mes parents. Je suis restée dans cette ville jusqu'à ces derniers jours et j'ai commencé mes écoles. C'est mes parents qui m'ont envoyée en Suisse pour venir rejoindre ma grand-mère. Ma maman était Suisse avant son mariage et elle m'a envyée en Suisse de crainte des bombardements. J' ai passé la frontière avec un convoi d'enfant organisé par le comité "OSE" et nous avons été accompagnés jusqu'à Annecy par une demoiselle . Ma maman est venue avec moi jusqu'à Annecy et de là je suis partie avec cette demoiselle jusqu'à St. Julien puis un Mr. Nous a accompagnés jusqu'à la frontière. Nous avons passé le 11.10.43 vers les 2230 dans la région de Certoux."

5149 **Abraham Cymerman**, 14, male, Sosnowiec (Poland), "par Simon":

"Born in Sosnowiec, I left that city at the age of 1 to come to Paris with my parents; since that time we always lived in Paris, until 1942. I did all my classes in Paris. My parents were deported in July 42; and, since then, we were arrested with my sister and taken to a camp. We were liberated and put in forced residence in Aux Bonnes [Eaux-Bonnes?]; then, afterwards, we were in Grenoble, where we joined our cousin. I came by myself to Switzerland to evade the measures taken by the Germans against the Jews. I crossed the border on October 11, 1943, around 2230 in the region of Certoux. It was with a convoy of children that I came to Switzerland, a convoy organized by the committee "OSE"; we were taken as far as Annemasse—Annecy [sic], and from there, by bus to Saint-Julien. At Saint-Julien a gentleman was waiting for us and led us up to the barbed wire."

"Né à Sosnowiec je suis parti de cette ville èà l'âge de 1 an, pour venir à Paris avec mes parents depuis cette date nous avons toujours habité à Paris jusqu'en 1942. J'ai fait toutes mes classes à Paris. Mes parents ont été déportés au mois de juillet 42 et depuis nous avons été arrêtés avec ma soeur et conduit dans un camp. Nous avons été libéré et mis en résidence forcée à Aux Bonnes puis nous avons été par la suite à Grenoble rejoindre notre cousin. Je suis venu seul en Suisse pour éviter les mesures prises par les Allemands contre les juifs. J'ai passé la frontière le 11.10.43. vers les 2230 dans la région de Certoux. C'est avec un convoi d'enfant que je suis venu en Suisse organisé par le comité "OSE" nous avons été conduits jusqu'à Annemasse –Annecy et de là le car jusqu'à St. Julien. A St. Julien un Mr. nous attendait et nous a conduits jusqu'au barbelés."

Profile of the Convoy of October 12, 1943
MJS Convoy Number 17

Summary Information:

Border Guard Post: Certoux
Place where Arrest was made: Plaine du Loup
Time of Arrest: 2125 (9:25 p.m.)

Place and Time of Crossing: "on foot between the *bornes* 51 and 52 at 21:25 [9:25 p.m.]"
Number of Persons: 8
Composition of convoy: 8 unaccompanied children
Correspondence with OSE list: All children's names appear on OSE list as "par Simon"

List of Children Comprising the Convoy and Excerpts from Declarations:

5123 **David Hirsch**, 15, male, Mayence (Germany), "par Simon":

"I lived in Germany until 1940, and, from 1940, in France. My parents have been in Argentina since 1937; my father is a woodworker. I come to Switzerland to avoid being deported to Germany. I came with a convoy of 8 children; we crossed the border clandestinely in the region of Certoux at around 2200. We crossed the border alone; a person just showed us the direction to follow."

"J'ai habité en l'Allemagne jusqu'en 1940 et dès 1940 en France. Mes parents sont en Argentine depuis 1937, mon père est menuisier. Je viens en Suisse pour éviter d'être déporté en Allemagne. Je suis venu avec un convoi de 8 enfants, nous avons franchi la frontière clandestinement dans la région de certoux à 2200 environ. Nous avons passé la frontière seul, une personne nous a indiqué la direction à suivre uniquement."

5143 **Maurice Szwed**, 12, male, Paris: "par Simon"

"We have always lived in Paris. My father is a tailor. Presently, he is deported since May 14, 1941; my mother is hiding in Paris. We come to Switzerland so as not to be deported. A person took us from Paris to Annecy; then afterwards two men [took us] to a house near the border. We crossed the border on October 12, 1943, in the area of Certoux and were arrested immediately . . ."

"Nous avons toujourd habité Paris. Mon père est tailleur. Actuellement il est déporté depuis le 14.5.41, ma mère se cache à Paris. Nous venons en Suisse pour ne pas être déportés. Une personne nous a conduit de Paris à Annecy, puis ensuite deux hommes jusqu'à une maison près de la frontière. Nous avons passé la frontière le 12.10.43 dans la région de Certoux et avons été arrêtés immediatement . . ."

5143 **Marcel Szwed**, 9, male, Paris. He is Maurice's brother. "par Simon" "rue Amelot"

5145 **Heinz Diewald**, 15, male, Trèves (Trier) (Germany), "par Simon":

"Born in 1928 in Germany, I stayed there until 1939. I did the beginning of my primary schooling there. From 1939 to 1940, we took refuge in Brussels with my parents. From 1940 to 1942, in Marseille and finally in Chabannes, which was my last place of residence. My parents were deported in 1942, from Marseille. I made my way to Switzerland to evade the measures taken by the German authorities against the Israelites. We crossed the Swiss border on October 12, 1943, at 2215 in the region of Certoux. It was a relief organization that took care of our crossing. We were with another comrade going by bus as far as Saint-Julien; and from there two *passeurs* had us cross the border. I do not know these *passeurs*."

"Né en 1928 en Allemagne, j'y suis resté jusqu'en 1939. J'y ai fait le commencementde mes écoles primaires. En 1939 jusqu'en 1940, nous nous sommes réfugiés à Bruxelles avec mes parents. de 1940 à 1942 à Marseille et enfin à Chabannes qui fut mon dernier domicile. Mes parents ont été déportés en 1942 depuis Marseille. J'ai gagné la Suisse pour éviter les mesures prises par les autorités allemandes contre les israelites. Nous avons franchi la frontière suisse le 12.10.43 à 2215 dans la région de Certoux. C'est une organisation de secours qui s'est occupée de notre passage. Nous avons été avec un autre camarade jusqu'à St-Julien en car et delà deux passeurs nous ont fait traverser la frontière. Je ne connais pas ces passeurs."

5146 **Madeleine Rozenberg**, 15, female, Tomasow (Poland) "par Simon":

"Born in 1928 in Poland, we came in 1931 to France, to Paris, where we all did or began our primary schooling. We stayed there until 1942. We were on vacation in the Sarthe [department], where our mother and our older brother were deported. Then we were in a boarding school in Clamard (Seine). [Perhaps this refers to Clamart in the department of the Hauts-de-Seine.] Then we returned on vacation in the Sarthe, which is where we came from. We made our way to Switzerland to evade the measures taken by the German authorities against the Israelites. We crossed the Swiss border on October 12, 1943, at 2215 in the region of Certoux. Our crossing was organized by the Social Assistance Committee of Paris, and [we] were passed from hand to hand among different people whom we do not know. Since Saint-Julien, two men served as *passeurs*."

"Née 1928 en Pologne, nous sommes venus en 1931 en France à Paris où nous avons tous fait ou commencé nos écoles primaires. Nous y sommes restés jusqu'en 1942. Nous avons été en vacances dans la Sarthe où nous notre mère et notre grand frère ànt été déportés . Puis nous avons été en Pension à Clamard (Seine). Puis, nous sommes retournés en vacances dans la Sarthe d'où nous venons présentement. Nous avons gagné la Suisse pour éviter les mesures prises par les autorités allemandes contre les israelites. Nous avons franchi la frontière suisse le 12.10.43 à 2215 dans la région de Certoux. Notre passage a été organisé par un comité d'Assistance Sociale de Paris et avons été remis mains en mains à différentes personnes que nous ne connaissons pas. Depuis St.Julien, 2 hommes ont fait fonction de passeurs."

5146 **Suzanne Rozenberg**, 13, female, Tomasow (Poland). She is Madeleine's sister. "par Simon"

5146 **Rachèle Rozenberg**, 5, female, Paris. She is Madeleine's sister. "par Simon"

5146 **Bernard Rozenberg**, 9, male, Paris. He is Madeleine's brother. "par Simon"

Profile of the Convoy of October 13, 1943
MJS Convoy Number 18

Summary Information:

Border Guard Post: Cornières
Place where Arrest was made: Vignes de Bran
Time of Arrest: 1700 (5:00 p.m.)
Place and Time of Crossing: "through the barbed wire"
Number of Persons: 8
Composition of convoy: 8 unaccompanied children
Correspondence with OSE list: All children's names appear on the OSE list as "par Simon"

List of Children Comprising the Convoy and Excerpts from Declarations:

5153 **Fanny Zilberg**, 12, female, Paris, "par Simon":

"Born in 1930 in Paris, I stayed there continually until 1942, as did my sisters. I did my primary schooling there. In 1942, my mother was deported with all of our identity papers. My father is now in South America. Since my mother was deported, I have been in a foster home with my sisters, the home of Mrs. PICCOT, in Fontenay-Saint-Père. We made our way Switzerland to evade the measures taken by the German authorities against the Israelites. We crossed the Swiss border on October 13, 1943, at 1830 in the region of Cornières. It was the Israelite Relief Committee in Paris that organized our convoy, comprised of

8 children. From Paris, it was a woman whom I do not know who took us as far as Lyon. From Lyon to Annecy, it was Monsieur Roland who took us. Similarly, he took care of us from Annecy to Annemasse aided by Mademoiselle Jeanne. For the clandestine crossing, two *passeurs* led us, but I do not know them."

"Née en 1930 à Paris j'y suis restée constamment jusqu-en 1942 ainsi que mes soeurs. J'y ai fait mes écoles primaires. En 1942, ma mère a été déportée avec tous les papiers d'identité. Mon père se trouve actuellement en Amérique du Sud. Depuis la déportation de ma mère, j'ai été ennourice avec mes soeurs chez une Dame PICCOT, à Fontenay St.Père. Nous avons gagné la Suisse pour éviter les mesures prises par les autorités allemandes contre les israelites. Nous avons franchi la frontière suisse le 13.10.43 à 1830 dans la région de Cornières. C'est le Comité Israelite de Secours à Paris qui a organisé notre convoi composé de 8 enfants. Depuis Paris, c'est une dame que je ne connais pas qui nous a conduits jusqu'à Lyon. De lyon à Annecy, c'est M. ROLAMD qui nous conduisait . Egalement il s'est occupé de nous de puis à Annecy à Annemasse aidé de Mlle Jeanne. Pour le passage clandestin, 2 passeurs nous ont conduits mais je ne les connais pas."

5153 **Anette Zilberg**, 11, female, Paris. She is Fanny's sister. "par Simon"

5153 **Lili Zilberg**, 7, female, Paris. She is Fanny's sister. "par Simon"

5155 **Jacques Rosenberg**, 13, male, Paris, "par Simon":

"Born in 1930 in Paris, I stayed there continually, as did my brother and my sister. I did my primary schooling in Paris, the same as my sister. My mother is still living in Paris, Montreuil-sous-Bois (Seine). My father has been a prisoner in Germany since June 6, 1941. We made our way to Switzerland to evade the measures taken by the German authorities against the Israelites and the bombardments. We crossed the Swiss border on October 13, 1943, at 1830 in the region of Cornière. It was the Israelite Relief Committee of Paris that organized this trip for a convoy of 8 children. From Paris, it was a woman who took us as far as Lyon. From Lyon to Annecy, it was a certain Monsieur ROLAND, who also accompanied us as far as Annemasse with Mademoiselle JEANNE. From Annemasse, 2 *passeurs* had us cross the border. I do not know these two people."

"Né en 1930 à Paris, j'y suis resté constamment, ainsi que mon frère et ma soeur. J'ai fait mes écoles primaires à Paris de même que ma soeur. Ma mère habite toujours Paris, Montreuill-s.Bois Seine. Mon père est prisonnier en Allemagne depuis le 6.6.41. Nous avons gagné la Suise pour éviter les mesures prises par les autorités allemandes contre les israelites et les bombarements. Nous avons franchi la frontière suisse le 13.10.43 à 1830 dans la région Cornière. C'est le Comité Israelite de Secours à Paris qui a organisé ce voyage pour un convoi de 8 enfants. Depuis Paris, c'est une dame qui nous a conduits jusqu'à Lyon- De Loyn à Annecy, c'est un certain M. ROLAND qui nous a également accompagnés jusqu'à Annemasse avec Mlle JEANNE. Depuis Annemasse, 2 passeurs nous ont fait traverser la frontière. Je ne connais pas ces deux personnes."

5155 **Victor Rosenberg**, 5, male, Paris. He is Jacques' brother. "par Simon"

5155 **Jeanne Rosenberg**, 11, female, Paris. She is Jacques' sister. "par Simon"

5158 **Charles Beinart**, 14, male, Paris, "par Simon":

"We always lived in Paris with our parents. My father was a taxi driver; now he has been deported for about two years. My mother is in Paris. We left Paris with a convoy of 8 children under the supervision of a certain Monsieur Roland, who took us as far as Annecy. Then two men and a woman—who must have been named Denis, François, and Suzanne—led us to a *passeur* whose name I do not know. We crossed the border on October 13, 1943, in the region of Chêne, and, once on Swiss [soil], we were immediately arrested . . ."

"Nous avons toujours habité Paris avec nos parents. Mon père était chauffeur de ta xis, actuellement il est déporté depuisenviron deux ans. Ma mère est à Paris. Nous avons quitté Paris avec un convoi de 8 enfants sous la conduite d'un certain M. Roland qui nous a amené jusqu'à Annecy. Puis deux hommes et une dame qui doivent s'appeler Denis, François et Suzanne nous conduisirent jusqu'au passeur dont je ne sais pas le nom. Nous avons franchi la frontière le 13.10.43 dans la région de Chêne et sur Suisse nous avons été arrêté tout de suite . . ."

5158 **Maurice Beinart,** 9, male, Paris. He is Charles' brother. "par Simon"

Profile of the Convoy of October 14 (1), 1943
MJS Convoy Number 19

Summary Information:

Border Guard Post: Cornières
Place where Arrest was made: Chemin des Vignes
Time of Arrest: 1915 (7:15 p.m.)
Place and Time of Crossing: "through the barbed wire"
Number of Persons: 9

Composition of convoy: 9 unaccompanied children
Correspondence with OSE list: All children's names appear on OSE list as "par Simon"

List of Children Comprising the Convoy and Excerpts from Declarations:

5176 **Jacques Jungerman**, 12, male, Paris, "par Simon":

"I lived in Paris until May 1943. My parents have been deported since about two weeks ago. My father was a tailor. My parents were taken in Nice by the Germans, as that was the last city in which I lived. I came with a convoy of children; we were 9. The two *passeurs* led us up to the barbed wire; and, once on Swiss [soil], we were arrested, then taken to the Gendarmerie post, then to Cropettes. We crossed the border on October 14, 1943, around 2000 in the region of Cornières."

"J'ai habité Paris jusqu'au mois de mai 1943. Mes parents sont déportés depuis environ deux semaines. Mon père était tailleur. Mes parents ont été pris à Nice par les allemands, car c'est dans cette ville q ue j'ai habité en dernier lieu. Je suis venu avec un convoi d-enfants, nous étions 9. Les deux pa sseurs nous conduisirent jusqu'aux barbelés et sur Suisse nous avons été arrêtés puis conduits au poste de Gendarmerie, puis aux Cropette Nous avons passé la frontière le 14.10.43 à 2000 environ, dans la région de Cornières."

5177 **Lucie Kuhn**, 15, female, Luxembourg, "par Simon":

"Born in Luxembourg, we stayed in that city until 1940. We then came to France with our mom to join our father, who was already in France, in Nice. We were not able to cross the line of demarcation; we were in forced residence in Montélimar until 1942. We were seized in a roundup and taken to a camp. An Israelite committee succeeded in getting out all of the children younger than 16; we left and we went to meet up with an aunt in Nice, then in Lyon, and finally I went to a convent; then, afterwards, we were put in a private school in Nice. From there, our aunt was taken by the Germans; and, since then, I do not know the whereabouts of her or my mother. We had no means of support, and we came to Switzerland. We came to Switzerland because we had no more means of support in France and for fear of German reprisals against the Jews. We crossed the border on October 14, 1943, around 1930 in the region of Cornières. We came with a convoy of children accompanied by a young girl, Mademoiselle Mila, as far as Annecy; and from there we went to Annemasse with two young people who placed us in the hands of *passeurs*."

"Nées à Luxembourg nous sommes restées dans cette ville jusqu'en 1940. Nous sommes alors venues en France avec notre maman pour rejoindre notre père qui se rouvait déjà en France à Nice. Nous n'avons pas pû passer la ligne de démarcation et nous avons été en résidence forcés à Montélimar jusqu'en 1942. Nous avons été prises dans une refle et conduite dans un camp. Un comité israelite réussi à faire sortir tous les enfants en dessous de 16 ans, nous sommes sorties et nous avons été rejoindre une tante à Nice puis à Lyon et ensuite je suis allée dans un couvent puis par lasuite nous avons été mises dans une école privée à Nice. De là notre tante a été prise par les Allemands et depuis je ne sais plus où elle se trouve ainsi que ma mère. Nous étions sans ressourses et nous sommes venues en Suisse. Nous sommes venues en Suisse car nous n'avions plus de ressourses en France et de crainte des représailles Allemandes contre les juifs. Nous avons passée la frontière le 14.10.43. vers les 1930 dans la région de Cornièes. Nous sommes venues avec un convoi d'enfant accompagné par une jeune fille, Melle Mila, jusqu'à Annecy et de là nous sommes allées à Annemasse avec deux jeunes gens qui nous ont remises en tre les mains de passeurs."

5177 **Sonia Kuhn**, 6, female, Luxembourg. She is Lucie's sister. "par Simon"

5179 **Edith Salik**, 15, female, Vienna, "par Simon":

"Born in Vienna in 1928, I stayed in that city until 1939; I did all my classes and I came to France. And, afterwards, my parents left for America, where my father died. In France, I went to a children's home, where I stayed until 1942; then I went to join a cousin in Voiron, where I stayed until recently. I came to Switzerland to evade the measures taken by the Germans against the Jews. I crossed the border on October 14, 1943, around 1930 in the region of Cornières. I left Voiron accompanied by a young lady Ruth as far as Annecy. There two young people accompanied us as far as Annemasse with some other children who were in Annecy. We were then placed in the hands of *passeurs* who accompanied us as far as the border."

"Née à Vienne en 1928 je suis restée dans cette ville jusqu'en 1939, j'ai fait toutes mes classes et je suis venue en France . Et par la suite mes parents sont partis pour l'Amérique où mon père est mort. EnFrance je suis allée dans une maison d'enfant où je suis restée jusqu'en 1942 puis je suis allée rejoindre un cousin à Voiron où je suis restée jusqu'à ces derniers jours, Je suis venue en Suisse pour éviter les mesures prises par les Allemands contre les juifs. J'ai passé la frontière le 14.10.43. vers les 1930 dans la région de Cornières. Je suis partie de Voiron accompagnéed 'une demoiselle Ruth, jusqu'à Annecy. Là deux jeunes gens nous ont accompagés jusqu'à Annemasse avec d'autre enfants que l'on a trouvés à Annecy. Nous avons été ensuite remis en tre les mains de passeurs qui nous ont accompagés jusqu'à la frontière."

5180 Fernande Valigora, 12, male, Paris, "par Simon":

"Born in Paris in 1931, I stayed in that city until 1942. I began my schooling, and I left Paris with my mother and my sister. We went to Rodès to meet up with my uncle, where I stayed until recently. My mom sent me to Switzerland for fear of German reprisals against the Israelites. I left Rodès with a young girl, Mademoiselle Andrée, who accompanied me as far as Annecy. There, I joined a group of children and we were taken as far as Annemasse by a young man; then he placed us into the hands of *passeurs*. I crossed the border on October 14, 1943, around 1930 in the region of Cornières."

"Née à Paris en 1931 je suis restée dans cette ville jusqu'en 1942. J'ai commencé mes écoles et je suis partie de Paris avec ma mère et ma soeur. Nous avons été à Rodès rejoindre mon oncle, où je suis restée jusqu'à ces derniers temps. Ma mère m'a envoyée en Suisse de crainte des représailles Allemandes contre les israelites Je suis partie de Rodès avec une jeune fille, Melle Andrée, qui m'a accompagnée jusqu'à Annecy. Là j'ai rejoint un groupe d'enfants et nous avons été conduits jusqu'à Annem sse par un jeune homme, puis il nous a remis en tre les mains de passeurs. J'ai passé la frontière le 14.10.43. vers les 1930 dans la région de Cornières."

5184 Louis Folbaum, 11, male, Paris, "par Simon":

"Born in Paris, we left that city in 1942. We went to Nice with our parents, and it was there that our parents were taken by the Germans; we do not know where they are now. From that time on, we stayed in the home of a woman who raised us. From Nice, we came to Switzerland. We came to Switzerland to evade the measures taken by the Germans against the Jews. We crossed the border on October 14, 1943, around 1930 in the area [of] Cornières. We came with a convoy of children; and, from Nice, we were accompanied by a young woman, Mademoiselle Mila, as far as Annecy; from there, by two young people as far as Annemasse and by some *passeurs* up to the barbed wire."

"Nés à Paris nous avons quitté cette ville en 1942. Nous sommes allés à Nice avec nos parents et c' est là que nos parents ont été pris par les Allemands nous ne savons pas où ils se trouvent actuellement. De cette date nous sommes restés chez une dame qui nous élevait. De Nice nous sommes venus en Suisse. Nous sommes venus en Suisse pour éviter les mesures prises par les Allemands contre les juifs. Nous avons passé la frontière 14.10.43. vers les 1930 dans la région Cornières. Nous sommes venus avec un convoi d'enfants et de Nice nous avons été accompagnés par une demoiselle, Melle Mila,jusqu'à Annecy de là avec deux jeunes gens jusqu'à Annemasse et par des passeurs jusqu'au barbelés."

5184 **Bernard Folbaum**, 4, male, Paris. He is Louis' brother. "par Simon"

5185 **Alain Charas**, 7, male, Paris, "par Simon":

[Note: The crossing date stated on the Declaration appears to be incorrect, as it does not correspond with the crossing date stated on the arrest report.]

"Born in Paris in 1936, we left that city with our parents to go to many villages and then to Marseille. From there, we were at Moirons [Moirans] (Isère), and from there we came to Switzerland. Our parents stayed in hiding in Moirons and sent us to Switzerland to evade the measures taken by the Germans against the Jews. We crossed the border on October 15, 1943, around 1930 in the region of Cornières. We came with a convoy of children accompanied by some girls, who placed us into the hands of *passeurs*."

"Nés à Paris en 1936 nous avons quitté cett e ville avec nos parents pour nous rendre dans plusieurs villages et ensuite à Marseile. De là nous acons été à Moirons (Isère) et de là nous sommes venus en Suisse. Nos parents sont restés ca chés à Moirons et nous ont envoyé en Suisse pour éviter les mesures prises par les Allemands contre les juifs. Nous avons passé la frontière le 15.10.43. vers les 1930 dans la région de Cornières. Nous sommes venus avec un convoi d'enfants accompagnés par des jeunes filles, qui nous ont remis entre les mains de passeurs."

5185 **Martine Charas**, 7, female, Paris. She is Alain's twin sister. "par Simon"

Profile of the Convoy of October 14 (2), 1943
MJS Convoy Number 20

Summary Information:

Border Guard Post: Certoux
Place where Arrest was made: Plaine du Loup
Time of Arrest: 2230 (10:30 p.m.)
Place and Time of Crossing: "under the barbed wire between *bornes* 51 and 52 at 22:30h"
Number of Persons: 8
Composition of convoy: 4 unaccompanied children and one family of 4 (parents and 2 children)
Correspondence with OSE list: 3 of 6 children's names appear on OSE list as "par Simon" and one name appears as "par OSE"

List of Children Comprising the Convoy and Excerpts from Declarations:

5174 **Louis Salomons**, 55, male, Amsterdam:

"Born in 1888 in Holland, I stayed there until 1893. From then on, I lived continually in Paris, where I did my primary schooling and my studies. I married two times. The last time was in 1939. I left Paris at the end of 1941. Beginning in 1942, we took refuge in Montauban and, lately, in Nice, which I left eight days ago. We made our way to Switzerland to evade the measures taken by the German authorities against the Israelites. We crossed the Swiss border on October 14, 1943, at 2200 in the region of Certoux. It was an Israelite organization that provided us with *passeurs*, whom we do not know. One accompanied us from Annecy to Saint-Julien by bus, and two others came from Saint-Julien for the crossing. I paid 15,000 French francs."

"Né en 1888 en Hollande, j'y suis resté jusqu'en 1893. Dès lors j'ai habité constmment à Paris où j'ai fait mes écoles primaires et mes études. Je me suis marié deux fois. La derrière en 1939. J'ai quitté Paris fin 1941. Nous nous sommes réfugiés dès 1942 à Montauban et à Nice dernièrement que j'ai quitté il y a 8 jours. Nous avons gagné la Suisse pour éviter les mesures prises par les autorités allemandes contre les israelites. Nous avons franchi la frontière suisse le 14.10.43 à 2200 dans la région de Certoux. C'est une organisation israelite qui nous a fourni des passeurs que nous ne connaissons pas. Un nous a accompgné de Annecy à St-Julien en car et les deux autres sont venus de St-Julien pour le passage. J'ai payé fr.f. 15.000."

5174 **Alice Salomons**, 44, female, Paris. She is Louis' wife.

5174 **Philippe Salomons**, 3, male, Paris. He is Louis' son.

5174 **Anne Ischwall**, 13, female, Peterborough (England). She is Alice's daughter from a previous marriage.

5183 **Marcel Morgenstern**, 4, male. Place of birth and date of birth are not indicated. "par Simon":

"My parents stayed in Nice, where they are hiding and expect to come to join me shortly in Switzerland."

"Mes parensts sont restés à Nice où ils se cachent et compte venir me rejoindre prochaibement en Suisse."

5203 Hélène Junger, 15, female, Sighet (Romania), "par Simon":

"Born in Romania in 1928, we left that country to go to Antwerp (Belgium) at the age of one year. We stayed in that city until 1940; we did all of our schooling and we came to France with our parents, to Péraclos. After a stay of two weeks, we were arrested and taken to a camp. After three months, we were in Draguignan, where we stayed until September 1943. We then went to Aix-en-Provence, and from there, to Nice, and from there, to Switzerland. We came to Switzerland because our parents were deported and we fear the measures taken by the Germans against the Israelites. We crossed the border on October 14, 1943, around 2230 in the region of Certoux. We came with a convoy organized by an Israelite committee; and we were accompanied by a young man as far as Saint-Julien; and there he placed us in the hands of *passeurs*."

"Nées en Roumanie en 1928 nous avons quitté ce pays pour aller à Anvers (BE) à l'âge d'un an. Nous sommes restées dans cette ville jusqu'en 1940, nous avons fait toutes nos écoles et nous sommes venues en France avec nos parents à Péraclos. Après un séjour de deux semaines nous avons été arrêtés et conduites dans un camp. Après 3 mois nous a vons été à Draguignan où nous sommes restées jusqu'en mois de septembre 43. Nous avons été ensuite à Aix-en-Provence et de là à Nice et de là en Suisse. Nous sommes venues en Suisse car nos parents ont été déportés et nous avons craint les mesures prises par les Allemands, contre les israelites. Nous avons passé la frontière le 14.10.43. vers les 2230 dans la région de Certoux. Nous sommes venues avec un convoi organisé par un comité israelite et nous avons été accompagnées par un jeune homme jusqu'à St. Julien et là il nous a remises entre les mains de passeur."

5203 Berthe Junger, 15, female, Sighet (Romania). She is Hélène's twin sister. "par Simon"

5204 Lydia Merwitzer, 15, Milan, "par OSE":

"Born in Milan in 1928, I left that city with my parents to go to Nice, in 1939. I did a part of my studies in Milan, and I continued them for two years in Nice. I left Nice at the beginning of the year to go into forced residence in Vance [Vence]; then I left with the Italians to go to La Bollène [-Vésubie]. I came again to Nice; and, from that city, I came to Switzerland. I came to Switzerland because my parents were deported and I no longer have relatives in France. I came because I fear the measures taken by the Germans against the Israelites. I crossed the border on October 14, 1943, around 2200 in the region of Certoux. I came with a convoy organized by a Jewish committee. We left Nice accompanied as far as Saint-Julien by a young man; and there he placed us in the hands of *passeurs*."

"Née à Milan en 1928 j'ai quitté cette ville avec mes parents pour aller à Nice, en 1939. J'ai fait une partie de mes études à Milan et j'ai encore continué deux ans à Nice. J'ai quitté Nice au début de l'année pour aller en résidence forcée à Vance puis je suis partie avec les Italiens pour aller à la Bollène. Je suis à nouveau venue à Nice et de cete ville je suis venue en Suisse. Je suis venue en Suisse car mes parents ont été déportés et je n'ai plus de parents en France. JE suis venue dans la crainte des mesures prises par les Allemands contre les israelites. J'ai passé la frontière le 14.10.43. vers les 2200 dans la région de Certoux. Je suis venue avec un convoi organisé par un comité juif. Nous sommes parties de Nice accompagnées jusqu'à St. Julien par un jeune homme et là il nous a remises entre les mains de passeurs."

Profile of the Convoy of October 18, 1943 MJS Convoy Number 21

Summary Information:

Border Guard Post: Certoux
Place where Arrest was made: Plaine du Loup
Time of Arrest: 2100 (9:00 p.m.)
Place and Time of Crossing: "beneath the barbed wire between *bornes* 51 and 52 at 21:00 [9:00p.m.]"
Number of Persons: 9
Composition of convoy: 7 unaccompanied children and one mother and child
Correspondence with OSE list: 5 of 8 children's names appear on OSE list as "par Simon" and one name appears on list as "par OSE"

List of People Comprising the Convoy and Excerpts from Declarations:

5217 **Berthe Weinstein**, 6, female, Antwerp, date of birth not indicated, "par Simon":

"Born in Antwerp, we came to France with our parents. We lived in Saint-Gervais, then in Nice. My mom came to Switzerland, and she is now in the camp of Champel. Not of an age to give precise information. Could have come to Switzerland to join her mother, who recently came to Switzerland with another child. They came from Nice with a convoy of children and crossed the border on October 18, 1943, in the region of Certoux."

"Nés à Anvers nous sommes venus en France avec nos parents . Nous avons habit é à St. Gervais puis à Nice. Ma maman est venue en Suisse et elle est actuellement au camp de Champel. N'est pas en âge de donner des renseignements précis. Serait venue en Suisse pour rejoindre sa maman qui est entrée dernièrement en Suisse avec un autre enfant. Il sont venus de Nive avec un convoi d'engant et ont passé la frontière le 18.10.43. dans la région de Certoux."

5217 **Robert Weinstein,** 4, male, Antwerp. Date of birth not indicated. He is Berthe's brother. "par Simon"

5218 **Sarah Kalmanowicz**, 39, female, Wyschcow (Poland):

"Born in 1904 in Poland, I stayed there until 1926. I did my primary schooling there. From 1926 to 1933, in Belgium, in Antwerp. From 1933 to 1939, in Italy, in Trieste, where I was married in 1934. From 1939 on, I was in Nice. My husband was deported in 1942. We made our way to Switzerland to evade the measures taken by the German authorities against the Israelites. We crossed the Swiss border on October 18, 1943, at 2100 in the region of Certoux. I made the trip from Nice to Annecy by train in the company of a few children that I met at the train station in Nice. From Annecy as far as Saint-Julien, by bus. A gentleman gave us information in Annecy, but I do not know him. From Saint-Julien to the border, we had two *passeurs*."

"Née en 1904 en Pologne, j'y suis resté jusqu'en 1926. J-y ai fait mes écoles primaires. De 1926 à 1933 en Belgique à Anvers. de 1933 à 1939 en Italie à Trieste où je me suis mariée en 1934. Dès 1939, je suis à Nice. Mon mari a été déporté en 1942. Nous avons gagné la Suisse pour éviter les mesures prises par les autorités allemandes contre les israelites. Nous avons franchi la frontière suisse le 18.10.43 à 2100 dans la région de Certoux. J'ai fait le trajet de Nice à Annecy en train en compagnie de quelques enfants que j'ai rencontré en Gare de Nice. Depuis Annecy jusqu'à St. Julien en car. Un monsieur nous a donné des renseignements à Annecy, mais je ne le connais pas. Dès St. Julien à la frontière nous avonsneu deux passeurs."

5218 **Paulette Kalmanowicz**, 9 months, female, Nice. She is Sarah's daughter.

5222 **Henri Wander**, 14, male, Lvov (Poland), "par OSE":

"Born in Lvov in 1929, I left that city with my parents to come to France. We went to Paris, and, in that city, I began my schooling. I then went to Nice, where I continued my schooling and stayed until recently. My parents stayed in Nice and sent me to Switzerland for fear of German reprisals against the Israelites. I crossed the border on October 18, 1943, around 2130 in the region of Certoux. I came with a convoy organized by an Israelite committee. We were accompanied by a young girl as far as Annecy. From there, we took the bus as far as Saint-Gervais [sic], and four gentlemen who were in the bus accompanied us as far as the border."

"Né à Lwow en 1929 j'ai quitté cette ville avec mes parents pour venir en France. Nous sommes allés à Paris et dans cette ville j'ai commencé mes écoles. Je suis ensuite venu à Nice où j'ai contunué mes écoles et suis resté jusqu'à ces derniers j ours. Mes parents sont restés à Nice et m'ont envoyé en Suisse de crainte des représailles Allemandes contre les israelites. J'ai passé la frontière le 18.10.43. vers les 2130 dans la région de Certoux. Je suis venu avec un convoi organisé par un comité israelite. Nous avons été accompagné par une jeune fille jusqu'à Annecy . De là nous avons pris le car jusqu'à St. Gervais et quatre Mr. qui se trouvaient dans le car nous ont accompagné jusqu'à la frontière."

5224 **Dora Chimon**, 11, female, Milan:

"Born in 1932 in Milan, I stayed there until the middle of 1938. Beginning in 1938, I lived in Nice with my parents. My mother and my sister were deported in the spring. My father is still hiding in Nice. I made my way to Switzerland to evade the measures taken by the German authorities against the Israelites. I crossed the Swiss border on October 18, 1943, at 2030 in the region of Certoux. I was part of a convoy of children, a convoy organized by an Israelite committee. A person whom I do not know accompanied us to Annecy; then from there two gentlemen whom I do not know took us by bus to the border."

"Née en 1932 à Milan, j'y suis restée jusqu'au milieu 1938. Dès 1938, j'ai habité Nice avec mes parents. Ma mère et ma soeur ont été déportées ce printemps. Mon père est toujours caché à Nice. J'ai gagné la Suisse pour éviter les mesures prises par les autorités allemandes contre les israelites. J'ai franchi la frontière suisse le 18.10.43 à 2030 dans la région de Certoux. J'ai fait partie d'un convoi d'enfants, convoir organisé par un Comité Israelite. Une personne que je ne connais pas nous a acconpagnées jusqu'à Annecy, puis de là deux messieurs que je ne connais pas nous ont conduits en car à la frontière."

5226 **Louise Tchoukran**, 16, Trieste (Italy), "par Simon":

"Born in 1927 in Trieste, I stayed there until 1936, where I began my primary schooling; then in Milan until 1939, where I continued my primary schooling. Since 1939, we have been in Nice, where my parents are still living. We made our way to Switzerland to evade the measures taken by the German authorities against the Israelites. We crossed the Swiss border on October 18, 1943, at 2000 in the region of Certoux. It was an organization that took care of our convoy, in which there were several children. We were accompanied from Nice to Annecy by a woman whom I do not know. Then, from Annecy to the border, by two *passeurs* (trip by bus). We do not know them."

"Née en 1927 à Trieste, j'y suis restée jusqu'en 1936 où j'ai commencé mes écoles primaires, puis à Milan jusqu'en 1939 où j'ai continue mes écoles primaires. Dès 1939, nous nous trouvons à Nice où mes parents habitent encore. Nous avons gagné la Suisse pour éviter les mesures prises par les autorités allemandes contre les israelites. Nous avons franchi la frontière suisse le 18.10.43 à 2000 dans la région de Certoux. C'est une organisation qui s'est occupé de notre convoi où nous étions plusieurs enfants. Nous avons été accompagné de Nice à Annecy par une dame que je ne connais pas. Puis de de Annecy à la frontière par deux passeurs(voyage en car). Nous ne les connaissons pas."

5226 **Nisso Tchoukran,** 12, male, Trieste. He is Louise's brother. "par Simon"

5227 **Simon Rozen**, 13, male, Paris, "par Simon"::

"I always lived in Paris; since the war began, in Clermont-Ferrand [sic]. My parents have been deported since this year. My father was an independent welder. I am his only son. I come to Switzerland to avoid being deported and because now I am alone in France, my mother having been deported on September 29, 1943. I came with a convoy of children from Nice. I do not know exactly how many we were. A young woman, then a man led us up to the barbed wire. We crossed on October 18, 1943, in the evening in the region of Certoux; we were arrested on Swiss soil immediately . . ."

"J'ai toujours habité Paris,depuis la guerre à Clermont Ferrand. Mes parents sont déportés depuis cette année. Mon père était soudeur en autogène. Je suis fils unique. Je viens en Suisse pour éviter d'être déporté et maintenant je seul en France, mamère étant déportée le 29.9.43. Je suis venu avec un convoi d'enfants depuis Nice, je ne sais pas exactement combien on était. Unedemoiselle, puis ensuite un homme nous on conduit jusqu'aux barbelés. Nous avons passé le 18.10.43 au soir dans la région de Certoux, nous avons été arrêtés sur Suisse immédiatement . . ."

Profile of the Convoy of October 20, 1943
MJS Convoy Number 22

Summary Information:

Border Guard Post: Cornières
Place where Arrest was made: Les Huteaux
Time of Arrest: 2000 (8:00 p.m.)
Place and Time of Crossing: Les Huteaux, 20:00 (8:00 p.m.)
Number of Persons: 9
Composition of convoy: 6 unaccompanied children and one mother and two children
Correspondence with OSE list: 5 of 8 children's names, including those of the 2 children who crossed with their mother, appear on OSE list as "par Simon"

List of People Comprising the Convoy and Excerpts from Declarations:

5235 Dora Israel, 37, female, Constantinople (Turkey):

"Born in Constantinople, I stayed in that city until 1916. I did all my classes there, and I left for Bologna (Italy). I was married in Bologna in 19287 [sic]; I stayed in that city with my husband until 1928; then we left for Milan, where we stayed until 1939; then went to Nice, where we stayed until recently. My husband fought with France and is now a prisoner of war in Metz. I came to Switzerland to evade the measures taken by the Germans against the Israelites. We crossed the border on October 20, 1943, around 2000 in the region of Cornières. I came from Nice to Annecy with my children; there a gentleman entrusted me with several children and told me to take them to Annemasse; there a gentleman told us to follow him, and he showed us the way to the border."

"Née à Constantinople je suis restée dans cette villejusqu'en 1916. J'y ai fait toutes mes écoles et je suis partie pour Bologne (IT) . Je me suis mariée à Bologne en 19287(sic), je suis restée dans cette ville avec mon mari jusqu'en 1928 puis nous sommes partis pour Milan où nous sommes restés jusqu'en 1939 pour aller à Nice, où nous sommes restés jusqu'à ces derniers jours. Mon mari à fait la campagne avec la france et est actuellement prisonnier de guerre à Metz. Je suis venue en Suisse pour éviter les mesures prises par les Allemands contre les israelites. Nous avons passé la frontière le 20.10.43. vers les 2000 dans la région de Cornières. Je suis venue de Nice jusqu'à Annecy avec mes enfants et là un Mr. m'a remis plusieurs enfants en me disant de les conduire jusqu'à Annemasse, là un Mr. nous dit de le suivre et il nous a indiqué le chemin jusqu'à la frontière."

5235 Robert Israel, 14, male, Milan. He is Dora's son. "par Simon"

5235 Fortunée Israel, 3, female, Nice. She is Dora's daughter. "par Simon"

5238 Mylan Isaack, 6, male, Milan. The Declaration states that he is not of an age to give precise information on his background. It also states that his parents are in Nice. "par Simon"

5239 Suzanne Sobelman, 7, female, Paris:

"Born in Paris in 1936, I stayed in that city until 1941. I then went to Lyon with my parents, and from there, to Vizille. From Vizille, I came to Switzerland. I began my schooling in Paris, and I continued it in the various towns where I spent time. My parents are still in Vizille, and I came to Switzerland to evade the measures taken by the Germans against the Israelites. I crossed the border on October 20, 1943, around 2030 in the region of Cornières. We were accompanied by a gentleman as far as Annecy. Then we went to Annemasse with Madame ISRAEL; from there, a gentleman showed us the way to the border."

"Née à Paris en 1936 je suis restée dans cette ville jusqu'en 1941. Je suis ensuite allée à Lyon avec, mes parents et de là à Vizille. De Vizille je suis venue en Suisse. J'ai commencé mes écoles à Paris et je les ai continuées dans les différents villages où je suis apssée. Mes parents sont restée à Vizille et je suis venue en Suisse pour éviter les mesures prises par les Allemands contre les israelites. J'ai passé la frontière le 20.10.43. vers les 2030 dans la région de Cornières. Nous avons, été accompagnées par un Mr. jusqu'à Annecy Puis nous sommesallés jusqu'à Annemasse avec Mme. ISRAEL, et là un Mr. nous a montré le chemin jusqu'à la frontière."

5240 **Jeanette Wahl**, 8, female, Antwerp, "par Simon":

"Born in Antwerp, I left that city with my parents at the age of 4 years to come to France. We were arrested and taken to a camp; then we were released and we settled in Nîmes, where I stayed for one year; after that, I went to Montpellier and Nice; then we were in forced residence at Megève; then we came to Nice again; from there, I came to Switzerland. My father, my mother, then my uncle and my aunt were deported; and I came to Switzerland to evade the measures taken by the Germans against the Israelites. I came to Switzerland on October 20, 1943, around 2030 in the region of Cornières. We came from Nice with a convoy, accompanied by a young woman as far as Annecy; and from there we went with Madame ISRAEL to Annemasse and a gentleman showed us the way to cross the barbed wire."

"Née à Anvers j'ai quitté cette v lle avec mes parents à l'âge de 4 ans pour venir en France. Nous avons été arrêtés et conduits dans un camp puis nous avons été relarchés et nous nous sommes instalés à Nimes où je suis restée une année de là j'ai été à Montpellier et Nice, puis nous avons été en résidence forcée à Mègève puis nous sommes venus à nouveau à Nice de de là je suis venue en Suisse, Mon papa, ma maman, puis mon oncle et ma tante ont été déportés et je suis venue en Suisse pour éviter les mesures prises par les Allemands contre les israelites. Je suis venue en Suisse le 20.10.43. vers les 2030 dans la région de Cornières. Nous sommes venus de Nice avec un convoi accompagné par une demoiselle jusqu'à Annecy et de là nous sommes allés avec Mme. ISRAEL jusqu'à Annemasse et un Mr. nous a montré le chemin pour passer les barbelés."

5244 Liba Rosenberg, 13, female, Tomastow (Poland):

"Born in Poland; I left that country with my parents at the age of three to come to Paris. In that city, I did my classes until recently. We left Paris in 1942 to go to Decines [possibly Décines-Charpieu], then to Vizille, and from there, to Switzerland. My parents stayed in Vizille and may come to join us in Switzerland; we came to Switzerland to evade the measures taken by the Germans against the Israelites. We crossed the border on October 20, 1943, around 2030 in the region of Cornières. We left Grenoble alone as far as Annecy; there, we found Madame Israel, who came with us to Switzerland. We went to Annemasse, and there a gentleman showed us the way."

"Née en Pologne j'ai quitté ce pays avec mes parents à l'âge de trois ans pour venir à Paris. Dans cette ville j'ai fait mes classes jusqu'à ces derniers temps. Nous avons quitté Paris en 1942 pour aller à Decines puis à Vizille et de là en Suisse. Mes oarenst sont restée à Vizille et viendrons peut-être nous rejoindre en Suisse, nous sommes venus en Suisse pour éviter les mesures prises par les Allemands contre les israelites. Nous avons passé la frontière le 20.10.43. vers les 2030 dans la région de Cornières. Nous sommes partis de Grenoble seuls jusqu'à Annecy là nous avons trouvé Mme. ISRAEL qui est venue avec nous jusqu'en Suisse . Nous sommes allé jusqu'à Annemasse et là un Mr. nous a montré le chemin."

5244 Paul Rosenberg, 8, male, Paris. He is Liba's brother.

5245 Lisette Palestrant, 13, female, Warsaw, "par Simon":

"Born in Warsaw, I left that city with my parents at the age of 1 year to come to Paris. In that city, I did all my classes and stayed until recently. My dad has been deported, and my mother is hiding in Paris; I came to Switzerland to evade the measures taken by the Germans against the Israelites. I crossed the border on October 20, 1943, around 1930 in the region of Cornières. I came to Switzerland, sent by my mom, who entrusted me to a gentleman who took me as far as Annecy. From there, he led me to a woman where there were already some other children. This woman came with us to Switzerland."

"Née à Varsovie je suis partie de cette ville avec mes parents à l'âge de 1 an pour venir à Paris. J'ai fait, dans cette ville, toutes mes écoles et suis restée jus qu'à ces derniers hours. Mon papa est déporté et ma maman est cachée à Paris, je suis venue en Suisse pour éviter les mesures prises par les Allemands contre les israelités. J'ai passé la frontière le 20.10.43. vers les 1930 dans la région de Cornières. Je suis venue en Suisse envoyée par ma maman qui m'a confiée à un Mr. qui m'a conduit jusqu 'à Annecy. De là il m'a conduite à une dame où se trouvait déjà d'autre enfants. Cette dame est venue avec nous jusqu'en Suisse."

Profile of the Convoy of October 20, 1943
MJS Convoy Number 23

Summary Information:

Border Guard Post: Certoux
Place where Arrest was made: Plaine du Loup
Time of Arrest: 2230 (10:30 p.m.)
Place and Time of Crossing: between *bornes* 51 and 52 at 20:00 (8:00 p.m)
Number of Persons: 8
Composition of convoy: Two families, related to one another (6 adults and 2 children)
Correspondence with OSE list: No names appear on OSE list as "par Simon"

List of People Comprising the Convoy and Excerpts from Declarations:

5242 **Adam Rapaport**, 28, male, Vienna:

"Born in 1915 in Vienna, I stayed there until 1923, when [I] began my primary school. From 1925 to 1940, in Antwerp. I was married in 1939 in Antwerp. From 1935 to 1937, I stayed in Palestine. From 1940, we took refuge in France, first in Montpellier, then on the outskirts of Nice, and, finally, in Saint-Martin-Vésubie. We made our way to Switzerland to evade measures taken by the German military authorities against the Israelites. We crossed the Swiss border on October 20, 1943, at 2230 in the region of Certoux. A farmer pointed out to us the way to the border."

"Né en 1915 à Vienne, j'y suis resté jusqu'en 1923 où commencé mes écoles primaires. Dès 1925 à 1940 à Anvers. Je me suis marié en 1939 à Anvers. De 1935 à 1937 j'ai fait un séjour en Palestine. Dès 1940, nous nous sommes réfugiés en France à Montpellier d'abord, puis aux environs de Nice et enfin à S.Martin Vésubié. Nous avons gagné la Suisse pour éviter les mesures prisespar les autorités militaires allemandes contre les israelites. Nous avons franchi la frontière suiss ele 20.10.43 à 2230 dans la région de Certoux. Un paysans nous a indiqué le chemin de la frontière."

5242 **Mirjam Rapaport**, 25, female, Lodz (Poland). She is Adam's wife.

5242 **Sylvie Rapaport**, 2, female, Montpellier (France). She is Adam's daughter.

5246 Mager Lubelski, 65, male, Ivanowicz (Poland):

"Born in 1878 in Poland, I stayed there until 1930. There I did my apprenticeship as a baker-pastry cook. From 1930 to 1940, I came to take up residence in Antwerp with my family. I practiced my trade with my son. Beginning in 1940, we took refuge in France, first in Montpellier, then on the outskirts of Nice, and finally lastly in Chambéry. We made our way to Switzerland to evade measures taken by the German military authorities against the Israelites. We crossed the Swiss border on October 20, 1943, at 2230 in the region of Certoux. A farmer showed us the way at the border."

"Né en 1878 en Pologne, j'y suis resté jusqu'en 1930. J'y ai fait mon apprentissagede boulanger-pâtissier. Dès 1930 à 1940, je suis venu m'établir à Anvers avec ma famille. J'y ai exercé mon métier avec mon fils. Dès 1940, nous nous sommes réfugiés en France, d'abord à Montpellier, puis dans les environs de Nice et enfin dernièrement à Chambéry Nous avons gagné la Suisse pour éviter les mesures prises par les autorités militaires allemandes contre les israelites. Nous avons franchi la frontière suisse le 20.10.43 à 2230 dans la région de Certoux. Un paysan nous a montré le chemin à la frontière."

5246 Hinda Lubelski, 61, female, Lodz (Poland). She is Mager's wife.

5246 Maurice Lubelski, 23, male, Lodz (Poland). He is Mager's son.

5246 Nadia Lubelski, 22, female, Lodz (Poland). She is Mager's daughter-in-law.

5246 Elly Lubelski, 2, female, Montpellier. She is Mager's granddaughter.

Profile of the Convoy of October 21, 1943
MJS Convoy Number 24

Summary Information:

Border Guard Post: Cornières
Place where Arrest was made: Les Huteaux
Time of Arrest: 1915 (7:15 p.m.)
Place and Time of Crossing: "through the barbed wire"
Number of Persons: 8 (Note: Arrest reports indicate group size as 10, although I identified 8.)
Composition of convoy: Two families (4 adults and 4 children)
Correspondence with OSE list: No names appear on OSE list as "par Simon"

List of People Comprising the Convoy and Excerpts from Declarations:

5254 Zajwel Djament, 39, male, Tirobin [Turobin] (Poland):

"Born in Poland, I left that country in 1928 to come to France. I did all of my schooling and my apprenticeship in Poland. My wife stayed in Poland until 1929; she did all of her classes in Poland. We were married in France, in Saint-Léger-des-Vignes, in 1939 (sic). [It appears that this is an error and should have been 1929.] We came to Paris, and we stayed in that city until 1939. I did my military service, and my wife was evacuated to Saint-Léger. We returned to Paris, and, in 1941, came to Nice. And, from there, to Switzerland. We came to Switzerland for fear of deportation, being of the Jewish race. We crossed the border on October 21, 1943, around 1930 in the region of Cornières."

"Né en Pologne j'ai quitté ce ays en 1928 pour venir en France. J'ai fait toutes mes écoles et mon apprentissage en Pologne. Ma femme est restée en Pologne jusqu'en 1929 elle a fait toutes ses classes en Pologne. Nous nous sommes mariée en France à St. Léger-des-Vignes en 1939. Nous sommes venus à Paris et nous sommes restés dans cette ville jusqu'en 1939. J'ai fait mon régiment et ma femme a été évacuée sur St. Léger. Nous sommes retournés à Paris et en 1941 venus à Nice. Et de là en Suisse. Nous sommes venus en Suisse de crainte de la déportation étant de race juive. Nous avons assé la frontière le 21.10.43. vers les 1930 dans la région de Cornières."

5254 Rywka Djament, 34, female, Stawiezyn [Stawiszyn] (Poland). She is Zajwel's wife.

5254 Henri Djament, 10, male, Paris. He is Zajwel's son.

5254 Paul Djament, 4, male, Paris. He is Zajwel's son.

5257 Srul Engel, 38, male, Kaluszyn (Poland).

"Born in Poland, I left that country to go to Germany, where I stayed for awhile; then I went to Belgium and to France. I did all of my studies in Poland and my apprenticeship. I met my wife in the village of my birth, which was also hers. She left her country in 1927 to come to join me in Paris, where I had been for 1 year. We were married in 1928 in Paris. We stayed in Paris until 1941; then we went to Nice; from there, we were in assigned residence in La Turbie; and, after 9 months, we again came to Nice, where we stayed until a few days ago. We came to Switzerland to evade measures taken by the Germans against the Jews. We crossed the border on October 21, 1943, around 1930 in the region of Chêne."

"Né en Pologne, j'ai quitté ce pays pour aller en Allemagne où je suis resté quelques temps puis je suis allé en Belgique et en France. J'ai fait toutes mes études en Pologne et mon apprentissage. J'ai fait la connaissance de ma femme dans le village de ma naissance qui est aussi le sien . Elle a quitté san pays en 1927 pour venir me rejoindre à Paris où j'étais depuis 1 année. Nous nous sommes mariés en 1928 à Paris. Nous sommes restés à Paris jusqu'en 1941 puis nous sommes allés à Nice, de là nous avons été en résidence assignée à La Turbie, et après 9 mois nous sommes à nouveau venus à Nice où nous s mmes restés jusqu'à ces derniers jours. Nous sommes venus en Suisse pour eviter les mesures prises parles Allemands contre les juifs. Nous avons passé la frontière le 21.10.43 vers les 1930 dans la région de Chêne ."

5257 **Léa Engel**, 37, female, Kaluszyn (Poland). She is Srul's wife.

5257 **Rachèle Engel**, 14, female, Paris. She is Srul's daughter.

5257 **Yvonne Engel**, 4, female, Paris. She is Srul's daughter.

Appendix 3: Accommodation of Jewish Children in Switzerland

by Samantha Lakin, Fulbright Full Research Grantee, University of Lausanne, Switzerland, 2011–2012

Jewish children who entered Switzerland illegally during the Second World War and who were allowed to remain in the country found themselves housed in a variety of accommodations that differed in terms of location, type, sponsor, and quality. This appendix seeks to provide a brief overview of such accommodations.

Immediately after having entered Switzerland and been arrested by Swiss border guards, refugees were taken to a nearby guard post and questioned. Although some spent the first few days in prison, many were taken directly to installations known as a *camps d'accueil* (reception camps). (An individual in need of medical care might be taken to a quarantine camp.) The refugee was confined to the reception camp for an undetermined period of time—generally, a few days to a few weeks—while awaiting a permanent placement. Organized and supervised by the army for the EJPD (Eidgenössisches Justiz- und Polizeidepartment; Federal Department of Justice and Police), the reception camps were set up in various types of structures, including single-family residences, hotels, factories, and military barracks. *Camps d'acceuil* situated in the canton of Geneva included Champel, Charmilles, and Bout du Monde, a place whose name means "End of the World."

While in a reception camp, Jewish children typically experienced feelings of relief mixed with those of anxiety and uncertainty. They were out of imminent danger of arrest and deportation and had their basic needs met. After months of concealing their true identities, they could finally speak openly about who they were. Some reunited with friends and acquaintances and/or found people to whom they could relate by virtue of common country of origin or language. At the same time, many lacked information on the whereabouts of immediate family members and feared for their safety. Awaiting permanent placement, some worried that they might yet be expelled from Switzerland.

The refugee child would eventually be assigned a permanent placement in a foster family or institutional setting. Children who had crossed the border unaccompanied by parents or other close relatives and who were younger than twelve would generally be placed with foster families. The non-denominational woman's organization known as the SHEK (*Schweizerisches Hilfswerk für Emigrantenkinder*; Swiss Relief Work for Refugee Children) was the organization primarily responsible for arranging the placement of Jewish children in foster families. Many child survivors whom I interviewed recalled their experiences of living with Swiss families. The experiences were quite varied. Some enjoyed the months or years that they spent with their hosts and developed lasting attachments with family members. Others did not feel well-integrated and suffered feelings of alienation and anxiety. In some cases, a placement did not work out, and it was necessary to transfer the child to a different family or to an institution. I should also note that it was not only children without parents in Switzerland who were placed in foster families. Some children were separated from parents or other close relatives with whom they had crossed the border. The children were placed in foster families, and the adults were sent to work camps.

Adolescents were generally placed in institutional settings, mainly children's homes. (As used here, the term "children's homes" encompasses orphanages.) Children's homes were established, sponsored, and and/or operated by various religious and secular organizations and by private benefactors. The Jewish organizations OSE (Oeuvre de Secours aux Enfants; Children's Rescue Network), HaShomer HaTza'ir, and VSJF (Verband Schweizerischer Jüdischer Fürsorgen; Association of Swiss-Jewish Welfare Organizations) played a prominent role, as did the SHEK and the Swiss Croix Rouge (Red Cross). A small number of Jewish refugee children were placed in convents.

The Institut Monnier, Les Mureilles, and the Home de la Forêt were the key Jewish children's homes located in the canton of Geneva. In these facilities, teachers and administrators sought not only to care for and educate refugee children but to also reinforce, re-establish, or establish the child's connection to Judaism. Shabbat was observed and Jewish holidays celebrated. The Institut Monnier, located in Versoix and operated by the HaShomer HaTza'ir, was inspired by the Zionist ideal, organized like a kibbutz, and prepared children to make *aliyah*. Educators and children were all refugees, which allowed them to form strong connections to one another and to Judaism.

Reflecting the realities of the wartime situation, living conditions in the children's homes were far from luxurious. Meals provided little more than sustenance, and heat and hot water were strictly limited. However, the men and women responsible for administering the homes and instructing the children were, for the most part, professionally trained teachers, nurses, and social workers. They genuinely cared about the children and sought to meet their needs—physical, psychological, and educational—to the greatest extent possible.

As a Fulbright Full Research Grantee from September 2011 to July 2012, Samantha Lakin conducted research on the experiences of Jewish refugee children who entered Switzerland between 1942 and 1944 and who resided there for some period of time. She conducted 60 oral history interviews with such child survivors, men and women now liv-

ing in Switzerland, France, Israel, the Netherlands, England, and the United States. She also conducted archival research in cantonal, Federal, and international archives. Currently enrolled at the Fletcher School of Law and Diplomacy at Tufts University, Ms. Lakin will continue her research on the subject addressed here.

Glossary of Foreign Words and Terms

Fr. = French; It. = Italian; He. = Hebrew; Gr. = German; Yd. = Yiddish.

Anschluss The invasion and forced annexation of Austria by Germany that took place on March 12, 1938. Literally, "connection." *Gr.*

aliyah A cultural term used by Jews to signify a coreligionist's immigration to Israel. Literally, "ascent." *He.*

Appell The name given to the very lengthy process of roll call conducted each morning and evening in Ravensbrück and other concentration camps. *Gr.*

Aufseherin Female overseer in a German concentration camp. *Gr.*

Bunker Name given to the prison in Ravensbrück concentration camp. *Gr.*

bif A type of forged identity paper that created a false Aryan identity for the holder, one not based on the identity of an actual person and, therefore, not verifiable. *Fr.*

Carabinieri Italian military police. Sometimes called "*La Benemerita*" ("The Meritorious"). *It.*

chutzpah Audacity. *Yd.*

département An administrative unit in France. The country is divided into twenty-two regions, which are subdivided into ninety-five departments. *Fr.*

disponible Available. *Fr.*

douane Customs house. *Fr.*

duce Leader. Il Duce refers to Benito Mussolini. *It.*

erev Eve. In Judaism, the day is measured from sundown to sundown. Thus, the Jewish holiday begins at sundown. *He.*

gdoud Brigade. Plural form is *gdoudim. He.*

haimish Homey; cozy and unpretentious. *Yd.*

chaverim Friends. *He.*

Eretz Israël Land of Israel. *He.*

jeunesse Youth. *Fr.*

juif n.m. Jew; adj. Jewish *Fr.*

juive n.f. Jew; adj. Jewish (fem. juive). *Fr.*

Judenrein Cleansed of Jews. *Gr.*

Kristallnacht Literally, "Crystal Night," which was the term used contemporaneously by German-speaking Aryans to refer to the widespread attacks on Jews and Jewish property organized and executed by the Nazi regime throughout Germany, Austria, and the Sudetenland on the night of November 9–10, 1938. Nearly all of the synagogues in Germany and Austria—more than fifteen hundred—were destroyed. Thousands of Jewish businesses were destroyed, more than thirty thousand Jewish males were taken to concentration camps, and an estimated one hundred Jews were beaten to death. The night of destruction was originally called Kristallnacht because, in many places, the sidewalks and streets were littered with the broken glass of shop windows. The term is not generally used in Germany today because it cynically misrepresents the horrific nature of the event. The term Pogromnacht (Pogrom Night) is more commonly used. *Gr.*

Magen David Star of David or Shield of David. This is the traditional name for the six-pointed Jewish star. *He.*

maréchal Marshall. *Le Maréchal* refers to Philippe Pétain. *Fr.*

minyan The quorum of ten men required when performing certain Jewish religious functions, such as a prayer service. *He.*

passeur A term used in France during the war to refer to a professional guide or smuggler who, in exchange for money or goods, effected the passage of individuals across the line of demarcation or across an international border. *Fr.*

patrie Homeland. *Fr.*

pension Boardinghouse, boarding school, or room and board. *Fr.*

Polizia Razziale Italian Race Police. *It.*

préfet Prefect; chief administrative official of a French department. *Fr.*

rafle Roundup. *Fr.*

refoulement Driving back; the term has been used to mean the turning back of aliens, whether they are seeking entry at a border or have entered. *Fr.*

réseau Network. *Fr.*

résidence forcée Forced residence; also called *résidence assignée* (assigned residence). A French law passed in October 1940 authorized prefects to intern foreign Jews in special camps, send them to designated places for stays of indeterminate length, and keep them under police surveillance. *Fr.*

Saint-Gervolains Residents of Saint-Gervais. *Fr.*

secours Help; assistance; aid; relief; rescue. *Fr.*

séjour Stay. *Fr.*

Shemini Atzeret A Jewish festival immediately following the seven days of Sukkot and whose name literally means "the eighth day of assembly." The festival does not commemorate a specific event. Rather, the sages interpreted it as an "extra" day that God set aside as a festival day because, like a host who does not want his guests to leave just yet, he wished to extend the fall festival season. *He.*

siddur Jewish prayerbook. *He.*

stagiaire Trainee; apprentice; intern. *Fr.*

synthé Name given to a type of false identity paper based on the identity of an actual person and, therefore, verifiable. *Fr.*

tefillin Two small black boxes with black straps attached to them that observant Jewish men put on each morning except on the Sabbath. One box and strap is affixed to the arm, and one, to the head. The boxes contain the handwritten text of four Biblical verses. *He.*

thermalisme The use of warm, underground springs for their therapeutic and healthful benefits. *Fr.*

tricolore Literally, three-colored, but used to refer to the three-colored French flag. *Fr.*

Vel d'Hiv Shortened form of Vélodrome d'Hiver, the winter bicycling stadium. This large indoor sports arena stood on the boulevard de Grenelle in the Fifteenth Arrondissement. It was here that thousands of men, women, and children were imprisoned after being arrested throughout Paris on July 16–17, 1942. The massive roundups executed on those two days were large and unlike those carried out previously, and they marked a clear turning point. The name "Vel d'Hiv" became synonymous with that tragic event. *Fr.*

Verfügbar Available. In Ravensbrück, the word stood for a prisoner who was not assigned to a permanent work detail. The plural form was "*Verfügbaren.*" *Gr.*

Zone libre Free Zone, i.e. that part of France not occupied by German personnel, military and civilian, prior to November 1942. Also called the Zone nonoccupée (the Unoccupied Zone) and the Zone sud (southern zone). *Fr.*

Zone occupée Occupied Zone, i.e., that part of France occupied by German troops and officials in June 1940; also called the Zone nord (northern zone). *Fr.*

Bibliography

1. Books

Adler, Jacques. *Face à la persécution: les organisations juives à Paris de 1940 à 1944*. Paris: Calmann-Lévy, 1985. Translated and published as *The Jews of Paris and the Final Solution: Communal Response and Internal Conflicts, 1940–1944*. New York: Oxford University Press, 1987. Name of translator not indicated.

Agarossi, Elena. *Une nazione allosbando*. Bologna: Mulino, 1993. Translated by Harvey Fergusson II and published as *A Nation Collapses: The Italian Surrender of September 1943*. Cambridge: Cambridge University Press, 2006.

Amicale de Ravensbrück and Assocation des Déportées et Internées de la Résistance. *Les Françaises à Ravensbrück*. Paris: Gallimard, 1965.

Anciens de la Résistance juive en France (ARJF). *Organisation juive de combat: Résistance/sauvetage France 1940–1945*. Paris: Editions Autrement, 2002.

Archives d'État de Genève. *Le passage de la frontière durant la Seconde Guerre mondiale: Sources et méthodes*. Genève: État de Genève, Archives d'État, 2002.

Baldran, Jacqueline, and Claude Bochurberg. *David Rapoport,"La Mère et l'enfant", 36 rue Amelot*. Paris: Mémorial de la Shoah, 2007.

Bergier, Jacques ("Verne"). *Agents secrets contre armes secrètes*. Paris: Éditions Arthaud, 1955. Translated by Edward Fitzgerald and published as *Secret Weapons—Secret Agents*. London: Hurst & Blackett, 1956.

Bikales, Gerda. *Through the Valley of the Shadow of Death*. Lincoln, Nebraska: iUniverse, Inc., 2004.

Bodénès, Stéphane. *Promenades sur la frontière Franco-Genevoise*. Genève: Éditions Slatkine, 2001.

Bower, Tom. *Klaus Barbie: The Butcher of Lyons*. New York: Pantheon Books, 1984.

Buber-Newmann, Margarete. *Under Two Dictators*. New York: Dodd, Mead, 1949.

Carpi, Daniel. *Between Mussolini and Hitler: The Jews and the Italian Authorities in France and Tunisia*. Waltham, Massachusetts: Brandeis University Press, 1994.

Chombart de Lauwe, Marie-Jo. *Toute une vie de résistance*. Paris: Éditions Graphein: FNDIRP, 1998.

Cohen, Richard I. *The Burden of Conscience: French Jewish Leadership during the Holocaust.* Bloomington: Indiana University Press, 1987.

Croquet, Jean-Claude. *Chemins de passage: Les passages clandestins entre la Haute-Savoie et la Suisse de 1940 à 1944.* Saint-Julien-en-Genevois: La Salévienne, 1996.

Curé de Douvaine. *Résistance non violente: la filière de Douvaine: l'abbé Jean Rosay, Joseph Lançon, François Périllat: morts en déportation.* Douvaine (Haute-Savoie): Le Curé de Douvaine, 1987.

Dereymez, Jean-William (ed.). *Être jeune en Isère (1939–1945).* Paris: L'Harmattan, 2001.

Doulut, Alexandre, and Labeau, Sandrine. *Les 473 déportés Juifs de Lot-et-Garonne: Histoires individuelles et archives.* No place of publication indicated. Published by Après l'oubli in association with Les fils et filles des déportés juifs de France, 2010.

Dufournier, Denise. *La maison des mortes, Ravensbrück.* Republished with new prefatory material. Paris: Julliard, 1992. Originally published by Hachette, 1945. Translated and published as *Ravensbrück: The Women's Camp of Death.* London: George Allen & Unwin, Ltd., 1948. Name of translator not indicated. Page references cited here refer to the 1992 edition, and translations of excerpts presented are those of N. Lefenfeld.

Dupraz, Pierre. *Bientôt, la liberté: Une chronique de la Seconde Guerre mondiale à Passy, Saint-Gervais, Les Contamines, et Servox.* Passy: Pierre Dupraz, 1997.

Estèbe, Jean. *Les Juifs à Toulouse et en Midi toulousain au temps de Vichy.* Toulouse: Presses universitaires du Mirail, 1996.

Fabre, Emile C. (ed.). *Les clandestins de Dieu: CIMADE, 1939–1945.* Collected by Jeanne Merle d'Aubigné and Violette Mouchon. Paris: Librairie Arthème Fayard, 1968. Translated by William and Patricia Nottingham and published as *God's Underground: Accounts of the Activity of the French Protestant Church during the German Occupation of the Country in World War II.* St. Louis: The Bethany Press, 1970.

Fivaz-Silbermann, Ruth. *Le refoulement de réfugiés civils juifs à la frontière Franco-Genevoise durant la Seconde Guerre mondiale.* Paris: Beate Klarsfeld Foundation, 2000.

Flückiger, Pierre, and Gérard Bagnoud. *Les réfugiés civils et la frontière genevoise durant la Deuxième Guerre mondiale: Fichiers et archives.* Genève: Archives d'État, 2000.

Fondation pour la mémoire de la déportation. *Livre-mémorial des déportés de France.* Volume 1, no date.

Freihammer, Josef. *Heimat Amstetten VI.* Amstetten: Medieninhaber und Verleger, 2001.

Gamzon, Robert. *Les eaux claires: Journal 1940–1944*. Paris: Eclaireuses Eclaireurs Israélites de France, 1981.

Gaulle-Anthonioz, Geneviève de. *La traversée de la nuit*. Paris: Éditions du Seuil, 1998. Translated by Richard Seaver and published as *The Dawn of Hope: A Memoir of Ravensbrück*. New York: Arcade Publishing, Inc., 1999.

Germain, Michel. *Mémorial de la déportation: Haute-Savoie 1940/1945*. Montmélian: La Fontaine de Siloé, 1999.

Gildea, Robert. *Marianne in Chains: Daily Life in the Heart of France during the German Occupation*. New York: Henry Holt and Company, First Picador Edition, 2004.

Gorce, Nelly. *Journal de Ravensbrück*. Arles: Actes Sud, 1995.

Gorgiel-Sercarz, Hélène. *Memoirs of a Jewish Daughter*. Tel-Aviv: H. Gorgiel-Sercarz, 1990. This is an unpublished manuscript contained in various libraries, including the USHMM in Washington, DC, and the CJDC in Paris. The USHMM lists the 1990 date followed by a question mark.

Grandjacques, Gabriel. *La montagne-refuge: Les Juifs au pays du Mont-Blanc*. Montmélian: La Fontaine de Siloé, 2007.

Grove-Pollak, Fay (ed.). *The Saga of a Movement: WIZO 1920–1970*. No place or date of publication indicated in the text. (The Library of Congress record indicates that the book was published in Tel Aviv by the Department of Organisation and Education of WIZO and cites 1970 as a possible publication date.)

Gurewitsch, Brana (ed.). *Mothers, Sisters, Resisters: Oral Histories of Women who Survived the Holocaust*. Tuscaloosa: The University of Alabama Press, 1998.

Hammel, Frédéric Chimon. *Souviens-toi d'Amalek: Témoignage sur la lutte des Juifs en France, 1938–1944*. Paris: C.L.K.H., 1982.

Häsler, Alfred A. *Das Boot ist voll . . .* Zürich: Stuttgart, Fretz & Wasmuth, 1967. Translated by Charles Lam Markmann and published as *The Lifeboat is Full: Switzerland and the Refugees, 1933–1945*. New York: Funk & Wagnalls, 1969.

Haymann, Emmanuel. *Le camp du bout du monde 1942: des enfants juifs de France à la frontière suisse*. Lausanne: Éditions Pierre-Marcel Favre, 1984.

Henry, Patrick. *We Only Know Men: The Rescue of Jews in France during the Holocaust*. Washington, DC: The Catholic University of America Press, 2007.

Herbermann, Nanda. *Der gesegnete Abgrund: Schutzhäftling Nr. 6582 im Frauenkonzentrationslager Ravensbrück*. Nürnberg: Glock und Lutz, 1948. Translated by Hester Baer and published as *The Blessed Abyss: Inmate #6582 in Ravensbrück Concentration Camp for Women*. Edited by Hester Baer and Elizabeth R. Baer. Detroit: Wayne State University Press, 2000.

Höss, Rudolph. *Death Dealer, the memoirs of the SS Kommandant at Auschwitz*. Translated by Andrew Pollinger. Edited by Steven Paskuly. New York: Da Capo Press, 1996.

Independent Commission of Experts Switzerland—Second World War. *Die Schweiz und die Flüchtinge zur Zeit des Nationalsozialismus*. Bern: BBL/EDMZ, 1999. Generally referred to as the *Bergier Report*. Translated by several individuals and published as *Switzerland and Refugees in the Nazi Era*. Bern: BBL/EDMZ, 1999. See www.uek.ch/en/index.htm

Israel, Gérard. *Heureux comme Dieu en France, 1940–1944*. Paris: Editions Robert Laffont, 1975.

Jacoubovitch, Jules. *Rue Amelot: Aide et résistance*. Translated from the Yiddish by Gabrielle Jacoubovitch-Bouhana. Paris: Éditions du Centre Medem, 2006.

Kapel, René S. *Un rabbin dans la tourmente (1940–1944)*. Paris: CDJC, 1986.

Kedward, H. R. *In Search of the Maquis: Rural Resistance in Southern France, 1942–1944*. Oxford: Clarendon Press, 1994; New York: Oxford University Press, 1994.

Klarsfeld, Serge. *Nice: Hotel Excelsior: Les rafles des Juifs par la Gestapo à partir du 8 septembre 1943*. Paris: Les Fils et Filles des Déportés Juifs de France, 1998.

Klarsfeld, Serge. *Le calendrier de la persécution des juifs en France 1940–1944*. Paris: Beate Klarsfeld Foundation, 1993. An updated version of this work was published in two volumes under the title *Le calendrier de la déportation*. Paris: Fayard, 2001. The updated version constitutes Volume II of the series *La Shoah en France*. Page references cited here are from the original (1993) publication.

Klarsfeld, Serge. *Le mémorial de la déportation des juifs en France*. Paris: Klarsfeld, 1978.

Klarsfeld, Serge. *Vichy-Auschwitz: La "solution finale" de la question juive en France*. Paris: Fayard, 2001. Volume I of the series *La Shoah en France*. This is an updated version of *Vichy-Auschwitz: le rôle de Vichy dans la solution finale de la question juive en France*. Paris: Fayard, 1983 and 1985. Page references cited here refer to the updated (2001) publication.

Knout, David. *Contribution à l'histoire de la Résistance Juive en France, 1940–1944*. Paris: Éditions du Centre, 1947.

Kott, Aline and Jacques Kott. *Roanne: Enquête sur les origines d'une communauté juive atypique . . .* Paris: Édition Wern, 1998.

Lapidus, Serge. *Étoiles jaunes dans la France des années noires: Onze récits parallèles de jeunes rescapés*. Paris: Harmattan, 2000.

Laqueur, Walter. *The First News of the Holocaust*. Leo Baeck Memorial Lecture 23. New York: Leo Baeck Institute, 1979.

Latour, Anny. *Résistance juive en France, 1940–1944*. Paris: Stock, 1970. Translated by Irene R. Ilton and published as *The Jewish Resistance in France (1940–1944)*. New York: Holocaust Library, distributed by Schocken Books, 1981.

Lazare, Lucien. *La résistance juive en France*. Paris: Stock, 1987. Translated by Jeffrey M. Green and published as *Rescue as Resistance: How Jewish Organizations Fought the Holocaust in France*. New York: Columbia University Press, 1996.

Lazare, Lucien. *Le livre des Justes*. Paris: Éditions Jean-Claude Lattès, 1993.

Lazarus, Jacques. *Juifs au combat: Témoignage sur l'activité d'un mouvement de résistance*. Paris: Editions du Centre, 1947.

Lévitte, Simon. *Le Sionisme: Quelques pages de son histoire*. Paris: Éditions des Cahiers Juifs, 1936.

Lewi, Monique, *Histoire d'une communauté juive, Roanne: Étude historique et sociologique d'un judaïsme*. Roanne: Horvath, 1976.

Marrus, Michael R., and Robert O. Paxton. *Vichy et les juifs*. Paris: Éditions Calmann-Lévy, 1981. Translated and published as *Vichy France and the Jews*. Stanford, California: Stanford University Press, 1995. First English edition published by Basic Books in 1981 and a paperback edition published by Schocken Books in 1983. Name of translator not indicated.

Marzac, Jacques, and Denise Rey Jouenne. *Irma Jouenne: Disparue à Ravensbrück*. Paris: Editions N. C., 1995.

Maurice, Violette. *Les murs éclatés*. Saint-Etienne, France: Action Graphique, 1990.

Maurice, Violette. *N. N.* With a preface by Jean Nocher. Saint-Etienne: S. P. E. R., 1946. This book was republished, with a preface by Marcel Conche, by La Versanne in 1991 under the same title. Page references cited here refer to the original (1946) publication.

Mazower, Mark. *Salonica, City of Ghosts: Christians, Muslims and Jews, 1430–1950*. New York: Vintage Books, 2006.

Morgan, Ted. *An Uncertain Hour: The French, the Germans, the Jews, the Klaus Barbie Trial, and the City of Lyon, 1940–1945*. New York: Arbor House/William Morrow, 1990.

Morrison, Jack G. *Ravensbrück: Everyday Life in a Women's Concentration Camp, 1939–45*. Princeton: Markus Wiener Publishers, 2000.

Mouthon, Pierre. *Résistance, occupation, collaboration: Haute-Savoie 1940–1945*. Épinal: Éditions de Sapin d'Or, 1993.

Munos-du Peloux, Odile. *Passer en Suisse: Les passages clandestins entre la Haute-Savoie et la Suisse, 1940–1944*. Grenoble: Presses Universitaires de Grenoble, 2002.

Najman, Judith, and Emmanuel Haymann. *Claude Kelman: Une ambition pour le judaïsme*. Paris: Alliance israélite universelle (AIU), 2001.

Ofer, Dalia, and Lenore J. Weitzman (eds.). *Women in the Holocaust*. New Haven: Yale University Press, 1998.

Ousby, Ian. *Occupation: The Ordeal of France, 1940–1944*. New York: Cooper Square Press, 2000.

Panczer, André. *Je suis né dans l'faubourg Saint-Denis . . .* Treignac, France: Le Loubanel, Éditions "Les Monédières," 2007.

Picard, Jacques. *On the Ambivalence of Being Neutral: Switzerland and Swiss Jewry Facing the Rise and Fall of the Nazi State*. Joseph and Rebecca Meyerhoff Annual Lecture, Number 23, delivered September 23, 1997. Washington, DC: USHMM, Center for Advanced Holocaust Studies, 1998.

Poliakov, Leon. *La condition des Juifs en France sous l'occupation italienne*. Paris: Éditions du Centre, 1946. Translated and published, with second author, Jacques Sabille, as *Jews Under the Italian Occupation*. New York: Howard Fertig, 1983. Name of translator not indicated.

Poznanski, Renée. *Les Juifs en France pendant la Seconde Guerre mondiale*. Paris: Hachette, 1997. Translated by Nathan Bracher and published as *Jews in France During World War II*. Waltham, Massachusetts: Brandeis University Press in association with the USHMM, 2001.

Rayski, Adam. *Le choix des Juifs sous Vichy: Entre soumission et résistance*. Paris: Éditions La Découverte, 1992. Translated by Will Sayers and published in association with the United States Holocaust Memorial Museum as *The Choice of the Jews Under Vichy: Between Submission and Resistance*. Notre Dame, Indiana: University of Notre Dame Press, 2005.

Reynaud, Michel, and Fondation pour la mémoire de la déportation. *Livre-mémorial des déportés de France arrêtés par mesure de répression et dans certains cas par mesure de persécution, 1940–1945*. Paris: Éditions Tirésias, 2004.

Rittner, Carol, and John K. Roth (eds.). *Different Voices: Women and the Holocaust*. New York: Paragon House, 1993.

Rochlitz, Joseph. *The Righteous Enemy: Document Collection*. Rome: Edizione in proprio, 1988.

Rutkowski, Adam. *La lutte des juifs en France à l'époque de l'occupation, 1940–1944: Recueil de documents*. Paris: CDJC, 1975.

Sachar, Howard M. *A History of Israel from the Rise of Zionism to Our Time*. New York: Alfred A. Knopf, 2007.

Saidel, Rochelle G. *The Jewish Women of Ravensbrück Concentration Camp*. Madison, Wisconsin: The University of Wisconsin Press, 2004.

Salon, Jacques. *Trois mois dura notre bonheur: Journal 1943–1944*. Paris: Fondation pour la mémoire de la Shoah, 2005.

Samuel, Vivette. *Sauver les enfants*. Paris: Liana Levi, 1995. Translated by Charles B. Paul and published as *Rescuing the Children: A Holocaust Memoir*. Madison: University of Wisconsin Press, 2002.

Shirer, William L. *The Rise and Fall of the Third Reich: A History of Nazi Germany*. New York: A Fawcett Crest Book, 1960.

Szajkowski, Zosa, *Analytical Franco-Jewish Gazetteer, 1939–1945: With an Introduction to Some Problems in Writing the History of the Jews in France During World War II*. New York: Published privately with the assistance of the American Academy for Jewish Research, the Lucius N. Littauer Foundation, and the Gustav Wurzweiler Foundation, 1966.

Tillion, Germaine. *Ravensbrück*. Third edition. Paris: Éditions du Seuil, 1988. This edition is greatly expanded over previous editions and contains three lengthy appendices on gas chambers at Ravensbrück, Hartheim, Mauthausen, and Gusen: "*Les exterminations par gaz à Ravensbrück*" by Anise Postel-Vinay; "*Les exterminations par gaz à Hartheim*" and "*Les exterminations par gaz à Mauthausen et Gusen*" by Pierre Serge Choumoff.

Tillion, Germaine. *Ravensbrück*. Second edition. Paris: Éditions du Seuil, 1973. Translated by Gerald Satterwhite and published as *Ravensbrück: Eyewitness Account of a Women's Concentration Camp*. Garden City, New York: Anchor Press/Doubleday, 1975.

Vielcazat-Petitcol, Marie-Juliette. *Lot-et-Garonne: Terre d'exil, terre d'asile: les réfugiés Juifs pendant la Seconde Guerre mondiale*. Narosse: Éditions d'Albret, 2006.

Vigée, Claude. *La lune d'hiver: Récit – journal – essai*. Paris: Flammarion, 1970.

Villermet, Christian. *A noi Savoia: Histoire de l'occupation italienne en Savoie, novembre 1942-septembre 1943*. Les Marches: La Fontaine de Savoisiennes Siloé, 1991.

Vulliez, Hyacinthe. *Camille Folliet: Prêtre et résistant*. Paris: Les Éditions de l'Atelier/ Les Éditions Ouvrières, 2001, and Annecy: Éditions Le Vieil Annecy, 2001.

Yagil, Limor. *Chrétiens et Juifs sous Vichy, 1940–1944: Sauvetage et désobéissance civile*. Paris: Cerf, 2005.

Zeitoun, Sabine. *L'Oeuvre de secours aux enfants (O.S.E.) sous l'Occupation en France: Du légalisme à la résistance 1940–1944*. Paris: Éditions L'Harmattan, 1990.

Zuccotti, Susan. *The Holocaust, the French, and the Jews*. New York: BasicBooks, 1993.

Zuccotti, Susan. *Holocaust Odysseys: The Jews of Saint-Martin-Vésubie and Their Flight Through France and Italy*. New Haven: Yale University Press, 2007.

Zuccotti, Susan. *Under His Very Windows: The Vatican and the Holocaust in Italy*. New Haven and London: Yale University Press, 2000.

2. *Essays*

Ariel, Joseph. "Jewish Self-Defence and Resistance in France During World War II." *Yad Vashem Studies on the European Catastrophe and Resistance* 6 (1967): 221–250.

Diamant, Zanvel. "Jewish Refugees on the French Riviera." *YIVO Annual of Jewish Social Science* 8 (1953): 264–280.

Kieval, Hillel J. "Legality and Resistance in Vichy France: The Rescue of Jewish Children." *Proceedings of the American Philosophical Society* 124, no. 5 (October 1980): 339–366.

Panicacci, Jean-Louis. "Les Juifs et la Question Juive dans les Alpes-Maritimes de 1939 à 1945." *Recherches Régionales, Côte d'Azur et Contrées Limitrophes: Bulletin Trimestriel* 4 (October-December 1983): 239–331.

Roby. "Dans les mains de la police allemande sous l'occupation." *Le Républicain Savoyard,* no. 37 (September 13, 1986): 1–4.

Rutkowski, Adam. "Les évasions de Juifs de trains de déportation de France." *Le Monde Juif,* no. 73 (1974): 10–29.

Schnek, Georges. "Etre jeune en France, 1939–1945." Address presented at the Colloque international de Grenoble 23/01/1997 au 25/01/1997. Printed copy given to N. Lefenfeld by Georges Schnek. This address appears, with very minor changes, in Dereymez, Jean-William (ed.), *Être jeune en Isère (1939–1945),* 60–61. Paris: L'Harmattan, 2001.

Vernay, Denise ("Miarka"). Printed copy of speech delivered November 20, 1981. Private collection of Emmanuel Racine. This speech also appeared under the title "J'ai le Devoir, l'Obligation Douloureuse de Témoigner sur Mila," in *Revue de la WIZO,* November-December 1981.

3. *Other*

Commission de réhabilitation sur son activité pendant les années 2004 à 2008. *Rapport: Réhabilitation de personnes ayant aidé des fugitifs à fuir les persécutions nazis.* March 2, 2009. See www.admin.ch/ch/f/ff/2009/2903.pdf

Fivaz-Silbermann, Ruth. Doctoral dissertation in progress, *La fuite en Suisse: Migrations, stratégies, fuite, accueil, refoulement et destin des réfugiés juifs venus de France durant la Seconde Guerre mondiale.* Geneva: University of Geneva.

Ludwig, Carl. *La politique pratiquée par la Suisse à l'égard des réfugiés au cours des années 1933 à 1955. Annexe au rapport du Conseil fédéral à l'Assemblée fédérale sur la politique pratiquée par la Suisse à l'égard des réfugiés au cours des années 1933 à nos jours.* Bern, 1957. The German version of this book is *Die Flüchtlingspolitik der Schweiz in den Jahren 1933 bis 1955: Bericht an den Bundesrat zuhanden der eidgenössischen Räte*. Bern, 1957.

4. Archives Consulted

AFHRA	Air Force Historical Research Agency, Maxwell Air Force Base, Alabama
ADHS	Archives départmentales de la Haute-Savoie, Annecy
AEG	Archives de l'État de Genève, Geneva, Switzerland
AIU	Alliance israélite universelle, Paris
CDJC	Mémorial de la Shoah Musée/Centre de documentation juive contemporaine, Paris
ICJ-OH	Oral History Division, Institute of Contemporary Jewry, Hebrew University, Jerusalem
JDC	American Jewish Joint Distribution Committee Archives, New York
MAU	Archiv der KZ-Gedenkstätte Mauthausen, Vienna
USHMM	United States Holocaust Memorial Museum, Washington
YIVO	YIVO Institute for Jewish Research, Center for Jewish History, New York
YV	Yad Vashem, Jerusalem

5. Interviews and Correspondence Conducted by the Author

Gerda Bikales (née Bierzonski)
Marie-Claude Bonaldi (née Mion)
Miriam Brinbaum (née Wajntrob)
Jeanne Brousse-Maurier
Jacques Charmatz
Marie-Jo Chombart de Lauwe
Jean and Germaine Cochet
Sonia Constant (née Veissid)
Claude Emerich
Nadine Gill (née Racine)
Maurice Glazman
Alice Gliklich (née Gryn)
Cécile Gostynski
Gabriel Grandjacques
Sara Grunberg
Tito Gryn
Edgar Kleinberger
Bernard Kott

Georges Loinger
Sacha Maidenberg (née Racine)
Violette Maurice
Father François Mercier
Helen Mirkine (née Racine)
Robert Moos
André Panczer
Lili Racine Peyser
Anise Postel-Vinay
Myriam Pupier (née Charmatz)
Emmanuel Racine
Lucia Rombaut
Georges Schnek
Eliane Suernick (née Neoussikhin)
Denise Vernay (née Jacob)
Wolf Wapniarz
Frida Wattenberg
Esther Weil (née Constant)
Daniella Marianne Wexler (née Racine)
Renée Wiener (née Kurz)
Lydie Weissberg

Many of the individuals listed above allowed me to consult their privately-held archival documents.

Index